W9-CXW-670

MARKET SHARE REPORTER

ISSN 1052-9578

MARKET SHARE REPORTER

AN ANNUAL COMPILATION

OF REPORTED MARKET SHARE

DATA ON COMPANIES,

PRODUCTS, AND SERVICES

2 0 0 5

Volume 2
ROBERT S. LAZICH, Editor

NOV 2 3 2004

THOMSON
★
GALE

Detroit • New York • San Francisco • New Haven, Conn. • Waterville, Maine • London • Munich

THOMSON

GALE

Market Share Reporter 2005
Robert S. Lazich

Project Editor
Virgil L. Burton III

Editorial
Joyce Piwowarski, Susan Turner

Imaging and Multimedia
Michael Logusz

Manufacturing
Rita Wimberley

ISBN 0-7876-9414-2 (2 vol. set)
ISBN 0-7876-7444-3 (Vol. 1)
ISBN 0-7876-7368-4 (Vol. 2)
ISSN 0071-0210

Printed in the United States of America
10 9 8 7 6 5 4 3 2 1

TABLE OF CONTENTS

TABLE OF TOPICS

The *Table of Topics* lists all topics used in *Market Share Reporter* in alphabetical order. One or more page references follow each topic; the page references identify the starting point where the topic is shown. The same topic name may be used under different SICs; therefore, in some cases, more than one page reference is provided. Roman numerals indicate volume number.

SIC 38 - Instruments and Related Products

★ 2048 ★
Avionics
SIC: 3812; NAICS: 334511
Avionics Market in Taiwan

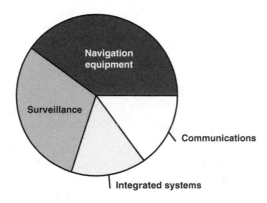

Market shares are shown in percent.

Navigation equipment	40.0%
Surveillance	30.0
Integrated systems	15.0
Communications	15.0

Source: "Avionics." [online] from http:// www.usatrade.gov [accessed January 5, 2004], from U.S. Commercial Service.

★ 2049 ★
Car Navigation Systems
SIC: 3812; NAICS: 334511
Top Car Navigation System Makers in Japan, 2002

Market shares are shown based on domestic shipments of 1.01 million units.

Pioneer	33.0%
Matsushita Electric Industrial	24.4
Fujitsu Ten	9.9
Sony	5.9
Clarion	5.1
Other	21.7

Source: "Market Share Survey Report 2002." [online] from http://www.nni.nikkei.co.jp [accessed January 20, 2004], from Nikkei estimates.

★ 2050 ★
Defense Electronics
SIC: 3812; NAICS: 334511
Leading ASW Sensor Companies Worldwide

The market for anti-submarine warfare sensors will generate an estimated $4.7 billion in sales from 2001-2011. Not included in the top 5 is the multi-contractors category with $1.07 billion in sales and a 22.78% share.

	($ mil.)	Share
Thomson-CSF	$ 1,174.4	24.95%
Raytheon	834.2	17.73
BAE Systems	376.3	8.00
L-3 Communications	371.0	7.88
Ultra Electronics	224.5	4.77

Source: "Changing World for Airborne Anti-Submarine Warfare." [online] available from http:// www.forecast1.com [accessed March 7, 2003], from Forecast International.

★ 2051 ★

Defense Electronics

SIC: 3812; NAICS: 334511

Leading Defense Electronics Makers

Market shares are projected for 2003-2012. Over the decade, the industry is projected to be worth $181 billion, much of this coming from the United States' war on terrorism.

Raytheon Company 12.68%
BAE Systems 8.80
Lockheed Martin 6.86
Northrop Grumman 4.95
Boeing 4.09
Other 37.38

Source: "US Defense Electronics Market to Explode." [Online] from http://www.forecast1.com/press/press85.htm [accessed September 24, 2003], from Forecast International.

★ 2052 ★

Marine Voyage Recorders

SIC: 3812; NAICS: 334511

Worldwide Maritime Voyage Recorder Market, 2003

L-3 Communications Aviation Recorders

Other

Market shares are shown in percent.

L-3 Communications Aviation Recorders . . . 81.0%
Other 19.0

Source: *Sarasota Herald Tribune*, April 1, 2004, p. D1.

★ 2053 ★

Radar and Search Equipment

SIC: 3812; NAICS: 334511

Leading Radar Companies Worldwide

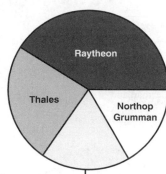

BAE Systems/Ericsson

The market for military radar will generate an estimated $22 billion in sales from 2001-2011.

	($ bil.)	Share
Raytheon	$ 7.1	32.2%
Thales	4.2	18.8
BAE Systems/Ericsson	3.1	13.9
Northop Grumman	2.9	13.1

Source: "Military Radar Market Woth More than $22 Billion." [online] available from http://www.forecast1.com [accessed March 7, 2003], from Forecast International.

★ 2054 ★

Radar and Search Equipment

SIC: 3812; NAICS: 334511

Surveillance and Recon Systems Worldwide

Market shares are shown in percent.

Northrop Grumman 15.8%
Raytheon 9.1
Lockheed Martin 9.0
Other 66.1

Source: *Aviation Week & Space Technology*, April 28, 2003, p. 13, from Frost & Sullivan.

★ 2055 ★
Machine Vision
SIC: 3820; NAICS: 334519

Machine Vision Industry, 2001

The world market had turnover of 7 billion euros.

	(bil.)	Share
Japan	2.3	32.39%
North America	2.3	32.39
Europe	1.8	25.35
Germany	0.7	9.86

Source: ''The German and European Machine Vision Market.'' [online] from http://www.machinevisiononline.org [accessed May 23, 2004].

★ 2056 ★
Machine Vision
SIC: 3820; NAICS: 334519

Machine Vision Industry in Germany, 2000

The industry is shown by segment.

Systems	66.9%
Cameras	14.8
Frame grabbers	8.5
Optics	3.3
Illuminations	2.8
Processors	1.3
Intelligent cameras	0.6
Other	2.2

Source: ''The German and European Machine Vision Market.'' [online] from http://www.machinevisiononline.org [accessed May 23, 2004].

★ 2057 ★
Machine Vision
SIC: 3820; NAICS: 334519

Machine Vision Industry in North America, 2002

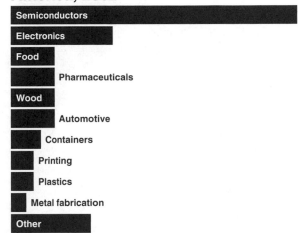

Data show revenues in millions of dollars.

	($ mil.)	Share
Semiconductors	$ 474	39.27%
Electronics	169	14.00
Food	76	6.30
Pharmaceuticals	73	6.05
Wood	72	5.97
Automotive	69	5.72
Containers	48	3.98
Printing	35	2.90
Plastics	35	2.90
Metal fabrication	24	1.99
Other	132	10.94

Source: *Advanced Manufacturing Technology*, July 15, 2003, p. 11, from Frost & Sullivan.

★ 2058 ★
Machine Vision
SIC: 3820; NAICS: 334519

Machine Vision Market in Europe, 2002

The European market was worth about $1.3 billion, behind Japan's $1.9 billion and North America's $1.5 billion industries. Distribution is shown based on revenues.

Cameras	51.7%
Frame grabbers	22.2
Smart cameras	12.9
Compact vision systems	9.8
Smart sensors	3.4

Source: *Vision Systems Design*, August 2003, p. 5, from IMS Research.

★ 2059 ★
Laboratory Instruments
SIC: 3821; NAICS: 339111

HPLC Market Shares Worldwide

The leading end markets for the global industry are shown.

Pharmaceuticals	43.0%
Academic	10.0
Agriculture/food/beverage	8.0
Biotechnology	8.0
Chemical	5.0
Environmental testing	5.0
Other	21.0

Source: *LCGC North America*, October 2003, p. 954.

★ 2060 ★
Laboratory Instruments
SIC: 3821; NAICS: 339111

Laser-based Analytical Equipment, 2002

The market for laboratory analytical techniques that incorporate laser technology was nearly $3 billion for the year. Combined annual growth has been estimated at 13% through 2006.

DNA sequencers	34.0%
Microarrays	21.0
Flow cytometry	11.0
Atomic force microscopy	7.0
Other	27.0

Source: *Spectroscopy*, April 2003, p. 12.

★ 2061 ★
Weather Measuring Equipment
SIC: 3822; NAICS: 334512

World Disposable Sondes Market, 2003

Sondes are small devices that measure temperature, electricity and air pressure in the upper atmosphere.

InterMet	80.0%
Other	20.0

Source: *Grand Rapids Press*, June 10, 2003, p. A17.

★ 2062 ★
Building Control Systems
SIC: 3823; NAICS: 334513

Building Control Systems Industry in North America, 2002

The North American market fell 5% over the previous year and another 5-10% in 2003.

BCS maintenance	37.6%
BCS installations	29.8
Building control systems	10.8
Instruments & actuators	10.1
Other	0.1

Source: *Energy User News*, September 2003, p. 18.

★ 2063 ★
Control Equipment
SIC: 3823; NAICS: 334513

Global Temperature Controller Uses, 2002 and 2005

The level of temperature controller use is expected to fall as more control users employ PLCs (programmable logic controllers), DCSs (distributed control systems) and PCs (personal computers) to manage their own processes. Data for 2005 are forecasts.

	2002	2005
Temperature controllers	56.2%	48.4%
PLCs	25.1	29.2
DCSs	11.2	13.0
Personal computers	7.5	9.4

Source: *Process Heating*, September 2003, p. 12, from Venture Development Corp.

★ 2064 ★
Automatic Meter Readers
SIC: 3824; NAICS: 334514

AMR Market by Type in North America

By the end of 2002, 49.3 million AMR units were shipped to all utilities in North America. By 2002, more water AMR units were shipped than gas.

Mobile RF	64.0%
PLC	18.0
Fixed RF	17.0
Telephone	1.0

Source: *Water World*, July-August 2003, p. 33.

★ 2065 ★
Voting Machines
SIC: 3824; NAICS: 333313

Voting Machine Market, 2002

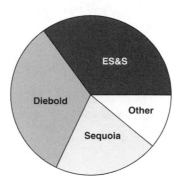

Sales of direct recording electronic vendors totaled $345 million in 2002. The category ''other'' includes Hart InterCivic, VoteHere.com, and Unilect.

ES&S	35.0%
Diebold	33.0
Sequoia	21.0
Other	11.0

Source: *Austin Chronicle*, February 20, 2004, p. NA, from Diebold's 2003 annual shareholder report.

★ 2066 ★
Analytical Instruments
SIC: 3826; NAICS: 334516

Analytical Instrumentation Market Worldwide, 2002

Shares are by end use industry for the laser-based analytical instruments market.

DNA sequencers	34.0%
Microarrays	21.0
Flow cytometry	11.0
Atomic force microscopy	7.0
MALDI-TOF MS	6.0
Biosensors	4.0
Particle characterization	4.0
Raman	3.0
Confocal microscopes	3.0
Other	7.0

Source: *Spectroscopy*, February 2004, p. 43, from Strategic Directions International.

★ 2067 ★
Analytical Instruments
SIC: 3826; NAICS: 334516

Process Control Market Worldwide

Shares are by process control type used in the food and pharmaceutical industries.

Inspection	64.0%
Spectroscopy	17.0
Water analysis	14.0
Other	5.0

Source: *Spectroscopy*, February 2004, p. S42, from Process Analytics Consulting.

★ 2068 ★
Bar Coding
SIC: 3827; NAICS: 333314

Bar Code Hardware Sales, 2002

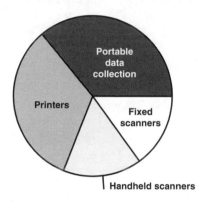

The industry will soon shift from the standard 12 digit bar code (in place for three decades) to a 13 digit bar code.

Portable data collection terminals	36.1%
Printers	32.9
Handheld scanners	15.7
Fixed scanners	15.3

Source: *Investor's Business Daily*, December 1, 2003, p. A8, from company reports, First Call, and Raymond James & Associates.

★ 2069 ★
Bar Coding
SIC: 3827; NAICS: 333314

Bar Coding Printers Worldwide, 2003 and 2007

Total sales worldwide are forecasted to grow from $1.5 billion in 2003 to $2.1 billion in 2007.

	2002	2007
Stationary thermal	64.1%	67.6%
Non-thermal	28.0	23.2
Portable thermal	7.9	9.2

Source: *Modern Materials Handling*, September 2003, p. 1, from VDC Corp.

★ 2070 ★
Biometrics
SIC: 3827; NAICS: 333314

Biometric Technology Market Shares, 2002

Market revenues are projected to climb from $277.8 million in 2002 to $1.37 billion in 2005.

Finger-scan	52.1%
Middleware	13.2
Facial-scan	12.4
Hand-scan	10.0
Iris scan	5.9
Voice scan	4.4
Signature scan	2.1

Source: *Security Director's Report*, June 2003, p. 5, from International Biometric Group.

★ 2071 ★

Biometrics

SIC: 3827; NAICS: 333314

Sensor Fingerprint Market Worldwide, 2002

The silicon sensor fingerprint market was worth $9.1 million in 20002, although the market has been forecasted to reach $1 billion in 2009 by Frost & Sullivan.

AuthenTec	65.0%
Other	35.0

Source: *Electronic Business*, January 2004, p. 58, from Frost & Sullivan.

★ 2072 ★

Testing Instruments

SIC: 3827; NAICS: 333314

Global Spectroscopy Software Market, 2003

Spectroscopes are measuring instruments that are almost always connected to computers which run specialized software to manage the instrument's operation and data collection. The total world market for spectroscopy software was estimated to be about $525 million in 2003. Shares are shown for the three types of spectrometry.

Molecular spectrometry	55.0%
Atomic spectroscopy	33.0
Mass spectrometry	12.0

Source: *Spectroscopy*, February 2004, p. 14.

★ 2073 ★

Testing Instruments

SIC: 3827; NAICS: 333314

Raman Spectroscopy Demand by Industry, 2002

Shares are by industrial application of Raman spectroscopy.

Polymers	18.0%
Pharmaceuticals	15.0
Government	14.0
Organic chemicals	12.0
Academic	11.0
Metals	10.0
Hospital / Clinical	6.0
Biotechnology	4.0

Semi electronics	3.0%
Other	7.0

Source: *Spectroscopy*, November 2003, p. 12, from Strategic Directional International.

★ 2074 ★

Aquaculture Equipment

SIC: 3829; NAICS: 334519

Aquaculture Market in Mindanao, Philippines

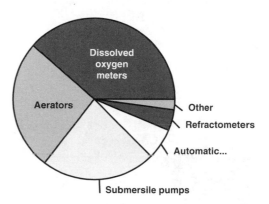

Mindanao is a vital agricultural region of the Philippines. It accounts for 25% of total Philippine aquaculture equipment. Total market size was $7.3 million.

Dissolved oxygen meters	37.0%
Aerators	25.0
Submersile pumps	22.0
Automatic feeders	6.0
Refractometers	4.0
Other	2.0

Source: "Aquaculture Equipment and Supplies Market in Mindanao." [online] from http://www.usatrade.gov [accessed June 1, 2004].

★ 2075 ★
Fuel Testing Equipment
SIC: 3829; NAICS: 334519

Contracted Fuel Testing Industry

The company has over 75% of the market for contracted fuel quality testing and, according to the source "a track record of 600,000 samples, since pioneering this service in 1980."

DNVPS 75.0%
Other 25.0

Source: "DNV Petroleum Services Opens Laboratory in Algeciras." [online] available from http://www2.dnv.com [accessed April 9, 2003].

★ 2076 ★
Thermometers
SIC: 3829; NAICS: 334514

Top Thermometers (Personal), 2004

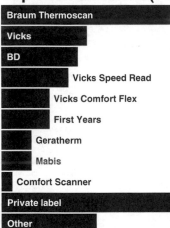

Brands are ranked by sales at supermarkets, drugstores and discount stores (but not Wal-Mart) for the year ended January 25, 2004.

	($ mil.)	Share
Braum Thermoscan	$ 20.2	18.18%
Vicks	10.3	9.27
BD	9.3	8.37
Vicks Speed Read	7.7	6.93
Vicks Comfort Flex	5.6	5.04
First Years	5.3	4.77
Geratherm	3.4	3.06
Mabis	2.9	2.61
Comfort Scanner	1.4	1.26
Private label	33.7	30.33
Other	11.3	10.17

Source: *MMR*, April 19, 2004, p. 59, from Information Resources Inc.

★ 2077 ★
Medical Equipment
SIC: 3841; NAICS: 339113

Assistive Technology Market in Switzerland

The assistive technology market for mobility and speech impairments is a $1.6 million market. FST stands for Swiss Foundation for Electronic Aids for Handicapped People.

FST 75.0%
Other 25.0

Source: "Advanced Assistive Technology Market." [online] from http://www.export.gov [accessed May 4, 2004].

★ 2078 ★
Medical Equipment
SIC: 3841; NAICS: 339112

Dry-Powder Inhaler Market

Market shares are shown in percent.

Advair Diskus 82.0%
Other 18.0

Source: *Investor's Business Daily*, December 8, 2003, p. A9.

★ 2079 ★
Medical Equipment
SIC: 3841; NAICS: 339112

Home Healthcare Market in Japan

Japan's population is aging more quickly than any other developed nations. By 2025, a quarter of the population is thought to be over the age of 65 years of age. The home health care market was valued at 1.9 trillion yen in 2001 ($9.9 billion). Market sizes are shown in billions of yen.

Diapers . . . . ¥ 61.2
Wheelchairs 19.3
Bedsore preventing disorders 5.4
Stair lifts 4.1
Push carts 3.1
Sitting furniture 1.8
Walking frames 1.2
Walking sticks 1.2

Source: "Home Healthcare Market." [online] from http://www.usatrade.gov [accessed February 1, 2004], from GOJ Ministry of Economy, Trade and Industry, Japan.

★ 2080 ★
Medical Equipment
SIC: 3841; NAICS: 339112

Imaging Agent Market Shares Worldwide, 2000

North America had 41% of the $3.7 billion industry, followed by Japan at 35% of sales.

Amersham Health	35.0%
Bracco	19.0
Tyco	15.0
Schering	13.0
DuPont	10.0
Other	8.0

Source: *Medical Devices & Surgical Technology Week*, April 7, 2002, p. 21, from Decision Resources.

★ 2081 ★
Medical Equipment
SIC: 3841; NAICS: 334510

In-Patient Medical Monitors in the U.K., 2003

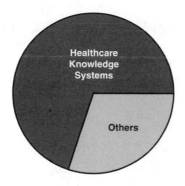

Market shares are shown in percent.

Healthcare Knowledge Systems International Ltd.	70.0%
Others	30.0

Source: *The Daily Deal*, April 8, 2004, p. NA.

★ 2082 ★
Medical Equipment
SIC: 3841; NAICS: 339112

Insulin Pump Market

Medtronic has 75 - 80% of the market. Insulin pump sales reached $370 million in 2002.

Medtronic	80.0%
Other	20.0

Source: *The Business Journal (Minneapolis - St. Paul)*, October 27, 2003, p. NA.

★ 2083 ★
Medical Equipment
SIC: 3841; NAICS: 339112

Pacemaker Market Shares

Market shares are shown in percent. St. Jude or Guidant typically claim second place.

Medtronic	52.0%
Other	48.0

Source: *Hospital Materials Management*, June 2003, p. 1.

★ 2084 ★
Medical Equipment
SIC: 3841; NAICS: 339112

Patient Monitoring Industry, 2003

Market sizes are shown in millions of dollars.

Diabetes	$ 2,923
Sleep apnea	639
Anesthesia	529
Defib	437
Telemetry	423
Blood pressure	415
Cardiovascular	306
TM monitoring	242
Blood gas	169
Fetal	131
Respiratory gases	97
EEG monitoring	96

Source: *Healthcare Purchasing News*, December 2003, p. 40, from Frost & Sullivan.

★ 2085 ★
Medical Equipment
SIC: 3841; NAICS: 339113

Safety Needle and Syringe Market

Market shares are shown in percent.

BD 98.0%
Other 2.0

Source: *Hospital Materials Management*, June 2003, p. 6.

★ 2086 ★
Medical Equipment
SIC: 3841; NAICS: 339112

Sleep Apnea Market

People with sleep apnea stop breathing during the night — in some cases as frequently as 100 times. The National Institute of Health believes 18 million are afflicted. Market shares are estimated.

Respironics 37.0%
ResMed 31.0
Tyco/Mallinckrodt 13.0
Fisher & Paykel 5.0
Vital Signs 3.0
Sunrise Medical 3.0
Other 8.0

Source: *Investor's Business Daily*, May 21, 2003, p. A7, from company reports, SG Cowen, and First Call.

★ 2087 ★
Medical Equipment
SIC: 3841; NAICS: 339112

Top Pacemaker/ICD Makers

The total market is valued at $4.9 billion.

Medtronic 50.0%
Guidant 31.0
St. Jude Medical 16.0
Biotronik 2.5
ELA Medical 0.5

Source: *Hospital Materials Management*, September 2003, p. 2, from Biotronik.

★ 2088 ★
Medical Equipment
SIC: 3841; NAICS: 339112

Top Trocar Makers

Trocars are instruments used to puncture body cavities and drain fluid. The company has 65-70% of the market.

Johnson & Johnson 70.0%
Other 30.0

Source: *Hospital Materials Management*, September 2003, p. 2.

★ 2089 ★
First Aid Products
SIC: 3842; NAICS: 339113

Top First Aid Kit Brands, 2004

Brands are ranked by sales at supermarkets, drugstores and discount stores (but not Wal-Mart) for the year ended January 25, 2004.

	($ mil.)	Share
Johnson & Johnson	$ 5.7	38.26%
First Aid Only	5.4	36.24
Total Resources	0.7	4.70
J&J 1st Aid To Go	0.7	4.70
Band Aid	0.5	3.36
Coleman	0.4	2.68
Curad	0.3	2.01
Swab Plus	0.2	1.34
3M Nexcare	0.2	1.34

Continued on next page.

★ 2089 ★

[Continued]
First Aid Products
SIC: 3842; NAICS: 339113

Top First Aid Kit Brands, 2004

Brands are ranked by sales at supermarkets, drugstores and discount stores (but not Wal-Mart) for the year ended January 25, 2004.

	($ mil.)	Share
Little Remedies	$ 0.1	0.67%
Other	0.7	4.70

Source: *MMR*, April 19, 2004, p. 59, from Information Resources Inc.

★ 2090 ★

First Aid Products
SIC: 3842; NAICS: 339113

Top First Aid Ointment Brands, 2004

Brands are ranked by sales at supermarkets, drug stores and discount stores (but not Wal-Mart) for the year ended January 25, 2004.

	($ mil.)	Share
Neosporin Plus	$ 47.0	12.35%
Neosporin	38.7	10.17
Mederma	21.4	5.62
Bactine	11.3	2.97
Aquaphor	11.3	2.97
Solarcaine	10.5	2.76
Polysporin	8.2	2.16
Becton Dickinson	7.2	1.89
Betadine	5.8	1.52
Private label	138.5	36.40
Other	80.6	21.18

Source: *MMR*, April 19, 2004, p. 59, from Information Resources Inc.

★ 2091 ★

First Aid Products
SIC: 3842; NAICS: 339113

Top First Aid Tape/Bandage/Gauze Brands, 2003

Market shares are shown based on drug store sales.

Johnson & Johnson	15.50%
Band-Aid	13.90

Nexcare	3.50%
New Skin	2.60
J&J Kling	2.30
J&J Hurt-Free	1.90
Nexcare Active Strips	1.60
Curity Curad	1.50
Curad	1.50
Curity Kerlix	1.40
Private label	22.48
Other	31.82

Source: *Chain Drug Review*, January 5, 2004, p. 45.

★ 2092 ★

First Aid Products
SIC: 3842; NAICS: 339113

Top Heat/Ice Pack Brands, 2004

Brands are ranked by sales at supermarkets, drugstores and discount stores (but not Wal-Mart) for the year ended January 25, 2004.

	($ mil.)	Share
Therma Care	$ 58.2	46.08%
Thera-Med	9.2	7.28
Ace	7.4	5.86
Bed Buddy	6.5	5.15
3M Nexcare	4.2	3.33
Playtex Heat Therapy	3.6	2.85
Faultless	3.0	2.38
Tru Fit Polar Preene	2.6	2.06
Other	31.6	25.02

Source: *MMR*, April 19, 2004, p. 59, from Information Resources Inc.

★ 2093 ★

First Aid Products

SIC: 3842; NAICS: 339113

Top Insect First Aid Treatments, 2004

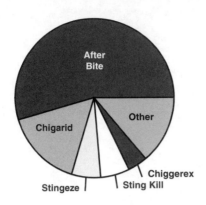

Brands are ranked by sales at supermarkets, drugstores and discount stores (but not Wal-Mart) for the year ended January 25, 2004.

	($ mil.)	Share
After Bite	$ 2.8	54.90%
Chigarid	0.8	15.69
Stingeze	0.3	5.88
Sting Kill	0.3	5.88
Chiggerex	0.2	3.92
Other	0.7	13.73

Source: *MMR*, April 19, 2004, p. 59, from Information Resources Inc.

★ 2094 ★

Hearing Aids

SIC: 3842; NAICS: 334510

Hearing Aid Sales by State, 2003

Sales are for the first nine months of the year. Total for the period was 1,554,654 units. ITE's (in the ear) share of sales was 62%, BTE (behind the ear) 23.6%, full-shell 27.3%.

	Units	Share
California	142,568	7.21%
Florida	96,722	4.89
Texas	74,358	3.76
New York	64,721	3.27
Pennsylvania	60,804	3.08
Michigan	59,052	2.99
Ohio	52,534	2.66
Illinois	49,154	2.49
Washington	35,607	1.80
Indiana	33,307	1.68

	Units	Share
New Jersey	30,604	1.55%
Other	1,277,591	64.62

Source: *The Hearing Journal*, December 2003, p. 11, from Hearing Industries Association.

★ 2095 ★

Hearing Aids

SIC: 3842; NAICS: 334510

Top Hearing Aid Makers Worldwide, 2001

Shares are shown based on a market of 6 million devices.

Siemens	21.0%
William Demant	15.0
Sarkey	15.0
Phonak	15.0
GN Resound	15.0
Widex	8.0
Other	11.0

Source: "Franchising in Hearing Aid Business." [online] available from http://www.export.gov [accessed December 1, 2003].

★ 2096 ★

Orthopedic Appliances

SIC: 3842; NAICS: 339113

Fixation Market, 2003

Distribution of the $1.17 billion market has been estimated.

	($ mil.)	Share
Internal fixation	$ 460	39.28%
Craniomaxillofacial fixation	185	15.80
Allograft & bone substitute materials	176	15.03
External fixation	165	14.09
Electrical simulation	160	13.66
Growth factor platelets	25	2.13

Source: "2003 Market Graphs." [online] available from http://www.biomet.com/financials/market_graphs.cfm, from Biomet.

★ 2097 ★
Orthopedic Appliances
SIC: 3842; NAICS: 339113
Leading Hip Implant Makers Worldwide, 2002

Market shares are estimated in percent.

Zimmer/Centerpulse 30.0%
Stryker Howmedica Osteonics 24.0
DePuy Orthopedics 22.0
Biomet 13.0
Smith & Nephew Orthopedics 6.0
Wright Medical 2.0
Other 3.0

Source: *Financial Times*, June 4, 2003, p. 17, from HealthPoint.

★ 2098 ★
Orthopedic Appliances
SIC: 3842; NAICS: 339113
Leading Knee/Hip/Spine Implant Makers Worldwide

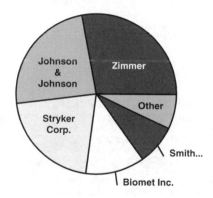

Market shares are shown in percent.

Zimmer 28.0%
Johnson & Johnson 24.0
Stryker Corp. 21.0
Biomet Inc. 12.0
Smith & Nephew 8.0
Other 7.0

Source: *Indianapolis Star*, October 3, 2003, p. NA, from ThinkEquity Partners.

★ 2099 ★
Orthopedic Appliances
SIC: 3842; NAICS: 339113
Leading Knee Implant Makers Worldwide, 2002

Market shares are estimated in percent.

Zimmer/Centerpulse 29.0%
DePuy Orthopedics 25.0
Stryker Howmedica Osteonics 21.0
Biomet 12.0
Other 25.0

Source: *Financial Times*, June 4, 2003, p. 17, from HealthPoint.

★ 2100 ★
Orthopedic Appliances
SIC: 3842; NAICS: 339113
Leading Knee Joint Makers in South Korea

The market was worth about $89.2 million in 2002. According to the source, 100% of the market is from imports. Knee and hip implants make up 98-99% of demand (knees 63%, hips 35%). Stryker/Howmedica lead the hip joint market with a 25.5% share.

DePuy 32.8%
Stryker/Howmedica 29.5
Zimmer 23.2
Other 14.5

Source: "Orthetics." [online] from http://www.usatrade.gov [accessed January 5, 2004], from U.S. Commercial Service.

★ 2101 ★
Orthopedic Appliances
SIC: 3842; NAICS: 339113
Musculoskeletal Product Market, 2003

Distribution of the $9.53 billion market has been estimated.

	($ mil.)	Share
Reconstructive devices	$3,810	39.98%
Spinal products	2,180	22.88
Fixation	1,170	12.28
Arthroscopy	770	8.08

Continued on next page.

★ 2101 ★
[Continued]
Orthopedic Appliances
SIC: 3842; NAICS: 339113

Musculoskeletal Product Market, 2003

Distribution of the $9.53 billion market has been estimated.

	($ mil.)	Share
Softgoods & bracing	$ 525	5.51%
Dental reconstructive implants . .	390	4.09
O.R. supplies	300	3.15
Powered surgical equipment . . .	205	2.15
Bone cements & accessories . . .	180	1.89

Source: "2003 Market Graphs." [online] available from http://www.biomet.com/financials/market_graphs.cfm, from Biomet.

★ 2102 ★
Orthopedic Appliances
SIC: 3842; NAICS: 339113

Orthopedic Reconstruction Market, 2003

Distribution of the $3.81 billion market has been estimated.

	($ mil.)	Share
Knees	$ 2,035	53.41%
Hips	1,625	42.65
Shoulder	100	2.62
Other	50	1.31

Source: "2003 Market Graphs." [online] available from http://www.biomet.com/financials/market_graphs.cfm, from Biomet.

★ 2103 ★
Orthopedic Appliances
SIC: 3842; NAICS: 339113

Orthopedic Reconstruction Market Worldwide

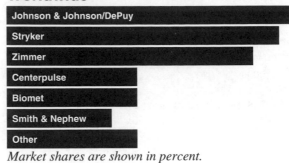

Market shares are shown in percent.

Johnson & Johnson/DePuy	22.0%
Stryker	21.0
Zimmer	19.0
Centerpulse	10.0
Biomet	10.0
Smith & Nephew	8.0
Other	10.0

Source: *Financial Times*, August 7, 2003, p. 13, from Thomson Datastream and Dresdner Kleinwort Wasserstein.

★ 2104 ★
Orthopedic Appliances
SIC: 3842; NAICS: 339113

Orthopedics Industry, 2002

The U.S. is the world's largest market for orthopedics. The market was valued at $3 billion in 2002, having grown about 4% during the previous four years.

Knee implants	30.5%
Hip implants	26.2
Trauma devices	22.7
Spinal implants	20.6

Source: *Datamonitor Industry Market Research*, November 1, 2003, p. NA, from Datamonitor.

★ **2105** ★

Orthopedic Appliances

SIC: 3842; NAICS: 339113

Orthopedics Industry in Belgium, 2002

The orthopedics market in Belgium was valued at $61.2 million in 2002. It has about 2.5% of the European market.

Hip implants	43.7%
Knee implants	34.9
Trauma devices	14.1
Spinal implants	7.3

Source: *Datamonitor Industry Market Research*, November 1, 2003, p. NA, from Datamonitor.

★ **2106** ★

Orthopedic Appliances

SIC: 3842; NAICS: 339113

Orthopedics Industry in Canada, 2002

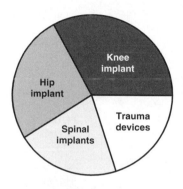

The market was valued at $166.4 million in 2002. Canada represented about 2% of the global market.

Knee implant	32.7%
Hip implant	26.3
Spinal implants	21.2
Trauma devices	19.8

Source: *Datamonitor Industry Market Research*, November 1, 2003, p. NA, from Datamonitor.

★ **2107** ★

Orthopedic Appliances

SIC: 3842; NAICS: 339113

Orthopedics Industry in France, 2002

The orthopedics market in France was valued at $433.8 million in 2002. It is the largest market in Europe and takes in more than one quarter of global orthopedic revenue.

Hip implants	40.0%
Knee implants	35.2
Trauma devices	15.7
Spinal implants	9.2

Source: *Datamonitor Industry Market Research*, November 1, 2003, p. NA, from Datamonitor.

★ **2108** ★

Orthopedic Appliances

SIC: 3842; NAICS: 339113

Orthopedics Industry in Spain

The market was worth about $12 million in 2002. Growth is about 7-8% annually. The market is split between 65% tailored and 35% premanufactured devices.

Thoracic	20.0%
Knee	16.0
Hip	14.0
Elbow	14.0
Shoulder	12.0
Leg	12.0
Wrist and ankle	10.0
Cranial	2.0

Source: "Orthetics." [online] from http://www.usatrade.gov [accessed January 5, 2004], from U.S. Commercial Service.

★ 2109 ★

Orthopedic Appliances

SIC: 3842; NAICS: 339113

Spinal Product Market, 2003

Distribution of the $2.18 billion market has been estimated.

	($ mil.)	Share
Plates, rods, screws	$ 830	38.07%
Machined allograft	325	14.91
Growth factors platelets, vertebroplasty	295	13.53
Fusion cages	295	13.53
Allograft/bone substitute materials	235	10.78
Electrical stimulation	200	9.17

Source: "2003 Market Graphs." [online] available from http://www.biomet.com/financials/market_graphs.cfm, from Biomet.

★ 2110 ★

Orthopedic Appliances

SIC: 3842; NAICS: 339113

Top Orthopaedic Leaders Worldwide, 2001

Market shares are shown in percent.

Johnson & Johnson/DePuy	16.6%
Stryker	14.2
Smith & Nephew/Centerpulse	12.3
Zimmer	9.2
Biomet	7.9
Synthes Stratec	6.7
B Braun	6.2
Medtronic	4.6
Other	22.3

Source: *Financial Times*, March 21, 2003, p. 25, from Morgan Stanley.

★ 2111 ★

Stents

SIC: 3842; NAICS: 339113

Coronary Stent Market

Market shares are shown based on dollars.

Cordis Corp.	69.2%
Other	30.8

Source: *Cardiovascular Week*, February 2, 2004, p. 62, from CathTrak Market Watch.

★ 2112 ★

Stents

SIC: 3842; NAICS: 339113

Drug-Coated Stent Market, 2006

A stent is a medical device, a metal mesh device, that is designed to be implanted in an artery to keep it open. Market shares are forecasted in percent. Boston Scientific's share is estimated to fall from 65% in 2004. Data are forecasted.

Boston Scientific	40.0%
Johnson & Johnson	31.0
Other	29.0

Source: *Investor's Business Daily*, September 11, 2003, p. A7, from Morgan Stanley.

★ 2113 ★

Stents

SIC: 3842; NAICS: 339113

Stent Graft Market

Medtronic's had its stent-graft device approved in 1999. Recent competitors include W.L. Gore & Assoc. of Delaware and Cook of Indiana. Market shares are shown in percent.

Medtronic	65.0%
Other	35.0

Source: *San Jose Mercury News*, July 13, 2003, p. NA.

★ 2114 ★
Surgical Gloves
SIC: 3842; NAICS: 339113
Occupational Glove Market

The market is valued at $1.9 billion.

Ansell	18.0%
Best	6.0
Other	76.0

Source: *European Rubber Journal*, November 2003, p. 18, from Neilson, IMS, and internal estimates.

★ 2115 ★
Surgical Gloves
SIC: 3842; NAICS: 339113
Surgical Glove Market

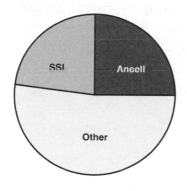

The market is valued at $600 million.

Ansell	25.0%
SSL	23.0
Other	52.0

Source: *European Rubber Journal*, November 2003, p. 18, from Neilson, IMS, and internal estimates.

★ 2116 ★
Surgical Gloves
SIC: 3842; NAICS: 339113
Surgical Glove Market, 2002

The market has been valued at $302 million with $211 million of that coming from sales to acute care facilities and $91 million coming from alternative care sites (such as surgicenters). 308 million units are thought to be sold each year.

Regent	36.3%
Cardinal	31.8
Ansell	25.8
Other	6.1

Source: *Healthcare Purchasing News*, June 2003, p. 26, from IMS Health and Cardinal Health.

★ 2117 ★
Surgical Supplies
SIC: 3842; NAICS: 339113
Disposable Surgical Drapes Market

The United States has 37% of the $544 million global market.

Kimberly-Clark	38.0%
Allegiance	24.0
Medline	19.0
Johnson & Johnson	13.0
Maxxim Medical	6.0

Source: *Hospital Materials Management*, January 2004, p. 11, from Kalorama Information.

★ 2118 ★
Surgical Supplies
SIC: 3842; NAICS: 339113
Implantable Device Demand, 2002 and 2007

Overall sales are forecasted to increase from $14.6 billion in 2002 to $24.35 billion in 2007. Strongest gains in demand are expected to be cardiac resynchronization devices, implantable cardioverter defibrillators and drug-eluting stents.

	2002	2007	Share
Cardiac implants	$ 7,080	$ 13,740	56.43%
Orthopedic implants . . .	6,410	8,730	35.85
Other implantable devices .	1,120	1,880	7.72

Source: *Health Care Strategic Management*, March 2004, p. 4, from Freedonia Group.

★ 2119 ★
Surgical Supplies
SIC: 3842; NAICS: 339113
Implantable Device Market

Demand for implantable devices will increase 11% annually. Data are in millions of dollars.

	2002	2007
Cardiac implants	$ 7,080	$ 13,740
Orthopedic implants	6,410	8,730
Other	1,120	1,880

Source: *Hospital Materials Management*, March 2004, p. 3, from Freedonia Group.

★ 2120 ★
Surgical Supplies
SIC: 3842; NAICS: 339113
Leading Ear Implant Makers Worldwide

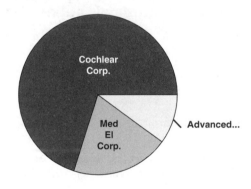

Market shares are estimated in percent.

Cochlear Corp.	70.0%
Med El Corp.	20.0
Advanced Bionics	10.0

Source: *San Fernando Valley Business Journal*, August 18, 2003, p. 12.

★ 2121 ★
Surgical Supplies
SIC: 3842; NAICS: 339112
Manual Ligation Clip Market Worldwide

Ligation clips are used as replacements for sutures to block off blood vessels cut during surgery. Market shares are shown in percent.

Weck Closure Systems	70.0%
Other	30.0

Source: *Packaging Digest*, September 2002, p. 32.

★ 2122 ★
Surgical Supplies
SIC: 3842; NAICS: 339113
Men's Bladder Control Market Worldwide

American Medical has the lion's share of the world market.

American Medical	90.0%
Other	10.0

Source: *Investor's Business Daily*, April 23, 2004, p. A5.

★ 2123 ★
Surgical Supplies
SIC: 3842; NAICS: 339113
Sterilization Wrap Market

Data show the company's estimate of its own share. Some analysts believe this figure to be high.

Kimberly-Clark	95.0%
Other	5.0

Source: *Healthcare Purchasing News*, May 2003, p. 54.

★ 2124 ★
Surgical Supplies
SIC: 3842; NAICS: 339113
Top Suture Makers

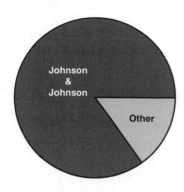

The company has 80-85% of the market.

Johnson & Johnson 85.0%
Other 15.0

Source: *Hospital Materials Management*, September 2003, p. 2.

★ 2125 ★
Surgical Supplies
SIC: 3842; NAICS: 339113
Ventricular Support Systems

The BVS-500 has 70% market shares in hospitals that perform more than 500 open heart hospitals annually.

BVS 5000 . . . . 70.0%
Other 30.0

Source: *Surgical Litigation & Law Weekly*, May 28, 2004, p. 2.

★ 2126 ★
Dental Equipment
SIC: 3843; NAICS: 339114
Artificial Teeth Market

The company has 75-80% of the market based on revenues and 67% of the market based on units.

Dentsply 80.0%
Other 20.0

Source: *Mondaq Business Briefing*, November 18, 2003, p. NA.

★ 2127 ★
Dental Equipment
SIC: 3843; NAICS: 339114
Dental Equipment Industry in Japan, 2001

Figures show total sales. There were about 64,297 dental clinics in the country. There were 90,857 dentists, 37,244 lab technicians and 67,376 hygienists.

	($ mil.)	Share
Dental materials	$ 966.7	66.21%
Dental devices	419.7	28.74
X-ray equipment	55.2	3.78
Dental film	12.2	0.84
X-ray related equipment	6.3	0.43

Source: ''Building Products.'' [online] from http://www.usatrade.gov [accessed January 5, 2004], from U.S. Commercial Service, *Annual Production Statistics of Pharmaceuticals Etc.*, and Ministry of Health Labor and Welfare.

★ 2128 ★
Dental Equipment
SIC: 3843; NAICS: 339114
Dental Laser Market

Market shares are shown in percent. In April 2003, Forbes named Biolase among the top ten fastest growing technology copmanies.

Biolase Technology 80.0%
Other 20.0

Source: *Knight Ridder/Tribune Business News*, July 13, 2003, p. NA.

★ 2129 ★
Dental Equipment
SIC: 3843; NAICS: 339114

Dental Reconstructive Implants Worldwide

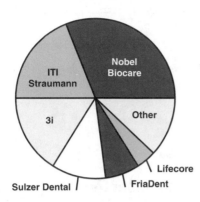

The $740 million market is shown by company.

Nobel Biocare	31.0%
ITI Straumann	19.0
3i	16.0
Sulzer Dental	11.0
FriaDent	7.0
Lifecore	4.0
Other	12.0

Source: "Biomet 2001 Annual Report." [Online] from http://www.biomet.com/investors/2001/3i.html [accessed Janaury 8, 2003].

★ 2130 ★
Dental Equipment
SIC: 3843; NAICS: 339114

Intraoral Camera Market

Dentists insert these cameras to show the inside of a patient's mouth to the patient. Market shares are shown in percent.

RF	85.0%
Other	15.0

Source: *Japan Inc.*, July 2003, p. 10.

★ 2131 ★
Screening Equipment
SIC: 3844; NAICS: 334517

Luggage and Parcel Screening Market

Figures are in millions of dollars.

2010	$ 3,500
2006	1,200
2003	700

Source: *Business Wire*, April 28, 2004, p. NA.

★ 2132 ★
Electromedical Equipment
SIC: 3845; NAICS: 334510, 334517

Market for MRI Result Readers

The company also has 80% of the worldwide market for monitors used for magnetic resonance imagine reader results.

Invivo Corp.	90.0%
Other	10.0

Source: *Mergers & Acquisitions*, December 8, 2003, p. NA.

★ 2133 ★
Electromedical Equipment
SIC: 3845; NAICS: 334510

Medical Robotics Market

The market for medical robotics and computer-assisted surgical equipment grew from $105 million in 1999 to an estimated $245 million in 2002. By 2007, it is forecasted to reach $673 million.

	2002	2007
Surgical navigation systems	61.2%	52.0%
Surgical robots	20.4	32.6

Source: *Industries in Transition*, June 2003, p. NA, from Business Communications Inc.

★ 2134 ★
Electromedical Equipment
SIC: 3845; NAICS: 334517

Top MRI System Makers Worldwide, 2002

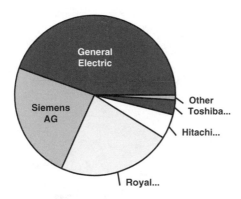

Market shares are shown based on total worldwide sales of 346 billion yen.

General Electric	45.0%
Siemens AG	24.0
Royal Philips Electronics	23.0
Hitachi Medical Corp.	5.0
Toshiba Corp.	2.5
Other	0.5

Source: ''Market Share Survey Report 2002.'' [online] from http://www.nni.nikkei.co.jp [accessed January 20, 2004], from Nikkei estimates.

★ 2135 ★
Contact Lenses
SIC: 3851; NAICS: 339115

Cosmetic Contact Lens Market Worldwide

CIBA Vision has a lock on the cosmetic lens market because of its acquisition of Wesley Jessen Vision Care in 2001.

CIBA Vision	85.0%
Other	15.0

Source: ''Contact Lens Market.'' [online] available from http://www.optistock.com [accessed December 1, 2003].

★ 2136 ★
Contact Lenses
SIC: 3851; NAICS: 339115

New Contact Lens Patients, 2002

Figures show new soft contact lens patients by type.

Planned replacement	20.0%
Reusable/traditional	16.0
1-day disposable	2.0
Other disposable	62.0

Source: *Investor's Business Daily*, June 24, 2003, p. A10, from OptiStock MarketWatch and Health Products Research Inc.

★ 2137 ★
Contact Lenses
SIC: 3851; NAICS: 339115

Top Contact Lens Makers

Market shares are shown in percent.

J&J	48.0%
Ocular Sciences	23.0
Other	29.0

Source: *Optistock Market Watch*, October 2003, p. NA, from FTN Midwest Research.

★ 2138 ★
Contact Lenses
SIC: 3851; NAICS: 339115

Top Toric Lens Makers

Market shares are shown in percent.

CooperVision	34.0%
CIBA Vision	30.0
Other	36.0

Source: *Optistock Market Watch*, October 2003, p. NA, from FTN Midwest Research.

★ 2139 ★
Optical Goods
SIC: 3851; NAICS: 339115
Lens Sales by Type, 2003

Figures are projected.

	2001	2003
Conventional plastic	57.5%	56.6%
Polycarbonates	29.0	31.9
Mid/high-latex	10.5	10.0
Glass	3.0	1.5

Source: *20/20 Magazine*, January 1, 2003, p. NA, from Jobson Optical Research.

★ 2140 ★
Optical Goods
SIC: 3851; NAICS: 339115
Optical Goods Sales, 2003

Market shares are shown in percent.

Lenses/treatments	54.5%
Ophthalmic frames	31.5
Contact lenses	11.8
Plano sunglasses and sunclips	3.7

Source: *Vision Monday*, March 10, 2004, p. NA, from Jobson Optical Research.

★ 2141 ★
Optical Goods
SIC: 3851; NAICS: 339115
Visco-Elastic Market

Visco-elastic products are used in occular surgery.

Alcon	50.0%
Pfizer	15.0
Other	35.0

Source: *Mergers & Acquisitions Report*, August 4, 2003, p. NA.

★ 2142 ★
Cameras
SIC: 3861; NAICS: 333315
Camera Market in France

The camera market is worth about 222 million units annually.

35-mm compact cameras	56.0%
35-mm reflex cameras	27.0
APS cameras	12.0
Digital cameras	5.0

Source: *Echos*, April 11, 2002, p. 11.

★ 2143 ★
Cameras
SIC: 3861; NAICS: 333315
Camera Sales by Type, 2003

APS (Advanced Photo System) camera sales have fallen from 10.5 million to less than 2 million. Canon and Fuji each have about 30% of the APS market. Kodak also had 30% of the segment although it has decided to leave the U.S. 35mm camera market and focus on overseas markets.

	(mil.)	Share
Digital	12.8	56.14%
35mm	8.4	36.84
APS	1.6	7.02

Source: *USA TODAY*, January 14, 2004, p. 5B, from Photo Marketing Association International.

★ 2144 ★
Cameras
SIC: 3861; NAICS: 339115
Digital Camera Market Worldwide

The 27.5 million digital camera sold represented 30% of the total 90.5 million still cameras sold worldwide.

	1999 (bil.)	2002 (bil.)	Share
United States	2.0	9.9	35.87%
Japan	1.8	6.9	25.00
Europe	1.1	8.0	28.99
Other	0.6	2.8	10.14

Source: *Photo Marketing*, June 2003, p. 41, from GfK Marketing Services.

★ 2145 ★
Cameras
SIC: 3861; NAICS: 333315

Leading Digital Camera Makers Worldwide, 2003

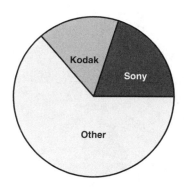

Market shares are shown in percent.

Sony	22.0%
Kodak	18.0
Other	70.0

Source: *Wall Street Journal*, March 10, 2004, p. B4, from International Data Corp.

★ 2146 ★
Cameras
SIC: 3861; NAICS: 333315

Movie Camera Market

Panaflex cameras were used in 75 percent of all films produced last year.

Panaflex	75.0%
Other	25.0

Source: *San Fernando Valley Business Journal*, September 29, 2003, p. 6.

★ 2147 ★
Cameras
SIC: 3861; NAICS: 333315

Top Compact Camera Producers, 2002

Market shares are shown based on total worldwide sales of 20.23 million units.

Canon Inc.	21.0%
Fuji Photo Film Co.	14.9
Olympus Optical Co.	13.1
Minolta Co.	9.7
Pentax Corp.	7.8
Other	33.5

Source: "Market Share Survey Report 2002." [online] from http://www.nni.nikkei.co.jp [accessed January 20, 2004], from iSuppli Corp.

★ 2148 ★
Cameras
SIC: 3861; NAICS. 333315

Top Disposable Camera Makers, 2003

Market shares are shown based on sales at supermarkets, drug stores and mass merchandisers (but not Wal-Mart) for the year ended May 18, 2003.

Kodak	61.9%
Fuji Photo Film	18.7
Konishiroku Photo	0.7
Jazz Photo Corp.	0.4
Private label	18.0
Other	0.3

Source: *Grocery Headquarters*, August 2003, p. S6, from Information Resources Inc.

★ 2149 ★
Cameras
SIC: 3861; NAICS: 333315

Top One-Time Use Cameras, 2003

Brands are ranked by sales in millions of dollars at drug stores, supermarkets and discount stores for the year ended December 28, 2003. Figures exclude Wal-Mart.

	($ mil.)	Share
Kodak Max Flash	$ 189.0	26.63%
Fuji Quicksnap Flash	110.0	15.50
Kodak Max HQ	97.0	13.67
Kodak Fun Saver	81.3	11.46

Continued on next page.

★ 2149 ★
[Continued]
Cameras
SIC: 3861; NAICS: 333315

Top One-Time Use Cameras, 2003

Brands are ranked by sales in millions of dollars at drug stores, supermarkets and discount stores for the year ended December 28, 2003. Figures exclude Wal-Mart.

	($ mil.)	Share
Kodak	$ 36.6	5.16%
Kodak Max	17.1	2.41
Kodak Advantix Switchable . . .	11.0	1.55
Fuji Quicksnap	8.7	1.23
Fuji Quicksnap Waterproof	5.8	0.82
Private label	120.0	16.91
Other	33.1	4.66

Source: *MMR*, February 9, 2004, p. 24, from Information Resources Inc.

★ 2150 ★
Copy Machines
SIC: 3861; NAICS: 333315

Copy Machine Market and the Federal Government, 2002

Market shares are shown based on total purchases of $249.5 million.

Xerox Corp.	24.72%
Chenega Management	11.04
ASRC Communications LTD.	11.04
Verizon Communications	9.63
National Micrographics System	6.00
Other	37.57

Source: *Government Executive*, September 4, 2003, p. NA.

★ 2151 ★
Copy Machines
SIC: 3861; NAICS: 333315

Copy Machine Market in Europe, 2001

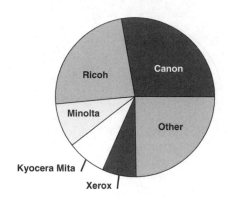

Market shares are shown in percent.

Canon	27.7%
Ricoh	23.6
Minolta	8.8
Kyocera Mita	7.7
Xerox	7.3
Other	24.9

Source: *Computerwoche*, April 19, 2002, p. 24, from International Data Corp.

★ 2152 ★
Copy Machines
SIC: 3861; NAICS: 333315

Copy Machine Market in Hungary

Canon Hungaria
Minolta
Ricoh
Other

Shares refer to photocopiers and digital printer-copier systems.

Canon Hungaria	22.50%
Minolta	17.06
Ricoh	17.00
Other	43.44

Source: *Europe Intelligence Wire*, April 26, 2004, p. NA, from International Data Corp.

★ **2153** ★
Copy Machines
SIC: 3861; NAICS: 333315
Leading Plain Copier Makers in Japan, 2002

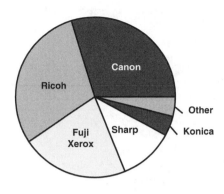

Market shares are shown based on total domestic shipments.

Canon	29.7%
Ricoh	29.5
Fuji Xerox	22.0
Sharp	10.6
Konica	4.2
Other	4.0

Source: "Market Share Survey Report 2002." [online] from http://www.nni.nikkei.co.jp [accessed January 20, 2004], from Nikkei estimate and Japan Business Machine and Information Systems Industries Association.

★ **2154** ★
Photographic Equipment
SIC: 3861; NAICS: 325992
Digital Photo Processing Equipment

The company's share is estimated to be 60-70% of the market.

Fuji	70.0%
Other	30.0

Source: *Wall Street Journal*, May 19, 2003, p. R17.

★ **2155** ★
Photographic Equipment
SIC: 3861; NAICS: 325992
Film Market in China

Kodak has more than 70% of the market. Fujifilm and Konica have less than 25% combined.

Kodak	75.0%
Fujifilm/Konica	25.0

Source: *Asia Africa Intelligence Wire*, February 24, 2004, p. NA.

★ **2156** ★
Photographic Equipment
SIC: 3861; NAICS: 325992
Leading Photo Brands in Drug Stores, 2002

Brands are ranked by drug store sales in millions of dollars for the 52 weeks ended December 29, 2002.

Kodak Max Flash (dis. camera)	$ 104.6
Kodak Gold (film)	85.7
Kodak Advantix (film)	62.6
Kodak Gold Max (film)	48.9
Kodak Max HQ (dis. camera)	39.0
Fuji Quick Snap Flash (dis. camera) . . .	32.5
Kodak Max (film)	25.7
Kodak Fun Saver (dis. camera)	25.6
Fuji Super HQ (film)	22.9
Fuji Color Superia (film)	17.4

Source: *Drug Store News*, May 19, 2003, p. 60, from Information Resources Inc.

★ **2157** ★
Photographic Equipment
SIC: 3861; NAICS: 325992
Top Film Brands, 2003

Brands are ranked by sales in millions of dollars at drug stores, supermarkets and discount stores for the year ended December 28, 2003. Figures exclude Wal-Mart.

	($ mil.)	Share
Kodak Gold	$ 143.0	23.84%
Kodak Max	97.4	16.24
Kodak Advantix	92.1	15.35
Kodak Gold Max	56.5	9.42

Continued on next page.

★ 2157 ★

[Continued]
Photographic Equipment
SIC: 3861; NAICS: 325992

Top Film Brands, 2003

Brands are ranked by sales in millions of dollars at drug stores, supermarkets and discount stores for the year ended December 28, 2003. Figures exclude Wal-Mart.

	($ mil.)	Share
Fuji Super HQ	$ 39.6	6.60%
Fuji Superia Xtra	31.7	5.28
Kodak	24.6	4.10
Fuji Color Superia	19.7	3.28
Kodak Max Zoom	17.5	2.92
Kodak Select Black & White . . .	12.2	2.03
Other	65.6	10.94

Source: *MMR*, February 9, 2004, p. 24, from Information Resources Inc.

★ 2158 ★

Photographic Equipment
SIC: 3861; NAICS: 325992

Top Film Makers, 2003

Market shares are shown based on sales at supermarkets, drug stores and mass merchandisers (but not Wal-Mart) for the year ended May 18, 2003.

Eastman Kodak Co.	74.5%
Fuji Photo Film	19.1
Konishiroku Photo	0.2
Agfa-Gevaert	0.1
Private label	6.1

Source: *Grocery Headquarters*, August 2003, p. S6, from Information Resources Inc.

★ 2159 ★

Photographic Equipment
SIC: 3861; NAICS: 325992

Top Instant/Polaroid Film Brands, 2003

Market shares are shown based on sales at supermarkets, drug stores and mass merchandisers (but not Wal-Mart) for the year ended May 18, 2003.

600	75.7%
Spectra	9.0
i-Zone	8.9
500 Captiva	4.4
600 Alter Image	1.3
Other	0.7

Source: *Grocery Headquarters*, August 2003, p. S6, from Information Resources Inc.

★ 2160 ★

Projectors
SIC: 3861; NAICS: 333315

Leading Projector Makers Worldwide, 2002

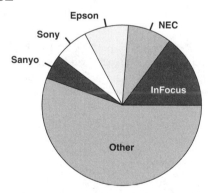

Shares are shown based on units shipped for the first six months of the year. Digital projectors offer high quality pictures and are becoming increasingly popular in business and home theaters, according to the source. Shipments may hit 3.5 million units in 2006.

InFocus	14.8%
NEC	9.0
Epson	8.5
Sony	6.8
Sanyo	5.1
Other	55.8

Source: *Investor's Business Daily*, November 26, 2002, p. A4, from International Data Corp.

★ 2161 ★
Theater Screens
SIC: 3861; NAICS: 333315

Large Theater Screen Makers in North America

Market shares are for North America.

Imax	73.0%
Iwerks	10.7
MegaSystems	8.7
Kinoton	3.1
Ballantyne	1.5
CDC	1.0
Other	2.0

Source: *Screen Digest*, May 2003, p. 159.

★ 2162 ★
Theater Screens
SIC: 3861; NAICS: 333315

Large Theater Screen Makers Worldwide

Market shares are shown in percent. Imax is the leading producer of large theater screens. Its share in selected regions: 78.6% in Africa and the Middle East, 40.4% in Asia, 100% in Central and Eastern Europe and 61.1% in Latin America.

Imax	63.7%
Iwerks	13.6
Goto Optical	6.4
MegaSystems	5.9
Kinoton	2.5
CDC	1.5
Christie	1.2
Ballantyne	0.7
Other	2.5

Source: *Screen Digest*, May 2003, p. 159.

★ 2163 ★
Watches
SIC: 3873; NAICS: 334518

Leading Watch Makers in Japan, 2002

Market shares are shown based on domestic output of 528.6 million units.

Citizen Watch	54.6%
Seiko	35.9
Ricoh Elemex	1.3
Casio Computer	0.7
Orient Watch	0.1
Other	7.4

Source: "Market Share Survey Report 2002." [online] from http://www.nni.nikkei.co.jp [accessed January 20, 2004], from Nikkei estimate and Ministry of Economy, Trade and Industry.

★ 2164 ★
Watches
SIC: 3873; NAICS: 334518

Top Watch Movement Producers Worldwide, 2002

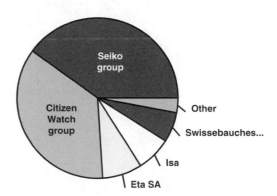

Market shares are shown based on total worldwide output of 785 million units.

Seiko group	40.3%
Citizen Watch group	36.0
Eta SA	8.0
Isa	6.8
Swissebauches Ltd.	5.5
Other	3.4

Source: "Market Share Survey Report 2002." [online] from http://www.nni.nikkei.co.jp [accessed January 20, 2004], from Nikkei estimates.

★ 2165 ★
Watches
SIC: 3873; NAICS: 334518

Watch Sales by Type, 2003

Figures show share of retail sales in October 2003.

Steel-look 44.9%
Steel/18-karat gold 17.7
Two-tone 11.8
Gold-plated 10.9
18-karat gold 8.6
Titanium 3.0
14-karat gold 1.6
Other 1.4

Source: *National Jeweler*, January 1, 2004, p. 28, from LGI
Network.

SIC 39 - Miscellaneous Manufacturing Industries

★ 2166 ★

Diamond Grading

SIC: 3911; NAICS: 339911

Who Issues Diamond Grading Reports

The diamond jewlery market absorbs roughly 10.5 million new diamond grading reports.

International Gemological Institute	33.0%
Gem Trade Laboratory	29.0
HRD Certificates	11.0
Euroepan Gemological Laboratory	10.0
American Gem Society Laboratory	8.0

Source: *Israel Diamonds*, April 2004, p. 38, from Israel Diamond Exchange.

★ 2167 ★

Jewelry

SIC: 3911; NAICS: 339911

Diamond Jewelry Sales Worldwide, 2002

The U.S. market continues to drive the industry. The U.S. market in turn was driven by the engagement ring segment ($4.3 billion up from $4.2 billion in 2001). Total sales reached $48.1 billion.

	($ bil.)	Share
United States	$ 27.4	57.0%
Japan	8.2	17.0
Europe	6.2	13.0
Asia Pacific	3.4	7.0
Asia Arabia	2.9	6.0

Source: *Israel Diamonds*, June 2003, p. 54, from Diamond Information Center.

★ 2168 ★

Jewelry

SIC: 3911; NAICS: 339911

Jewelry Industry Sales, 2001-2003

The United States accounts for 15% of global watch and jewelry sales. Retail sales in the United States are shown in billions of dollars. Figures are projected for 2002 and 2003.

	2001 ($ bil.)	2002 ($ bil.)	2003 ($ bil.)
Fine jewelry and watches	$ 40.600	$ 42.300	$ 45.200
Diamonds and diamond jewelry	18.676	19.458	20.792
Karat gold jewelry	4.710	4.910	5.240
Colored stone jewelry	3.740	3.890	4.160
Platinum jewelry	0.930	0.970	1.040

Source: *WWD*, October 20, 2003, p. 2B, from U.S. Department of Commerce, Jewelers of America, and Davenport and Co.

★ 2169 ★
Jewelry
SIC: 3911; NAICS: 339911

Largest Jewelry/Watch Markets

■ New York City, NY

■ Chicago, IL

■ Los Angeles, CA

■ Washington D.C./MD/VA/WV

■ Philadelphia, PA/NJ

■ Atlanta, GA

■ Detroit, MI

■ Houston, TX

■ Dallas, TX

Other

Total jewelry and watch sales are expected to grow from $52.1 billion in 2002 to $61.8 billion in 2007.

	2002	2007	Share
New York City, NY	$ 2,300	$ 2,500	4.05%
Chicago, IL	2,000	2,500	4.05
Los Angeles, CA	1,800	1,900	3.07
Washington D.C./MD/ VA/WV	1,500	1,900	3.07
Philadelphia, PA/NJ	1,100	1,300	2.10
Atlanta, GA	979	1,300	2.10
Detroit, MI	970	1,100	1.78
Houston, TX	922	1,200	1.94
Dallas, TX	869	1,200	1.94
Other	39,660	46,900	75.89

Source: *Jewelers Circular Keystone*, June 2003, p. 86, from Claritas Inc. and *Bureau of Labor Statistics Consumer Expenditure Survey*.

★ 2170 ★
Jewelry
SIC: 3911; NAICS: 339911

Women's Diamond Jewelry Sales, 2002

Diamond sales at retail hit $27.4 billion in 2002, up 5% from 2001. Sales of women's diamond jewelry are shown by occassion for the purchase. The category "other special" includes Valentine's Day and Mother's Day.

Christmas	24.0%
Other special	22.2
No special	20.2
Anniversary	19.0
Birthday	14.0

Source: *New York Diamonds*, May 2003, p. 34, from Diamond Information Center.

★ 2171 ★
Flatware
SIC: 3914; NAICS: 332211

Retail Flatware Sales, 2001-2002

Sales are shown in millions of dollars. Mass merchants and clubs represent 40% of the market.

	2001	2002
Flatware	$ 868.83	$ 855.00
Stainless steel	683.79	680.00
Sterling silver	131.36	125.45
Silver plate	53.68	50.00

Source: *HFN*, September 8, 2003, p. 14S.

★ 2172 ★
Musical Instruments
SIC: 3931; NAICS: 339992

Cymbal Market Shares

Market shares are estimated in percent.

Zildjian	65.0%
Other	35.0

Source: *Los Angeles Times*, May 12, 2003, p. C6.

★ 2173 ★
Musical Instruments
SIC: 3931; NAICS: 339992
Global Organ Market

The company has instruments in 81 nations and on all seven continents.

Allen Organ Co.	75.0%
Other	25.0

Source: *Reading Eagle*, March 9, 2003, p. NA.

★ 2174 ★
Musical Instruments
SIC: 3931; NAICS: 339992
Leading Saxophone Makers in Switzerland

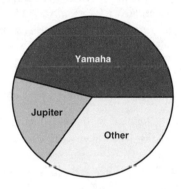

Market shares are shown in percent. Yahama has 32% of the brass market (trumpets and trombones).

Yamaha	46.0%
Jupiter	19.0
Other	35.0

Source: "Musical Instruments." [online] from http://www.usatrade.gov [accessed January 5, 2004], from U.S. Commercial Service.

★ 2175 ★
Musical Instruments
SIC: 3931; NAICS: 339992
Mandolin Market, 2003

The company claims 30% of the market.

Sound to Earth	30.0%
Other	70.0

Source: *Export America*, January 2004, p. 6.

★ 2176 ★
Musical Instruments
SIC: 3931; NAICS: 339992
Music Industry Shipments, 2003

The top music categories are shown based on whole-sale shipments, shown in millions, for the year. General accessories includes instrument care products, metronomes, reeds and polishers.

	($ mil.)	Share
Electric guitars	$ 305.92	4.39%
Acoustic guitars	289.37	4.15
Printed music	271.31	3.89
Speaker enclosures	233.66	3.35
Instrument amplifier	220.30	3.16
Grand pianos	207.86	2.98
Cabled microphones	198.05	2.84
General accessories	182.17	2.61
Power amplifiers	142.78	2.05
Fretted instrument strings	116.36	1.67
Vertical pianos	100.77	1.45
Other	4,698.45	67.44

Source: *Music Trades*, April 2004, p. 70.

★ 2177 ★
Musical Instruments
SIC: 3931; NAICS: 339992
School Music Sales, 2003

Clarinets were the top selling instruments with 154,025 in unit sales, followed by 135,876 flutes, 130,610 trumpets and 121,313 violas, violins and cellos.

	2002	2003	Share
Woodwind	$ 302.04	$ 269.4	50.63%
Brass	214.60	207.9	39.07
Stringed	55.10	54.8	10.30

Source: *Music Trades*, April 2004, p. 70.

★ 2178 ★
Dolls
SIC: 3942; NAICS: 339931
Fashion Doll Market

At the height of her popularity in 1997, Barbie and related merchandise sales claimed 90% of the category. Its chief competitor is now the Bratz dolls.

Barbie	70.0%
Other	30.0

Source: *Wall Street Journal*, July 18, 2003, p. A6, from Gerard Klauer Mattison.

★ 2179 ★
Toys and Games
SIC: 3944; NAICS: 339932
Building Toy Market in North America

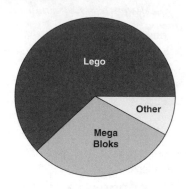

Shares are for the North American market. A few years ago Lego had 80% of the industry. Mega Blok's share basically doubled during the same period.

Lego	62.0%
Mega Bloks	30.0
Other	8.0

Source: *Wall Street Journal*, February 4, 2004, p. B1.

★ 2180 ★
Toys and Games
SIC: 3944; NAICS: 339932
Card Game Market

Hasbro has 65% of the board game market and 60% of the figure market.

Hasbro	75.0%
Other	25.0

Source: "Play for the Long Haul With 10 Year Stocks." [online] from http://www.thestreet.com [accessed March 8, 2004].

★ 2181 ★
Toys and Games
SIC: 3944; NAICS: 339932
Electronic Dartboard Market in Japan

Market shares are shown in percent.

Medalist Marketing 95.0%
Other 5.0

Source: *Asia Africa Intelligence Wire*, October 2, 2003, p. NA.

★ 2182 ★
Toys and Games
SIC: 3944; NAICS: 339932
Electronic Toy Market

$800 million was spent on educational toys in 2002. Market shares are shown in percent.

Leapfrog Enterprises 80.0%
Other 20.0

Source: *Los Angeles Times*, December 24, 2003, p. NA.

★ 2183 ★
Toys and Games
SIC: 3944; NAICS: 339932
Global Shuffleboard Industry

Market shares are shown in percent.

Champion Shuffleboard 95.0%
Other 5.0

Source: *The Plain Dealer*, January 31, 2003, p. 15.

★ 2184 ★
Toys and Games
SIC: 3944; NAICS: 339932
Global Toy Market

Figures include video games.

	1998	2000
North America	$ 28,371	$ 30,949
Asia	17,971	16,942
Europe	17,137	16,059
Latin America	2,808	2,768
Oceania	1,385	1,370
Middle East	1,040	972
Africa	379	433

Source: "Toy Sales at Retail." [online] from http://www.toy-icti.org/publications/wtf&f_2001/03.html [accessed May 25, 2004], from NPD Group Worldwide.

★ 2185 ★
Toys and Games
SIC: 3944; NAICS: 339932
Global Toy Sales, 2000

Figures include video games.

Infant/preschool 13.0%
Games/puzzles 12.0
Dolls 12.0
Activities 12.0
Male action 10.0
Vehicles 9.0
Ride-ons 8.0
Plush 8.0
Other 16.0

Source: "Toy Sales at Retail." [online] from http://www.toy-icti.org/publications/wtf&f_2001/03.html [accessed May 25, 2004], from NPD Group Worldwide.

★ 2186 ★
Toys and Games
SIC: 3944; NAICS: 339932

Leading Toy Firms

Market shares are shown in percent.

Mattel/Hasbro	35.0%
Other	65.0

Source: *Philadelphia Inquirer*, December 23, 2003, p. NA.

★ 2187 ★
Toys and Games
SIC: 3944; NAICS: 339932

Role Playing Game Market

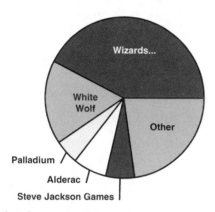

Market shares are shown in percent.

	2001	2002
Wizards of the Coast	45.0%	43.0%
White Wolf	19.0	17.0
Palladium	9.0	5.0
Alderac	8.0	7.0
Steve Jackson Games	5.0	5.5
Other	14.0	23.0

Source: "State of the Gaming Industry." [online] available from http://www.hubhobbyshop.com/press96.htm [accessed January 5, 2004], from *Comic & Games Retailer's Market Beat* data.

★ 2188 ★
Toys and Games
SIC: 3944; NAICS: 339932

Top Toy Brands in Argentina

Data show the top brands in the market. The top local producers are Yoly Bel S.A., Plastigal Juegos SRL and Kipo's S.A.

Hasbro	45.0%
Mattel	39.0
Lego	16.0

Source: "Toys and Games." [online] available from http://www.export.gov [accessed December 1, 2003].

★ 2189 ★
Toys and Games
SIC: 3944; NAICS: 339932

Top Toy Licenses in the U.K.

Licenses are ranked by sales in millions of British pounds for 1994-2002. The toy market overall was valued at 3.16 billion pounds in 2002, the largest in Europe (Germany and France came in next with 2.38 billion and 2.54 billion respectively).

Thomas and Friends	£ 312.8
Winnie and Pooh	255.4
Power Rangers	250.2
Star Wars	212.4
Teletubbies	152.2
Pokemon	150.3
Bob the Builder	147.5
Barbie	144.7
Toy Story	132.5
Harry Potter	126.9

Source: *Brand Strategy*, December 4, 2003, p. 36, from NPD Consumer Panel Service.

★ 2190 ★
Toys and Games
SIC: 3944; NAICS: 339932

Top Toy Makers in the U.K.

Sales of toys and games fell slightly from 2 billion pounds to 1.88 billion pounds in 2002, infant and pre-school toys was the toy segment. The second segment was activity and construction games.

	2001	2002
Mattel	10.7%	10.9%
Hasbro	10.1	8.5

Continued on next page.

★ 2190 ★

[Continued]
Toys and Games
SIC: 3944; NAICS: 339932

Top Toy Makers in the U.K.

Sales of toys and games fell slightly from 2 billion pounds to 1.88 billion pounds in 2002, infant and pre-school toys was the toy segment. The second segment was activity and construction games.

	2001	2002
Vivid Imaginations	4.8%	5.2%
Lego	2.3	2.9
Tomy	2.2	2.2
Character Options	2.0	2.6
Smoby	1.8	1.7
Bandai	1.6	1.5
Zapf	1.5	1.7
Halsall	1.2	1.6
Other	61.8	61.2

Source: "U.K. Toy Market Facts & Figures." [online] from http://www.mailorderexpress.com/media/factsandfigures1.html [accessed May 25, 2004].

★ 2191 ★

Toys and Games
SIC: 3944; NAICS: 339932

Toy Industry in Europe, 2002

The table shows market distribution with and without the video game segment. With video games, the market was valued at 17.31 billion euros. Without this segment, the total market falls to 12.7 billion euros.

	With Video	Without
Video games	27.7%	0.0%
Infant/pre-school	12.0	16.6
Activity toys	11.4	15.7
Dolls	10.5	14.5
Games/puzzles	9.6	13.3
Vehicles	8.6	11.8
Plush	4.2	5.8
Action figures	3.4	4.8
Ride-ons	2.8	3.8
Other	9.8	13.7

Source: *Toy Industries of Europe*, July 2003, p. NA, from NPD Group Worldwide.

★ 2192 ★

Toys and Games
SIC: 3944; NAICS: 339932

Toys and Game Sales

Department store sales are shown in millions of dollars.

	($ mil.)	Share
Action figures, access., robots	$ 2,012	17.36%
Dolls, accessories, houses	1,568	13.53
Games, puzzles	1,428	12.32
Plush	1,198	10.34
Infants, pre-school	978	8.44
Educational	531	4.58
Crafts	528	4.56
Kids' sporting goods	421	3.63
Books	348	3.00
Kids' riding vehicles	347	2.99
Playground equipment	134	1.16
Other	2,098	18.10

Source: *Retail Merchandiser*, July 2003, p. 20, from *Retail Merchandiser*.

★ 2193 ★

Toys and Games
SIC: 3944; NAICS: 339932

Toys and Game Sectors, 2002

The toy industry saw $21 billion in sales. Mass merchandisers take 41% of sales by channel.

	($ mil.)	Share
Infant/preschool learning	$ 2,900	13.6%
Dolls	2,700	12.5
Outdoor/sports	2,500	11.8
Vehicles	2,300	11.0
Arts and crafts	2,300	10.6
Games/puzzles	2,200	10.3
Plush	1,500	6.9
Action figures	1,400	6.7
Building sets	765	3.6
Learning/exploration	457	2.2

Source: *Supermarket News*, October 20, 2003, p. 25, from NPD Group, NPD Funworld, and Consumer Panel.

★ 2194 ★
Toys and Games
SIC: 3944; NAICS: 339932

Trading Card Game Market Shares, 2002

Market shares are shown in percent.

Wizards of the Coast 42.0%
Upper Deck 21.0
Decipher 17.0
Other 20.0

Source: "State of the Gaming Industry." [online] available
from http://www.hubhobbyshop.com/press96.htm
[accessed January 5, 2004], from *Comic & Games Retailer's Market Beat* data.

★ 2195 ★
Video Game Consoles
SIC: 3944; NAICS: 339932

Top Video Game Console Makers in Asia

Xbox has not seen the success it has hoped for in Europe and Japan. Sales are shown in millions of units.

	2004	2005	Share
Game Boy Advance	6.0	4.0	38.46%
Playstation 2	4.0	4.0	38.46
GameCube	3.0	2.0	19.23
Xbox	0.5	0.4	3.85

Source: *Financial Times*, August 7, 2002, p. 2, from UBS
Warburg.

★ 2196 ★
Video Game Consoles
SIC: 3944; NAICS: 339932

Top Video Game Console Makers in Japan, 2002

Market shares are shown based on domestic shipments of 5.04 million units.

Sony 78.2%
Nintendo 17.9
Microsoft 3.9

Source: "Market Share Survey Report 2002." [online]
from http://www.nni.nikkei.co.jp [accessed January 20,
2004], from Nikkei estimates.

★ 2197 ★
Video Game Consoles
SIC: 3944; NAICS: 339932

Top Video Game Console Makers Worldwide, 2002

Market shares are shown in percent.

Sony 74.0%
Nintendo 14.0
Microsoft 12.0

Source: "World Leisure Software Sales Forecast to Pass
$18 Billion." [online] from http://www.screendigest.com
[Press release March 10, 2003].

★ 2198 ★
Video Game Consoles
SIC: 3944; NAICS: 339932

Top Video Game Consoles, 2003

Market shares are shown in percent.

Playstation/Playstation 2 . . . . 50.0%
Microsoft Xbox 18.0
Nintendo Game Boy 18.0
Nintendo GameCube 14.0

Source: *Business 2.0*, May 2004, p. 30.

★ **2199** ★
Video Game Consoles
SIC: 3944; NAICS: 339932

Top Video Game Consoles in Australia

Playstation is in about 424,000 households, Xbox is in 209,000 homes and GameCube is in 67,000 households. Market shares are shown in percent.

Playstation	65.0%
Xbox	29.0
Nintendo GameCube	6.0

Source: *Herald Sun (Melbourne, Australia)*, May 14, 2003, p. C3, from InForm.

★ **2200** ★
Video Game Consoles
SIC: 3944; NAICS: 339932

Top Video Game Consoles in Western Europe, 2002

Market shares are shown based on units sold.

Sony PlayStation 2	80.9%
Microsoft Xbox	10.1
Nintendo GameCube	9.1

Source: *Wall Street Journal*, August 29, 2003, p. B6, from *Screen Digest*.

★ **2201** ★
Video Game Consoles
SIC: 3944; NAICS: 339932

Top Video Game Consoles Worldwide, 2003

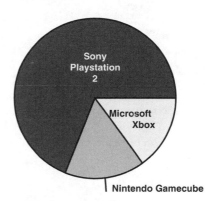

Market shares are as of December 31, 2003. Both Microsoft and Sony are planning to launch the next generation of their consoles. Playstation 3 may hit Japan in spring 2006 and then North America six months later. Xbox might be able to introduce its new version a year earlier than this, claiming market share and ownership of "hot" titles.

Sony Playstation 2	69.0%
Nintendo Gamecube	16.0
Microsoft Xbox	15.0

Source: *BusinessWeek*, May 10, 2004, p. 44, from DFC Intelligence.

★ **2202** ★
Video Games
SIC: 3944; NAICS: 339932

Best-Selling Computer Game Genres

Sales are shown by genre.

Strategy	27.4%
Children	15.9
Shooter	11.5
Family	9.6
Other	35.6

Source: *Florida Today*, August 31, 2003, p. 1, from Entertainment Software Association.

★ 2203 ★
Video Games
SIC: 3944; NAICS: 339932

Best-Selling Video Game Genres

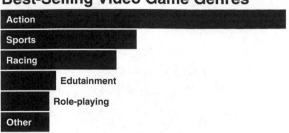

According to the source, 28.5% of players are women. About 38% of players are below 18 years of age. 18% of gamers played online. In 2002, the figure stood at 37%.

Action	42.1%
Sports	19.5
Racing	16.6
Edutainment	7.6
Role-playing	7.4
Other	6.8

Source: *Newsweek*, September 8, 2003, p. E6, from ELSPA.

★ 2204 ★
Video Games
SIC: 3944; NAICS: 339932

Best-Selling Video Game Sales (Console), 2003

Figures show percent of total sales. Total sales were $5.8 billion and 186.4 million units.

Action	27.1%
Sports	17.6
Racing titles	15.7
Role-playing games	8.7
Fighting games	6.9
Family entertainment	4.7
Shooter games	4.6
Other	14.7

Source: *Computer Graphics World*, March 2004, p. 12, from Entertainment Software Association and NPD Group.

★ 2205 ★
Video Games
SIC: 3944; NAICS: 339932

Best-Selling Video Game Sales (PC), 2003

Computer game sales were $1.2 billion and 52.8 million units.

Strategy games	27.1%
Children's entertainment	14.5
Shooter games	13.5
Family entertainment	9.5
Role-playing games	8.7
Sports titles	5.8
Racing	4.4
Adventure	3.9
Simulation	3.5
Other	9.1

Source: ''Computer and Video Game Software Sales Break $7 Billion.'' [online] from http://www.theesa.com/ pressroom.html, from Entertainment Software Association and NPD Group.

★ 2206 ★
Video Games
SIC: 3944; NAICS: 339932

Best-Selling Video Games

The best selling games of all time are ranked by millions of unit sales.

Super Mario Bros.	40.0
Tetris	33.0
Super Mario Bros. 3	18.0
Super Mario World	17.0
Super Mario Land	14.0
Super Maria 64	11.0
Super Mario Bros. 2	10.0
The Sims	10.0
Grand Theft Auto: Vice City	8.5
Harry Potter & The Sorcerer's Stone	8.0

Source: *Los Angeles Business Journal*, October 6, 2003, p. 15, from NPD.

★ 2207 ★
Video Games
SIC: 3944; NAICS: 339932

Best-Selling Video Games, 2003

Titles are ranked by unit sales for January - November 2003.

Madden Football '04	2,400,000
Pokemon Ruby	1,500,000
Pokemon Sapphire	1,400,000
Zelda: The Wind Waker	1,300,000
Grand Theft Auto: Vice City	1,100,000
Enter the Matrix	1,000,000
The Getaway	829,000
NCAA Football '04	811,000
NBA Street Vol. 2	790,000
The Sims	707,000

Source: *Variety*, January 12, 2004, p. A15, from NPD Funworld.

★ 2208 ★
Video Games
SIC: 3944; NAICS: 339932

Leading Game Publishers in France, 2002

Market shares are shown for the first half of the year based on revenues.

Electronic Arts	26.0%
Activision	10.0
Take 2	7.0
THQ	6.0%
Konami	5.0
Infogrames	5.0
Capcom	5.0
Acclaim	5.0
Squaresoft	4.0
Midway	4.0
Namco	2.0
Eidos	2.0
Other	17.0

Source: *Games Analyst*, December 13, 2002, p. 12, from Chart Track, NPD TRST, and GfK.

★ 2209 ★
Video Games
SIC: 3944; NAICS: 339932

Leading Game Publishers in Germany, 2002

Market shares are shown for the first half of the year based on revenues.

Electronic Arts	19.0%
Infogrames	10.0
Ubi Soft	9.0
Take 2	7.0
Eidos	7.0
Vivendi	6.0
Activision	6.0
THQ	4.0
Konami	4.0
Virgin	3.0
Other	25.0

Source: *Games Analyst*, December 13, 2002, p. 12, from Chart Track, NPD TRST, and GfK.

★ 2210 ★
Video Games
SIC: 3944; NAICS: 339932

Leading Video Game Publishers

Market shares are shown in percent.

Electronic Arts	19.0%
Take-Two Interactive	8.0
Nintendo of America	7.0

Continued on next page.

★ 2210 ★
[Continued]
Video Games
SIC: 3944; NAICS: 339932

Leading Video Game Publishers

Market shares are shown in percent.

Activision	7.0%
THQ	6.0
Sony	6.0
Atari (Infogrames)	6.0
Vivendi Universal	5.0
Microsoft	4.0
Sega of America	3.0
Other	29.0

Source: *USA TODAY*, July 22, 2003, p. 3B, from Wedbush Morgan.

★ 2211 ★
Video Games
SIC: 3944; NAICS: 339932

Mature Rated Game Sales by Age

18 and over	78.0%
18 and younger	22.0

Source: *Investor's Business Daily*, April 25, 2003, p. A5, from NPD.

★ 2212 ★
Video Games
SIC: 3944; NAICS: 339932

Sports Video Market

Sports titles represent about 27% of the game market in North America. The two titles are the top selling titles in the football category. Market shares are shown in percent.

Madden NFL 2004/NCAA Football 2004	82.1%
Other	17.9

Source: *Business Wire*, September 2, 2003, p. NA.

★ 2213 ★
Video Games
SIC: 3944; NAICS: 339932

Video and PC Game Sales, 2002

Sales reached $7.4 billion.

New	94.0%
Used	6.0

Source: *Investor's Business Daily*, June 5, 2003, p. A7, from Interactive Digital Software Association.

★ 2214 ★
Video Games
SIC: 3944; NAICS: 339932

Video Game Rentals by Platform, 2002

Video stores saw $721.6 million in rentals for the year. There were 162.9 million turns (rentals). The average video store makes 10% of its revenue from games.

Playstation 2	48.8%
Playstation	14.9
Xbox	13.0
Nintendo 64	12.7
Nintendo GameCube	8.2
Other	2.4

Source: *Electronic Gaming Business*, August 27, 2003, p. NA, from Video Software Dealers Association.

★ 2215 ★
Video Games
SIC: 3944; NAICS: 339932

Video Game Sales by Rating, 2003

The distribution is roughly the same as in 2002: 55.7% for E, 27.6% for T and 13.2% for M.

E (for Everyone)	54.0%
T (Teen)	30.5
M (Mature)	11.9

Source: "Computer and Video Game Software Sales Break $7 Billion." [online] from http://www.theesa.com/pressroom.html, from Entertainment Software Association and NPD Group.

★ 2216 ★
Video Games
SIC: 3944; NAICS: 339932

Video Game Sales Worldwide, 2004 and 2010

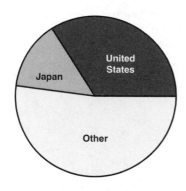

Japanese companies have a 30% share of the U.S. market down from 50% a few years ago.

	2004	2010
United States	30.0%	34.0%
Japan	14.0	14.0
Other	56.0	52.0

Source: *Wall Street Journal*, June 3, 2004, p. B5, from Informedia Group.

★ 2217 ★
Sporting Goods
SIC: 3949; NAICS: 33992

Baseball and Softball Equipment Sales

Total annual sales reach $440 million.

Bats	41.0%
Gloves/mitts	25.0
Balls	21.0
Batting gloves	8.0
Protective gear	5.0

Source: *American Demographics*, June 2003, p. 48, from Sporting Goods Manufacturers Association.

★ 2218 ★
Sporting Goods
SIC: 3949; NAICS: 33992

Bat Market

Market shares are estimated in percent.

Hillerich & Bradsby	60.0%
Other	40.0

Source: *The Seattle Times*, June 21, 2003, p. D5.

★ 2219 ★
Sporting Goods
SIC: 3949; NAICS: 33992

Bicycle Helmet Market

The company has the lion's share of the $254 million market.

Bell Helmets	63.0%
Other	37.0

Source: "What Ever Happened to Bell Helmets?" [online] available at http://www.snowmobile.ca/mha_internal/article [accessed November 1, 2003].

★ 2220 ★
Sporting Goods
SIC: 3949; NAICS: 33992

Blade Holders on NHL Skates

According to company literature, 80% of National Hockey League players use the TUUK blade holders. 60% of players wear Bauer or Nike skates.

TUUK	80.0%
Other	20.0

Source: *The Business Journal - Portland*, July 14, 2003, p. NA.

★ 2221 ★
Sporting Goods
SIC: 3949; NAICS: 33992
Freshwater Fishing in Florida

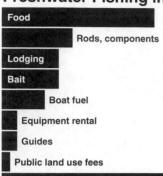

A total of $666 million is spent on freshwater fishing in Florida. Black bass fishing takes the bulk of spending. According to the source, the average bass fisherman is white, 41.4 years of age and has an average household income of $52,885. Data are in millions of dollars.

	($ mil.)	Share
Food	$ 145.5	21.85%
Rods, components	68.8	10.33
Lodging	53.2	7.99
Bait	52.9	7.94
Boat fuel	40.6	6.10
Equipment rental	16.0	2.40
Guides	14.3	2.15
Public land use fees	3.9	0.59
Other	270.8	40.66

Source: *Florida Trend*, November 2003, p. 42, from Southwick Associates.

★ 2222 ★
Sporting Goods
SIC: 3949; NAICS: 33992
Golf Ball Industry in Japan, 2002

Market shares are shown based on domestic shipments of 9.5 million dozen.

Bridgestone Sports	36.4%
Sumitomo Rubber Industries	30.8
Acsinet Japan	11.2
Callaway Golf	3.3
Kasco	2.8
Other	15.5

Source: "Market Share Survey Report 2002." [online] from http://www.nni.nikkei.co.jp [accessed January 20, 2004], from Nikkei estimate.

★ 2223 ★
Sporting Goods
SIC: 3949; NAICS: 33992
Golf Club Market in Japan

Market shares are shown in percent.

Sumitomo Rubber Industries	18.0%
Bridgestone Sports	11.0
Salomon & Taylormade	10.7
Other	60.3

Source: *Nikkei Weekly*, July 21, 2003, p. 1, from Nihon Keizai Shimbun.

★ 2224 ★
Sporting Goods
SIC: 3949; NAICS: 33992
Golf Industry Market Shares, 2001-2003

Unit shares are shown by category for the top 5 companies at on- and off-course shops.

	2001	2002	Sep. 2003
Footwear	89.1%	90.8%	90.0%
Balls	84.0	87.5	88.5
Wedges	69.0	69.0	69.9
Woods	61.9	57.6	61.6
Irons	48.2	45.4	45.8
Putters	48.2	45.4	45.8

Source: *Golf World Business*, January 2004, p. 9, from Golf Datatech.

★ 2225 ★
Sporting Goods
SIC: 3949; NAICS: 33992
Golf Industry Sales

Data show sales at on and off course shops during September 2003. Figures are in millions of dollars.

Golf balls	$ 46.6
Irons	32.4
Shoes	16.7
Putters	15.8
Wedges	6.6

Source: *Golf World*, November 14, 2003, p. S1, from Golf Datatech.

★ 2226 ★
Sporting Goods
SIC: 3949; NAICS: 33992
Golf Industry Sales, 2002-2003

Figures are in millions of dollars for off-course equipment sales.

	2002	2003
Woods	$ 418.0	$ 376.9
Irons	310.8	273.5
Balls	235.3	172.7
Putters	77.2	71.0
Wedges	34.8	31.2

Source: *Golf World Business*, January 2004, p. 23.

★ 2227 ★
Sporting Goods
SIC: 3949; NAICS: 33992
Golf Iron Market

Market shares are shown in percent.

Callaway	17.9%
TaylorMade	8.3
Cobra	7.9
Other	65.9

Source: *Brandweek*, October 13, 2003, p. 21, from Golf Datatech.

★ 2228 ★
Sporting Goods
SIC: 3949; NAICS: 33992
Golf Shaft Market

Market shares are shown in percent.

Tru Temper	70.0%
Other	30.0

Source: *The Daily Deal*, October 13, 2003, p. NA.

★ 2229 ★
Sporting Goods
SIC: 3949; NAICS: 33992
Hockey Equipment Market Worldwide

The worldwide market is valued at $700 million.

Hockey Co.	30.0%
Nike (Bauer brand)	15.0
Other	55.0

Source: *Boston Herald*, April 9, 2004, p. 33.

★ 2230 ★
Sporting Goods
SIC: 3949; NAICS: 33992
Kayak Sales

Figures show percent of sales at specialty shops in April 2003.

Recreational	73.0%
Touring	20.0
Whitewater	7.0

Source: *Knight Ridder/Tribune Business News*, July 16, 2003, p. NA, from Leisure Trends Goup.

★ 2231 ★
Sporting Goods
SIC: 3949; NAICS: 33992

Leading Camping Equipment Brands in Argentina

There are over 60 companies in the field, most of which are small, mom & pop operations. The market includes utensils, cookware and storage items.

Doitte	25.0%
Northland	22.0
Columbia	10.0
Montagne	9.0
Cacique	6.0
Ferrino	4.0
Outside	3.0
Other	21.0

Source: "Outdoor Equipment: Camping, Fishing, Hunting." [online] from http://www.usatrade.gov [accessed January 5, 2004], from U.S. Commercial Service.

★ 2232 ★
Sporting Goods
SIC: 3949; NAICS: 33992

Leading Fishing Equipment Brands in Argentina

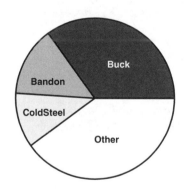

Total demand was $8.69 million. The breakdown of the market: $3.44 million for fishing poles, $3.67 million reels, $21 million for hooks and $370,000 for fishing lines.

Buck	35.0%
Bandon	14.0
ColdSteel	11.0
Other	40.0

Source: "Outdoor Equipment: Camping, Fishing, Hunting." [online] from http://www.usatrade.gov [accessed January 5, 2004], from U.S. Commercial Service.

★ 2233 ★
Sporting Goods
SIC: 3949; NAICS: 33992

Leading Sports Brands, 2002

Market shares are shown in percent.

Nike	20.96%
Reebok	5.97
Adidas	5.48
New Balance	4.69
Champion	2.12
Columbia	1.74
Coleman	1.70
Russell	1.48
Nutmeg	1.34
Icon	1.23
Wilson	1.21
Other	52.08

Source: *Sporting Goods Business*, July 2003, p. 21, from Sportscaninfo.

★ 2234 ★
Sporting Goods
SIC: 3949; NAICS: 33992

NFL Helmet Market

The share refers to the professional helmet market (National Football League). The company has about half of the football helmet market.

Riddell	85.0%
Other	15.0

Source: *Financial Times*, July 4, 2003, p. 15.

★ 2235 ★
Sporting Goods
SIC: 3949; NAICS: 33992

NHL Stick Market

Roughly 60% of NHL players use Eaton sticks.

Eaton	60.0%
Other	40.0

Source: *Los Angeles Business Journal*, June 23, 2003, p. 29.

★ 2236 ★
Sporting Goods
SIC: 3949; NAICS: 33992
Popular Sports/Recreational Activities, 2002

Data show millions of people (age seven and older) who participated in each activity more than once.

Exercise walking	82.2
Camping (vacation/overnite)	55.4
Swimming	54.7
Exercising with equipment	50.2
Fishing	44.2
Bowling	43.9
Bicycle riding	41.4
Billiards/pool	35.3
Hiking	30.5
Aerobic exercising	29.0

Source: "2002 Participation." [online] available at http://www.nsga.org/public/pages/index.cfm?pageid150 [accessed November 1, 2003], from National Sporting Goods Association.

★ 2237 ★
Sporting Goods
SIC: 3949; NAICS: 33992
Roller Hockey Equipment Market

Market shares are estimated in percent. Nike, which also owns Bauer, has between 15-20% of the market.

Mission	60.0%
Nike	20.0
Other	20.0

Source: *News-Press*, July 26, 2003, p. 1C, from Nike.

★ 2238 ★
Sporting Goods
SIC: 3949; NAICS: 33992
Snow Shoe Market in North America

WinterQuest is the leading maker of lightweight aluminum, traditional wood and molded plastic snowshoes in North America. It has 75-80% of the market.

WinterQuest	80.0%
Other	20.0

Source: *The Burlington Free Press*, October 22, 2003, p. A4.

★ 2239 ★
Sporting Goods
SIC: 3949; NAICS: 33992
Snowboarding Equipment Market

The top four companies have 75% of the market.

Burton/K2/Rossignol/Salomon	75.0%
Other	25.0

Source: "Here and Now." [online] available at http://www.surfpulse.com/ben4.shtml [accessed November 3, 2003].

★ 2240 ★
Sporting Goods
SIC: 3949; NAICS: 33992
Snowshoe Market

Market shares are shown in percent.

Tubbs	85.0%
Other	15.0

Source: *Eagle Times*, April 21, 2004, p. NA.

★ 2241 ★
Sporting Goods
SIC: 3949; NAICS: 33992
Soccer Equipment Market

Soccer equipment includes jerseys, balls and cleats. Nike's share could reach 30% by the time of the World Cup tournament in 2006.

Adidas 31.0%
Nike 20.0
Other 49.0

Source: *Globe & Mail*, June 14, 2002, p. B12, from Morgan Stanley Dean Witter.

★ 2242 ★
Sporting Goods
SIC: 3949; NAICS: 33992
Sporting Goods Industry in Malaysia

The market is seen as having very bright prospects with a 20% growth between 2003 and 2004. This translates into a $8-10 million industry. The commercial portion is shown below.

Treadmills 50.0%
Elliptical cross trainers 25.0
Steppers 20.0
Exercise/stationary bikes 3.0
Rowers 2.0

Source: "Sporting Goods." [online] from http://www.usatrade.gov [accessed January 5, 2004], from U.S. Commercial Service.

★ 2243 ★
Sporting Goods
SIC: 3949; NAICS: 33992
Top Sports Equipment Markets

Sales are shown in billions of dollars. Categories that saw the top sales gains were snowboards (up 12% to $168 million), paintball (up 10.4% to $370 million), ice skates/hockey (up 8.5% to $255 million) and optical goods (up 8.5% to $575 million).

	($ bil.)	Share
Fitness machines	$ 3.78	21.24%
Golf	2.38	13.37
Firearms/hunting	1.90	10.67
Camping	1.71	9.61
Team sports	1.55	8.71
Fishing	1.00	5.62
Other	5.48	30.79

Source: *Mergers & Acquisitions*, September 1, 2003, p. 1, from Sporting Goods Manufacturers Association.

★ 2244 ★
Sporting Goods
SIC: 3949; NAICS: 33992
Top Tennis Racket Makers in Japan, 2002

Market shares are shown based on domestic shipments.

Amer Sports Japan 24.5%
Yonex 24.0
Daiwa Seiko 21.8
Sumitomo Rubber Industries 13.2
World Commerce 10.9
Other 5.6

Source: "Market Share Survey Report 2002." [online] from http://www.nni.nikkei.co.jp [accessed January 20, 2004], from Nikkei estimate.

★ 2245 ★
Writing Instruments
SIC: 3950; NAICS: 339941, 339942

Top Writing Instrument Firms Worldwide, 2001

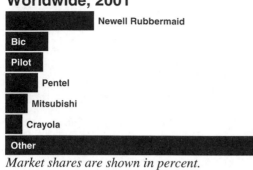

Market shares are shown in percent.

Newell Rubbermaid	17.0%
Bic	8.0
Pilot	7.0
Pentel	6.0
Mitsubishi	4.0
Crayola	3.0
Other	55.0

Source: "Bic's Updated Stationery Presentation." [online] from http://www.bicworld.com [Published May 2003], from Bic.

★ 2246 ★
Writing Instruments
SIC: 3950; NAICS: 339941, 339942

Writing Instrument Industry, 2001

The world market is shown by segment.

Pens	51.0%
Markers	15.0
Pencils	14.0
Coloring	13.0
Correction	7.0

Source: "Bic's Updated Stationery Presentation." [online] from http://www.bicworld.com [Published May 2003], from Bic.

★ 2247 ★
Pens
SIC: 3951; NAICS: 339941

Correction Pen Industry in Thailand

The industry is valued at Bt300 million market. The company also has 20% of the market.

Liquid Paper	70.0%
Other	30.0

Source: *Worldsources Online*, May 13, 2004, p. NA.

★ 2248 ★
Pens
SIC: 3951; NAICS: 339941

Luxury Writing Instruments Worldwide

The company has 60-70% of the market.

Montblanc	70.0%
Other	30.0

Source: *Daily News Record*, May 12, 2003, p. 10.

★ 2249 ★
Pencils
SIC: 3952; NAICS: 339942

Blacklead Pencil Market in Turkey

Adel Kalemcilik Ticaret ve Sanayl A.S. has 84% of the wood-cased blacklead pencil market, 78% of the color pencil market and 75% in fiber pens.

Adel	84.0%
Other	16.0

Source: "Writing Instruments and Stationery Group." [online] from http://www.anadolugroup.com/english/inf05_writing.htm [accessed April 27, 2004].

★ 2250 ★
Pencils
SIC: 3952; NAICS: 339942
Premium Pencil Market

The company has at least half of the premium market. This segment, however, is only about a fifth of the entire pencil industry.

Ticonderoga 50.0%
Other 50.0

Source: *Florida Trend*, December 2003, p. 72.

★ 2251 ★
Zippers
SIC: 3965; NAICS: 339993
Global Zipper Industry

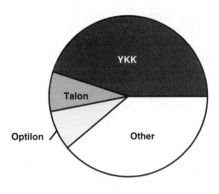

The market has been valued at $4.3 billion. Tapilo and Talon have between 7-8% of the market.

YKK 45.0%
Talon 8.0
Optilon 8.0
Other 39.0

Source: *Forbes Global*, November 24, 2003, p. 89.

★ 2252 ★
Brooms and Brushes
SIC: 3991; NAICS: 339994
Leading Stick Goods Makers

Market shares are shown in percent.

O-Cedar 17.8%
FHP 9.3
Other 72.9

Source: *HFN*, December 15, 2003, p. 49.

★ 2253 ★
Signs
SIC: 3993; NAICS: 33995
Illuminated Product Industry, 2002

Data show the types of products used by sign dealers. Neon is the most used, although it's at its lowest level in four years. Figures are based on a survey by the source with 113 respondents.

Neon 49.7%
Fluorescent 36.7
LEDs 4.7
Incandescent 3.6
HID 2.6
Fiberoptics 1.4
Other 1.5

Source: *Signs of the Times*, June 2004, p. 88, from *Electronic State of the Industry Report*.

★ 2254 ★
Flooring
SIC: 3996; NAICS: 326192, 31411
Floor Covering Sales

Data show share of total flooring.

Carpet/area rugs 47.0%
Sheet vinyl flooring 13.0
Ceramic tile 13.0
Hardwood 12.0
Laminates 10.0
Vinyl 3.0
Stone 2.0

Source: *National Floor Trends*, August 2003, p. 14.

★ 2255 ★
Flooring
SIC: 3996; NAICS: 326192
Top Selling Vinyl Flooring Brands, 2003

Vinyl flooring has about 14% of the flooring market. Carpets and area rugs have 50% of the flooring market.

Mannington 31.0%
Armstrong 27.0
Congoleum 23.0
Domco 8.0
Tarkett 5.0
Nafco 3.0
Other 3.0

Source: *National Floor Trends*, June 2003, p. 10, from *2003 Vinyl Flooring Study*.

★ 2256 ★
Laminates
SIC: 3996; NAICS: 326192
Laminate Flooring Industry in the U.K.

Laminate and wood flooring have a strong presence in the U.K. market. Laminate's growth rate was close to 50% in 2001. The market segments are shown in pounds.

	1999	2001	Share
DIY retail	49.2	138.3	60.60%
Flooring retailers	39.6	46.2	20.25
Building merchants	7.2	35.2	15.43
Contract	5.4	8.5	3.72

Source: *Carpet & Floorcoverings Review*, October 7, 2002, p. 44, from MZA floorcovering industry database.

★ 2257 ★
Laminates
SIC: 3996; NAICS: 326192
Popular Laminate Brands

Figures show the top brands based on a survey.

Wilsonart 22.0%
Columbia 13.0
QuickStep 10.0
Shaw 9.0
Mannington 9.0
Alloc 8.0
Pergo 7.0
Armstrong 5.0
Witex 4.0
Mohawk 3.0
Other 10.0

Source: *National Floor Trends*, August 2003, p. 14, from *2003 Laminate Flooring Market Study*.

★ 2258 ★
Artificial Turf
SIC: 3999; NAICS: 326199

Artificial Turf Market

Data show the estimated share of the market held by the top two companies.

FieldTurf/SRI Sports 80.0%
Other 20.0

Source: *Crain's Detroit Business*, April 14, 2003, p. 3, from General Sports Turf.

★ 2259 ★
Baby Products
SIC: 3999; NAICS: 326199, 332999, 339999

Top Baby Care/Safety Access Product Makers, 2003

Market shares are shown based on sales at super-markets, drug stores and mass merchandisers (but not Wal-Mart) for the year ended May 18, 2003.

	($ mil.)	Share
Cosco Inc.	$ 85.3	28.2%
Evenflo Inc.	41.2	13.6
Graco Children's Pdts. Inc.	32.2	10.7
First Years	26.9	3.7
Playtex Products Inc.	24.3	8.0

Source: *Grocery Headquarters*, August 2003, p. S6, from Information Resources Inc.

★ 2260 ★
Bath Products
SIC: 3999; NAICS: 326199

Top Bath Scrubber/Massager Brands, 2004

Brands are ranked by sales at supermarkets, drugstores and discount stores (but not Wal-Mart) for the year ended January 25, 2004.

	($ mil.)	Share
The Bathery	$ 7.1	12.52%
Body Image	6.3	11.11
Lady Elizabeth	4.1	7.23
Botany Bay	3.6	6.35
O Cel O Sponge Bob	1.6	2.82
Spa Paradiso	1.4	2.47
Pleasure Puff	1.2	2.12

	($ mil.)	Share
Body Image Body Benefits	$ 1.1	1.94%
Lady Elizabeth Leponge	0.8	1.41
Body Benefits	0.7	1.23
Private label	18.8	33.16
Other	10.0	17.64

Source: *MMR*, April 19, 2004, p. 59, from Information Resources Inc.

★ 2261 ★
Candles
SIC: 3999; NAICS: 339999

Top Candle Brands, 2003

Brands are ranked by supermarket sales for the year ended December 28, 2003.

	($ mil.)	Share
Glade Candle Scents	$ 37.9	11.22%
Glade	24.4	7.22
Fragrance de Lite	24.3	7.19
Reeds	22.8	6.75
Guild House	12.9	3.82
Candle Lite	9.9	2.93
Betty Crocker	8.9	2.63
Private label	11.7	3.46
Other	185.0	54.77

Source: *MMR*, May 31, 2004, p. 33, from Information Resources Inc.

★ 2262 ★
Card Shuffling Devices
SIC: 3999; NAICS: 333319

Automatic Playing Card Shuffling Market

Market shares are shown in percent.

Shuffle Master 90.0%
Other 10.0

Source: *Investor's Business Daily*, June 9, 2003, p. A6.

★ 2263 ★
Firelogs
SIC: 3999; NAICS: 325998, 339999

Top Firelog Brands, 2003

Market shares are shown based on sales at super-markets, drug stores and mass merchandisers (but not Wal-Mart) for the year ended May 18, 2003.

Duraflame 24.5%
Pine Mountain 8.8
Duraflame Crackleflame 5.5
Pine Mountain Superlog 4.4
The Chimney Sweeping Log 4.2
Duraflame Colorlog 3.3
Pine Mountain Cracklelog 3.1
Northland 1.4
Hearthlogg 0.7
Private label 21.6
Other 22.5

Source: *Grocery Headquarters*, August 2003, p. S6, from Information Resources Inc.

★ 2264 ★
Firelogs
SIC: 3999; NAICS: 325998, 339999

Top Firelog Vendors, 2003

Market shares are shown based on sales at super-markets, drug stores and mass merchandisers (but not Wal-Mart) for the year ended May 18, 2003.

Duraflame Inc. 33.5%
Conros Corp. 19.2
Joseph Enterprises Inc. 4.2
Canadian Firelog Co. Ltd. 0.2
Private label 21.6
Other 21.3

Source: *Grocery Headquarters*, August 2003, p. S6, from Information Resources Inc.

★ 2265 ★
Flashlights
SIC: 3999; NAICS: 339999

Top Flashlight Brands, 2003

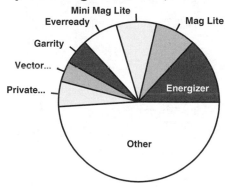

Brands are ranked by supermarket, drug store and discount store (excluding Wal-Mart) sales for the year ended December 28, 2003.

	($ mil.)	Share
Energizer	$ 12.6	13.13%
Mag Lite	8.1	8.44
Mini Mag Lite	8.0	8.33
Everready	7.1	7.40
Garrity	5.0	5.21
Vector Sport Spot	4.2	4.38
Private label	4.5	4.69
Other	46.5	48.44

Source: *MMR*, May 31, 2004, p. 33, from Information Resources Inc.

★ 2266 ★
Halloween Costumes
SIC: 3999; NAICS: 339999

Halloween Costume Sales

The Halloween costume industry is valued at $1.5 billion.

Children's	65.0%
Adult-size	35.0

Source: *Daily Herald*, October 26, 2003, p. 1.

★ 2267 ★
Holiday Decorations
SIC: 3999; NAICS: 339999

Christmas Decoration Spending

According to the survey of 3,000 adults, the youngest households (ages 18 to 24 year olds) were the top spenders. This group's average spending stood at $195. Not too surprisingly, women were the primary customers of home decorations.

$1 to $49	29.0%
$50 to $99	24.0
$100 to $199	21.0
$200 to $499	14.0
Over $500	7.0

Source: *Supermarket News*, November 10, 2003, p. 26, from *Gifts & Decorative Accents Report, 2003* by Unity Marketing.

★ 2268 ★
Holiday Decorations
SIC: 3999; NAICS: 339999

Holiday Decoration Spending

Seasonal decorations rose 6.4% from 2001 to 2002, increasing from $4.37 billion to $4.65 billion.

	($ mil.)	Share
Christmas decorations	$ 2,050	44.09%
Thanksgiving/home harvest	571	12.28
Halloween	458	9.85
Other	1,571	33.78

Source: *Supermarket News*, November 10, 2003, p. 26, from *Gifts & Decorative Accents Report, 2003* by Unity Marketing.

★ 2269 ★
Lighters
SIC: 3999; NAICS: 339999

Lighter Sales by Type

Sales are shown in millions of dollars. Bic is the most well known brand.

Disposable	950
Refillable	15

Source: *Tobacco Retailer*, June 2003, p. 20, from Lighter Association.

★ 2270 ★
Pet Care
SIC: 3999; NAICS: 326199, 339999

Top Pet Care Brands, 2003

Market shares are shown based on sales at supermarkets, drug stores and mass merchandisers (but not Wal-Mart) for the year ended May 18, 2003.

Hartz Mad-Maddogs	5.8%
Hartz Advanced Care	5.8
Van Ness	4.4
Hartz Health Measures	4.4
Hartz Control Pet Care System	3.3
Hartz Wacky Cats	3.2
Hartz Groomer's Best	3.1
Alliance	2.9
Hartz	2.8
Private label	6.7
Other	57.6

Source: *Grocery Headquarters*, August 2003, p. S6, from Information Resources Inc.

★ 2271 ★
Pet Care
SIC: 3999; NAICS: 326199, 339999

Top Pet Care Makers, 2003

Market shares are shown based on sales at super-markets, drug stores and mass merchandisers (but not Wal-Mart) for the year ended May 18, 2003.

Hartz Mountain Corp. 36.7%
Van Ness Plastic Molding Co. 4.8
Coastal Pet Products Inc. 4.0
Sergeants Pet Products 3.5
Private label 6.7

Source: *Grocery Headquarters*, August 2003, p. S6, from Information Resources Inc.

★ 2272 ★
Pet Care
SIC: 3999; NAICS: 326199, 339999

Top Pet Need (Non Dog/Cat) Brands, 2003

Market shares are shown based on sales at super-markets, drug stores and mass merchandisers (but not Wal-Mart) for the year ended May 18, 2003.

Perky-Pet 13.2%
Nature's Gold 7.0
Pet Pick 6.2
Bag Balm 6.0
Hartz 5.7
Penn-Plax 3.4
Brown's 2.5
Artline 2.5
Private label 3.1
Other 50.4

Source: *Grocery Headquarters*, August 2003, p. S6, from Information Resources Inc.

★ 2273 ★
Pet Products
SIC: 3999; NAICS: 326199, 339999

Pet Product Sales, 2003

Sales are shown at food/drug/mass stores (but not Wal-Mart) for the year ended December 27, 2003.

Cat and dog litter . . . . $ 743.5
Rawhide bones & chews 262.7
Flea collars 72.4
Flea and tick products 52.8
Pet treatments external 23.7
Pet treatments internal 19.5

Source: *Retail Merchandiser*, February 2004, p. 16, from ACNielsen Strategic Planner.

★ 2274 ★
Squeegees
SIC: 3999; NAICS: 339999

Consumer Squeegee Market

The company also has 75% of the professional window cleaning market.

Ettore 80.0%
Other 20.0

Source: *Knight Ridder/Tribune Business News*, April 6, 2004, p. NA.

★ 2275 ★
Tanning Beds
SIC: 3999; NAICS: 339999

Tanning Bed Industry in Germany

JK-Holding manufactures the Ergoline and Soltron brands.

JK-Holding 65.0%
Other 35.0

Source: "New Directors for Distributors." [online] from http://en-us.ergoline.de [Press release October 2003].

SIC 40 - Railroad Transportation

★ 2276 ★
Railroads
SIC: 4011; NAICS: 482111
Largest Railroads in North America, 2002

Groups are ranked by revenues in billions of dollars.

Union Pacific	$ 12.5
Burlington Northern Santa Fe	9.0
CSX	8.2
Norfolk Southern	6.3
Canadian National Railway	3.9
Canadian Pacific Railway	2.3

Source: *Wall Street Journal*, October 21, 2003, p. A22, from companies and Mergent.

★ 2277 ★
Railroads
SIC: 4011; NAICS: 482111
Rail Fleet Ownership in North America, 2003

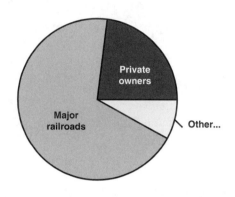

	U.S.	Canada	Mexico
Private owners	53.0%	17.0%	23.0%
Major railroads	37.0	80.0	69.0
Other railroads	10.0	3.0	8.0

Source: *Trains*, January 2004, p. 58.

★ 2278 ★
Railroads
SIC: 4011; NAICS: 482111
Rail Traffic, 2003

Figures show number of originated carloads for the 28 weeks ended July 12, 2003.

	Num.	Share
Coal	113,904	37.48%
Nonmetallic min. & prod.	41,077	13.52
Agricultural products	40,062	13.18
Chemicals	35,404	11.65
Metallic ores & minerals	30,507	10.04

Continued on next page.

586

★ 2278 ★

[Continued]
Railroads
SIC: 4011; NAICS: 482111

Rail Traffic, 2003

Figures show number of originated carloads for the 28 weeks ended July 12, 2003.

	Num.	Share
Forest products	17,722	5.83%
Motor vehicles & equipment	11,291	3.72
Other	13,958	4.59

Source: *Railway Age*, August 2003, p. 1, from *Weekly Railroad Traffic* and Association of American Railroads.

★ 2279 ★

Railroads
SIC: 4011; NAICS: 482111

Rail Traffic in Canada, 2003

Figures show number of originated carloads for the 28 weeks ended July 12, 2003.

	No.	Share
Chemicals	13,535	23.62%
Agricultural products	12,378	21.60
Forest products	10,247	17.88
Coal	7,896	13.78
Nonmetallic min. & prod.	4,810	8.40
Metallic ores and min.	3,672	6.41
Motor vehicles & equipment	2,944	5.14
Other	1,812	3.16

Source: *Railway Age*, August 2003, p. 1, from *Weekly Railroad Traffic* and Association of American Railroads.

SIC 41 - Local and Interurban Passenger Transit

★ 2280 ★
Bus Companies
SIC: 4111; NAICS: 485113
Largest Bus Operators in London

Arriva	
Go Ahead	
FirstGroup	
Stagecoach	
Metroline	
London United	
Other	

Market shares are shown in percent.

Arriva	20.0%
Go Ahead	18.0
FirstGroup	17.0
Stagecoach	15.0
Metroline	12.0
London United	10.0
Other	8.0

Source: *Knight Ridder/Tribune Business News*, September 22, 2003, p. NA.

★ 2281 ★
Mass Transit
SIC: 4111; NAICS: 485112
Boston-New York Market

Figures are for the first quarter of 2003. In the quarter following the September 11, 2001 attacks Amtrak had as much 49% of the traffic.

Airlines	67.0%
Amtrak	33.0

Source: *The Boston Globe*, July 14, 2003, p. NA.

★ 2282 ★
Mass Transit
SIC: 4111; NAICS: 485112
London-Paris Travel Market, 2003

Market shares are shown for November 2003.

Eurostar	65.96%
BA	13.18
Air France	11.46
EasyJet	5.03
bmi	4.25
Other	0.12

Source: *PR Newswire*, January 12, 2004, p. NA, from Civil Aviaiton Authority data.

★ 2283 ★
Mass Transit
SIC: 4111; NAICS: 485112
Subway Traffic

Cities are ranked by annual subway traffic.

New York City	5,616,200
Washington D.C.	860,100
Chicago, IL	509,100
Boston, MA	419,400
San Francisco, CA	319,300
Philadelphia, PA	286,200
Atlanta, GA	231,600
Los Angeles, CA	108,500
Miami, FL	49,400
Baltimore, MD	40,400

Source: *USA TODAY*, April 6, 2004, p. 3A, from American Public Transportation Association.

SIC 42 - Trucking and Warehousing

★ 2284 ★
Logistics
SIC: 4200; NAICS: 484122

Largest Logistics/Freight Transport Groups Worldwide, 2002

The top firms worldwide are ranked by group revenues in millions of dollars. Industry sectors include shipping, logistics, trucking, forwarding and rail.

Deutsche Post/DHL/Danzas	$ 40,891
UPS	31,272
FedEx	22,487
Deutsche Bahn/Stinnes/Scheiner	19,464
Nippon Express	12,824
Union Pacific	12,491
TPG/TNT group	12,273
A.P. Moller/Maersk group	11,567
NYK	10,393
BNSF	8,979
CSX	8,152
Mitsui O.S.K. Lines	7,573

Source: *American Shipper*, October 2003, p. 26.

★ 2285 ★
Logistics
SIC: 4200; NAICS: 49312, 49313

Value-Added Warehousing in North America

The top providers have been ranked by share of North American gross revenues.

	($ mil.)	Share
Exel plc Americas	$ 2,200	24.59%
UPS	1,600	17.88
Tibbett & Britten Group	914	10.21
APL Logistics	869	9.71
TNT Logistics	750	8.38
Caterpillar Logistics Services	700	7.82

	($ mil.)	Share
Americold Logistics	$ 700	7.82%
Menlo Worldwide	415	4.64
GENCO Distribution System	377	4.21
DSC Logistics	280	3.13
Other	143	1.60

Source: *TrafficWorld*, January 19, 2004, p. 22.

★ 2286 ★
Moving Companies
SIC: 4212; NAICS: 484122

Leading Household Movers

North American Van Line

United Van Lines

Atlas Van Lines

Covan World-Wide Moving Inc.

Firms are ranked by net income in millions of dollars.

North American Van Line	$ 33.9
United Van Lines	22.8
Atlas Van Lines	10.8
Covan World-Wide Moving Inc.	3.2

Source: *Mississippi Business Journal*, August 11, 2003, p. 9.

★ 2287 ★
Trucking
SIC: 4212; NAICS: 48411, 48421, 48422
Largest Trucking Firms, 2002

Firms are ranked by revenues in millions of dollars.

United Parcel Svc. Trkg . . . . . . $ 20,273.05
FedEx Ground 3,413.00
Roadway Express Inc. 2,627.00
Yellow Trptn. Inc. 2,522.29
J.B. Hunt Transport Inc. 2,247.88
FedEx Freight 2,120.00
Swift Transportation Co. 2,101.47
Con-Way Trptn. Svcs. 1,935.21
Ryder Integrated Logistics 1,553.50
Werner Enterprises 1,341.45
Overnite Transportation 1,332.52

Source: *Commercial Carrier Journal*, August 2003, p. 36.

★ 2288 ★
Trucking
SIC: 4213; NAICS: 484122
Long-Haul LTL Market

LTL stands for less-than-truckload. Yellow Freight, the number one firm, recently acquired Roadway Express the number two firm.

Yellow Freight/Roadway Express 60.0%
Other 40.0

Source: *Workboat*, September 2003, p. 12.

★ 2289 ★
Package Delivery Services
SIC: 4215; NAICS: 49211, 49221
Courier Market in the U.K.

Market shares are shown bsed on volume.

DHL 32.0%
UPS 20.0
TNT 10.0
FedEx 4.0
Other 34.0

Source: "Pactrac Parcels & Packets Market." [online] from http://www.andrew-lester.com/AlaNew/ongoing-pactrac-release.html [Press release June 17, 2002].

★ 2290 ★
Package Delivery Services
SIC: 4215; NAICS: 49211, 49221
Ground-Parcel Industry

Market shares are shown in percent.

UPS . . . . SIC . . 70.3%
FedEx Ground 15.3
U.S. Postal Service 9.8
Airborne 1.7
Other 3.0

Source: *Cincinnati Enquirer*, September 7, 2003, p. D1, from UBS Investment Research.

★ 2291 ★
Package Delivery Services
SIC: 4215; NAICS: 49211, 49221

Leading Package Delivery Firms, 2003

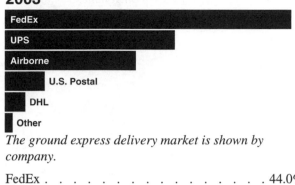

The ground express delivery market is shown by company.

FedEx 44.0%
UPS 26.0
Airborne 20.0
U.S. Postal 6.0
DHL 3.0
Other 1.0

Source. *Wall Street Journal*, October 6, 2003, p. A14, from Goldman Sachs.

★ 2292 ★
Package Delivery Services
SIC: 4215; NAICS: 49211, 49221

Leading Package Delivery Firms Worldwide, 2003

The ground express delivery market is shown by company.

DHL 40.0%
FedEx 19.0
UPS 15.0
TNT 12.0
Express Mail 1.0
Airborne 1.0
Other 6.0

Source: *Wall Street Journal*, October 6, 2003, p. A14, from Goldman Sachs.

★ 2293 ★
Package Delivery Services
SIC: 4215; NAICS: 49211, 49221

Leading Parcel Delivery Firms in Japan, 2002

Market shares are shown based on total domestic parcels delivered of 2.95 billion units.

Yamato Transport 33.7%
Sagawa Express 30.1
Nippon Express 13.6
Fukuyama Transporting 8.9
Japan Post 5.7
Other 8.0

Source: "Market Share Survey Report 2002." [online] from http://www.nni.nikkei.co.jp [accessed January 20, 2004], from Ministry of Land, Infrastructure and Transport and Japan Post.

★ 2294 ★
Refrigerated Storage
SIC: 4222; NAICS: 49312

Refrigerated Storage Capacity in Australia

Companies are ranked by share of total storage capacity.

John Swire & Sons 24.8%
P & O Logistics 16.7
TDG Cold Storage 9.7
Cleland Cold Storage 8.0
Montague Cold Stores 7.8
Other 33.0

Source: *Quick Frozen Foods International*, April 2002, p. 118.

SIC 43 - Postal Service

★ 2295 ★
Postal Service
SIC: 4311; NAICS: 49111

Mail Delivery in Hungary, 2003

Market shares are shown in percent.

Magyar Posta	75.0%
Others	25.0

Source: *The Budapest Sun*, March 18, 2004, p. NA.

★ 2296 ★
Postal Service
SIC: 4311; NAICS: 49111

Postal Service Providers in the U.K., 2004

*The United Kingdom's postal service will be gradu-
ally deregulated until 2007.*

Royal Mail	99.0%
Other	1.0

Source: *Europe Intelligence Wire*, April 1, 2004, p. NA,
from *Die Welt*.

SIC 44 - Water Transportation

★ 2297 ★
Shipping
SIC: 4412; NAICS: 483111

Chemical Hauling Market Worldwide, 2001

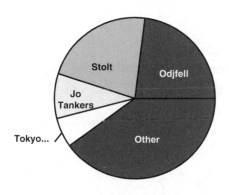

Market shares are for the shipment of liquid chemicals by seagoing parcel tankers.

Odjfell	23.0%
Stolt	22.0
Jo Tankers	9.0
Tokyo Marine Co.	6.0
Other	40.0

Source: *Wall Street Journal*, February 20, 2003, p. A1, from Odfjell annual report.

★ 2298 ★
Shipping
SIC: 4412; NAICS: 483111

Leading Exporters, 2003

Market shares are for the first six months of the year.

Columbus Line	43.0%
Maersk Sealand	12.7
Hanjin Shipping	5.6

Mediterranean Shipping Co.	4.7%
P&O Nedlloyd	4.6
Hapag-Lloyd	4.0
Crowley Liner Services	4.0
Hyundai	3.5
Yang Ming	3.3
K Line	3.2
Westwood Shipping	3.1
Other	8.3

Source: *Journal of Commerce*, September 1, 2003, p. 22, from Port Import/Export Reporting Service.

★ 2299 ★
Shipping
SIC: 4412; NAICS: 483111

Leading Importers, 2003

Market shares are for the first six months of the year.

Maersk Sealand	13.1%
Hanjin Shipping	7.0
Evergreen	7.0
APL	6.5
P&O Nedlloyd	4.6
NYK Line	4.3
OOCL	4.2
Mediterranean Shipping Co.	4.1
Hyundai	3.9
Hapag-Lloyd	3.6
Yang Ming	3.4
Other	38.3

Source: *Journal of Commerce*, September 1, 2003, p. 22, from Port Import/Export Reporting Service.

★ 2300 ★
Shipping
SIC: 4412; NAICS: 483111

Top 10 Merchant Fleets of the World, 2003

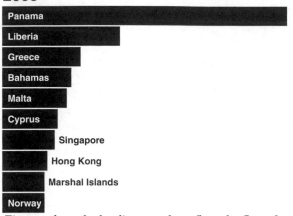

Figures show the leading merchant fleets by flag of registry. Figures include tankers, dry bulk, containers, and are based on the deadweight value of self propelled oceangoing vessels that are at least 1,000 gross tons or greater in size. These data are as of July 1, 2003.

	Ships	Deadweight
Panama	4,820	188,472
Liberia	1,448	77,335
Greece	740	50,602
Bahamas	1,018	44,979
Malta	1,244	42,279
Cyprus	1,098	36,192
Singapore	857	33,859
Hong Kong	583	29,145
Marshal Islands	388	27,441
Norway	605	26,983

Source: "Top 20 Merchant Fleets of the World." [online] from http://www.marad.dot.gov/Marad-Statistics/mfw-703.htm [accessed March 24, 2004], from Lloyd's Registry Fairplay, U.S. Department of Transportation, and Maritime Administration.

★ 2301 ★
Shipping
SIC: 4412; NAICS: 483111

Top Waterbourne Trading Partners of the U.S.

Countries are ranked in metric tons traded with the United States. The top 20 firms have 73% of trade.

Mexico	1,137,210
Venezuela	116,684

Canada	96,429
Saudi Arabia	78,798
Japan	60,008
China	56,627
Brazil	35,482
United Kingdom	33,134
Nigeria	33,128
Colombia	31,570
Korea, South	24,567
Iraq	23,673

Source: "Top 20 Leading Partners." [online] from http://www.marad.dot.gov [accessed March 24, 2004], from U.S. Maritime Administration Waterborne Databank, 2002.

★ 2302 ★
Helicopter Transportation
SIC: 4424; NAICS: 483113

Helicopter Transportation in the Gulf of Mexico

The top two companies hold 70% of the business of transporting crews and supplies.

Petroleum Helicopter Inc.	40.0%
AirLog	30.0
Era Aviation (Rowan Cos.)	10.0
Other	20.0

Source: *Oil & Gas Investor*, May 2004, p. 37.

★ 2303 ★
Cruise Lines
SIC: 4481; NAICS: 483112

Cruise Line Industry

Florida is the state that most benefits from the cruise line industry, receiving nearly 127,000 jobs and $4.5 billion in direct spending on goods and services.

Florida	45.3%
California	14.4
Other	40.3

Source: *Knight Ridder/Tribune Business News*, August 29, 2003, p. NA, from International Council of Cruise Lines.

★ 2304 ★
Cruise Lines
SIC: 4481; NAICS: 483112, 483114

Cruise Line Market Worldwide

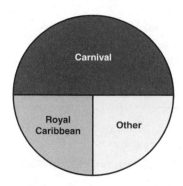

Market shares are shown in percent.

Carnival	50.0%
Royal Caribbean	25.0
Other	25.0

Source: *The Times*, February 16, 2004, p. 22.

★ 2305 ★
Cruise Lines
SIC: 4481; NAICS: 483112, 483114

Top Cruise Lines in North America, 2003

Crusie lines are ranked by thousands of passengers transported during the year. The industry saw 8.2 million passengers take 3,840 cruises in 2003.

	No.	Share
Carnival Cruise Line	2,868	34.6%
Royal Caribbean International . . .	2,233	27.0
Norwegian Cruise Line	798	9.6
Princess Crusies	699	8.4
Celebrity Cruises	603	7.3
Holland America Line	545	6.6
Disney Cruise Line	399	4.8
Costa Cruise Line	34	0.4
Crystal Cruises	28	0.3

Source: "Cruise Passenger Statistics." [online] from http://www.marad.dot.gov [accessed June 1, 2004], from U.S. Maritime Administration.

★ 2306 ★
Ferries
SIC: 4482; NAICS: 483114, 483212

Ferry Passenger Traffic Worldwide, 2002

Asia	28.0%
Americas	22.0
Baltic	21.0
Mediterranean	14.0
North Sea	12.0
Pacific	3.0

Source: *Duty-Free News International*, Annual 2003, p. 78, from ShipPax Information.

★ 2307 ★
Ferries
SIC: 4482; NAICS: 483114, 483212

Private Ferry Riders in New York City

Figures show share of 67,702 riders per day that used private ferries from May 19-May 23, 2003.

NY Waterway	92.9%
Seastreak	4.7
New York Water Taxi	1.2
Liberty Park Water Taxi	1.2

Source: *New York Times*, July 22, 2003, p. A20, from companies.

★ 2308 ★
Ports
SIC: 4491; NAICS: 48831, 48832

Container Traffic In North Atlantic Ports

Market shares are shown in percent.

Port of Montreal	38.0%
Port of New York	35.0
Other	27.0

Source: *Montreal Gazette*, January 5, 2004, p. NA.

★ 2309 ★

Ports

SIC: 4491; NAICS: 48831

Top Container Ports in China, 2003

Ports are ranked by annual traffic measured in twenty foot equivalent units (TEUs), a standard form of measure for shipping containers. Shanghai is the world's third largest container port.

Shanghai	11.3
Shenzhen	10.6
Qingdao	4.2
Tianjin/Xingang	3.0
Ningo	2.8
Guangzhou	2.8
Xiamen	2.3
Dalian	1.7

Source: *American Shipper*, March 2004, p. 16, from OOCL.

★ 2310 ★

Ports

SIC: 4491; NAICS: 48831

Top Container Ports Worldwide, 2002

Hong Kong, China
Singapore
Pusan, South Korea
Kaohsiung, Taiwan
Shanghai, China
Rotterdam, Netherlands
Los Angeles, CA
Shenzen, China
Hamburg, Germany
Long Beach, CA
Antwerp, Belgium
Port Kelang, Malaysia

Ports are ranked by traffic in millions of twenty-foot equivalent units. Shares are shown for the top 50 ports.

	2001	2002
Hong Kong, China	17.83	19.14
Singapore	15.57	16.94
Pusan, South Korea	8.07	9.45
Kaohsiung, Taiwan	7.54	8.47
Shanghai, China	6.34	8.61
Rotterdam, Netherlands	6.10	6.52
Los Angeles, CA	5.18	6.11
Shenzen, China	5.08	7.62
Hamburg, Germany	4.69	5.37
Long Beach, CA	4.46	4.53
Antwerp, Belgium	4.22	4.87
Port Kelang, Malaysia	3.76	4.53

Source: *Journal of Commerce*, September 29, 2003, p. 14A, from port websites.

★ 2311 ★

Ports

SIC: 4491; NAICS: 48831

Top Port Groups Worldwide, 2002

Port groups are ranked by TEU throughput (twenty-foot equivalent units).

Hutchinson	35.8
PSA	24.5
APM Terminals	18.5
P&O Ports	12.3
Eurogate	9.5
Stevedoring Services of America	6.6
NYK/Ceres	6.0
CSX World Terminals	3.7

Source: *American Shipper*, May 2003, p. 18.

★ 2312 ★

Ports

SIC: 4491; NAICS: 48831

Top Ports for Cruises in North America, 2003

The industry saw 8.2 million passengers take 3,840 cruises in 2003.

	No.	Share
Miami, FL	1,865	22.5%
Port Canaveral, FL	1,116	13.5
Fort Lauderdale, FL	1,078	13.0
San Juan, PR	571	6.9
Los Angeles, CA	515	6.2
Vancouver, BC	460	5.6
New York City, NY	424	5.1
Tampa, FL	418	5.0

Continued on next page.

★ 2312 ★

[Continued]
Ports
SIC: 4491; NAICS: 48831

Top Ports for Cruises in North America, 2003

The industry saw 8.2 million passengers take 3,840 cruises in 2003.

	No.	Share
Galveston, TX	377	4.6%
New Orleans, LA	297	3.6

Source: "Cruise Passenger Statistics." [online] from http://www.marad.dot.gov [accessed June 1, 2004], from U.S. Maritime Administration.

★ 2313 ★

Terminal Operation
SIC: 4491; NAICS: 48831, 48832

Leading Terminal Operators Worldwide, 2002

Market shares are shown based on throughput in twenty foot equivalent units. Only two of the top twenty firms are U.S. based.

	(mil.)	Share
Hutchison Port Holdings	36.7	13.3%
PSA	26.2	9.5
APM Terminals	17.2	6.2
Eurogate	9.5	3.5
Evergreen	5.7	2.1
Dubai Ports Authority	5.3	1.9
Hanjin	4.7	1.7
COSCO	4.7	1.7
P&O Ports	1.0	4.6

Source: *American Shipper*, November 2003, p. 82, from Drewery Shipping Consultants.

SIC 45 - Transportation by Air

★ 2314 ★

Air Routes

SIC: 4512; NAICS: 481111

Air Travel Market Worldwide, 2002

Distribution is shown based on passengers.

United States	37.73%
Europe	28.88
Asia/Pacific	22.69
Latin America/Caribbean	4.39
Africa/Middle East	4.02
Canada	2.29

Source: *Air Transport World*, July 2003, p. 33, from *Air Transport World* research and direct reports.

★ 2315 ★

Air Routes

SIC: 4512; NAICS: 481111

Houston - Los Angeles Market

Market shares are shown in percent.

Continental	52.0%
Southwest	22.0
America West	12.0
American	7.0
United	4.0
Other	3.0

Source: *Aviation Daily*, December 9, 2003, p. 1, from Seabury/Airline Planning Group - APGDat.

★ 2316 ★

Air Routes

SIC: 4512; NAICS: 481111

Las Vegas - Boston Air Market, 2002

Figures are for the fourth quarter of 2002.

America West	77.5%
JetBlue	8.7
Other	13.8

Source: *Aviation Daily*, June 20, 2003, p. 6, from U.S. Department of Transportation.

★ 2317 ★

Air Routes

SIC: 4512; NAICS: 481111

United States - Germany Flight Leaders

Data show share of seats flown between the two countries for November 2003.

Lufthansa	51.4%
United	16.2
Delta	11.5
US Airways	8.0
American	3.6
Other	9.2

Source: *New York Times*, November 6, 2002, p. C1, from ECLAT Consulting.

★ 2318 ★
Air Routes
SIC: 4512; NAICS: 481111

United States - Great Britain Flight Leaders

Data show share of seats flown between the two countries for November 2003.

British Airways 38.1%
Virgin 15.7
American 14.3
United 10.9
Continental 5.1
Delta 4.2
Other 11.7

Source: *New York Times*, November 6, 2002, p. C1, from ECLAT Consulting.

★ 2319 ★
Air Routes
SIC: 4512; NAICS: 481111

Washington - Los Angeles Market

Market shares are shown in percent.

United 33.0%
American 18.0
Southwest 13.0
JetBlue 12.0
America West 8.0
US Airways 5.0
Delta 5.0
Other 8.0

Source: *Aviation Daily*, January 6, 2004, p. 1, from Seabury/Airline Planning Group and APGDat.

★ 2320 ★
Air Routes
SIC: 4512; NAICS: 481111

Washington - Seattle Air Market

Market shares are shown for the first quarter of 2003.

United 37.0%
Alaska Airlines 15.0
US Airways 12.0
Delta 8.0
American 8.0
Southwest 5.0
Other 7.0

Source: *Aviation Daily*, November 25, 2003, p. 1, from Seabury/Airline Planning Group and Internet Aviation Data Portal.

★ 2321 ★
Airlines
SIC: 4512; NAICS: 481111

Airline Market at Denver International Airport, 2003

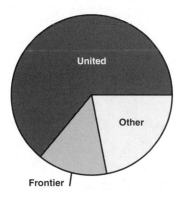

Market shares are shown in percent. In 1999 United's share was 74% and Frontier's was 6%.

United 64.0%
Frontier 14.0
Other 22.0

Source: *New York Times*, August 5, 2003, p. C1, from Denver International Airport.

★ 2322 ★
Airlines
SIC: 4512; NAICS: 481111
Airline Market in Canada

Market shares are shown as of November 2003.

Air Canada/Jazz	65.0%
WestJet	27.0
Jetsgo	9.0

Source: *Times Colonist (Victoria)*, January 7, 2004, p. NA.

★ 2323 ★
Airlines
SIC: 4512; NAICS: 481111
Airline Market in New York, 2002

Shares are based on revenues from flights from LaGuardia, Kennedy and Newark to domestic locations. Figures are for fourth quarter.

Continental	25.0%
American	24.0
Delta	16.0
United	11.0
JetBlue	10.0
US Airways	5.0
Northwest	5.0
Other	4.0

Source: *USA TODAY*, August 13, 2003, p. 3B, from J.P. Morgan estimates.

★ 2324 ★
Airlines
SIC: 4512; NAICS: 481111
Airline Market Shares

Market shares are shown in percent.

	1992	2003
Big six	72.0%	56.0%
Regionals	11.0	15.0
Low cost	10.0	23.0
Other	7.0	6.0

Source: *Consumers' Research Magazine*, September 2003, p. NA, from *USA Today*.

★ 2325 ★
Airlines
SIC: 4512; NAICS: 481111
Largest Airline Groups Worldwide, 2002

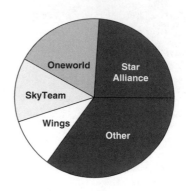

Shares are shown based on revenue passenger kilometers.

Star Alliance	23.9%
Oneworld	18.1
SkyTeam	12.7
Wings	9.9
Other	35.4

Source: *Financial Times*, September 17, 2003, p. 24, from Star Alliance.

★ 2326 ★
Airlines
SIC: 4512; NAICS: 481111
Largest Airlines Worldwide, 2002

Airlines are ranked by millions of passengers.

American	94.14
Delta	89.86
United	68.58
Southwest	63.04
Northwest	52.66
US Airways	47.16
Lufthansa Group	43.94
All Nippon	43.29

Continued on next page.

★ 2326 ★
[Continued]
Airlines
SIC: 4512; NAICS: 481111

Largest Airlines Worldwide, 2002

Airlines are ranked by millions of passengers.

Continental	41.01
Air France	38.04
British Airways	34.44
JAL	33.63

Source: *Air Transport World*, July 2003, p. 33, from *Air Transport World* research and direct reports.

★ 2327 ★
Airlines
SIC: 4512; NAICS: 481111

Leading Airlines for Federal Travelers, 2002

Market shares are shown based on total spending of $2.4 billion. Figures are based on charges made on travel charge cards issued by the govenment and its contractors.

United	25.6%
Delta	23.0
American Airlines	13.9
U.S. Airways	10.9
Northwest	7.3
Continental	4.8
Alaska Airlines	3.0
Southwest	2.8
America West	1.5
Trans World Airlines	0.3
Other	7.0

Source: *Government Executive*, September 4, 2003, p. NA, from General Services Administration.

★ 2328 ★
Airlines
SIC: 4512; NAICS: 481111

Low-Cost Air Market

Market shares are shown in percent.

Southwest	70.0%
Other	30.0

Source: *Europe Intelligence Wire*, July 3, 2003, p. NA.

★ 2329 ★
Airlines
SIC: 4512; NAICS: 481111

Top Airlines, 2003

Shares are for major and low-cost airlines through October 2003. Data are for domestic routes.

	1995	2003
Delta	15.1%	13.3%
United	12.8	9.6
American	12.0	12.4
US Airways	10.5	6.4
Southwest	9.5	12.8
Northwest	7.8	7.4
Continental	6.1	5.3
America West	3.2	3.3
Alaska	1.8	2.2

Source: *New York Times*, March 7, 2004, p. 9, from BACK Aviation Solutions.

★ 2330 ★
Airlines
SIC: 4512; NAICS: 481111

Top Airlines at Detroit Metropolitan Airport

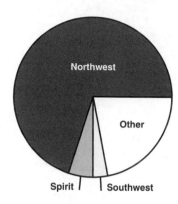

Figures show share of passengers transported.

Northwest	70.0%
Spirit	5.4
Southwest	2.8
Other	21.8

Source: *Detroit News*, October 26, 2003, p. B4.

★ 2331 ★
Airlines
SIC: 4512; NAICS: 481111

Top Airlines at Louis Armstrong New Orleans International Airport, 2004

Market shares are shown for year-to-date as of February 2004.

Southwest Airlines	29.7%
Delta	13.3
American	12.3
Other	44.7

Source: *New Orleans CityBusiness*, April 12, 2004, p. NA, from Air Transport Association.

★ 2332 ★
Airlines
SIC: 4512; NAICS: 481111

Top Airlines at Richmond International Airport

Market shares are estimated based on passengers.

US Airways	32.0%
Delta	28.2
United	13.0
American Airlines	11.0
Other	15.8

Source: *Times Dispatch*, December 17, 2003, p. NA.

★ 2333 ★
Airlines
SIC: 4512; NAICS: 481111

Top Airlines at Tampa International

Market shares are shown in percent.

Delta	21.5%
Southwest	21.3
US Airways	11.3
Other	45.9

Source: *St. Petersburg Times*, October 29, 2003, p. 2E.

★ 2334 ★
Airlines
SIC: 4512; NAICS: 481111

Top Airlines by Available Seat Miles

Market shares are shown based on available seat miles.

American	20.3%
United	16.2
Delta	15.0
Northwest	11.1
Continental	9.2
Southwest	8.5
US Airways	6.4
America West	2.4

Continued on next page.

★ 2334 ★

[Continued]

Airlines

SIC: 4512; NAICS: 481111

Top Airlines by Available Seat Miles

Market shares are shown based on available seat miles.

ATA 2.2%
Other 4.1

Source: *New York Times*, April 20, 2004, p. C6.

★ 2335 ★

Airlines

SIC: 4512; NAICS: 481111

Top Airlines by Passenger Traffic, 2003

Data show scheduled passenger traffic for January - December 2003.

	(mil.)	Share
American Airlines	193,608	20.99%
United Airlines	168,083	18.22
Delta Air Lines	158,766	17.21
NorthWest Airlines	110,178	11.95
Continental Airlines	96,196	10.43
Southwest Airlines	77,140	8.36
US Airways	60,725	6.58
America West Airlines	34,264	3.71
Alaska Airlines	23,417	2.54

Source: *Airline Business*, March 1, 2004, p. 24.

★ 2336 ★

Airlines

SIC: 4512; NAICS: 481111

Top Airlines in Albuquerque, NM, 2002

Airlines are ranked by share of enplaned passengers at Albuquerque New Mexico airports.

Southwest 51.44%
American 11.95
Delta 7.83
America West 7.50
United 6.33
Other 14.95

Source: *Aviation Daily*, August 5, 2003, p. 7, from U.S. Department of Transportation.

★ 2337 ★

Airlines

SIC: 4512; NAICS: 481111

Top Airlines in Atlanta, GA, 2002

Airlines are ranked by share of enplaned passengers at Atlanta, Georgia airports.

Delta 71.62%
AirTran 10.50
ASA 8.78
American 1.90
Northwest 1.20
Other 6.00

Source: *Aviation Daily*, August 5, 2003, p. 7, from U.S. Department of Transportation.

★ 2338 ★

Airlines

SIC: 4512; NAICS: 481111

Top Airlines in Australia

Market shares are shown for the year ended March 2003. Qantas has 65-70% of the market. Virgin Blue's share has jumped to 27.7% from 17.1% in August 2000.

Qantas 70.0%
Virgin Blue 27.7
Other 2.3

Source: *Air Transport World*, October 2003, p. 28.

★ 2339 ★

Airlines

SIC: 4512; NAICS: 481111

Top Airlines in Boston, MA, 2002

Airlines are ranked by share of enplaned passengers at Boston, Massachusetts airports.

Delta 22.11%
American 18.04
US Airways 14.90
United 10.08
Foreign Flag 8.51
Other 26.36

Source: *Aviation Daily*, August 5, 2003, p. 7, from U.S. Department of Transportation.

★ 2340 ★

Airlines

SIC: 4512; NAICS: 481111

Top Airlines in Brazil, 2003

Market shares are shown based on traffic for the first nine months.

Varig 34.4%
TAM 32.5
Gol 18.9
Vasp 12.5
Other 1.7

Source: *Air Transport World*, November 2003, p. 18.

★ 2341 ★

Airlines

SIC: 4512; NAICS: 481111

Top Airlines in Charlotte, NC, 2002

US Airways
Commuter Carriers
American
Delta
Northwest
Other

Airlines are ranked by share of enplaned passengers at Charlotte, North Carolina airports.

US Airways 78.48%
Commuter Carriers 13.31
American 1.76
Delta 1.70
Northwest 1.13
Other 3.62

Source: *Aviation Daily*, August 5, 2003, p. 7, from U.S. Department of Transportation.

★ 2342 ★

Airlines

SIC: 4512; NAICS: 481111

Top Airlines in Chicago O'Hare, 2002

Airlines are ranked by share of enplaned passengers at Chicago O'Hare airports.

United 42.52%
American 30.09
American Eagle 5.62
Foreign Flag 5.27
Commuter Carriers 4.46
Other 12.04

Source: *Aviation Daily*, August 5, 2003, p. 7, from U.S. Department of Transportation.

★ 2343 ★
Airlines
SIC: 4512; NAICS: 481111
Top Airlines in Cleveland, OH, 2002

Airlines are ranked by share of enplaned passengers at Cleveland, Ohio airports.

Continental	32.37%
ExpressJet	28.25
Southwest	10.95
United	4.92
American	4.38
Other	19.13

Source: *Aviation Daily*, August 5, 2003, p. 7, from U.S. Department of Transportation.

★ 2344 ★
Airlines
SIC: 4512; NAICS: 481111
Top Airlines in Denver, CO, 2002

Airlines are ranked by share of enplaned passengers at Denver, Colorado airports.

United	54.79%
Frontier	10.87
Air Wisconsin	6.56
American	5.56
Delta	4.68
Other	17.54

Source: *Aviation Daily*, August 5, 2003, p. 7, from U.S. Department of Transportation.

★ 2345 ★
Airlines
SIC: 4512; NAICS: 481111
Top Airlines in Detroit, MI, 2002

Airlines are ranked by share of enplaned passengers at Detroit, Michigan airports.

Northwest	67.86%
Mesaba	7.40
Spirit	4.27
American	3.41
Commuter Carriers	3.40
Other	13.66

Source: *Aviation Daily*, August 5, 2003, p. 7, from U.S. Department of Transportation.

★ 2346 ★
Airlines
SIC: 4512; NAICS: 481111
Top Airlines in Fort Lauderdale, FL, 2002

Airlines are ranked by share of enplaned passengers at Fort Lauderdale, Florida airports.

Delta	24.10%
Southwest	13.56
American	10.91
US Airways	10.25
Continental	8.09
Other	33.09

Source: *Aviation Daily*, August 5, 2003, p. 7, from U.S. Department of Transportation.

★ 2347 ★
Airlines
SIC: 4512; NAICS: 481111

Top Airlines in Honolulu, Hawaii, 2002

Airlines are ranked by share of enplaned passengers at Honolulu, Hawaii airports.

Hawaiian	27.45%
Aloha	20.40
Foreign Flag	18.03
United	8.50
Northwest	7.68
Other	17.94

Source: *Aviation Daily*, August 5, 2003, p. 7, from U.S. Department of Transportation.

★ 2348 ★
Airlines
SIC: 4512; NAICS: 481111

Top Airlines in India, 1998-2003

Market shares are shown in percent.

	1998-99	2000-01	2002-03
Indian Airlines	61.2%	50.9%	43.3%
Jet	33.7	42.4	43.4
Sahara	5.2	6.8	13.3

Source: *Business World*, September 15, 2003, p. NA.

★ 2349 ★
Airlines
SIC: 4512; NAICS: 481111

Top Airlines in Japan, 2002

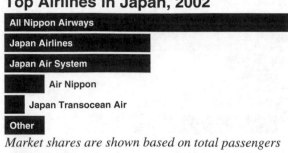

Market shares are shown based on total passengers of 96.37 million for the year ended March 2002.

All Nippon Airways	42.6%
Japan Airlines	21.6
Japan Air System	21.6
Air Nippon	6.1
Japan Transocean Air	2.5
Other	5.6

Source: *Nikkei Weekly*, August 18, 2003, p. 12, from *Nikkei Business Daily*.

★ 2350 ★
Airlines
SIC: 4512; NAICS: 481111

Top Airlines in Kansas City, 2002

Airlines are ranked by share of enplaned passengers at Kansas City airports.

Southwest	30.70%
American	14.54
Delta	9.30
Vanguard	8.63
Northwest	7.69
Other	29.14

Source: *Aviation Daily*, August 5, 2003, p. 7, from U.S. Department of Transportation.

★ 2351 ★
Airlines
SIC: 4512; NAICS: 481111

Top Airlines in Las Vegas, NV, 2002

Airlines are ranked by share of enplaned passengers at Las Vegas, NV airports.

Southwest	34.59%
America West	17.12
United	8.09
Delta	7.68
American	7.17
Other	25.35

Source: *Aviation Daily*, August 5, 2003, p. 7, from U.S. Department of Transportation.

★ 2352 ★
Airlines
SIC: 4512; NAICS: 481111

Top Airlines in Los Angeles County

- United Airlines
- Southwest Airlines
- American Airlines
- Delta Airlines
- Alaska Airlines
- Skywest Airlines
- Northwest Airlines
- America West Airlines
- Continental Airlines
- US Airways
- Other

The top 25 airlines have 89% of all airline traffic in the country. Airlines are ranked by millions of passengers transported.

United Airlines	10.38
Southwest Airlines	10.01
American Airlines	8.37
Delta Airlines	4.28
Alaska Airlines	2.66
Skywest Airlines	2.18
Northwest Airlines	2.01

America West Airlines	1.90
Continental Airlines	1.72
US Airways	1.22
Other	65.28

Source: *Los Angeles Business Journal*, August 4, 2003, p. 26.

★ 2353 ★
Airlines
SIC: 4512; NAICS: 481111

Top Airlines in Memphis, TN, 2002

Airlines are ranked by share of enplaned passengers at Memphis, Tennessee airports.

Northwest	60.29%
Commuter Carriers	12.19
Mesaba	10.21
Delta	5.71
AirTran	1.93
Other	9.67

Source: *Aviation Daily*, August 5, 2003, p. 7, from U.S. Department of Transportation.

★ 2354 ★
Airlines
SIC: 4512; NAICS: 481111

Top Airlines in New Orleans, LA, 2002

Airlines are ranked by share of enplaned passengers at New Orleans, Louisiana airports.

Southwest	31.56%
Delta	16.41
Continental	11.69
American	10.98
US Airways	8.51
Other	20.85

Source: *Aviation Daily*, August 5, 2003, p. 7, from U.S. Department of Transportation.

★ 2355 ★
Airlines
SIC: 4512; NAICS: 481111
Top Airlines in New York (Kennedy), 2002

Airlines are ranked by share of enplaned passengers at New York Kennedy Airport airports.

Foreign Flag	31.39%
American	22.71
JetBlue	17.22
Delta	13.98
United	5.42
Other	9.28

Source: *Aviation Daily*, August 5, 2003, p. 7, from U.S. Department of Transportation.

★ 2356 ★
Airlines
SIC: 4512; NAICS: 481111
Top Intra-Europe Airlines, 2002

Market shares are shown in percent.

Air France	15.5%
Lufthansa	11.4
British Airways	9.0
Iberia	8.6
SAS	6.7
Alitalia	6.4
Ryanair	4.8
EasyJet	4.4
Swiss	3.3
FinnAir	2.4
Other	27.5

Source: *Airline Business*, November 1, 2003, p. 30, from AEA statistics and company reports.

★ 2357 ★
Frequent Flier Programs
SIC: 4512; NAICS: 481111
Largest Frequent Flier Programs

Membership is shown in millions.

American AAdvantage	45
United Mileage Plus	40
Delta SkyMiles	29
Northwest WorldPerks	22
Continental OnePass	19

Source: *BusinessWeek*, June 2, 2003, p. 101.

★ 2358 ★
Air Cargo
SIC: 4513; NAICS: 49211
Air Cargo Industry, 2002

The volume of air freight is forecasted to grow from 15.3 million metric tons in 2002 to hit 20.5 million metric tons in 2007.

Perishables	11.8%
Construction & engineering	11.2
Textiles & wearing apparel	10.5
Documents & small packages	9.1
Computers, peripherals & spare parts	7.8
Other	49.6

Source: *Transportation & Distribution*, May 2003, p. 40, from MergeGlobal Inc. statistics in Lufthansa Cargo's Planet 2003.

★ 2359 ★
Air Cargo
SIC: 4513; NAICS: 49211
Air Cargo Market in Reno, NV

Market shares are shown for Reno-area businesses.

FedEx	23.6%
UPS	22.5
U.S. Postal Service	19.5
Airborne Express	10.0
Other	24.4

Source: *Reno Gazette-Journal*, August 17, 2003, p. E1, from Nevada Small Business Development and Reno/Tahoe International Airport.

★ 2360 ★

Air Cargo

SIC: 4513; NAICS: 49211

Air Cargo Market Worldwide, 2002

| D.H.L. Worldwide Express |
| Federal Express |
| UPS |
| T.N.T. |
| Other |

Market shares are shown in percent.

D.H.L. Worldwide Express	38.0%
Federal Express	21.0
UPS	13.0
T.N.T.	12.0
Other	16.0

Source: *New York Times*, June 1, 2003, p. 10, from D.H.L. Worldwide Express.

★ 2361 ★

Air Cargo

SIC: 4513; NAICS: 49211

Air Freight Industry Worldwide, 2002

Data are estimated.

High tech	19.0%
Intermediate manufacturers	17.0
Industrial machinery	15.0
Perishables	12.0
Apparel & footwear	9.0
Other	27.0

Source: *Air Cargo World*, May 2003, p. 28, from MergeGlobal inc. Airflow Model.

★ 2362 ★

Air Cargo

SIC: 4513; NAICS: 49211

Iraq and Military Cargo

A total of $574 million was spent on getting equipment to the Middle East for war with Iraq. Figures include passenger transportation. Entire mobilization spending was $1.2 billion.

	($ mil.)	Share
Atlas	$ 144	25.99%
Evergreen	109	19.68
Polar	70	12.64
Gemini	67	12.09
World	41	7.40
Other	123	22.20

Source: *New York Times*, December 26, 2003, p. C3, from Pentagon.

★ 2363 ★

Air Cargo

SIC: 4513; NAICS: 49211

Leading Air Cargo Carriers in Europe, 2002

Shares are shown based on freight tonne-kilometers.

Lufthansa	25.2%
Air France	17.2
British Airways	14.5
KLM	14.1
Cargolux	13.9
Alitalia	4.9
Iberia	2.8
Other	7.4

Source: *Air Cargo World*, April 2003, p. 54, from Association of European Airlines.

★ 2364 ★
Air Cargo
SIC: 4513; NAICS: 49211

Leading Air Cargo Carriers in Europe, 2003

Shares are based on freight ton kilometers flown during 2003.

Lufthansa	23.0%
Air France	15.5
KLM	13.8
British Airways	13.4
Cargolux	12.8
Alitalia	4.3
Swiss Air	4.1
Virgin	3.2
Others	9.9

Source: *Air Cargo World*, March 2004, p. 78, from Association of European Airlines.

★ 2365 ★
Air Cargo
SIC: 4513; NAICS: 49211

Leading Air Couriers for the Federal Government, 2002

Market shares are shown based on total purchases of $1.6 billion.

North American Airlines	38.45%
Federal Express	23.80
Wallenius Holdings Inc.	12.73
Atlas Air Inc.	6.63
Air Transport International	5.02
Other	13.37

Source: *Government Executive*, September 4, 2003, p. NA.

★ 2366 ★
Air Cargo
SIC: 4513; NAICS: 49211

Leading Cargo Airline Groups Worldwide, 2001

Market shares are shown based on freight-tonne kilometers.

WOW	21.9%
Skyteam	17.2
FedEx	13.8
Wings	8.5
UPS	7.6
Other	31.0

Source: *Air Cargo World*, January 2003, p. 41, from International Air Transport Association.

★ 2367 ★
Air Cargo
SIC: 4513; NAICS: 49211

Top Asian Airports for Cargo Traffic, 2003

Airports are ranked by tonnage moved through the airport between January and September of 2003.

Hong Kong (HKG)	1,883,717
Tokyo-Narita (NRT)	1,536,333
Seoul (ICN)	1,502,152
Singapore (SIN)	1,190,445
Taipei (TPE)	1,064,379
Shanghai (PUG)	833,098
Bangkok (BKK)	690,612
Osaka (KIX)	566,302
Tokyo-Haneda (HND)	508,350
Beijing (PEK)	450,343
Kuala Lumpur (KUL)	429,370

Source: *Air Cargo World*, March 2004, p. 26, from Airport Council International.

★ 2368 ★

Air Cargo

SIC: 4513; NAICS: 49211

Top Cargo Airlines, 2002

Airlines are ranked by share of total traffic of 199.79 billion in freight tonne-kilometers. When considering solely international traffic (about 94.13 billion FTKs), Lufthansa has the lead with 7.6% share.

JAL	3.7%
China Airlines	3.7
UPS	3.5
SIA	3.5
Lufthansa	3.5
Korean Air	3.5
FedEx	3.5
Cathay Pacific	3.5
Cargolux	3.5
Air France	3.5
Other	48.0

Source: *Air Cargo World*, September 2003, p. 26, from International Air Transport Association.

★ 2369 ★

Airports

SIC: 4513; NAICS: 49211

Top Cargo Airports in North America

Airports are ranked by traffic in tons.

Memphis, TN	3,390,299
Anchorage, AK	2,027,754
Los Angeles, CA	2,001,824
Miami, FL	1,624,240
New York, NY	1,574,462
Louisville, KY	1,523,880
Chicago, IL	1,279,178
Indianapolis, IN	866,014
Newark, NJ	821,537
Atlanta, GA	732,532

Source: *Air Cargo World*, July 2003, p. 24, from Airports Council International.

★ 2370 ★

Airports

SIC: 4513; NAICS: 49211

Top Cargo Airports Worldwide, 2002

Airports are ranked by traffic in tons.

Memphis International Airport	3,390,299
Hong Kong International Airport	2,516,441
Anchorage International Airport	2,027,754
Los Angeles International Airport	2,001,824
Tokyo Narita International Airport	2,001,824
Seoul Incheon International Airport	1,705,880
Singapore Changi Airport	1,660,404
Frankfurt Airport	1,631,489
Miami International Airport	1,624,240
John F. Kennedy International Airport	1,574,462

Source: *Air Cargo World*, July 2003, p. 24, from Airports Council International.

★ 2371 ★

Airports

SIC: 4513; NAICS: 49211

Top Cargo Airports Worldwide, 2003

Airports are ranked by freight traffic in millions of metric tons.

Memphis, TN	3.39
Hong Kong	2.66
Tokyo Narita, Japan	2.14
Anchorage, AK	2.09
Seoul, South Korea	1.84
Los Angeles, CA	1.80
Frankfurt, Germany	1.65
Singapore	1.63
New York City, NY	1.63
Miami, FL	1.63
Louisville, KY	1.61
Chicago, IL	1.60

Source: *Air Cargo World*, May 2004, p. 78, from Airports Council International.

★ 2372 ★
Airports
SIC: 4581; NAICS: 481111

Leading Airports in Africa, 2002

Airports are ranked by number of international passengers passing through an airport during 2002.

Cairo	6,269,742
Johannesburg	5,810,698
Monastir	3,007,145
Tunis	2,921,163
Nairobi	2,519,589
Casablanca	2,476,653
Plaine Magnien	1,784,403
Algeria	1,776,966
Djerba	1,558,273
St. Denis-Gillot	1,437,149

Source: *Duty-Free News International*, Annual 2003, p. 52, from Airport Council International.

★ 2373 ★
Airports
SIC: 4581; NAICS: 481111

Leading Airports in Asia/Pacific Region, 2002

Airports are ranked by number of international passengers passing through an airport during 2002.

Hong Kong International	33,454,000
Singapore Changi	27,374,329
Tokyo	24,760,468
Seoul	20,552,659
Taipei Chiang Kai-shek	16,999,357
Kuala Lumpur	10,345,432
Osaka	10,019,000
Sydney	8,487,139
Manila	7,466,379
Jakarta	5,025,383

Source: *Duty-Free News International*, Annual 2003, p. 52, from Airport Council International.

★ 2374 ★
Airports
SIC: 4581; NAICS: 481111

Leading Airports in Europe, 2002

Airports are ranked by number of international passengers passing through an airport during 2002.

London Heathrow	56,336,150
Paris Charles de Gaulle	43,664,118
Schiphol (Amsterdam)	40,956,845
Frankfurt	40,276,944
London Gatwick	26,089,733
Zurich	16,900,694
Madrid	16,865,805
Copenhagen	16,428,024
Manchester	15,885,153
Brussels	14,292,649

Source: *Duty-Free News International*, Annual 2003, p. 52, from Airport Council International.

★ 2375 ★
Airports
SIC: 4581; NAICS: 481111

Leading Airports Worldwide, 2002

Airports are ranked by number of movements.

Chicago, IL	923.55
Atlanta, GA	889.97
Dallas/Ft. Worth, TX	761.10
Los Angeles, CA	645.42
Phoenix, AZ	545.77
Paris, France	510.09

Continued on next page.

★ 2375 ★

[Continued]
Airports
SIC: 4581; NAICS: 481111

Leading Airports Worldwide, 2002

Airports are ranked by number of movements.

Minneapolis/St. Paul, MN	506.65
Los Angeles, CA	498.47
Las Vegas, NV	496.84
Denver, CO	493.84
Detroit, MI	490.88
Cincinnati, OH	486.65

Source: *Air Transport World*, July 2003, p. 33, from *Air Transport World* research and direct reports.

★ 2376 ★

Airports
SIC: 4581; NAICS: 481111

Top Airports in Russia, 2003

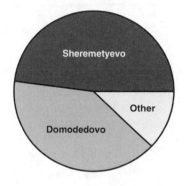

Shares are based on total passengers.

	2000	2003
Sheremetyevo	64.0%	48.0%
Domodedovo	16.0	40.0
Other	20.0	12.0

Source: *Aviation Week & Space Technology*, February 2, 2004, p. 50, from Domodedovo.

SIC 46 - Pipelines, Except Natural Gas

★ 2377 ★

Pipelines

SIC: 4612; NAICS: 48611

Leading Liquid Pipelines, 2002

Shell Pipeline Company	
Marathon Ashland Pipe Line	
Colonial Pipeline Co.	
Exxon/Mobil Pipeline Co.	
LOOP LLC	
Enbridge Energy	
	BP Pipelines North America
SFPP L.P.	
LOCAP Inc.	
Sunoco Pipeline	

Companies are ranked by millions of barrels delivered out of system.

Shell Pipeline Company	1,173.13
Marathon Ashland Pipe Line	858.22
Colonial Pipeline Co.	806.50
Exxon/Mobil Pipeline Co.	672.29
LOOP LLC	510.08
Enbridge Energy	487.83
BP Pipelines North America	420.07
SFPP L.P.	408.51
LOCAP Inc.	393.23
Sunoco Pipeline	368.23

Source: *Pipeline & Gas Journal*, November 2003, p. 59.

SIC 47 - Transportation Services

★ 2378 ★
Tourism
SIC: 4720; NAICS: 71399

State Tourism Spending

Spending is shown in millions of dollars.

Hawaii	$ 56
Illinois	50
Pennsylvania	35
Texas	31
Florida	29

Source: *USA TODAY*, July 29, 2003, p. B1, from Travel Industry Association of America.

★ 2379 ★
Tourism
SIC: 4720; NAICS: 71399

Top Nations for Tourism, 2003

Countries are ranked by revenues generated from international travel in billions of dollars.

United States	$ 65.8
Spain	34.9
France	32.3
Italy	26.2
Germany	19.0
United Kingdom	17.7

China	$ 17.5
Austria	11.6
Turkey	10.1
Mexico	9.5

Source: *Wall Street Journal*, April 28, 2004, p. A15, from World Tourism Organization and Mexico Central Bank.

★ 2380 ★
Tourism
SIC: 4720; NAICS: 71399

Tourism in Japan, 2002

In the previous year, 35.3% of foreign tourists were men and 44.7% of women. Tokyo was the most visited area (56.5%) and Osaka (25.2%).

Tourists	58.0%
Business	25.0
Shore excursionists	3.0
Other	14.0

Source: *Country Reports*, Autumn 2003, p. NA, from JNTO Overseas visitors survey.

★ 2381 ★
Tourism
SIC: 4720; NAICS: 71399

Visitors to the United States, 2002

Nations are ranked by number of visitors to the United States for 2002.

	Visitors	Share
Canada	12,968,103	30.96%
Mexico	9,807,000	23.41
United Kingdom	3,816,736	9.11
Japan	3,627,264	8.66
Germany	1,189,856	2.84
France	734,260	1.75

Continued on next page.

★ 2381 ★

[Continued]
Tourism
SIC: 4720; NAICS: 71399

Visitors to the United States, 2002

Nations are ranked by number of visitors to the United States for 2002.

	Visitors	Share
South Korea	638,697	1.52%
Australia	407,130	0.97
Italy	406,160	0.97
Brazil	405,094	0.97
Venezuela	395,913	0.95
Other	7,495,597	17.89

Source: ''Arrivals to the U.S.'' [online] from http://www.tinet.ita.doc.gov [accessed May 31, 2004], from Office of Travel & Tourism Industries, U.S. Department of Commerce.

★ 2382 ★

Travel
SIC: 4720; NAICS: 71399

Leading Travel Spenders

Data show the top states for spending by domestic travelers. Figures are in billions of dollars.

California	$ 60
Florida	40
Texas	31
New York	27
Illinois	21

Source: *USA TODAY*, January 21, 2004, p. B1, from Travel Industry Association of America.

★ 2383 ★

Travel
SIC: 4720; NAICS: 71399

Leisure Travel Market, 2002

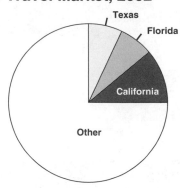

Market shares are shown in percent. Data are based on leisure trips, with a trip being one person traveling at least 50 miles one way or staying overnight somewhere regardless of distance.

California	11.4%
Florida	6.8
Texas	6.6
Other	75.2

Source: *Fort-Worth Star Telegram*, September 10, 2003, p. NA, from Office of the Governor, Economic Development and Tourism in Texas.

★ 2384 ★

Travel Agencies
SIC: 4724; NAICS: 56151

Largest Travel Agencies

Companies are ranked by gross sales in billions of dollars.

American Express	$ 15.5
Carlson Wagonlit Travel	12.5
Navigant International	5.3
Expedia	5.3
Rosenbluth International	5.2
WorldTravel	4.2
Travelocity	3.5
AAA Travel	3.2
Orbitz	2.5
TQ3 Maritz Travel Solutions	1.6
Liberty Travel	1.4
Cendant Retail Travel Services	1.4

Source: *Travel Weekly*, June 23, 2003, p. 26, from *Travel Weekly's Top 50*.

★ 2385 ★

Travel Agencies

SIC: 4724; NAICS: 56151

Largest Travel Agencies in Utah

Companies are ranked by revenue in millions of dollars.

Morris Murdock Travel	$ 128
Christopherson Business Travel	80
Travel Zone Inc.	28
HessTravel Inc.	22
Get Away Today Vacations	18
Cruise & Travel Masters	17
Thomas Travel	15
Clawson Travel Inc.	15

Source: *Utah Business*, July 2003, p. 76.

★ 2386 ★

Travel Agencies

SIC: 4724; NAICS: 56151

Leading Overseas Travel Arrangers in Japan, 2002

Market shares are shown based on total revenues of 2.83 trillion.

JTB	17.7%
Kinki Nippon Tourist	7.9
Hankyu Express International	7.3
H.I.S.	7.2
Nippon Travel	5.1
Other	54.8

Source: "Market Share Survey Report 2002." [online] from http://www.nni.nikkei.co.jp [accessed January 20, 2004], from Nikkei estimates.

★ 2387 ★

Travel Arrangements

SIC: 4724; NAICS: 56151

Corporate Travel Bookings

Shares are shown based on the corporate travel 100 list.

Sabre	52.0%
ND	21.0
TRX	12.0

CWT	5.0%
Amadeus	4.0
Travelport	3.0
WorldSpan	2.0
KDS	1.0

Source: *Business Travel News*, September 8, 2003, p. 14, from *Business Travel News Corporate Travel 100*.

★ 2388 ★

Travel Arrangements

SIC: 4724; NAICS: 56151

CRS Market Shares

CRS firms sold 58% of airline tickets through travel agents. Market shares are shown in percent

Sabre	44.7%
Worldspan	26.5
Galileo	19.7
Amadeus	9.2

Source: *Airline Financial News*, January 12, 2004, p. NA, from U.S. Department of Transportation.

★ 2389 ★

Travel Arrangements

SIC: 4724; NAICS: 56151

Global Distribution Systems, 2003

A total of 1.1 billion reservations were booked for domestic travel using global distribution systems. Figures are estimated and Sabre has less than 40% of the market.

	(mil.)	Share
Sabre	323	40.0%
Worldspan	180	30.0
Galileo	245	20.0
Amadeus	356	10.0

Source: *Airline Business*, March 1, 2004, p. 34.

★ 2390 ★
Travel Arrangements
SIC: 4724; NAICS: 56151

Largest Corporate Travelers, 2002

Companies are ranked by volume of air travel in millions of dollars. Shares are based on booked air volume for the top 40 companies. There was a 27% fall in spending between 2000 and 2002 amoung the top 100 companies. Larger companies are thought to have cut back more than medium sized companies.

	($ mil.)	Share
General Electric	$ 270	5.32%
IBM	270	5.32
Deloitte & Touche	225	4.44
The Boeing Co.	215	4.24
Lockheed Martin	202	3.98
PriceWaterhouseCoopers	197	3.88
Johnson & Johnson	183	3.61
ExxonMobil	164	3.23
Accenture	160	3.15
KPMG	160	3.15
Raytheon	160	3.15
Other	2,867	56.51

Source: *Business Travel News*, July 21, 2003, p. 3, from *Business Travel News Corporate Travel 100*.

★ 2391 ★
Travel Arrangements
SIC: 4724; NAICS: 56151

Leading Online Travel Agencies, 2003

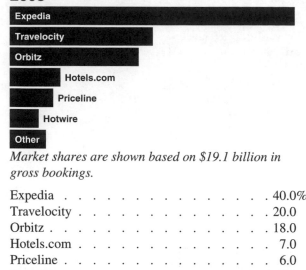

Market shares are shown based on $19.1 billion in gross bookings.

Expedia	40.0%
Travelocity	20.0
Orbitz	18.0
Hotels.com	7.0
Priceline	6.0
Hotwire	4.0
Other	5.0

Source: *Wall Street Journal*, March 25, 2004, p. D5, from PhoCusWright.

★ 2392 ★
Travel Arrangements
SIC: 4724; NAICS: 56151

Online Travel Industry, 2001, 2003, and 2005

Air travel reservations are forecasted to take 56.2% of the $55.6 billion market in 2005. Online travel agencies represent $40 billion in the U.S., a small part of the $40 billion spent globally in travel each year. Sales are shown in millions of dollars by segment.

	2001	2003	2005
Air	$ 13,965	$ 21,641	$ 31,296
Lodging	4,081	7,854	12,827
Car rental	2,353	4,303	6,998
Cruise/vacation	155	2,158	4,492

Source: *Airline Business*, March 1, 2004, p. 24, from ME-TA Group Research.

★ 2393 ★
Travel Arrangements
SIC: 4724; NAICS: 56151

Travel Arrangements in Colombia, 2003

The company took over 70% of the market during the first three months of 2003.

Amadeus	70.49%
Other	29.51

Source: *America's Intelligence Wire*, December 1, 2003, p. NA.

★ 2394 ★
Tour Operators
SIC: 4725; NAICS: 56152

Leading Tour Operators in the U.K., 2003

Firms are ranked by licensed capacity as of December 2003. Libra Holdings Group includes Sky Holdings. InterActive Corp. includes Expedia, TV Travel Shop Holidays and Interval Travel.

TUI Group	4,826,943
MyTravel Group	4,157,754
Thomas Cook Group	3,312,121
First Choice Group	2,608,097
Cosmos Group	1,183,938
Gold Medal Travel Group	654,848
Libra Holidays Group	618,870
Trailfinders	549,950
InterActive Corp.	536,605
Lotus Group	420,302

Source: *Travel Trade Gazette UK & Ireland*, January 12, 2004, p. 8, from CAA.

★ 2395 ★
Tour Operators
SIC: 4725; NAICS: 56152

Top Tour Operators in Europe, 2001

Companies are ranked by total business in millions of euros.

TUI	12.8
My Travel	8.2
Thomas Cook	7.9
Rewe Touristik	4.7
First Choice	3.9
Kuoni	2.7
Club Med	2.0
Hotelplan	1.5
Alltours	1.1
Alpitour	1.1

Source: *Der Spiegel*, no. 37, 2002, p. 89, from fvy.

★ 2396 ★
Tour Operators
SIC: 4725; NAICS: 56152

Top Tour Operators in Germany, 2002

Companies are ranked by turnover in millions of euros.

TUI Deutschland	4,800
Thomas Cook	3,729
Rewe-Touristik	3,404
Alltours	1,115
FTI	686
Oger	576

Source: *Der Spiegel*, October 17, 2003, p. 105, from FVW International.

★ 2397 ★
Tour Operators
SIC: 4725; NAICS: 56152

Top Tour Operators in the U.K.

Market shares are shown in percent.

Airtours	28.0%
Thomson	27.0
Thomas Cook	20.0
First Choice	18.0
Other	7.0

Source: *Travel Trade Gazette UK & Ireland*, April 7, 2003, p. 21.

★ 2398 ★
Freight Forwarding
SIC: 4731; NAICS: 48851, 541614

Freight Forwarding Industry in China

Foreign firms took three quarters of the worldwide forwarding industry with the balance held by domestic firms.

China Post	90.0%
Other	10.0

Source: *Asia Africa Intelligence Wire*, May 28, 2004, p. NA.

★ 2399 ★
Freight Forwarding
SIC: 4731; NAICS: 48851, 541614

Leading Air Freight Forwarders Worldwide

Firms are ranked by shares of international freight, which reached 15.7 million metric tons.

Danzas (DPWN)	11.6%
Panalpina	7.9
Kuehne & Nagel	4.4
Nippon Express	4.4
Schenker (Stinnes)	4.4
BAX Global	4.2

Emery/Menlo	3.7%
Kintetsu	3.5
Exel	3.3
Expeditors	3.2

Source: *Aviation Week & Space Technology*, March 31, 2003, p. 46, from MergeGlobal Inc.

★ 2400 ★
Freight Forwarding
SIC: 4731; NAICS: 48851, 541614

Leading Freight Forwarders in North America

The top providers have been ranked by North American gross revenues.

	($ mil.)	Share
Eagle Global Logistics	$ 1,869	24.75%
DHL Danzas Air & Ocean	1,445	19.13
UPS	673	8.91
BAX Global	597	7.90
Expeditors International of Washington	566	7.49
Wilson Logistics	536	7.10
Uti Worldwide	317	4.20
Panalpina	300	3.97
Kuehne & Nagel	300	3.97
Maersk Logistics USA Inc.	280	3.71
Other	670	8.87

Source: *TrafficWorld*, January 19, 2004, p. 22.

★ 2401 ★
Toll Collections
SIC: 4785; NAICS: 48849
Toll Collections by State, 2000

Collections are in millions of dollars for fiscal year 2000. Toll roads increased from 4,138 miles in 1993 to 5,100 miles in 2003.

New Jersey	$ 2,600
Florida	915
New York	619
Pennsylvania	495
Massachusetts	419
Illinois	367
Ohio	209
Oklahoma	172
Texas	135
Kansas	71

Source: *USA TODAY*, April 8, 2004, p. 3A, from Federal Highway Administration.

★ 2402 ★
Toll Operators
SIC: 4785; NAICS: 48849
Largest Toll Road Operators in Spain, 2000

Market shares are shown in percent.

Acesa	33.3%
Aurea	18.1
Europistas	13.4
Avasa	7.6
Audasa	6.5
Iberpistas	5.7
Aucat	4.1
Audenasa	2.0
Ausol	1.8
Aucalsa	1.8
Autema	1.4
Other	4.3

Source: *Expansion*, April 27, 2002, p. 3, from Informe 2000.

SIC 48 - Communications

★ 2403 ★

Mobile Gaming

SIC: 4812; NAICS: 513321, 513322, 51333

Mobile Entertainment Market, 2003, 2005 and 2007

Figures are in millions of dollars and are projections for 2005 and 2007. The global market measured $5 billion in 2003 and is expected to reach $10 billion in 2006.

	2003	2005	2007
Ringtones	$ 50	$ 300	$ 500
Games	30	200	400
Graphics/animations	15	100	300
Videos	1	20	100
SMS voting/polling	1	50	200
Advertising	1	30	200
Other	1	20	100

Source: *Mobile Messaging Analyst*, August 2003, p. 10, from Zingy.

★ 2404 ★

Mobile Gaming

SIC: 4812; NAICS: 513321, 513322, 51333

Mobile Game Market

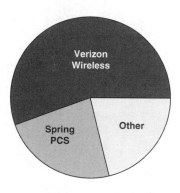

Mobile gaming revenues stood at $77 million in 2003.

Verizon Wireless	49.9%
Spring PCS	21.2
Other	18.9

Source: *Mobile Games Analyst*, February 6, 2004, p. 1, from Zelos Group and Spring PCS.

★ 2405 ★

Telecommunications

SIC: 4812; NAICS: 51333, 513322

Leading Telecom Firms in China, 2002

Telcom firms invested $25.4 billion in telecom infrastructure, down slightly from 2001. The carriers acquired nearly 96 million new subscribers which generated $55.36 billion in revenues. Market shares are shown based on revenues.

China Mobile 37.4%
China Telecom 32.5
China Netcom 16.6
China Unicom 12.1
China Railcom and ChinaSat 1.4

Source: "Telecommunications Equipment Market in China." [online] from http://www.usatrade.gov [accessed January 5, 2004], from U.S. Commercial Service.

★ 2406 ★

Telecommunications

SIC: 4812; NAICS: 51333, 513322

Telecom Market in Denmark

Market shares are shown in percent.

TDC 79.0%
Cybercity 11.0
Tiscali 8.0
Orange 1.0

Source: *Boersen*, October 29, 2002, p. NA, from Danish IT and Telecom Agency.

★ 2407 ★

Telecommunications

SIC: 4812; NAICS: 51333, 513322

Telecom Services to Large Companies

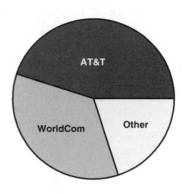

The market for providing data and telephone services to large companies is a lucrative one. AT&T has between 40-45% of the market. WorldCom's share is also estimated.

AT&T 45.0%
WorldCom 35.0
Other 20.0

Source: *International Herald Tribune*, March 4, 2004, p. NA.

★ 2408 ★

Telecommunications

SIC: 4812; NAICS: 51333, 513322

Telecommunications Industry in Moscow, Russia

Data are for 2001.

Golden Telecom 32.0%
MTU 17.0
Comstar 13.0
Combellga 12.0
Equant 8.0
Telmos 5.0
Other 13.0

Source: *Investor's Business Daily*, August 11, 2003, p. A5, from company reports, Pyramid Research, and First Call.

★ 2409 ★
Telecommunications
SIC: 4812; NAICS: 51333, 513322

Telecommunications Industry Spending

Total telecommunications spending increased nearly 5% from 2002 to reach an estimated $720.5 billion in 2003. Network equipment providers may see revenues increase to $18.5 billion in 2007 from the addition of VoIP and data transport services. Videoconferencing was the fastest growing segment of the enterprise equipment market.

Transport services	$ 285,000
Enterprise equipment	94,000
Network equipment	14,000
Broadband services	13,000

Source: *Fiber Optics Weekly Update*, January 16, 2004, p. 7, from Telecommunication Industry Association 2004 Telecommunications Market Review.

★ 2410 ★
Wireless Services
SIC: 4812; NAICS: 513322

Business Broadband Market

The U.S. business broadband data services market is shown by segment. Virtual protocol networks (VPNs) are seen as a hot market by some analysts in the industry. VPNs are perceived as a secure (and financially reasonable) way to send data by companies.

Private line	44.0%
Frame relay	35.0
ATM	10.0
DSL	4.0
Internet protocol VPN	4.0
Other	3.0

Source: *Investor's Business Daily*, June 23, 2003, p. A4, from Vertical Systems Group, International Data Corp., and Infonetics Research.

★ 2411 ★
Wireless Services
SIC: 4812; NAICS: 513322

GSM-based Technology Contracts Worldwide

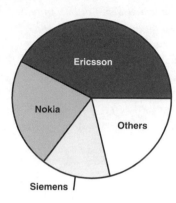

Total value of new GSM-based technology awards during the second half of 2003 totalled $5.23 billion. Leading award winners are listed in the table. GSM-based stands for Global System for Mobile-Communications.

Ericsson	42.30%
Nokia	22.25
Siemens	14.20
Others	21.25

Source: *Global Mobile*, February 11, 2004, p. 14, from Global Mobile survey.

★ 2412 ★
Wireless Services
SIC: 4812; NAICS: 513322

Largest CDMA Markets Worldwide

Countries are ranked by number of CDMA (code division multiple access) subscribers as of September 2003.

United States	67,681,800
Korea	33,320,500
Japan	15,318,100
China	13,702,700
Brazil	12,078,000
Canada	5,976,800
India	5,295,130
Mexico	5,242,700
Venezuela	2,593,900

Source: *World CDMA Report*, October 2003, p. 102.

★ 2413 ★
Wireless Services
SIC: 4812; NAICS: 513322

Largest CDMA Wireless Firms Worldwide

CDMA stands for Code Division Multiple Access and is a systems used in wireless communications. CDMA is a system different from GSM-based technology (Global System Mobile-Communications based technology). Unlike GSM-based technology, CDMA does not assign a specific frequency to each user. Instead, every channel uses the full available spectrum. Individual conversations are encoded with a pseudo-random digital sequence.

Nortel	45.1%
Lucent	40.4
Ericsson	8.0

Source: *Global Mobile*, February 11, 2004, p. 14, from Global Mobile survey.

★ 2414 ★
Wireless Services
SIC: 4812; NAICS: 513322

Leading CDMA2000 1X Service Providers Worldwide

CDMA stands for code division multiple access. By region, U.S. and Canada have 43.2% of subscribers, followed by Asia/Pacific with 39.1%. Data are for June 2003.

SK Telecom	32.0%
KDDI	32.0
KTF	17.0
Sprint PCS	6.0
LG Telecom	5.0
Telesp	2.0
Other	6.0

Source: *World CDMA Report*, October 2003, p. 4, from EMC World Cellular Database.

★ 2415 ★
Wireless Services
SIC: 4812; NAICS: 513322

Leading Cellular Phone Firms, 2002

Market shares are shown based on subscribers.

	(mil.)	Share
Verizon	32.4	23.9%
Cingular	21.9	16.2
AT&T	20.9	15.4
Sprint	14.8	10.9
Nextel	10.6	7.8
T-Mobile	10.0	7.4
Alltel	7.6	5.6

Source: *New York Times*, June 25, 2003, p. C6, from The Yankee Group.

★ 2416 ★
Wireless Services
SIC: 4812; NAICS: 513322

Leading IP-VPN Carrier Managed Services, 2002

Shares are based on estimated revenues. IP-VPN stands for Internet Protocol - Virtual Protocol Network.

	($ mil.)	Share
AT&T	$ 173.2	25.90%
WorldCom	150.3	22.48
Savvis	133.5	19.97
Sprint	109.4	16.36
Genuity	102.2	15.29

Source: *Telecommunications Americas*, April 2003, p. 10, from International Data Corp.

★ 2417 ★
Wireless Services
SIC: 4812; NAICS: 513322

Leading Mobile Phone Firms in France, 2002

Market shares are shown as of December 31, 2002.

Orange	49.8%
SFR	35.1
Bouygues Telecom	15.1

Source: *EuropeMedia*, January 30, 2003, p. NA.

★ 2418 ★
Wireless Services
SIC: 4812; NAICS: 513322

Leading Wireless Firms, 2003

The top 7 firms have nealy 93% of the market and 130 million subscribers in the United States. Figures are as of September 30, 2003.

Verizon	25.9%
Cingular	16.8
AT&T Wireless	15.6
Sprint PCS	11.1
Nextel	8.9
T-Mobile	8.7
Alltel	5.7
Other	7.1

Source: *USA TODAY*, November 24, 2003, p. 2B, from Yankee Group and J.D. Power & Associates.

★ 2419 ★
Wireless Services
SIC: 4812; NAICS: 513322

Leading Wireless Firms in Argentina

Market shares are shown in percent.

Telecom Personal	30.0%
Unifon (Telefonica)	26.0
Movicom	25.0
CTI	17.0
Nextel	2.0

Source: *New York Times*, January 15, 2003, p. W1, from Pyramid Research.

★ 2420 ★
Wireless Services
SIC: 4812; NAICS: 513322

Leading Wireless Firms in Australia

The Australian mobile industry had more than A$5 billion in revenues. Market shares are shown in percent.

Telstra	46.0%
Singtel Optus	34.0
Vodafone	18.0
Hutchinson Australia (Orange)	2.0

Source: *New Media Age*, November 27, 2003, p. S10.

★ 2421 ★
Wireless Services
SIC: 4812; NAICS: 513322

Leading Wireless Firms in Austria

Market shares are shown based on subscribers for the third quarter of 2003.

Mobilkom	39.6%
Connect	26.9
T-Mobile (Maxmobil)	26.0
tele.ring	6.6
H3G	0.8

Source: *Global Mobile*, November 19, 2003, p. 10, from Global Mobile Subscriber Database.

★ 2422 ★
Wireless Services
SIC: 4812; NAICS: 513322

Leading Wireless Firms in Belarus

*Market shares are shown based on subscribers for
the first quarter of 2003.*

Belcel 82.4%
Mobile Digital Comms 14.3
Other 3.3

Source: *Global Mobile*, June 18, 2003, p. 10, from Global
Mobile Subscriber.

★ 2423 ★
Wireless Services
SIC: 4812; NAICS: 513322

Leading Wireless Firms in Belgium

*Market shares are shown based on subscribers for
the third quarter of 2003.*

Belgacom Mobile 53.4%
Mobistar 31.8
Base (KPN Orange Belgium) 14.8

Source: *Global Mobile*, November 19, 2003, p. 10, from
Global Mobile Subscriber Database.

★ 2424 ★
Wireless Services
SIC: 4812; NAICS: 513322

Leading Wireless Firms in Estonia

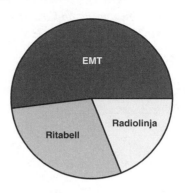

*Market shares are shown based on subscribers for
the first quarter of 2003.*

EMT 52.0%
Ritabell 29.0
Radiolinja 19.0

Source: *Global Mobile*, June 18, 2003, p. 10, from Global
Mobile Subscriber Database.

★ 2425 ★
Wireless Services
SIC: 4812; NAICS: 513322

Leading Wireless Firms in Finland

*Market shares are shown based on subscribers for
the third quarter of 2003.*

Sonera 53.8%
Radiolinja 30.3
Suomen 2G (Finnet Group) 15.9

Source: *Global Mobile*, November 19, 2003, p. 10, from
Global Mobile Subscriber Database.

★ 2426 ★
Wireless Services
SIC: 4812; NAICS: 513322

Leading Wireless Firms in Georgia

Market shares are shown based on subscribers for the first quarter of 2003.

Magticom	49.7%
Geocell	47.7
Megacom	2.6

Source: *Global Mobile*, June 18, 2003, p. 10, from Global Mobile Subscriber.

★ 2427 ★
Wireless Services
SIC: 4812; NAICS: 513322

Leading Wireless Firms in Germany, 2002

Market shares are shown in percent.

D1	39.7%
D2	37.6
E-Plus	13.7
Viag Interkom	6.6
MobilCom	1.4
Quam	1.0

Source: *Financial Times*, July 26, 2002, p. 18, from Bear Stearns.

★ 2428 ★
Wireless Services
SIC: 4812; NAICS: 513322

Leading Wireless Firms in Greece

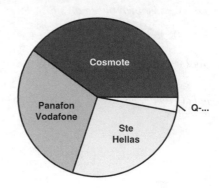

Market shares are shown based on subscribers for the third quarter of 2003.

Cosmote	40.3%
Panafon Vodafone	29.8
Ste Hellas	27.0
Q-Telecom	2.8

Source: *Global Mobile*, November 19, 2003, p. 10, from Global Mobile Subscriber Database.

★ 2429 ★
Wireless Services
SIC: 4812; NAICS: 513322

Leading Wireless Firms in Hong Kong

Shares are for the third quarter.

Hutchison	25.0%
Smartone	17.0
CSL	17.0
Peoples Phone	16.0
New World Mobility	15.0
Sunday	10.0

Source: *Asia-Pacific Mobile Communications Report*, August 2003, p. 4, from EMC World Cellular Database.

★ 2430 ★
Wireless Services
SIC: 4812; NAICS: 513322

Leading Wireless Firms in Hungary

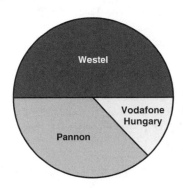

Market shares are shown based on subscribers for the first quarter of 2003.

Westel	50.3%
Pannon	37.0
Vodafone Hungary	12.6

Source: *Global Mobile*, June 18, 2003, p. 10, from Global Mobile Subscriber Database.

★ 2431 ★
Wireless Services
SIC: 4812; NAICS: 513322

Leading Wireless Firms in Mexico

The entire telecom industry was valued at $12 billion. Mobile phone subscriptions may reach 45 million in 2008 (currently 26 million).

	($ mil.)	Share
Telcel	$4,212	74.69%
Telefonica Moviles	552	9.79
Lusacell	499	8.85
Unefon	331	5.87
Nextel	45	0.80

Source: *Business Mexico*, August 2003, p. 22, from International Data Corp.

★ 2432 ★
Wireless Services
SIC: 4812; NAICS: 513322

Leading Wireless Firms in Poland

Market shares are shown based on subscribers for the first quarter of 2003.

Era	35.1%
Centertel	32.5
Plus (Polkomtel)	32.4

Source: *Global Mobile*, June 18, 2003, p. 10, from Global Mobile Subscriber Database.

★ 2433 ★
Wireless Services
SIC: 4812; NAICS: 513322

Leading Wireless Firms in Portugal

Market shares are shown based on subscribers for the third quarter of 2003.

TMN	48.5%
Vodafone (Telecel)	28.2
Optimus	23.2

Source: *Global Mobile*, November 19, 2003, p. 10, from Global Mobile Subscriber Database.

★ 2434 ★
Wireless Services
SIC: 4812; NAICS: 513322

Leading Wireless Firms in Spain

There were 50 operators in 2001. The number of fixed lines increased 2.5%, fixed traffic increased 32.3% and fixed revenue increased 6.35%.

Telefonica Moviles	56.6%
Vodafone	25.7
Armena	17.6
Other	0.1

Source: *Expansion*, July 26, 2002, p. NA.

★ 2435 ★

Wireless Services

SIC: 4812; NAICS: 513322

Leading Wireless Firms in Tatarstan, Russia

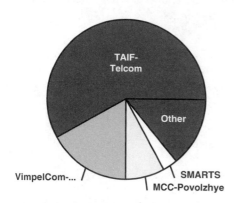

Market shares are shown in percent.

TAIF-Telcom	58.0%
VimpelCom-Region	16.9
MCC-Povolzhye	8.3
SMARTS	2.9
Other	13.9

Source: *Communications & Electronic Report*, October 20, 2003, p. NA.

★ 2436 ★

Wireless Services

SIC: 4812; NAICS: 513322

Leading Wireless Firms in the Middle East & Africa, 2003

Wireless operators in the Middle East and African are listed in order of the number of wireless phone subscribers they had as of the third quarter 2003.

Turkcell	18,180
Vodacom	7,185
Telsim	6,120
MTN	5,360
Marco Telecom	4,999
Saudi Telecom	3,640

TCI	2,905
MobiNil	2,784
Click Vodafone	2,503
Cellcom Israel	2,443

Source: *Global Mobile*, January 28, 2004, p. 14, from Global Mobile survey.

★ 2437 ★

Wireless Services

SIC: 4812; NAICS: 513322

Leading Wireless Firms in the Netherlands

Market shares are shown based on 12 million clients.

KPN Mobile	41.8%
Vodafone	27.1
T-Mobile	11.8
O2	10.7
Dutchstone (Orange)	8.5

Source: *Tarifica Alert*, October 14, 2003, p. NA, from Market Monitor Telecom 2002 and OPTA.

★ 2438 ★

Wireless Services

SIC: 4812; NAICS: 513322

Leading Wireless Firms Worldwide

Companies are ranked by millions of mobile subscribers. Cingular recently purchased AT&T Wireless.

China Mobile	153.6
Vodafone	118.9
Chian Unicom	86.6
Cingular/AT&T Wireless	67.1
Deutsche Telekom	65.8
NTT DoCoMo	50.8
France Telecom	41.9
America Movil	36.7
Telefonica	29.9
Verizon	28.8

Source: *Financial Times*, February 18, 2004, p. 1, from EMC.

★ **2439** ★

Wireless Services

SIC: 4812; NAICS: 513322

Leading Wireless Service Firms in Moscow, Russia

Market shares are shown in percent for 2002. Outside of Moscow, Mobile Telesystems has the largest market share.

Vimpel	52.0%
MTS	42.0
Megafon	5.0
Other	1.0

Source: *Investor's Business Daily*, October 28, 2003, p. A9, from company reports and Citigroup.

★ **2440** ★

Wireless Services

SIC: 4812; NAICS: 513322

Wholesale Broadband Market in Ireland

Share is for the entire broadband market, including fixed wireless and cable operators.

Eircom	79.0%
Other	21.0

Source: ''ComReg Proposes SMP Label for Eircom.'' [online] http://www.electricnews.net/ print.html?code9397559 [accessed March 31, 2004], March 8, 2004, p. NA.

★ **2441** ★

Wireless Services

SIC: 4812; NAICS: 513322

Wireless Subscribers by Region

Figures are for 2003 and 2004 are forecasted.

	2003	2003	2004
Asia Pacific	434.8	531.0	616.0
Western Europe	304.0	309.0	312.0
South America	75.3	86.3	97.4
Eastern Europe	74.4	93.6	108.6
Middle East	47.0	55.5	61.8
Africa	36.9	46.9	57.7

Source: *European Telecom*, August 2003, p. 1, from U.S. Bancorp. Piper Jaffray.

★ **2442** ★

Wireless Services

SIC: 4812; NAICS: 513322

Wireless Subscribers in the Middle East and Africa

Data show both analogue and digital subscribers.

	Subscribers	Share
South Africa	15,915,600	24.14%
Morocco	6,942,500	10.53
Saudi Arabia	6,935,400	10.52
Egypt	5,170,500	7.84
UAE	2,781,300	4.22
Iran	2,339,900	3.55
Nigeria	2,199,300	3.34
Kenya	2,077,200	3.15
Kuwait	1,609,250	2.44
Tunisia	1,379,300	2.09
Jordan	1,278,300	1.94
Cote d'Ivoire	1,225,200	1.86
Other	16,069,600	24.38

Source: *African and Middle East Mobile Communications Report*, October 2003, p. 50.

★ **2443** ★

Wireless Services

SIC: 4812; NAICS: 513322

Wireless Subscribers Worldwide by Format, 2003

Shares are for the third quarter. CDMA stands code division multiple access. TDMA stands for time division multiple access. GSM stands for global system for mobile communications. CDMA is the fastest-growing technology worldwide. It added 39 million subscribers between September 2002 - September 2003.

CDMA	44.0%
TDMA	26.0
GSM	15.0
Other	15.0

Source: *PrimeZone Media Network*, November 20, 2003, p. NA, from EMC database.

★ 2444 ★
Telephone Services
SIC: 4813; NAICS: 513322, 51333

Cable Telephone Subscriptions

Data show the estimated number of subscribers by the end of the year.

	No.	Share
Comcast	1,300,000	54.99%
Cox	976,173	41.29
Mediacom	55,000	2.33
Charter	24,533	1.04
Cablevision	5,006	0.21
Time Warner	2,000	0.08
Other	1,250	0.05

Source: *USA TODAY*, December 10, 2003, p. 7B, from MRG.

★ 2445 ★
Telephone Services
SIC: 4813; NAICS: 51331

IDD Market Shares in the U.K.

Market shares are shown in percent.

BT	32.0%
C&W	5.7
Ntl & Telewest	5.6
Kingston	0.1
Other	56.6

Source: *Tarifica Alert*, September 2, 2003, p. NA.

★ 2446 ★
Telephone Services
SIC: 4813; NAICS: 51333

Leading Service Providers in the U.K. 2001-2002

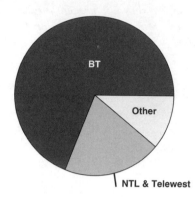

Market shares for residential service are shown based on revenues.

BT	69.1%
NTL & Telewest	20.4
Other	10.5

Source: *Financial Times*, December 24, 2003, p. 14, from ABG Sundai Collier and Oftel.

★ 2447 ★
Telephone Services
SIC: 4813; NAICS: 51331

Local-Phone Service Market, 2003

Data show share of all households.

Verizon	25.0%
SBC	23.0
BellSouth	11.0
Qwest	9.0
Sprint	5.0
Other	27.0

Source: *Fortune*, May 31, 2004, p. 124.

★ 2448 ★
Telephone Services
SIC: 4813; NAICS: 51331
Long-Distance Market, 2003

Data show share of all households.

AT&T	25.0%
Verizon	15.0
SBC	13.0
MCI	11.0
Sprint	8.0
Other	28.0

Source: *Fortune*, May 31, 2004, p. 124.

★ 2449 ★
Telephone Services
SIC: 4813; NAICS: 51331
Long-Distance Market, 2004

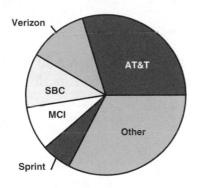

Market shares are shown in percent.

AT&T	30.0%
Verizon	12.0
SBC	11.0
MCI	9.0
Sprint	5.5
Other	32.5

Source: *Wall Street Journal*, June 10, 2004, p. 1, from
Yankee Group.

★ 2450 ★
Telephone Services
SIC: 4813; NAICS: 51331
Long-Distance Market in Argentina

Market shares are shown in percent.

Telefonica	48.0%
Telecom Personal	43.0
Movicom (BellSouth)	4.0
CTI (Verizon)	2.0
Other	3.0

Source: *New York Times*, January 15, 2003, p. W1, from
Pyramid Research.

★ 2451 ★
Telephone Services
SIC: 4813; NAICS: 51331
Long-Distance Market in Brazil, 2003

Market shares are shown in percent.

Embratel	25.15%
Telemar	24.45
Telefonica	24.10
Other	26.40

Source: *South American Business Information*, April 28,
2004, p. NA, from Agencia Nacional de
Telecommunicacoes.

★ 2452 ★
Telephone Services
SIC: 4813; NAICS: 51331
Long-Distance Market in Mexico

Market shares are shown in percent.

Telmex	85.0%
Other	15.0

Source: *Latin America Telecom*, March 2004, p. 7.

★ 2453 ★
Telephone Services
SIC: 4813; NAICS: 51331

Long-Distance Phone Service in Bolivia

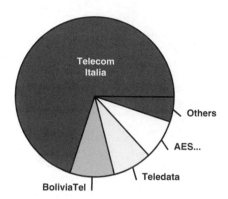

Market shares are for the third quarter of 2003.

Telecom Italia	70.0%
BoliviaTel	9.0
Teledata	8.0
AES Communications Bolivia	8.0
Others	5.0

Source: *Latin American Telecom*, September 2003, p. 4.

★ 2454 ★
Telephone Services
SIC: 4813; NAICS: 51331

Residential Service Market in the Mid-Atlantic States, 2002

Market shares are shown based on sample data.

AT&T	39.2%
MCI	18.2
Verizon	11.7
Sprint	7.1
Qwest	2.2
Other	21.8

Source: ''Trends in Telephone Service'' [Online] from http://www.fcc.gov [accessed October 1, 2003], from industry analysts, Technology Divison staff using survey data from TNS, and *Bill Harvesting*.

★ 2455 ★
Telephone Services
SIC: 4813; NAICS: 51331

Residential Service Market in the Midwest, 2002

Market shares are shown based on sample data.

AT&T	40.9%
MCI	15.4
Verizon	7.9
Sprint	7.2
Qwest	2.8
SBC	0.3
Other	25.5

Source: ''Trends in Telephone Service'' [Online] from http://www.fcc.gov [accessed October 1, 2003], from industry analysts, Technology Divison staff using survey data from TNS, and *Bill Harvesting*.

★ 2456 ★
Telephone Services
SIC: 4813; NAICS: 51331

Residential Service Market in the Northeastern United States, 2002

Market shares are shown based on sample data.

AT&T	29.9%
Verizon	28.4
MCI	12.1
SBC	6.7
Sprint	2.6
Qwest	1.3
Other	19.1

Source: ''Trends in Telephone Service'' [Online] from http://www.fcc.gov [accessed October 1, 2003], from industry analysts, Technology Divison staff using survey data from TNS, and *Bill Harvesting*.

★ 2457 ★
Telephone Services
SIC: 4813; NAICS: 51331

Residential Service Market in the Southeastern United States, 2002

Market shares are shown based on sample data.

AT&T 41.3%
MCI 16.6
Sprint 10.9
Verizon 5.4
Qwest 2.1
BellSouth 1.2
SBC 0.1
Other 22.4

Source: "Trends in Telephone Service" [Online] from http://www.fcc.gov [accessed October 1, 2003], from industry analysts, Technology Divison staff using survey data from TNS, and *Bill Harvesting*.

★ 2458 ★
Telephone Services
SIC: 4813; NAICS: 51331

Residential Service Market in the Southwest, 2002

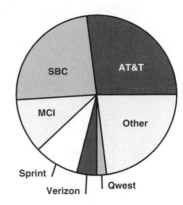

Market shares are shown based on sample data.

AT&T 27.3%
SBC 23.9
MCI 10.8
Sprint 8.5
Verizon 4.3
Qwest 1.9
Other 23.3

Source: "Trends in Telephone Service" [Online] from http://www.fcc.gov [accessed October 1, 2003], from industry analysts, Technology Divison staff using survey data from TNS, and *Bill Harvesting*.

★ 2459 ★
Telephone Services
SIC: 4813; NAICS: 51331

Residential Service Market in the Western United States, 2002

Market shares are shown based on sample data.

AT&T 33.9%
MCI 18.1
Sprint 6.6
Qwest 4.6
Verizon 4.0
Other 32.8

Source: "Trends in Telephone Service" [Online] from http://www.fcc.gov [accessed October 1, 2003], from industry analysts, Technology Divison staff using survey data from TNS, and *Bill Harvesting*.

★ 2460 ★
Telephone Services
SIC: 4813; NAICS: 51331

Residential Service Market on the West Coast, 2002

Market shares are shown based on sample data.

AT&T	39.5%
MCI	17.3
Verizon	10.7
Sprint	8.1
Qwest	2.2
SBC	0.7
Other	21.5

Source: "Trends in Telephone Service" [Online] from http://www.fcc.gov [accessed October 1, 2003], from industry analysts, Technology Divison staff using survey data from TNS, and *Bill Harvesting*.

★ 2461 ★
Telephone Services
SIC: 4813; NAICS: 51331

Telephone Market in Arizona

Data reflect both residential and business.

Qwest	79.0%
Other	21.0

Source: *Arizona Daily Star*, March 30, 2004, p. NA.

★ 2462 ★
Electronic Commerce
SIC: 4822; NAICS: 51331

Leading eBay Auction Categories

Data show millions of unique users.

Collectibles	11.50
Home	10.30
Motors	9.42
Electronics	7.87
Toys	7.70
Sports	7.67
Half (fixed price)	7.37
Entertainment	6.95

Clothing	6.50
Stores	6.25

Source: *Investor's Business Daily*, August 11, 2003, p. A4, from Nielsen/NetRatings Inc.

★ 2463 ★
Electronic Commerce
SIC: 4822; NAICS: 51331

Leading Online Travel Agencies

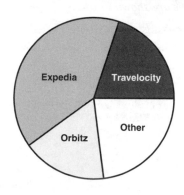

Market shares are shown in percent.

	2001	2004
Travelocity	32.0%	20.0%
Expedia	30.0	40.0
Orbitz	8.0	17.0
Other	30.0	23.0

Source: *New York Times*, January 5, 2004, p. C5, from PhoCusWright.

★ 2464 ★
Electronic Commerce
SIC: 4822; NAICS: 51331

Online Gaming Market in China, 2002

Market shares are shown in percent.

Shanda Networking	31.0%
Waei	17.0
Enix Softstar	12.0
Online-game	7.0
Other	33.0

Source: *Financial Times*, May 21, 2004, p. 16, from Morgan Stanley.

★ 2465 ★
Electronic Commerce
SIC: 4822; NAICS: 51331

Top E-Commerce Sites in Hong Kong

Figures are in thousands of home users in November 2003.

Yahoo Shopping	399
Yahoo Auctions	262
EBay	153
Amazon	109
YesAsia	98
Go2HK	82
Red-dots	80
ESD Life Shopping	50
ICare	49
Shopping.com	45
JUSCO	37

Source: *Investor's Business Daily*, January 29, 2004, p. A6, from Nielsen/NetRatings.

★ 2466 ★
Electronic Commerce
SIC: 4822; NAICS: 51331

Top E-commerce Web Sites

Figures show the millions of unique visitors for August 2003.

eBay	42.4
Amazon	26.1
Yahoo! Shopping	15.1
DealTime	11.9
Wal-Mart	9.2
Target	7.6
AOL Shopping	7.5
Bizrate.com	7.4
Sears	5.3

Source: *Wall Street Journal*, September 23, 2003, p. B1, from Nielsen/NetRatings.

★ 2467 ★
Electronic Commerce
SIC: 4822; NAICS: 51331

Top E-Retailers, 2002

Companies are ranked by sales in millions of dollars.

QVC	$ 4,381.00
Amazon.com	3,932.93
Home Shopping Network	1,900.00
Columbia House	1,000.00
ValueVision	550.90
Barnesandnoble.com	422.82

Source: *Stores*, July 2003, p. S16.

★ 2468 ★
Electronic Commerce
SIC: 4822; NAICS: 51331

Top Online Retailers in Europe

Sites are ranked by millions of unique visitors for September 2003.

Ebay	22.5
Amazon	11.7
Kelkoo	5.4
Expedia	2.5
Otto	2.2

Source: *New Media Age*, November 27, 2003, p. 14, from Nielsen/NetRatings.

★ 2469 ★
Electronic Commerce
SIC: 4822; NAICS: 51331

Top Sites for Used Book Purchases, 2003

In 2003, over half (54.4%) of all used book sales took place online. The top sites are shown below. Bookstores had the second largest share of used book sales with 29.5% of purchases and then book fairs with 3.9% of purchases.

Abebooks	39.2%
Amazon.com	17.3
Alibris	12.9
eBay	9.0
Dealer sites	8.6

Source: *New York Times*, May 17, 2004, p. C7, from Book Hunter Press.

★ 2470 ★
Internet
SIC: 4822; NAICS: 51331

Adults and Internet Use, 2002

At the end of 2002, 59% of American adults were on the Internet. According to the study, income and education play a significant role in Internet access and use.

Pacific Northwest	68.0%
New England	66.0
California	65.0
Mountain states	64.0
Nation's capital region	64.0
Border states	60.0
Upper Midwest	59.0
Mid-Atlantic	58.0
Southeast	57.0
Industrial Midwest	56.0
Midwest	55.0
South	48.0

Source: *USA TODAY*, August 28, 2003, p. 4D, from Pew Internet & American Life Project.

★ 2471 ★
Internet
SIC: 4822; NAICS: 51331

Internet Households, 2003

Figures are in millions for June 2003.

	(mil.)	Share
Cable modem	12.30	65.92%
Digital subscriber line	5.90	31.62
Satellite	0.40	2.14
Other	0.06	0.32

Source: *New York Times*, July 31, 2003, p. E1, from Yankee Group.

★ 2472 ★
Internet
SIC: 4822; NAICS: 51331
Internet Users by Country

The U.S. has about 50% of the global Internet access market, followed by Europe with 23% and Asia-Pacific 13%. The average user spends about 12 hours a month online according to Nielsen/NetRatings. Figures show millions of users.

United States	182.1
China	68.0
Japan	56.0
Germany	44.1
United Kingdom	34.3
South Korea	25.6
France	21.8
Italy	19.3
Russia	18.0
Canada	16.8
Spain	14.0

Source: *Stores*, January 2004, p. G26, from various sources.

★ 2473 ★
Internet
SIC: 4822; NAICS: 51331
Leading Internet Search Firms

About 245 million searches are performed daily in the United States. 550 million are performed worldwide. Information and reference make up 65% of searches, 20% entertainment, 15% commerce. Companies are ranked by search revenues in millions of dollars.

Overture Services	$ 688
Google	294
Yahoo	140
MSN	138
AOL	92
LookSmart	75
AskJeeves	74
AltaVista	55
Inktomi	46
Lycos	43
InfoSpace	43

Source: *Internet Business Daily*, May 2, 2003, p. A6, from U.S. Bancorp Piper Jaffray and Jupiter Research.

★ 2474 ★
Internet
SIC: 4822; NAICS: 51331
Leading Search Engines in Austria

There were about 4.1 million Austrians using the Internet in 2002. Some concerns about Internet use among Austrians are telephone and ISP fees and data security. However, electronic commerce appears to be a growing market with sales increasing from $3.6 billion in 2001 to $6.5 billion in 2002. Surfing is the most popular activity (45%) followed by email (40%). Netscape has a 90% share of the Web browser market.

Google	19.6%
Yahoo	19.2
Lycos	11.6
Fireball	8.9
web.de	7.6
Altavista	6.7
Other	26.4

Source: "Trends in the ICT-Sector in Austria." [online] from http://www.export.gov [accessed February 1, 2004].

★ 2475 ★
Internet
SIC: 4822; NAICS: 51331
Online Auction Market in China

The company has about 4 million users (eBay in the U.S. has about 62 million, by way of comparison) and is seeing healthy growth in its revenues.

Eachnet	85.0%
Other	15.0

Source: *Chief Executive*, August-September 2003, p. 31.

★ 2476 ★
Internet
SIC: 4822; NAICS: 51331
Online Job Market, 2003

Figures are for the first half of the year based on revenues. In August 2003, Monster.com had 15.2 million visitors, HotJobs.com 8.5 million and CareerBuilder.com 6.4 million.

Monster.com	38.0%
HotJobs.com	11.6
CareerBuilder.com	10.0

Source: *Crain's New York Business*, September 15, 2003, p. 4, from Jupiter Research.

★ 2477 ★
Internet
SIC: 4822; NAICS: 51331

Online Movie Tickets

The company has 70% of the market of theaters wired for online ticketing.

Fandango Inc. 70.0%
Other 30.0

Source: *Hollywood Reporter*, May 13, 2003, p. 6.

★ 2478 ★
Internet
SIC: 4822; NAICS: 51331

Spending for Online Content

Spending is shown in millions of dollars for the second quarter of 2003. The source points out that while online users will pay for some content — such as entertainment and dating — they are unwilling to pay for other forms of content (compare credit help to the dating category). According to surveys cited in the source users will pay for services that improve their online experience.

	($ mil.)	Share
Personals/dating	$ 109.7	28.87%
Business/investment	83.5	21.97
Entertainment/lifestyles	52.1	13.71
Research	24.7	6.50
Personal growth	22.3	5.87
General news	21.3	5.61
Community directories	20.6	5.42
Games	18.8	4.95
Greeting cards	10.1	2.66
Credit help	9.3	2.45
Other	7.6	2.00

Source: *Adweek*, September 15, 2003, p. 26, from Online Publishers Association, comScore Networks, and *Paid Online Content U.S. Market Spending Reports*.

★ 2479 ★
Internet
SIC: 4822; NAICS: 51331

Top Auto Dealer Sites

Data refer to web sites of specific car and vehicle dealers and licensed car dealers. Market shares are shown for September 2003. Chevrolet had the largest market share of auto makers' web sites (Ford, shown here, ranked fourth after Toyota and Cadillac).

CarMax.com 51.34%
Ford Direct 21.22
InvoiceDealers 15.44
Volvo Direct 2.85
www.autodealers-usa.com 1.26

Source: "$1.3B Expected for Online Auto Ads." [online] from http://www.clickz.com/news/print.php/3101211 [accessed April 29, 2004], from Hitwise.

★ 2480 ★
Internet
SIC: 4822; NAICS: 51331

Top Digital Sheet Music Sites

Musicnotes.com dominates the field of downloading of digital sheet music, guitar tablature and lyrics.

Musicnotes 93.0%
Other 7.0

Source: *Capital Times*, February 5, 2004, p. 6E.

★ 2481 ★
Internet
SIC: 4822; NAICS: 51331

Top Encyclopedia Sites

Sites are ranked by millions of vistors in April 2004.

AOL Research & Learn 7.2
Reference.com 6.6
MSN Encarta 5.7
Encyclopedia Britannica 3.4
HighBeam 2.7

Continued on next page.

★ 2481 ★

[Continued]
Internet
SIC: 4822; NAICS: 51331

Top Encyclopedia Sites

Sites are ranked by millions of vistors in April 2004.

Wikipedia.org	2.4
Questia.com	1.4
Scholastic.com	1.4

Source: *Investor's Business Daily*, June 7, 2004, p. A4, from comScore Media Metrix.

★ 2482 ★

Internet
SIC: 4822; NAICS: 51331

Top Game Sites, 2004

Data show share of traffic in the games category as of February 2004.

GameFaqs	2.47%
Cheat Planet	1.02
GameSpot	1.01
GameWinners.com	0.90
Cheat Code Central	0.72
IGN	0.48
CheatCodes.com	0.31
Game Revolution.com	0.27
Other	92.82

Source: *Electronic Gaming Business*, March 24, 2004, p. NA, from Hitwise.

★ 2483 ★

Internet
SIC: 4822; NAICS: 51331

Top Internet Sites

Figures show unique visitors for home, work and university locations during March 2004.

Yahoo! Sites	154,051
Time Warner Network	110,754
MSN-Microsoft Sites	109,660
eBay	69,701
Google Sites	65,029
About/Primedia	38,961
Terra Lycos	37,339
Amazon Sites	35,526
Viacom Online	26,906
Walt Disney Internet Group	25,236

Source: *PR Newswire*, April 22, 2004, p. NA, from Media Metrix.

★ 2484 ★

Internet
SIC: 4822; NAICS: 51331

Top Map Sites, 2004

Data show millions of unique visitors during February 2004.

Mapquest.com	29.37
Yahoo! Maps	14.92
Vicinity Sites	4.10
MSN MapPoint	2.75
Maps.com	1.45
Mapsonus.com	1.05
RandMcNally.com	0.91

Source: *Orange County Register*, March 25, 2004, p. NA, from ComSource Media Metrix.

★ 2485 ★
Internet
SIC: 4822; NAICS: 51331

Top Movie Sites, 2004

Yahoo Movies

IMDB.com

Moviefone.com

MSN Movies

iFilm Network

Figures show millions of visitors for the week ended February 22, 2004.

Yahoo Movies 3.04
IMDB.com 2.15
Moviefone.com 2.07
MSN Movies 1.76
iFilm Network 1.29

Source: *Investor's Business Daily*, March 1, 2004, p. A5, from comScore Media Metrix.

★ 2486 ★
Internet
SIC: 4822; NAICS: 51331

Top Music Sites

Figure show unique audience, in thousands, in August 2003.

Kazaa 10,397
Morpheus 722
BearShare 629
iMesh 586
Grokster 335
Napster 221

Source: *Financial Times*, October 16, 2003, p. 21, from Nielsen Ratings.

★ 2487 ★
Internet
SIC: 4822; NAICS: 51331

Top Online Gaming Sites

Share of users is for July 2003. Women over the age of 18 represent 26% of the gaming population, boys 6-17 represent 21%, girls 6-17 took 12% and men over the age of 18 took 38%.

Yahoo!Games 11.6%
Pogo 9.6
Yahoo!Sports Fantasy Baseball 5.0
Other 73.8

Source: *New Media Age*, September 4, 2003, p. 17, from Nielsen/NetRatings and Entertainment Software Association.

★ 2488 ★
Internet
SIC: 4822; NAICS: 51331

Top Personals Sites, 2003

Data show millions of unique visitors as of October 2003.

Yahoo! Personals 4.9
Match 3.9
AmericanSingles 3.7
MSN Dating & Personals 1.9
Netscape Love & Personals 1.5

Source: *USA TODAY*, December 5, 2003, p. A1, from Nielsen/NetRatings.

★ 2489 ★
Internet
SIC: 4822; NAICS: 51331

Top Search Engines

Data show share of searches conducted by U.S. users for May 2003.

Google 32.0%
Yahoo 25.0
AOL Time Warner 19.0
MSN-Microsoft 15.0
Ask Jeeves 3.0
Other 6.0

Source: *Wall Street Journal*, July 16, 2003, p. 1, from comScore Networks.

★ 2490 ★

Internet

SIC: 4822; NAICS: 51331

Top Search Engines Worldwide

Data show share of searches by Internet users world-wide for February 2004.

Google	43.3%
Yahoo sites	30.8
MSN microsoft sites	14.1
Time Warner Network	7.1
Ask Jeeves	1.7
Other	3.0

Source: *Financial Times*, May 1, 2004, p. 8.

★ 2491 ★

Internet

SIC: 4822; NAICS: 51331

Top Shopping Sites in the U.K.

Shares are for December 2003.

Ebay U.K.	25.92%
Amazon U.K.	8.21
Argos	2.31
E-bay Shops UK	2.23
Kelkoo UK	2.14
Play.com	1.60
Tesco.com	1.55
Argos Entretainment	1.01
Comet U.K.	0.99
Other	54.04

Source: *Retail Week*, January 30, 2004, p. 18, from Hitwise.

★ 2492 ★

Internet

SIC: 4822; NAICS: 51331

Top Sports Game Sites, 2003

Market share of destinations are for September 7 - 13, 2003.

Yahoo Sports Fantasy Football	11.73%
Yahoo Games	9.81
Pogo	8.91%
Yahoo Fantasy Sports	6.45
Yahoo Sports Fantasy Baseball	3.65
Neo Pets	3.02
ESPN Fantasy Games	2.61
MSN Gaming Zone	2.59
Gamefaqs	2.26
Other	48.97

Source: *Electronic Gaming Business*, September 24, 2003, p. NA, from Hitwise.

★ 2493 ★

Internet

SIC: 4822; NAICS: 51331

Top Travel Agency Sites in the U.K.

Market shares are for October 2003. There were 142.4 million holidays taken in 2002 at a cost of 35.7 billion pounds.

Lastminute	9.06%
Expedia	8.52
Ebookers	7.86
Teletext Holidays	4.34
My Travel UK	3.52
Other	66.70

Source: *Brand Strategy*, December 4, 2003, p. 26, from Mintel.

★ 2494 ★

Internet

SIC: 4822; NAICS: 51331

Top Travel Sites

According to the source, about two-thirds of travelers who bought tickets online visited 3 or more web sites. Figures show millions of visitors in June 2003.

Expedia	14.3
Travelocity	11.1
Orbitz	10.7
Hotels.com	6.4
Southwest Airlines	5.8
Yahoo! Travel	5.1

Continued on next page.

★ 2494 ★
[Continued]
Internet
SIC: 4822; NAICS: 51331
Top Travel Sites

According to the source, about two-thirds of travelers who bought tickets online visited 3 or more web sites. Figures show millions of visitors in June 2003.

American Airlines	5.1
AOL Travel	4.9
Priceline	4.5
Cheap Tickets	4.5

Source: *New York Times*, August 18, 2003, p. C8, from Nielsen NetRatings.

★ 2495 ★
Internet Phone Services
SIC: 4822; NAICS: 51331
Leading Online Phone Service Providers, 2003

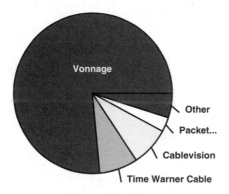

Residential Internet phone services include local and long-distance service using Internet protocol.

Vonnage	78.0%
Time Warner Cable	8.0
Cablevision	8.0
Packet 8	3.0
Other	5.0

Source: *New York Times*, February 15, 2004, p. 7.

★ 2496 ★
Internet Service Providers
SIC: 4822; NAICS: 51331
Broadband Market in Mexico

Shares are shown based on estimated revenues. DSL stands for digital subscriber line.

DSL	43.0%
Cable	41.0
Wireless	12.0
ISDN	4.0

Source: *Latincom*, September 19, 2003, p. 7.

★ 2497 ★
Internet Service Providers
SIC: 4822; NAICS: 514191
Broadband Market in South Sorea

Total subscribers reached 10.6 million.

KT Corp.	50.9%
Hanaro	28.3
Thrunet	10.4
Onse	4.4
Other	5.7

Source: *Financial Times*, October 20, 2003, p. 19, from Hanaro.

★ 2498 ★
Internet Service Providers
SIC: 4822; NAICS: 514191
DSL Subscribers by Region, 2004

Distribution of subscribers is shown by region.

Asia Pacific	44.0%
Europe	29.0
North America	24.0
Latin America	3.0

Source: *China Telecom*, October 2003, p. 1, from Jefferies & Company Inc.

★ 2499 ★
Internet Service Providers
SIC: 4822; NAICS: 514191

Largest Broadband Companies in Europe

Companies are ranked by millions of subscribers as of March 31, 2003.

T-Online	3,050
Wanadoo	1,613
Telefonica	806
Telecom Italia Media	584
America Online	488
BT	429
Terra Lycos	423
United Internet	400
Tiscali	360
Telia	350

Source: *Financial Times*, July 17, 2003, p. 16, from Jupiter Research and WestLB.

★ 2500 ★
Internet Service Providers
SIC: 4822; NAICS: 514191

Leading Dial-Up Access Firms

Companies are ranked by number of subscribers.

	Subscribers	Share
America Online	22,642,504	44.52%
MSN	5,069,220	9.97
EarthLink	4,046,322	7.96
United Online	3,805,402	7.48
AT&T	3,234,603	6.36
BellSouth	1,087,987	2.14
SBC	722,331	1.42
Citizens Communications	237,800	0.47
Alltel	227,068	0.45
Verizon	208,659	0.41
Other	9,578,645	18.83

Source: *New York Times*, November 24, 2003, p. C6, from ComScore Networks.

★ 2501 ★
Internet Service Providers
SIC: 4822; NAICS: 514191

Leading DSL Service Providers in Japan

Market shares are shown in percent.

Softbank BB	33.6%
NTT East	20.4
NTT West	16.1
Other	29.9

Source: *Nikkei Weekly*, July 21, 2003, p. 1, from Nihon Keizai Shimbun.

★ 2502 ★
Internet Service Providers
SIC: 4822; NAICS: 514191

Leading Internet Access Firms

Market shares are shown by household and revenue.

	Households	Revenues
America Online	24.0%	22.0%
MSN	8.0	7.0
EarthLink	6.0	6.0
Comcast	6.0	10.0
SBC Yahoo	5.0	7.0
Other	51.0	48.0

Source: *USA TODAY*, April 22, 2004, p. 3B, from TNS Telecoms.

★ 2503 ★
Internet Service Providers
SIC: 4822; NAICS: 514191

Leading Internet Access Providers

Market shares are shown in percent.

America Online 28.0%
Comcast 7.0
Microsoft 6.0
SBC Communications 6.0
United Online (Juno and NetZero) 6.0
Other 47.0

Source: *Wall Street Journal*, March 22, 2004, p. R2.

★ 2504 ★
Internet Service Providers
SIC: 4822; NAICS: 514191

Leading Internet Access Providers in Japan, 2002

Market shares are shown based on 39 million sub-scribers.

Nifty 13.7%
NEC 10.7
NTT Communications 9.0
Softbank BB 6.1
KDDI 6.1
Other 54.4

Source: "Market Share Survey Report 2002." [online] from http://www.nni.nikkei.co.jp [accessed January 20, 2004], from Nikkei estimate and Nikkei Market Access.

★ 2505 ★
Internet Service Providers
SIC: 4822; NAICS: 514191

Leading Services Providers in Norway

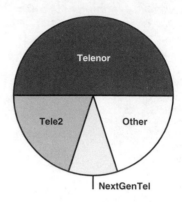

Market shares are shown in percent. Internet traffic generated turnover of $33.32 million for the first six months of 2002.

Telenor 50.0%
Tele2 . . . . 20.0
NextGenTel 10.0
Other 20.0

Source: *Dagens Naeringsliv*, October 15, 2002, p. 8.

★ 2506 ★
Internet Service Providers
SIC: 4822; NAICS: 514191

World Demand for Broadband Services, 2003

Estimates show that world broadband installations exeeded 100 million sites at the end of 2003. The table shows market shares by region. The Asia Pacific region is seeing a subscriber growth rate of 23%, Latin America 18%, Europe and the Middle East 13% and North America 8%. Global broadband industy is valued at $30 billion.

Asia Pacific 43.0%
North America 32.0
Europe, Middle East, Africa 23.0
Latin America 2.0

Source: *Telecom Asia*, January 2004, p. 8, from RHK.

★ 2507 ★

Wi-Fi

SIC: 4822; NAICS: 514191

Global Wi-Fi Revenues by Year, 2004-2008

Revenues are shown in millions of dollars. Wi-Fi stands for wireless fidelity.

2008	$ 1,591
2007	605
2006	197
2005	173
2004	33

Source: *U.S. News & World Report*, May 10, 2004, p. E10, from Pyramid Research.

★ 2508 ★

Wi-Fi

SIC: 4822; NAICS: 51331

Hotspot Market in New York City, NY

Hotspots are locations in which a wireless Internet connection is available to visitors and customers. Shares are for hotspots in the overall market.

Verizon	34.8%
T-Mobile	24.7
iPass	11.1
AT&T Wireless	10.0
Boingo	7.1
STSN	4.0
Surf and Sip	2.7
Other	5.5

Source: "North American Hotspot Deployments Exploding." [online] available from http://www.emediawire.com [accessed February 9, 2004], from ON World.

★ 2509 ★

Wi-Fi

SIC: 4822; NAICS: 51331

Hotspot Market in San Francisco, CA

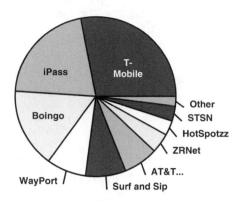

Hotspots are locations in which a wireless Internet connection is available to visitors and customers. Shares are for hotspots in the overall market.

T-Mobile	27.7%
iPass	21.0
Boingo	16.4
WayPort	7.9
Surf and Sip	7.6
AT&T Wireless	7.1
ZRNet	3.9
HotSpotzz	3.2
STSN	2.7
Other	2.4

Source: "North American Hotspot Deployments Exploding." [online] available from http://www.emediawire.com [accessed February 9, 2004], from ON World.

★ 2510 ★

Wi-Fi

SIC: 4822; NAICS: 51331

Hotspot Market in Seoul, South Korea

Hotspots are locations in which a wireless Internet connection is available to visitors and customers. These hotspots are usually cafes, restaurants or bars. Market shares are shown in percent.

Korea Telecom	86.0%
Other	14.0

Source: *Wireless News*, April 21, 2004, p. NA.

★ 2511 ★
Wi-Fi
SIC: 4822; NAICS: 51331

Hotspot Market in Tokyo, Japan

Hotspots are locations in which a wireless Internet connection is available to visitors and customers. These hotspots are usually cafes, restaurants or bars. Market shares are shown in percent.

NTT	69.0%
Other	31.0

Source: *Wireless News*, April 21, 2004, p. NA.

★ 2512 ★
Wi-Fi
SIC: 4822; NAICS: 51331

Wi-Fi Hot Spot Markets in Europe

Forrester Research forecasts 53 million wireless-enabled laptops and PDAs in Europe.

U.K.	27.0%
Germany	23.0
Other	50.0

Source: *Online Reporter*, August 20, 2003, p. NA, from Gartner Dataquest.

★ 2513 ★
Wi-Fi
SIC: 4822; NAICS: 51331

Wi-Fi Locations Worldwide

According to the source, Wi-Fi stands for wireless fidelity and is described as "a common term for the technology called 802.11 which enables short-range access to the Internet at high speeds." While growing tremendously, it remains to be seen if providers can make money with this service. Barnes & Noble planned to test Wi-Fi hot spots in some Seattle and Atlanta stores during the summer of 2003.

	2002	2004	Share
Retail outlets	11,109	82,149	62.01%
Hotels	2,274	22,021	16.62
Community hot spots . .	266	20,561	15.52
Enterprise guesting areas .	624	3,708	2.80
Stations and ports	88	2,143	1.62
Airports	152	378	0.29
Other	240	1,526	1.15

Source: *Wall Street Journal*, July 1, 2003, p. A3, from Gartner Inc.

★ 2514 ★
Wi-Fi
SIC: 4822; NAICS: 51331

Wi-Fi Users Worldwide, 2003

North America
Asia Pacific
Europe
Other

The number of public wireless local area networks (also called Wi-Fi hot spots) is expected to double by 2005.

North America	50.5%
Asia Pacific	29.0
Europe	18.3
Other	2.2

Source: *Investor's Business Daily*, July 10, 2003, p. A5, from Gartner Inc.

★ 2515 ★
Radio Broadcasting
SIC: 4832; NAICS: 513111, 513112

Leading Radio Broadcasters

Parent companies are ranked by share of revenues. According to a 2002 study by the source, the top two firms control 42% of listeners and 45% of industry revenues. In 1996, the Telecom Act was passed which allowed for the deregulation of radio station ownership.

Clear Channel Communications	27.5%
Viacom International	17.6
Cox Radio	3.7
Entercom	3.5
ABC Radio	3.4
Citadel Communications	2.6
Radio One	2.4
Cumulus Media	2.2
Hispanic Broadcasting Corp.	2.2
Emmis Communications	2.1
Other	32.7

Source: *American Demographics*, September 2003, p. 39, from Future of Music Coalition.

★ 2516 ★
Radio Broadcasting
SIC: 4832; NAICS: 513111, 513112

Leading U.K. Radio Stations, 2003

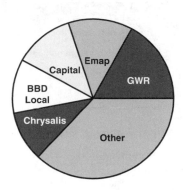

Shares are based on audience reach during the third quarter of 2003.

GWR	16.5%
Emap	13.4
Capital	11.9
BBD Local	10.8
Chrysalis	10.1
Other	37.3

Source: *Music Week*, November 1, 2003, p. 9.

★ 2517 ★
Radio Broadcasting
SIC: 4832; NAICS: 513111, 513112

Radio Market in Auckland, New Zealand

The Newstalk ZB program has about 204,600 listeners each week.

Newstalk ZB	12.3%
Mai	11.7
Classic Hits	10.0
ZM	5.5
Solid Gold	5.4

Source: *AdMedia (New Zealand)*, May 2004, p. 46, from Auckland 2004 Commercial Radio Measurement Surveys.

★ 2518 ★
Radio Broadcasting
SIC: 4832; NAICS: 513111, 513112
Radio Market in Denver, CO

Clear Channel Communications	
Jefferson-Pilot Communications	
Entercom Communications	
Infinity Broadcasting	
Entravision Communications	
Other	

Market shares are shown based on revenues.

Clear Channel Communications	41.4%
Jefferson-Pilot Communications	17.9
Entercom Communications	16.4
Infinity Broadcasting	9.9
Entravision Communications	4.2
Other	10.2

Source: *Mediaweek*, January 26, 2004, p. 16, from BIA Information Network.

★ 2519 ★
Radio Broadcasting
SIC: 4832; NAICS: 513111, 513112
Radio Market in Detroit, MI

Market shares are shown based on revenues.

Infinity Broadcasting	31.6%
Clear Channel Communications	29.3
Greater Media	17.7
ABC Radio	13.5
Radio One	4.9
Other	3.0

Source: *Mediaweek*, October 13, 2003, p. 12, from BIA Information Network.

★ 2520 ★
Radio Broadcasting
SIC: 4832; NAICS: 513111, 513112
Radio Market in Hartford-New Haven, CT

Market shares are shown based on revenues.

Infinity Broadcasting	46.3%
Clear Channel Communications	28.6
Buckley Broadcasting	9.1
Marlin Broadcasting	6.7
Mega Communications	2.4
Other	6.9

Source: *Mediaweek*, March 1, 2004, p. 12, from BIA Information Network.

★ 2521 ★
Radio Broadcasting
SIC: 4832; NAICS: 513111, 513112
Radio Market in Norfolk, VA

Market shares are shown based on ownership.

Entercom Communications	31.9%
Saga Communications	18.2
Barnstable Broadcating	18.2
Clear Channel Communications	15.9
Sinclair Telecable	11.9
Other	3.9

Source: *Mediaweek*, December 8, 2003, p. 12, from BIA Information Network.

★ 2522 ★
Radio Broadcasting
SIC: 4832; NAICS: 513111, 513112

Radio Market in Philadelphia, PA

Infinity Broadcasting	
Clear Channel Communications	
Greater Media	
	WEAZ-FM Radio
	Radio One
Other	

Market shares are shown based on ownership.

Infinity Broadcasting	34.0%
Clear Channel Communications	29.1
Greater Media	12.8
WEAZ-FM Radio	8.8
Radio One	6.1
Other	9.2

Source: *Mediaweek*, December 8, 2003, p. 12, from BIA Information Network.

★ 2523 ★
Radio Broadcasting
SIC: 4832; NAICS: 513111, 513112

Radio Market in Poland, 2003

Shares are shown for broadcasting companies based on advertising revenues.

RMF FM	23.6%
Radio ZET	18.9
Polish Radio Channel 1	16.1
Local Polish Radio	5.5
Polish Radio Channel 3	5.3
ZPR	4.9
Agora	4.7
Plus	1.6
Ad Point	1.4
Radio Wawa	1.1
Other	16.1

Source: *European Intelligence Wire*, February 13, 2004, p. NA.

★ 2524 ★
Radio Broadcasting
SIC: 4832; NAICS: 513111, 513112

Radio Market in Portland, OR

Market shares are shown based on revenues.

Entercom Communications	31.4%
Infinity Broadcasting	27.7
Clear Channel Communications	20.4
Salem Communications	8.2
Rose City Radio	7.5
Other	4.8

Source: *Mediaweek*, June 16, 2003, p. 12, from BIA Information Network.

★ 2525 ★
Radio Broadcasting
SIC: 4832; NAICS: 513111, 513112

Radio Market in Rochester, NY

Market shares are shown based on revenues.

Infinity Broadcasting	32.8%
Clear Channel Communications	30.0
Entercom Communications	19.1
Monroe County Broadcasting	4.6
North Coast Radio	1.7
Other	11.8

Source: *Mediaweek*, February 16, 2004, p. 10, from BIA Information Network.

★ 2526 ★

Radio Broadcasting
SIC: 4832; NAICS: 513111, 513112

Radio Market in San Diego, CA

Market shares are shown based on revenues.

Clear Channel Communications	29.2%
Midwest TV Inc.	13.6
XETRA	13.1
Jefferson Pilot Communications	13.0
Infinity Broadcasting	10.1
Other	21.0

Source: *Mediaweek*, May 5, 2003, p. 12, from BIA Information Network.

★ 2527 ★

Radio Broadcasting
SIC: 4832; NAICS: 513111, 513112

Radio Market in Spokane, WA

Market shares are shown based on revenues.

Clear Channel Communications	33.8%
Citadel Communications	32.6
Morgan Murphy Stations	26.9
Pamplin Communications	3.2
Blue Sky Broadcasting	1.1
Other	2.4

Source: *Mediaweek*, December 8, 2003, p. 12, from BIA Information Network.

★ 2528 ★

Radio Broadcasting
SIC: 4832; NAICS: 513111, 513112

Radio Market in Washington D.C.

Market shares are shown based on ownership.

Clear Channel	26.6%
Infinity Broadcasting	23.2
ABC Radio	14.8
Bonneville International	13.1
Radio One	11.8
Howard University Broadcasting	5.3
Other	5.2

Source: *Mediaweek*, October 20, 2003, p. 14, from Arbitron.

★ 2529 ★

Radio Broadcasting
SIC: 4832; NAICS: 513111, 513112

Radio Market in West Palm Beach, FL

Market shares are shown based on revenues.

Infinity Broadcasting	38.9%
Clear Channel Communications	32.2
Palm Beach Broadcasting	16.4
J Crystal Enterprises	5.9
Beasley Broadcast Group	1.8
Other	4.8

Source: *Mediaweek*, May 5, 2003, p. 12, from BIA Information Network.

★ 2530 ★

Radio Broadcasting
SIC: 4832; NAICS: 513111, 513112

Satellite Radio Industry

During the third quarter of 2003 the industry added 282,000 subscribers. Market shares are shown in percent.

XM	86.8%
Sirius	13.2

Source: *Satellite News*, December 15, 2003, p. NA.

★ 2531 ★

Radio Broadcasting

SIC: 4832; NAICS: 513111, 513112

Top Radio Groups, 2002

Groups are ranked by revenue in millions of dollars. Shares are shown based on the top 25 firms.

	($ mil.)	Share
Clear Channel Communications	$ 3,423.4	33.17%
Infinity Broadcasting	2,186.6	21.19
Cox Radio	466.8	4.52
Entercom	455.1	4.41
ABC Radio	424.6	4.11
Citadel	366.1	3.55
Radio One	338.1	3.28
Emmis	296.7	2.88
Cumulus	292.9	2.84
Univision	290.9	2.82
Other	1,778.4	17.23

Source: *Broadcasting & Cable*, September 29, 2003, p. 10.

★ 2532 ★

Television Broadcasting

SIC: 4833; NAICS: 51312

Digital Platforms Worldwide, 2008

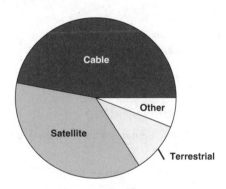

Satellite boxed currently have 61% of sales but they are expected to lose market share. Sales of digital TV set-top boxes is forecasted to grow from 50.3 million in 2004 to 121.8 million in 2008.

Cable	47.0%
Satellite	37.0
Terrestrial	10.0
Other	6.0

Source: *Business Wire*, December 16, 2003, p. NA, from Strategy Analytics.

★ 2533 ★

Television Broadcasting

SIC: 4833; NAICS: 51312

Hispanic TV Market in San Antonio, TX

Shares are for February 2003. Univision reached 75% of U.S. Hispanic homes.

Univision	70.8%
Telemundo	21.3
Other	7.9

Source: *San Antonio Business Journal*, May 5, 2003, p. NA.

★ 2534 ★

Television Broadcasting

SIC: 4833; NAICS: 51312

Leading Broadcast TV Firms, 2002

Companies are ranked by U.S. net revenues in millions of dollars.

Viacom	$ 7,490
NBC-TV (General Electric)	6,763
Walt Disney Co.	4,485
News Corp.	4,301
Tribune Co.	1,179
Univision	993
Gannett Co.	771
Sinclair Broadcast Group	731
Hearst Corp.	721
Belo	658

Source: *Advertising Age*, August 18, 2003, p. S-3, from BIA Financial Network and TNS Media Intelligence/Competitive Media Reporting.

★ 2535 ★
Television Broadcasting
SIC: 4833; NAICS: 51312

Leading TV Channels in the U.K.

Share of audience is for July 2003.

BBC1	25.1%
ITV	22.3
Channel 4	11.2
BBC2	10.9
Channel 5	6.7
Other	23.9

Source: *Wall Street Journal*, September 26, 2003, p. B1, from Broadcasters' Audience Research Board.

★ 2536 ★
Television Broadcasting
SIC: 4833; NAICS: 51312

Leading TV Networks

Figures show millions of prime-time average viewers for September 2002 - May 2003.

CBS	12.6
NBC	11.7
Fox	10.0
ABC	10.0
WB	4.1

Source: *New York Times*, September 3, 2003, p. C1, from Nielsen EDI and Nielsen Media Research.

★ 2537 ★
Television Broadcasting
SIC: 4833; NAICS: 51312

Leading TV Networks in South Korea, 2002

The South Korean Television industry is expected to see another year of growth (advertising revenues increased 23% in 2002). Programming sales are up and satellite TV is flourishing. Data show the top networks.

MBC	20.0%
SBS	19.0
KBS1	19.0
KBS2	16.0
Others	26.0

Source: *Hollywood Reporter*, March 18, 2003, p. 8, from Korean Broadcasting Advertising Corp.

★ 2538 ★
Television Broadcasting
SIC: 4833; NAICS: 51312

Leading TV Shows in Canada, 2002

Top three TV shows in Canada and the top three non-U.S. shows based on average total viewers, in thousands.

Survivor: Amazon	3,500
CSI: Crime Scene Investigation	2,700
The Simpsons	2,200
Hockey Night in Canada (Non-U.S.)	1,480
This Hour Has 22 Minutes (Non-U.S.)	860
Da Vinci's Inquest (Non-U.S.)	810

Source: *Hollywood Reporter*, March 18, 2003, pp. S-7, from BBM Canada Meter Service.

★ 2539 ★
Television Broadcasting
SIC: 4833; NAICS: 51312

Leading TV Shows in Mexico, 2002

Top three TV shows in Mexico and the top three non-U.S. shows based on average total households viewership, in thousands.

XHDerbez (Non-U.S.)	2,975
La Parodia (Non-U.S.)	2,791
La Hora Pico (Non-U.S.)	2,699
Sabrina, the Teenage Witch	910
Charmed	634
World's Wildest Police Videos	614

Source: *Hollywood Reporter*, March 18, 2003, pp. S-7, from IBOPE AGB Mexico.

★ 2540 ★
Television Broadcasting
SIC: 4833; NAICS: 51312

Leading TV Stations in France, 2003

Shares are listed by audience levels per TV station during 2003.

TF1	31.5%
France 2	20.5
France 3	16.1
M6	12.6
France 5	6.4
La 5	4.7
Canal+	3.7
Arte	3.4
Other	10.9

Source: *TV International*, January 30, 2004, p. 9, from *Mediametrie*.

★ 2541 ★
Television Broadcasting
SIC: 4833; NAICS: 51312

Leading TV Stations in Norway, 2002

Shares are for leading TV stations in Norway by viewership during 2002.

NRK1	39.2%
TV2	32.2
TVNorge	9.6
TV3	6.0
NRK2	3.0
Others	10.0

Source: *TV International*, December 5/, 204, p. NA, from MMI and Norsk TV-meterpanel.

★ 2542 ★
Television Broadcasting
SIC: 4833; NAICS: 51312

Leading TV Stations in Sweden, 2002

Shares are for leading TV stations in Sweden by viewership during 2002.

SVT1	27.0%
TV4	25.0
SVT2	16.0
TV3	10.0
Kanal 5	8.0
Others	14.0

Source: *TV International*, December 5/, 204, p. NA, from SVT.

★ 2543 ★
Television Broadcasting
SIC: 4833; NAICS: 51312
Prime-Time TV Market in Italy, 2002

Market shares are shown in percent. RAI's total was 45.06% compared to Mediaset's 44.68% share.

Canale 5	24.63%
RAI1	24.28
Italia 1	12.27
RAI2	10.67
RAI3	10.11
Rete 4	7.78
La 7	2.31
Other	7.95

Source: *TV International*, October 10, 2003, p. 5, from AGB and Informa Media Group.

★ 2544 ★
Television Broadcasting
SIC: 4833; NAICS: 51312
Spanish Language Television

Figures show the share of the prime time audience last year and over the previous 12 months.

	2002	2003
Univision/TeleFutura	79.0%	82.0%
Telemundo	21.0	18.0

Source: *Broadcasting & Cable*, September 8, 2003, p. 30, from Nielsen Media Research.

★ 2545 ★
Television Broadcasting
SIC: 4833; NAICS: 51312
Television Revenues

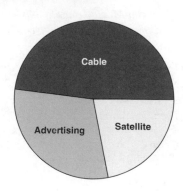

About 86% of U.S. households have a pay television service in 2004, up from 79% in 1998. Spending is expected to increase from $59 billion to $6.2 billion.

	1999	2004
Cable	49.6%	47.7%
Advertising	38.7	30.3
Satellite	11.7	22.0

Source: *Business 2.0*, September 2003, p. 38, from National Cable and Telecommunications Association, PriceWaterhouseCoopers, UniversalMcCann, and Wilkofsky Gruen Associates.

★ 2546 ★
Television Broadcasting
SIC: 4833; NAICS: 51312
Top Television Shows, 2003

Programs are ranked by millions of viewers for September 22, 2003 - December 7, 2003.

CSI	26.4
Survivor Pearl Islands	20.6
Friends	20.0
ER	19.8
Everybody Loves Raymond	18.8
CSI: Miami	17.9
Law & Order	16.8
Monday Night Football	16.7
Two and a Half Men	15.8
Without A Trace	15.7

Source: *Entertainment Weekly*, January 9, 2004, p. 71.

★ 2547 ★
Television Broadcasting
SIC: 4833; NAICS: 51312

Top TV Broadcasters in Mexico

Market shares are estimated. About 98% of Mexican households own a TV set.

Televisa	70.0%
TV Azteca	30.0

Source: *Wall Street Journal*, April 7, 2004, p. B2B.

★ 2548 ★
Television Broadcasting
SIC: 4833; NAICS: 51312

TV Advertising Market in the U.K., 2003

Shares are for net advertising revenues.

ITV1	51.0%
C4	20.0
Channel Five	8.0
GMTV	2.0
Other	19.0

Source: *Financial Times*, October 8, 2003, p. 22, from ZenithOptimedia.

★ 2549 ★
Television Broadcasting
SIC: 4833; NAICS: 51312

TV Sports Audiences

Figures show the average millions of viewers per game.

	2000	2001	2002
NFL	17.0	16.9	18.6
MLB	7.7	9.8	8.9
NBA	6.7	6.8	5.6
NHL	2.8	3.1	2.6

Source: *Wall Street Journal*, February 9, 2004, p. B4, from Nielsen Media Research.

★ 2550 ★
Broadcast Recording Services
SIC: 4841; NAICS: 51321, 51322

Broadcasting News/Recording Services

The industry provides clips on specific topics (health, insurance) to its clients. Close captioning from broadcasts may be uploaded to an internet site in the form of test files for downloading. Burrells/VMS controls the market.

Burrells/VMS	90.0%
Other	10.0

Source: *Knight Ridder/Tribune News Service*, June 20, 2003, p. NA.

★ 2551 ★
Cable Broadcasting
SIC: 4841; NAICS: 51321, 51322

Cable Market in Boston, MA

Market shares are shown in percent.

Comcast	76.0%
Other	24.0

Source: *Boston Herald*, April 8, 2004, p. NA.

★ 2552 ★
Cable Broadcasting
SIC: 4841; NAICS: 51321, 51322

Leading Cable Firms in Europe, 2001

Firms are ranked by total revenues in millions of euros.

NTL	1,480.96
Telewest	872.61
Kabel NRW	608.27
Kabel Baden Wurttemberg	318.62
UPC Netherlands	303.32
(Noos) Lyonnaise Cable	286.23
TeleColumbus	267.93
France Telecom Cable	262.42
TV Cabo	237.79
NC Numericable	234.83

Source: *Screen Digest*, October 2002, p. 309.

★ 2553 ★

Cable Broadcasting

SIC: 4841; NAICS: 51321, 51322

Leading Cable Markets Worldwide

China

United States

India

Germany

Japan

Countries are ranked by millions of cable subscribers as of December 2003.

China	98
United States	68
India	41
Germany	18
Japan	12

Source: *New York Times*, January 26, 2004, p. C8, from In-Stat/MDR.

★ 2554 ★

Cable Broadcasting

SIC: 4841; NAICS: 51321, 51322

Leading Cable TV Firms, 2002

Companies are ranked by U.S. net revenues in millions of dollars.

Comcast Corp.	$ 16,043
AOL Time Warner	14,192
Viacom	5,052
Cox Enterprises	5,040
Charter Communications	4,566
Walt Disney Co.	4,428
Adelphia Communications Corp.	3,426
Cablevision Systems Corp.	3,292
News Corp.	1,660
Advance Publications	1,455

Source: *Advertising Age*, August 18, 2003, p. S-3, from BIA Financial Network and TNS Media Intelligence/Competitive Media Reporting.

★ 2555 ★

Cable Broadcasting

SIC: 4841; NAICS: 51312

Top Cable Networks

Networks are ranked by millions of viewers as of February 8, 2004.

Nickelodeon	1.86
TNT	1.34
Disney	1.34
HBO	1.19
USA	1.14
The Cartoon Network	1.14
Lifetime	1.13
TBS	1.08
ESPN	0.81
Fox News Channel	0.80

Source: *Wall Street Journal*, February 12, 2004, p. B1, from Nielsen Media Research.

★ 2556 ★

Hospital Communications Services

SIC: 4841; NAICS: 51321, 51322

Hospital Bedside Communications in the U.K.

The company has over 60% of the market for bedside screens that allow patients to watch TV, make phone calls, send emails and surf the Web.

Patientline	62.0%
Other	38.0

Source: *Daily Mail*, June 12, 2004, p. 80.

★ 2557 ★
Pay Television
SIC: 4841; NAICS: 51321, 51322

Cable/Satellite Market, 2003

Data show share of all households.

Comcast	26.0%
Time Warner	12.0
DirecTV	12.0
Dish Network	10.0
Charter	8.0
Other	32.0

Source: *Fortune*, May 31, 2004, p. 124.

★ 2558 ★
Pay Television
SIC: 4841; NAICS: 51321, 51322

Digital TV Market in Canada

Market shares are shown in percent.

Bell ExpressVU/Star Choice	57.0%
Cable	41.0
Other	2.0

Source: *America's Intelligence Wire*, May 21, 2004, p. NA.

★ 2559 ★
Pay Television
SIC: 4841; NAICS: 51321, 51322

Largest Satellite Platforms Worldwide

Services are ranked by millions of subscribers.

DirecTV	11.23
Echostar's DISH Network	8.30
BSkyB	6.10
SkyPerfecTV	2.95
Canal Satellite Digital	2.04
DirecTV Satellite Digital	1.67
TelePiu	1.38
Premiere World	1.37
Canal Satellite Digital	1.23
Bell ExpressVu	1.12

Source: *Video Store*, April 6, 2003, p. 32, from Skyreport.com.

★ 2560 ★
Pay Television
SIC: 4841; NAICS: 51321, 51322

Leading Cable/Satellite Broadcasters, 2002

Companies are ranked by millions of basic subscribers.

Comcast Cable Comm.	21.40
DirecTV	11.90
Time Warner Cable	9.40
EchoStar Comm.	8.50
Charter Comm.	6.40
Cox Comm.	6.30
Adelphia Comm.	5.50
Cablevision Systems	3.00
Advance/Newhouse	2.10
Mediacom Comm.	1.60
Insight Comm.	1.30
Cable One	0.71

Source: *Broadcasting & Cable*, November 10, 2003, p. 32, from *Broadcasting & Cable's Top 15 MSOs* list.

★ 2561 ★
Pay Television
SIC: 4841; NAICS: 51321, 51322
Leading Cable/Satellite Providers

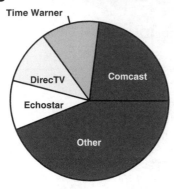

Market shares are shown in percent.

Comcast	23.0%
Time Warner	12.0
DirecTV	11.0
Echostar	10.0
Other	44.0

Source: *Financial Times*, February 11, 2004, p. 11, from Merrill Lynch.

★ 2562 ★
Pay Television
SIC: 4841; NAICS: 51321, 51322
Leading Channels in China

CCTV-1
Shandong Satellite
Liaoning Satellite
Guizhou Satellite
Other

China has 651 stations and 90 million cable sub-scribers. Channels are ranked by audience share.

CCTV-1	9.3%
Shandong Satellite	6.0
Liaoning Satellite	3.1
Guizhou Satellite	2.9
Other	73.6

Source: *Financial Times*, February 10, 2004, p. 20, from Access Asia Limited.

★ 2563 ★
Pay Television
SIC: 4841; NAICS: 51321, 51322
Multichannel TV Service, 2003

Shares are estimated.

Cable only	74.0%
Satellite only	23.0
C-band and other	2.0
Dual cable/satellite	1.0

Source: *Investor's Business Daily*, January 27, 2004, p. A6, from UBS AG.

★ 2564 ★
Pay Television
SIC: 4841; NAICS: 51321, 51322
Pay TV Operators in Brazil, 2003

Brazil had 178 pay TV operators. It is anticipated that after the purchase of Sky by DirecTV, the latter will holds a 32% share.

Net	38.0%
Sky	20.0
DirecTV	12.0
Horizon	9.0
TVA	8.0
Other	13.0

Source: *The America's Intellegence Wire*, April 1, 2004, p. NA, from Anatel.

★ 2565 ★
Pay Television
SIC: 4841; NAICS: 51321, 51322
Satellite Broadcasting Market by State

Data show subscribers by state as of third quarter 2002.

California	2,048,170
Texas	1,650,403
Florida	1,098,110
New York	857,336
Georgia	748,881
Illinois	744,759
North Carolina	719,761

Continued on next page.

★ 2565 ★

[Continued]
Pay Television
SIC: 4841; NAICS: 51321, 51322

Satellite Broadcasting Market by State

Data show subscribers by state as of third quarter 2002.

Ohio	656,881
Michigan	651,723
Pennsylvania	523,612

Source: *Investor's Business Daily*, June 26, 2003, p. A5, from Satellite Broadcasting and Communications Association.

★ 2566 ★

Pay Television
SIC: 4841; NAICS: 51321, 51322

Satellite TV Market Shares

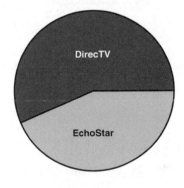

At the end of 2004, DirecTV had 12.2 million subscribers while EchoStar had 9.4 million. Market shares are estimated in percent.

DirecTV	56.5%
EchoStar	43.5

Source: *Satellite News*, March 1, 2004, p. NA.

SIC 49 - Electric, Gas, and Sanitary Services

★ 2567 ★
Energy
SIC: 4911; NAICS: 221111, 221112, 221113, 221122
Energy Consumption, 2002

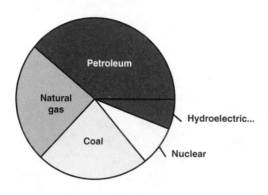

Figures show share of consumption.

Petroleum	39.0%
Natural gas	24.0
Coal	23.0
Nuclear	8.0
Hydroelectric and other	6.0

Source: *New York Times*, June 17, 2003, p. C3, from Energy Information Administration.

★ 2568 ★
Energy
SIC: 4911; NAICS: 221111, 221112, 221122
Energy Consumption in Germany

The U.K. and Germany are both predicted to see increased gas use in the coming decade. The reason is that the industry does not see viable alternatives. Gas may even be used for baseload generators.

	2002	2020
Oil	37.5%	34.3%
Gas	21.7	31.9
Hard coal	13.2	13.7
Nuclear	12.6	3.3
Lignite	11.6	9.4
Renewables	3.4	7.4

Source: *World Gas Intelligence*, January 6, 2004, p. NA.

★ 2569 ★
Energy
SIC: 4911; NAICS: 221119, 221121, 221122
Leading Energy Companies in Europe

Companies are ranked by installed capacity in Megawatt hours.

Electricite de France	117,000
Eon	49,000
Enel	46,400
Endessa	42,100
RWE Power	32,339
Vattenfall	31,596
Electrabel	24,896
Iberdrola	16,088
EnBW	14,461

Source: *Financial Times*, January 6, 2004, p. 22, from CEZ.

★ 2570 ★
Pipeline Trading
SIC: 4911; NAICS: 221121

Leading Forward Capacity Traders, 2004

There were 150 forward trading companies that traded nearly 1.3 trillion cubic feet (TCF) as of September 1, 2003. Figures are based on the trading of 2004 capacity.

Axia Energy	20.6%
Cargill Inc.	19.4
BP America Holding	9.9
EnCana Corporation	5.0
El Paso Corporation	3.2
Dominion Corporation	3.1
New Jersey Resources	2.8
ONEOK Energy Marketing and Trading Company	2.7
Sempra Energy	2.1
Cross Timbers Oil Company	2.1
Other	29.1

Source: *Electric Light & Power*, October 2003, p. 11.

★ 2571 ★
Utilities
SIC: 4911; NAICS: 221119, 221121, 221122

Electricity Demand in Australia, 2002

Overseas investors have begun to leave the country. These companies entered the market in the 1990s to bid on Victoria's energy sector. The companies ended up with large debts after misjudging the market. Market shares are shown based on customers.

AGL	29.0%
Origin	17.0
EnergyAust	14.0
Energex	10.0
TXU	9.0
Integral	7.0
Ergon	7.0
Country	7.0

Source: *Financial Times*, October 14, 2003, p. 24, from Thomson Datastream.

★ 2572 ★
Utilities
SIC: 4911; NAICS: 221119, 22121, 221122

Electricity Generation, 2002

Renewables refers to wind, solar, photovoltaics and geothermal.

Coal	50.0%
Nuclear	20.0
Natural gas	18.0
Renewables	9.0
Fuel oil	2.0

Source: *Natural Gas Week*, September 15, 2003, p. 10.

★ 2573 ★
Utilities
SIC: 4911; NAICS: 221119, 221121, 221122

Electricity Industry Revenues

Figures show percent of industry revenues of $224.2 billion for 2000 (latest year available). 64% of electricity firms are municipal/state owned.

Investor	75.6%
Municipal/state	14.7
Cooperative	9.1
Federal	0.6

Source: *Wall Street Journal*, July 31, 2003, p. A4, from U.S. Department of Energy.

★ 2574 ★
Utilities
SIC: 4911; NAICS: 221119, 221121, 221122

Houston's Residential Energy Market

Market shares are shown in percent.

Reliant Energy	85.0%
Other	15.0

Source: *Houston Chronicle*, April 1, 2004, p. NA.

★ 2575 ★
Utilities
SIC: 4911; NAICS: 221119, 221121, 221122
Leading Electricity Firms, 2002

Firms are ranked by sales in billions of dollars.

Duke Energy	$ 4.92
Calpine	4.03
El Paso Energy Corporation	3.71
FPL Group Inc.	3.26
PG&E	3.03
Dominion Resources	2.82
Southern Company	2.71
Xcel Energy Inc.	2.40
Public Service Enterprise Group	2.33

Source: *Electric Light and Power*, September 2003, p. 17.

★ 2576 ★
Utlities
SIC: 4911; NAICS: 221119, 221121, 221122
Leading Electricity Companies in the U.K.

Market shares are shown in percent.

Innogy	19.0%
Centrica	17.0
TXU	15.0
Scottish & Southern	14.0
ScottishPower	10.0

EdF (London, South Westrn)	10.0%
Powergen	8.0
SEEBOARD	6.0
Other	1.0

Source: *Financial Times*, March 22, 2002, p. 23, from Thomson Financial Data stream, UBS Warburg, and Ofgem.

★ 2577 ★
Wind Power
SIC: 4911; NAICS: 221119
Wind Energy Industry in Europe, 2002

Countries are ranked by total installed capacity at the end of 2002 in megawatts (MW). Wind power technology installed during the year was worth 5.8 billion British pounds.

	MW	Share
Germany	12,001	52.05%
Spain	4,830	20.95
Denmark	2,880	12.49
Italy	785	3.40
Netherlands	688	2.98
U.K.	552	2.39
Sweden	328	1.42
Greece	276	1.20
Portugal	194	0.84
France	145	0.63
Other	377	1.64

Source: "European Wind Industry." [online] from http://www.awea.org [accessed June 1, 2004], from European Wind Energy Association.

★ 2578 ★
Wind Power
SIC: 4911; NAICS: 221119
Wind Power Generation

States are ranked by capacity in megawatts (MW). From the source: "the United States added 1,687 megawatts of new wind power in 2003 for a total of 6,374 megawatts."

	Megawatts	Share
California	2,043	36.56%
Texas	1,293	23.14
Minnesota	563	10.08
Iowa	471	8.43
Wyoming	285	5.10

Continued on next page.

★ 2578 ★

[Continued]
Wind Power
SIC: 4911; NAICS: 221119

Wind Power Generation

States are ranked by capacity in megawatts (MW). From the source: "the United States added 1,687 megawatts of new wind power in 2003 for a total of 6,374 megawatts."

	Megawatts	Share
Oregon	259	4.63%
Washington	244	4.37
Colorado	223	3.99
New Mexico	207	3.70

Source: *Star Tribune*, April 2, 2004, p. 1D, from American Wind Energy Association.

★ 2579 ★

Gas Transmission
SIC: 4922, NAICS: 48621

Gas Transmission Market in Germany, 2001

Market shares are shown in percent.

Ruhrgas	57.1%
Wingas	14.4
Verbundnetz Gas	13.5
BEB Erdgas und Heinzol	6.0
Thyssengas	5.9
Other	3.1

Source: *Der Spiegel*, no. 27, 2002, p. 94, from Bundesverband der Ga und Wasserwirtschaft.

★ 2580 ★

Gas Transmission
SIC: 4922; NAICS: 48621

Leading Gas Companies in the U.K.

Market shares are shown in percent.

Centrica	67.0%
Innogy	11.0
TXU	6.0
ScottishPower	4.0
Scottish & Southern	4.0
Other	8.0

Source: *Financial Times*, March 22, 2002, p. 23, from Thomson Financial Data stream, UBS Warburg, and Ofgem.

★ 2581 ★

Gas Transmission
SIC: 4922; NAICS: 48621

Leading Gas Pipelines, 2002

Companies are ranked by miles of pipeline operated.

Duke Energy Field Services	60,000
ONEOK Inc.	21,700
Northern Natural Gas Co.	16,658
Tennessee Gas Pipeline Co.	14,140
El Paso Natural Gas Co.	10,629
Columbia Gas Transmission Co.	10,488
Transcontinental Gas Pipe Line Corp.	10,449
Natural Gas Pipeline Co. of America	9,784
ANR Pipeline Co.	9,615
Texas Eastern Transmission	8,913
Enogex Inc.	8,910
Southern Natural Gas Co.	7,933

Source: *Pipeline & Gas Journal*, November 2003, p. 59.

★ 2582 ★
Natural Gas
SIC: 4922; NAICS: 48621

Natural Gas Consumption, 2002

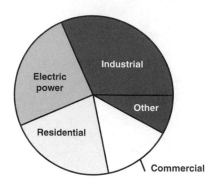

Figures show share of consumption.

Industrial	31.7%
Electric power	24.8
Residential	21.9
Commercial	14.0
Other	7.5

Source: *New York Times*, June 17, 2003, p. C3, from Energy Information Administration.

★ 2583 ★
Natural Gas
SIC: 4923; NAICS: 22121

Natural Gas Demand, 2004

Total demand is 60 billion cubic feet.

	(bil.)	Share
Industrial	22.9	38.23%
Residential	14.3	23.87
Commercial	8.9	14.86
Electric utility & other	7.5	12.52
Field usage/exports	6.3	10.52

Source: *Electric Light & Power*, June 2003, p. 20, from Energy Information Administration, Department of Energy, and A.G. Edwards & Sons Research.

★ 2584 ★
Recycling
SIC: 4953; NAICS: 562219, 56292

Leading Recycling Groups

Companies are ranked by recycling revenue in millions of dollars.

OmniSource	$ 808.6
Metal Management Inc.	806.0
Imco Recycling	687.2
Waste Management	635.0
Smurfit-Stone Container Corp.	563.2

Source: *Waste News*, September 15, 2003, p. 11, from *Waste News 2003 Recycling Rankings*.

★ 2585 ★
Waste Collection
SIC: 4953; NAICS: 562212, 562213

Garbage Market in Eugene, Oregon

The city's residential market is led by Sanipac. Sanipac has 70% of the city's commercial market.

Sanipac	80.0%
Other	20.0

Source: *Register-Guard*, June 23, 2003, p. NA.

★ 2586 ★
Waste Collection
SIC: 4953; NAICS: 562212, 562213, 562219

Industrial Waste Market in Utah

Market shares are shown in percent.

Metro Waste	60.0%
Other	40.0

Source: *Waste News*, February 16, 2004, p. 6.

★ 2587 ★

Waste Collection

SIC: 4953; NAICS: 562212, 562213

Leading Solid Waste Disposal Firms, 2003

Waste Management Inc.	
Allied Waste Industries Inc.	
	Republic Services Inc.
	Onyx N.A.
	PSC - Industrial Services
	Covanta Energy Corp.
	Safety-Kleen Systems
	Waste Connections Inc.
	Casella Waste Systems Inc.
	Stericycle
	Norcal Waste Systems
	Clean Harbors Environmental Services

Firms are ranked by revenues in millions of dollars.

Waste Management Inc.	$ 11,142.0
Allied Waste Industries Inc.	5,517.0
Republic Services Inc.	2,365.0
Onyx N.A.	1,300.0
PSC - Industrial Services	1,200.0
Covanta Energy Corp.	920.3
Safety-Kleen Systems	870.2
Waste Connections Inc.	499.0
Casella Waste Systems Inc.	420.8
Stericycle	401.5
Norcal Waste Systems	354.9
Clean Harbors Environmental Services	350.1

Source: *Waste Age*, June 2003, p. 40.

SIC 50 - Wholesale Trade - Durable Goods

★ 2588 ★

Wholesale Trade - Tires

SIC: 5014; NAICS: 42113

Passenger Tire Shipments, 2003

Market shares are shown in percent.

Local dealerships	44.0%
National dealerships	19.0
General merchandise distributors	18.0
Tire makers outlets	10.0
Regional dealerships	4.0
Other	5.0

Source: *Tire Business*, February 2, 2004, p. 9.

★ 2589 ★

Wholesale Trade - Construction

SIC: 5030; NAICS: 42131, 42132

Leading Construction Industry Suppliers

Companies are ranked by sales in millions of dollars.

Stock Building Supply	$ 2,595.4
84 Lumber Co.	2,196.4
ABC Supply Co.	1,924.4
Builders FirstSource	1,651.1
Lanoga Corp.	1,560.0
BMHC	1,415.0
Allied Building Products	990.0

Bradco Supply Corp.	$ 965.2
Beacon Roofing Supply	580.2
Hope Lumber & Supply Co.	500.4
White Cap Industries	485.1

Source: *Prosales*, May 2004, p. 46.

★ 2590 ★

Wholesale Trade - Electronics

SIC: 5060; NAICS: 421690

Largest Electrical Wholesalers, 2002

Firms are ranked by sales in billions of dollars.

Graybar Electric	$ 3.97
Wesco Distribution	3.30
Anixter Inc.	2.50
GE Supply	2.47
Rexel	2.10
Sonepar	1.40
W.W. Grainger	0.88
Hughes Supply	0.62

Source: *Electrical Wholesaling*, June 1, 2003, p. NA.

★ 2591 ★

Wholesale Trade - Electronics

SIC: 5060; NAICS: 421690

Largest Franchised Distributors in North America

Companies are ranked by North American sales in millions of dollars. Newark InOne ranked eighth, but its figure was unavailable.

Avnet Inc.	$ 5,141
Arrow Electronics Inc.	4,238

Continued on next page.

★ 2591 ★

[Continued]
Wholesale Trade - Electronics
SIC: 5060; NAICS: 421690

Largest Franchised Distributors in North America

Companies are ranked by North American sales in millions of dollars. Newark InOne ranked eighth, but its figure was unavailable.

Future Electronics Inc.	$ 2,400
Pioneer-Standard	2,000
Bell Microproducts	1,239
Memec Group Holdings	750
TTI Inc.	531
Digi-Key Corp.	350
All American	332
Reptron Electronics Inc.	320

Source: *Electronic Buyer's News*, May 12, 2003, p. 42.

★ 2592 ★

Wholesale Trade - Electronics
SIC: 5063; NAICS: 421690

Leading Electronics Distributors

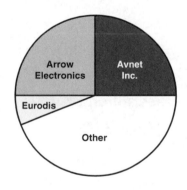

Market shares are shown in percent.

Avnet Inc.	25.0%
Arrow Electronics	25.0
Eurodis	6.0
Other	44.0

Source: *EBN*, February 4, 2002, p. 32, from analyst estimates.

★ 2593 ★

Wholesale Trade
SIC: 5080; NAICS: 42181, 42182, 44421

Largest Industrial Distributors in North America

Companies are ranked by sales in billions of dollars.

W.W. Grainger	$ 4.64
Hughes Supply Inc.	3.07
Motion Industries	2.25
Airgas Inc.	1.79
Hagemeyer NA Holdings Inc.	1.54
Applied Industrial Technologies	1.45
Ferguson Enterprises Inc.	1.07
Wilson Industries	0.90
Fastenal Co.	0.90
McJunkin Corp.	0.80
MSC Industrial Direct Co. Inc.	0.79
Interline Brands	0.64

Source: *Industrial Distribution*, June 2003, p. 41.

★ 2594 ★

Wholesale Trade - Bicycles
SIC: 5091; NAICS: 42191

Specialty Bike Sales

According to the source, bike sales are doing well but prices are falling. From 2002 to 2003 the average wholesale price fell from $830 to $780 million. The retail price fell from $1,200 to $1,118 for the same period. Shares are shown based on wholesale shipments.

	2002	2003
26" all	53.0%	51.0%
20/24"	30.0	30.0
Hybrid	10.0	10.0
Road	6.0	8.0

Source: *Bicycle Retailer and Industry News*, March 1, 2004, p. 1, from Bicycle Product Suppliers Association.

SIC 51 - Wholesale Trade - Nondurable Goods

★ 2595 ★
Wholesale Trade - Convenience Stores
SIC: 5100; NAICS: 42241, 42294

Leading Convenience Wholesalers

Companies are ranked by estimated fiscal sales in millions of dollars.

McLane Company	$ 18,100
Eby-Brown	3,800
Core-Mark International	3,100
H.T. Hackney	2,500
GSC Enterprises	1,215
Klein Candy Co.	1,022
S. Abraham & Sons	920
Harold Levinson Associates	820
Amcon Distributing	813
Spartan Stores/Convenience Stores	800

Source: *Convenience Store News*, October 12, 2003, p. 117.

★ 2596 ★
Office Supply Stores
SIC: 5112; NAICS: 42212, 45321

Home and Office Supply Market

The $324 billion market is shown by distribution channel. The direct mail/catalog and institutional sectors have between 1-2% of the market.

Retail	67.0%
Contract/commercial	22.0
E-Commerce	8.0
Institutional	2.0
Direct mail/catalog	2.0

Source: *DSN Retailing Today*, August 18, 2003, p. 17, from School, Home & Office Products Association.

★ 2597 ★
Office Supply Stores
SIC: 5112; NAICS: 45321

Leading Office Supply Stores

Staples

Office Depot

OfficeMax

Firms are ranked by sales in billions of dollars. Staples has 1,500 stores, Office Depot has 1,045 stores and Office Max has 1,000 stores.

Staples	$ 11.6
Office Depot	11.4
OfficeMax	4.8

Source: *USA TODAY*, July 15, 2003, p. 4B, from Hoovers and company reports.

★ 2598 ★
Prescription Drug Managers
SIC: 5122; NAICS: 42221

Leading Prescription Drug Managers

Market shares are shown by number of covered lines.

AdvancePCS	19.0%
Medco Health Solutions Inc.	15.0
Express Scripts Inc.	12.0
WellPoint Pharmacy Management	9.0
Caremark Rx, Inc.	6.0
MedImpact Healthcare Systems Inc.	6.0
Eckerd Health Services	4.0
PharmaCare Management Services Inc.	4.0
Other	25.0

Source: *Drug Cost Management Report*, August 29, 2003, p. 1.

★ 2599 ★
Wholesale Trade - Drugs
SIC: 5122; NAICS: 42221

Drug Wholesaling Markets

| Independent drug stores |
| Hospitals |
| Mass merchandisers and food stores |
| Chain drug stores |
| Clinics and nursing homes |
| Other |

End markets are shown based on sales.

Independent drug stores	33.5%
Hospitals	24.7
Mass merchandisers and food stores	11.1
Chain drug stores	9.8
Clinics and nursing homes	8.9
Other	12.0

Source: *Wall Street Journal*, September 29, 2003, p. 1, from Healthcare Distribution Management Association.

★ 2600 ★
Wholetrade Trade - Seafood
SIC: 5146; NAICS: 42246

Top Seafood Wholesalers

Companies are ranked by sales in millions of dollars.

Sysco Corp.	$ 1,300
U.S. Foodservice	760
Performance Food Group	295
Inland Seafood	150
East Coast Seafood	135
Supreme Lobster & Seafood Co.	129
Morey's Seafood International	125
Gordon Food Service	110
Reinhart FoodService	94
Southstream Seafoods	72

Source: *Seafood Business*, September 2003, p. 1.

★ 2601 ★
Wholesale Trade - Comic Books
SIC: 5192; NAICS: 42292

Popular Comics Titles

Data show estimated sales by Diamond Comics, the major comic distributor, to comic specialty shops for the month of October 2003.

Avengers/JLA #2	176,734
Amazing Spider-Man #500	162,176
Marvel 1602 #3	140,972
Ultimate Six #2	130,575
Ultimate Six #3	119,499
Ultimate X-Men #38	117,729
Batman #620	117,213
New X-Men #147	115,045
Batman/Superman #3	112,782
New X-Men #148	112,173

Source: "Top 300 Comics Actual." [online] available from http://www.icvs.com/articles/home/3873.html [accessed November 25, 2003], from Diamond Comics.

★ 2602 ★
Wholesale Trade - Pool Supplies
SIC: 5199; NAICS: 42299

Pool Supply Distribution Market

The company is the world's largest independent distributor of pool related products. The top four firms control about 50% of the market with 170 other local and regional firms holding the balance.

SCP	35.0%
Next 3 distributors	15.0
Other	50.0

Source: *BusinessWeek Online*, July 22, 2003, p. NA.

SIC 52 - Building Materials and Garden Supplies

★ 2603 ★

Home Improvement Stores

SIC: 5211; NAICS: 44411, 44419

Home Improvement Sales by Year, 2003-2007

Sales of home improvement products are forecasted for the United States.

2007	$ 247
2006	236
2005	225
2004	214
2003	204

Source: *Do-It-Yourself Retailing*, August 2003, p. 20, from Home Improvement Research Institute.

★ 2604 ★

Home Improvement Stores

SIC: 5211; NAICS: 44411, 44419

Home Improvement Spending

A total of $121.5 billion in home improvement spending took place during the year. The top categories are shown below. By larger category, alterations took $39.3 billion, major replacements of roofing, plumbing, siding and windows took $25.3 billion, maintenance and repairs took $23.6 billion, additions took $33 billion.

Room additions	$ 13,040
Kitchen remodeling	6,608
Roofing	5,974
Flooring	5,052
Bathroom remodeling	4,492
HVAC	4,314
Windows	3,861
Interior restructuring	3,558
Decks and porches	3,239
Finishing space	2,956

Source: *Research Alert*, March 5, 2004, p. 7, from National Association of Home Builders and U.S. Bureau of the Census.

★ 2605 ★

Home Improvement Stores

SIC: 5211; NAICS: 44411, 44419

Largest DIY Markets in Europe

The top markets in the do-it-yourself industry (DIY) are ranked by sales in billions of euros.

Germany	36.60
U.K.	34.80
France	16.80
Italy	8.20
Spain	3.05

Source: *LSA Libre Service Actualites*, July 11, 2002, p. 30, from Fideuram Wargny and the source.

★ 2606 ★

Home Improvement Stores

SIC: 5211; NAICS: 44411, 44419

Largest DIY Markets in Western Europe

The Western European market was worth 81.6 billion euros.

	(bil.)	Share
Germany	15.0	18.38%
France	12.4	15.20
Italy	11.7	14.34
U.K.	11.2	13.73
Spain	6.4	7.84
Other	24.9	30.51

Source: *Retail Week*, May 7, 2004, p. 5.

★ 2607 ★
Home Improvement Stores
SIC: 5211; NAICS: 44411, 44419

Leading DIY Chains in Israel

Retail sales were about $430 million 2002, in which 61% was for traditional DIY products and 39% was spent on electrical and non-DIY products.

Home Centers	54.0%
ACE	38.0
Hyper Rosenfeld	6.0
Other	2.0

Source: ''Do-It-Yourself (DIY) Hand Tools.'' [online] from http://www.usatrade.gov [accessed January 5, 2004], from U.S. Commercial Service.

★ 2608 ★
Home Improvement Stores
SIC: 5211; NAICS: 44411, 44419

Leading DIY Retailers in the U.K., 2002

Market shares are shown in percent.

B & Q Plc	49.0%
Focus Wickes	20.7
Homebase	18.9
Toppes Tiles	1.6
JH Leeke & Son	1.3
C Brewer & Sons Ltd.	1.1
Robert Dyas	1.0
Mica Ltd.	0.7
Machine Mart Ltd.	0.6
Glyn Webb Wallpaper Ltd.	0.6

Source: *UK Retail Briefing*, April 2004, p. 84, from Mintel.

★ 2609 ★
Home Improvement Stores
SIC: 5211; NAICS: 44411, 44419

Sales at Home Improvement Channels

Store types are ranked by sales in millions of dollars.

	2003	2005	2007
Home centers	$ 126.1	$ 140.5	$ 157.4
Lumberyards	56.5	62.1	66.0
Hardware stores	25.8	28.5	31.4

Source: *Do-It-Yourself Retailing*, November 2003, p. 30, from company reports and estimates by the source.

★ 2610 ★
Home Improvement Stores
SIC: 5211; NAICS: 44411, 44419

Top Home Improvement Chains, 2002

Companies are ranked by sales in millions of dollars.

Home Depot	$ 58,247
Lowe's Cos.	26,491
Menard Inc.	5,300
Stock Building Supply	2,700
84 Lumber	2,000
Sears Hardware	1,600
Lanoga	1,500
BMHC	1,161
Sutherland Lumber	835
Wickes	577

Source: *Do-It-Yourself Retailing*, November 2003, p. 30, from company reports and estimates by the source.

★ 2611 ★
Home Improvement Stores
SIC: 5211; NAICS: 44411, 44419

Top Home Improvement Stores, 2002

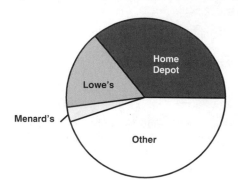

Market shares are shown in percent.

Home Depot	36.0%
Lowe's	16.0
Menard's	3.0
Other	45.0

Source: *The Indianapolis Star*, June 23, 2003, p. C1, from Farnsworth Group.

★ 2612 ★
Home Improvement Stores
SIC: 5211; NAICS: 44411, 44419

Top Home Improvement Stores in France, 2001

Market shares are shown based on total sales of $16.25 billion.

Castorama	18.2%
Leroy Merlin	15.7
Bricomarche	9.2
Mr. Bricolage	6.7
Domaxel	4.8
Tabur	2.2
BHV	1.0
Other	39.8

Source: *Home Channel News*, June 17, 2002, p. S12, from Unibal.

★ 2613 ★
Home Improvement Stores
SIC: 5211; NAICS: 44411, 44419

Top Home Improvement Stores in Japan

Market shares are shown in percent.

Cainz	5.74%
Konan Shoji	5.16
Homac	5.10
Nafuko	4.74
Kelyo	4.58
Komeri	3.94
Kahma	3.84
Shimachu	3.27
Joyful Honda	3.01
Tokyu Hands	2.87
Other	57.75

Source: *Home Channel News*, June 17, 2002, p. S21, from Diamond Friedman.

★ 2614 ★
Home Improvement Stores
SIC: 5231; NAICS: 44411, 44419

Big-Box Market Shares

Figures show the percent of customers making their last purchase at a Lowe's, Menard's and Home Depot.

Lumber	99.0%
Building materials	99.0
Lighting	94.0
Electrical supplies	90.0
Plumbing supplies	89.0
Hardware	87.0
Kitchen cabinets and counter tops	86.0
Bath vanity and bath remodeling	86.0
Windows and doors	84.0
Storage and shelving	84.0

Source: *Do-It-Yourself Retailing*, June 2003, p. 49, from *Home Improvement DATA*.

★ 2615 ★
Paint and Flooring Stores
SIC: 5231; NAICS: 44412

Largest Specialty Paint and Flooring Retailers, 2002

Firms are ranked by sales in millions of dollars.

CCA Global Partners	$ 6,100.0
Sherwin-Williams	3,358.6
Abbey Carpet	1,620.0
ICI Paints	1,555.0
Dal-Tile	1,134.2
Professional Paint Inc.	400.0
Duran Paints & Wallcoverings	327.0
Kelly-Moore Paint	323.0
Dunn-Edwards	292.0
M.A. Bruder & Sons	193.0
Porter Paints	180.0
Benjamin Moore & Co.	158.0

Source: *Home Channel News*, November 3, 2003, p. 12.

★ 2616 ★
Hardware Stores
SIC: 5251; NAICS: 44413

Leading Hardware Stores in Canada

| Rona |
| Home Depot Canada |
| Home Hardware |
| Canadian Tire |
| Other |

Market shares are shown in percent.

Rona	14.0%
Home Depot Canada	14.0
Home Hardware	13.0
Canadian Tire	12.0
Other	47.0

Source: *Home Channel News NewsFax*, February 9, 2004, p. 2, from Rona.

★ 2617 ★
Hardware Stores
SIC: 5251; NAICS: 44413

Sears and Tool Sales

Sears has 26% of overall tool sales and nearly 4% of the home improvement market. Its share is shown in selected categories.

Mechanics tool sales	44.0%
Tool storage	31.0
Benchtop tools	29.0
Portable electric tools	23.0

Source: *DSN Retailing Today*, September 8, 2003, p. NA.

★ 2618 ★
Lawn & Garden Industry
SIC: 5261; NAICS: 44421, 44422

Lawn & Garden Accessories Industry

Total sales of gifts & accessories was $1.65 billion.

Gifts & decorative	22.0%
Containers	17.9
Lawn decorations	11.6
Water features	10.6
Outdoor lighting	7.0
Weed barriers	4.5
Gloves	4.5
Sprayers	4.4
Play equipment	4.4
Lawn edging	3.7

Source: *Nursery Retailer*, January/February 2004, p. 84.

★ 2619 ★
Lawn & Garden Industry
SIC: 5261; NAICS: 44421, 44422

Lawn & Garden Sales by State, 2003

Total sales were $98.6 billion.

California	9.4%
Texas	6.2
Illinois	6.1
Minnesota	4.3
Iowa	4.2
Other	69.8

Source: *Nursery Retailer*, January/February 2004, p. 83.

★ 2620 ★
Lawn & Garden Industry
SIC: 5261; NAICS: 44421, 44422

Leading Lawn & Garden Retailers, 2002

An estimated 85 million households are thought to have participated in gardening activities during the year. The top 25 retailers generated sales of $1.39 billion (down slightly from $1.41 billion in 2001). Kmart and Wal-Mart, two of the nation's biggest retailers, hold less than 5% of the market together. Firms are ranked by sales in millions of dollars.

Frank's Nursery & Crafts	$ 315.1
Smith & Hawken	125.0
Barbeques Galore	102.1
Bachman's	90.0
Pike Family Nursery	89.0
Armstrong Garden Centers	75.0
Stein Garden & Gifts	67.0
Earl May Seed & Nursery	48.0
SummerWinds Garden Centers	45.0
Calloway's Nursery	43.3
Meadows Farms	38.0
Mahoney's Rocky Ledge Farm & Nursery	33.0

Source: *Home Channel News*, July 1, 2003, p. 11, from Home Improvement Research Institute.

SIC 53 - General Merchandise Stores

★ 2621 ★
Retailing
SIC: 5300; NAICS: 45211, 45291

Largest Retail Firms

Firms are ranked by sales in billions of dollars.

Wal-Mart	$ 246.53
Home Depot	58.25
Kroger	51.76
Target	42.72
Sears	41.37
Costco	37.99
Albertsons	35.63
Safeway	32.40
J.C. Penney	32.35
Kmart	30.76

Source: *Stores*, July 2003, p. S2, from National Retail Federation.

★ 2622 ★
Retailing
SIC: 5300; NAICS: 45211, 45299

Largest Retailers Worldwide, 2002

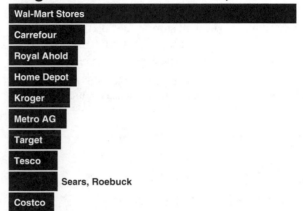

Firms are ranked by sales in billions of dollars.

Wal-Mart Stores	$ 244.52
Carrefour	64.94
Royal Ahold	59.22
Home Depot	58.24
Kroger	51.76
Metro AG	48.68
Target	43.91
Tesco	41.48
Sears, Roebuck	41.36
Costco	37.99

Source: *Chain Store Age*, December 2003, p. 41, from Cap Gemini Ernst & Young research.

★ 2623 ★
Retailing
SIC: 5300; NAICS: 45291, 44511, 44611

Retail Market

Sales are shown in millions of dollars.

	2001	2002
National & super regional grocers	$ 210,039	$ 216,572
Discount department stores . . .	128,783	124,893
Supercenters	100,853	119,448
Drug stores	87,068	93,398
DIY/home centers	76,813	85,749
Warehouse clubs	71,287	78,170
Mid-tier chains	70,663	72,006
Promotional department stores .	53,103	51,383
Apparel & accessories chains . .	46,016	49,165
Consumer electronics chains . .	38,519	42,474

Source: *DSN Retailing Today*, July 7, 2003, p. 15, from *DSN Retailing Today* research and industry sources.

★ 2624 ★
Retailing
SIC: 5300; NAICS: 45211, 45299

Seasonal Decoration Sales

Americans spent about $144 per household on Christmas and other seasonal decorations. Those 18 to 24 years old spent the most ($195, about one-third higher than average).

Discount department stores	52.0%
Traditional department stores	39.0
Other specialty (gift stores, etc.)	39.0
Home improvement/garden stores	20.0
Food and beverage retailers	6.0

Source: *Supermarket News*, November 10, 2003, p. 26, from *Gifts & Decorative Accents Report 2003*.

★ 2625 ★
Retailing
SIC: 5300; NAICS: 45211

Wal-Mart and Retail Sales

Data show the company's share in selected markets for 2002. Figures exclude Sam's Clubs.

Disposable diapers	32.0%
Hair care	30.0
Toothpaste	26.0
Pet food	20.0
Home textiles	13.0

Source: *BusinessWeek*, October 6, 2003, p. 104, from A.C. Nielsen, Retail Forward, and *Home Textiles Today*.

★ 2626 ★
Department Stores
SIC: 5311; NAICS: 45211

Top Department Stores, 2002

Companies are ranked by revenues in billions of dollars.

Sears	$ 23.03
J.C. Penney	17.70
Federated	15.54
May	13.49
Kohl's	9.12
Dillard's	8.23
Nordstrom	5.98
Saks	5.91
Mervyn's	3.82
Neiman Marcus	3.10

Source: *Footwear News*, November 24, 2003, p. 18.

★ 2627 ★
Department Stores
SIC: 5311; NAICS: 45211

Top Department Stores in the U.K., 2001

Market shares are shown in percent.

M&S	31.4%
John Lewis	16.2
Debenhams	14.6
HoF	8.5
Allders	4.9
Co-op	4.4
Harrods	4.0
Selfridges	3.6
Fnwick	2.6
Other	10.2

Source: *Retail Week*, August 23, 2002, p. 4, from Verdict Research.

★ 2628 ★
Convenience Stores
SIC: 5331; NAICS: 45299

Best-Selling Convenience Store Items, 2003

Figures show percentage of in-store sales.

Cigarettes	36.0%
Foodservice	12.3
Packaged beverages (non-alcoholic)	12.2
Beer	11.0
General merchandise	4.0
Candy	3.9
Fluid milk products	2.8
Salty snacks	2.7
Packaged sweet snacks	1.8
Other tobacco	2.7
Other	10.6

Source: *Beverage Dynamics*, January-February 2004, p. 9, from *National Association of Convenience Stores 2003 State of the Industry*.

★ 2629 ★
Convenience Stores
SIC: 5331; NAICS: 45299

Leading Convenience Store Companies

Companies are ranked by number of outlets.

7-Eleven Inc.	5,345
Shell Oil Products/Motive Enterprises	5,300
BP	5,050
Conoco Phillips Inc.	4,274
Exxon Mobil Corp.	4,000
ChevronTexaco Corp.	2,679
Speedway SuperAmerica	1,805
Casey's General Stores Inc.	1,345
The Pantry Inc.	1,274
Amerada Hess Corp.	1,205
Valero Energy Corp.	1,189
Clark Retail Enterprises Inc.	900

Source: *Convenience Store News*, August 25, 2003, p. 25, from *Convenience Store News Top 50 Report*.

★ 2630 ★
Discount Merchandising
SIC: 5331; NAICS: 45299

Close Out Retailing

Market shares are shown in percent. The company buys discontinued or overstocked items from companies and sells them at a discount.

Big Lots	70.0%
Other	30.0

Source: *Kipliner's Personal Finance Magazine*, November 2003, p. 62, from C&B Mid Cap Value fund.

★ 2631 ★
Discount Merchandising
SIC: 5331; NAICS: 45299

Discount Industry in Germany, 2001

Market shares are shown for the 45.02 billion industry.

Lidi	14.0%
Plus	12.0
Penny	12.0
Netto	7.0
Norma	5.0
Other	2.0

Source: *Quick Frozen Foods International*, January 2003, p. 123, from M+M Planet Retail.

★ 2632 ★
Discount Merchandising
SIC: 5331; NAICS: 45299

Leading Discount Clubs

Companies are ranked by revenues in millions of dollars.

Costco	$ 38,762
Sam's Club	32,536
BJ's Wholesale Club	5,859

Source: *DSN Retailing Today*, July 21, 2003, p. S6.

★ 2633 ★
Discount Merchandising
SIC: 5331; NAICS: 45299

Leading Discount Stores in South Korea, 2001

Market shares are shown in percent.

Homeplus	11.3%
Carrefour	10.0
Wal-Mart	5.0
Costco	3.6
Other	70.4

Source: "Discount Store Market." [online] from http://www.usatrade.gov [accessed January 5, 2004], from U.S. Commercial Service, *Ring Those Tills*, and Carrefour, Homeplus.

★ 2634 ★
Discount Merchandising
SIC: 5331; NAICS: 45299

Leading Discount Stores in the U.K.

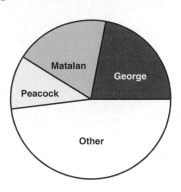

The sector is worth about 4.4 billion pounds.

George	22.0%
Matalan	18.7
Peacock	11.0
Other	48.3

Source: *The Evening Standard (London)*, October 28, 2003, p. 31.

★ 2635 ★
Discount Merchandising
SIC: 5331; NAICS: 45299

Leading Dollar Stores

Firms are ranked by sales in billions of dollars. The top five chains have 80% of the market. The other 20% are mom and pop stores.

Dollar General	$ 6.90
Family Dollar	4.80
Dollar Tree	2.80
Fred's	1.30
99c Only	0.57

Source: *HFN*, March 22, 2004, p. NA, from Bear Stearns.

SIC 54 - Food Stores

★ 2636 ★
Grocery Stores
SIC: 5411; NAICS: 44511

Grocery Store Market in Sweden

Market shares are shown in percent.

ICA	37.0%
Koopertiva Foerbundet	18.0
Axfood Group	17.0
Other	28.0

Source: *European Intelligence Wire*, April 4, 2004, p. NA.

★ 2637 ★
Grocery Stores
SIC: 5411; NAICS: 44511

Top Grocers Worldwide

Companies are ranked by sales in billions of dollars.

Wal-Mart	$ 218.95
Carrefour	62.53
Ahold	59.93
Kroger	50.36
Metro	44.57
Albertson's	38.50
Kmart	34.79
Safeway	34.48
Costco	34.31
Tesco	34.25

Source: *Candy Industry*, May 2002, p. 50, from M+M Planet Retail.

★ 2638 ★
Grocery Stores
SIC: 5411; NAICS: 44511

Top Grocery Chains, 2003

Total food sales, according to the Census Bureau and the Department of Commerce, reached $775 billion in 2003, an increase of 6.4% over $728.7 billion in 2002. If considering Wal-Mart's food sales only the share is 4.0%. Kroger and Albertsons' shares include nonfood items. Costco's food share only is 3.2%. Sam's Clubs food only share is 2.6%.

Wal-Mart Supercenters	13.3%
Kroger Co.	6.9
Costco	5.4
Albertsons	4.7
Safeway	4.3
Sam's Clubs	4.3
Ahold USA	3.5
Supervalu	2.6
Publix	2.2
Delhaize America	2.0
C&S Wholesale Grocers	1.5
Winn-Dixie	1.5
Other	47.8

Source: *Supermarket News*, January 12, 2004, p. 5S.

★ 2639 ★
Grocery Stores
SIC: 5411; NAICS: 44511

Top Grocery Stores, 2003

Companies are ranked by estimated sales in billions of dollars.

	($ bil.)	Share
Wal-Mart	$ 95	21.0%
Kroger	53	12.0
Albertsons	36	8.0
Safeway	31	7.0
Ahold USA	27	6.0
Publix	17	4.0
Delhaize America	16	3.0

Continued on next page.

★ 2639 ★
[Continued]
Grocery Stores
SIC: 5411; NAICS: 44511
Top Grocery Stores, 2003

Companies are ranked by estimated sales in billions of dollars.

	($ bil.)	Share
Winn-Dixie	$ 12	3.0%
Other	172	36.0

Source: *USA TODAY*, March 2, 2004, p. 2B, from Retail Forward Inc. and *USA Today* research.

★ 2640 ★
Grocery Stores
SIC: 5411; NAICS: 44511
Top Grocery Stores in Alabama, 2003

Market shares are shown in percent.

Wal-Mart	32.8%
Bruno's	18.0
Other	49.2

Source: *Birmingham Business Journal*, March 1, 2004, p. NA, from *Shelby Report*.

★ 2641 ★
Grocery Stores
SIC: 5411; NAICS: 44511
Top Grocery Stores in Albuquerque, NM

Market shares are shown in percent.

Smith's	27.0%
Wal-Mart	25.2
Albertsons	17.0
Raley's	9.9
Other	20.9

Source: *The Albuquerque Tribune*, December 1, 2003, p. B1, from *Shelby Report* and Trade Dimensions.

★ 2642 ★
Grocery Stores
SIC: 5411; NAICS: 44511
Top Grocery Stores in Argentina, 2003

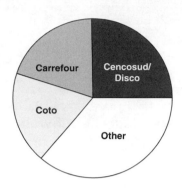

Total supermarket sales were 16,555 million pesos, a 9.6% increase over 2002.

Cencosud/Disco	22.7%
Carrefour	17.5
Coto	16.9
Other	32.9

Source: *South American Business Information*, May 10, 2004, p. NA.

★ 2643 ★
Grocery Stores
SIC: 5411; NAICS: 44511
Top Grocery Stores in Arkansas

Market shares are shown in percent. Wal-Mart saw its share increase 39% from 2001 to 2002.

Wal-Mart	43.64%
Kroger	12.76
Harps Food Stores	8.78
Hays Food Town	1.30
Town & Country	1.25
G&W Foods	0.85
Other	31.42

Source: *Arkansas Business*, June 30, 2003, p. 23, from Shelby Report Southwest.

★ 2644 ★
Grocery Stores
SIC: 5411; NAICS: 44511
Top Grocery Stores in Atlanta, GA

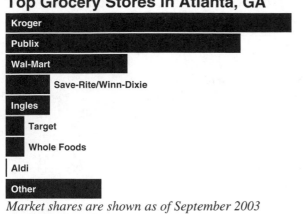

*Market shares are shown as of September 2003
based on store count.*

Kroger	32.6%
Publix	26.5
Wal-Mart	14.2
Save-Rite/Winn-Dixie	5.4
Ingles	5.4
Target	2.4
Whole Foods	1.9
Aldi	0.2
Other	11.4

Source: *Atlanta Journal-Constitution*, September 13, 2003, p. E1.

★ 2645 ★
Grocery Stores
SIC: 5411; NAICS: 44511
Top Grocery Stores in Austin/San Marcos, TX

*Market shares are shown based on area volume for
2002.*

H.E.B.	51.0%
Safeway's/Randall's	13.0
Albertsons	12.0
Wal-Mart	9.0
Other	15.0

Source: *MMR*, June 13, 2003, p. 26.

★ 2646 ★
Grocery Stores
SIC: 5411; NAICS: 44511
Top Grocery Stores in Australia

*Australians spend $60 billion each year in supermarkets. Market shares are shown in percent as of April
2003. Some stores operate only in certain regions of
the country.*

Woolworths/Safeway	35.5%
Coles/Bi-Lo	33.7
Action (WA, QLD)	2.3
Frankins (NSW)	2.2
Aldi (NSW, Vic)	1.2
Other	25.1

Source: *The Weekend Australian*, October 25, 2003, p. 26.

★ 2647 ★
Grocery Stores
SIC: 5411; NAICS: 44511
Top Grocery Stores in Baltimore, MD

*Market shares are shown based on area volume for
2002.*

Giant Food	28.0%
Safeway	10.0
Other	62.0

Source: *MMR*, June 13, 2003, p. 26.

★ 2648 ★
Grocery Stores
SIC: 5411; NAICS: 44511
Top Grocery Stores in Birmingham, AL

The local market is valued at $1.4 billion.

Bruno's	30.34%
Publix	26.46
Wal-Mart	22.89
Winn-Dixie	20.50
Piggly Wiggly	7.14

Source: *Birmingham Business Journal*, November 3, 2003, p. NA, from *Shelby Report*.

★ 2649 ★
Grocery Stores
SIC: 5411; NAICS: 44511

Top Grocery Stores in Brazil

Market shares are shown in percent.

Companhia Brasileria de Distribuicao (Pao de
   Acucar) 14.6%
Carrefour 12.6
Sonae Dist. Brasil 4.2
BomPreco 4.2
Sendas S/A 3.2
Wal-Mart Brasil 2.1
Cia Zaffari 1.3
G Barbosa Com Ltd. 1.0
COOP Coop de Consumo 0.9
Irmaos Bretas 0.8
Other 55.1

Source: "Brazil Retail Food Sector Report." [online] from
http://ffas.usda.gov [accessed January 1, 2004], p. NA,
from U.S. Department of Agriculture, ABRAS, and
ACNielsen.

★ 2650 ★
Grocery Stores
SIC: 5411; NAICS: 44511

Top Grocery Stores in Central New York

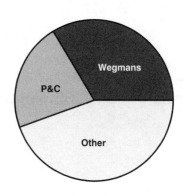

Market shares are shown in percent.

Wegmans 33.5%
P&C 21.7
Other 44.8

Source: *Post-Standard*, May 2, 2003, p. A1, from Market
Scope.

★ 2651 ★
Grocery Stores
SIC: 5411; NAICS: 44511

Top Grocery Stores in Chicago, IL

*Market shares are shown based on area volume for
2002.*

Jewel 43.0%
Safeway/Dominick's 18.0
Other 39.0

Source: *MMR*, June 13, 2003, p. 26.

★ 2652 ★
Grocery Stores
SIC: 5411; NAICS: 44511

Top Grocery Stores in Cincinnati, OH

Market shares are shown in percent.

Kroger 44.6%
Thriftway 7.6
Other 47.8

Source: *Cincinnati Post*, February 12, 2004, p. 1, from
Market Scope.

★ 2653 ★
Grocery Stores
SIC: 5411; NAICS: 44511

Top Grocery Stores in Columbia, SC

Market shares are shown in percent.

Wal-Mart 27.0%
Food Lion 15.3
Piggly Wiggly 14.3
Bi-Lo 14.2
Publix 10.0
Other 19.2

Source: *The State*, August 17, 2003, p. NA, from Trade
Dimensions.

★ 2654 ★
Grocery Stores
SIC: 5411; NAICS: 44511

Top Grocery Stores in Columbus, OH

Kroger's share is estimated.

Kroger	50.0%
Big Bear	15.0
Meijer	13.6
Wal-Mart	8.7
Other	12.7

Source: *Columbus Business First*, January 2, 2004, p. 1, from Market Scope.

★ 2655 ★
Grocery Stores
SIC: 5411; NAICS: 44511

Top Grocery Stores in Dallas-Ft. Worth, TX

Market shares are shown in percent.

Wal-Mart	25.1%
Albertsons	17.6
Tom Thumb	15.0
Kroger	12.7
Minyard Food Stores	9.1
SuperTarget	3.9
Other	16.6

Source: *Dallas Morning News*, February 5, 2004, p. NA, from *Market Scope*.

★ 2656 ★
Grocery Stores
SIC: 5411; NAICS: 44511

Top Grocery Stores in Denver, CO

Market shares are shown based on area volume for 2002.

King Soopers	38.0%
Safeway	20.0
Albertsons	12.0
Other	30.0

Source: *MMR*, June 13, 2003, p. 26.

★ 2657 ★
Grocery Stores
SIC: 5411; NAICS: 44511

Top Grocery Stores in Detroit, MI

Market shares are shown for 2003.

Farmer Jack	24.8%
Kroger	22.2
Meijer	18.7
Kmart	2.4
Save-A-Lot	1.9
Hiller's	1.3
Busch's	0.7
Whole Foods	0.2
Trader Joe's	0.2
Other	27.6

Source: *Detroit Free Press*, June 21, 2004, p. 24, from *Market Scope*.

★ 2658 ★
Grocery Stores
SIC: 5411; NAICS: 44511

Top Grocery Stores in Fort Lauderdale, FL

Market shares are shown based on area volume for 2002.

Publix	53.0%
Winn-Dixie's	17.0
Other	30.0

Source: *MMR*, June 13, 2003, p. 26.

★ 2659 ★
Grocery Stores
SIC: 5411; NAICS: 44511

Top Grocery Stores in France, 2002

Market shares are shown in percent.

Carrefour	21.0%
Leclerc	15.0
Intermarche	15.0
Casino	10.0
Other	39.0

Source: *Brand Strategy*, April 2004, p. 24.

★ 2660 ★
Grocery Stores
SIC: 5411; NAICS: 44511

Top Grocery Stores in Hartford, CT

Market shares are shown based on area volume for 2002.

Stop & Shop	39.0%
Shaw's	14.0
Big Y	12.0
Other	35.0

Source: *MMR*, June 13, 2003, p. 26.

★ 2661 ★
Grocery Stores
SIC: 5411; NAICS: 44511

Top Grocery Stores in Honolulu

Market shares are shown based on area volume for 2002.

Foodland	23.0%
Costco	17.0
Safeway	15.0
Times	12.0
Daiei	11.0
Other	22.0

Source: *MMR*, June 13, 2003, p. 26.

★ 2662 ★
Grocery Stores
SIC: 5411; NAICS: 44511

Top Grocery Stores in Houston, TX

Market shares are shown based on area volume for 2002.

Kroger	23.0%
H.E.B.	20.0
Safeway/Randall's	13.0
Wal-Mart	11.0
Fiesta Mart	9.0
Other	24.0

Source: *MMR*, June 13, 2003, p. 26.

★ 2663 ★
Grocery Stores
SIC: 5411; NAICS: 44511

Top Grocery Stores in Idaho

Market shares are shown in percent.

Albertsons	40.0%
Wal-Mart	28.0
Other	42.0

Source: *The Idaho Statesman*, November 12, 2003, p. 1, from Market Scope 2003.

★ 2664 ★

Grocery Stores

SIC: 5411; NAICS: 44511

Top Grocery Stores in Indianapolis, IN

Market shares are shown based on area volume for 2002.

Kroger	29.0%
Marsh	21.0
Meijer	12.0
Wal-Mart	10.0
Other	28.0

Source: *MMR*, June 13, 2003, p. 26.

★ 2665 ★

Grocery Stores

SIC: 5411; NAICS: 44511

Top Grocery Stores in Kansas City, MO

Market shares are shown based on area volume for 2002.

Ball's Super Foods	16.0%
Price Chopper	13.0
Wal-Mart	12.0
Hy-Vee	11.0
Other	48.0

Source: *MMR*, June 13, 2003, p. 26.

★ 2666 ★

Grocery Stores

SIC: 5411; NAICS: 44511

Top Grocery Stores in Lehigh Valley, PA

Market shares are shown in percent.

Giant	31.0%
Weis	17.0
Wegmans	13.8
ShopRite	11.3
Super Fresh	5.9
Other	21.0

Source: *The Morning Call*, July 13, 2003, p. D1, from Food Trade News.

★ 2667 ★

Grocery Stores

SIC: 5411; NAICS: 44511

Top Grocery Stores in London

Market shares are shown for the year ended December 8, 2002.

Sainsbury	30.9%
Tesco	28.3
Asda	10.5
Safeway	8.5
Morrisons	0.9
Other	20.9

Source: *Financial Times*, January 14, 2003, p. 11, from Taylor Nelson Sofres.

★ 2668 ★
Grocery Stores
SIC: 5411; NAICS: 44511

Top Grocery Stores in Long Island, NY

Market shares are shown in percent.

King Kullen	6.3%
A&P (Waldbaum's)	6.2
Stop & Shop	5.7
Pathmark	5.3
Costco	2.1
Shop Rite	1.5
BJ's WHolesale Club	1.1
Wal-Mart	0.7
C-Town	0.7
Associated Food Stores	0.7
Other	69.7

Source: *Long Island Business News*, June 13, 2003, p. 4A, from *Modern Grocer*.

★ 2669 ★
Grocery Stores
SIC: 5411; NAICS: 44511

Top Grocery Stores in Los Angeles/Long Beach, CA

Market shares are shown based on area volume for 2002.

Ralph's	22.0%
Safeway's/Von's	17.0
Albertson's	12.0
Costco	9.0
Other	40.0

Source: *MMR*, June 13, 2003, p. 26.

★ 2670 ★
Grocery Stores
SIC: 5411; NAICS: 44511

Top Grocery Stores in Mandarin, FL

Market shares are shown in percent.

Publix	32.20%
Winn-Dixie	27.15
Wal-Mart	14.28
Food Lion	9.28
Albertsons	3.98
Other	13.11

Source: *Florida Times Union*, April 10, 2004, p. D1, from Trade Dimensions.

★ 2671 ★
Grocery Stores
SIC: 5411; NAICS: 44511

Top Grocery Stores in Milwaukee, MN

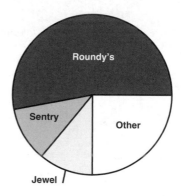

Market shares are shown in percent.

Roundy's	53.3%
Sentry	11.1
Jewel	10.9
Other	24.7

Source: *Supermarket News*, September 22, 2003, p. 6.

★ 2672 ★
Grocery Stores
SIC: 5411; NAICS: 44511

Top Grocery Stores in Minneapolis/ St. Paul

Market shares are shown based on area volume for 2002.

Super Valu	22.0%
Rainbow	21.0
Lund's/Byerley's	13.0
Jerry's	10.0
Other	34.0

Source: *MMR*, June 13, 2003, p. 26.

★ 2673 ★
Grocery Stores
SIC: 5411; NAICS: 44511

Top Grocery Stores in Nashville, TN

Market shares are shown based on area volume for 2002.

Kroger	38.0%
Wal-Mart	13.0
Food Lion	10.0
Publix	9.0
Other	30.0

Source: *MMR*, June 13, 2003, p. 26.

★ 2674 ★
Grocery Stores
SIC: 5411; NAICS: 44511

Top Grocery Stores in Nassau/ Suffolk, NY

Market shares are shown based on area volume for 2002.

A&P/Waldbaum	22.0%
Pathmark	18.0
King Kullen	16.0
Stop & Shop	14.0
Other	30.0

Source: *MMR*, June 13, 2003, p. 26.

★ 2675 ★
Grocery Stores
SIC: 5411; NAICS: 44511

Top Grocery Stores in New Orleans, LA

Market shares are shown based on area volume for 2002.

Winn-Dixie	29.0%
A&P	20.0
Wal-Mart	15.0
Other	36.0

Source: *MMR*, June 13, 2003, p. 26.

★ 2676 ★
Grocery Stores
SIC: 5411; NAICS: 44511

Top Grocery Stores in New York, NY

Market shares are shown based on area volume for 2002.

A&P	20.0%
Pathmark	18.0
Other	62.0

Source: *MMR*, June 13, 2003, p. 26.

★ 2677 ★
Grocery Stores
SIC: 5411; NAICS: 44511

Top Grocery Stores in Newark, NJ

Market shares are shown based on area volume for 2002.

Pathmark	19.0%
A&P	15.0
Village Shop Rite	12.0
Other	54.0

Source: *MMR*, June 13, 2003, p. 26.

★ 2678 ★
Grocery Stores
SIC: 5411; NAICS: 44511

Top Grocery Stores in North Carolina

Market shares are shown in percent.

Food Lion	32.8%
Wal-Mart	11.0
Other	46.2

Source: *Charlotte Business Journal*, February 10, 2003, p. NA, from *Shelby Report*.

★ 2679 ★
Grocery Stores
SIC: 5411; NAICS: 44511

Top Grocery Stores in Oklahoma City, OK

Market shares are shown based on area volume for 2002.

Wal-Mart	28.0%
Albertsons	11.0
Crest	10.0
Homeland	9.0
Other	42.0

Source: *MMR*, June 13, 2003, p. 26.

★ 2680 ★
Grocery Stores
SIC: 5411; NAICS: 44511

Top Grocery Stores in Omaha, NB

Market shares are shown based on area volume for 2002.

Dillon/Baker's	31.0%
Hy-Vee	16.0
Albertsons	10.0
Other	43.0

Source: *MMR*, June 13, 2003, p. 26.

★ 2681 ★
Grocery Stores
SIC: 5411; NAICS: 44511

Top Grocery Stores in Ontario

Market shares are shown in percent.

Loblaw	44.0%
A&P	23.0
Sobeys	17.0
Metro	3.0
Other	13.0

Source: *Canadian Business*, September 2, 2003, p. 27.

★ 2682 ★
Grocery Stores
SIC: 5411; NAICS: 44511

Top Grocery Stores in Philadelphia, PA

Market shares are shown for an eight county metropolitan region.

Acme	26.6%
Shop-Rite	12.9
Genuardi's	12.1
Other	48.4

Source: *Philadelphia Inquirer*, June 25, 2003, p. NA, from *Food Trade News*.

★ 2683 ★
Grocery Stores
SIC: 5411; NAICS: 44511

Top Grocery Stores in Phoenix, AZ

Market shares are shown in percent.

Fry's Food Stores	29.3%
Safeway	18.2
Bashas	16.8
Wal-Mart	12.8
Albertsons	12.6
Other	10.3

Source: *Arizona Republic*, October 22, 2003, p. A1, from Trade Dimensions.

★ 2684 ★
Grocery Stores
SIC: 5411; NAICS: 44511

Top Grocery Stores in Pittsburgh, PA

Market shares are shown based on area volume for 2002.

Giant Eagle	40.0%
Super Valu	21.0
Other	39.0

Source: *MMR*, June 13, 2003, p. 26.

★ 2685 ★
Grocery Stores
SIC: 5411; NAICS: 44511

Top Grocery Stores in Portland, ME

Market shares are shown based on area volume for 2002.

Hannaford	47.0%
Shaw's	32.0
Other	21.0

Source: *MMR*, June 13, 2003, p. 26.

★ 2686 ★
Grocery Stores
SIC: 5411; NAICS: 44511

Top Grocery Stores in Portland, OR/ Vancouver, WA

Market shares are shown based on area volume for 2002.

Safeway	28.0%
Fred Meyer	17.0
Albertsons	13.0
Winco	11.0
Other	31.0

Source: *MMR*, June 13, 2003, p. 26.

★ 2687 ★
Grocery Stores
SIC: 5411; NAICS: 44511

Top Grocery Stores in Richmond/ Petersburg, VA

Market shares are shown based on area volume for 2002.

Ukrop's	29.0%
Food Lion	20.0
Wal-Mart	11.0
Other	40.0

Source: *MMR*, June 13, 2003, p. 26.

★ 2688 ★
Grocery Stores
SIC: 5411; NAICS: 44511

Top Grocery Stores in Sacramento, CA

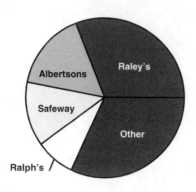

Market shares are shown based on area volume for 2002.

Raley's	31.0%
Albertsons	16.0
Safeway	13.0
Ralph's	8.0
Other	32.0

Source: *MMR*, June 13, 2003, p. 26.

★ 2689 ★
Grocery Stores
SIC: 5411; NAICS: 44511

Top Grocery Stores in St. Louis, MO

Market shares are shown based on area volume for 2002.

Schunk Markets	38.0%
Dierberg's	15.0
SuperValu	12.0
Other	35.0

Source: *MMR*, June 13, 2003, p. 26.

★ 2690 ★
Grocery Stores
SIC: 5411; NAICS: 44511

Top Grocery Stores in San Antonio, TX

Market shares are shown in percent.

H-E-B	67.0%
Wal-Mart	19.0
Other	14.0

Source: *San Antonio Express News*, January 6, 2004, p. NA, from *Shelby Report*.

★ 2691 ★
Grocery Stores
SIC: 5411; NAICS: 44511

Top Grocery Stores in San Diego County

Market shares are shown in percent.

Vons	30.9%
Albertsons	21.7
Ralph's	13.7
Other	33.7

Source: *San Diego Union-Tribune*, November 4, 2003, p. NA, from *San Diego Union-Tribune 2002 Grocery Store Study*.

★ 2692 ★
Grocery Stores
SIC: 5411; NAICS: 44511

Top Grocery Stores in Sarasota-Bradenton, FL

Shares are for February 2004. In February 2003, Wal-Mart had 8.8% of the market.

Publix	40.3%
Wal-Mart	16.1
Kash n' Karry	14.1
Other	29.5

Source: *Sarasota Herald Tribune*, March 1, 2004, p. 12, from *Market Scope*.

★ 2693 ★
Grocery Stores
SIC: 5411; NAICS: 44511
Top Grocery Stores in Scotland

Market shares are shown for the year ended December 8, 2002.

Tesco	24.0%
Asda	22.0
Safeway	21.3
Sainsbury	5.2
Morrisons	0.7
Other	26.8

Source: *Financial Times*, January 14, 2003, p. 11, from Taylor Nelson Sofres.

★ 2694 ★
Grocery Stores
SIC: 5411; NAICS: 44511
Top Grocery Stores in Seattle/ Bellevue/Everett, WA

Market shares are shown based on area volume for 2002.

Safeway	24.0%
Quality Food Centers	23.0
Albertsons	12.0
Other	41.0

Source: *MMR*, June 13, 2003, p. 26.

★ 2695 ★
Grocery Stores
SIC: 5411; NAICS: 44511
Top Grocery Stores in South Carolina

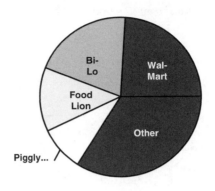

Market shares are shown in percent.

Wal-Mart	24.40%
Bi-Lo	20.45
Food Lion	12.90
Piggly Wiggly	8.56
Other	33.69

Source: *The Post and Courier*, February 23, 2004, p. NA, from *Shelby Report*.

★ 2696 ★
Grocery Stores
SIC: 5411; NAICS: 44511
Top Grocery Stores in Southeastern Wisconsin

Market shares are shown in percent.

Roundy's	60.0%
Other	40.0

Source: *Milwaukee Journal-Sentinel*, November 27, 2003, p. NA.

★ 2697 ★
Grocery Stores
SIC: 5411; NAICS: 44511

Top Grocery Stores in Tampa Bay, FL

Market shares are shown in percent.

Publix	34.9%
Kash n'Karry	15.9
Wal-Mart	14.5
Winn-Dixie	13.8
Albertsons	11.2
Other	9.7

Source: *St. Petersburg Times*, January 31, 2004, p. 1A, from Trade Dimensions Market Scope.

★ 2698 ★
Grocery Stores
SIC: 5411; NAICS: 44511

Top Grocery Stores in the U.K.

Market shares are shown in percent.

Tesco	27.1%
Asda	16.9
Sainsbury's	16.1
Morrisons	3.2
Other	36.7

Source: *The Guardian*, September 27, 2003, p. 26.

★ 2699 ★
Grocery Stores
SIC: 5411; NAICS: 44511

Top Grocery Stores in Toledo, OH

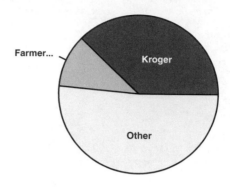

Market shares are shown in percent.

Kroger	38.0%
Farmer Jack	10.5
Other	51.5

Source: *The Blade*, January 13, 2004, p. NA.

★ 2700 ★
Grocery Stores
SIC: 5411; NAICS: 44511

Top Grocery Stores in Wales and Western Britain

Market shares are shown for the year ended December 8, 2002.

Tesco	29.5%
Asda	17.4
Sainsbury	11.7
Safeway	9.7
Morrisons	1.3
Other	30.4

Source: *Financial Times*, January 14, 2003, p. 11, from Taylor Nelson Sofres.

★ 2701 ★
Grocery Stores
SIC: 5411; NAICS: 44511

Top Grocery Stores in Washington D.C.

Market shares are shown based on area volume for 2002.

Giant Food	38.0%
Safeway	20.0
Other	42.0

Source: *MMR*, June 13, 2003, p. 26.

★ 2702 ★
Grocery Stores
SIC: 5411; NAICS: 44511

Top Grocery Stores in Western New York

Market shares are shown in percent.

Tops	53.4%
Wegmans	26.2
Other	30.3

Source: *The Buffalo News*, March 22, 2004, p. NA, from *Market Scope.*

★ 2703 ★
Grocery Stores
SIC: 5411; NAICS: 44511

Top Grocery Stores in Winston-Salem, NC

Market shares for the first three months of 2004.

Food Lion	30.82%
Wal-Mart	17.84
Harris Teeter	13.03
Lowes Foods	7.30
Winn-Dixie	6.93
Other	24.08

Source: *Winston-Salem Journal*, March 10, 2004, p. D1, from *Shelby Report*.

★ 2704 ★
Grocery Stores
SIC: 5411; NAICS: 44511

Top Specialty Food Retailers in Hampton Roads, Virginia

Market shares are shown in percent.

Food Lion	24.8%
Farm Fresh	17.5
Wal-Mart	9.5
Military commissaries	7.1
7-Eleven	6.3
Kmart	5.1
Eckerd	4.5
Kroger	3.4
Sam's Clubs	2.8
Harris Teeter	2.3
Other	16.7

Source: *The Virginian Pilot*, November 2, 2003, p. D1.

★ 2705 ★
Grocery Stores
SIC: 5411; NAICS: 44511

Top Supermarket Sectors in New Zealand

Sales of all scanned grocery products (including house brands) rose from $7.05 billion in 2002 to $7.48 billion in 2003. Alcohol, packaged snacks and stationery saw the largest growth in sales over the previous year (14.7%, 10.2% and 10.7% respectively). Goodman Fielder was the food company with the top sales for the year.

	($ mil.)	Share
Chilled food	$ 1,077.3	14.4%
Shelf stable other edibles	1,054.8	14.1
Shelf stable bakery biscuit	860.3	11.5
Alcohol	695.7	9.3
Beverages	665.8	8.9
Personal care	583.5	7.8
Packaged snacks	508.7	6.8
Frozen food	433.9	5.8
Household products	299.2	4.0
Tobacco	284.3	3.8
Paper products	261.8	3.5
Pet supplies	246.9	3.3
Other	509.0	6.8

Source: *New Zealand Marketing Magazine*, April 2004, p. 18, from ACNielsen ChannelScan.

★ 2706 ★
Retailing - Beverages
SIC: 5411; NAICS: 44511

Gourmet Beverage Sales

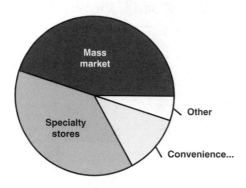

Sales are shown by channel. Bottled water and ready-to-drink beverages are included in the $14.7 billion category, which helped to give mass market channels control. Specialty stores include coffee and tea stores, cafes, bakeries and chocolatiers.

Mass market	45.0%
Specialty stores	38.0
Convenience stores	12.0
Other	5.0

Source: *Research Alert*, August 1, 2003, p. 8, from Packaged Facts.

★ 2707 ★
Retailing - Food
SIC: 5411; NAICS: 44511

Food and Drink Sales in the U.K., 2003

The food industry is the largest retail sector in the country. Grocers take the vast majority of sales. Large grocers grew 34.5% from 1997 - 2003. In the same period, fishmonger sales fell 34.1%.

Large grocers	78.0%
Small grocers	6.6
Tobacconists	4.7
Alcohol	2.7
Butchers	2.5
Bakers	2.1
Greengrocers	1.4
Fishmongers	0.2
Other	1.5

Source: *UK Retail Briefing*, March 2004, p. 65, from Mintel and national statistics.

★ 2708 ★
Retailing - Food
SIC: 5411; NAICS: 44511

Food Retail Sales in Bangladesh

Shares are presented by category of retail establishment.

Small grocery shops	75.0%
Municipal corporate markets	20.0
Convenience stores	5.0

Source: "Bangladesh Retail Food Sector Report 2004" [Online] http://www.usda.gov/ [accessed March 22, 2004], from U.S. Department of Agriculture and Foreign Agricultural Service.

★ 2709 ★
Retailing - Food
SIC: 5411; NAICS: 44511

Leading Food Retailers in Finland

Market shares are shown in percent.

Kesko	36.0%
S-Group	31.1
Tradeka/Elanto	12.9
Stockmann	8.1
Spar group	8.1
Wihuri	5.2

Source: "Finland Retail Food Sector Report 2003." [online] from http://www.fas.usda.gov [accessed January 7, 2004], from U.S. Department of Agriculture.

★ 2710 ★
Retailing - Food
SIC: 5411; NAICS: 44511

Leading Food Retailers in Sweden

There were 6,060 food retail outlets in 2000, down from 13,000 in 1970. Sales were $19 billion.

ICA Ahold	36.5%
Coop	18.5
Axfood	18.2
BergendahlsGruppen	2.4
Other	24.4

Source: "Finland Retail Food Sector Report 2003." [online] from http://www.fas.usda.gov [accessed January 7, 2004], from U.S. Department of Agriculture.

★ 2711 ★
Retailing - Food
SIC: 5411; NAICS: 44511

Non-Traditional Grocers in Canada

Non-traditional grocers take 14% ($9.2 billion) of the overall food retailing business.

Costco Wholesale Canada	5.9%
Wal-Mart Cnada Corp.	3.8
Zellers Inc.	2.7
Alimentation Couche-Tard Inc.	1.2
Shoppers Drug Mart Corp.	1.0
Other	85.4

Source: *Globe & Mail*, May 29, 2004, p. NA, from CIBC World Markets.

★ 2712 ★
Retailing - Food
SIC: 5411; NAICS: 44511

Retail Frozen and Chilled Food Sales, 2003

The frozen and chilled foods markets were valued at $26.4 billion and $18.9 billion respectively in 2003.

	Frozen	Chilled
Supermarket/hypermarkets . . .	61.8%	62.7%
Independence food stores	21.7	21.7
Discount stores	6.5	6.4
Convenience stores	2.0	4.8
Internet sales	0.1	0.3

Source: *Refrigerated & Frozen Foods*, October 2003, p. 60, from Euromonitor and *Global Packaged Foods Market System, 2003-2004*.

★ 2713 ★
Retailing - Food
SIC: 5411; NAICS: 44511, 44512, 45291

Retail Milk Sales

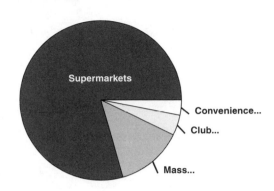

While supermarkets are still the primary vendors of milk, other outlets have begun to steal share. Analysts think there are several reasons for this, chief among them being the growth of various retail outlets as a primary shopping destination.

	June 2002	June 2003
Supermarkets	78.6%	77.4%
Mass merchants	12.6	13.0
Club stores	3.2	4.0
Convenience stores	2.5	2.6

Source: *Supermarket News*, November 17, 2003, p. 24, from Information Resources Inc.

★ 2714 ★
Retailing - Food
SIC: 5411; NAICS: 44511, 44512

Where We Shop for Food

Superstores are larger supermarkets with more services and non-food items. Supercenters include Super Target, Wal-Mart supercenters, Fred Meyer and Meijer.

	2002	2007
Superstore	25.8%	21.7%
Supermarkets	18.1	16.6
Food/drug	15.0	15.2
Supercenters	10.1	15.4
Wholesale clubs	8.5	9.2
Convenience stores	6.0	5.5

Source: *USA TODAY*, October 28, 2003, p. 6B, from Willard Bishop Consulting.

★ 2715 ★
Retailing - Pet Food
SIC: 5411; NAICS: 44511

Leading Cat and Dog Food Retailers in the U.K.

Market shares are shown for the year ended April 28, 2003.

Tesco	24.2%
Asda	13.6
Sainsbury	13.2
Safeway	8.0
Morrisons	6.2
All co-ops	4.3
All independents	3.4
Somerfield	2.9
Kwik Save	2.5
Waitrose	2.4
Other	19.3

Source: *Grocer*, July 19, 2003, p. 49, from TNS Superpanel.

★ 2716 ★
Retailing - Meat
SIC: 5421; NAICS: 44521

Retail Sausage Sales in Germany

1.05 million tons of sausage were sold in 2001.

	2000	2001
Discounters	30.0%	31.0%
Hypermarkets	26.0	27.0
Butcher's shops	25.0	27.0
Grocery stores	10.0	12.0
Other	6.0	6.0

Source: *Lebensmittel Zeitung*, June 7, 2002, p. 47, from ZMP/CMA.

★ 2717 ★
Retailing - Fruits & Vegetables
SIC: 5431; NAICS: 44523

Retail Produce Sales in Canada, 2002

Canadians consumed (CAN) $6 billion worth of fresh produce for the year. 75% of the fresh produce sold in the country is imported. (The top sources are the U.S., Mexico, Chile and the Netherlands).

Grocery chains	65.0%
Independent fruit & vegetable stores	29.0
Club stores	4.0
Farmers' markets	1.5
Roadside markets	0.4
Pick your own	0.1

Source: "Packaging & Retailing Trends for Fresh Produce in Canada." [online] from http://www.fas.usda.gov [accessed December 1, 2003], from Food and Agricultural Service, United States Department of Agriculture.

★ 2718 ★
Retailing - Ice Cream
SIC: 5451; NAICS: 445299

Retail Ice Cream Market

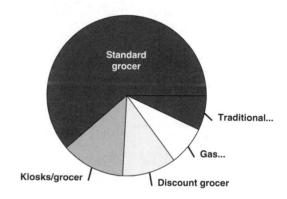

A traditional grocer included corner and family owned stores. Standard grocers include chains and co-ops.

Standard grocer	61.7%
Kiosks/grocer	13.2
Discount grocer	10.9
Gas station/convenience store	7.6
Traditional grocer	6.6

Source: *Wall Street Journal*, June 26, 2003, p. B1, from Datamonitor.

SIC 55 - Automotive Dealers and Service Stations

★ 2719 ★
Retailing - Autos
SIC: 5511; NAICS: 44111
Auto Retail Sector in Germany, 2001

The industry generated sales of 126.47 billion euros in 2001.

New car dealers	59.8
Garages and repair shops	22.9
Used car sales under finance	22.9
Other used car sales	7.8
New HGV sales	6.3
Used HGV sales	3.8

Source: *Handelsblatt*, April 8, 2002, p. 11, from ZDK.

★ 2720 ★
Retailing - Autos
SIC: 5511; NAICS: 44111
Largest Dealerships

Companies are ranked by number of dealerships.

AutoNation Inc.	267
United Auto Group	165
Sonic Automotive Inc.	150
Asbury Automotive Group	99
Lithia Motors Inc.	79
Group Automotive Inc.	76
V.T. Inc.	55
Hendrick Automotive Group	49
Larry H. Miller Group	35
Planet Automotive	33

Source: *WARD's DealerBusiness*, April 2004, p. 18.

★ 2721 ★
Retailing - Autos
SIC: 5511; NAICS: 44111
Largest Online Auto Dealers

Dealerships are ranked by unit sales. Locations are shown in parentheses.

Dave Smith Motors	5,307
Tyson's Toyota	3,095
Turnersville Auto Complex (NJ)	2,894
Burt Toyota (CO)	2,681
Bob Howard Automotive (OK)	2,460
Capital Ford (NC)	2,340
Conincelli Autoplex (PA)	2,324
Hudson Toyota (NJ)	2,101
Red McCombs Automotive (TX)	2,040
Power Toyota (CA)	1,914

Source: *Ward's Dealer Business*, April 1, 2004, p. 4.

★ 2722 ★
Retailing - Auto Supplies
SIC: 5531; NAICS: 44131
Motor Oil Sales, 2002

Market shares are shown type of chain. Total aftermarket sales were $4.9 billion for the year.

Discount store chains	48.0%
Automotive chains	38.0
Department store chains	3.0
Non-automotive chains	1.0

Source: *Aftermarket Business*, April 2003, p. 78, from *29th Annual Car Care Study*.

★ 2723 ★
Retailing - Auto Supplies
SIC: 5531; NAICS: 44131
Spark Plug Sales, 2002

Market shares are shown type of chain. Total aftermarket sales were $888 million for the year.

Automotive chains	52.0%
Discount store chains	40.0
Department store cahins	5.0
Non-automotive chains	3.0

Source: *Aftermarket Business*, April 2003, p. 78, from *29th Annual Car Care Study.*

★ 2724 ★
Retailing - Auto Supplies
SIC: 5531; NAICS: 44131
Top Auto Parts Stores

Companies are ranked by sales in millions of dollars.

AutoZone	$ 5,326
Advance Auto Parts	3,288
Pep Boys - Manny Moe & Jack	1,757
CSK Auto Corp.	1,507
O'Reilly Automotive	1,312

Source: *DSN Retailing Today*, July 9, 2003, p. 42.

★ 2725 ★
Retailing - Auto Supplies
SIC: 5531; NAICS: 44131
Touch-Up Paint Sales, 2002

Market shares are shown type of chain. Total aftermarket sales were $508 million for the year.

Automotive chains	63.0%
Discount store chain	34.0
Non-automotive chains	2.0
Department store chains	1.0

Source: *Aftermarket Business*, April 2003, p. 78, from *29th Annual Car Care Study.*

★ 2726 ★
Retailing - Auto Supplies
SIC: 5531; NAICS: 44131
Where Additives are Purchased

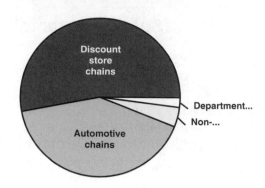

Total aftermarket additive sales were $3.5 billion.

Discount store chains	53.0%
Automotive chains	41.0
Non-automotive chains	4.0
Department store chains	2.0

Source: *Aftermarket Business*, April 2004, p. 26.

★ 2727 ★
Retailing - Auto Supplies
SIC: 5531; NAICS: 44131
Wiper Blade Sales, 2002

Market shares are shown type of chain. Total aftermarket sales were $837 million for the year.

Automotive chains	53.0%
Discount store chains	44.0
Department store chains	2.0
Non-automotive chains	1.0

Source: *Aftermarket Business*, April 2003, p. 78, from *29th Annual Car Care Study.*

★ 2728 ★

Tire Dealerships

SIC: 5531; NAICS: 44132

Top Independent Tire Dealerships, 2003

Companies are ranked by sales in millions of dollars. Data are for the U.S. and Canada.

Les Schwab Tire Centers	$ 254.9
Kal Tire	244.2
Tirecraft Auto Centers	141.1
Purcell Tire & Rubber Co.	139.4
Pomp's Tire Service inc.	116.0
Bauer Built Inc.	107.0
Snider Tire Inc.	101.0
Cross-Midwest Tire Inc.	98.5
Parkhouse Tire Inc.	96.0
McCarthy Tire Service Inc.	90.4

Source: *Tire Business*, April 12, 2004, p. 10.

★ 2729 ★

Tire Dealerships

SIC: 5531; NAICS: 44132

Top Tire Dealerships, 2002

Companies are ranked by sales in millions of dollars.

Discount Tire Co.	$ 1,539.0
Les Schwab Tire Centers	913.3
Tire Kingdom	299.0
Belle Tire Distributors	125.0

Kal Tire	$ 123.6
Fountain Tire	106.2
Somerset Tire Service	105.0
Peerless Tyre	87.2
V.I.P. Inc.	86.0
Dunlap & Kyle	80.8
Dobbs Tire & Auto	68.0
Sullivan Tire	63.0

Source: *Tire Business*, February 2, 2004, p. 9.

★ 2730 ★

Gas Stations

SIC: 5541; NAICS: 44711, 44719

Leading Gas Station Operators in Europe

Companies are ranked by number of stations. BP & Aral have about 15% of the market, Shell/Dea just under 14%.

BP & Aral	10,975
Total/FinaElf	9,908
Shell/Dea	9,869
Exxon	5,089
Repsol	3,540
Agip	1,341

Source: *Financial Times*, January 31, 2002, p. 25, from BP & Petrofinance and Deutsche Bank.

★ 2731 ★

Gas Stations

SIC: 5541; NAICS: 44711, 44719

Leading Gas Station Operators in Germany

Market shares are shown in percent.

BP & Aral	26.5%
Shell/Dea	24.5
Total/FinaElf	12.4
Esso	10.8
Jet (Conoco)	6.5
AVIA	3.5
Other	15.8

Source: *Financial Times*, January 31, 2002, p. 25, from BP & Petrofinance and Deutsche Bank.

★ 2732 ★
Gas Stations
SIC: 5541; NAICS: 44711, 44719

Leading Gas Station Operators in St. Petersburg, Russia

| PTK |
| Phaeton |
| LUKoil Petersburg Service |
| Slavneft |
| Neste-Petersburg |
| Other |

The number of gas stations in the city grew 45% between 1999 and 2002. Market shares are shown in percent.

PTK	28.0%
Phaeton	14.0
LUKoil Petersburg Service	11.0
Slavneft	9.0
Neste-Petersburg	9.0
Other	29.0

Source: *America's Intelligence Wire*, August 5, 2003, p. NA, from Worldsources.

★ 2733 ★
Gas Stations
SIC: 5541; NAICS: 44711, 44719

Top Fuel Retailers in South Africa, 2003

Shares are shown in percent.

Engen	27.0%
Royal Dutch/Shell	16.5
Chevron Texaco	16.5
British Petroleum	16.5
Other	23.5

Source: *International Petroleum Finance*, March 2004, p. 13.

SIC 56 - Apparel and Accessory Stores

★ 2734 ★
Retailing - Apparel
SIC: 5600; NAICS: 44812, 44811

Top Apparel Chains, 2002

Companies are ranked by sales in millions of dollars.

Gap	$ 14,454.70
Limited Brands	8,444.65
Ross Stores	3,531.34
Spiegel/Eddie Bauer	2,650.00
Charming Shoppes	2,412.40
Abercrombie & Fitch	1,595.75
Talbots	1,595.32
American Eagle Outfitters	1,463.14
Stein Mart	1,408.00
AnnTaylor	1,380.96

Source: *Stores*, July 2003, p. S16.

★ 2735 ★
Retailing - Apparel
SIC: 5611; NAICS: 44811, 44815

Boy's Apparel Sales in France

In 2000, the overall menswear industry had sales of roughly $3 billion. Shorts/bermudas, parkas and jeans were the top sellers by units. Market shares are estimated in percent.

Specialized chains	22.0%
Hypermarkets	16.2
Sporting goods stores	15.8
Franchises	13.0
Independent stores	10.6
Mail order catalogs	6.7
Supermarkets	5.1
Department stores	2.2
Popular stores	1.3
Other	7.1

Source: "Menswear Market." [online] from http://www.usatrade.gov [accessed January 5, 2004], from U.S. Commercial Service.

★ 2736 ★
Retailing - Apparel
SIC: 5611; NAICS: 44811, 44815

Leading Men's Apparel Retailers

Companies are ranked by annual sales in billions of dollars.

Wal-Mart	$ 247.0
Target Corp.	44.0
Sears, Roebuck & Co.	41.0
J.C. Penney Co.	32.0
Kmart Corp.	31.0
Federated Department Stores	15.4
The Gap Inc.	14.5
May Department Stores Co.	13.5
TJX Cos.	12.0
Dillard's Inc.	8.2

Source: *Daily News Record*, June 9, 2003, p. 36, from company reports.

★ 2737 ★

Retailing - Apparel

SIC: 5611; NAICS: 44811, 44815

Men's Apparel Sales

The $51.9 billion industry is shown by channel. Department stores have lost market share, falling from 19.7% to 18.8%.

	($ mil.)	2002	2003
Specialty stores	$ 13,599	26.2%	26.4%
Department stores	10,230	19.7	18.8
Mass merchants	8,494	16.3	16.0
National chains	7,646	14.7	15.7
Off-price retailers	4,475	8.6	9.3
Direct mail/e-tail pure plays	2,770	5.3	5.8
Factory outlets	1,372	2.6	2.4
Other	3,382	6.5	5.6

Source: *Daily News Record*, March 29, 2004, p. NA, from NPD.

★ 2738 ★

Retailing - Apparel

SIC: 5611; NAICS: 44811, 44815

Men's Apparel Sales in Canada, 2003

The apparel market overall was flat and the men's segment shrunk by 2%. Figures are based on a survey of 10,000 Canadian households. Menswear was $.3 billion of the $13.7 billion in apparel spending.

Sears	13.0%
Retail	9.7
The Bay	8.8
Moores	6.4
Wal-Mart	6.0%
Zellers	5.3
Marks WW	4.4
Winners	2.9
Catalog	2.8
Costco/Price	1.8
Tip Top	1.7
Old Navy	0.7
Other	48.8

Source: *Daily News Record*, June 7, 2004, p. 12, from Canadian Soft Goods Index.

★ 2739 ★

Retailing - Apparel

SIC: 5611; NAICS: 44811, 44815

Men's Casual Apparel Market, 2002

Menswear is a $52 billion segment of the $161 billion apparel market.

Wal-Mart/Wal-Mart Supercenter	24.0%
J.C. Penney	8.0
Kohl's	7.0
Kmart/Big K	6.0
Sears	4.0
Mervyn's	2.0
Other	49.0

Source: *USA TODAY*, July 7, 2003, p. 6B, from Retail Forward.

★ 2740 ★

Retailing - Apparel

SIC: 5611; NAICS: 44811, 44815

Men's Hosery Sales, 2003

Total sales were $457.14 million in 2003, up from $441.91 million in 2002.

	($ 000)	Share
Mass merchants	$ 690,612	37.20%
Specialty stores	289,010	15.57
National chains	236,053	12.71
Department stores	183,729	9.90
Other	457,144	24.62

Source: *Daily News Record*, April 12, 2004, p. 25, from NPD Group and NPD Fashionworld Consumer Data Estimates.

★ 2741 ★

Retailing - Apparel

SIC: 5611; NAICS: 44441, 44815

Men's Jeans Market, 2003

A total of $5.6 billion was spent on men's jeans in 2003 (by Americans 13 and over).

	2002	2003
J.C. Penney	9.7%	7.9%
Wal-Mart	8.7	9.6
Sears	5.3	6.5
Kmart	5.1	3.7
Gap	4.6	4.5
Old Navy	3.5	4.4
Kohl's	3.4	4.4
Macy's	2.9	3.9
Target	1.9	2.4
Other	54.9	52.7

Source: *Daily News Record*, March 29, 2004, p. 20, from STS Market Research.

★ 2742 ★

Retailing - Apparel

SIC: 5611; NAICS: 44811, 44815

Men's Sportswear Market, 2002

Data are for August 2002 - July 2003.

J.C. Penney	8.6%
Wal-Mart	6.9
Sears	4.3
Kohl's	4.2
Macy's	3.4
Old Navy	3.3
Kmart	3.2

Gap	2.8%
Target	2.5
Dillard's	2.5
Other	58.3

Source: *Daily News Record*, November 24, 2003, p. 16, from STS Market Research.

★ 2743 ★

Retailing - Apparel

SIC: 5611; NAICS: 44811, 44815

Men's Suit Market

Between June 2002 - June 2003 sales of men's suit increased 1 percent to 14.3 million. Men's Wearhouse is the largest retailer of tailored clothing in North America. Its share is shown below.

Mens' Wearhosue	21.0%
Other	79.0

Source: *Retail Traffic*, October 1, 2003, p. NA, from Johnson Rice & Co.

★ 2744 ★

Retailing - Apparel

SIC: 5611; NAICS: 44811, 44815

Specialty Big & Tall Business

Market shares are shown in percent.

Casual Male	55.0%
Other	45.0

Source: *Daily News Record*, August 11, 2003, p. 6.

★ 2745 ★

Retailing - Apparel

SIC: 5611; NAICS: 44811

Top Dress Shirt Retailers, 2003

Market shares are for the 12 months ended September 2003.

J.C. Penney	9.9%
Kohl's	5.4
Macy's	5.3
Sears	5.2

Continued on next page.

★ 2745 ★

[Continued]
Retailing - Apparel
SIC: 5611; NAICS: 44811

Top Dress Shirt Retailers, 2003

Market shares are for the 12 months ended September 2003.

Dillard's	3.3%
Wal-Mart	2.6
Nordstrom	2.4
Lands' End	2.2
Brooks Brothers	2.2
Foley's	1.8
Other	59.7

Source: *Daily News Record*, December 1, 2003, p. 10, from 2002-2003 STS Market Research.

★ 2746 ★

Retailing - Apparel
SIC: 5621; NAICS: 44812

Lingerie Sales in France, 2001

Lingerie sales for the year were up over the year with total sales at 1.52 billion euros and 150.6 million units.

Large food outlets/discount stores	33.4%
Specialized retail chains	17.5
Mail order	14.5
Independent retailers	13.3
Other	9.2

Source: *LSA*, May 10, 2002, p. 54, from Secodip.

★ 2747 ★

Retailing - Apparel
SIC: 5621; NAICS: 44812

Maternitywear Sales in the United Kingdom, 2001

Sales in each market are in millions of British pounds.

	(mil.)	Share
Fashion multiples	£ 26	24.53%
Maternity specialists	26	24.53
Mail order	21	19.81
Department stores	4	3.77
Other	29	27.36

Source: *Retail Week*, August 9, 2002, p. 14, from Mintel.

★ 2748 ★

Retailing - Apparel
SIC: 5621; NAICS: 44812

Where Women Buy Licensed Apparel

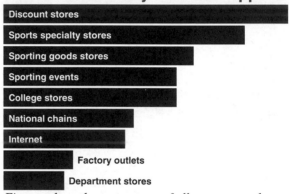

Figures show the percentage of all women purchasing licensed apparel at each channel.

Discount stores	33.0%
Sports specialty stores	28.0
Sporting goods stores	22.0
Sporting events	20.0
College stores	20.0
National chains	15.0
Internet	14.0
Factory outlets	8.0
Department stores	7.0

Source: *WWD*, September 25, 2003, p. 11, from NPD Fashionworld.

★ 2749 ★

Retailing - Apparel

SIC: 5621; NAICS: 44812

Where Women Shopped for Sportswear

Market shares are shown in percent.

Specialty stores	28.0%
Discount stores	19.0
Department stores	14.0
National chains	13.0
Off-price retailers	6.0
Direct mail	6.0
Factory outlet	2.0
Other	12.0

Source: *Display & Design Ideas*, June 2003, p. 20, from STS Market research.

★ 2750 ★

Retailing - Apparel

SIC: 5621; NAICS: 44812

Women's Retail Jeans Sales

The industry was valued at $4.5 billion in 2002.

Specialty chains	33.0%
Discount stores	18.0
National chains	15.0
Department stores	13.0
Other	21.0

Source: *WWD*, July 17, 2003, p. 6B.

★ 2751 ★

Retailing - Wedding Gowns

SIC: 5621; NAICS: 44812

Bridal Dress Market

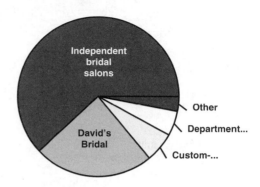

The number of women of typical marrying age (20 to 29) may hit 20 million in 2008. 28% of women under 25 purchased gowns at a chain; over 25 years of age, the figure dropped to 21%, according to Conde Nast. Figures show where brides buy their dresses.

Independent bridal salons	62.0%
David's Bridal	24.0
Custom-made dresses	6.0
Department or specialty store	5.0
Other	3.0

Source: *Wall Street Journal*, October 21, 2003, p. A17, from *Conde Nast Bridal Infobank American Wedding Study, 2002.*

★ 2752 ★

Retailing - Apparel

SIC: 5641; NAICS: 44813

Children's Apparel Retail Sales, 2003

Children's apparel sales grew to $29.4 billion in 2003 from $27.2 billion in 2002.

	($ mil.)	Share
Mass	$ 8.72	29.7%
Specialty	7.16	24.3
National chains	6.71	22.8
Department stores	2.94	10.0
Off-price	1.58	5.4
Other	2.27	7.8

Source: *Children's Business*, May 2004, p. 7, from NPD Data.

★ 2753 ★

Retailing - Apparel

SIC: 5651; NAICS: 44814

Apparel Sales in Mexico

Total retail clothing sales were $15-$17 billion.

Liverpool y Fabricas de Francia	10.7%
Suburbia	10.7
Sears	5.2
Aurerra	3.3
Palacio de Hierro	3.3
Wal-Mart	3.3
Zara	2.4
Comercial Mexicana	2.2
Aldo Conti	1.6
Gigante	1.6
Other	55.7

Source: *The America's Intelligence Wire*, December 8, 2003, p. NA, from Corporate Mexico and Kurt Salmon Associates.

★ 2754 ★

Retailing - Apparel

SIC: 5651; NAICS: 44814

Discount Apparel Market, 2003

The discount apparel industry grew over the last decade thanks to better selection, better quality, and better presentation of merchandise. The market is valued at $70.2 billion.

Wal-Mart	24.6%
T.J. Maxx/Marshall's	10.1
Target	8.4
Old Navy	7.8
Kmart	6.1
Ross	3.8
Charming Shops	3.2
Burlington Coat Factory	2.7
American Eagle Outfitters	1.9
Value City Dept. Stores	1.7
Other	29.6

Source: *DSN Retailing Today*, October 27, 2003, p. 6, from *Chain Store Guide*.

★ 2755 ★

Retailing - Apparel

SIC: 5651; NAICS: 44814

Discount Clothing Market in the U.K.

Market shares are shown in percent.

Matalan	16.5%
New Look	14.3
Primark	10.0
Brown & Jackson	8.5
TK Maxx	6.9
Peacocks	6.6
Bonmarche	3.5
QS Group	3.0
Mk One	3.0
Ethel Austin	3.0
Other	24.7

Source: *UK Retail Report*, May 2001, p. 90, from Retail Intelligence.

★ 2756 ★

Retailing - Apparel

SIC: 5651; NAICS: 44814

Leading Apparel Retailers in the U.K., 2003

Market shares are shown in percent.

Marks & Spencer	11.1%
Arcadia	7.1
Next	6.8
Debenhams	4.4
Asda	3.3
Bhs	2.2
Other	65.1

Source: *Financial Times*, May 29, 2004, p. 9, from Citigroup and Verdict Analysis.

★ 2757 ★
Retailing - Apparel
SIC: 5651; NAICS: 44814

Leading Off-Price Apparel Stores

Stores are ranked by sales in thousands of dollars.

TJX	$ 9,485,600
Ross Stores	3,531,349
Stein Mart	1,408,648
Men's Wearhouse	1,295,049
Dress Barn	717,136

Source: *Chain Store Age*, August 2003, p. 10A, from company reports and *Chain Store Age* research.

★ 2758 ★
Retailing - Apparel
SIC: 5651; NAICS: 44814

Leading Specialty Clothing Retailers in Europe

Firms are ranked by sales in millions of British pounds for 2001-2002.

Hennes & Mauritz	£ 4,486
Inditex	3,250
Next	3,019
Benetton	2,098
Arcadia	1,597
Coin	1,557

Source: *Financial Times*, September 18, 2002, p. 15, from companies.

★ 2759 ★
Retailing - Apparel
SIC: 5651; NAICS: 44814

Leading Youth Apparel Stores

Stores are ranked by sales in thousands of dollars.

Abercrombie & Fitch	$ 1,595,757
American Eagle Outfitters	1,463,141
Pacific Sunwear of California	846,393
Wet Seal	608,509
Hot Topic	443,250
Urban Outfitters	422,754

Buckle	$ 401,060
Gadzooks	325,521

Source: *Chain Store Age*, August 2003, p. 10A, from company reports and *Chain Store Age* research.

★ 2760 ★
Retailing - Apparel
SIC: 5651; NAICS: 44814

Retail Outerwear Sales

Sales are shown by model for the 12 months ended September 2003. Total sales are expected to reach $2.89 billion. Data are based on a poll of the top 12 outerwear manufacturers.

Specialty stores	32.5%
Department stores	22.7
Direct mail	15.3
Off-price stores	12.5
Chains	9.7
Mass	7.3

Source: *Daily News Record*, November 17, 2003, p. 22, from NPD Fashionworld.

★ 2761 ★
Shoe Stores
SIC: 5661; NAICS: 44821

Comfort Shoe Sales by Channel

Comfort shoes were a $4.6 billion industry in 2003, with women's shoes taking $3.4 billion of the pie, men's shoes taking $1.07 billion and children's shoes taking $58 million.

	($ mil.)	Share
Company/factory outlet	$ 981.6	21.84%
Shoe store	913.0	20.31
Department	872.9	19.42
National chain	404.6	9.00
Off-price	383.3	8.53
Catalog/direct mail	222.8	4.96
Pureplays (Internet only)	151.5	3.37
Clothing specialty	119.0	2.65

Continued on next page.

★ 2761 ★
[Continued]
Shoe Stores
SIC: 5661; NAICS: 44821
Comfort Shoe Sales by Channel

Comfort shoes were a $4.6 billion industry in 2003, with women's shoes taking $3.4 billion of the pie, men's shoes taking $1.07 billion and children's shoes taking $58 million.

	($ mil.)	Share
Athletic specialty/sporting goods . .	$ 91.8	2.04%
Other	353.9	7.87

Source: *Footwear News*, April 26, 2004, p. 30, from NPD Group and NPD Fashionworld.

★ 2762 ★
Shoe Stores
SIC: 5661; NAICS: 44821
Largest Sports Shoe Retailers

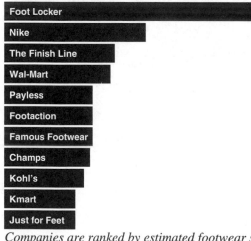

Companies are ranked by estimated footwear sales in millions of dollars.

Foot Locker	$ 1,600
Nike (retail only)	800
The Finish Line	625
Wal-Mart (athletic only)	600
Payless (athletic only)	500
Footaction	500
Famous Footwear	500
Champs	485
Kohl's (athletic only)	450
Kmart (athletic only)	400
Just for Feet	400

Source: *Sporting Goods Business*, June 2003, p. 52.

★ 2763 ★
Shoe Stores
SIC: 5661; NAICS: 44821
Leading Shoe Stores

The responses are shown to the question: "What shoe store do you msot often shop in most often." 23 % had no preference. The shoe industry is estimated at $40 billion.

Payless ShoeSource	16.4%
Wal-Mart	16.3
Kmart	3.9
JCPenney	2.7
Sears	2.6
Kohl's	2.0

Source: *Advertising Age*, July 28, 2003, p. 3, from BIGResearch.

SIC 57 - Furniture and Homefurnishings Stores

★ 2764 ★

Furniture Stores

SIC: 5712; NAICS: 44211

Top Furniture Retailers

Companies are ranked by estimated furniture and bedding sales in millions of dollars.

Wal-Mart	$ 1,240
Rooms To Go	1,235
Ethan Allen	1,006
Levitz Home Furnishings	950
La-Z-Boy Furniture Galleries	896
Office Depot	868
Sam's Club	850
Federated Department Stores	843
Berkshire Hathaway furniture division	836
Costco	750
Staples	702
Havertys	683

Source: *Furniture Today*, Winter 2003, p. 37, from *Furniture Today* market research.

★ 2765 ★

Furniture Stores

SIC: 5712; NAICS: 44211

Top Furniture Retailers in the U.K., 2003

Market shares are shown n percent.

	2002	2003
MFI	7.9%	8.2%
Argos	5.6	5.9
DFS	4.8	5.0
IKEA	4.6	4.8
Homestyle	3.3	3.2
Other	73.8	72.9

Source: *Marketing*, April 1, 2004, p. 13, from Verdict Research.

★ 2766 ★

Furniture Stores

SIC: 5712; NAICS: 44211

Top Furniture Stores

Companies are ranked by furniture, bedding and accessories sales in millions of dollars.

Rooms To Go	$ 1,300.0
Pier 1 Imports	1,238.1
Ethan Allen	1,156.1
Levitz Home Furnishings	965.0
La-Z-Boy Furniture Galleries	920.2
Berkshire Hathaway furniture division	878.8
Ikea	873.0
Havertys	704.0

Continued on next page.

★ 2766 ★
[Continued]
Furniture Stores
SIC: 5712; NAICS: 44211

Top Furniture Stores

Companies are ranked by furniture, bedding and accessories sales in millions of dollars.

Value City Furniture	$ 700.0
Rhodes	584.0
Art Van	560.0
Thomasville Home Furnishings Stores . . .	485.0

Source: *Furniture Today*, Winter 2003, p. 5, from *Furniture Today* market research.

★ 2767 ★
Carpet Stores
SIC: 5713; NAICS: 44221

Leading Carpet Retailers in the U.K.

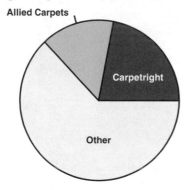

Allied Carpets

Carpetright

Other

Market shares are shown in percent.

Carpetright	22.0%
Allied Carpets	15.0
Other	63.0

Source: *Marketing Week*, February 14, 2002, p. 10.

★ 2768 ★
Retailing - Homefurnishings
SIC: 5713; NAICS: 44221

Rug Market Sales, 2003

Rug sales increased slightly to $4.8 billion. 69% are machine-made and 31% are hand-made. 60% are tufted.

Discount department stores	25.0%
Carpet/floor covering stores	11.0
Home improvement stores	10.0
Furniture stores	9.0
Direct-to-consumer	8.0
Mid-price chains	7.0
Department stores	7.0
Home textiles specialty stores	5.0
Gift/home accent stores	5.0
Other	13.0

Source: *Home Textiles Today*, January 12, 2004, p. 42.

★ 2769 ★
Retailing - Homefurnishings
SIC: 5719; NAICS: 442299

Home Furnishings Chain Leaders

Sales of household accessories and decor exceeded $78 billion in 2002.

Bath & Beyond/Linens N Things	7.0%
Pier 1	3.0
Kirkland's	1.0
Cost Plus World Market	1.0
Other	88.0

Source: *Retail Traffic*, November 1, 2003, p. 11, from Suntrust Robinson Humphrey.

★ 2770 ★
Retailing - Homefurnishings
SIC: 5719; NAICS: 442291, 442299
Leading Home Accent Retailers, 2002

Market shares are shown in percent.

Discount department stores 36.0%
Specialty stores 18.0
Furniture stores 17.0
Home improvement centers 12.0
Direct to consumer 8.0
Department stores 7.0
Warehouse clubs 2.0

Source: *Home Accents Today*, December 2003, p. 16.

★ 2771 ★
Retailing - Homefurnishings
SIC: 5719; NAICS: 442291, 442299
Leading Textile Retailers, 2002

Companies are ranked by revenues in millions of dollars. Department stores in the United States have been steadily losing market share to mass merchants, warehouse clubs, and specialty stores.

Wal-Mart . . . . $ 3,352.27
J.C. Penney 2,610.61
Target 2,210.38
Bed Bath & Beyond 2,016.00
Kmart 1,521.28
Linens 'n Things 1,289.15
Sears Hoffman 1,061.07
TJX 753.25
Kohl's 584.09
Costco 500.00

Source: *HFN*, August 18, 2003, p. 26.

★ 2772 ★
Retailing - Homefurnishings
SIC: 5719; NAICS: 442299
Retail Comforter Sales, 2003

Sales rose slightly from $1.42 billion in 2002 to $1.43 billion in 2003.

Mass merchants 51.0%
Department stores 25.0
Specialty stores 17.0
Catalogs 6.0
Other 1.0

Source: *HFN*, February 23, 2004, p. 30.

★ 2773 ★
Retailing - Homefurnishings
SIC: 5719; NAICS: 442299
Retail Flatware Sales, 2003

Sales fell slightly from $125.4 million in 2002 to $119.1 million in 2003.

Specialty and jewlery stores 48.0%
Catalogs 25.0
Department stores 23.0
Other 4.0

Source: *HFN*, February 23, 2004, p. 30.

★ 2774 ★
Retailing - Homefurnishings
SIC: 5719; NAICS: 442299
Retail Glassware Sales, 2003

Sales increased slightly from $1.2 billion in 2002 to $1.27 billion in 2003.

Mass merchants & clubs	61.0%
Specialty stores	30.0
Department stores	5.0
Other	4.0

Source: *HFN*, February 23, 2004, p. 30.

★ 2775 ★
Retailing - Homefurnishings
SIC: 5719; NAICS: 442299
Retail Quilt Sales, 2003

Sales rose slightly from $500 million in 2002 to $525 million in 2003.

Mass merchants and clubs	43.0%
Department stores	36.0
Specialty stores	15.0
Catalogs	5.5
Other	0.5

Source: *HFN*, February 23, 2004, p. 30.

★ 2776 ★
Retailing - Homefurnishings
SIC: 5719; NAICS: 442299
Retail Sheet Sales, 2003

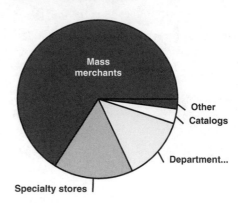

Sales fell slightly from $2.41 billion in 2002 to $2.38 billion in 2003.

Mass merchants	66.0%
Specialty stores	16.0
Department stores	13.0
Catalogs	3.0
Other	2.0

Source: *HFN*, February 23, 2004, p. 30.

★ 2777 ★
Retailing - Homefurnishings
SIC: 5719; NAICS: 442299
Top Bedding Retailers

Companies are ranked by bedding sales in millions of dollars.

Select Comfort	$ 311.8
The Mattress Firm	234.0
Sleepy's	227.0
Federated Department Stores	220.0
Sam's Club	210.0
Mattress Discounters	199.0
Mattress Giant	184.0
Rooms To Go	130.0
May Department Stores	130.0
Berkshire Hathaway furniture division	127.0

Source: *Furniture Today*, Winter 2003, p. 5, from *Furniture Today* market research.

★ 2778 ★
Retailing - Homefurnishings
SIC: 5719; NAICS: 442299

Top Lighting Retailers

Figures include residential light fixtures, portable lamps and ceiling fans. Figures don't include commercial lighting. Firms are ranked by revenues in millions of dollars.

Home Depot	$ 1,147.07
Lowe's	589.60
Lighting One	245.50
Wal-Mart	219.90
Lamps Plus	141.75
J.C. Penney	113.74
Target	99.20
Sears	72.40
TJX Cos.	71.20
Kmart	62.50

Source: *HFN*, August 18, 2003, p. 33, from *HFN* survey.

★ 2779 ★
Retailing - Homefurnishings
SIC: 5719; NAICS: 442299

Upstairs Dinnerware Sales, 2003

Sales increased from $749.48 million in 2002 to $805.04 million in 2003.

Department stores	49.0%
Specialty stores	37.0
Catalogs	6.0
Other	8.0

Source: *HFN*, February 23, 2004, p. 30.

★ 2780 ★
Retailing - Homefurnishings
SIC: 5719; NAICS: 442291

Wall Decor Sales

The industry was valued at $387 million.

Specialty stores	30.0%
Mass merchants	29.0
Furniture stores and chains	18.0
Department stores	15.0
Other	8.0

Source: *HFN*, October 13, 2003, p. 92.

★ 2781 ★
Retailing - Appliances
SIC: 5722; NAICS: 443111

Automatic Drip Coffeemaker Sales

Figures are for July - December 2002.

Traditional mass merchandiser	29.5%
Kitchen/home specialty stores	28.4
Department stores	26.6
General merchandiser	12.9
Drug stores	2.7

Source: "Some Like it Hot." [online] from http://www.npdhouseworldcom [accessed November 11, 2003], from NPD Group, NPD Houseworld, and POS Information.

★ 2782 ★
Retailing - Appliances
SIC: 5722; NAICS: 443111

Cooking Appliance Sales, 2002

Total sales rached $2.83 billion.

Appliance stores	41.0%
Sears	39.0
Home improvement centers	17.0
Mass	3.0

Source: *HFN*, October 20, 2003, p. 52.

★ 2783 ★

Retailing - Appliances

SIC: 5722; NAICS: 443111

Laundry Equipment Sales, 2002

Total sales rached $2.83 billion.

Sears	49.0%
Appliance stores	33.0
Home improvement centers	12.0
Mass	5.0
Other	1.0

Source: HFN, *October 20, 2003, p. 52.*

★ 2784 ★

Retailing - Appliances

SIC: 5722; NAICS: 443111

Leading Appliance Retailers, 2002

Companies are ranked by revenues in millions of dollars. The industry has enjoyed noticeable growth in the United States because of the strong housing market and low interest rates.

Sears	$ 7,112.64
Lowe's	2,635.79
Best Buy	1,256.76
Home Depot	1,200.00
Costco Wholesale	432.66
P.C. Richard & Son	385.00
Sam's Club	378.62
Berkshire Hathaway	267.00
Wal-Mart	257.66
H.H. Gregg	236.00

Source: HFN, August 18, 2003, p. 26.

★ 2785 ★

Retailing - Appliances

SIC: 5722; NAICS: 443111

Room Air Conditioner Market, 2002

Sales increased slightly from $1.41 billion in 2001 to $1.51 billion in 2002.

Mass merchants and clubs	37.0%
Home improvement centers	22.0
Appliance stores	20.0
Sears	16.0
Other	5.0

Source: *HFN*, January 12, 2004, p. 62, from Association of Home Appliance Manufacturers.

★ 2786 ★

Retailing - Appliances

SIC: 5722; NAICS: 443111

Top Appliance Vendors, 2002

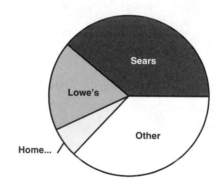

Market shares are shown in percent.

Sears	39.0%
Lowe's	18.0
Home Depot	6.0
Other	37.0

Source: *Do-It-Yourself Retailing*, May 2003, p. 16, from Midwest Research.

★ 2787 ★
Retailing - Electronics
SIC: 5731; NAICS: 443112
DVD Player Sales, 2002

Market shares are estimated.

Wal-Mart	26.2%
Best Buy	19.1
Circuit City	9.6
Sears	5.2
Target	5.0
Costco	4.4
Appliance/TV store	4.2
Sam's Club	4.1
Internet	4.1
Other	18.1

Source: *Dealerscope*, August 2003, p. 32, from
Dealerscope 81st Annual Statistical Survey and Report.

★ 2788 ★
Retailing - Electronics
SIC: 5731; NAICS: 443112
Projection TV Sales, 2002

Market shares are estimated.

Appliance/TV stores	24.6%
Circuit City	19.3
Best Buy	18.4
Sears	11.1
Hi-fi stereo stores	10.5

Wal-Mart	2.3%
Internet	2.1
Sam's Club	1.6
Other	10.1

Source: *Dealerscope*, August 2003, p. 32, from
Dealerscope 81st Annual Statistical Survey and Report.

★ 2789 ★
Retailing - Consumer Electronics
SIC: 5731; NAICS: 443112
Home Theater in a Box Sales, 2002

Market shares are estimated. Home theaters include receivers and speakers.

Best Buy	21.4%
Wal-Mart	14.3
Circuit City	12.8
Appliance/TV store	6.6
Sears	6.0
Sam's Club	5.3
Internet	5.2
Other	28.4

Source: *Dealerscope*, August 2003, p. 32, from
Dealerscope 81st Annual Statistical Survey and Report.

★ 2790 ★
Retailing - Computer Peripherals
SIC: 5734; NAICS: 44312
Portable MP-3 Player Sales, 2002

Market shares are estimated.

Best Buy	25.3%
Internet	17.2
Circuit City	11.4
Wal-Mart	9.1
Hi-fi/stereo store	5.7
Mail order	4.9
Radio shack	4.0
Computer store	4.0
Other	18.4

Source: *Dealerscope*, August 2003, p. 32, from
Dealerscope 81st Annual Statistical Survey and Report.

★ 2791 ★
Retailing - Video Games
SIC: 5734; NAICS: 44312

Leading Video Game Retailers, 2003

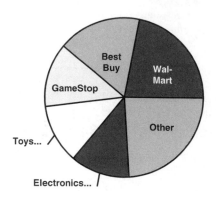

Market shares are shown in percent.

Wal-Mart	22.0%
Best Buy	17.0
GameStop	13.0
Toys R Us	12.0
Electronics Boutique	12.0
Other	24.0

Source: *Electronic Gaming Business*, December 3, 2003, p. NA, from U.S. Bancorp. Piper Jaffray.

★ 2792 ★
Retailing - Movies
SIC: 5735; NAICS: 45122

Leading DVD Sellthrough Leaders, 2003

Market shares are shown based on sales of $11.8 billion revenues.

Wal-Mart	27.6%
Target	12.1
Best Buy	11.0
Costco	6.4
Sam's Club	4.2
Circuit City	3.7

Blockbuster	3.2%
Musicland Stores	3.1
Suncoast Motion Picture Co.	1.8
Other	26.9

Source: *Video Store*, April 25, 2004, p. 18, from *Video Store* Magazine Market Research.

★ 2793 ★
Retailing - Movies
SIC: 5735; NAICS: 45122

Leading Online Video Retailers, 2003

Companies are ranked by estimated gross sales in millions of dollars.

Amazon.com	$ 350.2
Netflix	272.2
Buy.com	56.3
DVD.com	45.8
Best Buy	25.7
Target	18.9
DVDEmpire	18.6
Costco	18.0
Blockbuster	10.3

Source: *Video Store*, April 25, 2004, p. 18, from *Video Store* Magazine Market Research.

★ 2794 ★
Retailing - Movies
SIC: 5735; NAICS: 45122

Leading Sellthrough Leaders, 2003

Market shares are shown based on revenues.

Wal-Mart	31.0%
Target	12.0
Costco	5.9
Sam's Club	4.8
Kmart	2.0
Fred Meyer	0.6
BJ's Wholesale Club	0.5
ShopKo	0.3
Food 4 Less	0.2
Other	42.7

Source: *Video Store*, April 25, 2004, p. 18, from *Video Store Magazine* Market Research.

★ 2795 ★
Retailing - Movies
SIC: 5735; NAICS: 45122

Leading Video Revenue Generators, 2003

Market shares are shown based on revenues of $24.7 billion.

Wal-Mart	17.6%
Blockbuster	14.6
Target Stores	6.8
Hollywood Entertainment	5.5
Best Buy	5.4
Other	50.1

Source: *Video Store*, April 25, 2004, p. 18, from *Video Store* Magazine Market Research.

★ 2796 ★
Retailing - Movies
SIC: 5735; NAICS: 45122

Video Sellthrough Channels, 2003

Sellthrough revenues have increased from $10.8 billion in 2001, to $12.1 billion in 2002 to $14 billion in 2003.

Discount stores	57.0%
Video specialty stores	15.0
Warehouse/club stores	8.0
Electronic stores	8.0
Internet	4.0
Mail order	1.0
Grocery	1.0
Other	6.0

Source: *Video Store*, April 25, 2004, p. 15, from *2004 Consumer Home Entertainment Study*.

★ 2797 ★
Retailing - Music
SIC: 5735; NAICS: 45122

Album Sales by Outlet, 2002

Figures are in millions.

	(mil.)	Share
Music chain stores	347.2	50.99%
Mass merchants	230.0	33.78
Independent	81.0	11.90
Other	22.7	3.33

Source: *Wall Street Journal*, September 18, 2003, p. B1, from Nielsen Soundscan.

★ 2798 ★
Retailing - Music
SIC: 5735; NAICS: 45122

Leading Online Music Stores

Market shares are shown in percent. Other includes Wal-Mart, Buy Music, Real Netwroks, and Music Match.

iTunes	70.0%
Napster	15.0
Other	15.0

Source: *New York Post*, February 25, 2004, p. 35.

★ 2799 ★
Retailing - Music
SIC: 5735; NAICS: 45122

Music Sales in China

China is the fifth largest market in Asia. Privately owned stores and vendors account for some 50% of legal pre-recorded music sales. Xin Hua was a former state-run monopoly.

Xin Hua	70.0%
State run post office	15.0
Other	15.0

Source: *Music & Copyright*, October 29, 2003, p. 8.

★ 2800 ★
Retailing - Music
SIC: 5735; NAICS: 45122

Music Sales in the U.K.

Market shares are shown in percent.

	1998	2000	2002
Specialist multiple	48.0%	50.2%	46.9%
General multiple	26.7	23.8	20.3
Independents	14.1	12.4	12.7
Supermarkets	11.3	13.6	20.0

Source: *Music & Copyright*, September 17, 2003, p. 1, from Gallup, Millward Brown, and BPI.

★ 2801 ★
Retailing - Music
SIC: 5735; NAICS: 45122

Retail Music Sales

In September 2003 UMG reduced the wholesale price of its products by 24%. The reduced prices are a way to combat the company's falling sales, due in part to competition from music downloading online. The table shows the fall of the record store market share in recent years. Mail order includes record clubs.

	1998	2000	2002
Record store	50.8%	42.4%	36.8%
Mail order	11.9	10.0	6.0
Internet	1.1	3.2	3.4
Other	34.4	40.6	50.7

Source: *Music & Copyright*, September 17, 2003, p. 1, from Recording Industry Association of America.

★ 2802 ★
Retailing - Music Products
SIC: 5736; NAICS: 45114

Leading Music Product Retailers

Companies are ranked by estimated revenues in millions of dollars.

Guitar Center Inc.	$ 1,100.88
Sam Ash Music Corp.	368.00
Brook Mays / H&H	160.00
Hermes Music	86.50
Victor's House of Music	81.35
Music and Arts Center	70.00
Sweetwater Sound	60.27
J.W. Pepper & Son Inc.	57.00
Schmitt Music Company	$ 55.90
Washington Music Center	54.00
Pro Sound & State Lighting	52.00
Full Compass Systems	50.00

Source: *Music Trades*, August 2003, p. 86, from *Music Trade's Top 2003*.

★ 2803 ★
Retailing - Music Products
SIC: 5736; NAICS: 45114

Musical Instrument Purchases in Germany

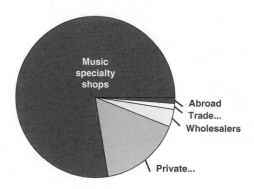

About 8% of all Germans play an instrument (although 10% of all households own at least one musical instrument). Those who own an instrument play for fun (94%) compared to those who play professionally (1%) or semi-professionally (3%).

Music specialty shops	66.0%
Private individuals	14.0
Wholesalers	3.0
Trade fairs/special exhibitions	1.0
Abroad	1.0

Source: ''Musical Instruments.'' [online] available from http://www.export.gov [accessed December 1, 2003].

SIC 58 - Eating and Drinking Places

★ 2804 ★
Catering
SIC: 5812; NAICS: 72231

Airline Catering Market Worldwide

Market shares are shown in percent.

Sky Chef	35.0%
Gate Gourmet	25.0
Other	40.0

Source: *Knight Ridder-Tribune Business News*, February 5, 2002, p. NA, from University of Surrey.

★ 2805 ★
Catering
SIC: 5812; NAICS: 72231

Leading Airline Catering Firms Worldwide, 2001

Companies are ranked by revenues in millions of dollars.

Sky Chefs	$ 3,315
GateGourmet	1,957
Servair	408
Alpha Flight Services	388
SATS	230

Source: *Airline Business*, January 1, 2003, p. 39.

★ 2806 ★
Catering
SIC: 5812; NAICS: 72231

School Meals in the U.K., 2004

In the United Kingdom school meals are provided to students and the local education authorities can choose to have the local authorities run the catering, do it themselves, or contract with an outside firm to provide the catering services. The market shares shown here are an estimate for 2003 and breakdown the catering services according to method.

In-house, council run	66.0%
Other private contractors	11.0
Contractor -- Compass Group	10.0
Contractor -- Initial Catering Services	8.0
Contractor -- Sodexho	3.0
Self-operated by the school	2.0

Source: *Caterer & Hotelkeeper*, March 25, 2004, p. 30.

★ 2807 ★
Catering
SIC: 5812; NAICS: 72232

Top Hospital Catering Firms in Japan, 2002

Market shares are shown based on value of services undertaken as 473 billion yen.

Nissin Healthcare Food Service Co.	25.3%
Fuji Sangyo	8.4
Shidax Food Service Corp.	5.7
Aim Services Co.	4.4
Mefos Ltd.	4.1
Other	52.1

Source: "Market Share Survey Report 2002." [online] from http://www.nni.nikkei.co.jp [accessed January 20, 2004], from Nikkei estimate.

★ 2808 ★
Coffee Shops
SIC: 5812; NAICS: 722213

Largest Coffee Shop Chains, 2001

Chains are ranked by number of stores. There were over 8,800 retail coffee shops in the United States in 2001, which generated sales of $4.06 billion.

	Outlets	Share
Starbucks	3,540	26.52%
Diedrich's	278	2.08
Coffee Beanery	198	1.48
Caribou Coffee	170	1.27
Barnie's Coffee	125	0.94
Seattle Coffee	121	0.91
Tully's	114	0.85
Other	8,803	65.95

Source: *New York Times*, November 29, 2003, p. B3, from Mintel.

★ 2809 ★
Foodservice
SIC: 5812; NAICS: 72231

Branded QSR Sales in Convenience Stores

The top selling types of quick service restaurant items are shown.

Sandwiches	29.3%
Pizza	23.0
Chicken	19.0
Burgers	13.5
Snacks	8.4
Seafood	0.2
Other	6.7

Source: *Restaurant & Institutions*, January 2004, p. 67, from Technomic Inc. research for National Association of Convenience Stores.

★ 2810 ★
Foodservice
SIC: 5812; NAICS: 72231

Foodservice Industry, 2003-2004

Total retail sales were $429.9 billion.

	($ mil.)	Share
Limited-service restaurants	$ 141,130	32.8%
Full-service restaurants	127,733	29.7
Business & industry	20,300	4.7
Convenience stores	15,448	3.6
Primary/secondary schools	13,592	3.2
Recreation	12,395	2.9
Lodging	11,292	2.6
Colleges/universities	9,721	2.3

Continued on next page.

★ 2810 ★
[Continued]
Foodservice
SIC: 5812; NAICS: 72231

Foodservice Industry, 2003-2004

Total retail sales were $429.9 billion.

	$ mil.)	Share
Hospitals	$ 6,656	1.5%
Nursing homes	5,816	1.4

Source: *Restaurants & Institutions*, January 2004, p. 53, from Technomic.

★ 2811 ★
Foodservice
SIC: 5812; NAICS: 72231

Foodservice Industry in Canada

Sales show actual and projected figures.

	2002	2003	Share
Full service	$ 16,316	$ 16,719.0	49.55%
Limited service	11,788	12,043.0	35.69
Caterers, taverns, bars .	5,030	4,982.6	14.77

Source: *Food in Canada*, September 2003, p. 48, from Canadian Restaurant & Food Association.

★ 2812 ★
Foodservice
SIC: 5812; NAICS: 72231

Foodservice Industry Worldwide

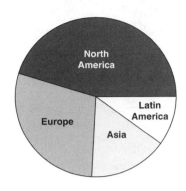

Total sales were 290 billion British pounds.

	(mil.)	Share
North America	£ 130.5	45.0%
Europe	84.1	29.0
Asia	46.4	16.0
Latin America	29.0	10.0

Source: *Financial Times*, July 30, 2001, p. 14, from Unilever.

★ 2813 ★
Foodservice
SIC: 5812; NAICS: 72211

Foodservice Market in Taiwan, 2003

> **Restaurants**
> **Coffee/tea shops**
> **Hotel restaurants**
> **Other**

Foodservice sales increased 3% over 2002 to $8.3 billion. The industry is being driven by a ''dining out'' culture and a high per capita income, according to the source.

	($ mil.)	Share
Restaurants	$ 6,852	77.35%
Coffee/tea shops	764	8.62
Hotel restaurants	420	4.74
Other	822	9.28

Source: ''HRI Food Service Director - Market Reports.'' [online] from http://fas.usda.gov [accessed June 10, 2004], from Foreign Agricultural Service, U.S. Department of Commerce.

★ 2814 ★
Foodservice
SIC: 5812; NAICS: 72231

Largest Contract Management Firms in North America

Companies are ranked by North American food & beverage sales in millions of dollars. The top 50 firms had aggregate had sals of $21.5 billion, of which the top three firms took about two thirds.

	($ mil.)	Share
Aramark	$ 5,700.0	26.51%
Sodexho	5,500.0	25.58
Compass Group North America	5,100.0	23.72
Delaware North Companies	1,600.0	7.44
HMSHost Corp.	1,400.0	6.51
Centerplate	577.2	2.68
Levy Restaurants Sports & Entertainment	313.0	1.46
HDS Services	297.0	1.38
Guckenheimer Enterprises	225.0	1.05
All Seasons Services	210.0	0.98
Guest Services	190.0	0.88
Other	387.8	1.80

Source: *Food Management*, April 2003, p. 36, from *Food Management's Top 50*.

★ 2815 ★
Foodservice
SIC: 5812; NAICS: 72231

Noncommercial Foodservice Market, 2002

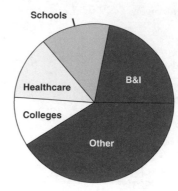

Other includes vending, office coffee, military and corrections. B&I stands for business and institutions.

	($ bil.)	Share
B&I	$ 21.48	22.41%
Schools	13.26	13.83
Healthcare	12.43	12.97
Colleges	9.48	9.89
Other	39.20	40.90

Source: *Restaurants & Institutions*, September 15, 2003, p. 40, from Technomic.

★ 2816 ★
Foodservice
SIC: 5812; NAICS: 72231

Retail Foodservice Industry, 2002

Retailers are ranked by estimated sales in millions of dollars.

Wal-Mart	$ 255.0
Kmart	250.0
Target	170.0
Barnes & Noble	170.0
Borders Books and Music	126.0
Nordstrom	105.0

Continued on next page.

★ 2816 ★

[Continued]
Foodservice
SIC: 5812; NAICS: 72231

Retail Foodservice Industry, 2002

Retailers are ranked by estimated sales in millions of dollars.

Marshall Field's	$ 105.0
Costco	90.0
Ikea North America	32.0
Neiman Marcus	25.7

Source: *Restaurants & Institutions*, June 1, 2003, p. 32, from company documents and Securities and Exchange Commission filings.

★ 2817 ★

Foodservice
SIC: 5812; NAICS: 72231

School Pizza Market

The company supplies 70% of the pizza served in school lunchrooms in the coutnry.

Schwan Food Co.	70.0%
Other	30.0

Source: *Pizza Marketing Quarterly*, August 25, 2003, p. NA.

★ 2818 ★

Foodservice
SIC: 5812; NAICS: 72231

Top Foodservice Contractors

Companies are ranked by food & beverage sales in millions of dollars.

Aramark Corp.	$ 6,545.4
Compass Group North America	6,376.0
Sodexho USA	5,800.0
Delaware North Companies	1,600.0
Autogrill Group	1,600.0

Source: *Restaurants & Institutions*, January 1, 2004, p. 51.

★ 2819 ★

Restaurants
SIC: 5812; NAICS: 722110

Doughnut Shop Market

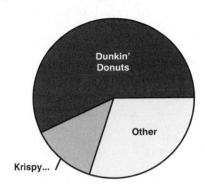

Market shares are shown in percent.

Dunkin' Donuts	57.0%
Krispy Kreme	13.0
Other	30.0

Source: *Grand Rapids Press*, September 24, 2003, p. B5.

★ 2820 ★

Restaurants
SIC: 5812; NAICS: 722211

Fast-Food Market Sizes

Figures are in billions of dollars.

Burgers	$ 47.5
Pizza	25.1
Sandwiches	15.8

Source: *Chain Leader*, October 2003, p. 43, from Technomic.

★ 2821 ★
Restaurants
SIC: 5812; NAICS: 722211, 722213

Largest Coffee and Donut Chains

Starbucks and Krispy Kreme are among the nation's fastest growing chains (among chains with sales over $200 million). Tim Horton's has 70% of Canada's coffee and baked goods market.

Starbucks	7,567
Dunkin' Donuts	5,800
Tim Hortons	2,527
Diedrich Coffee	430
Krispy Kreme	333
Caribou Coffee	251
Winchell's Donut House	200
Peet's Coffee & Tea	75

Source: *Restaurant Business*, February 15, 2004, p. 32.

★ 2822 ★
Restaurants
SIC: 5812; NAICS: 722211

Leading Bakery Cafe Chain Leaders

- Einstein Bros. Bagels
- Au Bon Pain
- Corner Bakery
- Bruegger's Bagel Bakery

Stores are ranked by systemwide sales in millions of dollars.

Einstein Bros. Bagels	$ 311.7
Au Bon Pain	203.1
Corner Bakery	186.0
Bruegger's Bagel Bakery	153.1

Source: *Nation's Restaurant News*, July 28, 2003, p. 74, from *Nation's Restaurant News*.

★ 2823 ★
Restaurants
SIC: 5812; NAICS: 72211

Leading Casual Dinnerhouse Chains

Data show share of aggregate sales of dinnerhouse chains in the source's top 100 list.

Applebee's	15.21%
Red Lobster	11.28
Outback Steakhouse	10.85
Chilis Grill & Bar	10.70
Olive Garden	9.27
T.G.I. Friday's	8.34
Ruby Tuesday	6.00
Bennigan's	3.25
Romano's Macaroni Grill	3.05
Hooters	3.01
Other	19.04

Source: *Nation's Restaurant News*, June 30, 2003, p. 116, from *Nation's Restaurant News* research.

★ 2824 ★
Restaurants
SIC: 5812; NAICS: 72211

Leading Chicken Chains

Data show share of aggregate sales of chicken chains in the source's top 100 list.

KFC	50.74%
Chick-fil-A	14.51
Popeye's Chicken & Biscuits	12.84
Church's Chicken	7.61
Boston Market	6.78
EL Pollo Loco	3.85
Bojangles	3.67

Source: *Nation's Restaurant News*, June 30, 2003, p. 116, from *Nation's Restaurant News* research.

★ 2825 ★
Restaurants
SIC: 5812; NAICS: 72211
Leading Grill-Buffet Chains

Data show share of aggregate sales of grill-buffet chains in the source's top 100 list.

Golden Corral	46.25%
Ryan's Family Steak House	32.47
Ponderosa Steakhouse	21.28

Source: *Nation's Restaurant News*, June 30, 2003, p. 116, from *Nation's Restaurant News* research.

★ 2826 ★
Restaurants
SIC: 5812; NAICS: 72211
Leading Independent Restaurants, 2003

Restaurants are ranked by food and beverage sales in millions of dollars.

Tavern on the Green	$ 34.41
Joe's Stone Crab	24.33
Hilltop Steak House	23.50
Tao Asian Bistro	21.85
Bob Chinn's Crab House	21.44
Spraks Steakhouse	18.60
Old Ebbitt Grill	17.77
Gibsons Bar Steakhouse	16.69
Fulton's Crab House	16.26
"21" Club	15.86

Source: *Restaurants & Institutions*, April 1, 2004, p. 58.

★ 2827 ★
Restaurants
SIC: 5812; NAICS: 72211
Leading Multiconcept Operators, 2002

Companies are ranked by sales in millions of dollars.

Restaurant Associates	$ 440.0
Levy Restaurants	382.0
Lettuce Entertain You	185.0

Restaurants Unlimited	$ 145.0
Back Bay Restaurant Group	119.6
Ark Restaurants Corp.	115.5
Kimpton Hotels & Restaurants	110.0
Specialty Restaurants Corp.	100.0
Restaurant Development Group	85.0

Source: *Restaurants and Institutions*, November 1, 2003, p. 48.

★ 2828 ★
Restaurants
SIC: 5812; NAICS: 722211
Leading Pizza Chain Leaders

Stores are ranked by systemwide sales in millions of dollars.

CiCi's Pizza	$ 334.0
Papa Murphy's Take 'N Bake Pizza	332.4
Godfather's Pizza	287.0
Hungry Howie's Pizza	220.0
Donatos Pizzeria	195.0
Mazzio's Pizza	164.0
Pizza Hut	157.6

Source: *Nation's Restaurant News*, July 28, 2003, p. 74, from *Nation's Restaurant News*.

★ 2829 ★
Restaurants
SIC: 5812; NAICS: 722211

Pizza Chain Leaders, 2003

Market shares are shown in percent.

Pizza Hut	13.4%
Domino's	8.4
Little Caesars	5.3
Papa John's	4.6
Other	68.3

Source: *USA TODAY*, January 16, 2004, p. B1, from *Advertising Age*.

★ 2830 ★
Restaurants
SIC: 5812; NAICS: 72211

Pizza Industry in Thailand, 2003

The pizza market in Thailand measured 2.5 billion Thai bahts.

The Pizza Company	70.0%
Others	30.0

Source: *Bangkok Post*, March 18, 2004, p. NA.

★ 2831 ★
Restaurants
SIC: 5812; NAICS: 72211

Pizza Market in Australia

Market shares are shown in percent.

Pizza Hut	40.0%
Domino's	25.0
Other	35.0

Source: *Daily Telegraph*, June 19, 2002, p. 38.

★ 2832 ★
Restaurants
SIC: 5812; NAICS: 722211

Quick-Service Traffic

Data show average share of quick service traffic over 21 quarters.

Burgers	42.8%
Pizza	17.9
Regional/other	16.8
Sandwiches	8.0
Chicken	7.4
Mexican	7.1

Source: *Chain Leader*, September 2003, p. 82, from Sandelman & Associates and Quick-Track.

★ 2833 ★
Restaurants
SIC: 5812; NAICS: 722211

Sandwich Market Leaders

The industry has benefited from the trend of healthy eating. Sandwich sales increased 8.5% to $15.8 billion (compared to a 2% growth for hamburgers).

Subway	32.8%
Arby's	17.0
Quiznos	3.9
Schlotzsky's Deli	2.5
Blimpie Subs & Salads	1.7
Other	43.1

Source: *Wall Street Journal*, October 6, 2003, p. B7, from Technomic.

★ **2834** ★
Restaurants
SIC: 5812; NAICS: 72211

Top Full-Service Chains

Chains are ranked by sales in millions of dollars.

Applebee's	$ 3,244.0
Red Lobster	2,340.0
Chili's Grill & Bar	2,310.2
T.G.I. Friday's	2,300.0
Outback Steakhouse	2,300.0
Denny's	2,217.8
Olive Garden	1,860.0
Cracker Barrel	1,825.7
IHOP	1,478.6
Ruby Tuesday	1,200.0

Source: *Restaurants & Institutions*, July 15, 2003, p. 19.

★ **2835** ★
Restaurants
SIC: 5812; NAICS: 72211

Top Italian Restaurants, 2002

Market shares are shown in percent.

	2001	2002
Olive Garden	17.3%	18.1%
Romano's Macaroni Grill	5.2	5.5
Pizzeria Uno	3.6	3.7
Carrabba's Italian Grill	2.7	3.2
Maggiano's	1.4	1.7
Other	69.8	67.8

Source: *ID Sales Pro*, July-August 2003, p. 12, from Technomic.

★ **2836** ★
Restaurants
SIC: 5812; NAICS: 72211

Top Seafood Restaurants

Companies are ranked by systemwide sales in millions of dollars.

Red Lobster	$ 2,430.0
Landry's	1,000.0
McCormick & Schmick's	180.0
Legal Sea Foods	148.1
Bubba Gump Shrimp	79.0

Source: *Restaurant Business*, March 1, 2004, p. 30.

★ **2837** ★
Retailing - Coffee
SIC: 5812; NAICS: 722211

Where We Buy Coffee

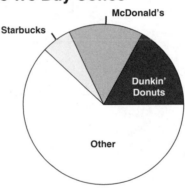

Dunkin' Donuts is the top seller of sales of regular, nonflavored brewed coffee (in fast-food chains). Starbucks has 5,439 locations in the country while Dunkin' Donuts has about 4,100 locations. The article points out that Starbucks has been looking for growth by opening outlets in numerous locations, including lower-income neighborhoods where Dunkin' Donuts tends to dominate.

Dunkin' Donuts	17.0%
McDonald's	15.0
Starbucks	6.0
Other	62.0

Source: *Wall Street Journal*, February 10, 2004, p. B1, from NPD Group.

★ 2838 ★

Bars & Taverns

SIC: 5813; NAICS: 72241

Leaders in Pub Operations in the U.K., 2004

The shares listed are for the leading bar operating companies in the U.K. after the early 2004 purchase of Unique Pub Company by Enterprise Inns. Almost one third of British pubs are managed by their independent owners and are referred to as "freehouses."

Freehouses	30.0%
Enterprise Inns	15.0
Punch Taverns	13.0
M&B	4.0
Spirit	4.0
Others	34.0

Source: *Financial Tmes*, March 13, 2004, p. 9, from Industry estimates.

★ 2839 ★

Bars & Taverns

SIC: 5813; NAICS: 72241

Leading Pub Operators in the U.K., 2003

Data show number of outlets.

Enterprise Inns	5,277
Punch Taverns	4,484
Unique Pub Co.	4,082
Pubmaster	3,288
Spirit (post acquisition)	2,478
Mitchells & Butlers	2,042
Wolverhampton & Dudley	1,628
Greene King	1,628
InnSpired Pubs	1,075
Wellington Pub Co.	833

Source: *Financial Times*, October 7, 2003, p. 26, from company, Mintel, and British Beer & Pub Association.

SIC 59 - Miscellaneous Retail

★ 2840 ★
Drug Stores
SIC: 5912; NAICS: 44611

Leading Categories at Drug Stores

Sales are shown in millions of dollars for the 52 weeks ended March 22, 2003. Figures refer to drug store with more than $1 million in sales.

Pain remedies, headache	$ 954.92
Nutritional supplements	838.29
Cold remedies, adult	806.31
Hair coloring, women's	596.01
Face cleaners/creams/lotions	531.03
Blood urine stool test products	510.35
Cosmetics/lipsticks	474.08
Laxatives	461.54
Antismoking products	412.11
Antacids	396.61

Source: *Retail Merchandiser*, June 2003, p. 27, from *AC Nielsen Health and Beauty Care Category Performance Study* and *Retail Merchandiser*.

★ 2841 ★
Drug Stores
SIC: 5912; NAICS: 44611

Top Drug Store Chains

Data show estimated number of outlets.

Walgreens	4,300
CVS	4,200
Rite Aid	3,400
Eckerd	2,700

Source: *USA TODAY*, April 6, 2004, p. B1, from Hoovers.

★ 2842 ★
Drug Stores
SIC: 5912; NAICS: 44611

Top Drug Stores, 2003

Companies are ranked by sales in millions of dollars. Shares are shown based on sales of $118.4 billion.

	($ mil.)	Share
Walgreens	$ 32,505	27.45%
CVS	26,590	22.46
Rite Aid	16,537	13.97
Eckerd	14,927	12.61
Albertsons	11,650	9.84
Longs Drug Stores	4,530	3.83
Medicine Shoppe International	2,240	1.89
Brooks Pharmacy	1,781	1.50
Duane Reade	1,384	1.17
Snyder's Drug Stores	730	0.62
Discount Drug Mart	550	0.46
Other	4,977	4.20

Source: *Drug Store News*, April 19, 2004, p. 72, from *Drug Store News* research.

★ 2843 ★
Drug Stores
SIC: 5912; NAICS: 44611

Top Drug Stores in Akron, OH

Companies are ranked by share of area volume in 2002.

CVS	22.0%
Marc's	21.0
Walgreen's	15.0
Rite Aid	9.0
Other	33.0

Source: *Chain Drug Review*, October 13, 2003, p. 52.

★ 2844 ★
Drug Stores
SIC: 5912; NAICS: 44611

Top Drug Stores in Albuquerque, NM

Companies are ranked by share of area volume in 2002.

Walgreens	55.0%
Wal-Mart/Sam's	12.0
Smith's Food & Drug	10.0
Other	23.0

Source: *Chain Drug Review*, October 13, 2003, p. 52.

★ 2845 ★
Drug Stores
SIC: 5912; NAICS: 44611

Top Drug Stores in Allentown Bethlehem/Easton, PA

Companies are ranked by share of area volume in 2002.

CVS	33.0%
Eckerd	19.0
Rite Aid	10.0
Walgreens	9.0
Other	29.0

Source: *Chain Drug Review*, October 13, 2003, p. 52.

★ 2846 ★
Drug Stores
SIC: 5912; NAICS: 44611

Top Drug Stores in Ann Arbor, MI

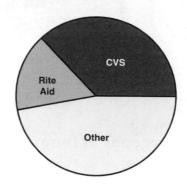

Companies are ranked by share of area volume in 2002.

CVS	37.0%
Rite Aid	16.0
Other	47.0

Source: *Chain Drug Review*, October 13, 2003, p. 52.

★ 2847 ★
Drug Stores
SIC: 5912; NAICS: 44611

Top Drug Stores in Atlanta, GA

Companies are ranked by share of area volume in 2002.

CVS	26.0%
Eckerd	23.0
Kroger	12.0
Walgreens	11.0
Other	28.0

Source: *MMR*, June 16, 2003, p. 30.

★ **2848** ★

Drug Stores

SIC: 5912; NAICS: 44611

Top Drug Stores in Austin/San Marcos, TX

Companies are ranked by share of area volume in 2002.

Walgreens	34.0%
H.E.B.	20.0
Eckerd	14.0
Other	32.0

Source: *MMR*, June 16, 2003, p. 30.

★ **2849** ★

Drug Stores

SIC: 5912; NAICS: 44611

Top Drug Stores in Baltimore, MD

Companies are ranked by share of area volume in 2002.

Rite Aid	36.0%
CVS	19.0
Other	45.0

Source: *MMR*, June 16, 2003, p. 30.

★ **2850** ★

Drug Stores

SIC: 5912; NAICS: 44611

Top Drug Stores in Birmingham, AL

Companies are ranked by share of area volume in 2002.

CVS	33.0%
Walgreens	13.0
Wal-Mart/Sam's	12.0
Other	42.0

Source: *Chain Drug Review*, October 13, 2003, p. 52.

★ **2851** ★

Drug Stores

SIC: 5912; NAICS: 44611

Top Drug Stores in Canada

Chains are ranked by number of outlets.

Walgreen	4,368
CVS	4,182
Rite Aid	3,382
Jean Coutu	2,196
Medicine Shoppe	1,100

Source: *Wall Street Journal*, April 30, 2004, p. B4, from *Wall Street Journal* research.

★ **2852** ★

Drug Stores

SIC: 5912; NAICS: 44611

Top Drug Stores in Chicago, IL

Companies are ranked by share of area volume in 2002.

Walgreens	49.0%
Osco	32.0
Other	19.0

Source: *MMR*, June 16, 2003, p. 30.

★ **2853** ★

Drug Stores

SIC: 5912; NAICS: 44611

Top Drug Stores in Cleveland/Lorain/ Elyria, OH

Companies are ranked by share of area volume in 2002.

CVS	20.0%
Marc's	19.0
Discount Drug Mart	14.0
Walgreens	13.0
Rite Aid	11.0
Other	23.0

Source: *MMR*, June 16, 2003, p. 30.

★ 2854 ★
Drug Stores
SIC: 5912; NAICS: 44611

Top Drug Stores in Columbus, OH

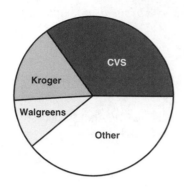

Companies are ranked by share of area volume in 2002.

CVS	35.0%
Kroger	16.0
Walgreens	10.0
Other	39.0

Source: *Chain Drug Review*, October 13, 2003, p. 52.

★ 2855 ★
Drug Stores
SIC: 5912; NAICS: 44611

Top Drug Stores in Dallas, TX

Companies are ranked by share of area volume in 2002.

Eckerd	27.0%
Walgreens	24.0
Albertsons	14.0
Wal-Mart/Sam's	10.0
Other	25.0

Source: *MMR*, June 16, 2003, p. 30.

★ 2856 ★
Drug Stores
SIC: 5912; NAICS: 44611

Top Drug Stores in Dayton/ Springfield, OH

Companies are ranked by share of area volume in 2002.

CVS	22.0%
Rite Aid	19.0
Walgreens	18.0
Kroger	10.0
Other	31.0

Source: *Chain Drug Review*, October 13, 2003, p. 52.

★ 2857 ★
Drug Stores
SIC: 5912; NAICS: 44611

Top Drug Stores in Denver, CO

Companies are ranked by share of area volume in 2002.

Walgreens	38.0%
Kings Soopers	18.0
Safeway	12.0
Other	32.0

Source: *MMR*, June 16, 2003, p. 30.

★ 2858 ★
Drug Stores
SIC: 5912; NAICS: 44611

Top Drug Stores in Flint, MI

Companies are ranked by share of area volume in 2002.

Rite Aid	50.0%
Walgreens	15.0
Other	35.0

Source: *Chain Drug Review*, October 13, 2003, p. 52.

★ 2859 ★
Drug Stores
SIC: 5912; NAICS: 44611

Top Drug Stores in Gary, IN

Companies are ranked by share of area volume in 2002.

Walgreens 62.0%
Osco 10.0
Other 28.0

Source: *Chain Drug Review*, October 13, 2003, p. 52.

★ 2860 ★
Drug Stores
SIC: 5912; NAICS: 44611

Top Drug Stores in Greensboro/ Winston-Salem/High Point, NC

Companies are ranked by share of area volume in 2002.

CVS 42.0%
Eckerd 30.0
Kerr Drug 9.0
Other 19.0

Source: *Chain Drug Review*, October 13, 2003, p. 52.

★ 2861 ★
Drug Stores
SIC: 5912; NAICS: 44611

Top Drug Stores in Harrisburg/ Lebanon/Carlisle, PA

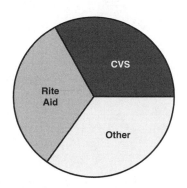

Companies are ranked by share of area volume in 2002.

CVS 33.0%
Rite Aid 32.0
Other 35.0

Source: *Chain Drug Review*, October 13, 2003, p. 52.

★ 2862 ★
Drug Stores
SIC: 5912; NAICS: 44611

Top Drug Stores in Hartford, CT

CVS
Walgreens
Other

Companies are ranked by share of area volume in 2002.

CVS 49.0%
Walgreens 14.0
Other 37.0

Source: *Chain Drug Review*, October 13, 2003, p. 52.

★ 2863 ★
Drug Stores
SIC: 5912; NAICS: 44611

Top Drug Stores in Honolulu, Hawaii

Companies are ranked by share of area volume in 2002.

Longs 73.0%
Times 11.0
Other 16.0

Source: *Chain Drug Review*, October 13, 2003, p. 52.

★ 2864 ★
Drug Stores
SIC: 5912; NAICS: 44611

Top Drug Stores in Huntington, WV

Companies are ranked by share of area volume in 2002.

Rite Aid 29.0%
CVS 28.0
Fruth Pharmacy 11.0
Wal-Mart/Sam's 10.0
Other 22.0

Source: *Chain Drug Review*, October 13, 2003, p. 52.

★ 2865 ★
Drug Stores
SIC: 5912; NAICS: 44611

Top Drug Stores in Indianapolis, IN

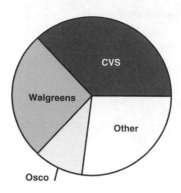

Companies are ranked by share of area volume in 2002.

CVS 37.0%
Walgreens 26.0
Osco 10.0
Other 27.0

Source: *MMR*, June 16, 2003, p. 30.

★ 2866 ★
Drug Stores
SIC: 5912; NAICS: 44611

Top Drug Stores in Los Angeles/ Long Beach, CA

| Osco/Sav-on |
| Rite Aid |
| Walgreens |
| Other |

Companies are ranked by share of area volume in 2002.

Osco/Sav-on 36.0%
Rite Aid 22.0
Walgreens 8.0
Other 34.0

Source: *MMR*, June 16, 2003, p. 30.

★ **2867** ★

Drug Stores

SIC: 5912; NAICS: 44611

Top Drug Stores in Middlesex/ Somerset/Hunterdon, NJ

Companies are ranked by share of area volume in 2002.

CVS	20.0%
Eckerd	15.0
Rite Aid	14.0
Walgreens	12.0
Drug Fair	10.0
Other	29.0

Source: *Chain Drug Review*, October 13, 2003, p. 52.

★ **2868** ★

Drug Stores

SIC: 5912; NAICS: 44611

Top Drug Stores in Milwaukee/ Waukesha, MN

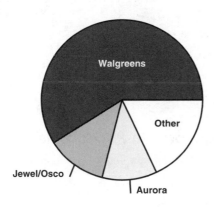

Companies are ranked by share of area volume in 2002.

Walgreens	59.0%
Jewel/Osco	12.0
Aurora	11.0
Other	18.0

Source: *MMR*, June 16, 2003, p. 30.

★ **2869** ★

Drug Stores

SIC: 5912; NAICS: 44611

Top Drug Stores in Minneapolis/St. Paul, MN

Companies are ranked by share of area volume in 2002.

Walgreens	46.0%
Snyder's	24.0
Other	30.0

Source: *MMR*, June 16, 2003, p. 30.

★ **2870** ★

Drug Stores

SIC: 5912; NAICS: 44611

Top Drug Stores in Monmouth/ Ocean, NJ

Companies are ranked by share of area volume in 2002.

CVS	22.0%
Rite Aid	18.0
Eckerd	14.0
Drug Fair	10.0
Other	36.0

Source: *MMR*, June 16, 2003, p. 30.

★ **2871** ★

Drug Stores

SIC: 5912; NAICS: 44611

Top Drug Stores in Nashville, TN

Companies are ranked by share of area volume in 2002.

Walgreens	37.0%
CVS	18.0
Kroger	12.0
Eckerd	11.0
Other	22.0

Source: *Chain Drug Review*, October 13, 2003, p. 52.

★ 2872 ★
Drug Stores
SIC: 5912; NAICS: 44611

Top Drug Stores in New York, NY

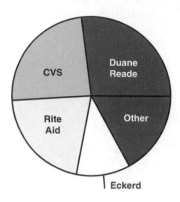

Companies are ranked by share of area volume in 2002.

Duane Reade	27.0%
CVS	24.0
Rite Aid	21.0
Eckerd	11.0
Other	17.0

Source: *MMR*, June 16, 2003, p. 30.

★ 2873 ★
Drug Stores
SIC: 5912; NAICS: 44611

Top Drug Stores in Oklahoma City, OK

Walgreens
Eckerd
Wal-Mart/Sam's
Other

Companies are ranked by share of area volume in 2002.

Walgreens	34.0%
Eckerd	25.0
Wal-Mart/Sam's	16.0
Other	25.0

Source: *Chain Drug Review*, October 13, 2003, p. 52.

★ 2874 ★
Drug Stores
SIC: 5912; NAICS: 44611

Top Drug Stores in Omaha, NB

Companies are ranked by share of area volume in 2002.

Walgreens	47.0%
Osco	12.0
Other	41.0

Source: *Chain Drug Review*, October 13, 2003, p. 52.

★ 2875 ★
Drug Stores
SIC: 5912; NAICS: 44611

Top Drug Stores in Philadelphia, PA

Companies are ranked by share of area volume in 2002.

CVS	27.0%
Rite Aid	22.0
Eckerd	18.0
Other	33.0

Source: *MMR*, June 16, 2003, p. 30.

★ 2876 ★
Drug Stores
SIC: 5912; NAICS: 44611

Top Drug Stores in Phoenix/Mesa, AZ

Companies are ranked by share of area volume in 2002.

Walgreens	54.0%
Osco	12.0
Fry's	10.0
Other	24.0

Source: *MMR*, June 16, 2003, p. 30.

★ 2877 ★
Drug Stores
SIC: 5912; NAICS: 44611

Top Drug Stores in Pittsburgh, PA

Companies are ranked by share of area volume in 2002.

Eckerd	36.0%
Rite Aid	16.0
CVS	14.0
Giant Eagle	11.0
Other	23.0

Source: *MMR*, June 16, 2003, p. 30.

★ 2878 ★
Drug Stores
SIC: 5912; NAICS: 44611

Top Drug Stores in Portland OR/ Vancouver, WA

Companies are ranked by share of area volume in 2002.

Walgreens	19.0%
Rite Aid	15.0
Hi-School Pharmacy	14.0
Safeway	13.0
Fred Meyer	11.0
Other	28.0

Source: *Chain Drug Review*, October 13, 2003, p. 52.

★ 2879 ★
Drug Stores
SIC: 5912; NAICS: 44611

Top Drug Stores in Providence/ Warwick/Pawtucket, RI

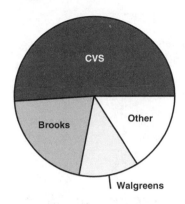

Companies are ranked by share of area volume in 2002.

CVS	51.0%
Brooks	21.0
Walgreens	12.0
Other	16.0

Source: *Chain Drug Review*, October 13, 2003, p. 52.

★ 2880 ★
Drug Stores
SIC: 5912; NAICS: 44611

Top Drug Stores in Richmond/ Petersburg, VA

Companies are ranked by share of area volume in 2002.

CVS	33.0%
Walgreens	20.0
Rite Aid	13.0
Other	34.0

Source: *Chain Drug Review*, October 13, 2003, p. 52.

★ 2881 ★
Drug Stores
SIC: 5912; NAICS: 44611

Top Drug Stores in St. Louis, MO

Companies are ranked by share of area volume in 2002.

Walgreens	59.0%
Schnuck Markets	12.0
Wal-Mart/Sam's	10.0
Other	19.0

Source: *MMR*, June 16, 2003, p. 30.

★ 2882 ★
Drug Stores
SIC: 5912; NAICS: 44611

Top Drug Stores in San Diego, CA

Companies are ranked by share of area volume in 2002.

Osco/Sav-on	24.0%
Longs	22.0
Rite Aid	20.0
Other	34.0

Source: *MMR*, June 16, 2003, p. 30.

★ 2883 ★
Drug Stores
SIC: 5912; NAICS: 44611

Top Drug Stores in San Francisco, CA

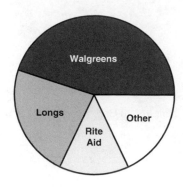

Companies are ranked by share of area volume in 2002.

Walgreens	45.0%
Longs	23.0
Rite Aid	14.0
Other	18.0

Source: *MMR*, June 16, 2003, p. 30.

★ 2884 ★
Drug Stores
SIC: 5912; NAICS: 44611

Top Drug Stores in Seattle/Bellevue/ Everett, WA

Companies are ranked by share of area volume in 2002.

Rite Aid	25.0%
Walgreens	17.0
Bartell	13.0
Safeway	11.0
Longs	10.0
Other	24.0

Source: *MMR*, June 16, 2003, p. 30.

★ 2885 ★
Drug Stores
SIC: 5912; NAICS: 44611

Top Drug Stores in Stockton/Lodi, CA

Companies are ranked by share of area volume in 2002.

Longs 33.0%
Walgreens 21.0
Rite Aid 17.0
Other 29.0

Source: *Chain Drug Review*, October 13, 2003, p. 52.

★ 2886 ★
Drug Stores
SIC: 5912; NAICS: 44611

Top Drug Stores in Syracuse, NY

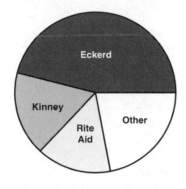

Companies are ranked by share of area volume in 2002.

Eckerd 46.0%
Kinney 17.0
Rite Aid 15.0
Other 22.0

Source: *Chain Drug Review*, October 13, 2003, p. 52.

★ 2887 ★
Drug Stores
SIC: 5912; NAICS: 44611

Top Drug Stores in Tampa Bay, FL

Market shares are shown in percent.

Walgreens 43.0%
Eckerd 27.0
Other 30.0

Source: *St. Petersburg Times*, April 11, 2004, p. 1D.

★ 2888 ★
Drug Stores
SIC: 5912; NAICS: 44611

Top Drug Stores in Toledo, OH

Companies are ranked by share of area volume in 2002.

Rite Aid 30.0%
Seaway Foodtown 12.0
CVS 11.0
Kroger 10.0
Other 37.0

Source: *Chain Drug Review*, October 13, 2003, p. 52.

★ 2889 ★
Drug Stores
SIC: 5912; NAICS: 44611

Top Drug Stores in Tulsa, OK

Companies are ranked by share of area volume in 2002.

May's Drug 24.0%
Walgreens 23.0
Wal-Mart/Sam's 15.0
Med-X 14.0
Other 24.0

Source: *Chain Drug Review*, October 13, 2003, p. 52.

★ 2890 ★
Drug Stores
SIC: 5912; NAICS: 44611

Top Drug Stores in Ventura, CA

Companies are ranked by share of area volume in 2002.

Longs 26.0%
Rite Aid 23.0
Osco/Sav-on 20.0
Other 31.0

Source: *Chain Drug Review*, October 13, 2003, p. 52.

★ 2891 ★
Drug Stores
SIC: 5912; NAICS: 44611

Top Drug Stores in Washington D.C.

Companies are ranked by share of area volume in 2002.

CVS 55.0%
Rite Aid 11.0
Giant Food 10.0
Safeway 9.0
Other 15.0

Source: *MMR*, June 16, 2003, p. 30.

★ 2892 ★
Drug Stores
SIC: 5912; NAICS: 44611

Top Drug Stores in Wilmington/ Newark, DE

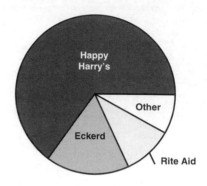

Companies are ranked by share of area volume in 2002.

Happy Harry's 65.0%
Eckerd 17.0
Rite Aid 10.0
Other 8.0

Source: *Chain Drug Review*, October 13, 2003, p. 52.

★ 2893 ★
Drug Stores
SIC: 5912; NAICS: 44611

Top Drug Stores in Youngstown/ Warren, OH

Companies are ranked by share of area volume in 2002.

Rite Aid 31.0%
Marc's 13.0
CVS 12.0
Walgreen's 11.0
Other 33.0

Source: *Chain Drug Review*, October 13, 2003, p. 52.

★ 2894 ★

Pharmacy Benefit Managers

SIC: 5912; NAICS: 44611

Pharmacy Benefit Manager Industry, 2002

Market shares are shown based on number of people covered.

AdvancePCS	16.0%
Merck-Medco	14.0
Express Scripts	11.0
Wellpoint Pharmacy	7.0
Caremark Rx	5.0
Other	47.0

Source: *New York Times*, July 19, 2003, p. B1, from The Health Strategies Consultancy.

★ 2895 ★

Prescription Filling

SIC: 5912; NAICS: 44611

Prescription Drug Channels, 2003

The industry had total sales of $216.4 billion. Sales include prescription products only at wholesale prices.

	($ mil.)	Share
Chain stores	$ 78.6	36.3%
Independents	31.6	14.6
Mail service	28.6	13.2
Non-federal hospitals	22.9	10.6
Clinics	19.5	9.0
Food stores	19.3	8.9
Long-term care	7.8	3.6
Federal facilities	3.4	1.6
Home health care	2.2	1.0
Other	2.4	1.1

Source: *Business Wire*, February 17, 2004, p. NA, from IMS National Sales Perspective.

★ 2896 ★

Prescription Filling

SIC: 5912; NAICS: 44611

Prescription Drug Management

Market shares are shown in percent.

Medco Health Services	19.3%
AdvancePCS	15.3
Caremark	4.6
Other	60.2

Source: *Nashville Business Journal*, October 13, 2003, p. NA, from Credit Suisse.

★ 2897 ★

Prescription Filling

SIC: 5912; NAICS: 44611

Prescription Market in Atlanta, GA

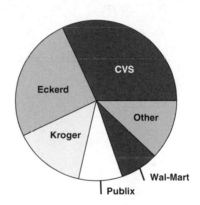

Market shares are shown in percent.

CVS	28.5%
Eckerd	22.9
Kroger	13.0
Publix	7.9
Wal-Mart	7.0
Other	10.7

Source: *Drug Store News*, June 9, 2003, p. 93, from *Chain Store Guide* and the source.

★ 2898 ★
Prescription Filling
SIC: 5912; NAICS: 44611

Prescription Market in Boston, MA

Market shares are shown in percent.

CVS	47.0%
Walgreens	16.2
Brooks	16.0
Stop & Shop	5.4
Other	15.4

Source: *Drug Store News*, June 9, 2003, p. 93, from *Chain Store Guide* and the source.

★ 2899 ★
Prescription Filling
SIC: 5912; NAICS: 44611

Prescription Market in Chicago, IL

Market shares are shown in percent.

Walgreens	51.8%
Jewel, Jewel Osco, Osco Drug	18.8
Dominick's	7.4
Wal-Mart	4.5
Other	17.5

Source: *Drug Store News*, June 9, 2003, p. 93, from *Chain Store Guide* and the source.

★ 2900 ★
Prescription Filling
SIC: 5912; NAICS: 44611

Prescription Market in Detroit, MI

Market shares are shown in percent.

CVS	37.1%
Rite Aid	20.3
Walgreens	13.2
Kroger	5.2
Other	24.2

Source: *Drug Store News*, June 9, 2003, p. 93, from *Chain Store Guide* and the source.

★ 2901 ★
Prescription Filling
SIC: 5912; NAICS: 44611

Prescription Market in Philadelphia, PA

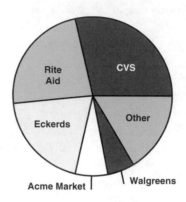

Market shares are shown in percent.

CVS	25.8%
Rite Aid	20.9
Eckerds	18.3
Acme Market	5.7
Walgreens	4.6
Other	15.3

Source: *Drug Store News*, June 9, 2003, p. 93, from *Chain Store Guide* and the source.

★ 2902 ★
Prescription Filling
SIC: 5912; NAICS: 44611

Prescription Market in Washington D.C.

Market shares are shown in percent.

CVS	48.7%
Giant Food	14.9
Rite Aid	11.0
Safeway	8.2
Other	17.2

Source: *Drug Store News*, June 9, 2003, p. 93, from *Chain Store Guide* and the source.

★ 2903 ★
Retailing - Sporting Goods
SIC: 5941; NAICS: 45111

Leading Athletic Apparel Retailers

Firms are ranked by apparel sales in millions of dollars. Industry sources estimate the retail athletic apparel market at $35 billion, according to the source. Shares are shown using that figure.

	($ mil.)	Share
Wal-Mart (athletic only)	$ 1,200	3.43%
Pacific Sunwear	761	2.17
The Sports Authority	386	1.10
Kmart (athletic only)	300	0.86
Dick's Sporting Goods	255	0.73
Kohl's (athletic only)	250	0.71
Champs Sports	245	0.70
Modell's	242	0.69
Academy Sports & Outdoors	240	0.69
Galyan's Trading Co.	227	0.65
Gart Sports	226	0.65
Nike (retail only)	200	0.57
J.C. Penney (athletic only)	200	0.57
Foot Locker	200	0.57
Other	30,068	85.91

Source: *Sporting Goods Business*, June 2003, p. 54.

★ 2904 ★
Retailing - Sporting Goods
SIC: 5941; NAICS: 45111

Leading Hunting/Camping/Fishing Retailers

Companies are ranked by sales in millions of dollars. Wal-Mart has about 10% of the market for camping, hunting and fishing gear sales.

Wal-Mart	$ 3,300
Cabela's	1,100
Bass Pro	880
Gander Mtn.	357
Sports Authority	250
REI	200

Source: *Star Tribune*, March 7, 2004, p. 1D.

★ 2905 ★
Retailing - Sporting Goods
SIC: 5941; NAICS: 45111

Leading Sporting Good Retailers

Firms are ranked by sales in billions of dollars.

Wal-Mart (athletic only)	$ 5.9
Foot Locker	1.8
Kmart (athletic only)	1.7
The Sports Authority	1.4
Bass Pro Shops	1.2
Cabela's	1.2
Dick's Sporting Goods	1.2
Famous Footwear	1.1
Gart Sports	1.1
L.L. Bean	1.1
Nike	1.0

Source: *Sporting Goods Business*, June 2003, p. 54.

★ 2906 ★
Retailing - Sporting Goods
SIC: 5941; NAICS: 45111
Retail Sporting Good Sales

Industry sales reached $370 billion.

Mass merchants	60.0%
Sporting good chains	10.0
Independent sporting goods stores	5.0
Other	25.0

Source: *Indianapolis Business Journal*, January 26, 2004, p. 1, from IBJ research, Dick's Sporting Goods inc., Galyan's Trading Co. Inc., and Sporting Goods Intelligence.

★ 2907 ★
Retailing - Sporting Goods
SIC: 5941; NAICS: 45111
Water Sports Sales in Canada

Retail sales stood at $50 million in 2002.

Sporting goods retail stores	40.0%
Sport specialist stores	36.0
Canadian Tire	13.0
Discount stores	5.0
Other	6.0

Source: "Canadian Water Sports Equipment Industry." [online] from http://www.export.gov [accessed November 1, 2003].

★ 2908 ★
Retailing - Books
SIC: 5942; NAICS: 451211
Children's Book Sales

22% of Americans purchased at least one book for some one under 14 years of age, down from 24% for the same period in 2002. Spending on children's books rose 10% to $840 million, although unit sales fell 6% to 188 million. Shares are for the first six months of each year.

	2002	2003
Book stores	16.3%	19.8%
Dollar stores	15.4	7.9
Mass	14.1	11.7
Other	54.2	60.6

Source: *Publishers Weekly*, September 22, 2003, p. 10, from Ipsos BookTrends.

★ 2909 ★
Retailing - Books
SIC: 5942; NAICS: 451211
Leading Book Chains, 2003

Chains are ranked by sales in millions of dollars.

Barnes & Noble	$ 4,372
Borders	3,731
Books-A-Million	460

Source: *Publishers Weekly*, March 29, 2004, p. 5.

★ 2910 ★
Retailing - Books
SIC: 5942; NAICS: 451211
Leading Book Retailers in the U.K., 2003-2004

Companies are ranked by projected sales in millions of British pounds for the period.

Waterstone's	£ 422.4
W.H. Smith	357.0
Amazon.co.uk	251.0
Borders UK	190.0
Ottakar's	158.0
BCA	125.0
Blackwell UK	88.0
The Book People	85.0

Continued on next page.

★ 2910 ★
[Continued]
Retailing - Books
SIC: 5942; NAICS: 451211

Leading Book Retailers in the U.K., 2003-2004

Companies are ranked by projected sales in millions of British pounds for the period.

British Bookshop	£ 39.0
David Flatman	25.0

Source: *The Bookseller*, December 19, 2003, p. 9.

★ 2911 ★
Retailing - Books
SIC: 5942; NAICS: 451211

Leading Book Store Chains in Norway

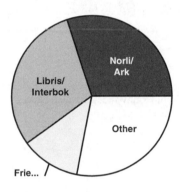

Market shares are shown in percent. Frie Bokhandlere is an association of independent book-stores.

Norli/Ark	30.0%
Libris/Interbok	30.0
Frie Bokhandlere	12.0
Other	28.0

Source: *Dagens Naeringsliv*, October 7, 2002, p. 8, from Bokhandlerforeningen.

★ 2912 ★
Retailing - Books
SIC: 5942; NAICS: 451211

Online Book Purchases in Australia

Data show the top two sites visited by Australians.

Amazon.com	52.20%
Amazon.co.uk	9.85
Other	37.95

Source: *B&T Weekly*, June 30, 2003, p. NA.

★ 2913 ★
Retailing - Books
SIC: 5942; NAICS: 451211

Top Book Store Chains

Market shares are shown in percent.

	1992	2002
Walden Books	9.5%	4.8%
B. Dalton	4.8	1.0
Barnes & Noble	1.9	9.4
Borders	1.0	4.5
Other	82.8	80.3

Source: *Detroit Free Press*, June 14, 2003, p. NA.

★ 2914 ★
Retailing - Cards
SIC: 5943; NAICS: 45321

Religious Card Sales

The size of the Christian retail industry is estimated at $3.75 billion.

Card/specialty stores	26.0%
Drug stores	19.0
Discount stores	18.0
Christian bookstores	15.0
Food stores	13.0
Other	9.0

Source: "Religious/Inspirational Card Market Overview." from http://pressroom.hallmark.com/ christian_products_overview.html [accessed April 27, 2004].

★ 2915 ★

Jewelry Stores

SIC: 5944; NAICS: 44831

Leading Jewelry/Watch Retailers, 2002

Companies and ranked by estimated watch and jewelry sales in billions of dollars.

Wal-Mart	$ 2,400.0
Zale Corp.	2,192.0
Sterling Jewelers	1,735.0
J.C. Penney Co.	1,000.0
QVC	1,000.0
Sears, Roebuck & Co.	1,000.0
Finlay Fine Jewelry Corp.	930.7
Tiffany & Co.	819.4
Helzberg Diamonds	550.0
Fred Meyer Jewelers	475.0
Target Stores	450.0
Friedman's	436.0

Source: *National Jeweler*, June 1, 2003, p. S3.

★ 2916 ★

Jewelry Stores

SIC: 5944; NAICS: 44831

Retail Jewelry Sales

Market shares are shown in percent.

	($ bil.)	Share
Jewelry stores	$ 21.7	49.43%
Apparel	7.0	15.95
Department stores	4.0	9.11
Non-store	3.8	8.66
Discounters/mass	3.0	6.83
Other general merchandise	2.9	6.61
Other	1.5	3.42

Source: *New York Diamonds*, July 2003, p. 40, from Unity Marketing and U.S. Census Bureau.

★ 2917 ★

Retailing - Hobbies

SIC: 5945; NAICS: 45112

Retail Hobby Sales

The percentage of households participating in crafts & hobbies increased from 2000 to 2001, increasing from 54% to 58%. The total industry increased from $23 billion to $25.7 billion for the same period.

Craft chains	24.0%
Discount stores	24.0
Other	52.0

Source: *Knight Ridder/Tribune Business News*, June 10, 2003, p. NA, from Hobby Industry Association.

★ 2918 ★

Retailing - Toys

SIC: 5945; NAICS: 45112

Collectible Card Game Sales

The market was estimated at $750 million in 2003, with a possible error of $150 in either direction. The Yu Gi Oh phenomenon is a significant part of this sector, although the size has proven hard to measure (Yu Gi Oh did not start shipping until March 2002).

	($ mil.)	Share
Mass merchants	$ 450	60.00%
Hobby stores	250	33.33
Specialty chains	50	6.67

Source: ''Game Market Up Dramatically in 2002.'' [online] from http://www.hubhobbyshop.com/press94.htm [Press release, undated].

★ 2919 ★
Retailing - Toys
SIC: 5945; NAICS: 45112
Retail Toy Industry

The toy and game market is worth $30 billion a year.

Discount stores	42.0%
Toy stores	21.0
Mail order	5.0
Hobby stores	4.0
Department stores	4.0
Food/drug	3.0
Variety	2.0
Internet	2.0
Card/gift stores	2.0
Other	15.0

Source: *Retail Merchandiser*, March 2004, p. 15.

★ 2920 ★
Retailing - Toys
SIC; 5945; NAICS: 45112
Retail Toy Industry in Europe, 2002

The table shows market distribution with and without the video game segment. With video games, the market was valued at 17.31 billion euros. Without this segment, the total market falls to 12.7 billion euros.

	With Video	Without
Toy specialists	30.5%	36.2%
Hyper/supermarkets . . .	22.2	22.5
General merchandise . . .	14.4	12.8
Department stores . . .	7.0	7.7
Mail order	6.3	5.3
Other	19.6	15.5

Source: *Toy Industries of Europe*, July 2003, p. NA, from NPD Group Worldwide.

★ 2921 ★
Retailing - Toys
SIC: 5945; NAICS: 45112
Top Toy Retailers, 2003

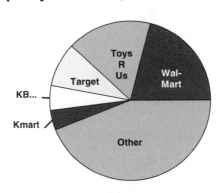

Market shares are shown in percent.

Wal-Mart	21.0%
Toys R Us	17.0
Target	9.0
KB Toys	5.0
Kmart	4.0
Other	44.0

Source: *Time*, December 8, 2003, p. 54, from NPD Group Inc. and Harris Nesbitt Gerard.

★ 2922 ★
Retailing - Video Games
SIC: 5945; NAICS: 45112
Electronic Game Sales in France, 2001

Video games represented 28.1% ($1.52 billion) of the $3.85 billion industry. The market is forecasteed to grow in the coming years.

Hypermarkets	43.8%
Specialized retailers	32.1
Mail-order companies	4.4
Department stores	2.6
Bazars, discount stores	2.1
Book stores, gift shops	0.9
Other	14.1

Source: "Electronic Games Market." [online] from http://www.usatrade.gov [accessed January 5, 2004], from U.S. Commercial Service.

★ 2923 ★
Retailing - Cameras
SIC: 5946; NAICS: 44313
Digital Camera Sales, 2002

Market shares are estimated.

Best Buy	14.3%
Wal-Mart	12.5
Internet	10.6
Circuit City	8.7
Camera/photo stores	5.0
Staples	4.5
Computer stores	4.2
Mail order	4.0
Sears	3.5
Office Max	3.5
CompUSA	3.5
Other	25.7

Source: *Dealerscope*, August 2003, p. 32, from *Dealerscope 81st Annual Statistical Survey and Report.*

★ 2924 ★
Embroidery Shops
SIC: 5949; NAICS: 45113
Embroidery Industry

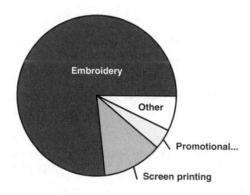

The 25,000 embroidery shops in the country repre-sent a $9.1 billion market. The size of the market reflects the changing industry, which includes screen printing, promotional products, sublimation and oth-er services. The average embroidery shop generates $363,000 in sales.

Embroidery	75.9%
Screen printing	12.0
Promotional products	4.0
Other	7.2

Source: *Embroidery Monogram Business*, May 1, 2004, p. NA.

★ 2925 ★
Catalogs
SIC: 5961; NAICS: 45411
Leading Catalog Firms

Firms are ranked by sales in millions of dolalrs.

Dell Computer Corp.	$ 35,404.0
IBM	6,820.8
W.W. Grainger	4,643.9
Corporate Express North America	4,630.2
CDW Corp.	4,264.6
Office Depot	3,913.9
Staples	3,389.6
Fisher Scientific International	3,238.0
Henry Schein	2,825.0
Boise Office Solutions	2,760.0

Source: *Catalog Age*, August 1, 2003, p. 9.

★ 2926 ★
Home Shopping
SIC: 5961; NAICS: 45411
Leading Home Shopping Firms in South Korea, 2002

The industry began in Korea in 1996. It saw roughly 60% annual growth from 2000 to 2002. By 2003, the industry saw $3.5 billion in sales. Firms are ranked by billions of Korean Won.

LG	1,805
CJ	1,427
Hyundai	408
Woori	305
Nongsusan	265

Source: "Korea's Television Homeshopping Industry." [online] from http://www.usatrade.gov [accessed February 1, 2004], from *Electronic Times*.

★ 2927 ★
Vending Machines
SIC: 5962; NAICS: 45421

Vending Industry in the U.K., 2002

Market research firm Key Note estimates that sales of vended products at 3.10 billion pounds sterling in 2002. Mars bar was the best-selling chocolate brand, and Fruit Pastilles was the best-selling sweet brand.

Automatic traditional drink vendors	40.0%
In-cup	30.0
Snack/food	15.0
Can vendor	15.0

Source: *just-food.com (Management Briefing)*, February 2004, p. 19, from Vending International.

★ 2928 ★
Vending Machines
SIC: 5962; NAICS: 45421

Vending Machine Installations, 2002

Total industry sales were $23.1 billion.

Manufacturing, fabrication or warehouse facilities	33.9%
Offices	22.4
Schools, colleges, universities	8.2
Hotels/motels	5.4
Hospitals, nursing homes	5.2
Restaurants, bars, clubs	4.9
Military bases	2.0
Correctional facilities	0.7
Other	7.6

Source: *Automatic Merchandiser*, August 2003, p. 31, from *2003 Automatic Merchandiser State of the Vending Industry Report*.

★ 2929 ★
Vending Machines
SIC: 5962; NAICS: 45421

Vending Machine Sales

Estimated sales have fallen from $25.6 billion in 2000 to $23.1 billion in 2002. Manufacturers announced price hikes at the end of 2002, with candy seeing the highest increase. The fall in sales is in part from changes in vending machines in public schools. Over concern for children's health, school officials are shifting from soft drinks and candy to healthier foods.

	2000	2002	Share
Manual foodservice . .	$ 5,430.0	$ 6,430.0	27.84%
Cold beverages	7,408.0	6,380.0	27.62
Candy/snacks/ confections	6,560.0	5,320.0	23.03
Vending food	1,490.0	1,500.0	6.49
Hot beverages	1,490.0	1,180.0	5.11
OCS (coffee)	1,080.0	924.9	4.00
Ice cream	281.8	254.3	1.10
Milk	461.2	208.1	0.90
Cigarettes	230.6	138.7	0.60
Other	819.8	763.0	3.30

Source: *Automatic Merchandiser*, August 2003, p. 31, from *Automatic Merchandiser State of the Industry Report*.

★ 2930 ★
Vending Machines
SIC: 5962; NAICS: 45421

Vending Machine Sales in Canada

Total sales were $1 billion. In the all purpose food segment, sandwiches had nearly half of sales, followed by juice and then salads.

	($ mil.)	Share
Beverages	$ 670	67.0%
Confections & snacks	210	21.0
All purpose food	70	7.0
Ice cream	20	2.0
Other	30	3.0

Source: "Vending Machine Food Distribution in Canada." [online] from http://www.usda.gov [accessed November 1, 2003], from *Canadian Vending & Office Coffee Service* magazine.

★ 2931 ★

Retailing - Propane

SIC: 5984; NAICS: 454312

Largest Propane Gas Retailers

Companies are ranked by millions of gallons sold for the fiscal year.

AmeriGas Partners	1,074.88
Ferrellgas Partners	898.60
Suburban Propane Partners	597.95
Cenex Propane Partners	590.08
Heritage Propane Partners	375.90
CornerStone Propane	246.00
Star Gas Propane	166.00
Inergy	150.17
MFA Oil	100.20
Southern States Cooperative	73.45
Blossman Gas	73.00
Dowdle Butane Gas	70.90

Source: *LP/Gas*, February 2004, p. 19.

★ 2932 ★

Retailing - Flowers

SIC: 5992; NAICS: 45311

Retail Flower Market in Greater Des Moines

Market share is estimated. The company listed has 5 freestanding stores and 8 through other locations.

Boesen	50.0%
Other	50.0

Source: *Business Record (Des Moines)*, August 18, 2003, p. 32.

★ 2933 ★

Tobacco Retailing

SIC: 5993; NAICS: 453991

Largest Tobacco Retailers

Companies are ranked by number of stores. Shares are shown based on a total for the top 40 establishments.

	Outlets	Share
Cigarettes Cheaper	428	21.07%
Smoker Friendly International	265	13.05

	Outlets	Share
Admiral Discount Tobacco	120	5.91%
Tobacco Central Inc.	119	5.86
Smokes For Less	89	4.38
Tobacco Superstore	80	3.94
Choice Tobacco Outlet	67	3.30
The Cigarette Outlets	48	2.36
Tobacco Outlet Plus	47	2.31
Discount Smoke Shop	45	2.22
Other	723	35.60

Source: *Tobaco Outlet Business*, May/June 2003, p. NA.

★ 2934 ★

Retailing - Magazines

SIC: 5994; NAICS: 451212

Magazine Sales in the U.K.

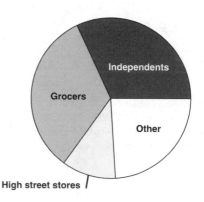

Magazine sales are on the rise, according to the source. Some have questioned if supermarkets' share of sales may go as high as 45%.

	1997	2001
Independents	45.0%	32.0%
Grocers	19.0	33.0
High street stores	15.0	11.0
Other	21.0	24.0

Source: *Marketing Week*, October 9, 2003, p. 17, from Periodical Publishers Association.

★ 2935 ★
Optical Good Stores
SIC: 5995; NAICS: 44613

Leading Optical Departments in Mass Merchants, 2002

Firms are ranked by domestic net sales in millions of dollars.

Wal-Mart	$ 1,032.5
Costco Wholeslae	240.8
ShopKo Stores	75.0
Sam's Club	71.5
Target/Super Target	38.3
BJ's Wholesale	36.1

Source: *Vision Monday*, May 12, 2003, p. NA, from Jobson Optical Research.

★ 2936 ★
Optical Good Stores
SIC: 5995; NAICS: 44613

Leading Optical Retailers, 2002

Firms are ranked by domestic net sales in millions of dollars. Shares are shown based on net sales of the top 50 retail lenses.

	($ mil.)	Share
LensCrafters	$ 1,352.0	23.11%
Cole Vision	1,135.0	19.40
Wal-Mart Stores	884.5	15.12
Eye Care Centers of America	363.7	6.22
National Vision	241.8	4.13
Costco Wholesale	240.8	4.12
U.S. Vision	145.0	2.48
Consolidated Vision Group	120.0	2.05
D.O.C. Optics	110.3	1.89
Emerging Vision	104.5	1.79
Empire Vision CentersDavis Vision	82.8	1.42
EyeMart Express	80.0	1.37
Cohen's Fashion Optical	80.0	1.37
Other	909.3	15.54

Source: *Vision Monday*, May 12, 2003, p. NA, from Jobson Optical Research.

★ 2937 ★
Optical Good Stores
SIC: 5995; NAICS: 44613

Optical Retail Channels, 2003

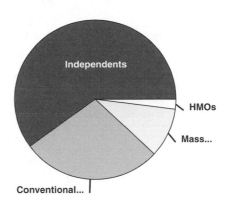

Market shares are shown in percent.

	2002	2003
Independents	60.4%	59.9%
Conventional optical chains	28.1	27.7
Mass merchants	9.3	10.0
HMOs	2.3	2.4

Source: *Vision Monday*, March 10, 2004, p. NA, from Jobson Optical Research.

★ 2938 ★
Retailing - Personal Care Products
SIC: 5999; NAICS: 446199

Healthy & Beauty Care Retailing in the U.K., 2002

Market shares are shown in percent.

Boots	26.2%
Tesco	14.3
Asda	7.6
Superdrug	7.0
J. Sainsbury	7.0
Safeway	4.8
Other	33.1

Source: *Financial Times*, March 28, 2003, p. 24, from Verdict Research and Thomson Datastream.

★ 2939 ★
Retailing - Personal Care Products
SIC: 5999; NAICS: 446199

Leading Hair Care Retailers in the U.K.

Market shares are shown for the year ended May 25, 2003.

Boots	21.6%
Tesco	18.9
Superdrug	12.4
Sainsbury	10.3
Asda	8.8
Safeway	5.7
Wilkinsons	4.4
Morrisons	3.9
Somerfield	1.2
All co-ops	0.9
Other	11.9

Source: *Grocer*, August 9, 2003, p. 31, from TNS Superpanel.

★ 2940 ★
Retailing - Personal Care Products
SIC: 5999; NAICS: 44612

Prestige Skin Care Market in Canada

Market shares are shown in percent.

	Face	Hand/body	Sun
Department stores	69.2%	49.7%	42.8%
Drug stores	20.0	36.7	46.1
Clothing stores	3.4	3.9	5.5
Cosmetic/beauty care stores	1.8	5.9	3.1
Other	5.6	3.8	2.5

Source: *Cosmetics Magazine Newsletter*, October 8, 2003, p. NA, from Trendex North America.

★ 2941 ★
Retailing - Personal Care Products
SIC: 5999; NAICS: 446199

Retail Antacid Sales, 2003

Market shares are shown based on sales at supermarkets, drugstores and mass merchandisers for the year ended May 18, 2003. Figures exclude Wal-Mart.

	($ mil.)	Share
Drug	$ 332.5	45.71%
Food	315.9	43.43
Mass	79.0	10.86

Source: *Grocery Headquarters*, August 2003, p. S14, from Information Resources Inc.

★ 2942 ★
Retailing - Personal Care Products
SIC: 5999; NAICS: 45211, 44611

Retail Cold/Allergy/Sinus Market, 2003

Market shares are shown based on sales at supermarkets, drugstores and mass merchandisers for the year ended May 18, 2003. Figures exclude Wal-Mart.

	($ mil.)	Share
Drug	$ 721.8	49.53%
Food	606.8	41.64
Mass	128.8	8.84

Source: *Grocery Headquarters*, August 2003, p. S14, from Information Resources Inc.

★ 2943 ★
Retailing - Personal Care Products
SIC: 5999; NAICS: 44612, 446199

Retail Cosmaceuticals Market

Cosmaceuticals are products especially formulated to enhance both health and beauty — moisturizers that protect from the sun and smooth wrinkles as well. Alternative includes Avon, health food stores, salons and mail order.

Drug stores/discount stores/supermarkets	59.0%
Alternative	24.0
Other	17.0

Source: *Global Cosmetic Industry*, May 2003, p. 69, from Packaged Facts.

★ 2944 ★
Retailing - Personal Care Products
SIC: 5999; NAICS: 45211, 44611

Retail Deodorant Market, 2003

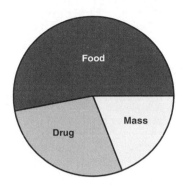

Market shares are shown based on sales at super-markets, drugstores and mass merchandisers for the year ended May 18, 2003. Figures exclude Wal-Mart.

	($ mil.)	Share
Food	$ 607.2	52.60%
Drug	325.2	28.17
Mass	221.9	19.22

Source: *Grocery Headquarters*, August 2003, p. S14, from Information Resources Inc.

★ 2945 ★
Retailing - Personal Care Products
SIC: 5999; NAICS: 45211, 44611

Retail Face Makeup Sales, 2003

Market shares are shown based on sales at super-markets, drug stores and mass merchandisers for the year ended May 18, 2003. Figures exclude Wal-Mart.

	($ mil.)	Share
Mass	$ 916.6	61.3%
Drug	447.0	29.9
Food	131.6	8.8

Source: *Grocery Headquarters*, August 2003, p. S14, from Information Resources Inc.

★ 2946 ★
Retailing - Personal Care Products
SIC: 5999; NAICS: 45211, 44611

Retail Toothpaste Market, 2003

Market shares are shown based on sales at super-markets, drug stores and mass merchandisers for the year ended May 18, 2003. Figures exclude Wal-Mart.

	($ mil.)	Share
Food	$ 738.8	59.71%
Drug	288.3	23.30
Mass	210.2	16.99

Source: *Grocery Headquarters*, August 2003, p. S14, from Information Resources Inc.

★ 2947 ★
Retailing - Personal Care Products
SIC: 5999; NAICS: 44612

Women's Prestige Fragrance Market in Canada

Market shares are shown in percent.

	2000	2002
Department stores	62.5%	58.0%
Drugstores	15.2	19.0
Cosmetic/beauty care stores	4.1	6.0
Clothing stores	0.4	2.0
Other	17.8	13.0

Source: *Cosmetics Magazine Newsletter*, August 6, 2003, p. NA, from Trendex North America.

★ 2948 ★
Retailing - Religious Products
SIC: 5999; NAICS: 453998

Christian Retail Market, 2003

The Christian market generates over $4 billion in sales annually.

Books/bibles	21.0%
Gift items	19.0
Music	15.0
Other	45.0

Source: *Research Alert*, March 5, 2004, p. 2, from EPM's *Guide to the Christian Marketplace*.

★ 2949 ★
Retailing - Religious Products
SIC: 5999; NAICS: 45299

Christian Retailing Industry

The Christian retailing industry grew from $1 billion in 1980 to $4.2 billion in 2004. Figures are in millions of dollars.

Christian retailers . . . . $ 2,400
Mainstream retailers 1,100
Direct-to-consumer/ministry sales channels . 725

Source: *DSN Retailing Today*, April 19, 2004, p. 4.

★ 2950 ★
Retailing - Supplements
SIC: 5999; NAICS: 446199

Dietary Supplement Market in New Zealand

There are roughly 300 companies involved in making dietary supplements, vitamins, natural products and other supplements. Total sales were $322 million.

	Sales	Share
Grocery/supermarkets	$ 76,000	34.0%
Health food stores	45,000	20.0
Pharmacy	41,000	18.0
Direct selling	30,000	14.0
Direct marketing	20,000	9.0
Internet	5,000	2.0
Practitioners	5,000	2.0

Source: "Complementary Medicines, Vitamins & Food Supplements." [online] from http://www.usatrade.gov [accessed February 1, 2004], from New Zealand Direct Sellers Association.

★ 2951 ★
Retailing - Swimming Pools
SIC: 5999; NAICS: 453998

Largest Builder/Pool Retailers

Paddock Pool Construction Co.

Shasta Industries

Aqua Quip

Patio Pools & Spas

Anthony & Sylvan

Barrington Pools

Pulliam Pools

Vaughan Pools

Sonco Pools & Spas

J. Tortorella Swimming Pools

Other

The top 10 built more than 9,000 pools in 2002. Companies are ranked by retail revenues in millions of dollars. Shares are shown based on total industry revenues of $446.2 million.

	($ mil.)	Share
Paddock Pool Construction Co.	$ 35.0	7.87%
Shasta Industries	18.0	4.05
Aqua Quip	7.5	1.69
Patio Pools & Spas	6.3	1.42
Anthony & Sylvan	5.2	1.17
Barrington Pools	3.8	0.85
Pulliam Pools	3.5	0.79
Vaughan Pools	3.4	0.76
Sonco Pools & Spas	3.0	0.67
J. Tortorella Swimming Pools	3.0	0.67
Other	355.9	80.05

Source: *Pool & Spa News*, September 5, 2003, p. 70.

SIC 60 - Depository Institutions

★ 2952 ★

Banking

SIC: 6021; NAICS: 52211

Largest Banks Worldwide, 2002

Banks are ranked by assets in billions of dollars as of December 31, 2002.

Mizuho Holdings	$ 1,135.6
Citigroup	1,097.2
Sumitomo Mitsui Financial Group	873.0
UBS	852.2
Allianz	850.4
Deutsche Bank	791.7
J.P. Morgan Chase	758.8
HSBC Holdings	757.4
ING Group	751.7
BNBP Paribas	744.6

Source: *New York Times*, March 23, 2004, p. C4, from *American Banker*.

★ 2953 ★

Banking

SIC: 6021; NAICS: 52211

Top Banks, 2003

Banks are ranked by deposits in billions of dollars as of October 27, 2003.

Bank of America/FleetBoston Financial	$ 541.03
Citigroup	454.24
J.P. Morgan Chase	313.63
Wells Fargo	253.48
Wachovia	203.50
Bank One	163.41
U.S. Bancorp	115.04
HSBC North America	80.88
SunTrust Banks	80.47
National City	70.28

Source: *Wall Street Journal*, November 4, 2003, p. C1, from SNL Financial.

★ 2954 ★

Banking

SIC: 6021; NAICS: 52211

Top Banks by Assets, 2003

Banks are ranked by assets in billions of dollars.

Citigroup	$ 1,208.9
Bank of America	933.5
J.P. Morgan Chase	792.7
Wells Fargo	393.9
Wachovia	388.8
Bank One	290.0
U.S. Bancorp.	188.8
ABN Amro	149.0
SunTrust Banks	126.7
HSBC	121.2

Source: *Wall Street Journal*, October 28, 2003, p. A1, from SNL Financial and companies.

★ 2955 ★

Banking

SIC: 6021; NAICS: 52211

Top Banks by Deposits, 2003

Banks are ranked by deposits in billions of dollars as of June 30, 2003. Bank of America and FleetBoston recently announed plans to merge.

Citigroup	$ 447.9
Bank of America	421.9
J.P. Morgan Chase	318.2
Wells Fargo	230.9
Wachovia	203.8
Bank One	172.0
FleetBoston	130.2
U.S. Bancorp	126.3
Washington Mutual	114.3
SunTrust Banks	77.3

Source: *New York Times*, October 28, 2003, p. C4.

★ 2956 ★
Banking
SIC: 6021; NAICS: 52211

Top Banks in Africa

Standard Bank Group
ABSA Group
Nedcor Group
First Rand Banking Group
Investec Group
Union Bank of Nigeria
Mauritius Commercial Bank
NMBZ Holdings
African Bank
State Bank of Mauritius

Banks are ranked by capital in millions of dollars.

Standard Bank Group	$ 2,971
ABSA Group	1,715
Nedcor Group	1,680
First Rand Banking Group	1,250
Investec Group	790
Union Bank of Nigeria	249
Mauritius Commercial Bank	220
NMBZ Holdings	215
African Bank	195
State Bank of Mauritius	164

Source: *African Business*, October 2003, p. 24.

★ 2957 ★
Banking
SIC: 6021; NAICS: 52211

Top Banks in Alabama, 2003

Market shares are shown based on deposits as of June 30, 2003.

Regions Bank	16.45%
SouthTrust Bank	15.49
AmSouth Bank	12.82
Compass Bank	8.55
Colonial Bank	5.66
First Commercial Bank	1.81
New South FSB	1.58
National Bank Com. Birmingham	1.35

The Bank	1.14%
First American Bank	1.14
Other	34.01

Source: ''Market Share Report.'' [online] available from http://www.fdic.gov [accessed December 18, 2003], from Federal Deposit Insurance Corp.

★ 2958 ★
Banking
SIC: 6021; NAICS: 52211

Top Banks in Alaska, 2003

Market shares are shown based on deposits as of June 30, 2003.

Wells Fargo Bank Alaska	45.09%
First National Bank Alaska	23.17
Northrim Bank	11.14
Keybank National Association	7.07
First Bank	4.70
Mt. Mckinley Bank	2.85
Denali State Bank	2.80
Alaska Pacific Bank	2.29
Alaska First B&T	0.90

Source: ''Market Share Report.'' [online] available from http://www.fdic.gov [accessed December 18, 2003], from Federal Deposit Insurance Corp.

★ 2959 ★
Banking
SIC: 6021; NAICS: 52211

Top Banks in Arizona, 2003

Market shares are shown based on deposits as of June 30, 2003.

Bank One National Association	27.86%
Bank of America	20.30
Wells Fargo Bank Arizona	19.82
National Bank of Arizona	4.65
World Savings Bank	3.54
Compass Bank	3.18
M&I Marshall & Illsley Bank	2.64
Northern Trust Bank	1.34
Washington FS&LA	1.32

Source: ''Market Share Report.'' [online] available from http://www.fdic.gov [accessed December 18, 2003], from Federal Deposit Insurance Corp.

★ 2960 ★

Banking

SIC: 6021; NAICS: 52211

Top Banks in Arkansas, 2003

Market shares are shown based on deposits as of June 30, 2003.

Regions Bank	10.78%
Arvest Bank	6.19
Bank of America	5.77
Bancorpsouth Bank	4.47
U.S. Bank National Assn.	2.64
Bank of the Ozarks	2.52
Superior Bank FSB	2.42
Simmons First National Bank	2.12
First Security Bank	1.85
Metropolitan National Bank	1.79
Other	59.45

Source: "Market Share Report." [online] available from http://www.fdic.gov [accessed December 18, 2003], from Federal Deposit Insurance Corp.

★ 2961 ★

Banking

SIC: 6021; NAICS: 52211

Top Banks in Australia, 2004

Shares are calculated based on the number of large commercial customers each bank serves. Large commercial customers are defined as those with an annual turnover of between $20 million and $100 million. Data are for February 2004.

Commonwealth Bank	22.3%
National Australia Bank	17.8
St. George Bank	5.8
Other	54.1

Source: *Sydney Morning Herald*, March 25, 2020, p. NA.

★ 2962 ★

Banking

SIC: 6021; NAICS: 52211

Top Banks in Brazil

Banks are ranked by assets under management in millions of reais.

BB	63,115
Bradesco	62,297
Itau	61,235

Citibank	34,503
BankBoston	26,618
HSBC Investment Bank	22,187
CEF	21,980
Unibanco	21,350
Santander Brasil	20,000
ABN Amro Real	14,652

Source: *The Banker*, April 2003, p. 164.

★ 2963 ★

Banking

SIC: 6021; NAICS: 52211

Top Banks in Brevard County, FL

Market shares are as of March 31, 2002.

Wachovia	24.92%
Bank of America	18.57
SunTrust	16.12
Washington Mutual	8.31
Riverside	6.51
Harbor Federal	3.77
Republic	3.62
InterBank	2.79
Fidelity	2.78
Other	12.61

Source: *Florida Today*, September 4, 2003, p. 1, from Florida Bankers Association.

★ 2964 ★

Banking

SIC: 6021; NAICS: 52211

Top Banks in California, 2003

Market shares are shown based on deposits as of June 30, 2003.

Bank of America	21.63%
Wells Fargo Bank	15.75
Washington Mutual Bank FA	12.84
Union Bank of California	5.44
Citibank	4.26
World Savings Bank	4.22
Comerica Bank	3.31
Bank of the West	2.66

Continued on next page.

★ 2964 ★

[Continued]
Banking
SIC: 6021; NAICS: 52211

Top Banks in California, 2003

Market shares are shown based on deposits as of June 30, 2003.

U.S. Bank National	1.82%
Other	28.07

Source: "Market Share Report." [online] available from http://www.fdic.gov [accessed December 18, 2003], from Federal Deposit Insurance Corp.

★ 2965 ★

Banking
SIC: 6021; NAICS: 52211

Top Banks in Charleston, SC

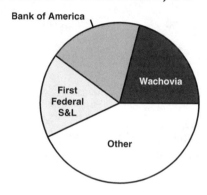

Market shares are shown based on deposits in June 30, 2003.

Wachovia	21.0%
Bank of America	18.6
First Federal S&L	17.0
Other	43.4

Source: *The Post and Courier*, January 15, 2003, p. B9, from Federal Deposit Insurance Corp.

★ 2966 ★

Banking
SIC: 6021; NAICS: 52211

Top Banks in Charlotte, NC

Market shares for the Charlotte area are shown based on deposits as of June 30, 2003.

Wachovia	21.0%
BofA	18.6
First Federal	17.0
Other	43.4

Source: *The Post and Courier*, November 15, 2003, p. B9, from Federal Deposit Insurance Corp.

★ 2967 ★

Banking
SIC: 6021; NAICS: 52211

Top Banks in Chicago, IL

Market shares are shown based on deposits as of June 30, 2003.

Bank One Corp.	19.52%
LaSalle Bank Corporation	13.83
EMO Financial Group	8.62
Citigroup Inc.	4.50
Northern Trust Corp.	4.23
Charter One Financial	3.54
HSBC Holdings	3.02
Fifth Third Bancorp	2.81
MAF Bancorp Inc.	2.43
Other	37.50

Source: *US Banker*, July 2003, p. 12, from Federal Deposit Insurance Corporation.

★ 2968 ★
Banking
SIC: 6021; NAICS: 52211

Top Banks in China

Shares are shown based on total assets.

Industrial and Commercial Bank of China	26.0%
China Construction Bank	16.0
Agriculture Bank of China	14.0
Bank of China	14.0
Rural credit and co-ops	12.0
Other	18.0

Source: *Financial Times*, December 19, 2003, p. 15, from CLSA Emerging Markets and Bloomberg.

★ 2969 ★
Banking
SIC: 6021; NAICS: 52211

Top Banks in Cleveland, OH

Market shares are shown based on deposits as of June 30, 2002.

Third Federal Savings & Loan Assn.	38.4%
Ohio Savings Bank	16.0
Dollar Bank	13.2
First Federal Savings & Loan Assoc.	7.1
Park View Federal Savings Bank	3.8
DeepGreen Bank	3.0
Northern Savings & Loan Co.	2.1
First Federal S&L Assn. of Lorain	1.9
North Akron Savings Bank	0.9
Century Bank	0.9
Other	19.7

Source: *Crain's Cleveland Business*, December 29, 2003, p. NA.

★ 2970 ★
Banking
SIC: 6021; NAICS: 52211

Top Banks in Colorado, 2003

Market shares are shown based on deposits as of June 30, 2003.

Wells Fargo Bank West	17.75%
U.S. Bank National Assn.	10.56
World Savings Bank	7.30
Bank One National Assn.	4.95
Commercial Fed Bank	3.33
Vectra Bank Colorado	3.05
Community First	2.02
First Trust Corp.	1.92
First National Bank	1.71
Other	47.41

Source: "Market Share Report." [online] available from http://www.fdic.gov [accessed December 18, 2003], from Federal Deposit Insurance Corp.

★ 2971 ★
Banking
SIC: 6021; NAICS: 52211

Top Banks in Connecticut, 2003

Market shares are shown based on deposits as of June 30, 2003.

Fleet National Bank	23.45%
Peoples Bank	12.69
Webster Bank	11.49
Wachovia Bank National Assn.	7.67
Citizens Bank of Connecticut	3.77
Banknorth National Assn.	3.65
JPMorgan Chase Bank	3.10
New Haven Savings Bank	2.66

Continued on next page.

★ 2971 ★
[Continued]
Banking
SIC: 6021; NAICS: 52211

Top Banks in Connecticut, 2003

Market shares are shown based on deposits as of June 30, 2003.

Liberty Bank	2.54%
Other	28.98

Source: "Market Share Report." [online] available from http://www.fdic.gov [accessed December 18, 2003], from Federal Deposit Insurance Corp.

★ 2972 ★
Banking
SIC: 6021; NAICS: 52211

Top Banks in Croatia

Banks are ranked by assets in millions of kuna.

Zagrebacka Banka	5,717
Privredna Banka Zagreb	3,767
Rijecka Banka	1,266
Raiffeisen Bank Croatia	1,176
Splitska Bank	1,169
Hypo Alpe-Adria-Bank	758
Dalmatinska Bank	630
Erste Et Steiermarkische Bank	588
HVB Bank Croatia	356

Source: *The Banker*, March 2003, p. 4, from *The Banker* research.

★ 2973 ★
Banking
SIC: 6021; NAICS: 52211

Top Banks in Delaware, 2003

Market shares are shown based on deposits as of June 30, 2003.

MBNA America Bank	33.33%
Discover Bank	14.10
ING Bank	13.54
Lehman Brothers Bank	7.99
Chase Manhattan Bank	6.85
Wilmington Trust Co.	6.63
Bank One Delaware	2.73

PNC Bank Delaware	2.06%
Citibank Delaware	1.78
Other	10.99

Source: "Market Share Report." [online] available from http://www.fdic.gov [accessed December 18, 2003], from Federal Deposit Insurance Corp.

★ 2974 ★
Banking
SIC: 6021; NAICS: 52211

Top Banks in Detroit, MI

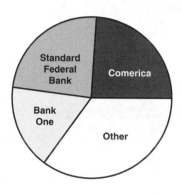

Market shares are for the five country Detroit metro area as of June 30, 2003.

Comerica	24.3%
Standard Federal Bank	23.7
Bank One	16.8
Other	35.2

Source: *Crain's Detroit Business*, January 19, 2004, p. 1.

★ 2975 ★
Banking
SIC: 6021; NAICS: 52211

Top Banks in Europe, 2003

Banks are ranked by assets in millions of dollars.

UBS	$ 851,686
Deutsche Bank	795,255
HSBC Holdings	759,246
BNP Paribas	744,882
HypoVereinsbank	724,787

Continued on next page.

★ 2975 ★
[Continued]
Banking
SIC: 6021; NAICS: 52211

Top Banks in Europe, 2003

Banks are ranked by assets in millions of dollars.

Credit Suisse Group	$ 689,109
Royal Bank of Scotland	649,402
Barclays Bank	637,946
Credit Agricole Groupe	609,055
ABN AMRO Bank	583,073

Source: *The Banker*, September 2003, p. 136.

★ 2976 ★
Banking
SIC: 6021; NAICS: 52211

Top Banks in Florida, 2003

Market shares are shown based on deposits as of June 30, 2003.

Bank of America	19.22%
Wachovia	15.73
SunTrust	11.38
Washington Mutual	4.02
SouthTrust	3.68
AmSouth	2.51
World Savings	2.23

Amtrust	1.93%
Colonial	1.57
Ocean Bank	1.43
Other	36.30

Source: *Sarasota Herald Tribune*, January 19, 2004, p. 12, from Florida Bankers Association.

★ 2977 ★
Banking
SIC: 6021; NAICS: 52211

Top Banks in Florida (FDIC), 2003

Market shares are shown based on deposits as of June 30, 2003.

Bank of America	20.10%
Wachovia Bank National Assn.	14.92
SunTrust Bank	10.96
SouthTrust Bank	3.87
Washington Mutual Bank	3.87
Amsouth Bank	2.45
World Savings Bank	2.14
Citibank	2.04
Ohio Savings Bank	1.86
Other	37.79

Source: "Market Share Report." [online] available from http://www.fdic.gov [accessed December 18, 2003], from Federal Deposit Insurance Corp.

★ 2978 ★
Banking
SIC: 6021; NAICS: 52211

Top Banks in Forsyth County/Triad, NC

Market shares are shown based on deposits.

BB&T	53.0%
Wachovia	22.0
Piedmont Federal Savings & Loan	6.6
Central Carolina Bank	5.0
Southern Community Bank	4.5
Other	8.9

Source: *Winston-Salem Journal*, November 6, 2003, p. D1, from Federal Deposit Insurance Corp.

★ 2979 ★
Banking
SIC: 6021; NAICS: 52211
Top Banks in Georgia

Market shares are shown based on deposits as of June 30, 2003.

Wachovia Bank National Assn.	15.99%
SunTrust Bank	14.07
Bank of America	12.41
Regions Bank	4.63
Southtrust Bank	4.49
Branch Banking & Trust Co.	4.40
Columbus Bank &Trust Co.	1.71
Netbank	1.68
United Community Bank	1.67
Other	43.44

Source: "Market Share Report." [online] available from http://www.fdic.gov [accessed December 18, 2003], from Federal Deposit Insurance Corp.

★ 2980 ★
Banking
SIC: 6021; NAICS: 52211
Top Banks in Greece

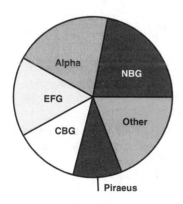

Market shares are shown based on assets.

NBG	22.0%
Alpha	20.0
EFG	16.0
CBG	13.0
Piraeus	10.0
Other	19.0

Source: *Retail Banker International*, February 28, 2003, p. 10, from Merrill Lynch estimates, Bank of Greece, and company data.

★ 2981 ★
Banking
SIC: 6021; NAICS: 52211
Top Banks in Greene County, MO

Market shares are shown based on deposits as of June 2002.

Great Southern Bank	19.47%
Commerce Bank	13.27
Bank of America	9.22
The Signature Bank	9.01
U.S. Bank	8.35
Guranty Bank	5.46
Liberty Bank	3.70
Citizens National Bank of Springfield	3.54
Metropolitan National Bank	2.58
Other	15.71

Source: *Springfield News-Leader*, October 31, 2003, p. A1, from Federal Deposit Insurance Corp.

★ 2982 ★
Banking
SIC: 6021; NAICS: 52211
Top Banks in Guam, 2003

Market shares are shown based on deposits as of June 30, 2003.

Citibank National Assn.	25.47%
Bank of Hawaii	22.45
Bank of Guam	20.88
First Hawaiian Bank	20.39
Citizens Security	6.23
Bankpacific	3.24
Other	1.34

Source: "Market Share Report." [online] available from http://www.fdic.gov [accessed December 18, 2003], from Federal Deposit Insurance Corp.

★ 2983 ★
Banking
SIC: 6021; NAICS: 52211

Top Banks in Hawaii, 2003

Market shares are shown based on deposits as of June 30, 2003.

Bank of Hawaii	29.98%
First Hawaiian Bank	29.82
American Savings Bank	18.44
Central Pacific Bank	8.13
City Bank	5.60
Territorial Savings Bank	3.66
Finance Factors	1.86
Other	2.51

Source: "Market Share Report." [online] available from http://www.fdic.gov [accessed December 18, 2003], from Federal Deposit Insurance Corp.

★ 2984 ★
Banking
SIC: 6021; NAICS: 52211

Top Banks in Idaho, 2003

Wells Fargo Bank
U.S. Bank National Assn.
Keybank National Assn.
Bank of America
Washington FS&LA
Bank of Commerce
Zions First National Bank
Idaho Independent Bank
Home FS&LA
Other

Market shares are shown based on deposits as of June 30, 2003.

Wells Fargo Bank	24.25%
U.S. Bank National Assn.	19.45
Keybank National Assn.	4.95
Bank of America	4.60
Washington FS&LA	3.90
Bank of Commerce	3.44

Zions First National Bank	2.88%
Idaho Independent Bank	2.44
Home FS&LA	2.23
Other	31.86

Source: "Market Share Report." [online] available from http://www.fdic.gov [accessed December 18, 2003], from Federal Deposit Insurance Corp.

★ 2985 ★
Banking
SIC: 6021; NAICS: 52211

Top Banks in Illinois, 2003

Market shares are shown based on deposits as of June 30, 2003.

Bank One National Assn.	15.66%
Lasalle Bank National Assn.	9.11
Harris Trust & Savings Bank	3.82
Citibank	3.02
Northern Trust Co.	2.97
Fifth Third Bank	2.26
Charter One Bank	2.16
National City Bank	2.05
U.S. Bank National Assn.	1.66
Other	57.29

Source: "Market Share Report." [online] available from http://www.fdic.gov [accessed December 18, 2003], from Federal Deposit Insurance Corp.

★ 2986 ★
Banking
SIC: 6021; NAICS: 52211

Top Banks in Indiana, 2003

Market shares are shown based on deposits as of June 30, 2003.

Bank One	12.97%
National City Bank of Indiana	9.83
Old National Bank	5.76
Fifth Third Bank Indiana	4.93
Irwin Union Bank & Trust Co.	3.40
Union Federal Bank of Indianapolis	3.20

Continued on next page.

★ 2986 ★
[Continued]
Banking
SIC: 6021; NAICS: 52211

Top Banks in Indiana, 2003

Market shares are shown based on deposits as of June 30, 2003.

1st Source Bank	3.15%
Union Planters Bank	2.41
Keybank National Assn	2.11
Other	52.24

Source: "Market Share Report." [online] available from http://www.fdic.gov [accessed December 18, 2003], from Federal Deposit Insurance Corp.

★ 2987 ★
Banking
SIC: 6021; NAICS: 52211

Top Banks in Iowa, 2003

Market shares are shown based on deposits as of June 30, 2003.

Wells Fargo Bank Iowa	14.35%
U.S. Bank National Assn.	7.94
Principal Bank	3.51
Commercial Fed Bank	2.06
Bankers Trust Co.	2.06
Bank of America	1.71
Hills Bank & Trust	1.62
First American Bank	1.26
West Des Moines & State Bank	1.07
Other	64.42

Source: "Market Share Report." [online] available from http://www.fdic.gov [accessed December 18, 2003], from Federal Deposit Insurance Corp.

★ 2988 ★
Banking
SIC: 6021; NAICS: 52211

Top Banks in Iraq, 2004

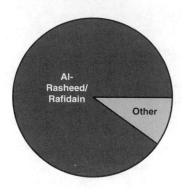

The top two state banks take the lion's share of the market.

Al-Rasheed / Rafidain	90.0%
Other	10.0

Source: *Daily Star*, March 23, 2004, p. NA.

★ 2989 ★
Banking
SIC: 6021; NAICS: 52211

Top Banks in Kansas, 2003

Market shares are shown based on deposits as of June 30, 2003.

Capitol Federal Savings Bank	9.81%
Bank of America	6.54
Intrust Bank National Assn.	4.23
Gold Bank	3.15
U.S. Bank National Assn.	2.46
World Savings Bank	2.35
Commerce Bank National Assn.	2.30
First National Bank of Kansas	2.10
Other	67.06

Source: "Market Share Report." [online] available from http://www.fdic.gov [accessed December 18, 2003], from Federal Deposit Insurance Corp.

★ 2990 ★
Banking
SIC: 6021; NAICS: 52211

Top Banks in Kentucky, 2003

Market shares are shown based on deposits as of June 30, 2003.

National City Bank of Kentucky	9.56%
Branch Banking & Trust Co.	7.29
U.S. Bank National Assn.	6.29
Bank One National Assn.	6.17
PNC Bank National Assn.	3.95
Fifth Third Bank of Kentucky	3.55
Community Trust Bank	3.46
Republic Bank & Trust Co.	2.04
Other	57.69

Source: "Market Share Report." [online] available from http://www.fdic.gov [accessed December 18, 2003], from Federal Deposit Insurance Corp.

★ 2991 ★
Banking
SIC: 6021; NAICS: 52211

Top Banks in Louisiana, 2003

Market shares are shown based on deposits as of June 30, 2003.

Hibernia National Bank	21.86%
Bank One National Assn.	17.21
Whitney National Bank	8.82
Regions Bank	6.24
Iberiabank	2.90
Amsouth Bank	2.90
Hancock Bank of Louisiana	2.54
Union Planters Bank	1.43

Fidelity Homestead Assn.	1.11%
Other	34.99

Source: "Market Share Report." [online] available from http://www.fdic.gov [accessed December 18, 2003], from Federal Deposit Insurance Corp.

★ 2992 ★
Banking
SIC: 6021; NAICS: 52211

Top Banks in Maine, 2003

Market shares are shown based on deposits as of June 30, 2003.

Banknorth National	18.98%
Keybank National Assn.	14.26
Fleet National Bank	8.17
Bangor Savings Bank	6.76
Camden National Bank	3.63
Norway Savings Bank	3.19
Kennebunk Savings Bank	2.92
Saco & Biddeford	2.28
Gardiner Svg Inst.	2.24
Other	37.57

Source: "Market Share Report." [online] available from http://www.fdic.gov [accessed December 18, 2003], from Federal Deposit Insurance Corp.

★ 2993 ★
Banking
SIC: 6021; NAICS: 52211

Top Banks in Maryland, 2003

Market shares are shown based on deposits as of June 30, 2003.

Bank of America	17.25%
Manufacturers & Traders	10.36
Chevy Chase Bank	7.83
SunTrust Bank	7.70
Wachovia Bank National Assn.	6.91
Mercantile-Safe Deposit	4.52
Branch Banking & Trust Co.	4.42
Provident Bank of Maryland	4.16
Other	36.85

Source: "Market Share Report." [online] available from http://www.fdic.gov [accessed December 18, 2003], from Federal Deposit Insurance Corp.

★ 2994 ★
Banking
SIC: 6021; NAICS: 52211
Top Banks in Massachusetts, 2003

Market shares are shown based on deposits as of June 30, 2003.

Fleet National Bank	24.08%
Citizens Bank of MA	10.76
State Street Bank & Trust	10.41
Sovereign Bank	5.13
Boston Safe Deposit & Trust Co.	3.64
BankNorth National Assn.	3.29
Investor's Bank & Trust Co.	2.07
Eastern Bank	2.07
Middlesex Savings Bank	1.58
Other	36.97

Source: ''Market Share Report.'' [online] available from http://www.fdic.gov [accessed December 18, 2003], from Federal Deposit Insurance Corp.

★ 2995 ★
Banking
SIC: 6021; NAICS: 52211
Top Banks in Mexico

Market shares are shown based on deposits.

BBVA-Bancomer	27.8%
Banamex	22.9
Santander Mexicano	13.2
Banorte	12.6
Bital	11.5
Other	12.0

Source: *Financial Times*, February 3, 2003, p. 17.

★ 2996 ★
Banking
SIC: 6021; NAICS: 52211
Top Banks in Michigan, 2003

Market shares are shown based on deposits as of June 30, 2003.

Standard Federal Bank	15.69%
Comerica Bank	15.56
Bank One National Assn.	13.03
Fifth Third Bank	8.55
National City Bank of MI	7.03
Flagstar Bank	3.85
Charter One Bank	3.76
Huntington National Bank	3.55
Citizens Bank	2.79
Other	26.19

Source: ''Market Share Report.'' [online] available from http://www.fdic.gov [accessed December 18, 2003], from Federal Deposit Insurance Corp.

★ 2997 ★
Banking
SIC: 6021; NAICS: 52211
Top Banks in Minnesota, 2003

Market shares are shown based on deposits as of June 30, 2003.

Wells Fargo Bank	37.87%
U.S. Bank National Assn	16.64
TCF National Bank	3.64
Bremer Bank National Assn	1.36
Associated Bank Minnesota	1.30
M&I Marshall & Ilsley Bank	0.94
Community First National Bank	0.68
Stearns Bank National Assn.	0.59
Other	36.98

Source: ''Market Share Report.'' [online] available from http://www.fdic.gov [accessed December 18, 2003], from Federal Deposit Insurance Corp.

★ 2998 ★

Banking

SIC: 6021; NAICS: 52211

Top Banks in Mississippi, 2003

Market shares are shown based on deposits as of June 30, 2003.

Trustmark National Bank	13.73%
BancorpSouth Bank	13.43
Union Planters Bank	7.49
Amsouth Bank	7.29
Hancock Bank	6.41
Peoples Bank &Trust Co.	3.51
Bankplus	2.83
Merchants & Farmers Bank	2.59
National Bank of Commerce	2.06
Other	38.66

Source: "Market Share Report." [online] available from http://www.fdic.gov [accessed December 18, 2003], from Federal Deposit Insurance Corp.

★ 2999 ★

Banking

SIC: 6021; NAICS: 52211

Top Banks in Missouri, 2003

Market shares are shown based on deposits as of June 30, 2003.

U.S. Bank National Assn.	19.25%
Bank of America	10.81
Commerce Bank National Assn.	8.38
UMB Bank National Assn.	4.06
Union Planters Bank	2.85
First Bank	2.09
Allegiant Bank	1.92
Bank Midwest National Assn.	1.75
Southwest Bank of St. Louis	1.62
Other	47.27

Source: "Market Share Report." [online] available from http://www.fdic.gov [accessed December 18, 2003], from Federal Deposit Insurance Corp.

★ 3000 ★

Banking

SIC: 6021; NAICS: 52211

Top Banks in Montana, 2003

Market shares are shown based on deposits as of June 30, 2003.

First Interstate Bank	16.27%
Wells Fargo Bank	11.53
U.S. Bank National Assn.	7.13
Stockman Bank of Montana	5.90
Mountain West Bank	3.06
Glacier Bank	3.06
First Security Bank Missoula	3.06
Rocky Mountain Bank	2.51
First Security Bank	2.51
Other	45.27

Source: "Market Share Report." [online] available from http://www.fdic.gov [accessed December 18, 2003], from Federal Deposit Insurance Corp.

★ 3001 ★

Banking

SIC: 6021; NAICS: 52211

Top Banks in Nebraska, 2003

Market shares are shown based on deposits as of June 30, 2003.

First National Bank of Omaha	12.63%
Wells Fargo Bank Nebraska	9.56
U.S. Bank National Assn.	7.29
Pinnacle Bank	4.56
Commercial Fed Bank	4.34
Tierone Bank	3.03
Union Bank & Trust	2.97
American National Bank	2.34

Continued on next page.

★ 3001 ★
[Continued]
Banking
SIC: 6021; NAICS: 52211
Top Banks in Nebraska, 2003

*Market shares are shown based on deposits as of
June 30, 2003.*

Great Western Bank	2.09%
Other	51.19

Source: ''Market Share Report.'' [online] available from
http://www.fdic.gov [accessed December 18, 2003], from
Federal Deposit Insurance Corp.

★ 3002 ★
Banking
SIC: 6021; NAICS: 52211
Top Banks in Nevada, 2003

*Market shares are shown based on deposits as of
June 30, 2003.*

Bank of America	19.00%
Wells Fargo Bank Nevada	18.84
Citibank Nevada	17.80
Nevada State Bank	7.97
U.S. Bank National Assn.	5.47
Citibank West	4.03
Bankwest of Nevada	2.68
Washington Mutual Bank	2.46
First National Bank of Nevada	1.86
Other	19.89

Source: ''Market Share Report.'' [online] available from
http://www.fdic.gov [accessed December 18, 2003], from
Federal Deposit Insurance Corp.

★ 3003 ★
Banking
SIC: 6021; NAICS: 52211
Top Banks in New Hampshire, 2003

*Market shares are shown based on deposits as of
June 30, 2003.*

Providian National Bank	36.76%
Citizens Bank New Hampshire	17.91
Banknorth National Assn.	13.24
Fleet National Bank	6.12
Granite Bank	2.68
Laconia Savings Bank	2.05
First Essex Bank	1.80
Sovereign Bank	1.68
Lake Sunapee Bank	1.18
Other	16.87

Source: ''Market Share Report.'' [online] available from
http://www.fdic.gov [accessed December 18, 2003], from
Federal Deposit Insurance Corp.

★ 3004 ★
Banking
SIC: 6021; NAICS: 52211
Top Banks in New Jersey, 2003

*Market shares are shown based on deposits as of
June 30, 2003.*

Fleet National Bank	18.04%
Wachovia Bank National Assn.	10.31
PNC Bank National Assn.	6.77
Merrill Lynch Bank & Trust Co.	6.23
Hudson City Savings Bank	5.11
Commerce Bank National Assn	4.04
Sovereign Bank	3.68
Valley National Bank	3.07

Continued on next page.

★ 3004 ★

[Continued]
Banking
SIC: 6021; NAICS: 52211

Top Banks in New Jersey, 2003

Market shares are shown based on deposits as of June 30, 2003.

TD Waterhouse Bank	2.92%
Other	39.83

Source: ''Market Share Report.'' [online] available from http://www.fdic.gov [accessed December 18, 2003], from Federal Deposit Insurance Corp.

★ 3005 ★

Banking
SIC: 6021; NAICS: 52211

Top Banks in New Mexico, 2003

Market shares are shown based on deposits as of June 30, 2003.

Wells Fargo Bank	22.81%
Bank of America	15.98
First State Bank	5.46
Los Alamos National Bank	5.10
Bank of Albuquerque	4.41
Bank of the West	4.00
First NB of Santa Fe	2.30
Charter Bank	2.05
Century Bank	1.79
Other	36.10

Source: ''Market Share Report.'' [online] available from http://www.fdic.gov [accessed December 18, 2003], from Federal Deposit Insurance Corp.

★ 3006 ★

Banking
SIC: 6021; NAICS: 52211

Top Banks in New York, 2003

Market shares are shown based on deposits as of June 30, 2003.

JPMorgan Chase Bank	23.82%
Citibank National Assn.	19.28
HSBC Bank	6.88
Bank of New York	5.78
Fleet National Bank	3.60
Manufacturers & Traders	2.51

North Fork Bank	2.41%
Greenpoint Bank	2.16
Other	33.56

Source: ''Market Share Report.'' [online] available from http://www.fdic.gov [accessed December 18, 2003], from Federal Deposit Insurance Corp.

★ 3007 ★

Banking
SIC: 6021; NAICS: 52211

Top Banks in North Carolina, 2003

Market shares are shown based on deposits as of June 30, 2003.

Wachovia Bank	27.40%
Bank of America	25.19
Branch Banking & Trust	13.61
First Citizens Bank & Trust Co.	5.95
National Bank of Commerce	5.16
RBC Centura Bank	4.54
First Charter Bank	1.76
First Bank	0.74
Fidelity Bank	0.64
Other	15.01

Source: ''Market Share Report.'' [online] available from http://www.fdic.gov [accessed December 18, 2003], from Federal Deposit Insurance Corp.

★ 3008 ★
Banking
SIC: 6021; NAICS: 52211

Top Banks in North Dakota, 2003

Market shares are shown based on deposits as of June 30, 2003.

Wells Fargo	11.78%
U.S. Bank National Asssn.	8.90
Gate City Bank	5.23
State Bank of Fargo	5.03
Community First	3.60
Alerus Financial	3.49
First International	3.43
Bremer Bank National Assn.	2.77
Other	55.77

Source: "Market Share Report." [online] available from http://www.fdic.gov [accessed December 18, 2003], from Federal Deposit Insurance Corp.

★ 3009 ★
Banking
SIC: 6021; NAICS: 52211

Top Banks in Ohio, 2003

Market shares are shown based on deposits as of June 30, 2003.

Fifth Third Bank	12.05%
National City Bank	11.23
Keybank National Assn.	10.17
Bank One National Assn.	8.50
U.S. Bank National Assn.	6.25
Huntington National Bank	5.03
Provident Bank	4.89
Charter One Bank	3.55
Firstmerit Bank	3.27
Other	35.06

Source: "Market Share Report." [online] available from http://www.fdic.gov [accessed December 18, 2003], from Federal Deposit Insurance Corp.

★ 3010 ★
Banking
SIC: 6021; NAICS: 52211

Top Banks in Oklahoma, 2003

Bank of Oklahoma
Bancfirst
Midfirst Bank
Bank of America
Bank One National Assn.
Arvest Bank
Local Oklahoma Bank
Stillwater NB&T Co.
F&M Bank & Trust
Other

Market shares are shown based on deposits as of June 30, 2003.

Bank of Oklahoma	13.35%
Bancfirst	5.66
Midfirst Bank	5.08
Bank of America	5.01
Bank One National Assn.	4.87
Arvest Bank	4.20
Local Oklahoma Bank	4.15
Stillwater NB&T Co.	2.67
F&M Bank & Trust	1.83
Other	53.18

Source: "Market Share Report." [online] available from http://www.fdic.gov [accessed December 18, 2003], from Federal Deposit Insurance Corp.

★ 3011 ★
Banking
SIC: 6021; NAICS: 52211

Top Banks in Oregon, 2003

Market shares are shown based on deposits as of June 30, 2003.

U.S. Bank National Assn.	24.15%
Washington Mutual Bank	13.83
Wells Fargo Bank	10.92
Bank of America	10.51
Keybank National Assn.	7.12
Umpqua Bank	5.98
Klamath First	2.87

Continued on next page.

★ 3011 ★
[Continued]
Banking
SIC: 6021; NAICS: 52211

Top Banks in Oregon, 2003

Market shares are shown based on deposits as of June 30, 2003.

West Coast Bank	2.73%
Other	21.89

Source: "Market Share Report." [online] available from http://www.fdic.gov [accessed December 18, 2003], from Federal Deposit Insurance Corp.

★ 3012 ★
Banking
SIC: 6021; NAICS: 52211

Top Banks in Pennsylvania, 2003

Market shares are shown based on deposits as of June 30, 2003.

PNC Bank	12.95%
Wachovia Bank	12.27
Citizens Bank of PA	8.96
National City Bank of PA	5.32
Mellon Bank	5.22
Manufacturers & Traders	3.77
Sovereign Bank	3.05
Northwest Savings Bank	1.91
Commercebank Pennsylvania	1.84
Other	44.71

Source: "Market Share Report." [online] available from http://www.fdic.gov [accessed December 18, 2003], from Federal Deposit Insurance Corp.

★ 3013 ★
Banking
SIC: 6021; NAICS: 52211

Top Banks in Pittsburgh, PA

Market shares are shown based on deposits.

PNC	24.00%
Mellon	19.00
National City	16.00
Citizens	10.00
Dollar Bank	4.75
Other	26.25

Source: *Pittsburgh Post-Gazette*, February 4, 2004, p. NA, from Federal Deposit Insurance Corp.

★ 3014 ★
Banking
SIC: 6021; NAICS: 52211

Top Banks in Portland, OR

Market shares are shown based on deposits as of June 30, 2003.

U.S. Bank	27.8%
Washington Mutual	16.5
Bank of America	14.3
Wells Fargo Bank	12.6
Other	28.8

Source: *The Business Journal - Portland*, December 15, 2003, p. NA, from Federal Deposit Insurance Corp.

★ 3015 ★
Banking
SIC: 6021; NAICS: 52211
Top Banks in Puerto Rico, 2003

Market shares are shown based on deposits as of June 30, 2003.

Banco Popular De Puerto Rico	31.56%
Westernbank Puerto Rico	12.09
Firstbank of Puerto Rico	11.82
Banco Santander Puerto Rico	9.47
Citibank National Assn.	6.70
R-G Premier Bank	6.69
Banco Bilbao Vizcaya Argenta	6.58
Other	15.09

Source: "Market Share Report." [online] available from http://www.fdic.gov [accessed December 18, 2003], from Federal Deposit Insurance Corp.

★ 3016 ★
Banking
SIC: 6021; NAICS: 52211
Top Banks in Rhode Island, 2003

Market shares are shown based on deposits as of June 30, 2003.

Citizens Bank of Rhode Island	40.70%
Fleet National Bank	23.40
Sovereign Bank	10.77
Washington TR Co of Westerly	6.10
Bank Rhode Island	4.41
Bank of Newport	3.66
Centreville Savings Bank	2.94
Metlife Bank	2.29
Other	5.73

Source: "Market Share Report." [online] available from http://www.fdic.gov [accessed December 18, 2003], from Federal Deposit Insurance Corp.

★ 3017 ★
Banking
SIC: 6021; NAICS: 52211
Top Banks in Russia

Banks are ranked by assets in millions of dollars.

Sberbank - Savings Bank	$ 25,601
Vneshtorgbank	6,128
Vnesheconombank	3,826
Gazprombank	3,811
International Industrial Bank	3,354
Alfa Bank	2,726
International Moscow Bank	2,467
Bank of Moscow	2,255
Surgutneftegazbank	2,092

Source: *The Banker*, December 2002, p. 57, from *The Banker*.

★ 3018 ★
Banking
SIC: 6021; NAICS: 52211
Top Banks in Slovenia

Banks are ranked by assets in millions of dollars.

Nova Ljubljanska Banka	$ 8,920
Nova Kreditna banka Maribor	2,327
Abanka Vipa	1,767
SKA banka d.d.	1,658
Banka Koper d.d.	1,277
Banka Celije d.d.	1,243
Gorenjska Banka d.d. Kranj	1,030

Source: *The Banker*, November 2003, p. 76.

★ 3019 ★
Banking
SIC: 6021; NAICS: 52211
Top Banks in South Africa

Market shares are shown based on deposits as of December 2001.

Absa	21.1%
Standard Bank	18.6

Continued on next page.

★ 3019 ★
[Continued]
Banking
SIC: 6021; NAICS: 52211

Top Banks in South Africa

Market shares are shown based on deposits as of December 2001.

Nedcor	18.1%
FirstRand	14.9
BOE Bank	6.5
Investec Bank Ltd.	6.0
Nedcor Investment Bank	2.5
Other	12.3

Source: *ABSA Bank Quarterly South African Economic Monitor*, August 8, 2002, p. 14.

★ 3020 ★
Banking
SIC: 6021; NAICS: 52211

Top Banks in South Carolina, 2003

Market shares are shown based on deposits as of June 30, 2003.

Wachovia Bank	18.56%
Bank of America	12.86
Branch B&T Co. of SC	9.74
Carolina First Bank	8.11
First-Citizens B&T Co. of SC	7.23
National Bank of SC	4.50
First FS&LA of Charleston	3.22
National Bank of Commerce	2.96
Regions Bank	1.88
Other	30.94

Source: "Market Share Report." [online] available from http://www.fdic.gov [accessed December 18, 2003], from Federal Deposit Insurance Corp.

★ 3021 ★
Banking
SIC: 6021; NAICS: 52211

Top Banks in South Dakota, 2003

Wells Fargo Bank
Citibank USA
Citibank South Dakota
First Premier Bank
Great Western Bank
Home Federal Bank
U.S. Bank National Assn.
Dacotah Bank
First NB in Sioux Falls
Other

Market shares are shown based on deposits as of June 30, 2003.

Wells Fargo Bank	15.74%
Citibank USA	8.85
Citibank South Dakota	8.01
First Premier Bank	4.46
Great Western Bank	4.06
Home Federal Bank	3.93
U.S. Bank National Assn.	3.91
Dacotah Bank	3.79
First NB in Sioux Falls	3.10
Other	44.15

Source: "Market Share Report." [online] available from http://www.fdic.gov [accessed December 18, 2003], from Federal Deposit Insurance Corp.

★ 3022 ★
Banking
SIC: 6021; NAICS: 52211

Top Banks in South Korea, 2003

Shares are based on total assets which are listed in billion Won.

Kookmin	184,100
Woori	103,300
Hana	80,600
Shinhan	70,100

Continued on next page.

★ 3022 ★
[Continued]
Banking
SIC: 6021; NAICS: 52211

Top Banks in South Korea, 2003

Shares are based on total assets which are listed in billion Won.

KEB	68,000
Chohung	59,200
KorAm	43,000
KFB	39,500

Source: *Financial Times*, March 4, 2004, p. 21, from *Fitch Ratings*.

★ 3023 ★
Banking
SIC: 6021; NAICS: 52211

Top Banks in Spain

	(bil.)	Share
Banco Bilboa Vizcaya Argentaria	194.5	31.5%
Santander Central Hispano	192.0	31.0
Banesto	59.4	9.6
Popular	34.8	5.6
Sabadell	28.5	4.6

Source: *Euromoney*, October 2003, p. 1.

★ 3024 ★
Banking
SIC: 6021; NAICS: 52211

Top Banks in Syracuse, NY

Market shares are shown in percent.

M&T Bank	19.18%
Fleet National Bank	11.81
HSBC Bank	11.65
KeyBank	11.13
J.P. Morgan Chase Bank	7.80

Solvay Bank	4.60%
Alliance Bank	4.00
First Niagara Bank	3.80
Other	26.03

Source: *The Post-Standard*, January 12, 2004, p. 3, from Federal Deposit Insurance Corp.

★ 3025 ★
Banking
SIC: 6021; NAICS: 52211

Top Banks in Tennessee, 2003

Market shares are shown based on deposits as of June 30, 2003.

First Tennessee Bank	17.56%
Amsouth Bank	10.68
Union Planters Bank	8.19
Suntrust Bank	7.83
Bank of America	6.86
National Bank of Commerce	5.66
U.S. Bank National Assn.	1.98
Home Federal Bank of Tennessee	1.46
Regions Bank	1.44
Other	38.84

Source: "Market Share Report." [online] available from http://www.fdic.gov [accessed December 18, 2003], from Federal Deposit Insurance Corp.

★ 3026 ★
Banking
SIC: 6021; NAICS: 52211

Top Banks in Texas, 2003

Market shares are shown based on deposits as of June 30, 2003.

JPMorgan Chase Bank	15.50%
Bank of America	11.43
Wells Fargo Bank	7.15
Bank One National Assn.	6.59
USAA Federal Savings Bank	3.49
Washington Mutual Bank	2.76

Continued on next page.

★ 3026 ★
[Continued]
Banking
SIC: 6021; NAICS: 52211

Top Banks in Texas, 2003

Market shares are shown based on deposits as of June 30, 2003.

Frost National Bank	2.68%
Treasury Bank National Assn.	2.64
Guaranty Bank	2.33
Other	45.43

Source: "Market Share Report." [onlinc] available from http://www.fdic.gov [accessed December 18, 2003], from Federal Deposit Insurance Corp.

★ 3027 ★
Banking
SIC: 6021; NAICS: 52211

Top Banks in the Philippines, 2003

Bankss are ranked by deposits outstanding in millions of Phillipine pesos.

	(mil.)	Share
Metropolitan Bank and Trust	362,318	15.0%
Bank of the Philippine Islands	314,919	13.0
Land Bank of the Philippines	175,720	7.0
Equitable-PCI Bank	169,509	7.0
Philippine National Bank	134,646	6.0
Rizal Commerical Bank	122,499	5.0
Allied Bank	100,834	4.0
Banco de Oro	92,425	4.0
United Coconut Planters Bank	84,243	4.0
Development Bank	34,177	1.0

Source: *European Intelligence Wire*, April 19, 2004, p. NA, from Philippine Central Bank, Moody's Investor Services, and Phillipine Deposit Insurance Corp.

★ 3028 ★
Banking
SIC: 6021; NAICS: 52211

Top Banks in the Triangle, TN

Market shares are shown based on deposits.

Wachovia	29.0%
National Bank of Commerce	17.0
BB&T	13.0
First Citizens	12.0
Bank of America	9.0
Other	20.0

Source: *Triangle Business Journal*, August 11, 2003, p. NA, from Federal Deposit Insurance Corp.

★ 3029 ★
Banking
SIC: 6021; NAICS: 52211

Top Banks in the Twin Cities, MN

Market shares are shown based on deposits as of June 30, 2003.

Wells Fargo	30.71%
U.S. Bank	28.00
TCF National Bank	6.54
Bremer Bank	2.37
Twin Cities	1.87
Other	30.51

Source: *The Business Journal (Minneapolis - St. Paul)*, November 17, 2003, p. NA, from Federal Deposit Insurance Corp.

★ 3030 ★
Banking
SIC: 6021; NAICS: 52211

Top Banks in the Twin Cities, MN

Market shares for 2002 are estimated based on deposits.

Wells Fargo Bank	33.0%
U.S. Bank	25.0
Other	42.0

Source: *Finance and Commerce Daily Newspaper*, August 23, 2003, p. NA, from Federal Deposit Insurance Corp.

★ 3031 ★
Banking
SIC: 6021; NAICS: 52211
Top Banks in the U.K.

HBOS	
RBS	
Lloyds TSB	
Barclays	
HSBC	
Abbey	
Other	

Market shares are shown based on total deposits of 545 billion pounds.

HBOS	22.0%
RBS	16.0
Lloyds TSB	12.0
Barclays	11.0
HSBC	9.0
Abbey	9.0
Other	21.0

Source: *Bank Marketing International*, December 31, 2003, p. 14, from IBM Business Consulting Services.

★ 3032 ★
Banking
SIC: 6021; NAICS: 52211
Top Banks in Tunisia

Banks are ranked by assets in millions of dollars.

Societe Tunisienne de Banque	$ 3,170
Banque Nationale Agricole	2,440
Banque Internationale Arabe de Tunisie . . .	2,099
Amen Bank	1,434
Banque du Sud	1,236
Banque de Tunisie	1,138

Source: *The Banker*, November 2003, p. 76.

★ 3033 ★
Banking
SIC: 6021; NAICS: 52211
Top Banks in Turkey

Banks are ranked by assets in millions of dollars.

TC Ziraat Bankasi	$ 20,036
Akbank	11,759
Turkiye is Bankasi	11,304
Turkiye Garanti Bankasi	11,160
Yapi ve Kredi Bankasi	10,585
Turkiye Halk Bankasi	10,585
VakifBank	6,454
Kocbank	3,927
Finans Bank	2,370
Disbank	2,051

Source: *The Banker*, May 2003, p. 136, from *The Banker*.

★ 3034 ★
Banking
SIC: 6021; NAICS: 52211
Top Banks in U.A.E.

Banks are ranked by assets in millions of dollars.

National Bank of Abu Dhabi	$ 10,632
National Bank of Dubai	9,575
Abu Dhabi Commercial Bank	7,538
Emirates Bank International	7,411
Mashreqbank	6,449
Dubai Islamic Bank	5,336
Union National Bank	4,007
Commercial Bank of Dubai	2,165
Arab Bank for Investment & Foreign Trade .	1,579
First Gulf Bank	1,357

Source: *The Banker*, November 2003, p. 76.

★ 3035 ★
Banking
SIC: 6021; NAICS: 52211

Top Banks in Utah, 2003

Market shares are shown based on deposits as of June 30, 2003.

Merrill Lynch Bank	63.99%
Zions First National Bank	7.46
Wells Fargo Bank	6.06
American Express Centurion	5.99
Bank One National Assn.	1.99
Providian Bank	1.60
Advanta Bank Corp.	1.53
U.S. Bank National Assn.	0.91
Keybank National Assn.	0.80
Other	9.67

Source: "Market Share Report." [online] available from http://www.fdic.gov [accessed December 18, 2003], from Federal Deposit Insurance Corp.

★ 3036 ★
Banking
SIC: 6021; NAICS: 52211

Top Banks in Vermont, 2003

Market shares are shown based on deposits as of June 30, 2003.

Chittenden Trust Co.	27.73%
Banknorth National Assn.	18.27
Charter One Bank	10.79
Merchants Bank	8.91
Keybank National	5.03
Northfield Savings Bank	3.43
Union Bank	3.25
Factory Bank NB Manchester	3.10

Passumpsic Savings Bank	2.80%
Other	16.69

Source: "Market Share Report." [online] available from http://www.fdic.gov [accessed December 18, 2003], from Federal Deposit Insurance Corp.

★ 3037 ★
Banking
SIC: 6021; NAICS: 52211

Top Banks in Virginia, 2003

Market shares are shown based on deposits as of June 30, 2003.

Wachovia Bank	15.62%
Bank of America	10.39
Suntrust Bank	9.41
Branch B&T Co. of Virginia	7.82
Capital One	7.79
E* Trade Bank	7.06
Capital One Bank	6.57
First Virginia Bank	3.09
Chevy Chase Bank	1.22
Riggs Bank	1.02
Other	30.01

Source: "Market Share Report." [online] available from http://www.fdic.gov [accessed December 18, 2003], from Federal Deposit Insurance Corp.

★ 3038 ★
Banking
SIC: 6021; NAICS: 52211

Top Banks in Washington, 2003

Market shares are shown based on deposits as of June 30, 2003.

Bank of America	21.21%
Washington Mutual Bank	18.63
U.S. Bank National Assn.	11.03
Keybank National Assn.	5.83
Wells Fargo Bank	3.96
Washington FS&LA	2.39
Sterling Savings Bank	2.20
Pacific Northwest Bank	2.14
Frontier Bank	2.06
Other	30.55

Source: "Market Share Report." [online] available from http://www.fdic.gov [accessed December 18, 2003], from Federal Deposit Insurance Corp.

★ 3039 ★
Banking
SIC: 6021; NAICS: 52211
Top Banks in Washington D.C., 2003

Market shares are shown based on deposits as of June 30, 2003.

Riggs Bank National Assn.	22.70%
Wachovia Bank National Assn.	21.87
Bank of America	17.01
SunTrust Bank	10.69
Citibank	8.83
Branch Banking & Trust Co.	5.80
Chevy Chase Bank	2.36
Manufacturers & Traders Trust Co.	1.76
United Bank	1.58
Other	7.40

Source: ''Market Share Report.'' [online] available from
http://www.fdic.gov [accessed December 18, 2003], from
Federal Deposit Insurance Corp.

★ 3040 ★
Banking
SIC: 6021; NAICS: 52211
Top Banks in Washoe County, NV

Market shares are shown based on deposts as of June 30, 2003.

Wells Fargo Nevada	28.95%
Bank of America	17.01
Nevada State Bank	9.72
US Bank	7.73
Citibank	6.56
First Independent Bank	3.83
Heritage Bank	2.42
Other	23.78

Source: *Reno Gazette-Journal*, November 30, 2003, p. E1,
from Federal Deposit Insurance Corp.

★ 3041 ★
Banking
SIC: 6021; NAICS: 52211
Top Banks in West Virginia, 2003

Market shares are shown based on deposits as of June 30, 2003.

Branch Banking & Trust Co.	17.34%
United Bank	9.78
Westbanco Bank Inc.	8.87
Bank One West Virginia	7.71
City NB of West Virginia	7.10
Huntington National Bank	6.69
First Community Bank	3.77
Putnam County Bank	1.89
Huntington FSB	1.56
Other	35.29

Source: ''Market Share Report.'' [online] available from
http://www.fdic.gov [accessed December 18, 2003], from
Federal Deposit Insurance Corp.

★ 3042 ★
Banking
SIC: 6021; NAICS: 52211
Top Banks in Wisconsin, 2003

Market shares are shown based on deposits as of June 30, 2003.

M&I Marshall & Illsley Bank	16.97%
U.S. Bank National Assn.	16.36
Associated Bank	6.34
Bank One National Assn.	5.04
Anchorbank	2.74
Wells Fargo Bank	2.37
Mutual Savings Bank	2.22
First Federal Capital Bank	2.06
Johnson Bank	1.82
Other	44.08

Source: ''Market Share Report.'' [online] available from
http://www.fdic.gov [accessed December 18, 2003], from
Federal Deposit Insurance Corp.

★ 3046 ★

Banking

SIC: 6021; NAICS: 52211

★ 3043 ★

Banking

SIC: 6021; NAICS: 52211

Top Banks in Wyoming, 2003

Market shares are shown based on deposits as of June 30, 2003.

First Interstate Bank	15.44%
Wells Fargo Bank	12.62
Community First	10.29
Jackson State Bank	5.46
American National Bank	3.54
Hilltop National Bank	3.50
Pinnacle Bank Wyoming	3.34
U.S. Bank National Assn.	3.29
Bank of Jackson Hole	2.63
Other	39.89

Source: "Market Share Report." [online] available from http://www.fdic.gov [accessed December 18, 2003], from Federal Deposit Insurance Corp.

★ 3044 ★

Banking

SIC: 6021; NAICS: 52211

Top Global Private Banks

UBS
Merrill Lynch
Credit Suisse
Deutsche Bank
HSBC
Citigroup
JPMorgan Chase
Dresdner
Morgan Stanley
ABN Amro

Banks are ranked by assets under management in billions of dollars.

UBS	$ 1,031.2
Merrill Lynch	935.0
Credit Suisse	394.0
Deutsche Bank	183.4
HSBC	169.0
Citigroup	145.0
JPMorgan Chase	138.0
Dresdner	133.6

Morgan Stanley	$ 130.0
ABN Amro	115.5

Source: *Financial Times*, May 27, 2004, p. 19, from Scorpio Partnership.

★ 3045 ★

Banking

SIC: 6021; NAICS: 52211

Top Private Commercial Banks in Germany, 2002

Countries are ranked by total assets in millions of euros. Shares of the top 10 banks are shown in percent. Savings banks take 29% of customer deposits, 18% co-ops and 14% of the big four commercial banks.

	(bil.)	% of Group
Deutsche Bank	758.4	24.7%
HVB	691.2	22.6
Commerzbank	422.1	13.8
Dresdner	413.4	13.5
Eurohypo	215.0	7.0
Bankgesellschaft Berlin	174.8	5.7
Postbank	141.1	4.6
Depfa	94.5	3.1
Allgemeine Hypotheken Rheinboden	79.3	2.5
HVB Real Estate	77.8	2.5

Source: *Financial Times*, May 13, 2004, p. 20.

★ 3046 ★

Banking

SIC: 6021; NAICS: 52211

U.K. Banking Market, 2003

Shares are average shares for the period March—December 2003 and includes banking services and mortgage services.

Lloyds TSB	16.7%
Barclays	13.1
Halifax	10.8
NatWest	10.6
HSBC	10.4
Abbey	6.7
Nationwide	3.9
Bank of Scotland	3.4
Royal Bank of Scotland	3.3

Continued on next page.

★ 3046 ★
[Continued]
Banking
SIC: 6021; NAICS: 52211

U.K. Banking Market, 2003

Shares are average shares for the period March—December 2003 and includes banking services and mortgage services.

Alliance & Leicester	2.9%
Other	18.2

Source: *Banking Marketing International*, February 2004, p. 4, from Martin Hamblin GfK and John Gilbert Associates.

★ 3047 ★
Credit Unions
SIC: 6061; NAICS: 52213

Top Credit Unions

Credit unions are ranked by assets in millions of dollars.

Navy Federal Credit Union	$ 19,349.78
State Employees Credit Union	10,807.51
Pentagon Federal Credit Union	5,868.21
Golden 1 Credit Union	4,598.97
Boeing Employees Credit Union	4,526.39
United Airlines Employees' Credit Union	4,467.79
Orange County Teachers Federal Credit Union	4,435.14
American Airlines Federal Credit Union	3,967.56
Suncoast Schools Federal Credit Union	3,823.83
Patelco Credit Union	3,177.10

Source: *American Banker*, November 11, 2003, p. 8.

★ 3048 ★
Foreign Banks
SIC: 6081; NAICS: 52211

Top Foreign Banks in Central and Eastern Europe

Market shares are shown in percent.

KBC	11.49%
Erste Bank	10.75
Bank Austria Creditanstalt	9.34
UniCredito Italiano	8.23%
Citigroup	6.04
Societe Generale	5.83
RZB	5.69
Banca Intesa	5.54
ING	4.96
Commerzbank	3.19
Other	28.94

Source: *European Banker*, October 2003, p. 1, from Bank Austria Creditanstal.

★ 3049 ★
Bank Cards
SIC: 6099; NAICS: 52232

Bank Card Industry

Market shares are shown for March 2003. The two companies were planning to merege although such a plan is in doubt. The Department of Justice fears a possible monopoly of the industry.

Concord	56.0%
First Data	10.0
Other	34.0

Source: *Oil Express*, November 3, 2003, p. 6.

★ 3050 ★
Bill Payment
SIC: 6099; NAICS: 52232

How Payments Are Made in New Zealand

	1998	2002
EFTPOS	31.0%	35.0%
Check & paper deposits	23.0	13.0
Electronic credits	20.0	18.0
ATM	14.0	12.0
Credit cards	8.0	17.0
Direct debits	4.0	5.0

Source: *The Reserve Bank of New Zealand*, June 2003, p. 5, from New Zealand Bankers Association.

★ 3051 ★
Financial Services
SIC: 6099; NAICS: 52232

Leading Financial Service Firms in Australia

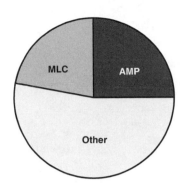

Market shares are shown in percent for 2002-2003. In the previous financial year, MLC had a 17.8% share and AMP had a 27% share.

AMP	25.0%
MLC	21.6
Other	53.4

Source: *Australian Business Intelligence*, September 24, 2003, p. Na, from DEXXS-R.

★ 3052 ★
Money Transfers
SIC: 6099; NAICS: 52232

Electronic Transfer Industry with Mexico

Bancomer has a dominant share of the electronic tranfer business due to its alliance with Wells Fargo and relationship with other banks. It recently announced plans to release a debit card for migrants to simplify the process of sending money home. The remittance business has been placed at $10 billion by some estimates.

	($ bil.)	Share
BBVA Bancomer	$ 4.8	54.5%
Other	4.0	45.5

Source: *Financial Times*, July 4, 2003, p. 18, from Banco de Mexico and BBVA Bancomer.

★ 3053 ★
Money Transfers
SIC: 6099; NAICS: 52232

Sending Money to Latin America

Figures show how Latinos in the United States send money to Latin America. Remittances to Latin America and the Caribbean were $20 billion in 2001.

Western Union	32.0%
People travelling	17.0
Money and money orders	16.0
Banks	16.0
MoneyGram	12.0
Credit unions	7.0

Source: *American Banker*, February 6, 2003, p. 6, from Celent Communications.

★ 3054 ★
Travelers Checks
SIC: 6099; NAICS: 52232

Travelers Check Industry

Market shares are shown in percent.

American Express	70.0%
Other	30.0

Source: *Houston Chronicle*, December 28, 2003, p. 3.

SIC 61 - Nondepository Institutions

★ 3055 ★
Credit Cards
SIC: 6141; NAICS: 52221
Consumer Credit Lending in the U.K., 2002

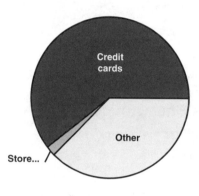

Consumer credit gross lending totalled 193,877 million pounds.

Credit cards	60.38%
Store cards	2.46
Other	37.16

Source: *Cards International*, April 2, 2004, p. 4, from Mastercard.

★ 3056 ★
Credit Cards
SIC: 6141; NAICS: 52221
Credit Card Market

Market shares are compared based on the number of general purpose cards and dollar amount of receivables.

	Accounts	Dollars
MasterCard	43.7%	43.8%
Visa	41.4	43.1
Other	14.9	13.1

Source: *Wall Street Journal*, April 27, 2004, p. D2, from SMR Research Corp.

★ 3057 ★
Credit Cards
SIC: 6141; NAICS: 52221
Credit Card Market in Asia/Pacific, 2002

In the region there were 448 million cards issued to people. This represents 6.3 billion transactions worth $874 billion. Market shares are shown based on retail transactions.

Visa	62.0%
Mastercard	22.3
JCB	8.9
American Express	4.6
Diner's Club	2.1

Source: *Financial Times*, February 2, 2004, p. 9.

★ 3058 ★
Credit Cards
SIC: 6141; NAICS: 52221
Credit Card Market Worldwide, 2002

Market shares are shown based on $273 billion in shopping transactions.

Visa	58.2%
MasterCard	28.2
American Express	11.3
JCB	1.3
Diners Club	1.0

Source: "Market Share Survey Report 2002." [online] from http://www.nni.nikkei.co.jp [accessed January 20, 2004], from Nikkei estimates.

★ 3059 ★
Credit Cards
SIC: 6141; NAICS: 52221
Credit Card Use in China, 2003

Figures show how card holders use their cards. According to the source, 38% of card holders are single, 61% and under 35 years of age, and 81.2% have a college degree.

Hotel accomodations	65.0%
Dining out	17.0
Entertainment	10.9
Shopping and other	7.1

Source: *Wall Street Journal*, March 10, 2004, p. C1, from Goldman Sachs Group and McKinsey & Company Management Company.

★ 3060 ★
Credit Cards
SIC: 6141; NAICS: 52221
Global Credit and Debit Card Spending

Spending is shown in billions of dollars.

United States	$ 1,200.0
U.K.	247.7
France	164.2
South Korea	104.6
Canada	90.6

Source: *Wall Street Journal*, December 4, 2003, p. B1, from The Nilson Report.

★ 3061 ★
Credit Cards
SIC: 6141; NAICS: 52221
Leading Credit Card Holders

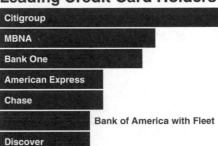

Citigroup
MBNA
Bank One
American Express
Chase
Bank of America with Fleet
Discover
Capital One
Other

About $662 billion was owed on general purpose credit cards during the third quarter of the year. Shares are shown for outstanding balances. Bank One and Chase announced plans to merge.

	($ bil.)	Share
Citigroup	$ 114.1	17.2%
MBNA	81.7	12.3
Bank One	74.2	11.2
American Express	55.4	8.4
Chase	50.9	7.7
Bank of America with Fleet	49.2	7.4
Discover	47.9	7.2
Capital One	44.7	6.8
Other	143.9	21.7

Source: *New York Times*, January 16, 2004, p. C3, from Nilson Report.

★ 3062 ★
Credit Cards
SIC: 6141; NAICS: 52221
Payment Card Networks in Spain

Market shares are shown based on cards issued by group members.

ServiRed	52.0%
Euro 6000	25.0
Sistema 4B	23.0

Source: *Cards International*, April 27, 2004, p. 28, from ServiRed.

★ 3063 ★
Credit Cards
SIC: 6141; NAICS: 52221

Top Credit Card Issuers, 2003

Institutions are ranked by aggregate card loans in billions of dollars as of December 31, 2003.

Citigroup	$ 119.8
MBNA	85.8
Bank One	76.3
J.P. Morgan Chase	52.3
Discover	48.4
Capital One	46.3
American Express	38.5
Bank of America	36.6
Household	17.9
Fleet	17.0

Source: *Caribbean Business*, April 29, 2004, p. 21, from CardData.

★ 3064 ★
Credit Cards
SIC: 6141; NAICS: 52221

Top Credit Card Issuers in Australia, 2002

In terms of issuing, Commonwealth Bank has 21.6% of the market. In 2002 Australians spent $2 on credit cards for every $1 on debit cards. Roughly $65 billion was spent on credit cards during the year. Just under half of all credit cards are linked to consumer reward programs which helps motivate spending. Market shares of acquirers are shown based on value.

Commonwealth Bank	30.0%
ANZ Bank	24.0
National	19.0
Westpac	18.0
St. George	3.0
Other	6.0

Source: *Cards International*, March 7, 2003, p. 17, from Card Smart Consulting.

★ 3065 ★
Credit Cards
SIC: 6141; NAICS: 52221

Top Credit Card Issuers in Canada

Data show outstanding debt in billions of Canadian dollars for the year ended October 31, 2003. On average Canadians have 3 bank citicards.

	2001	2002	Share
CIBC	8.7	9.5	21.59%
Royal Bank of Canada	6.2	6.4	14.55
Scotiabank	4.9	6.0	13.64
TD	4.4	5.0	11.36
Bank of Montreal	4.0	4.2	9.55
MBNA	2.9	3.6	8.18
Other	7.7	9.3	21.14

Source: *Cards International*, April 23, 2003, p. 23.

★ 3066 ★
Credit Cards
SIC: 6141; NAICS: 52221

Top Credit Card Issuers in Denmark

Market shares take into account only international cards and AcceptFinancs and Magasin retailer cards.

Danske Bank	36.6%
AcceptFinancs	32.3
SEB Kort	16.4
Other	14.7

Source: *Cards International*, February 23, 2004, p. 20, from issuers.

★ 3067 ★
Credit Cards
SIC: 6141; NAICS: 52221

Top Credit Card Issuers in France, 2002

Market shares of merchant acquirers are shown based on number of transactions.

Credit Mutuel	21.3%
Credit Agricole	19.5
Credit Lyonnais	11.8
Banques Populaires	11.8
BNP Paribas	9.0

Continued on next page.

★ 3067 ★
[Continued]
Credit Cards
SIC: 6141; NAICS: 52221

Top Credit Card Issuers in France, 2002

Market shares of merchant acquirers are shown based on number of transactions.

Societe Generale 8.7%
Credit Industriel et Commercial 6.3
Caisses d'Espargne 5.2
Other 6.4

Source: *Cards International*, February 2, 2004, p. 12, from Groupement des Cartes Bancaires.

★ 3068 ★
Credit Cards
SIC: 6141; NAICS: 52221

Top Credit Card Issuers in Germany, 2002

Market shares of merchant acquirers are shown based on 322.67 million transactions.

B+S Card Service 34.4%
Euro Kartensystems 27.0
Citibank 18.6
Other 20.0

Source: *Cards International*, February 2, 2004, p. 12, from Euro Kartensysteme.

★ 3069 ★
Credit Cards
SIC: 6141; NAICS: 52221

Top Credit Card Issuers in Greece, 2002

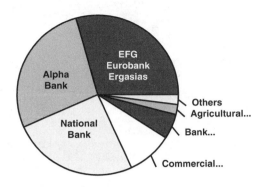

Credit card firms in Greece are ranked by share of 5.7 million cards issued. Cards included are deferred debit, charge cards, co-branded and store cards.

EFG Eurobank Ergasias 29.0%
Alpha Bank 27.1
National Bank of Greece 25.2
Commercial Bank of Greece 9.4
Bank of Piraeus 5.3
Agricultural Bank of Greece 2.3
Others 1.7

Source: *Cards International*, April 2, 2004, p. 18.

★ 3070 ★
Credit Cards
SIC: 6141; NAICS: 52221

Top Credit Card Issuers in Indonesia, 2002

Credit card firms in Indonesia are ranked by share of 2.65 million cards issued.

Bank Central Asia 14.3%
GE Capital 10.9
Bank Mandiri 10.3
Other 64.5

Source: *Cards International*, April 2, 2004, p. 20, from Lafferty estimates and company reports.

★ 3071 ★
Credit Cards
SIC: 6141; NAICS: 52221

Top Credit Card Issuers in Malaysia, 2002

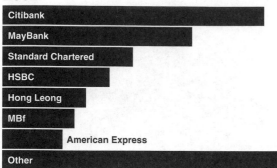

According to the source, cash is still the preferred means of payment in Malaysian society. This is changing in urban areas. Also, the government is working to stimulate domestic activity as the nation struggless to recover from the 1997 Asean economic crisis. Market shares are shown based on 4.36 million cards issued.

Citibank	22.0%
MayBank	16.0
Standard Chartered	11.0
HSBC	9.0
Hong Leong	7.0
MBf	6.0
American Express	5.0
Other	24.0

Source: *Cards International*, June 18, 2003, p. 18, from Lafferty estimates and company estimates.

★ 3072 ★
Credit Cards
SIC: 6141; NAICS: 52221

Top Credit Card Issuers in Norway

Market shares are shown in percent. There were 4.65 million credit cards in the Norwegian market in 2002. Many cards are ''combined'' credit but also cash and debit cards.

Oil companies	34.8%
DnB Kort	10.2
SEB Kort Norway	9.1
Other	46.1

Source: *Cards International*, February 23, 2004, p. 20, from issuers.

★ 3073 ★
Credit Cards
SIC: 6141; NAICS: 52221

Top Credit Card Issuers in Poland

Market shares are shown in percent.

Pekao Bank	30.0%
PKO Bank Polski	21.0
ING Bank Slaski	15.0
BPH BPK2	8.0
Bank Zachodnil	8.0
Kredyt Bank	5.0
Citibank/Hanlowy	5.0
Other	13.0

Source: *Cards International*, August 11, 2003, p. 21, from company reports.

★ 3074 ★
Credit Cards
SIC: 6141; NAICS: 52221

Top Credit Card Issuers in South Korea, 2002

Market shares are shown in percent.

BC Card	28.0%
LG Card	23.0
Samsung Card	22.0
Kookmin Card	14.0
KEB Credit Services	5.0
Other	8.0

Source: *Retail Banker International*, March 10, 2004, p. 12, from FSS and companies.

★ 3075 ★
Credit Cards
SIC: 6141; NAICS: 52221

Top Credit Card Issuers in Sweden

Market shares are shown in percent.

SEB Kort	19.0%
ForeningSparbanken	17.0
Other	64.0

Source: *Cards International*, February 2, 2004, p. 22.

★ 3076 ★
Credit Cards
SIC: 6141; NAICS: 52221

Top Credit Card Issuers in Switzerland, 2002

A total of 3.3 million cards were issued during the year. Master Card has 60% of the market and Visa 40%.

UBS	31.0%
Viseca	27.0
Swisscard	25.0
ConFr Bank	17.0

Source: *Cards International*, November 10, 2003, p. 20.

★ 3077 ★
Credit Cards
SIC: 6141; NAICS: 52221

Top Credit Card Issuers in Thailand

Largely because of low income in the population, only about 3.5 million out of 40 million adults carry credit cards. Shares are shown based on number of cards issued.

Krung Thai Cards	17.0%
Bank of Ayudhya	14.0
Citibank	13.0
Bangkok Bank	13.0
Kasikorn Bank	11.0
Standard Chartered Nakanthorn	6.0
Bank of Asia	4.0
Other	20.0

Source: *Cards International*, October 24, 2003, p. 20, from Thailand National Statistics Office.

★ 3078 ★
Credit Cards
SIC: 6141; NAICS: 52221

Top Credit Card Issuers in the U.K.

Market shares are shown based on cards issued.

Barclaycard	19.0%
RBS Group	17.0
HSBC + Household	13.0
Lloyds	12.0
MBNA	10.0
HBOS	10.0
Capital One	4.0
Other	15.0

Source: *Bank Marketing International*, February 26, 2003, p. 13, from Datamonitor.

★ 3079 ★
Credit Cards
SIC: 6141; NAICS: 52221

Top Credit Card Issuers in Turkey, 2002

Turkey is the fourth largest card market in Europe and one of the fastest growing markets worldwide. Market shares are shown based on number of cards issued.

Yapi Kredi Bankasi	29.0%
Garanti Bank	17.0
Isbank	12.0
Akbank	10.0
Other	32.0

Source: *Cards International*, July 1, 2003, p. 17, from companies.

★ 3080 ★
Credit Cards
SIC: 6141; NAICS: 52221

Top Credit Card Issuers Worldwide, 2002

Firms are ranked by estimated consumer credit-related net income worldwide.

	($ bil.)	Share
Citigroup	$ 6.23	28.0%
Citigroup (cards only)	3.11	14.0

Continued on next page.

★ 3080 ★
[Continued]
Credit Cards
SIC: 6141; NAICS: 52221

Top Credit Card Issuers Worldwide, 2002

Firms are ranked by estimated consumer credit-related net income worldwide.

	($ bil.)	Share
HSBC	$ 2.06	9.0%
GE Capital	1.94	9.0
JP Morgan Chase/Bank One	1.83	8.0
MBNA	1.77	7.0
American Express	1.52	7.0
Capital One	1.02	5.0
DBS Holdings	0.95	4.0
UOB	0.89	4.0

Source: *Cards International*, February 23, 2004, p. 16, from Morgan Stanley research and company reports.

★ 3081 ★
Credit Cards
SIC: 6141; NAICS: 52221

Top Credit Card Markets in Europe, 2002

Countries are ranked by outstanding debt in billions of dollars.

U.K.	$ 1,414
Germany	1,196
France	682
Spain	445
Netherlands	398
Italy	383

Source: *European Banker*, March 2004, p. 8, from Morgan Stanley Research.

★ 3082 ★
Credit Cards
SIC: 6141; NAICS: 52221

Top Credit Cards in Germany

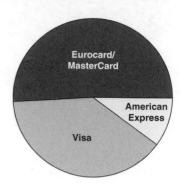

Shares are shown based on cards in circulation. There are 21 million cards in the German market but usage is low.

Eurocard/MasterCard	51.0%
Visa	39.0
American Express	10.0

Source: *European Banker*, July 16, 2003, p. 2, from Euro Kartensysteme.

★ 3083 ★
Debit Cards
SIC: 6141; NAICS: 52221

Debit Card Industry

Market shares are shown in percent.

	1998	2002
Visa	77.5%	78.1%
MasterCard	22.5	21.9

Source: *USA TODAY*, November 17, 2003, p. 6B.

★ 3084 ★
Debit Cards
SIC: 6141; NAICS: 52221
Debit Card Market in Indonesia, 2002

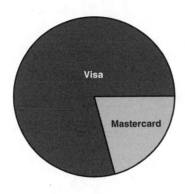

Shares are shown based on $1.6 billion in spending. Transactions include spending and cash advances/ withdrawals.

Visa 79.4%
Mastercard 20.6

Source: *Cards International*, April 2, 2004, p. 21, from company reports and Lafferty estimates.

★ 3085 ★
Debit Cards
SIC: 6141; NAICS: 52221, 522298
Online Debit Card Processing

The two companies are planning to merge and figures show estimates of the market of the new company.

First Data/Concord 67.0%
Other 33.0

Source: *Rocky Mountain News*, September 27, 2003, p. 3C.

★ 3086 ★
Gas Cards
SIC: 6141; NAICS: 52221
Leading Gas Card Issuers

The number of proprietary consumer and commercial credit cards fell 4.6% to 1.7 billion transactions. Proprietary cards had a market share of 17.1%. Universal cards and card-lock plastic by third party firms took 19.1%. Companies are ranked by volume of sales in millions of dollars.

	($ mil.)	Share
Shell	$ 4,654.0	20.88%
ExxonMobil	4,630.0	20.78
BPAmoco	3,250.0	14.58
Chevron	3,180.0	14.27
ConPhil	2,480.0	11.13
Citgo	1,150.0	5.16
Valero	853.0	3.83
Sunoco	655.0	2.94
Speedway	379.0	1.70
Marathon Ashland	324.0	1.45
Other	730.2	3.28

Source: *Oil Express*, September 22, 2003, p. 5, from Nilson Report.

★ 3087 ★
Agricultural Lending
SIC: 6150; NAICS: 52232
Leading Agricultural Banks

Banks are ranked by value of loans in millions of dollars for the quarter ended December 31, 2002. Shares are shown based on $27.15 billion in loans made by the top 100 banks.

	($ mil.)	Share
Wells Fargo	$ 3,335.00	12.28%
US Bank	2,056.97	7.58
Bank of America	1,536.00	5.66
Bank of the West	1,076.27	3.96
Wachovia Bank	963.00	3.55
Union Planters	847.53	3.12
Regions Bank	804.75	2.96
Bank One	698.00	2.57
Keybank	691.16	2.55
M&I Marshall & Ilsley	660.90	2.43
Other	14,480.47	53.33

Source: *Ag Lender*, April 2003, p. 10, from Federal Reserve System.

★ 3088 ★
Agricultural Lending
SIC: 6150; NAICS: 52232
Who Makes Farm Loans, 2002

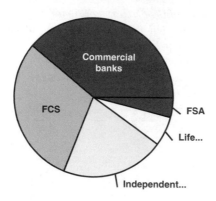

FCS's total farm debt has increased 72% in the last decade while total farm debt has increased only 42%, giving it a larger piee of the pie.

Commercial banks	39.4%
FCS	30.3
Independent and others	20.7
Life insurance companies	6.1
FSA	3.5

Source: *Ag Lender*, April 2003, p. 9, from Economic Research Service and U.S. Department of Agriculture.

★ 3089 ★
Business Loans
SIC: 6150; NAICS: 522, 52232
Largest SBA Lenders

Lenders are ranked by number of loans for the 12 months ended September 2003. SBA stands for small business administration.

Bank of America Corp.	9,406
Citizens Financial Group Inc.	5,899
Wells Fargo & Co.	3,174
Innovative Bank	2,212
FleetBoston Financial Corp.	2,130
Capital One Financial Corp.	2,106
U.S. Bancorp	1,653
CIT Small Business Lending Corp.	1,540
National City Corp.	1,410
Zions Bancorp.	1,322

Source: *American Banker*, November 12, 2003, p. 21A.

★ 3090 ★
Business Loans
SIC: 6159; NAICS: 522292
80-20 Rental Market in Manhattan, NY

80-20 refers to the financing of large rental apartment buildings in Manhattan. 20% of the apartments are set aside for low-income tenants. The segment of the banking is seeing growth, unlike many other segments.

Fleet National Bank	75.0%
Other	25.0

Source: *Crain's New York Business*, November 3, 2003, p. 10.

★ 3091 ★
Lease Financing
SIC: 6159; NAICS: 532
Top Leasing Firms in Poland, 2003

The movable asset leasing business in Poland in 2003 was valued at 10.5 billion PLN (Polish New Zloty).

Europejski Fundusz Leasingowy (EFL)	18.5%
Raiffeisen Leasing	9.9
Other	71.6

Source: *Poland Business News*, January 29, 2004, p. NA.

★ 3092 ★
Loan Arrangers
SIC: 6162; NAICS: 522292
Largest Real Estate Lenders, 2003

Companies are ranked by value of direct real estate loans for January 1 - June 30, 2003.

Bank of America	$ 15.7
GMAC Commercial Mortgage Corp.	14.0
Wachovia	7.6
Lehman Brothers	6.0
KeyBank Real Estate Capital	5.3
Credit Suisse First Boston	4.3
Washington Mutual	4.0
Freddie Mac	3.8
Morgan Stanley	3.1
Prudential Mortgage Capital	2.5

Source: *Commercial Property News*, December 2003, p. 33.

★ **3093** ★

Loan Arrangers

SIC: 6162; NAICS: 52239

Largest Syndicated Loan Arrangers in Western Europe, 2003

Shares are shown for the top banks involved in organizing and distributing syndicated loans in Western Europe from January 1 - December 10, 2003.

Citigroup	15.06%
J.P. Morgan Chase	9.56
Deutsche Bank	8.51
Barclays Bank	8.11
BNP Paribas	7.18
Other	51.58

Source: *Wall Street Journal*, December 17, 2003, p. C1.

★ **3094** ★

Loan Arrangers

SIC: 6162; NAICS: 52231

Loan Industry in Mexico

Market shares are shown in percent.

Commercial	41.0%
State agencies	29.0
Housing	15.0
Consuemr	11.0
Interbank	4.0

Source: *Wall Street Journal*, July 18, 2003, p. A7, from International Monetary Fund and National Banking Commission of Mexico.

★ **3095** ★

Mortgage Loans

SIC: 6163; NAICS: 52231

Largest Mortgage Bankers, 2003

Companies are ranked by their transaction volume in millions of dollars for the period between October 1, 2002 - September 30, 2003.

Holiday Fenoglio Fowler	$ 15,500
L-J Melody & Co.	10,000
Meridian Capital Group	7,500
Wachovia	7,400
GMAC Commercial Mortgage Corp.	5,400
PNC Real Estate Finance	3,900

Northmarq Capital	$ 3,700
Bear, Stearns & Co.	3,600
Icap Reality Advisors	3,400
Berkshire Mortgage Finance	3,300

Source: *Commercial Property News*, February 1, 2004, p. 16.

★ **3096** ★

Mortgage Loans

SIC: 6163; NAICS: 52231

Largest Residential Servicers, 2003

Market shares are shown based on servicing volume as of December 31, 2003.

Washington Mutual	10.26%
Wells Fargo Home Mortgage	9.38
Countrywide Financial	9.11
Chase Home Finance	6.64
Bank of Amcrica	3.48
ABN Amro Mortgage	2.93
CitiMortgage Inc.	2.89
GMAC Residential	2.84
National City Mortgage	2.15
Cendant Mortgage	1.96
Principal Residential Mortgage	1.68
Homecomings/GMAC-RFC	1.13
Other	45.55

Source: *Mortgage Servicing News*, March 2004, p. 1, from Mortgage Servicing News Quarterly Data Report.

★ **3097** ★

Mortgage Loans

SIC: 6163; NAICS: 52231

Leading Home Mortgage Originators, 2003

Market shares are shown in percent.

Wells Fargo	12.01%
Washington Mutual	11.12
Countrywide Financial Corp.	11.11
Chase Home Finance	7.26
Bank of America	3.34
ABN Amro Mortgage	3.17
GMAC Residential Holdings	2.92

Continued on next page.

★ 3097 ★

[Continued]
Mortgage Loans
SIC: 6163; NAICS: 52231

Leading Home Mortgage Originators, 2003

Market shares are shown in percent.

CitiMortgage Inc.	2.77%
National City Mortgage	2.70
Other	43.60

Source: *American Banker*, April 22, 2004, p. 16, from *National Mortgage News*.

★ 3098 ★

Mortgage Loans
SIC: 6163; NAICS: 52231

Leading Mortgage Banks in France

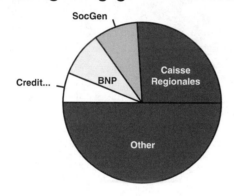

Market shares are estimated for June 2003.

Caisse Regionales	26.0%
SocGen	9.0
BNP	9.0
Credit Lyonnais	6.0
Other	50.0

Source: *Financial Times*, November 3, 2003, p. 18, from Morgan Stanley.

★ 3099 ★

Mortgage Loans
SIC: 6163; NAICS: 52231

Leading Subprime Servicers, 2003

Market shares are as of December 31, 2003.

Household Finance	8.36%
CitiFinancial	7.55
HomeComings	6.63
Option One	6.20
Fairbanks Capital	6.14
Countrywide Financial Corp.	5.90
Ocwen Financial Corp.	5.62
Homeq Servicing Corp.	4.34
Chase Home Finance	4.19
Other	45.07

Source: *National Mortgage News*, April 5, 2004, p. 1, from National Mortgage News/Quarterly Data Report.

★ 3100 ★

Mortgage Loans
SIC: 6163; NAICS: 522292

Mortgage Market in Mexico

Demand for housing and mortgages is expected to increase dramatically in the coming decade. Half of the population is less than 25 years of age.

Infonavit	65.0%
Other	35.0

Source: *Country ViewsWire*, December 3, 2003, p. NA.

★ 3101 ★

Mortgage Loans
SIC: 6163; NAICS: 52231

Online Mortgage Maket in Europe

The online mortgage market was worth 70 billion euros in 2003. By 2008, it has been forecasted to reach 230 billion euros.

U.K.	29.0%
Germany	17.0
Netherlands	10.0
Other	44.0

Source: *European Banker*, October 2003, p. 15.

★ 3102 ★

Mortgage Loans

SIC: 6163; NAICS: 52231

Top Counties for Existing Home Sales, 2003

Market shares are shown based on value of existing home transactions during the first six months of the year. Total transactions were worth $52.61 billion.

	($ mil.)	Share
Los Angeles, CA	$ 16.65	5.93%
Orange, CA	7.09	2.16
San Diego, CA	6.73	2.28
Maricopa, AZ	3.95	2.26
Broward, FL	3.59	1.97
Riverside, CA	3.36	1.61
Dade, FL	3.34	1.73
Clark, NV	3.01	1.67
San Bernadino, CA	2.87	1.60
Harris, TX	2.55	1.76

Source: *Mortgage Banking*, November 2003, p. 108, from First American Real Estate Solutions.

★ 3103 ★

Mortgage Loans

SIC: 6163; NAICS: 52231

Top Counties for New Homes, 2003

Clark, NV
Harris, TX
Maricopa, AZ
Riverside, CA
Tarrant, TX
Sacramento, CA
San Diego, CA
Meckleburg, NC
Collin, TX
Palm Beach, FL

Market shares are shown based on the number of new home transactions during the first six months of the year. Total transactions were worth $52.61 billion.

	Transactions	Share
Clark, NV	11,106	3.57%
Harris, TX	9,931	3.19
Maricopa, AZ	9,446	3.04
Riverside, CA	9,245	2.97

	Transactions	Share
Tarrant, TX	5,857	1.88%
Sacramento, CA	5,453	1.75
San Diego, CA	5,394	1.73
Meckleburg, NC	4,636	1.49
Collin, TX	4,455	1.43
Palm Beach, FL	4,330	1.39

Source: *Mortgage Banking*, November 2003, p. 108, from First American Real Estate Solutions.

★ 3104 ★

Mortgage Loans

SIC: 6163; NAICS: 52231

U.K. Mortgage Loan Providers, 2002

In 2001 the firm Halifax merged with Bank of Scotland to create the new firm, HBOS.

HBOS	26.0%
Abbey	10.4
Other	63.6

Source: *Money Marketing*, January 29, 2004, p. NA, from Council of Mortgage Lenders.

SIC 62 - Security and Commodity Brokers

★ 3105 ★
Investment Banking
SIC: 6211; NAICS: 52311
529 Plan Leaders

A "529 Plan" is a financial savings tool with tax benefits. It allows users to set aside money for a child's education on a tax free basis. Not a bad idea since on year at a state school, including room and board, is approximately $10,636. At a private school the cost much higher, $26,854. Providers of 529 Plans are ranked by assets in billions of dollars.

	($ bil.)	Share
TIAA-CREF	$ 4.3	16.0%
American Funds	3.4	13.0
Alliance	3.3	13.0
Fidelity	3.1	12.0
Putnam	2.4	9.0
Merrill Lynch	1.7	6.0
Citigroup	1.6	6.0
Vanguard	0.6	2.0
American Express	0.5	2.0
Manulife	0.5	2.0

Source: *USA TODAY*, October 24, 2003, p. 3B, from Cerulli Associates.

★ 3106 ★
Investment Banking
SIC: 6211; NAICS: 52311
529 Plans and States

Figures show assets held in 529 plans for the first quarter.

	($ mil.)	Share
Rhode Island	$ 2,801	13.1%
Virginia	2,722	12.8
Ohio	2,027	9.5
New Hampshire	1,660	7.8
New York	1,605	7.5

Source: *Wall Street Journal*, May 27, 2003, p. 1, from Financial Research Corp.

★ 3107 ★
Investment Banking
SIC: 6211; NAICS: 52311
College and University Underwriting

Schools must spend high sums on state-of-the-art facilities to remain competitive. However, with alumni contributions and endowments down, some schools have to turn elsewhere for dollars. Market shares are shown in percent.

	($ bil.)	Share
Lehman Bros.	$ 3.40	20.9%
Citigroup	3.08	19.2

Source: *Investment Dealers' Digest*, September 8, 2003, p. NA.

★ 3108 ★
Investment Banking
SIC: 6211; NAICS: 52311
ETF Fund Managers, 2002

In 2002, exchange traded funds (ETF) pulled in $17 billion in new assets. Trading volume nearly doubled. The largest ETF (by asset) is S&P 500 SPDR.

	Assets ($ bil.)	Share
State Street Global Advisors . . .	$ 54	45.0%
Barclays Global Investors	34	28.5
The Bank of New York	23	20.0

Source: *Alternative Investment News*, August 2003, p. S1, from Morgan Stanley.

★ 3109 ★
Investment Banking
SIC: 6211; NAICS: 52311

Largest Convertible Bond Bookrunners, 2003

Banks are ranked by volume of deals in billions of dollars for January - June 27, 2003.

JPMorgan	$ 8.1
Citigroup	7.7
Goldman Sachs	7.6
Morgan Stanley	7.2
Merrill Lynch	6.5
BofA Securities	5.1
CSFB	3.9
UBS	2.7
Deutsche Bank	2.7
Lehman Brothers	1.9

Source: *Euromoney*, July 2003, p. 36, from Convertbond.com.

★ 3110 ★
Investment Banking
SIC: 6211; NAICS: 52311

Largest Corporate Securities Underwriters, 2003

Market shares are shown in percent.

	($ bil.)	Share
Citigroup	$ 408.81	12.0%
Lehman Brothers	314.03	9.3
Merrill Lynch	304.03	9.0
Morgan Stanley	301.99	8.9
J.P. Morgan Chase	264.59	7.8
Credit Suisse First Boston	250.51	7.4
Goldman Sachs	241.49	7.1
UBS Warburg	208.59	6.1
Banc of America Securities	198.19	5.8
Bear Stearns	180.25	5.3

Source: *New York Times*, January 1, 2004, p. C4, from Thomson Financial.

★ 3111 ★
Investment Banking
SIC: 6211; NAICS: 52311

Leading Asset Managers in Spain

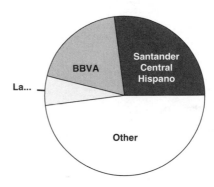

Spain is the seventh largest fund market in Europe. Assets for local funds reached $210 million by the end of May 2003.

Santander Central Hispano	27.0%
BBVA	19.0
La Craixa	6.0
Other	48.0

Source: *Global Fund News*, September 2003, p. 14, from INVERCO.

★ 3112 ★
Investment Banking
SIC: 6211; NAICS: 52311

Leading Brokerage Businesses in Thailand, 2004

Shares are shown for the first four months of 2004.

Kim Eng Securities Thailand Plc	12.07%
ABN Amro Asia Plc	6.90
Seamico Securities Plc	6.50
KGI Thailand Securities Plc	4.79
SCB Securities Plc	3.90
Other	65.93

Source: *Asia Africa Intelligence Wire*, May 6, 2004, p. NA, from Seamico Securities Plc (ZMICO).

★ 3113 ★
Investment Banking
SIC: 6211; NAICS: 52311

Leading Foreign Exchange Firms, 2003

Market shares are shown in percent.

UBS	11.53%
Citigroup	9.87
Deutsche Bank	9.79
JPMorgan Chase	6.79
Goldman Sachs	5.56
Credit Suisse First Boston	4.23
HSBC	3.89
Morgan Stanley	3.87
Barclays Capital	3.84
ABN Amro	3.63
Merrill Lynch	2.98
Royal Bank of Scotland	2.85
Other	68.83

Source: *Euromoney*, May 2003, p. 46, from *2003 Euromoney Forex Poll*.

★ 3114 ★
Investment Banking
SIC: 6211; NAICS: 52311

Leading Independent Brokers

Companies are ranked by gross revenue in millions of dollars.

AIG Advisors Group	$ 810.4
LPL Financial Services	776.0
ING Advisors Network Inc.	713.7
Raymond James	601.0
Lincoln Financial	537.0
Signator Investors Inc.	253.7
MML Investor Srvices Inc.	227.7
Securities America Inc.	220.0
NYLIFE Securities Inc.	199.6
Walnut Street	195.2

Source: *Investment News*, December 15, 2003, p. 28.

★ 3115 ★
Investment Banking
SIC: 6211; NAICS: 52311

Leading Merger Advisers in Europe, 2003

Financial advisers of any European involvement are shown based on deals announced from January 1, 2003 - June 30, 2003. Energy & power represented 18% of all deals, followed by telecommunications with 15%.

Goldman Sachs & Co.	22.4%
Lazard	20.7
JP Morgan	19.4
Citigroup	15.8
UBS	14.8
Merrill Lynch & Co. Inc.	12.8
Credit Suisse First Boston	12.2
Deutsche Bank	12.0
Morgan Stanley	10.4
Rothschild	8.0

Source: *Acquisitions Monthly*, September 2003, p. S3.

★ 3116 ★

Investment Banking

SIC: 6211; NAICS: 52311

Leading Merger Advisers Worldwide

Market shares are shown for global deals since the beginning of the year. Value of deals are shown in billions of dollars.

	($ bil.)	Share
Goldman Sachs	$467.8	29.2%
Morgan Stanley	386.1	24.1
J.P. Morgan	343.5	21.4
Merrill Lynch	268.9	16.8
Citigroup	242.3	15.1

Source: *Wall Street Journal*, February 12, 2004, p. C4, from Thomson Financial.

★ 3117 ★

Investment Banking

SIC: 6211; NAICS: 52311

Private Placement Market, 2003

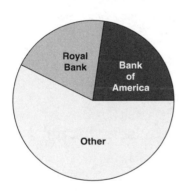

Traditional private placement topped the $20 billion market for the first time since the 1990s. Placements were valued at $21.33 billion for the first six months of 2003. Royal Bank of Scotland has a 9.5% for the same period in 2002.

Bank of America	22.7%
Royal Bank of Scotland	19.7
Other	57.6

Source: *Private Placement Market*, September 8, 2003, p. NA.

★ 3118 ★

Investment Banking

SIC: 6211; NAICS: 52311

Separate Account Managers

Market shares are shown in percent.

Smith Barney	32.8%
Merrill Lynch & Co.	23.5
Morgan Stanley	8.2
UBS Financial Services Inc.	7.2
Prudential Financial Inc.	3.8
Raymond James	2.5
Charles Schwab & Co. Inc.	2.4
A.G. Edwards & Sons Inc.	2.4
Deutsche Bank Alex. Brown	2.3
Wachovia Securities	1.9
Other	13.0

Source: *Investment News*, December 15, 2003, p. 44, from Cerulli Associates.

★ 3119 ★

Investment Banking

SIC: 6211; NAICS: 52311

Separately Managed Accounts, 2003 and 2006

Figures are based on a survey conducted electronically. More than 50 managed account program sponsors participate as well as more than 150 asset managers. Data for 2006 are forecasts.

	2003	2006
Wirehouses	68.0%	60.0%
Third-party vendors	9.0	12.0
Independent broker dealers	8.0	12.0

Source: *On Wall Street*, November 1, 2003, p. NA, from *Managed Accounts 2003 Asset Managers* and Cerulli Associates.

★ 3120 ★
Investment Banking
SIC: 6211; NAICS: 52311

Top Bookrunners in Latin America/ Caribbean, 2003

The top bookrunners of Latin American and Caribbean are ranked by issuances in billions of dollars.

JP Morgan . . . . $ 9.21
CSFB 6.24
Citigroup 4.62
Deutsche Bank 4.00
Morgan Stanley 3.53
UBS 2.92
Merrill Lynch 2.26
Wachovia Securities 2.15
ABN AMRO 2.01
ING 1.83

Source: *LatinFinance*, March 2004, p. 62.

★ 3121 ★
Investment Banking
SIC: 6211; NAICS: 52311

Top Bookrunners of Corporate Bonds in Mexico, 2003

Total issurances were $6.78 billion.

BBVA Bancomer 24.7%
ING 14.0
J.P. Morgan 13.7
Accival (Citigroup) 7.6
Ixe 6.8
Santander Serfin 6.6

Inversora Bursatil 6.5%
Scotia Inverlat 5.1
Other 15.0

Source: *LatinFinance*, March 2004, p. 27, from Dealogic.

★ 3122 ★
Investment Banking
SIC: 6211; NAICS: 52311

Top IPO Underwriters, 2003

Companies are ranked by amount raised in billions of dollars.

Goldman Sachs . . . . $ 3.94
CS First Boston 3.87
Friedman Billings 2.05
Citigroup 2.03
Morgan Stanley 1.93
Merrill Lynch 1.42
Bank of America 1.25
UBS 0.99
Lehman Bros. 0.74

Source: *Investor's Business Daily*, March 11, 2004, p. A7, from company reports and Equidesk.

★ 3123 ★
Investment Banking
SIC: 6211; NAICS: 52311

Top M&A Advisers in Latin America

Advisers are ranked by value of deals in billions of dollars.

Citigroup/Salomon Smith Barney . . . . . $ 9.24
JP Morgan 8.15
Credit Suisse First Boston 8.05
Goldman Sachs & Co. 6.92
Merrill Lynch & Co. 6.69
Morgan Stanley 3.87
UBS Warburg 1.96
Credit Lyonnais 1.68
Santander Central Hispano 1.58
Dresdner Kleinwort Wasserstein 1.57

Source: *Latin Trade*, April 2003, p. 38.

★ 3124 ★
Investment Banking
SIC: 6211; NAICS: 52311

Top Money Managers Worldwide

Managers are ranked by global institutional assets under management in millions of dollars.

State Street Global	$ 1,097,350
Barclays Global	958,165
Fidelity Investments	729,738
Mellon Financial	467,904
Deutsche Asset Mgmt.	467,065
AIG Global Investment	416,397
Wellington Management	393,756
Northern Trust Global	343,668
Vanguard Group	328,543
PIMCO	321,125
J.P. Morgan Fleming	317,217
TIAA-CREF	302,271

Source: *Pensions & Investments*, May 31, 2004, p. 22.

★ 3125 ★
Investment Banking
SIC: 6211; NAICS: 52311

Top Stock and Bond Underwriters Worldwide, 2002

The top firms worldwide are ranked by undisclosed fees.

	($ mil.)	Share
Citigroup	$ 1,760.2	12.17%
Morgan Stanley	1,195.4	8.27
J.P. Morgan	1,013.4	7.01
Goldman Sachs	1,002.6	6.93
Merrill Lynch	982.0	6.79
Credit Suisse F.B.	908.1	6.28
UBS	816.1	5.64
Lehman Brothers	636.7	4.40
Deutsche Bank	631.9	4.37
Nomura	574.3	3.97
Other	4,939.8	34.16

Source: *Wall Street Journal*, January 2, 2004, p. R17, from Thomson Financial.

★ 3126 ★
Investment Banking
SIC: 6211; NAICS: 52311

Who Controls the IRA Market

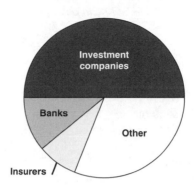

The IRA market is valued at $2.4 trillion.

Investment companies	50.0%
Banks	11.0
Insurers	8.0
Other	31.0

Source: *Annuity Market News*, August 1, 2003, p. NA, from Conning Research.

★ 3127 ★
Investment Banking
SIC: 6211; NAICS: 52311

Who Owns Stock

Households own more than a third of $11.1 billion in corporate stock. Figures are for the third quarter of 2002.

Household sector	37.0%
Mutual funds	18.0
Private pension funds	13.0
Rest of world	11.0
State/local govt. retirement funds	9.0
Life insurance companies	6.0
Other	6.0

Source: *USA TODAY*, September 5, 2003, p. 3B, from Federal Reserve.

★ 3128 ★

Mutual Funds

SIC: 6211; NAICS: 52311

Largest Mutual Fund Companies

Fund managers are ranked by assets in millions of dollars.

Fidelity Management & Research Co.	$ 664,394
The Vanguard Group Inc.	573,446
Capital Research & Management Co.	349,404
Merrill Lynch & Co.	180,973
Federated Investors Inc.	165,627
Mellon Financial Corp.	163,176
Morgan Stanley	155,482
Charles Schwab & Co. Inc.	154,653
Franklin Templeton Investments	153,736
Bank of America Corporation	148,066

Source: *American Lawyer*, April 2003, p. 125.

★ 3129 ★

Mutual Funds

SIC: 6211; NAICS: 52311

Largest Mutual Fund Managers

The top fund managers are shown as of December 2003. Figures include open- and closed-end funds. They exclude sub-advisory relationships and variable annuities.

	($ bil.)	Share
Fidelity Management & Research Co.	$ 788	11.63%
The Vanguard Group Inc.	683	10.09
Capital Group	495	7.30
Bank of America/Fleet	208	3.07
JP MorganChase/Bank One	208	3.07
Franklin Resources	199	2.94
Merrill Lynch	188	2.78
Morgan Stanley	179	2.65

Source: *Europe Intelligence Wire*, February 28, 2004, p. NA, from Strategic Insights.

★ 3130 ★

Mutual Funds

SIC: 6211; NAICS: 52311

Top Mutual Fund Companies in Greece

Market shares are shown in percent.

EFG Mutual Funds Management Company	25.85%
Diethniki	25.56
Alpha Mutual Funds	14.63
Ermis	7.55
Intertrust	7.08
Other	19.33

Source: *Europe Intelligence Wire*, May 10, 2004, p. NA, from Athens News Agency.

★ 3131 ★

Securites Exchanges

SIC: 6231; NAICS: 52321

Equity Option Trades

International Securities Exchange was launched in mid 2000 and rapidly claimed market share.

CBOE	31.0%
International Securites Exchange	30.0
Other	39.0

Source: *Chicago Tribune*, October 30, 2003, p. NA.

★ 3132 ★

Securites Exchanges

SIC: 6231; NAICS: 52321

Online Broker Market

Data show percent of average revenue trades.

Ameritrade	22.0%
Schwab	20.0
E-Trade	17.0
TD Waterhouse	11.0

Continued on next page.

★ 3132 ★

[Continued]
Securites Exchanges
SIC: 6231; NAICS: 52321

Online Broker Market

Data show percent of average revenue trades.

Fidelity	9.0%
Scottrade	8.0
TradeStation	3.0
Other	10.0

Source: *Investor's Business Daily*, September 26, 2003, p. A6, from company reports and Advest Inc.

★ 3133 ★

Securities Exchanges
SIC: 6231; NAICS: 52321

Derivative Exchanges Industry in Europe, 2001

Exchanges are ranked by number of contracts traded. CBOE stands for Chicago Board of Trade. CBOE stands for Chicago Board of Exchange.

	No.	Share
Korea SE	855	19.99%
Eurex	674	15.76
Euronext-Liffe	615	14.38
CME	412	9.63
CBOE	307	7.18
CBOT	260	6.08
Other	1,155	27.00

Source: *Financial Times*, January 13, 2003, p. 18, from UBS Warburg and FIBV.

★ 3134 ★

Securities Exchanges
SIC: 6231; NAICS: 52321

Equity Options Market

Market shares for equity options are for April 2004.

ISE	33.0%
CBOE	26.6
AMEX	18.2
PHLX	12.3
PCX	8.9
BOX	1.0

Source: *Securities Industry News*, May 10, 2004, p. 31, from Options Clearing Corp.

★ 3135 ★

Securities Exchanges
SIC: 6231; NAICS: 52321

NASDAQ Trading Volume

NASDAQ has less than 20% of trading volume.

NYSE	80.0%
NASDAQ	20.0

Source: *Business Week Online*, October 1, 2003, p. NA.

★ 3136 ★

Securities Exchanges
SIC: 6231; NAICS: 52321

Trading of Nasdaq-listed Companies

Market shares are shown in percent. ECN stands for electronic communication network.

ECNs and other firms	31.0%
Instinet and Island ECNs	26.0
ArcaEx	26.0
Nasdaq	17.0

Source: *Wall Street Journal*, September 19, 2003, p. A1, from companies.

★ 3137 ★

Securities Exchanges
SIC: 6231; NAICS: 52321

Trading of NYSE-listed Companies

Market shares are shown in percent. ECN stands for electronic communication network.

NYSE	80.0%
Nasdaq	13.0
ECNs and other firms	7.0

Source: *Wall Street Journal*, September 19, 2003, p. A1, from companies.

★ 3138 ★

Securities Exchanges
SIC: 6231; NAICS: 52321

Trading on the New York Stock Exchange

Figures are percent of volume figures as of September 30, 2003.

LaBranche	28.0%
Spear Leeds & Kellogg	21.0
Fleed Specialist	18.0
Bear Wagner	16.0
Van Der Moolen	12.0
Other	5.0

Source: *BusinessWeek*, November 3, 2003, p. 101, from New York Stock Exchange.

★ 3139 ★

Financial Information
SIC: 6289; NAICS: 523999

Financial Services Data Market Worldwide

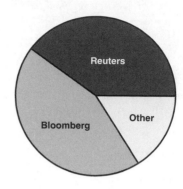

The industry is increasingly becoming a commoditized business. Also, a consortium of banks recently formed EBS to compete in the market and break the banking industry's dependence on Reuters (most of Reuter's customers are in the financial industry). Employers have also been trying to force employees to cut the use of data terminals which in turn cuts into the terminal firms revenues. The global industry has been valued at $6.5 billion.

	1991	2002	2003
Reuters	55.0%	40.0%	40.0%
Bloomberg	4.0	41.0	44.0
Other	41.0	19.0	16.0

Source: *BusinessWeek*, February 9, 2004, p. 8, from Shore Communications Inc.

★ 3140 ★

Financial Information
SIC: 6289; NAICS: 523999

Leading Financial Information Services, 2002 and 2003

Data show number of subscribers.

	2002	2003
Dow Jones Newswires	308,000	293,000
Reuters 300 Xtra	295,000	262,000
Bloomberg L.P.	250,000	263,000
Thomson ONE	110,000	102,500
S&P MarketScope	101,000	98,000

Continued on next page.

★ 3140 ★
[Continued]
Financial Information
SIC: 6289; NAICS: 523999

Leading Financial Information Services, 2002 and 2003

Data show number of subscribers.

	2002	2003
FTInteractive Data	83,000	86,000
RealMoney.com	82,000	85,000
myTrack	62,000	56,000
MultexNet	38,000	35,800

Source: *Electronic Information Report*, February 23, 2004, p. NA, from Simba Information and company reports.

SIC 63 - Insurance Carriers

★ 3141 ★
Insurance
SIC: 6300; NAICS: 524126
Commercial Insurance Market

The commerical insurance market is shown by distribution system. Shares are based on direct premiums written. In the personal line industry, regional companies were also growing in share: 21.81% in 2000, 22.18% in 2001 and 23.05% in 2002. National agencies fell from 14.96% in 2000 to 13.22% in 2002. Captive agencies had 54.75% in 2000, 55.24% in 2001 and then fell to 55.19% in 2002.

	2000	2001	2002
National agency companies	47.25%	47.17%	46.10%
Regional agency companies	31.47	31.91	32.72
Captive agency companies	20.88	20.53	20.81
Direct response companies	0.41	0.39	0.38

Source: *National Underwriter*, March 29, 2004, p. 12, from *IIABA 2002 P-C Insurance Maket Report*.

★ 3142 ★
Insurance
SIC: 6300; NAICS: 524126
Insurance Market in South Korea

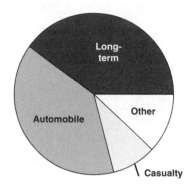

South Korea's non-life business was worth $17.9 billion, making it the world's tenth largest market.

Long-term (Non-life)	39.6%
Automobile	39.1
Casualty	8.9
Other	12.4

Source: *Reinsurance Magazine*, May 1, 2004, p. 31, from Korea Non-life Insurance Association.

★ 3143 ★
Insurance
SIC: 6300; NAICS: 524126

Largest Insurance Markets Worldwide, 2001

The industry is shown by country.

United States	30.0%
Japan	24.0
United Kingdom	10.0
Germany	3.8
Switzerland	1.3
Other	30.9

Source: *Reactions*, August 2003, p. 11.

★ 3144 ★
Insurance
SIC: 6300; NAICS: 524126

Leading Insurance Firms in Kenya

Market shares are estimated in percent. Workers compensation has the largest share of the premiums market at 40%.

Kenindia	13.0%
Alico	9.0
United	7.0
Heritage-All	5.0
UAP Provincial	4.0
Lion of Kenya	4.0
Kenyan Alliance	4.0
ICEA	4.0
PAN Africa	3.0
Jubilee	3.0
Other	44.0

Source: "Insurance Services." [online] from http://www.usatrade.gov [accessed January 5, 2004], from U.S. Commercial Service and Commissioner of Insurance.

★ 3145 ★
Insurance
SIC: 6300; NAICS: 524126

Leading Insurers in Latin America

Total premiums were $33 billion. Mexico, Brazil and Chile took 70% of volume. Companies are ranked by direct premiums in millions of dollars.

	($ mil.)	Share
ING Comercial America	$ 2,316	7.02%
Grupo Nacional Provincial	1,851	5.61
MetLife Mexico	1,772	5.37
Seguros Inbursa	1,519	4.60
Bradesco Vida e Previdencia	770	2.33
Bradesco Seguros	478	1.45
Porto Seguros Cia de Seguros Generais	466	1.41
Unibanco AIG Seguros	451	1.37
Itau Seguros	440	1.33
Monterrey New York Life	413	1.25
Other	22,524	68.25

Source: *Reactions*, October 2003, p. 56.

★ 3146 ★
Insurance
SIC: 6300; NAICS: 524126

Leading Non-Life Insurance Firms in India

New India
United India
National
Oriental
Bajaj Alliance
ICICI Lombard
Tata AIG
ECGC
Other

Market shares are shown in percent.

New India	23.71%
United India	20.43
National	19.96
Oriental	19.53
Bajaj Alliance	2.85

Continued on next page.

★ 3146 ★

[Continued]
Insurance
SIC: 6300; NAICS: 524126

Leading Non-Life Insurance Firms in India

Market shares are shown in percent.

ICICI Lombard	2.79%
Tata AIG	2.45
ECGC	2.34
Other	5.94

Source: *Reinsurance Magazine*, October 1, 2003, p. 26.

★ 3147 ★

Insurance
SIC: 6300; NAICS: 524126, 524128

Top Commercial Insurers in Michigan, 2002

Market shares are shown in percent.

Auto-Owners Insurance Group	9.6%
Allmerica	7.4
Chubb Group	6.2
Hartford Insurance Group	5.7
Zurich/Farmers Group	5.6
Other	65.5

Source: *A.M. Best Newswire*, September 18, 2003, p. NA, from A.M. Best & Co.

★ 3148 ★

Insurance
SIC: 6300; NAICS: 524126

Top Insurance Firms in Poland, 2003

Shares are for nonlife business insurance policies in place in Poland in 2003.

Powszechny Zaklad Ubezpieczen (PZU) . . .	53.3%
Warta	13.3
Other	33.4

Source: *A.M. Best Newswire*, May 3, 2004, p. NA.

★ 3149 ★

Insurance
SIC: 6300; NAICS: 524126

Top Insurers in Estonia, 2003

Shares are for the nonlife insurance sector in Estonia.

If Eesti Kindlustus	37.1%
Ergo Kindlustus	27.2
Seesam Rahvusvaheline Kindlustus	13.7
Other	22.0

Source: *A.M. Best Newswire*, May 6, 2020, p. NA.

★ 3150 ★

Insurance
SIC: 6300; NAICS: 524126

Top Insurers in the U.K., 2000

Market shares are shown in percent.

Royal & Sun Alliance	15.40%
Norwich Union	9.60
CGU International	9.40
Axa	8.09
Direct Line	4.65
Cornhill	4.12
Bupa	3.68
Zurich UK	3.23
Eagle Star	3.01
Other	38.82

Source: *Europe Intelligence Wire*, November 28, 2002, p. NA, from *Post Magazine*.

★ 3151 ★
Life Insurance
SIC: 6311; NAICS: 524113

Largest Life Insurers in Korea

Market shares are shown in percent.

Samsung Life Insurance	36.2%
Korea Life Insurance	18.6
Kyobo Life Insurance	17.4
Other	27.8

Source: *Asia Pacific Intelligence Wire*, February 10, 2004, p. NA.

★ 3152 ★
Life Insurance
SIC: 6311; NAICS: 524113

Leading Life/Health Insurance Firms

Shares are shown for the world market. The market is expected to increase from $1.8 trillion to $2.1 trillion.

Nippon Life Insurance	2.6%
ING Group	2.2
AXA	2.0
Aviva	1.5
Assicurazioni Generali	1.5
Other	9.8

Source: *Datamonitor Industry Market Research*, October 1, 2003, p. NA, from Datamonitor.

★ 3153 ★
Life Insurance
SIC: 6311; NAICS: 524113

Leading Variable Annuity Firms in Japan

Market shares are shown in percent.

Hatford Life Insurance	24.3%
ING Life	13.6
Mitsui Life	12.0
Sumitomo Life	7.4
Alico Japan	7.4
Skandia Life	7.3
Nippon Life	6.3

T&D Financial Life	5.7%
Daiichi Life	5.7
Mitsui Sumitomo Citi Insurance	3.6
Other	6.6

Source: *Best's Review*, December 2003, p. 88, from Hartford Life and Hoken Mainichi Shinbun.

★ 3154 ★
Life Insurance
SIC: 6311; NAICS: 524113

Top Life Insurers

American International Group Inc.
AEGON USA Inc.
Metropolitan Life Insurance Co.
Netherlands Insurance Company
The Hartford Financial Services Group Inc.
Principal Financial Group
Prudential Insurance Co. of America
New York Life Insurance Co.
CIGNA Corp.
Nationwide Life Insurance Co.
Citigroup inc.
Massachusetts Mutual Life Insurance Co.
Other

Market shares are shown based on direct premiums written.

American International Group Inc.	7.34%
AEGON USA Inc.	5.19
Metropolitan Life Insurance Co.	4.97
Netherlands Insurance Company (W.I.) Ltd.	4.55
The Hartford Financial Services Group Inc.	3.55
Principal Financial Group	3.21
Prudential Insurance Co. of America	2.84
New York Life Insurance Co.	2.84
CIGNA Corp.	2.66
Nationwide Life Insurance Co.	2.58
Citigroup inc.	2.44
Massachusetts Mutual Life Insurance Co.	2.12
Other	55.71

Source: *Investment News*, December 15, 2003, p. 53, from National Association of Insurance Commissioners.

★ 3155 ★
Life Insurance
SIC: 6311; NAICS: 524113
Top Life Insurers in Belgium

Market shares are shown for gross premium income for the first nine months of 2001.

State Insurance	38.78%
Institute/DZI/Orel Life	30.84
Vitosha Life	9.73
Allianz Bulgaria Life	7.89
Bulgarski Imoti	3.32
Bulstrad DZK Life	3.26
AIG Life	2.67
GRAVE Bulgaria	1.44
Dobrudzha-M Life	1.37
Medic Centre	0.70

Source: *European Banker*, January 23, 2002, p. 19.

★ 3156 ★
Life Insurance
SIC: 6311; NAICS: 524113
Top Life Insurers in China

The Chinese insurance market overall has grown 25% annually since 1996. In the non-life market the People's Insurance Company of China has a 70.5% share.

	2000	2002
China Life	65.0%	57.0%
Ping An	22.0	23.0
China Pacific	8.0	11.0
New China Life	2.0	4.8
AIA (AIG)	2.0	2.0
Taikang Life	0.0	2.0

Source: *Best's Review*, January 2004, p. 12, from Benfield Group, *Almanac of China's Insurance*, Swiss Re, and A.M. Best.

★ 3157 ★
Life Insurance
SIC: 6311; NAICS: 524113
Top Life Insurers in Estonia, 2003

Shares are for the life insurance sector in Estonia.

Hansapanga Kindlustus	42.7%
Eesti Uhispanga Elukindlustus	25.5
Other	31.8

Source: *A.M. Best Newswire*, May 6, 2020, p. NA.

★ 3158 ★
Life Insurance
SIC: 6311; NAICS: 524113
Top Life Insurers in Latvia

Market shares are shown in percent.

Ergo	34.1%
Baltikums Dziviba	25.0
Balta Dziviba	18.2
Other	32.7

Source: *A.M. Best Newswire*, May 6, 2004, p. NA.

★ 3159 ★
Life Insurance
SIC: 6311; NAICS: 524113

Top Life Insurers in Vietnam

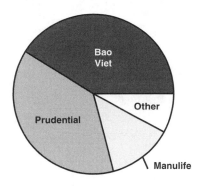

Overall, insurance companies saw sales of 10 trillion Vietnamese dollars.

Bao Viet	41.0%
Prudential	38.0
Manulife	12.6
Other	8.4

Source: *Saigon Times Magazine*, February 27, 2004, p. NA, from Finance Minestry's insurance department.

★ 3160 ★
Life Insurance
SIC: 6311; NAICS: 524113

Top Life Insurers Worldwide, 2000

Firms are ranked by premiums in millions of dollars.

Swiss Re	$ 5,091
Munich Re	3,443
Employers Re	3,007
General Re	2,264
Hannover Re	1,550
Transamerica Corp.	891
ING Re	844
Lincoln Re	841

Source: *Reinsurance Magazine*, February 1, 2002, p. 17, from Standard & Poor's.

★ 3161 ★
Auto Insurance
SIC: 6321; NAICS: 524126

Top Auto Insurers in Colorado

Market shares are shown in percent.

State Farm	23.5%
Farmers	15.6
American Family	9.3
Allstate	8.3
U.S. Auto Association	6.4
Progressive	5.3
Geico	3.9
Hartford	2.8
Safeco	2.4
Other	22.5

Source: *Rocky Mountain News*, May 15, 2003, p. 1B, from A.M. Best & Co.

★ 3162 ★
Auto Insurance
SIC: 6321; NAICS: 524126

Top Auto Insurers in Florida, 2002

Shares are for the private passenger market.

State Farm Group	24.3%
Allstate Insurance Group	14.6
Berkshire Hathaway Insurance	11.3
Progressive Insurance Group	9.1
USAA Group	4.6
Other	36.1

Source: *A.M. Best Newswire*, February 25, 2004, p. NA, from A.M. Best & Co.

★ 3163 ★
Auto Insurance
SIC: 6321; NAICS: 524126

Top Auto Insurers in Massachusetts, 2002

Market shares are shown in percent. Figures are for the private passenger market.

Commerce Group 25.5%
Arbella Insurance Group 10.5
MetLife Auto & Home Group 7.9
Liberty Mutual Insurance 7.3
Other 48.8

Source: *A.M. Best Newswire*, January 9, 2004, p. NA, from A.M. Best & Co.

★ 3164 ★
Auto Insurance
SIC: 6321; NAICS: 524126

Top Auto Insurers in Missouri, 2002

State Farm Group

American Family Insurance Group

Zurich/Farmers Group

Shelter Insurance

Allstate Insurance Group

Other

Market shares are shown in percent. Figures are for the private passenger market.

State Farm Group 23.9%
American Family Insurance Group 19.3
Zurich/Farmers Group 6.3
Shelter Insurance 6.3
Allstate Insurance Group 5.8
Other 38.4

Source: *A.M. Best Newswire*, January 30, 2004, p. NA, from A.M. Best & Co.

★ 3165 ★
Auto Insurance
SIC: 6321; NAICS: 524126

Top Auto Insurers in New Jersey, 2002

Market shares are shown in percent.

State Farm 15.1%
Allstate Insurance Group 12.3
NJM Insurance Group 12.1
Liberty Mutual Insurance 10.8
Prudential of America 7.2
Other 42.5

Source: *A.M. Best Newswire*, October 8, 2003, p. NA, from A.M. Best & Co.

★ 3166 ★
Auto Insurance
SIC: 6321; NAICS: 524126

Top Auto Insurers in North Carolina, 2002

Market shares are shown in percent.

Nationwide 20.1%
State Farm 14.1
Allstate 10.6
N.C. Farm Bureau 9.0
GMAC Integon 8.3
Other 48.5

Source: *A.M. Best Newswire*, March 1, 2004, p. NA, from A.M. Best & Co.

★ 3167 ★

Auto Insurance

SIC: 6321; NAICS: 524126

Top Auto Insurers in Texas, 2002

State Farm
Allstate
Zurich/Farmers
Progressive
USAA
Nationwide
Other

Market shares are shown in percent.

State Farm	23.0%
Allstate	16.2
Zurich/Farmers	13.3
Progressive	7.1
USAA	6.3
Nationwide	4.1
Other	30.0

Source: *Insurance Journal*, September 22, 2003, p. NA.

★ 3168 ★

Aviation Insurance

SIC: 6321; NAICS: 524114

Aviation Insurance Market in Saudi Arabia

NCCI also has 82.3% of the energy market and 65.3% of the marine hull market.

NCCI	86.7%
Other	13.3

Source: *A.M. Best Newswire*, May 25, 2004, p. NA.

★ 3169 ★

Health Insurance

SIC: 6321; NAICS: 524114

Largest Health Insurers, 2003

Companies are ranked by millions enrolled. WellChoice and Oxford Health Plans are planning to merge. Oxford has 1.5 million members.

UnitedHealthcare	18.7
WellPoint	15.0
Aetna	13.0
Anthem	11.9
Cigna	4.2
Humana	3.9
Health Net	3.9
PacifiCare	2.9
Coventry	2.4

Source: *New York Times*, April 6, 2004, p. C1, from Citigroup/Smith Barney.

★ 3170 ★

Health Insurance

SIC: 6321; NAICS: 524114

Leading Health Insurers

Groups are ranked by millions of customers. Anthem announced plans to acquire WellPoint in October 2003.

Anthem and WellPoint	25.8%
UnitedHealth and Mid Atlantic	20.3
Aetna	13.0
Cigna	12.0
Kaiser Permanente	8.1
Other	20.8

Source: *New York Times*, October 28, 2003, p. C9, from J.P. Morgan.

★ 3171 ★

Health Insurance

SIC: 6321; NAICS: 524114

Leading Health Insurers in New York/ New Jersey/Connecticut

Market shares are shown based on total enrollment as of July 2003. WellChoice and Oxford Health Plans are planning to merge.

WellChoice	12.0%
Aetna	12.0

Continued on next page.

★ 3171 ★

[Continued]
Health Insurance
SIC: 6321; NAICS: 524114

Leading Health Insurers in New York/ New Jersey/Connecticut

Market shares are shown based on total enrollment as of July 2003. WellChoice and Oxford Health Plans are planning to merge.

UnitedHealthcare	9.0%
Oxford	9.0
Cigna	8.0
Blue Cross Blue Shield	7.0
Anthem	6.0
Health Net	5.0
Other	32.0

Source: *New York Times*, April 6, 2004, p. C4, from Citigroup/Smith Barney.

★ 3172 ★

Health Insurance
SIC: 6324; NAICS: 524114

Health Insurance Market in California

Figures are for 2001-2002. There were 43.6 million people without health insurance in the United States during the period 2001-2002. This was up from 35.4 million people uninsured in 1992.

Private employer	59.7%
Uninsured	23.5
Medicare	8.0
Private individual	7.0
Public other	1.8

Source: *Governing*, February 2004, p. 74.

★ 3173 ★

Health Insurance
SIC: 6324; NAICS: 524114

Health Insurance Market in Indiana, 2002

Market shares are shown in percent.

Anthem	35.0%
UnitedHealthcare	15.0
Other	50.0

Source: *Indianapolis Star*, March 24, 2004, p. NA.

★ 3174 ★

Health Insurance
SIC: 6324; NAICS: 524114

Health Insurance Market in Southeast Pennsylvania

Market shares are shown in percent.

Independence	70.0%
Other	30.0

Source: *Philadelphia Inquirer*, November 20, 2003, p. NA.

★ 3175 ★

Health Plans
SIC: 6324; NAICS: 524114

Health Insurance Market in Rhode Island

Market shares are shown for 2002.

Blue Cross	71.0%
Other	29.0

Source: *Providence Journal*, March 8, 2004, p. NA.

★ 3176 ★
Health Plans
SIC: 6324; NAICS: 524114

HMO Enrollment by Region, 2002

In terms of market penetration Rochester, NY saw the highest rate (71.7%) followed by Buffalo-Niagara, NY (67.6%).

Los Angeles-Long Beach, CA	5,184,513
Riverside-San Bernadino, CA	1,870,548
Oakland, CA	1,599,739
San Diego, CA	1,516,775
Sacramento, CA	1,139,600
San Jose, CA	929,755
San Francisco, CA	900,271
Buffalo-Niagra Falls, NY	786,548
Rochester, NY	786,041

Source: *Managed Healthcare Executive*, April 2003, p. 43, from InterStudy Competitive Source.

★ 3177 ★
Health Plans
SIC: 6324; NAICS: 524114

Largest Health Plans in Michigan

Market shares are shown in percent.

Blue Cross and Blue Shield of Michigan	70.0%
Other	30.0

Source: *Modern Healthcare*, July 28, 2003, p. NA.

★ 3178 ★
Health Plans
SIC: 6324; NAICS: 524114

Largest HMOs in the Houston Area, 2002 and 2003

Plans are ranked by enrollment at the end of 2003.

	2002	2003
Cigna Healthcare of Texas	315,670	290,338
Southwest Texas HMO	280,168	178,995
Aetna	212,976	161,429
Amerigroup Texas	138,467	144,523
Texas Children's Health Plan	100,610	118,644

	2002	2003
Humana Health Plan of Texas	95,748	95,429
Community Health Choice	33,364	46,810
Evercare of Texas	29,105	31,701

Source: *Houston Chronicle*, March 24, 2004, p. q1.

★ 3179 ★
Health Plans
SIC: 6324; NAICS: 524114

Largest Medicaid Plans in Ohio

Market shares are shown as of October 1, 2003.

CareSource	66.0%
QualChoice	13.0
SummaCare	8.0
Paramount	6.0
Family Health Plan	5.0
MediPlan	2.0

Source: *Managed Care Week*, October 6, 2003, p. 3, from *AIS's Managed Medicare and Medicaid Factbook*.

★ 3180 ★
Health Plans
SIC: 6324; NAICS: 524114

Top Health Plans in South Jersey

Aetna has been losing market share to Blue Cross over the last five years.

Aetna	44.0%
Blue Cross	26.0
Other	30.0

Source: *Philadelphia Business Journal*, June 30, 2003, p. NA, from DGA Partners.

★ 3181 ★
Fire & Allied Insurance
SIC: 6331; NAICS: 524126
Top Fire/Allied Insurers, 2002

Market shares are shown based on direct premiums written.

Zurich/Farmers Group	7.3%
FM Global Group	7.0
Amer Intl Group	7.0
Ace INA Group	4.5
Allianz of America	4.4
Travelers PC Group	4.0
Royal & SunAlliance	3.7
Acceptance Ins Cos.	3.0
St. Paul Cos.	2.9
Hartford Ins Cos.	2.7
Other	53.5

Source: *Best's Review*, December 2003, p. 59, from A.M. Best Statement Products.

★ 3182 ★
Fire & Allied Insurance
SIC: 6331; NAICS: 524126
Top Fire/Allied Insurers in California, 2002

Market shares are shown based on direct premiums written.

California Earthquake	15.1%
Zurich/Farmers Group	10.3
Other	74.6

Source: *Best's Review*, December 2003, p. 59, from A.M. Best Statement Products.

★ 3183 ★
Fire & Allied Insurance
SIC: 6331; NAICS: 524126
Top Fire/Allied Insurers in Montana, 2002

Market shares are shown based on direct premiums written.

Ace INA Group	22.1%
Acceptance Ins Cos.	14.4
Other	63.5

Source: *Best's Review*, December 2003, p. 59, from A.M. Best Statement Products.

★ 3184 ★
Home Owners Insurance
SIC: 6331; NAICS: 524126
Top Home Owner Insurers in California, 2002

Market shares are estimated in percent.

State Farm	23.3%
Zurich/Farmers	19.3
Allstate	13.9
California State Auto Group	5.0
USAA Group	4.2
Other	34.3

Source: *A.M. Best Newswire*, May 6, 2004, p. NA, from A.M. Best & Co.

★ 3185 ★
Home Owners Insurance
SIC: 6331; NAICS: 524126

Top Home Owner Insurers in Colorado, 2002

Market shares are estimated in percent.

State Farm Group 23.35%
Zurich/Farmers Group 20.05
American Family Insurance Group 13.22
Allstate Insurance Group 8.83
USAA Group 5.14
Other 29.51

Source: *A.M. Best Newswire*, April 6, 2004, p. NA, from A.M. Best & Co.

★ 3186 ★
Home Owners Insurance
SIC: 6331; NAICS: 524126

Top Home Owner Insurers in Florida, 2002

Market shares are estimated in percent.

State Farm Group 23.5%
Allstate Insurance Group 11.2
HDI US Group 6.9
USAA Group 5.3
Nationwide Group 4.8
Other 48.3

Source: *A.M. Best Newswire*, December 19, 2003, p. NA, from A.M. Best & Co.

★ 3187 ★
Home Owners Insurance
SIC: 6331; NAICS: 524126

Top Home Owner Insurers in Hurricane-Prone State

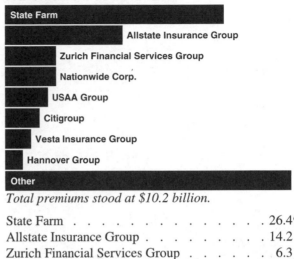

Total premiums stood at $10.2 billion.

State Farm 26.4%
Allstate Insurance Group 14.2
Zurich Financial Services Group 6.3
Nationwide Corp. 5.6
USAA Group 5.3
Citigroup 3.6
Vesta Insurance Group 2.5
Hannover Group 2.3
Other 33.7

Source: *Business Wire*, September 18, 2003, p. NA, from Weiss Ratings.

★ 3188 ★
Home Owners Insurance
SIC: 6331; NAICS: 524126

Top Home Owner Insurers in Texas, 2002

Market shares are shown in percent.

State Farm	30.2%
Allstate	17.3
Zurich/Farmers	12.0
USAA	6.2
Travelers	4.6
Testa	4.4
Other	25.3

Source: *Insurance Journal*, September 22, 2003, p. NA.

★ 3189 ★
Liability Insurance
SIC: 6331; NAICS: 524126

Leading D&O Insurers, 2002

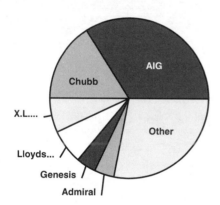

Leaders in the directors and officers liability insurance market are ranked by share of total premiums.

AIG	34.0%
Chubb	16.0
X.L. Insurance	7.0
Lloyds of London	7.0
Genesis	4.0
Admiral	4.0
Other	28.0

Source: *Wall Street Journal*, July 31, 2003, p. C1, from Tillinghast-Towers Penn.

★ 3190 ★
Liability Insurance
SIC: 6331; NAICS: 524126

Leading EPLI Insurers, 2003

Market shares are shown based on premiums written for employment practice liability coverage.

AIG	38.7%
XL	23.7
Chubb	15.7
Zurich	10.0
Hartford	2.6
Royal & SunAlliance	1.7
St. Paul	1.6
Kemper	1.2
Other	4.8

Source: *Best's Reveiew*, April 2004, p. 21, from *2003 RIMS Benchmark Survey* by the Risk and Insurance Management Society and Advisen Inc.

★ 3191 ★
Marine Insurance
SIC: 6331; NAICS: 524126

Top Inland Marine Insurers, 2002

Market shares are shown based on direct premiums written.

Amer Intl Group	9.1%
Zurich/Farmers Group	7.4
CNA Ins Cos.	5.6
FM Global Group	5.5
State Farm Group	4.8
Hartford Ins Group	4.4
Allianz of America	4.3
Assurant Group	4.2
Chubb Group of Ins Cos.	4.0
Travelers PC Group	3.9
Other	46.8

Source: *Best's Review*, December 2003, p. 59, from A.M. Best Statement Products.

★ 3192 ★
Marine Insurance
SIC: 6331; NAICS: 524126
Top Inland Marine Insurers in Florida

Market shares are shown in percent.

Zurich/Farmers Group	10.0%
CNA Insurance Cos.	8.1
State Farm Group	7.4
American International Group	7.3
Assurant Group	5.9
Other	61.3

Source: *A.M. Best Newswire*, October 20, 2003, p. NA, from A.M. Best & Co.

★ 3193 ★
Marine Insurance
SIC: 6331; NAICS: 524126
Top Inland Marine Insurers in Hawaii, 2002

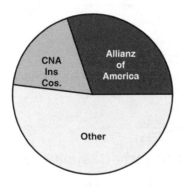

Market shares are shown based on direct premiums written.

Allianz of America	29.7%
CNA Ins Cos.	18.3
Other	52.0

Source: *Best's Review*, December 2003, p. 59, from A.M. Best Statement Products.

★ 3194 ★
Marine Insurance
SIC: 6331; NAICS: 524126
Top Inland Marine Insurers in Michigan, 2002

Market shares are shown based on direct premiums written.

Auto-Owners Ins Group	8.1%
Amer Intl Group	7.4
Other	84.5

Source: *Best's Review*, December 2003, p. 59, from A.M. Best Statement Products.

★ 3195 ★
Marine Insurance
SIC: 6331; NAICS: 524126
Top Inland Marine Insurers in New York, 2002

Market shares are shown based on direct premiums written.

Amer Intl Group	13.1%
Chubb Group of Ins Cos.	13.0
Other	73.9

Source: *Best's Review*, December 2003, p. 59, from A.M. Best Statement Products.

★ 3196 ★
Marine Insurance
SIC: 6331; NAICS: 524126
Top Ocean Marine Insurers, 2002

Market shares are shown based on direct premiums written.

CNA Ins. Cos.	11.9%
Amer Intl Group	11.3
Ace INA Group	6.6
Allianz of America	6.4
White Mtns. Group	5.5
St. Paul Cos.	4.9
Zurich/Farmers Group	4.1
XL America Group	4.0
Chubb Group of Ins. Cos.	3.8
Royal & SunAlliance	3.6

Continued on next page.

★ 3196 ★

[Continued]
Marine Insurance
SIC: 6331; NAICS: 524126

Top Ocean Marine Insurers, 2002

Market shares are shown based on direct premiums written.

Liberty Mutual	3.5%
Atlantic Mutual	3.0
Other	31.4

Source: *Best's Review*, December 2003, p. 59, from A.M. Best Statement Products.

★ 3197 ★

Marine Insurance
SIC: 6331; NAICS: 524126

Top Ocean Marine Insurers in Louisiana, 2002

Market shares are shown based on direct premiums written.

CNA Ins Cos.	17.1%
XL America Group	14.5
Other	68.4

Source: *Best's Review*, December 2003, p. 59, from A.M. Best Statement Products.

★ 3198 ★

Marine Insurance
SIC: 6331; NAICS: 524126

Top Ocean Marine Insurers in Maine, 2002

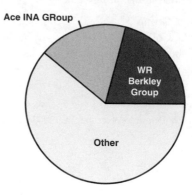

Market shares are shown based on direct premiums written.

WR Berkley Group	21.3%
Ace INA GRoup	17.6
Other	61.1

Source: *Best's Review*, December 2003, p. 59, from A.M. Best Statement Products.

★ 3199 ★

Property Insurance
SIC: 6331; NAICS: 524126

Largest Property/Casualty Insurers

Market shares are shown in percent.

AIG	8.8%
St. Paul Travelers	7.6
Zurich/Farmers	6.5
Travelers	4.4
CNA	3.8
Liberty Mutual	3.7
St. Paul	3.2
Chubb	3.1
Hartford	2.9
CA Comp Fund	2.7
ACE	2.3
Other	51.0

Source: *Financial Times*, November 18, 2003, p. 17, from A.M. Best & Co.

★ 3200 ★

Property Insurance

SIC: 6331; NAICS: 524126

Leading Fire & Peril Insurers in the Czech Republic

Market shares are shown in percent.

Ceska Pojistovna	51.0%
Kooperativa	18.4
Ceske Sporiteiny	7.3
Allianz	5.9
IPB	3.9
AIG Czech Republic	2.6
CSOB	2.1
Uniqa	2.0
Other	6.8

Source: *Reinsurance Magazine*, November 16, 2002, p. 26.

★ 3201 ★

Property Insurance

SIC: 6331; NAICS: 524126

Property/Casualty Insurance Market in China, 2001

Premiums stood at $8.3 billion in 2001, up from $5.8 billion in 1997.

Auto and third party liability	60.0%
Enterprise property	18.0
Cargo	6.0
Liability	4.0
Household property	3.0
Gurantee	1.0
Other	8.0

Source: *Best's Review*, February 2003, p. 27, from *Yearbook of China's Insurance* and Swiss Re.

★ 3202 ★

Workers Compensation Insurance

SIC: 6331; NAICS: 524126

Top Workers Comp Insurers, 2002

State Comp Fund California
Liberty Mutual Ins. Cos.
American Intl. Group
Zurich/Farmers Group
Travelers PC Group
Hartford Ins. Group
CNA Ins. Cos.
Kemper Ins. Cos.
Royal & SunAlliance
St. Paul Cos.
ACE INA Group
Everest Reins. US Group
Other

Market shares are shown in percent.

State Comp Fund California	12.7%
Liberty Mutual Ins. Cos.	8.8
American Intl. Group	7.3
Zurich/Farmers Group	4.9
Travelers PC Group	3.6
Hartford Ins. Group	3.5
CNA Ins. Cos.	3.3
Kemper Ins. Cos.	3.1
Royal & SunAlliance	2.7
St. Paul Cos.	2.2
ACE INA Group	1.7
Everest Reins. US Group	1.5
Other	44.7

Source: *Risk Management*, January 2004, p. 8, from A.M. Best & Co.

★ 3203 ★
Workers Compensation Insurance
SIC: 6331; NAICS: 524126

Top Workers Comp Insurers in California, 2002

Market shares are estimated in percent.

State Compensation Insurance Fund of
   California 50.4%
American International Group 4.7
Everest Re 4.6
Kemper Insurance Cos. 3.7
Zurich/Farmers 3.6
Other 33.0

Source: *A.M. Best Newswire*, November 12, 2003, p. NA, from A.M. Best & Co.

★ 3204 ★
Workers Compensation Insurance
SIC: 6331; NAICS: 524126

Top Workers Comp Insurers in Massachusetts

Market shares are shown in percent.

Travelers/Citigroup 10.7%
Liberty Mutual Insurance Cos. 10.4
Eastern Casualty Group 8.8
A.I.M. Mutual Insurance Cos. 7.4
American International Group Inc. 5.5
Other 57.2

Source: *A.M. Best Newswire*, May 19, 2003, p. NA, from A.M. Best & Co.

★ 3205 ★
Workers Compensation Insurance
SIC: 6331; NAICS: 524126

Top Workers Comp Insurers in Missouri

Market shares are shown in percent.

Travelers Property/Casualty Group 13.1%
Liberty Mutual Insurance Cos. 10.0
American International Group 9.1
Zurich/Farmers Group 7.8
Royal and Sun Alliance 4.3
Other 55.7

Source: *A.M. Best Newswire*, October 20, 2003, p. NA, from A.M. Best & Co.

★ 3206 ★
Workers Compensation Insurance
SIC: 6331; NAICS: 524126

Top Workers Comp Insurers in Texas, 2002

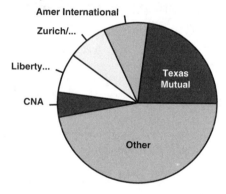

Market shares are shown in percent.

Texas Mutual 23.2%
Amer International 8.5
Zurich/Farmers 8.3
Liberty Mutual 8.2
CNA 5.1
Other 46.7

Source: *Insurance Journal*, September 22, 2003, p. NA.

★ 3207 ★
Workers Compensation Insurance
SIC: 6331; NAICS: 524126

Top Workers Comp Insurers in Washington, 2002

Market shares are estimated in percent.

Kemper Insurance Co.	23.1%
Liberty Mutual Insurance Cos.	20.8
Safety National	9.7
Majestic Insurance Co.	8.8
St. Paul	7.9
Other	29.7

Source: *A.M. Best Newswire*, December 3, 2003, p. NA, from A.M. Best & Co.

★ 3208 ★
Home Warranties
SIC: 6351; NAICS: 524126

Home Warranty Sales in California

HWAC stands for Home Warranty Association of California.

HWAC	91.0%
Other	9.0

Source: *Business Wire*, March 31, 2004, p. NA.

★ 3209 ★
Liability Insurance
SIC: 6351; NAICS: 524126

RRG Premiums

Premiums for risk retention groups (RRGs) are forecasted to grow from $1.2 billion in 2002 to $1.7 billion in 2003.

Health care	$ 898.3
Professional services	420.1
Government/institutions	194.3
Property development	86.0

Manufacturing & commerce	$ 54.3
Transportation	34.4
Environmental	32.9
Leisure	5.2

Source: *National Underwriter*, October 13, 2003, p. 28, from *Risk Retention Reporter 2003 Survey*.

★ 3210 ★
Medical Malpractice Insurance
SIC: 6351; NAICS: 524126

Leading Medical Malpractice Insurers, 2002

Market shares are shown in percent.

MLMIC Group	10.7%
American International Group Inc.	7.2
GE Global	7.1
ProAssurance Group	5.0
Zurich/Farmers	4.7
Other	65.2

Source: *Best Wire*, April 2, 2004, p. NA, from A.M. Best Co.

★ 3211 ★
Medical Malpractice Insurance
SIC: 6351; NAICS: 524126

Top Medical Liability Insurers in California

Market shares are shown in percent.

Norcal Group	20.6%
SCPIE Cos.	16.1
Doctors Company Insurance Group	15.2
Zurich/Farmers Group	7.3
American International Group	5.0
Other	35.8

Source: *A.M. Best Newswire*, September 3, 2003, p. NA, from A.M. Best & Co.

★ 3212 ★

Medical Malpractice Insurance

SIC: 6351; NAICS: 524126

Top Medical Liability Insurers in Colorado

Market shares are shown in percent.

COPIC 80.0%
Other 20.0

Source: *Denver Post*, September 25, 2003, p. C8.

★ 3213 ★

Medical Malpractice Insurance

SIC: 6351; NAICS: 524126

Top Medical Liability Insurers in Connecticut

Market shares are shown in percent.

Connecticut Medical Insurance Co. 31.51%
ProMutual Group 14.11
GE Global Insurance Group 8.85
Zurich/Farmers Group 8.07
Doctors Company Insurance Group 5.92
Other 31.54

Source: *A.M. Best Newswire*, September 18, 2003, p. NA, from A.M. Best & Co.

★ 3214 ★

Medical Malpractice Insurance

SIC: 6351; NAICS: 524126

Top Medical Liability Insurers in Florida, 2002

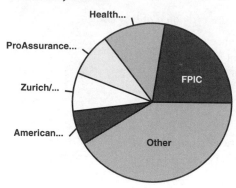

Market shares are estimated in percent.

FPIC 22.6%
Health Care Indemnity 13.0
ProAssurance Group 8.7
Zurich/Farmers Group 7.5
American International Group 6.5
Other 41.7

Source: *A.M. Best Newswire*, February 23, 2004, p. NA, from A.M. Best & Co.

★ 3215 ★

Medical Malpractice Insurance

SIC: 6351; NAICS: 524126

Top Medical Liability Insurers in Kentucky, 2002

Market shares are estimated in percent.

GE Global Insurance Group 23.4%
APCapital Group 13.0
State Volunteer Mutual Insurance 8.9
American International Group 6.6
Reciprocal Group 5.6
Other 42.5

Source: *A.M. Best Newswire*, November 12, 2003, p. NA, from A.M. Best & Co.

★ 3216 ★
Medical Malpractice Insurance
SIC: 6351; NAICS: 524126

Top Medical Liability Insurers in Maryland, 2002

Market shares are estimated in percent.

Medical Mutual Group	42.6%
MLMIC Group	17.3
American International Group	8.8
GE Global Insurance Group	6.7
Doctors Company Insurance Group	5.0
Other	19.6

Source: *A.M. Best Newswire*, December 19, 2003, p. NA, from A.M. Best & Co.

★ 3217 ★
Medical Malpractice Insurance
SIC: 6351; NAICS: 524126

Top Medical Liability Insurers in Nevada, 2002

Market shares are estimated in percent.

St. Paul	16.5%
Health Care Indemnity	14.3
Doctors Company Insurance Group	10.8
PIC Wisconsin Group	10.3
Allianz of America	8.1
Other	40.0

Source: *A.M. Best Newswire*, January 30, 2004, p. NA, from A.M. Best & Co.

★ 3218 ★
Medical Malpractice Insurance
SIC: 6351; NAICS: 524126

Top Medical Liability Insurers in New Jersey, 2002

Market shares are estimated in percent.

MLMIC Group (includes Princeton)	49.2%
Miix Group	18.3
ProMutual Group	7.4
Mixx Advantage	4.4
GE Global Insurance Group	4.4
Other	16.3

Source: *A.M. Best Newswire*, October 3, 2003, p. NA, from A.M. Best & Co.

★ 3219 ★
Medical Malpractice Insurance
SIC: 6351; NAICS: 524126

Top Medical Liability Insurers in Oklahoma, 2002

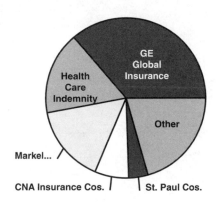

Market shares are estimated in percent.

GE Global Insurance Group	36.6%
Health Care Indemnity Inc.	16.7
Markel Corp. Group	15.5
CNA Insurance Cos.	6.6
St. Paul Cos.	3.5
Other	21.1

Source: *A.M. Best Newswire*, November 12, 2003, p. NA, from A.M. Best & Co.

★ 3220 ★
Medical Malpractice Insurance
SIC: 6351; NAICS: 524126

Top Medical Liability Insurers in West Virginia, 2002

Market shares are estimated in percent.

St. Paul	29.0%
ProAssurance	20.9
American International Group	19.0
Everest Re U.S. Group	7.8
NCRIC Group	7.5
Other	15.8

Source: *A.M. Best Newswire*, October 3, 2003, p. NA, from A.M. Best & Co.

★ 3221 ★
Surety Insurance
SIC: 6351; NAICS: 524126

Top Multiperil Insurers in Texas, 2002

Market shares are shown in percent.

Zurich/Farmers	13.0%
Travelers	9.8
CNA	7.6
Chubb	6.5
Hartford	5.7
State Farm	4.1
Other	53.3

Source: *Insurance Journal*, September 22, 2003, p. NA.

★ 3222 ★
Title Insurance
SIC: 6361; NAICS: 524127

Largest Title Insurers in Los Angeles County, 2002

Market shares are shown in percent.

Fidelity National Title	14.40%
First American Title	12.45
Chicago Title	10.19

Southland Title	6.27%
American Title	5.48
Stewart Title	5.27
Equity Title	5.24
Investors Title	4.03
Gateway Title	3.97
Other	32.70

Source: *San Fernando Valley Business Journal*, June 23, 2003, p. 33.

★ 3223 ★
Title Insurance
SIC: 6361; NAICS: 524127

Leading Title Insurers in Virginia

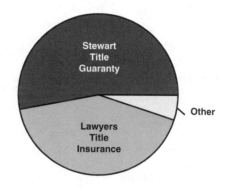

Market shares are shown in percent.

Stewart Title Guaranty Co.	53.3%
Lawyers Title Insurance	41.6
Other	5.0

Source: *Dolan's Virginia Business*, May 19, 2003, p. NA.

★ 3224 ★
Title Insurance
SIC: 6361; NAICS: 524127

Top Title Insurers in Los Angeles, CA

Market shares are shown in percent for 2003.

Fidelity National Title	14.5%
First American Title	11.0

Continued on next page.

★ 3224 ★

[Continued]
Title Insurance
SIC: 6361; NAICS: 524127

Top Title Insurers in Los Angeles, CA

Market shares are shown in percent for 2003.

Chicago Title	10.4%
Southland Title	7.1
Ticor Title	6.3
Stewart Title	5.3
Equity Title	4.7
LandAmerica Lawyers Title	4.5
Investors Title	4.1
Other	32.1

Source: *Los Angeles Business Journal*, March 1, 2004, p. 24.

★ 3225 ★

Pensions
SIC: 6371; NAICS: 52511

Largest Segregated Pension Fund Managers in the U.K., 2002

Firms are ranked by value of segregated funds under management in millions of Britihs pounds.

Barclays Global Investors	£ 30,071
Deutsche Asset Management	29,502
Merrill Lynch Investment Managers	29,212
Schroder Investment Management	29,100
UBS Global Asset Management	19,461
Goldman Sachs Asset Management	18,586
Henderson Global Investors	17,940
Capital International	16,049
Threadneedle Asset Management	14,205
Fidelity Pensions Management	14,176

Source: *Financial Times*, May 21, 2003, p. 1.

★ 3226 ★

Pensions
SIC: 6371; NAICS: 52511

Pension Bond Managers in the Midwest

Market shares are shown in percent.

UBS	13.2%
Citigroup	11.3
Bear Stearns	6.3
Other	69.2

Source: *The Bond Buyer*, August 13, 2003, p. 28.

★ 3227 ★

Banking Insurance
SIC: 6399; NAICS: 524128

Leading BHC Insurers

Companies are ranked by bank holding company insurance premiums written in 2002. Figures are in millions.

MetLife	$ 19,085,896
Citigroup	3,479,000
Countrywide Financial	561,868
Wells Fargo & Company	399,000
J.P. Morgan Chase & Co.	220,000
Bank One	157,000
Bank of America	133,000
U.S. Bancorp	40,200
National City Corp.	31,151
Wachovia	30,000

Source: *National Underwriter*, January 12, 2004, p. 30, from Michael D. White & Associates.

SIC 64 - Insurance Agents, Brokers, and Service

★ 3228 ★

Reinsurance

SIC: 6411; NAICS: 52421

Largest Reinsurers, 2002

Munich Re	
Swiss Re	
Berkshire Hathaway Re Group	
Hannover Re Group	
Employers Re Group	
Lloyd's	
SCOR Re Group	
Allianz Re Group	
Gerling Global Re Group	
XL Re Group	
Converium Re Group	

Firms are ranked by net reinsurance premiums written in billions of dollars.

Munich Re	$ 24.92
Swiss Re	21.60
Berkshire Hathaway Re Group	13.08
Hannover Re Group	8.52
Employers Re Group	7.89
Lloyd's	6.80
SCOR Re Group	4.69
Allianz Re Group	4.58
Gerling Global Re Group	4.46
XL Re Group	3.54
Converium Re Group	3.32

Source: *Reactions*, September 2003, p. SS10.

★ 3229 ★

Reinsurance

SIC: 6411; NAICS: 52421

Largest Reinsurers in Canada, 2002

Firms are ranked by net premiums written in millions of Canadian dollars.

Munich Re	480.0
Axa Re	358.9
Scor Canada Re	190.3
ERC	174.8
Partner Re	159.0
Swiss Re Canada	132.2
Everest Re	122.5
Hannover Re	101.4
Gerling Global Re	100.2

Source: *Reinsurance Magazine*, August 11, 2003, p. 22.

★ 3230 ★

Reinsurance

SIC: 6411; NAICS: 52421

Leading Reinsurers in Japan, 2000

Market shares are shown in percent.

Toa Re	16.3%
Earthquake Re	13.7
Tokio	13.1
Yasuda	8.9
Mitsui	6.0
Chiyoda	6.0
Sumitomo	5.6
Nissan	3.8
Nippon	3.6
Dowa	2.5
Other	20.5

Source: *Reinsurance Magazine*, May 1, 2002, p. 22, from Insurance Research Institute Hoken Kenkyujo.

SIC 65 - Real Estate

Shopping Centers
SIC: 6512; NAICS: 53112

Largest Shopping Center Brokers, 2003

Total brokered space was $7.1 billion. Market shares are shown in percent.

CB Richard Ellis	22.9%
Eastdil Realty	18.3
Cushman & Wakefield	10.8
Grubb & Ellis	6.1
Holliday Fenoglio Fowler	5.7
Secured Capital	5.0
Marcus & Millichap	4.7
Sperry Van Ness	3.9
Colliers International	3.9
Other	18.7

Source: *Real Estate Alert*, February 11, 2004, p. 1, from Real Estate Alert's Deal Database.

Shopping Centers
SIC: 6512; NAICS: 53112

Top Shopping Center Managers

Simon Property Group
Kimco Realty Corp.
Westfield America Inc.
CBL & Associates Properties Inc.
Inland Real Estate Corp.
The Macerich Co.
CB Richard Ellis Investors
New Plan Excel Realty Trust
Benderson Development Co. Inc.
The Rouse Co.

Groups are ranked by millions of gross leaseable area managed.

Simon Property Group	198.00
Kimco Realty Corp.	83.54
Westfield America Inc.	66.76
CBL & Associates Properties Inc.	63.10
Inland Real Estate Corp.	62.50
The Macerich Co.	60.00
CB Richard Ellis Investors	59.60
New Plan Excel Realty Trust	55.71
Benderson Development Co. Inc.	40.00
The Rouse Co.	39.80

Source: *Retail Traffic*, April 2004, p. 54.

★ 3233 ★

Shopping Centers

SIC: 6512; NAICS: 53112

Top Shopping Center Owners

Groups are ranked by millions of gross leaseable area owned.

Simon Property Group	183.30
General Growth Properties Inc.	109.63
Kimco Realty Corp.	74.63
Westfield America	63.50
The Macerich Company	57.90
New Plan Excel Realty Trust	52.00
The Rouse Co.	45.21
Benderson Development Co.	40.00
Developers Diversified Realty	39.72
Cafaro Co.	33.88

Source: *Shopping Center World*, April 2003, p. 44.

★ 3234 ★

Apartments

SIC: 6513; NAICS: 53111

Largest Apartment Managers, 2004

- Apartment Investment and Management Company
- Equity Residential
- American Management Services
- Lincoln Property Company
- Archstone-Smith
- United Dominion Realty Trust Inc.
- Lefrak Organization
- Trammell Crow Residential
- Alliance Holdings
- Sentinel Real Estate Corporation
- Wachovia
- Greystar Real Estate Partners
- Other

Companies are ranked by current units owned as of January 1, 2004. Shares are shown based on the top 50 companies.

	Units	Share
Apartment Investment and Management Company	239,875	9.74%
Equity Residential	209,124	8.49

	Units	Share
American Management Services	125,136	5.08%
Lincoln Property Company	110,236	4.48
Archstone-Smith	82,644	3.36
United Dominion Realty Trust Inc.	76,804	3.12
Lefrak Organization	71,000	2.88
Trammell Crow Residential	70,966	2.88
Alliance Holdings	63,519	2.58
Sentinel Real Estate Corporation	62,008	2.52
Wachovia	60,218	2.44
Greystar Real Estate Partners	55,488	2.25
Other	1,235,929	50.18

Source: "Top 50 Apartment Managers." [online] from http://www.nmhc.org [accessed April 27, 2004], from National Multi Housing Council.

★ 3235 ★

Apartments

SIC: 6513; NAICS: 53111

Largest Apartment Owners, 2004

Companies are ranked by current units owned as of January 1, 2004. Shares are shown based on the top 50 apartment owners.

	Units	Share
CharterMac	309,292	10.74%
Apartment Investment and Management Company	278,657	9.67
Equity Residential	207,506	7.20
MMA Financial	182,343	6.33
Boston Capital Corporation	129,660	4.50
SunAmerica Affordable Housing Partners Inc.	127,000	4.41
Archstone-Smith	82,644	2.87
United Dominion Realty Trusts	76,337	2.65
Lefrak Organization	71,000	2.46
Alliance Holdings	65,237	2.26
Sentinel Real Estate Corporation	62,008	2.15
Morgan Stanley	53,525	1.86
Other	1,235,660	42.89

Source: "Top 50 Apartment Owners." [online] from http://www.nmhc.org [accessed April 27, 2004], from National Multi Housing Council.

★ 3236 ★
Office Space
SIC: 6531; NAICS: 53121

Largest Office Brokers, 2003

A total of $20.5 billion in retail properties was brokered in 2003, up 53% from $13.4 billion in 2002. Market shares are shown in percent.

Eastdil Realty	31.7%
Goldman Sachs	19.3
Rockwood Realty	15.1
HI Group	8.6
Merrill Lynch	4.4
CB Richard Ellis	4.1
Sperry Van Ness	3.7
Morgan Stanley	2.5
Faris Lee	2.5
Other	8.1

Source: *Real Estate Alert*, February 11, 2004, p. 1, from Real Estate Alert's Deal Database.

★ 3237 ★
Property Management
SIC: 6531; NAICS: 53121, 531311

Top Property Managers Worldwide, 2002

Data show total space managed worldwide in millions of square feet as of December 31, 2002.

Jones Lang LaSalle	735.0
CB Richard Ellis	705.7
Trammell Crow Co.	515.1
Colliers International	332.5
Cushman & Wakefield	320.1
Insignia/ESG Inc.	251.0
NAI	210.6

Simon Property Group	190.8
Lincoln Property Group	184.0

Source: *National Real Estate Investor*, July 27, 2003, p. 24.

★ 3238 ★
Real Estate
SIC: 6531; NAICS: 531311

Condominium Sales in Thailand, 2002

After being down in recent years, the market has recently begun to take off. Several large, high profile projects are being planned. Data show estimated shares of condomium sales for the year.

LPN	32.0%
LH Property Fund	8.0
Bangkae City	6.0
Pacific Group	5.0
Manon Development	5.0
Guest Inn	5.0
Other	39.0

Source: *Financial Times*, December 2, 2003, p. 20, from *Thailand Property Guide*.

★ 3239 ★
Real Estate
SIC: 6531; NAICS: 531311, 531312

Cross Border Real Estate Investment in Europe, 2002

Paris is the most active property market in Europe. Paris and London have led the market for the last three years. Figures are for the first six months of the year.

U.K.	27.0%
France	22.0
Sweden	15.0
Spain	11.0
Italy	9.0

Source: *Urban Land Europe*, Winter 2003, p. 20.

★ 3240 ★
Real Estate
SIC: 6531; NAICS: 53121

Largest Real Estate Companies

Companies are ranked by sales volume in millions of dollars.

NRT	149,596.7
HomeServices of America Inc.	36,721.8
Weichert	24,500.0
Long & Foster Real Estate	21,993.3
Prudential Fox & Roach	7,747.3
Alain Pinel	6,491.0
Real Living Inc.	5,966.0
John L. Scott Real Estate	5,495.8
Realty Executives Inc.	5,405.1

Source: *Realtor Magazine*, July 2003, p. NA, from *Realtor Magazine Top 100 survey*.

★ 3241 ★
Real Estate
SIC: 6531; NAICS: 53112

Leading Industrial Owners

Companies are ranked by millions of square feet owned. Shares are shown based on the top 45 firms.

	(mil.)	Share
ProLogis	226.0	14.87%
RREEF	129.0	8.49
AMB Property Corp.	96.5	6.35
Duke Realty Corp.	82.6	5.43
First Industrial Realty Trust Inc. . .	74.0	4.87
Majestic Realty Co.	55.0	3.62
Principal Real Estate Investors . . .	50.2	3.30
LaSalle Investment Management . .	40.0	2.63
Lend Lease Real Estate Investments	37.7	2.48

	(mil.)	Share
Catellus Development Corp.	37.4	2.46%
Other	691.7	45.50

Source: *Commercial Property News*, October 1, 2003, p. 35.

★ 3242 ★
Real Estate
SIC: 6531; NAICS: 531311

Leading Letting Agents in Central London, 2003

Market shares are shown in percent.

	Sq. ft.	Share
CB Richard Ellis	1,339,350	10.0%
DTZ Debenham Tie Leung . .	1,014,628	7.0
Jones Lang LaSalle	768,171	6.0
ATIS Real Weatheralls	700,914	5.0
Cushman & Wakefield Healey & Baker	663,398	5.0
Knight Frank	639,444	5.0
FPDSavills	517,817	4.0
BH2	511,037	4.0
EA Shaw	496,620	4.0

Source: *Estates Gazette*, January 17, 2004, p. 28, from London Office Database.

SIC 67 - Holding and Other Investment Offices

★ 3243 ★

Bank Holding Companies

SIC: 6712; NAICS: 551111

Largest Holding Companies, 2003

The largest bank and thrift holding companies are ranked by deposits in millions of dollars as of December 31, 2003.

Citigroup	$ 474.01
Bank of America Corp.	414.81
J.P. Morgan Chase & Co.	326.49
Wells Fargo & Co.	247.52
Wachovia Corp.	224.45
Bank One Corp.	164.62
FleetBoston Financial	137.76
Washington Mutual Inc.	119.59
U.S. Bancorp.	119.05

Source: *American Banker*, April 15, 2004, p. 8.

★ 3244 ★

Trusts

SIC: 6730; NAICS: 523991, 52592

Largest Trust Operations

State Street Bank and Trust Co.

JP Morgan Chase Bank

The Bank of New York

Citibank

Deutsche Bank Trust Company

The Northern Trust Co.

Mellon Bank

Investors Bank and Trust Co.

Mellon Trust of New England

Wachovia Bank

Banks are ranked by assets in billions of dollars.

State Street Bank and Trust Co.	$ 6.89
JP Morgan Chase Bank	6.81
The Bank of New York	3.81
Citibank	2.24
Deutsche Bank Trust Company	2.11
The Northern Trust Co.	1.35
Mellon Bank	0.95
Investors Bank and Trust Co.	0.76
Mellon Trust of New England	0.65
Wachovia Bank	0.64

Source: *Investment News*, December 15, 2003, p. 51.

★ 3245 ★
Franchising
SIC: 6794; NAICS: 53311

Leading Franchisors in Australia

The franchising industry is worth $80 billion, or 12% of the nation's economy. It employs 600,000 people. Companies are ranked by store count.

Australia Post	2,919
Jim's Corp	2,196
Fastway	1,278
VIP Home Services	728
McDonald's	728
LJ Hooker	640
Baker's Delight	640
Subway	575
Video Ezy	540
Jani King	540

Source: *Business Review Weekly*, January 22, 2004, p. 36.

★ 3246 ★
Patents
SIC: 6794; NAICS: 53311

Top Patent Holders, 2003

Figures show number of patents.

IBM	3,415
Canon	1,992
Hitachi	1,893
Matsushita Electric	1,786
Hewlett-Packard	1,759

Source: *USA TODAY*, January 13, 2004, p. A1.

★ 3247 ★
Trademarks
SIC: 6794; NAICS: 53311

Trademark Applications

According to the source, the Atkins plan and similar diets have fueled the demand for trademark protection. Nearly 12 firms filed forms with variations of "low carb lifestyle" and another five "smartcarb" or "carbsmart".

	1999	2001	2003
United States	267,200	222,800	227,000
European Union	41,274	48,894	57,637

Source: *Financial Times*, May 3, 2004, p. 22, from Office for the Harmonisation of the Internal Market and Dechert.

★ 3248 ★
Real Estate Investment Trusts
SIC: 6798; NAICS: 52593

REITs by Sector

Data are based on share of $185 billion in market capitalization as of July 2003.

Industrial/offices	28.0%
Retail	25.0
Residential	17.0
Diversified	8.0
Health care	5.0
Other	17.0

Source: *Appraisal Journal*, October 2003, p. 351.

★ 3249 ★
Real Estate Investment Trusts
SIC: 6798; NAICS: 52593

Who Owns Public Real Estate

*According to the source, the public market's owner-
ship of income producing property in the United
States ranges from 7.6% of office assets to roughly a
third of all regional shopping malls. Total real estate
was $4.734 billion in value. Traded real estate was
valued at $552 billion, representing 12% of the total.*

	($ bil.)	Share
North America	$ 1,598	33.76%
Europe	1,262	26.66
Southeast Asia	825	17.43
Japan	600	12.67
United Kingdom	361	7.63
South America	50	1.06
Australia	38	0.80

Source: *Urban Land*, May 2003, p. 19.

SIC 70 - Hotels and Other Lodging Places

★ 3250 ★
Hotels
SIC: 7011; NAICS: 72111

Hotel Industry Leaders

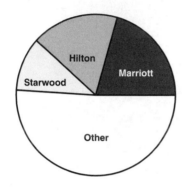

Market shares are shown based on revenues.

Marriott	21.0%
Hilton	18.0
Starwood	11.0
Other	52.0

Source: *Forbes*, May 10, 2004, p. 113, from Smith Travel Research and company fillings.

★ 3251 ★
Hotels
SIC: 7011; NAICS: 72111

How Hotel Rooms Are Booked

About 13% of hotel rooms and 26% of airline tickets were booked online in 2003. Online sales by hotels increased 50% between 2001 and 2002.

	2002	2005
Hotel call centers	60.0%	53.0%
Traditional travel agency	20.0	18.0
Walk-in	10.0	9.0
Online travel agency	5.0	9.0
Hotel Web site	5.0	11.0

Source: *USA TODAY*, June 20, 2003, p. 4D, from PhoCusWright.

★ 3252 ★
Hotels
SIC: 7011; NAICS: 72111

Largest Extended-Stay Hotels

Hotels are ranked by number of rooms.

Extended Stay America	37,692
Homestead Studio Suites	16,842
Candlewood Suites	12,720
TownePlace Suites	11,463
Suburban Extended Stay	8,793
InTown Suites	8,590
Studio Plus	7,722
Villager Lodge	7,504
Studio 6	5,082
Crossland Suites	5,072

Source: *New York Times*, April 21, 2004, p. C10, from Smith Travel Research.

★ 3253 ★
Hotels
SIC: 7011; NAICS: 72111

Largest Hotel Companies

Companies are ranked by number of guestrooms.
Shares are shown for the top 50 firms.

	Rooms	Share
Utell	762,000	15.60%
Cendant Corp.	528,437	10.82
Marriott International	471,275	9.65
Choice Hotels International . . .	383,592	7.86
Hilton Hotels	341,051	6.98
InterContinental hotels Group . .	330,000	6.76
Best Western International . . .	310,561	6.36
Starwood Hotels & Resorts Worldwide	228,215	4.67
VIP International	207,740	4.25
Carlson Hospitality Worldwide .	148,046	3.03
Other	1,172,142	24.00

Source: *Hotel & Motel Management*, September 15, 2003, p. 34.

★ 3254 ★
Hotels
SIC: 7011; NAICS: 72111

Largest Hotel Companies Worldwide

Companies are ranked by systemwide revenues in
billions of dollars. Cendant leads in terms of number
of hotels (6,513) and number of rooms (536,097).

Six Continents	$ 10.00
Marriott International	8.44
Accor	7.48
Carlson Hospitality	6.60

Best Western	.$ 5.90
Cendant	4.80
Hilton International	4.28
Starwood	3.87
Hilton Hotels Corp.	3.84
Choice	3.65
Hyatt Hotels Corp.	3.50

Source: *Business Travel News*, May 26, 2003, p. 54.

★ 3255 ★
Hotels
SIC: 7011; NAICS: 72111

Largest Hotel Owners, 2002

Data show total number of rooms as of December 31,
2002.

Accor North America	134,225
Host Marriott Corp.	59,176
Hilton Hotels	54,296
FelCor Lodging Trust	47,416
MeriStar Hospitality Corp.	26,603
Equity Inns Inc.	12,460
Baymont Innes & Suites	10,500
Boykin Lodging Co.	9,252

Source: *National Real Estate Investor*, July 2003, p. 54.

★ 3256 ★
Hotels
SIC: 7011; NAICS: 72111

Leading Hotels for Federal Travelers, 2002

Market shares are shown based on total spending of
$5.7 billion. Figures are based on charges made on
travel charge cards issued by the govenment and its
contractors.

Holiday Inn	8.0%
Marriott	5.5
Residence Inn	4.5
Hilton Hotels	3.6
Embassy Suites	3.3
Sheraton	3.1
Hampton Inns	2.4
Comfort Hotel Intl.	2.4
Best Western Hotels	2.4

Continued on next page.

★ 3256 ★

[Continued]
Hotels
SIC: 7011; NAICS: 72111

Leading Hotels for Federal Travelers, 2002

Market shares are shown based on total spending of $5.7 billion. Figures are based on charges made on travel charge cards issued by the govenment and its contractors.

Hyatt Hotels Intl.	2.0%
Doubletree Hotel	2.0
Other	60.8

Source: *Government Executive*, September 4, 2003, p. NA, from General Services Administration.

★ 3257 ★

Hotels
SIC: 7011; NAICS: 72111

Leading Hotels in Kyoto, Japan

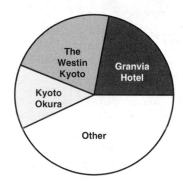

Market shares are shown in percent.

Granvia Hotel	22.4%
The Westin Kyoto	21.5
Kyoto Okura	13.4
Other	42.7

Source: *Japan Inc.*, October 2003, p. 40.

★ 3258 ★

Hotels
SIC: 7011; NAICS: 72111

Top Hotel Companies in the U.K. and Ireland, 2003

Maket shares are shown in percent.

Hilton	7.7%
Whitbread	6.8
InterContinental	5.2
DeVere	2.9
Thistle	2.1
Other	75.3

Source: *Marketing*, April 28, 2004, p. 18, from Datamonitor.

★ 3259 ★

Hotels
SIC: 7011; NAICS: 72111

Top Hotel Firms in Japan, 2002

Market shares are shown based on domestic operating revenues.

Prince Hotels	8.9%
Tokyu Hotels	8.1
Imperial Hotel	3.9
Hotel New Otani	3.6
Fujia Kanko	3.2
Other	72.3

Source: "Market Share Survey Report 2002." [online] from http://www.nni.nikkei.co.jp [accessed January 20, 2004], from Nikkei estimate.

SIC 72 - Personal Services

★ 3260 ★
Portrait Studios
SIC: 7221; NAICS: 541921

Who Sits for Portraits

According to the report, 37% of all portrait sittings took place at school. 21% of sittings took place at department and discount stores.

K-11 school photos	32.0%
Portraits of children (not at school)	17.0
Sports and team photos	7.0
Nursery and day care	5.0
High school senior photos	3.0
High school yearbook	2.7
Wedding photos	1.6
Cruise ship photos	1.5
Adult portraits	1.5
High school prom	1.4

Source: *Photo Marketing*, September 2003, p. 29, from *Photo Marketing Association's U.S. Consumer Photo Buying Report*.

★ 3261 ★
Salons
SIC: 7231; NAICS: 611511, 812112, 812113

How Salons Describe Themselves

Data show how salon owners describe their establishments. There are 220,000 barbers nationwide. Half are women.

Full service	59.4%
Haricutting	17.9
Barber	4.5
Nail	4.3
Day spa	4.0
Skin care	0.5
Other	6.6

Source: *USA TODAY*, June 28, 2004, p. 2D, from National Accrediting Commission of Cosmeotology and Sciences.

★ 3262 ★
Crematories
SIC: 7261; NAICS: 81222

Crematories by State

Two decades ago 4 in 10 chose cremation. It is now 1 in 4. There are now 1,835 crematories, up from 1,058 during the same period.

	No.	Share
California	177	9.65%
Florida	160	8.72
Pennsylvania	78	4.25
Illinois	75	4.09
Washington	72	3.92
North Carolina	68	3.71
Oregon	62	3.38
Arizona	46	2.51
Indiana	44	2.40
Georgia	43	2.34
Other	1,010	55.04

Source: *USA TODAY*, December 12, 2003, p. 3A, from Cremation Association of North America.

★ 3263 ★
Funeral Services
SIC: 7261; NAICS: 81221

Funeral Arrangements, 2010

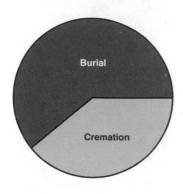

Figures show the forecasted split between services in the United States by 2010. In 2000, only 26.19% of people chose cremation.

Burial 61.0%
Cremation 39.0

Source: "Why a Funeral Home: Funeral Homes vs. Cemeteries and Others." [Online] http://www.nsm.org [accessed May 26, 2004], p. NA.

★ 3264 ★
Funeral Services
SIC: 7261; NAICS: 81221

Funeral Service Companies in the U.K., 2003

The funeral services market in the United Kingdom is dominated (65%) by independently owned operations.

Independent operators 65.0%
Co-operative Group 13.8
Dignity 11.7
Other groups 9.5

Source: *The Birmingham Post*, March 13, 2004, p. 15.

★ 3265 ★
Funeral Services
SIC: 7261; NAICS: 81221

Leading Funeral Service Providers

Market shares are shown in percent.

Service Corp. International 12.0%
Alderwoods Group 6.0
Stewart 3.0
Other 79.0

Source: *Adweek*, November 3, 2003, p. 13, from Johnson Rice & Co.

★ 3266 ★
Funeral Services
SIC: 7261; NAICS: 81221

Top Funeral Providers in the U.K.

Market shares are shown based on number of funerals conducted in 2003.

Co-operative Group 13.8%
Dignity 11.7
Other 74.5

Source: "Funerals Company Valued at pounds 200m." [online] from http://www.funeralwire.com [accessed June 8, 2004].

★ 3267 ★
Tax Preparation
SIC: 7291; NAICS: 541213

Tax Preparation Market Shares

Jackson Hewitt has less than 4% of the market.

H&R Block 21.0%
Jackson Hewitt 4.0
Other 75.0

Source: *Newsday*, March 16, 2004, p. NA.

★ 3268 ★
Tax Preparation
SIC: 7291; NAICS: 541213

Who Prepares Our Tax Returns

Paid preparers field 60% of all tax returns in 2003, up from 50% in 1996. The category ''other'' refers to other paid preparers.

	(mil.)	Share
Prepared by taxpayers	54.0	41.0%
H&R Block	16.3	12.4
Jackson Hewitt	2.8	2.1
Other	57.9	44.5

Source: *BusinessWeek*, April 26, 2004, p. 120.

SIC 73 - Business Services

★ 3269 ★
Advertising
SIC: 7311; NAICS: 54181
Largest Marketers Worldwide

Companies are ranked by media ad spending is shown in millions of dollars.

Procter & Gamble Co.	$ 4,479
Unilever	3,315
General Motors Corp.	3,218
Toyota Motor Corp.	2,405
Ford Motor Co.	2,387
Time Warner	2,349
DaimlerChrysler	1,800
L'Oreal	1,683
Nestle	1,547
Sony Corp.	1,513
Johnson & Johnson	1,453
Walt Disney Co.	1,428

Source: *Advertising Age*, November 10, 2003, p. 28, from TNS Media Intelligence, Niselsen Media Services, and Competitive Media Reporting.

★ 3270 ★
Advertising
SIC: 7311; NAICS: 54181
Largest Marketing Firms

Firms are ranked by revenues in millions of dollars. Revenues do not include non-advertising and subsidiary shops.

J. Walter Thompson Co.	$ 456.2
Leo Burnett Worldwide	404.2
McCann Erickson Worldwide	300.4
BBDO Worldwide	279.1
Grey Worldwide	270.5

DDB Worldwide Communications	$ 252.3
Ogilvy & Mather Worldwide	235.6
Foote Cone & Belding Worldwide	221.6
Y&R Advertising	215.7

Source: *Advertising Age*, April 19, 2004, pp. S-2, from research by source.

★ 3271 ★
Advertising
SIC: 7311; NAICS: 54181
Largest Marketing Firms Worldwide

Firms are ranked by revenues in millions of dollars.

Omnicom Group	$ 8,612.4
WPP Group	6,756.1
Interpublic Group of Cos.	5,863.4
Publicis Groupe	4,408.9
Dentsu	2,545.0
Havas	1,877.5
Grey Global Group	1,307.3
Hakuhodo DY Holdings	1,208.1
Aegis Group	1,067.4
Asatsu-DK	413.9

Source: *Advertising Age*, April 19, 2004, pp. S-2, from research by source.

★ 3272 ★
Advertising
SIC: 7311; NAICS: 54181
Top Ad Firms, 2002

Firms are ranked by share of the $10.33 billion spent on advertising & media during the year.

Interpublic Group of Cos.	18.2%
Publicis Groupe	14.3
Omnicom	10.8
WPP Group	10.1
Other	46.6

Source: *Advertising Age*, May 19, 2003, pp. S-1, from *Advertising Age* research.

★ 3273 ★
Advertising
SIC: 7311; NAICS: 54181
Top Ad Firms in Germany, 2002

Firms are ranked by gross income in millions of dollars.

BBDO Gruppe	$ 316
Grey Global Group	150
Publicis-Gruppe	125
McCann Ericson Gruppe	110
Ogilvy & Mather	105
Young & Rubicam	80
Springer & Jacobi	70
Scholz & Friends	70
TBWA Deutschland	60
J. Walter Thomspon Co.	60

Source: "Online Advertising." [online] from http://www.usatrade.gov [accessed January 5, 2004], from U.S. Commercial Service, GWA, and *Horizont*.

★ 3274 ★
Advertising
SIC: 7311; NAICS: 54181
Top Ad Firms in Japan, 2002

Market shares are shown based on total billing of 5.7 trillion yen.

Dentsu	24.0%
Hakuhodo	12.2
Asatsu-DK	5.9
Tokyu Agency	3.2
Daiko Advertising	2.8
Other	51.9

Source: "Market Share Survey Report 2002." [online] from http://www.nni.nikkei.co.jp [accessed January 20, 2004], from Nikkei estimates and Dentsu.

★ 3275 ★
Advertising
SIC: 7311; NAICS: 54181
Top Media Buying Groups Worldwide, 2001

Publicis became the largest purchaser of media space and airtime during 2001. Firms are ranked by billings in billions of dollars.

Publicis	$ 34.5
Interpublic	33.6
WPP	32.3
Omnicom	22.1
Aegis	16.1
Grey Global	10.9
Havas	9.4

Source: *Financial Times*, June 13, 2020, p. 20, from RECMA Institute.

★ 3276 ★
Advertising
SIC: 7312; NAICS: 54185

Leading Outdoor Advertisers

Figures show the estimated share held by the top 3 firms.

JCDecaux/Clear Channel/Viacom 35.0%
Other 65.0

Source: *Forbes Global*, October 13, 2003, p. 64.

★ 3277 ★
Advertising
SIC: 7313; NAICS: 54184

Ad Spending on News Programs

Spending is shown in millions of dollars. CNBC holds the top spot in news networks, with $507.8 million in 2002, followed by CNN with $352.4 million.

NBC Nightly News . . . . $ 157.3
CBS Evening News 151.0
ABC World News Tonight 147.1
60 Minutes - CBS 98.5
20/20 . . . . 94.7
60 Minutes II 64.3
The O'Reilly Factor 40.0
Hannity & Colmes 25.0

Source: *USA TODAY*, July 17, 2003, p. 3B, from TNS Media Intelligence and Competitive Media Reporting.

★ 3278 ★
Advertising
SIC: 7313; NAICS: 54184

Top Brands on Network TV

Ad spending is shown in millions of dollars.

McDonald's . . . . $ 255.62
Verizon Wireless 245.71
Home Depot 152.01
Wendy's 150.51
Burger King 140.36
KFC 133.88
Ford F-series trucks 128.13
Subway 126.42

MasterCard . . . . $ 120.11
Sprint PCS 114.31

Source: *Wall Street Journal*, March 24, 2004, p. B5, from TNS Media Intelligence/Competitive Media Reporting.

★ 3279 ★
Advertising
SIC: 7319; NAICS: 54185

Ad Market in Canada

Marketers expect to spend $7 billion in advertising. There are about 5,000 companies in the advertising sector which generate annual revenues of $2.9 billion.

Television 38.5%
Newspapers 38.1
Radio 12.2
Magazines 6.0
Outdoor 3.2
Internet 2.0

Source: "Advertising Services." [online] from http://www.export.gov [February 11, 2004], from Association of Canadian Advertisers.

★ 3280 ★
Advertising
SIC: 7319; NAICS: 54185

Ad Spending by the Financial Industry, 2003

Figures are for January - August, 2003.

	($ mil.)	Share
Credit cards	$ 856.3	23.04%
Banks, savings and loans assns. . .	839.8	22.60
Finance and mortgage companies	568.5	15.30
Investment brokers	551.8	14.85
Financial products and services . .	490.8	13.21
Credit-counseling services . . .	126.3	3.40
Tax-preparation services	112.2	3.02

Continued on next page.

★ 3280 ★

[Continued]

Advertising

SIC: 7319; NAICS: 54185

Ad Spending by the Financial Industry, 2003

Figures are for January - August, 2003.

	($ mil.)	Share
Mutual funds	$ 94.2	2.53%
Other	76.7	2.06

Source: *Wall Street Journal*, November 5, 2003, p. B4, from TNS Media Intelligence and Competitive Media Reporting.

★ 3281 ★

Advertising

SIC: 7319; NAICS: 54185

Ad Spending in China

Total ad spending in China was $10 billion in 2002. Figures are for the first four months of 2003.

Television	77.0%
Newspapers	21.0
Magazines	2.0

Source: *Television Asia*, October 2003, p. 61, from Nielsen Media Research.

★ 3282 ★

Advertising

SIC: 7319; NAICS: 54181

Advertising Spending

Magazine and broadcast television have yet to see their market shares return to 1999 levels.

	1999	2003
Local newspapers	19.0%	23.8%
Broadcast TV	21.2	19.3
Magazines	18.5	17.4
Cable TV	10.3	11.9
Other TV	21.6	18.7
Other	9.4	8.8

Source: *New York Times*, May 3, 2004, p. C6, from Publishers Information Bureau, TNS Media Intelligence, and Competitive Media Reporting.

★ 3283 ★

Advertising

SIC: 7319; NAICS: 54181

Advertising Spending, 2003

Total spending on advertisements in the U.S. grew 6.1% to $128.3 billion.

	($ bil.)	Share
Newspapers (local)	$ 22.8	17.77%
Network TV	20.4	15.90
Consumer magazines	18.3	14.26
Local TV	16.2	12.63
Cable TV	12.3	9.59
B-to-B magazines	7.3	5.69
Local radio	6.7	5.22
Intenet	6.5	5.07
Syndication (national)	3.4	2.65
National newspapers	3.0	2.34
Outdoor	2.7	2.10
Other	8.7	6.78

Source: *Wall Street Journal*, March 9, 2004, p. B6, from TNS Media Intelligence and Competitive Media Reporting.

★ 3284 ★
Advertising
SIC: 7319; NAICS: 54181

Advertising Spending in the U.K., 2002

Distribution is based on a total of $16.84 billion.

	($ bil.)	Share
Print	$ 9.42	55.94%
TV	5.22	31.00
Outdoor	0.98	5.82
Radio	0.69	4.10
Internet	0.27	1.60
Cinema	0.26	1.54

Source: *Wall Street Journal*, October 9, 2003, p. B6, from ZenithOptimedia.

★ 3285 ★
Advertising
SIC: 7319; NAICS: 54185

Leading Alcohol Advertisers for College Sports, 2002

Spending on college sports television is shown in millions of dollars.

Bud Light	$ 10.7
Miller Lite	10.2
Coors Light	6.5
Budweiser	6.2
Skyy Blue Malt Beverages	3.2

Source: *Wall Street Journal*, November 12, 2003, p. B1, from Center on Alcohol Marketing and Youth.

★ 3286 ★
Advertising
SIC: 7319; NAICS: 54185

Leading Apparel Advertisers, 2002

Companies are ranked by ad spending in millions of dollars.

	($ mil.)	Share
Nike Inc.	$ 66.9	5.14%
Gap Inc.	43.6	3.35
VF Corp.	40.0	3.08
Sara Lee Corp.	$ 38.7	2.98%
LVMH SA	34.9	2.68
Levi Strauss & Co.	30.0	2.31
De Beers	29.7	2.28
Tommy Hilfiger Corp.	26.0	2.00
Polo Ralph Lauren Corp.	24.7	1.90
Skechers USA Inc.	24.0	1.85
Other	941.9	72.43

Source: *Brandweek*, November 13, 2003, p. SR14, from TNS Media Intelligence and Competitive Media Reporting.

★ 3287 ★
Advertising
SIC: 7319; NAICS: 54181

Leading Cinema Advertisers in the U.K.

Market shares are shown in percent.

	2000	2001
Carlton Screen Advertising	69.8%	55.6%
Pearl and Dean	30.2	44.4

Source: *Screen Digest*, May 2002, p. 137.

★ 3288 ★
Advertising
SIC: 7319; NAICS: 54185

Leading Drug Advertisers

Figures show share of advertising for the first six months of the year. SSRI/SNRIs were the most advertised drug category (8.83% of the total) and Lexapro was the most advertised product.

Pfizer	9.01%
Forest Pharmaceuticals	6.39
GlaxoSmithKline	5.45
AstraZeneca	3.96
Merck	3.26
Novartis	3.25
Ortho-McNeil	2.36

Continued on next page.

★ 3288 ★

[Continued]

Advertising

SIC: 7319; NAICS: 54185

Leading Drug Advertisers

Figures show share of advertising for the first six months of the year. SSRI/SNRIs were the most advertised drug category (8.83% of the total) and Lexapro was the most advertised product.

Abbott Laboratories	2.21%
Wyeth Pharmaceuticals	2.15
Aventis	2.07
Other	59.89

Source: *Medical Marketing & Media*, October 2003, p. 45, from PERQ/HCI Journal Ad Review.

★ 3289 ★

Advertising

SIC: 7319; NAICS: 54181

Leading Internet Advertisers, 2002

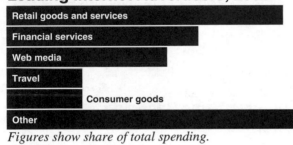

Figures show share of total spending.

Retail goods and services	26.0%
Financial services	18.0
Web media	15.0
Travel	7.0
Consumer goods	7.0
Other	27.0

Source: *USA TODAY*, June 2, 2003, p. B1, from Nielsen and NetRatings.

★ 3290 ★

Advertising

SIC: 7319; NAICS: 54185

Leading Online Advertisers, 2003

Spending is shown in millions of dollars for the first six months of the year.

Internet community, content and portals	$ 257.9
Video rental, CD and record stores	142.7
Investment brokers	134.0
Travel service companies	100.6
Consumer electronic stores	89.9

Source: *Business 2.0*, December 2003, p. 42, from TNS Media Intelligence and Competitive Media Reporting.

★ 3291 ★

Advertising

SIC: 7319; NAICS: 54185

Leading Toiletries/Cosmetics Advertisers, 2002

Companies are ranked by ad spending in millions of dollars.

	($ mil.)	Share
Procter & Gamble	$ 232.8	18.76%
L'Oreal	162.0	13.06
Estee Lauder Cos.	91.2	7.35
Johnson & Johnson	86.2	6.95
Unilever	80.5	6.49
Reckitt Benckiser	79.0	6.37
Beiersdorf	62.3	5.02
Kimberly-Clark Corp.	44.0	3.55
MacAndrews & Forbes	41.0	3.30
Kao Corp.	38.6	3.11
Other	323.1	26.04

Source: *Brandweek*, November 13, 2003, p. SR14, from TNS Media Intelligence and Competitive Media Reporting.

★ 3292 ★
Advertising
SIC: 7319; NAICS: 51331

Local Online Advertising Market, 2002

The source points out that HotJobs, Monster, Autotrader and similar online sites are threatening to steal newspaper's local ad share.

	($ mil.)	Share
Daily newspapers	$ 655	40.0%
Online Yellow Pages	388	23.0
Web portals	352	21.0
TV/radio stations	55	3.0

Source: *Dolan's Virginia Business Observer*, May 12, 2003, p. NA, from Borrell Associates.

★ 3293 ★
Advertising
SIC: 7319; NAICS: 54185

Most Avertised Brands, 2002

Spending is shown in millions of dollars.

Verizon wireless services	$ 660.99
McDonalds restaurants	537.60
Cingular wireless services	427.23
Home Depot home center	382.29
AT&T mlife wireless service	356.13
Burger King restaurant	334.41
Best Buy	293.53
Wendy's restaurant	270.23
Lowe's	263.99
Valassis coupons	259.85

Source: *Brandweek*, June 23, 2003, p. S68, from Competitive Media Reporting.

★ 3294 ★
Advertising
SIC: 7319; NAICS: 54185

Online Advertising in Poland, 2003

Online advertising market shares by company. The online advertising market in Poland in 2003 totalled 48 to 50 million Zloties.

Onet.pl	38.0%
WP	16.0

Ad.Net	14.0%
Gazeta.pl	12.0
Interia	10.0
IDM.net	3.0
o2.pl	2.0
ARBO Media	2.0
Others	3.0

Source: *Europe Intelligence Wire*, February 10, 2004, p. NA, from Gazeta Wyborcza, Ad.Net/CR Media.

★ 3295 ★
Advertising
SIC: 7319; NAICS: 54185

Online Advertising Market Worldwide

United States	81.6%
Western Europe	8.9
Asia Pacific	6.8
Latin America	1.2
Other	1.5

Source: *Investor's Business Daily*, July 9, 2003, p. A5.

★ 3296 ★
Advertising
SIC: 7319; NAICS: 54185

POP Advertising Spending Worldwide

Global spending has been estimated at $44 billion in 2002. Shares are shown based on print technology.

Screen	46.0%
Inkjet	18.0
Other	36.0

Source: *Photo Marketing Newsline*, June 25, 2003, p. 2, from Photo Marketing Association International.

★ 3297 ★
Advertising
SIC: 7319; NAICS: 54185

Screen Advertising Market in Los Angeles

The company has more than 60% of the market in Los Angeles and New York City. It also has 55% of the national market.

Screenvision	60.0%
Other	40.0

Source: *Business Wire*, January 20, 2004, p. NA.

★ 3298 ★
Advertising
SIC: 7319; NAICS: 54185

Theater Advertising Market in New York City, NY

The company has a 55% of the national market.

Screenvision	60.0%
Other	40.0

Source: *Hollywood Reporter*, January 20, 2004, p. 8.

★ 3299 ★
Advertising
SIC: 7319; NAICS: 54185

Top Ad Spenders in the Apparel Industry

Companies are ranked by print and outdoor spending in millions of dollars.

Nike	$ 17.47
LVMH Mort Hennessey	10.43
Adidas	7.14

Source: *Photo District News*, August 2003, p. 30, from Nielsen Monitor-Plus and *Adweek Directory 2002*.

★ 3300 ★
Advertising
SIC: 7319; NAICS: 54185

Top Ad Spenders in the Financial Industry

Companies are ranked by print and outdoor spending in millions of dollars.

Citigroup	$ 10.25
Charles Schwab	10.15
Merrill Lynch	9.37

Source: *Photo District News*, August 2003, p. 30, from Nielsen Monitor-Plus and *Adweek Directory 2002*.

★ 3301 ★
Advertising
SIC: 7319; NAICS: 54185

Top Ad Spenders in the Insurance/ Real Estate Industry

Companies are ranked by print and outdoor spending in millions of dollars.

Cendant Corp.	$ 31.51
Prudential Financial	12.04
Re/Max	7.96

Source: *Photo District News*, August 2003, p. 30, from Nielsen Monitor-Plus and *Adweek Directory 2002*.

★ 3302 ★
Advertising
SIC: 7319; NAICS: 54185

Top Pop-up Advertisers

The market share of pop-up/pop-under ads has fallen with the rise of software to block such advertising. In July 2003, 8.7% of Web ads were pop-ups while in December 2003 only 6.2% of ads were pop-ups. Data show millions of ads in December 2003. Orbitz was teh leader in the pop-under segment.

Bank One	248.1
LowerMyBills.com	215.3
Travelzoo.com	136.1
Ameriquest Mortgage Company	118.4
Yahoo	91.6

Source: *New York Times*, January 19, 2003, p. C4, from Nielsen/NetRatings and AdRelevance.

★ 3303 ★
Advertising
SIC: 7319; NAICS: 54185

Yellow Pages Advertising Market Worldwide, 2002

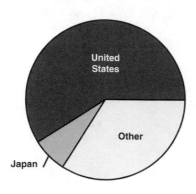

Simba estimates that the global yellow pages ad market grew 2.3% to $24.53 billion in 2002. India was the fastest growing market.

	($ bil.)	Share
United States	$ 14.584	59.45%
Japan	1.639	6.68
Other	8.310	33.87

Source: *Yellow Pages & Directory Report*, December 12, 2003, p. NA, from Simba Information.

★ 3304 ★
Pre-Paid Industry
SIC: 7319; NAICS: 54185, 54187

Pre-Paid Industry, 2003

Data show the industries in which pre-paid funds were loaded onto some sort of instrument (often a card). The report defines a pre-paid solution as a "process, card or other instrument that electronically stores provide access to a specified amount of funds selected by the holder of the instrument and available for making payments to others."

	($ bil.)	Share
Gift cards	$ 40.00	25.32%
Government	39.00	24.68
Telecommunications	21.00	13.29
Cash access	17.35	10.98
Payroll and benefits	15.00	9.49
Campus	12.00	7.59
Travel and entertainment	8.90	5.63

	($ bil.)	Share
Digital content	$ 3.30	2.09%
Purchasing	0.80	0.51
Petroleum	0.60	0.38
Other	0.05	0.03

Source: *ATM & Debit News*, April 1, 2004, p. 1, from *Prepaid 2003: Prepaid Market Segments Benchmarked.*

★ 3305 ★
Credit Rating Agencies
SIC: 7323; NAICS: 56145

Credit Rating Industry, 2001

Market shares are shown in percent.

Standard & Poor's	41.0%
Moody's	38.0
Fitch	14.0
Other	6.0

Source: *Wall Street Journal*, January 6, 2003, p. C1, from Moody's estimates.

★ 3306 ★
Advertising
SIC: 7331; NAICS: 54186

Leading Direct Marketing Firms, 2002

Firms are ranked by estimated share of the $2.50 billion spent on direct marketing during the year.

WPP Group	16.4%
Omnicom Group	14.2
Interpublic Group of Cos.	13.4
Publicis Groupe	0.2
Other	55.8

Source: *Advertising Age*, May 19, 2003, pp. S-1, from *Advertising Age* research.

★ 3307 ★
Direct Marketing
SIC: 7331; NAICS: 54186
Telephone Marketing Industry

Spending is shown in millions of dollars. The educational category includes elementary, high schools, colleges, vocational schools and even cooking schools and driving schools. Such organizations are at the top of the list because they are exempt from the Do-Not-Call list that was recently approved.

Educational services	$ 2,160
Real estate	1,860
Depository institutions	1,830
Insurance carriers and agents	1,760
Wholesale trade	1,490
Personal & repair services	1,400
Social services	1,330
Security & commodity brokers	1,320
Health services	1,310

Source: *DM News*, July 21, 2003, p. 1, from Direct Marketing Association's 2002 Economic Impact U.S. Direct Marketing Today.

★ 3308 ★
Direct Marketing
SIC: 7331; NAICS: 54186
Top Direct Mailers in the U.K.

Firms are ranked by spending in millions of British pounds.

MBNA Europe	65.96
Capital One	42.53
Lloyds TSB	41.32
BCA	26.22
Loans.co.uk	25.22
Barclays	24.01
Direct Wines	20.73
Redcats	19.55
Liverpool Victoria Friendly Society	19.40
Damart	18.81

Source: *Marketing*, February 26, 2004, p. 24, from Nilesen Media Research.

★ 3309 ★
Quick Printing
SIC: 7334; NAICS: 323114, 561439
Quick Print Industry

Figures are in billions of dollars.

	($ bil.)	Share
Independent quick printers	$ 6.6	55.46%
Franchises and chain quick printers	3.6	30.25
Mail services	1.7	14.29

Source: "Cap Ventures White Paper Defines and Sizes the Quick Print Market." [online] from http://www.capv.com [Press release May 19, 2004], from Cap Ventures and Infotrends.

★ 3310 ★
Heavy Equipment Rental
SIC: 7353; NAICS: 532412
Who Rents Heavy Equipment in North America

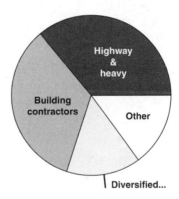

According to annual reports, the North American rental industry has annual revenues of $25 billion. The industry has been growing 15% compounded annually since 1982.

Highway & heavy contractors	36.0%
Building contractors	34.0
Diversified building and heavy contracctors	15.0
Other	15.0

Source: *Construction Equipment*, July 2003, p. 22, from *Construction Equipment Universe Studies*.

★ 3311 ★
Leasing
SIC: 7353; NAICS: 23499, 532412

Leasing Industry in India

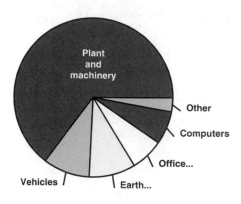

Market shares are estimated. Earth moving equipment has 8-10%, office equipment and computers each have 5-7%.

Plant and machinery	68.0%
Vehicles	10.0
Earth moving equipment	10.0
Office equipment	7.0
Computers	7.0
Other	3.0

Source: "Leasing Industry." [online] from http://www.usatrade.gov [accessed January 5, 2004], from U.S. Commercial Service.

★ 3312 ★
Railcar Leasing
SIC: 7359; NAICS: 532411

Tankcar Leasing Market

Market shares are shown in percent.

GATX	36.0%
Union Tank Car	33.0
GE Railcar	18.0
Other	13.0

Source: "GATX Overview." [online] from http://www.gatx.com/downloads/brochure/rail_cust_care.html [Report dated November 2002].

★ 3313 ★
Temp Agencies
SIC: 7363; NAICS: 56132

Leading Temp Agencies Worldwide, 2002

Firms are ranked by sales in billions of dollars.

Adecco	$ 18.2
Manpower	10.6
Vedior	6.5
Randstad	5.7
Kelly Services	4.3

Source: *USA TODAY*, January 13, 2004, p. B1, from Hoovers.com.

★ 3314 ★
Temp Agencies
SIC: 7363; NAICS: 56132

Temp Market in Europe

The value of the market is shown in billions of British pounds. Globally, the United States had 48% of the 94 billion pound market with Europe taking 38% of the industry.

	(bil.)	Share
U.K.	£ 17.6	49.0%
France	8.0	22.0
Netherlands	3.6	10.0
Germany	2.9	8.0
Belgium	1.4	4.0
Switzerland	0.8	2.0
Spain	0.5	2.0
Other	0.9	3.0

Source: *Financial Times*, February 22, 2002, p. 10, from CIETT and WestLB Panmure.

★ 3315 ★
Software
SIC: 7372; NAICS: 334611, 51121

Antivirus Market in Europe

Market shares are shown in percent.

Symantec	24.3%
Network Associates	21.5
Trend Micro	9.3
Sophos	6.8
Panda Software	4.4
Other	33.7

Source: "Les Differences Marches des SE." [online] from http://www.bruno.duffet.free.fr/technique/pdf/marche_des_OS.pdf [accessed June 1, 2004].

★ 3316 ★
Software
SIC: 7372; NAICS: 334611, 51121

Antivirus Market Leaders in France, 2003

Market shares are shown based on September 2003 estimates.

Symantec	55.0%
Network Associates/McAfee	22.0
Computer Associates	8.0
Trend Micro	5.0
F-Secure	3.0
Sophos	1.0
Panda	1.0
F-Prot	1.0
Other	4.0

Source: *Decision Distribution*, January 12, 2004, p. 14, from Compubase.

★ 3317 ★
Software
SIC: 7372; NAICS: 334611, 51121

Antivirus Software Companies in Europe, 2003

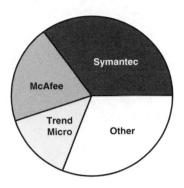

Market shares are shown in percent.

Symantec	35.0%
McAfee	20.0
Trend Micro	14.0
Other	31.0

Source: *International Herald Tribune*, May 13, 2004, p. 18, from Gartner.

★ 3318 ★
Software
SIC: 7372; NAICS: 334611, 51121

Antivirus Software Market

The industry is valued at $2.2 billion.

Symantec	36.0%
Network Associates	24.0
Trend Micro	14.0
Computer Associates	5.0
Sophos	3.0
Other	18.0

Source: *BusinessWeek*, September 29, 2003, p. 48, from International Data Corp.

★ 3319 ★
Software
SIC: 7372; NAICS: 334611, 51121

Application Development Market, 2002

Market shares are shown in percent.

IBM 23.0%
Microsoft 14.0
Compuware 10.0
Other 53.0

Source: *Computer Reseller News*, January 12, 2004, p. 12, from Gartner Dataquest.

★ 3320 ★
Software
SIC: 7372; NAICS: 334611, 51121

Application Software for Mobile Devices

Retail sales of application software for mobile devices fell from about $25 million to $20 million, a drop of roughly 20%. Business has 33% of software sales, followed by games with 31%.

Handmark 24.0%
Cosmi 15.0
DataViz 12.0
Palm/MDM 10.0
Other 39.0

Source: *Investor's Business Daily*, March 10, 2004, p. A5, from Handmark Inc. and NPD Group Inc.

★ 3321 ★
Software
SIC: 7372; NAICS: 334611, 51121

Application Software Licenses, 2003

Market shares are estimated in percent.

SAP 53.0%
Siebel 16.0
Oracle 12.0
PeopleSoft 12.0
JD Edwards 5.0
Other 2.0

Source: *Financial Times*, June 7, 2003, p. 1.

★ 3322 ★
Software
SIC: 7372; NAICS: 334611, 51121

Business Software Market

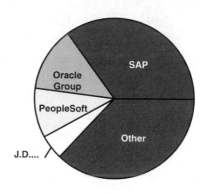

Market shares are shown in percent.

SAP 35.0%
Oracle Group 13.0
PeopleSoft 10.0
J.D. Edwards 5.0
Other 37.0

Source: *New York Times*, June 3, 2003, p. C4, from AMR Research.

★ 3323 ★
Software
SIC: 7372; NAICS: 334611, 51121

Content Management Software, 2002

Contact management license revenues were just under $1.5 billion in 2002. By 2007, this figure should rise to $2 billion.

IBM/Lotus 13.0%
Microsoft 9.0
Filenet 8.0
Documentum 8.0
IXOS 4.0
Other 58.0

Source: *Investor's Business Daily*, June 20, 2003, p. A7, from Ovum and First Call.

★ 3324 ★
Software
SIC: 7372; NAICS: 334611, 51121

E-Learning Software Market

Market shares are shown in percent.

Docent 13.1%
Saba 9.3
Other 76.6

Source: *Lifelong Learning Market Report*, October 31, 2003, p. NA, from Simba Information.

★ 3325 ★
Software
SIC: 7372; NAICS: 334611, 51121

EBPP Market Shares

The company is the leader in the Electronic Bill Presentment and Payment industry.

CheckFree 80.0%
Other 20.0

Source: *Electronic Payments International*, April 2004, p. 14.

★ 3326 ★
Software
SIC: 7372; NAICS: 334611, 51121

Encyclopedia Software Market

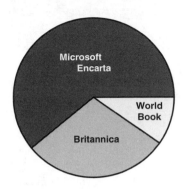

Market shares are shown in percent.

Microsoft Encarta 55.5%
Britannica 26.5
World Book 9.0

Source: *USA TODAY*, July 15, 2004, p. 4B, from NPD Group.

★ 3327 ★
Software
SIC: 7372; NAICS: 334611, 51121

Enterprise Resource Planning Market

Market shares are shown based on revenues.

SAP 18.1%
PeopleSoft 5.4
Oracle 5.4
J.D. Edwards 2.6
Other 68.5

Source: *USA TODAY*, June 19, 2003, p. B1, from International Data Corp.

★ 3328 ★
Software
SIC: 7372; NAICS: 334611, 51121
ERP Market in France, 2002

Shares are for the enterprise resource planning (ERP) market.

SAP	40.0%
PeopleSoft	11.0
Oracle	9.0
Intentia Consulting	7.0
JD Edwards	5.0
Adonix	4.0
Generix	2.0
Other	22.0

Source: ''Packaged Software.'' [online] from http://www.usatrade.gov [accessed January 5, 2004], from U.S. Commercial Service.

★ 3329 ★
Software
SIC: 7372; NAICS: 334611, 51121
ESL Design Market, 2001

Market shares are shown in percent.

Cadence	55.0%
CoWare	17.0
Other	28.0

Source: *Electronic Engineering Times*, September 15, 2003, p. 39, from *2002 Market Statistics Survey* by Gartner Dataquest.

★ 3330 ★
Software
SIC: 7372; NAICS: 334611, 51121
Global Server Software Market, 2002

Market shares are shown in percent.

Windows	44.0%
Linux	26.0
Unix	12.0
Novell NetWare	12.0
Other	6.0

Source: *New York Times*, May 15, 2003, p. C1, from International Data Corp.

★ 3331 ★
Software
SIC: 7372; NAICS: 334611, 51121
IMS Software Market

Data show the market shares of the top vendors of instructional management systems software.

Renaissance Learning	34.8%
Plato Learning	9.9
CompassLearning	8.1
Other	47.2

Source: *Electronic Education Report*, October 10, 2003, p. NA, from Simba Information.

★ 3332 ★
Software
SIC: 7372; NAICS: 334611, 51121
Instructional Software Market

Market shares are shown in percent. Data are for K-12.

	($ mil.)	Share
Pearson Digital Learning	$ 226.0	15.37%
Renaissance Learning	131.9	8.97
Riverdeep	111.0	7.55
Other	1,001.1	68.10

Source: *Educational Marketer*, January 12, 2004, p. NA, from Simba.

★ 3333 ★
Software
SIC: 7372; NAICS: 334611, 51121
Intrusion Detection and Prevention Worldwide, 2002

The global market for intrusion detection and prevention systems generated $383 million in revenues for 2002. North America has 62% of the market. Network-based hardware took 46% of the market followed by host-based software with 26%.

ISS	23.0%
Cisco	18.0
Other	59.0

Source: *PR Newswire*, March 3, 2003, p. NA, from Infonetics Research.

★ 3334 ★
Software
SIC: 7372; NAICS: 334611, 51121

Legal Reference Systems Market in Altai Region, Russia

Market shares are shown in percent.

Consultants plus (Jurcom)	70.0%
Garant	20.0
Codex (Information Technologies Center)	5.0
Other	5.0

Source: "Information Technology and Telecommunications." [online] from http://www.bisnis.doc.gov [accessed May 10, 2004].

★ 3335 ★
Software
SIC: 7372; NAICS: 334611, 51121

Linux Market Leaders Worldwide

Market shares are shown in percent.

Hewlett-Packard	28.0%
Dell	22.0
IBM	20.0
Other	30.0

Source: *Forbes*, June 7, 2004, p. 90, from International Data Corp.

★ 3336 ★
Software
SIC: 7372; NAICS: 334611, 51121

Magazine Design Software Market

The company has more than 90% of the market.

Quark	90.0%
Other	10.0

Source: *Folio*, November 1, 2003, p. NA.

★ 3337 ★
Software
SIC: 7372; NAICS: 334611, 51121

Operating Systems Market

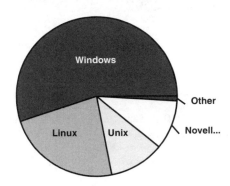

Market shares are shown in percent.

Windows	55.1%
Linux	23.1
Unix	11.0
Novell NetWare	9.9
Other	0.9

Source: *Investor's Business Daily*, November 5, 2003, p. 1, from International Data Corp.

★ 3338 ★
Software
SIC: 7372; NAICS: 334611, 51121

Operating Systems Market by Unit Shipments

Figures are in thousands of units.

	2002	2005	Share
Windows	3,169	3,992	69.47%
UNIX	484	387	6.74
Linux	425	1,018	17.72
Other	532	349	6.07

Source: *Christian Science Monitor*, December 4, 2003, p. 14, from Gartner.

★ 3339 ★
Software
SIC: 7372; NAICS: 334611, 51121
Operating Systems Market Worldwide, 2002

Market shares are shown in percent.

Microsoft 93.0%
Apple 3.0
Linux 3.0
Other 1.0

Source: *USA TODAY*, June 30, 2003, p. 3B, from International Data Corp.

★ 3340 ★
Software
SIC: 7372; NAICS: 334611, 51121
Professional Graphics Software Worldwide, 2003

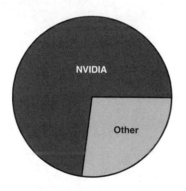

NVIDIA is the leading supplier worldwide in the sale of 2D and 3D professional graphics workstations in the 2nd quarter of 2003.

NVIDIA 73.0%
Other 27.0

Source: *Computer Workstations*, November 1, 2003, p. NA, from International Data Corporation.

★ 3341 ★
Software
SIC: 7372; NAICS: 334611, 51121
Relational Database Market Worldwide

The global industry is valued at $13 billion.

Oracle 39.0%
IBM 34.0
Microsoft 11.0
Sybase 4.0
Other 12.0

Source: *Informationweek*, October 13, 2003, p. NA, from International Data Corp.

★ 3342 ★
Software
SIC: 7372; NAICS: 334611, 51121
Software Quality Tool Market

Market shares are shown in percent.

Mercury Interactive 55.0%
Rational/IBM 22.0
Compuware 9.0
Segue Software 4.0
Other 10.0

Source: *Investor's Business Daily*, October 13, 2003, p. A6.

★ 3343 ★
Software
SIC: 7372; NAICS: 334611, 51121
Speech Recognition Market

Market shares are shown in percent.

Nuance Communications 36.0%
SpeechWorks 22.6
ScanSoft 13.1
IBM 5.7
Telisma 4.8
Other 17.8

Source: *Investor's Business Daily*, October 29, 2003, p. A4, from Gartner Inc.

★ 3344 ★
Software
SIC: 7372; NAICS: 334611, 51121
Supply Chain Industry

Market shares are shown in percent.

SAP 26.0%
Oracle 10.0
i2 . . . . 9.0
PeopleSoft 7.0
Other 48.0

Source: *MSI*, May 2003, p. NA, from AMR Research.

★ 3345 ★
Software
SIC: 7372; NAICS: 334611, 51121
Tax Preparation Software, 2003

Market shares are shown based on box units. During 2003, 6.2 million units were sold.

TurboTax 71.0%
TaxCut 28.0
Other 1.0

Source: *Investor's Business Daily*, March 31, 2004, p. A6, from NPD Group.

★ 3346 ★
Software
SIC: 7372; NAICS: 334611, 51121
Web Browser Market

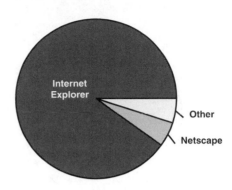

Netscape once dominated the market but now has less than 5% of the market.

Internet Explorer 90.0%
Netscape 5.0
Other 5.0

Source: *Seattle Post-Intelligencer*, May 30, 2003, p. E1.

★ 3347 ★
Software
SIC: 7372; NAICS: 334611, 51121
Web Browser Market Worldwide, 2003

Netscape had 80% of the market in 1995.

Microsoft 95.9%
Netscape 3.2
Other 0.9

Source: *Business 2.0*, June 2004, p. 105, from WebSideStory.

★ 3348 ★
Software
SIC: 7372; NAICS: 334611, 51121
Web Conferencing Market Worldwide, 2002

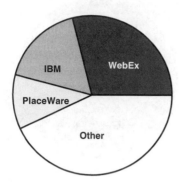

Market shares are shown based on revenues.

WebEx	29.0%
IBM	17.0
PlaceWare	11.0
Other	43.0

Source: *Investor's Business Daily*, September 25, 2003, p. A10, from Frost & Sullivan and International Data Corp.

★ 3349 ★
Software
SIC: 7372; NAICS: 334611, 51121
Web Conferencing Market Worldwide, 2002

The global market has doubled in the last two years.

WebEx	63.9%
Placeware	19.5
Raindance	5.7
Genesys Conferencing	3.9
Other	7.0

Source: *Wall Street Journal*, February 9, 2004, p. B8, from Frost & Sullivan.

★ 3350 ★
Software
SIC: 7372; NAICS: 334611, 51121
Worldwide Enterprise Software Package Market, 2003

Shares are shown for the world's largest enterprise software companies based on annual revenue.

SAP	37.0%
Oracle	11.0
PeopleSoft	11.0
Best Software	4.0
JD Edwards	2.0
Other	35.0

Source: *Investor's Business Daily*, March 8, 2004, p. A5, from AMR Research Inc.

★ 3351 ★
Servers
SIC: 7373; NAICS: 541512
Intel-based Server Market

Market shares are shown for the third quarter.

Dell	28.3%
Hewlett-Packard	28.1
IBM	11.9
Other	31.7

Source: *Computer Reseller News*, November 24, 2003, p. 39, from Gartner Dataquest Inc.

★ 3352 ★

Servers

SIC: 7373; NAICS: 541512

Largest Network Server Producers Worldwide, 2002-2003

Shares are shown based on sales revenue for network servers in 2002 and 2003.

	2002	2003
IBM	30.4%	32.0%
Hewlett-Packard	27.0	27.2
Sun Microsystems	14.6	11.8
Dell	7.4	8.6
Fujitsu Siemens	5.2	5.6
Other	15.4	14.8

Source: *Wall Street Journal*, April 5, 2004, p. 1, from Gartner Dataquest.

★ 3353 ★

Servers

SIC: 7373; NAICS: 541512

Leading Linux Server Makers, 2003

Shares are shown for the first six months of the year.

Hewlett-Packard	29.4%
Dell	22.9
IBM	17.3
NEC	1.6
Fujitsu Siemens	1.6
Other	27.2

Source: *Investor's Business Daily*, February 4, 2004, p. A6, from Gartner Dataquest.

★ 3354 ★

Servers

SIC: 7373; NAICS: 541512

Leading Server Makers in Japan, 2003

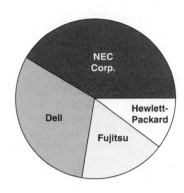

Companies are ranked by unit shipments.

	Units	Share
NEC Corp.	83,300	24.1%
Dell	63,100	18.3
Fujitsu	58,900	10.3
Hewlett-Packard	51,800	6.4

Source: *Asia Pulse*, February 20, 2004, p. NA, from Multimedia Research Institute.

★ 3355 ★

Servers

SIC: 7373; NAICS: 541512

Server Market, 2003

Market shares are shown based on revenues.

	Q3	Q4
IBM	29.8%	32.7%
HP	26.3	25.2
Dell	13.2	13.0
Sun	12.5	13.4
Other	16.2	15.7

Source: *Investor's Business Daily*, February 27, 2004, p. A4, from Gartner Inc.

★ 3356 ★
Servers
SIC: 7373; NAICS: 541512
Server Sales by Region, 2003

Data are for the fourth quarter.

	Units	Share
United States	653,365	41.06%
Europe (incl. Middle East/ Africa)	527,216	33.13
Asia/Pacific (incl. Japan) . . .	310,730	19.53
Canada	54,957	3.45
Latin America	44,898	2.82

Source: *Computergram International*, February 5, 2004, p. NA, from Gartner.

★ 3357 ★
Servers
SIC: 7373; NAICS: 541512
Top Server Makers in France

Market shares are shown in percent for the second quarter of 2003.

IBM	36.6%
Hewlett-Packard	23.3
Groupe Bull	12.7
Sun Microsystems	12.1
Dell	5.3
Other	10.0

Source: ''French Server Market Generated Unit Shipment and Revenues Growth.'' [online] from http://www.idc.com [May 26, 2004], from Intenational Data Corp.

★ 3358 ★
Servers
SIC: 7373; NAICS: 541512
Top Server Makers Worldwide, 2003

Companies are ranked by revenue in millions of dollars.

	($ mil.)	Share
IBM	$ 14,439	31.6%
Hewlett-Packard	12,497	27.3
Sun Microsystems	5,371	11.8
Dell	4,171	9.1
Fujitsu/Fujitsu Siemens	2,823	6.2
Other	6,403	14.0

Source: *Business Wire*, February 27, 2004, p. NA, from International Data Corp.

★ 3359 ★
Servers
SIC: 7373; NAICS: 541512
Top Unix Server Firms in Japan, 2002

Market shares are shown based on domestic shipments of 47,787 units.

Sun Microsystems	55.4%
Hewlett-Packard Japan	15.5
Fujitsu	14.0
IBM Japan	9.2
Apple Computer	2.3
Other	3.6

Source: ''Market Share Survey Report 2002.'' [online] from http://www.nni.nikkei.co.jp [accessed January 20, 2004], from Nikkei estimates.

★ 3360 ★

Servers
SIC: 7373; NAICS: 541512

Top Unix Server Makers Worldwide

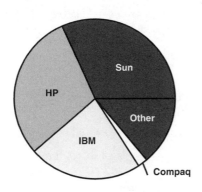

Global shares are shown for 2002.

Sun	32.3%
HP	29.9
IBM	22.5
Compaq	1.8
Other	13.5

Source: *Investor's Business Daily*, April 29, 2003, p. A4, from International Data Corp.

★ 3361 ★

Information Technology
SIC: 7375; NAICS: 514191

IT Services Industry

The overall industry grew from $536.2 billion in revenues in 2002 to $584.1 billion in 2004. Much of this market growth is attributed to offshore outsourcing.

	2002	2004	Share
North America . . .	$ 252,450	$ 276,258	47.29%
Western Europe	158,316	165,442	28.32
Japan	65,210	74,702	12.79
Asia/Pacific	29,081	33,257	5.69
Latin America . . .	17,411	18,788	3.22
Middle East and Africa	8,802	10,000	1.71
Eastern Europe	4,984	5,717	0.98

Source: *Technology Decisions*, August 2003, p. 36, from Gartner Dataquest Inc.

★ 3362 ★

Information Technology
SIC: 7375; NAICS: 514191

Leading IT Federal Contractors

Firms are ranked by total contracts in millions of dollars. Shares are shown based on contract value of the top 50 companies.

	($ mil.)	Share
Lockheed Martin Corp.	$ 4,858.87	15.95%
Northrop Grumman Corp. . . .	3,508.16	11.51
Science Applications International Corp.	1,992.98	6.54
Boeing Co.	1,922.76	6.31
Computer Sciences Corp. . . .	1,853.64	6.08
Raytheon Co.	1,491.94	4.90
General Dynamics Corp.	1,265.55	4.15
WorldCom Inc.	772.44	2.54
Electronic Data Systems Corp. .	660.32	2.17
BAE Systems	638.69	2.10
Other	11,501.75	37.75

Source: *Washington Technology*, May 12, 2003, p. 26.

★ 3363 ★

Information Technology
SIC: 7375; NAICS: 514191

Leading IT Vendors, 2002

Market shares are shown based on revenues.

IBM	6.5%
EDS	4.5
Accenture	2.8
CSC	2.5
Fujitsu	2.1
ADP	1.6
Cap Gemini	1.5
First Data	1.5
Lockheed Martin	1.5
Hewlett-Packard (inc. Compaq)	1.4
Northrop (incl. TRW)	1.4
Other	72.7

Source: *Investor's Business Daily*, October 27, 2003, p. A9, from Soundview Technology Group.

★ 3364 ★
Computer Services
SIC: 7378; NAICS: 44312, 811212

Top Computer Service Firms Worldwide

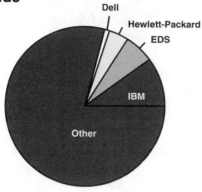

Market shares are shown in percent.

IBM	10.0%
EDS	6.0
Hewlett-Packard	4.0
Dell	1.0
Other	79.0

Source: *Time*, December 2, 2002, p. 50, from International Data Corp. and Gartner.

★ 3365 ★
Consulting Services
SIC: 7379; NAICS: 541512, 541519

Leading IT/Systems Integration Consultants in Germany

Market shares are shown in percent.

Gedas	4.8%
CSC	4.7
Accenture	4.6
Lufthansa Systems Group	4.3
IBM	4.0
Bearingpoint	3.8
Cap Gemini Ernst & Young	3.6

SAP	2.3%
Atos Origin	1.9
Plaut	1.7
Other	64.3

Source: *Management Consultant International*, September 2003, p. S6, from source estimates.

★ 3366 ★
Airport Security
SIC: 7381; NAICS: 561612

Airport Security Market

The annual security market stood at about $300 million. After September 11, 2001, the market roughly tripled. Primary applications are detection of explosives, weapons, narcotics and the identification of terrorists.

United States	65.0%
Europe	26.0
Other	9.0

Source: *Spectroscopy*, June 2003, p. 12, from Strategic Directions International.

★ 3367 ★
Private Investigators
SIC: 7381; NAICS: 561611

Private Investigators in California

There are are roughly 10,000 registered investigators in California.

	No.	Share
Los Angeles	2,165	21.65%
Orange County	976	9.76
San Diego	697	6.97
Riverside	543	5.43
San Bernadino	542	5.42
Other	5,077	50.77

Source: *New York Times*, December 8, 2003, p. C7, from California Department of Affairs.

★ 3368 ★

Security Industry

SIC: 7381; NAICS: 561612

Security Industry in Quebec

Market share is estimated.

Secur	68.0%
Other	32.0

Source: *Canadian Corporate News*, May 12, 2003, p. NA.

★ 3369 ★

Security Industry

SIC: 7382; NAICS: 561621

Top Security Firms, 2003

Companies are ranked by gross revenue in millions of dollars. Shares are shown based on $5.9 billion in revenues for the top firms.

	($ mil.)	Share
ADT Security Services Inc. . .	$ 3,580.00	60.68%
Brank's Home Security Inc. . . .	310.40	5.26
Protection One	277.09	4.70
Honeywell Security	200.00	3.39
Monitronics International Inc. . .	126.40	2.14
Slomin's Security	113.12	1.92
Vector Security Inc.	112.80	1.91
Ranger American	70.99	1.20
Sonitrol Management Corp. . . .	67.94	1.15
Bay Alarm Co.	59.90	1.02
Other	981.36	16.63

Source: *Security Distribution & Marketing*, March 2004, p. 45, from *2004 Security Distribution & Marketing 100*.

★ 3370 ★

News Syndicates

SIC: 7383; NAICS: 51411

Price-Sensitive News Distribution

RNS stands for Regulatory News Service.

RNS	85.0%
PRNewswire	10.5
Other	4.5

Source: *Financial News*, August 22, 2002, p. NA.

★ 3371 ★

Primary Information Services

SIC: 7383; NAICS: 51411

Primary Information Providers to Companies

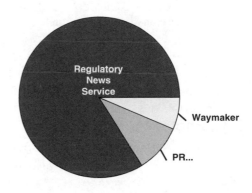

Data are based on a survey of primary information providers that is published bi-annually. Figures are for the six months ended September 5, 2003.

Regulatory News Service	78.00%
PR Newswire	9.20
Waymaker	6.32

Source: *PR Week*, September 5, 2003, p. 4, from Knowledge Technology Solutions.

★ 3372 ★
Photofinishing
SIC: 7384; NAICS: 812921, 812922

Digital Printing

The number of rolls of film processed declined for the third straight year in 2003. Film processing may be on the decline but the article points out that digital film is bringing new business to photo development firms. For example, in January there was a 535% increase in prints made at self-service kiosks from January 2003.

	2003	2004	Share
Home	1,757	2,348	68.06%
Local store	151	447	12.96
Ordered over Internet . . .	140	274	7.94
Kiosks	42	303	8.78
Other	74	78	2.26

Source: *New York Times*, April 5, 2004, p. C3, from Photo Marketing Association Marketing Research.

★ 3373 ★
Photofinishing
SIC: 7384; NAICS: 812921, 812922

Kiosk Photo Printing

Figures show where photo users made prints from kiosks. According to the survey, 11% of households used a self-service kiosk in 2002.

Discount stores/warehouse clubs	38.0%
Drugstores	36.0

Source: *Photo Marketing*, December 2003, p. 26, from *2003 PMA U.S. Consumer Photo Buying Report*.

★ 3374 ★
Call Centers
SIC: 7389; NAICS: 561422

Call Centers in the United States

According to the source, the entire call center market (worldwide) was worth $60 billion.

Outsourced call centers	60.0%
In-house centers	40.0

Source: *Europe Intelligence Wire*, November 17, 2003, p. NA, from International Data Corporation.

★ 3375 ★
Check Processing
SIC: 7389; NAICS: 52232

Check Processing Market in the U.K.

iPSL stands for Intelligent Processing Solutions Ltd.

iPSL	75.0%
Other	25.0

Source: *Business Wire*, April 6, 2004, p. NA.

★ 3376 ★
Conventions
SIC: 7389; NAICS: 56192

Top Convention Markets, 2001

Market shares are shown in business. Atlana held a 9% share in 1995. Las Vegas held a 15% share the same year.

Las Vegas	20.0%
Chicago	11.0
Orlando	8.0
New York City	8.0
New Orleans	8.0
Atlanta	7.0
Other	38.0

Source: *Atlanta Business Chronicle*, March 10, 2003, p. NA, from Atlanta Convention & Visitors Bureau and McKinsey & Co.

★ 3377 ★
Interior Design
SIC: 7389; NAICS: 54141

Leading Interior Design Firms, 2003

Firms are ranked by design fees in millions of dollars.

Gensler	$ 112.00
Hellmuth, Obata & Kassabaum	72.20
Perkins & Will	44.00
Leo A. Daly	41.91
Skidmore, Owings & Merrill	40.50
Pavlik Design Team	40.25
IA Interior Architects	35.49
NBBJ	33.75

Continued on next page.

★ 3377 ★

[Continued]
Interior Design
SIC: 7389; NAICS: 54141

Leading Interior Design Firms, 2003

Firms are ranked by design fees in millions of dollars.

Jacobs . . . .$ 31.50
Callison Architecture 31.41

Source: *Interior Design*, January 2004, p. 75.

★ 3378 ★

Mergers & Acquisitions
SIC: 7389; NAICS: 52232

Largest Bank Mergers, 2003 and 2004

Deals announced in 2003 and 2004 are ranked in billions of dollars. Acquirers are shown in parentheses.

Bank One (JP Morgan Chase) . . . . . $ 57,402
FleetBoston (Bank of America) 47,833
Concord (First Data) 6,749
Union Planters (Royal Bank of Scotland) . . 5,913
First Virginia Bank (BB&T) 3,030
Roslyn Bancorp (New York Community
    Bancorp) 2,126
Staten Island Bancorp (Independence
    Bancorp) 1,415

Source: *CFO*, March 2004, p. 31.

★ 3379 ★

Mergers & Acquisitions
SIC: 7389; NAICS: 52232

Largest Banking Mergers Worldwide

Banks are ranked by value of deals in billions of dollars, excluding net debt of target company. Mergers were announced between March 1995 and January 2004. Acquirers are shown in parentheses.

Citicorp. (Travelers Group) . . . . . . $ 72.56
BankAmerica (NationsBank) 61.63
Bank One (JP Morgan Chase) 60.00
FleetBoston Financial (Bank of America) . . 49.26
Sakura Bank (Sumitomo Bank) 45.49
Dai-Ichi Kangyo Bank (Fuji Bank) 40.10

National Westminster (Royal Bank of
    Scotland) . . . . $ 38.52
Wells Fargo (Norwest Corp.) 34.35
Bank of Tokyo (Mitsubishi Bank) 33.79

Source: *Wall Street Journal*, January 15, 2004, p. A10, from Thomson Financial.

★ 3380 ★

Mergers & Acquisitions
SIC: 7389; NAICS: 52232

Largest e-commerce Mergers

Data show the top U.S. deals since 2001. Value of deal is in millions of dollars. Acquirers are shown in parentheses.

Expedia (USA Interactive) . . . . . . $ 2,867.7
Galileo International (Cendant) 2,797.5
PayPal (eBay) 1,486.0
Expedia (USA Networks) 1,372.0
Datek Online Holdings (Ameritrade) . . . 1,360.8
Hotels.com (USA Interactive) 1,237.2
Ticketmaster (USA Interactive) 841.1
CSFBdirect (Bank of Montreal) 830.0
Lending Tree (USA Interactive) 722.0

Source: *Financial Times*, May 6, 2003, p. 1, from Thomson Financial.

★ 3381 ★

Mergers & Acquisitions
SIC: 7389; NAICS: 52232

Largest Financial Mergers

The value of deal is shown in billions of dollars. Acquirers are shown in parentheses.

Citicorp (Travelers Group) . . . . $ 72.6
BankAmerica (NationsBank) 61.6
FleetBoston Financial (Bank of America) . . . 47.0
Wells Fargo Capital (Norwest) 34.4
J.P. Morgan (Chase Manhattan) 33.6
Associates First Capital (Citigroup) 31.0
First Chicago NBD (Bank One) 29.6
Associates First Capital (Shareholders) . . . 26.6
American General (AIG) 23.4
General (Berkshire Hathaway) 22.3

Source: *USA TODAY*, October 28, 2003, p. 2B, from Thomson Financial.

★ 3382 ★
Mergers & Acquisitions
SIC: 7389; NAICS: 52232

Largest M&A Bankers in Europe

Banks are ranked by deal value in billions of dollars. Data are for January 1, 2003 - November 6, 2003.

	($ bil.)	Share
Goldman Sachs	$ 142	25.21%
Lazard	130	22.98
Merrill Lynch	126	22.30
J.P. Morgan Chase	120	21.24
Citigroup	82	14.57
UBS	78	13.87
Morgan Stanley	67	11.92
Rothschild	61	10.86
Credit Suisse First Boston	58	10.27
Lehman Brothers	57	10.13

Source: *BusinessWeek*, November 24, 2003, p. 56, from Dealogic.

★ 3383 ★
Mergers & Acquisitions
SIC: 7389; NAICS: 52232

Largest Mergers, 2003

Data show value of deals announced in billions of dollars in 2003. Acquirers are shown in parentheses.

FleetBoston (Bank of America)	$ 47.83
WellPoint (Anthem)	16.35
QVC (Liberty Media)	7.90
Concord EFS (First Data)	7.56
Biogen (IDEC Pharma.)	7.51

Source: *Wall Street Journal*, October 28, 2003, p. C1, from Dealogic and Thomson Financial.

★ 3384 ★
Mergers & Acquisitions
SIC: 7389; NAICS: 52232

Largest Mergers Worldwide, 2003

The top deals announced since the beginning of 2003 are shown in billions of dollars. Acquirers are shown in parentheses.

Aventis (Sanofi-Synthelabo)	$ 60.4
Bank One (J.P. Morgan)	58.8
FleetBoston Financial (Bank of America)	49.3
Walt Disney (Comcast)	48.7
Telecom Olivetti (Ing C. Oivetti)	27.8

Source: *Wall Street Journal*, February 12, 2004, p. C4, from Thomson Financial.

★ 3385 ★
Mergers & Acquisitions
SIC: 7389; NAICS: 52232

Largest Telecom Mergers

Figures show the top deals during the previous 12 months. Acquirers are shown in parentheses.

Telecom Italia (Ing C Olivetti & Co.)	$ 27.84
Orange (France Telecom)	7.09
Hughes Electronics (News Corp.)	6.88
China Telecom fixed line (China Telecom)	5.56
Koninklije KPN (Investor group)	2.31
Japan Telecom (Ripplewood Holdings)	2.22
Wind Telecommunicazioni (ENEL)	1.41
Nextwave wireless licenses (Cingular Wireless)	1.40
Loral Space satellites (Intelsat)	1.10

Source: *Wall Street Journal*, January 21, 2004, p. C4, from Thomson Financial.

★ 3386 ★
Reposessions
SIC: 7389; NAICS: 561491
Powersport Repossession Industry

The powersport reposession vehicle market is a small industry forecasted to see significant growth. Powersport vehicles include personal watercraft and all-terrain vehicles.

National Powersport Auctions 85.0%
Other 15.0

Source: *Buyouts*, March 1, 2004, p. NA.

★ 3387 ★
Trade Shows
SIC: 7389; NAICS: 561591
Leading Service Contractors, 2003

Market shares are shown in percent.

Freeman Decorating Company 49.5%
GES Exposition Services 28.5
George E Fern Company 4.0
Shepard Exposition Services 3.0
Champion Exposition Services 2.5
The Expo Group 1.5
Rosemont Exposition Services 1.5
Other 9.5

Source: *Tradeshow Week*, May 2004, p. 3, from *Tradeshow Week 200*.

★ 3388 ★
Trade Shows
SIC: 7389; NAICS: 56192
Leading Trade Show Management Groups, 2003

Market shares are shown in percent.

Reed Exhibitions 7.0%
George Little Management 6.0
VNU Expositions 5.5
VS&A Communications Partners 3.0
Advanstar Communications Inc. 3.0
dmg World Media 2.0
Western Exhibitors 1.5
Society of Manufacturing Engineers 1.5
SmithBucklin Corporation 1.5
AMC Inc. 1.5
Other 67.5

Source: *Tradeshow Week*, May 2004, p. 3, from *Tradeshow Week 200*.

★ 3389 ★
Trade Shows
SIC: 7389; NAICS: 56192
Top Trade Show Organizers in Canada

In 2003, net square feet of paid exhibition space totaled 5.4 million. There were 18,500 contracted exhibitors and professional attendance was 452,374. Shares are shown based on the top 50 shows organized.

dmg World Media 24.0%
George Little Management 16.0
Reed Exhibitions 8.0
Other 52.0

Source: *Tradeshow Week*, April 2004, p. 69.

★ 3390 ★
Trade Shows
SIC: 7389; NAICS: 561591

Where Trade Shows Are Held, 2003

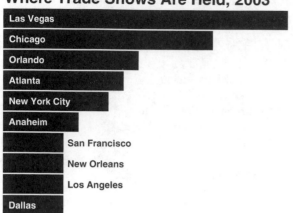

Cities are ranked by number of trade shows in the top 200.

	No.	Share
Las Vegas	38	19.0%
Chicago	27	13.5
Orlando	17	8.5
Atlanta	16	8.0
New York City	14	7.0
Anaheim	10	5.0
San Francisco	8	4.0
New Orleans	8	4.0
Los Angeles	8	4.0
Dallas	8	4.0

Source: *Tradeshow Week*, May 2004, p. 3, from *Tradeshow Week 200*.

★ 3391 ★
Training
SIC: 7389; NAICS: 561499

Leading Corporate Trainers

Companies are ranked by estimated revenues in millions of dollars.

New Horizons Worldwide	$ 550.0
Institute for International Research	400.0
Thomson Learning	283.4
Global Knowledge	248.8
SkillSoft	190.0
Learning Tree	168.0
ExecuTrain	141.0

American Management Association	$ 135.0
Franklin Covey	130.6

Source: *Lifelong Learning Market Report*, June 27, 2003, p. NA, from Simba Information.

★ 3392 ★
Training
SIC: 7389; NAICS: 561499

Leading Project Management Trainers

In spite of layoffs and what the source notes as a "perceived lack of urgency" among corporations, the management training industry is expected to see continued growth. The industry is currently valued at $1.4 billion. Hot training areas include the telecom, finance, drug and high tech industries. Companies are ranked by estimated revenues in millions of dollars.

Management Concepts	$ 33.0
ESI International	17.5
International Institute for Learning	16.5
PM Solutions	15.0

Source: *Lifelong Learning Market Report*, June 27, 2003, p. NA, from Simba Information.

★ 3393 ★
Training
SIC: 7389; NAICS: 561499

Leading USA Patriot Act Trainers

The market for training related to compliance with the anti-money laundering component of the USA Patriot Act was estimated to be $99.7 million in 2002. Companies are ranked by estimated revenues in millions of dollars.

Sheshunoff	$ 25
Emind	11
Training & Consulting Co.	10

Source: *Lifelong Learning Market Report*, June 27, 2003, p. NA, from Simba Information.

★ 3394 ★
Training
SIC: 7389; NAICS: 54199

Spending on Federal IT Training

An estimated $40.3 million has been awarded for year-to-date for non-degree IT and soft skill programs.

	($ mil.)	Share
Off-the-shelf content	$ 30.50	75.5%
E-learning infrastructure	8.80	21.8
Custom content	0.54	1.3

Source: *Lifelong Learning Market Report*, September 19, 2003, p. NA, from *Lifelong Learning Marekt Report* research.

★ 3395 ★
Training
SIC: 7389; NAICS: 54199, 561499

Who Leads Training Spending

Firms are ranked by annual budgets in millions of dollars.

IBM	$ 700
Lockheed Martin	350
Intel Corp.	336
Dept of Defense	324
Hewlett-Packard	260
United Airlines	225
Dow Chemical	144
Verizon Communications	135
Continental Airlines	113
Wachovia Corp.	102

Source: *Training*, March 2004, p. 42.

★ 3396 ★
Translation Services
SIC: 7389; NAICS: 54193

Language Services

Translation service industry saw demand drop after September 11. The industry is now starting to recover and is expected to grow from $9.5 billion to $13 billion in 2007. Lanugage-service companies are starting to grow in share.

Independent interpretors and translators . . .	70.0%
Other	30.0

Source: *Knight Ridder/Tribune Business News*, June 12, 2003, p. NA, from Allied Business Intelligence.

★ 3397 ★

Auto Rental

SIC: 7514; NAICS: 532111

Car Rental Industry at Jacksonville International Airport, 2002

Jacksonville International Airport is in Florida. Market shares are shown based on 2002 gross revenues.

Hertz	27.5%
Avis	22.0
Alamo/National	21.3
Budget	14.4
Dollar	8.2
Enterprise	6.4

Source: *Florida Times Union*, May 19, 2003, pp. FB-14, from Jacksonville International Airport.

★ 3398 ★

Auto Rental

SIC: 7514; NAICS: 532111

Car Rental Industry in Boston, MA

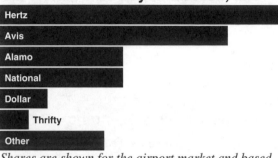

Shares are shown for the airport market and based on reported revenues from July 2002 - June 2003. Figures include on-airport and off-airport concessionaires to airport authorities.

Hertz	30.13%
Avis	24.31
Alamo	13.09
National	12.65
Dollar	5.36
Thrifty	3.47
Other	10.99

Source: *Auto Rental News*, Annual 2003, p. NA.

★ 3399 ★

Auto Rental

SIC: 7514; NAICS: 532111

Car Rental Industry in Charlotte, NC

Shares are shown for the airport market and based on reported revenues from July 2002 - June 2003. Figures include on-airport and off-airport concessionaires to airport authorities.

Hertz	32.91%
Avis	24.40
National	13.09
Budget	7.61
Alamo	7.30

Continued on next page.

★ 3399 ★

[Continued]
Auto Rental
SIC: 7514; NAICS: 532111

Car Rental Industry in Charlotte, NC

Shares are shown for the airport market and based on reported revenues from July 2002 - June 2003. Figures include on-airport and off-airport concessionaires to airport authorities.

Dollar	7.11%
Enterprise	5.47
Thrifty	2.10

Source: *Auto Rental News*, Annual 2003, p. NA.

★ 3400 ★

Auto Rental
SIC: 7514; NAICS: 532111

Car Rental Industry in Chicago, O'Hare Airport

Shares are shown for the airport market and based on reported revenues from July 2002 - June 2003. Figures include on-airport and off-airport concessionaires to airport authorities.

Hertz	32.78%
Avis	25.96
National	12.27
Budget	10.50
Alamo	7.20
Other	11.29

Source: *Auto Rental News*, Annual 2003, p. NA.

★ 3401 ★

Auto Rental
SIC: 7514; NAICS: 532111

Car Rental Industry in Denver, CO

Shares are shown for the airport market and based on reported revenues from July 2002 - June 2003. Figures include on-airport and off-airport concessionaires to airport authorities.

Hertz	30.00%
Avis	20.24
Alamo	10.24
Budget	9.71
National	9.25
Other	20.56

Source: *Auto Rental News*, Annual 2003, p. NA.

★ 3402 ★

Auto Rental
SIC: 7514; NAICS: 532111

Car Rental Industry in Detroit, MI

Shares are shown for the airport market and based on reported revenues from July 2002 - June 2003. Figures include on-airport and off-airport concessionaires to airport authorities.

Hertz	33.13%
Avis	22.36
National	13.85
Budget	10.94
Alamo	7.45
Dollar	6.19
Enterprise	3.87
Thrifty	2.21

Source: *Auto Rental News*, Annual 2003, p. NA.

★ 3403 ★

Auto Rental

SIC: 7514; NAICS: 532111

Car Rental Industry in Los Angeles, CA

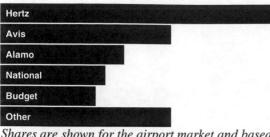

Shares are shown for the airport market and based on reported revenues from July 2002 - June 2003. Figures include on-airport and off-airport concessionaires to airport authorities.

Hertz	29.54%
Avis	17.52
Alamo	13.32
National	10.58
Budget	10.38
Other	18.46

Source: *Auto Rental News*, Annual 2003, p. NA.

★ 3404 ★

Auto Rental

SIC: 7514; NAICS: 532111

Car Rental Industry in Miami, FL

Shares are shown for the airport market and based on reported revenues from July 2002 - June 2003. Figures include on-airport and off-airport concessionaires to airport authorities.

Hertz	31.55%
Avis	18.39
Alamo	14.91
Dollar	11.04
Budget	7.78
Other	16.33

Source: *Auto Rental News*, Annual 2003, p. NA.

★ 3405 ★

Auto Rental

SIC: 7514; NAICS: 532111

Car Rental Industry in Nashville, TN

Shares are shown for the airport market and based on reported revenues from July 2002 - June 2003. Figures include on-airport and off-airport concessionaires to airport authorities.

Hertz	30.15%
Avis	21.69
Budget	12.21
National	11.43
Alamo	9.37
Thrifty	5.83
Dollar	5.05
Enterprise	4.21
Other	24.48

Source: *Auto Rental News*, Annual 2003, p. NA.

★ 3406 ★

Auto Rental

SIC: 7514; NAICS: 532111

Car Rental Industry in New Orleans, LA

Shares are shown for the airport market and based on reported revenues from July 2002 - June 2003. Figures include on-airport and off-airport concessionaires to airport authorities.

Hertz	27.67%
Avis	24.23
National	13.57
Budget	10.44
Alamo	9.07
Other	15.02

Source: *Auto Rental News*, Annual 2003, p. NA.

★ 3407 ★
Auto Rental
SIC: 7514; NAICS: 532111

Car Rental Industry in Orlando, FL

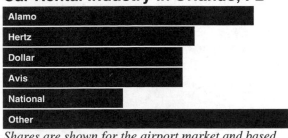

Shares are shown for the airport market and based on reported revenues from July 2002 - June 2003. Figures include on-airport and off-airport concessionaires to airport authorities.

Alamo	20.55%
Hertz	15.71
Dollar	15.13
Avis	14.69
National	9.88
Other	24.04

Source: *Auto Rental News*, Annual 2003, p. NA.

★ 3408 ★
Auto Rental
SIC: 7514; NAICS: 532111

Car Rental Industry in Philadelphia, PA

Shares are shown for the airport market and based on reported revenues from July 2002 - June 2003. Figures include on-airport and off-airport concessionaires to airport authorities.

Hertz	33.72%
Avis	26.31
National	14.03
Budget	10.67
Alamo	8.25
Dollar	7.02

Source: *Auto Rental News*, Annual 2003, p. NA.

★ 3409 ★
Auto Rental
SIC: 7514; NAICS: 532111

Car Rental Industry in Reno, NV

Shares are shown for the airport market and based on reported revenues from July 2002 - June 2003. Figures include on-airport and off-airport concessionaires to airport authorities.

Hertz	26.02%
Avis	15.96
Budget	12.32
Alamo	11.27
Dollar	10.49
Thrifty	7.82
National	6.89
Enterprise	5.54
Other	3.69

Source: *Auto Rental News*, Annual 2003, p. NA.

★ 3410 ★
Auto Rental
SIC: 7514; NAICS: 532111

Car Rental Industry in Seattle, WA

Shares are shown for the airport market and based on reported revenues from July 2002 - June 2003. Figures include on-airport and off-airport concessionaires to airport authorities.

Hertz	25.17%
Avis	22.71
National	12.48
Alamo	11.22
Budget	9.08
Other	19.34

Source: *Auto Rental News*, Annual 2003, p. NA.

★ 3411 ★
Auto Rental
SIC: 7514; NAICS: 532111

Leading Car Rental Firms for Federal Travelers, 2002

Market shares are shown based on total spending of $358 million. Figures are based on charges made on travel charge cards issued by the govenment and its contractors.

Hertz	15.8%
Avis	15.0

Continued on next page.

★ 3411 ★

[Continued]
Auto Rental
SIC: 7514; NAICS: 532111

Leading Car Rental Firms for Federal Travelers, 2002

Market shares are shown based on total spending of $358 million. Figures are based on charges made on travel charge cards issued by the govenment and its contractors.

Enterprise	13.9%
Budget	11.8
National	10.1
Dollar	9.6
Thrifty	8.7
Alamo	6.3
Other	8.8

Source: *Government Executive*, September 4, 2003, p. NA, from General Services Administration.

★ 3412 ★

Auto Rental
SIC: 7514; NAICS: 532111

Top Auto Rental Firms

Market shares are shown in percent.

Hertz	28.5%
Alamo/National	23.0
Avis	21.0
Budget	10.4
Dollar	8.1
Enterprise	4.2
Other	4.8

Source: *Atlanta Journal-Constitution*, May 25, 2004, p. D1, from *Auto Rental News*.

★ 3413 ★

Tire Retreading
SIC: 7534; NAICS: 326212

Largest Medium/Heavy Truck Tire Retreaders, 2002

Companies are ranked by millions of pounds per year used.

Wingfoot Commercial Tire Systems	$ 45.50
Tire Distribution Systems Inc. (Bandag)	21.50

Tire Centers L.L.C. (Michelin)	$ 16.20
Bridgestone/Firestone	12.20
Premier Bandag Inc.	10.40
Les Schwab Tire Centers	9.17
Snider Tire Inc.	7.00
Purcell Tire & Rubber Co.	7.00
Pomp's Tire Service Inc.	7.00
Kal Tire	7.00

Source: *Tire Business*, February 2, 2004, p. 15.

★ 3414 ★

Tire Retreading
SIC: 7534; NAICS: 326212

Truck Tire Retreading Market, 2003

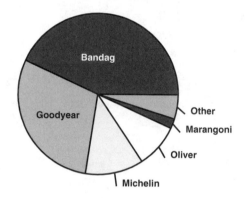

Market shares are shown in percent.

Bandag	43.5%
Goodyear	30.0
Michelin	11.5
Oliver	9.0
Marangoni	1.5
Other	4.5

Source: *Modern Tire Dealer*, Annual Fact Book 2004, p. 8, from *Modern Tire Dealer* estimates.

★ 3415 ★
Aftermarket Services
SIC: 7538; NAICS: 811111

Aftermarket Services in the U.K.

Parts, materials and labor charges generated $22 billion in revenues for the garage industry in 2002. The average car, acccording to the source, generates a revenue stream equal to its purchase price during its lifetime (the average car price is $16,000). Luxury cars and SUVs generate more because they typically last longer than the average car and are typically driven more miles.

	($ bil.)	Share
Tires	$ 8.5	38.64%
Brake friction pads and shoes	4.0	18.18
Brake disks and drums	2.8	12.73
Batteries	1.8	8.18
Oil filters	1.3	5.91
Shock absorbers	1.0	4.55
Air filters	1.0	4.55
Spark plugs	0.8	3.64
Fuel filters	0.8	3.64

Source: "Automotive Aftermarket Parts." [online] from http://www.export.gov [accessed February 1, 2004], from industry survey.

★ 3416 ★
Auto Repair Services
SIC: 7538; NAICS: 811111

Automotive Repair Industry in France, 2002

Shares are shown based on number of vehicles serviced.

	(000)	Share
Brakes	1,372	9.01%
Lights/signaling	1,165	7.65
Tires/traction	1,071	7.03
Emissions	746	4.90
Mechanical	353	2.32
Visibility	257	1.69
Electrical	253	1.66
Steering	233	1.53

Source: "French Automotive Repair Services." [online] from http://www.usatrade.gov [accessed June 1, 2004], from *Inspection Year End Report, 2002.*

★ 3417 ★
Auto Repair Services
SIC: 7538; NAICS: 811111

Largest Auto Repair Markets Worldwide

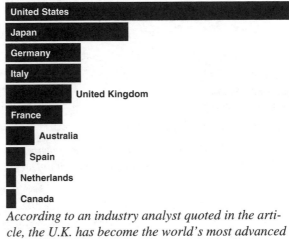

According to an industry analyst quoted in the article, the U.K. has become the world's most advanced auto body repair market but also its least profitable. Markets are shown in billions of dollars.

United States	$ 30.0
Japan	13.0
Germany	8.0
Italy	7.8
United Kingdom	7.3
France	5.5
Australia	2.9
Spain	2.4
Netherlands	1.1
Canada	1.1

Source: *Auto Body Repair News*, January 2002, p. 28, from NACE 2001 International Issues in Colliseum Repair Panel.

★ 3418 ★

Postal Bag Repair

SIC: 7699; NAICS: 81131

Who Fixes Postal Bags

FPI stands for Federal Prison Industries Program, which has 98% of the market for the repair of postal bags.

FPI	98.0%
Other	2.0

Source: ''Re: Oppose Attaching Federal Prison Industries.'' [online] from http://archive.aclu.org/congress/ 1091602b.html [Dated September 16, 2002].

SIC 78 - Motion Pictures

★ 3419 ★
DVDs and Videos
SIC: 7812; NAICS: 51211
Best-Selling Animated DVDs

Titles are ranked by millions of units sold.

Finding Nemo	21.5
Monsters Inc.	12.0
Shrek	11.5
Ice Age	9.4
Lion King: Special Edition	8.9
Lilo & Stitch	7.5
Lion King 1 1/2	5.7
Brother Bear	5.4
Beauty and the Beast	4.7
Snow White and the Seven Dwarfs	3.5

Source: *USA TODAY*, May 11, 2004, p. 6D, from *Video Store*.

★ 3420 ★
DVDs and Videos
SIC: 7812; NAICS: 51211
Best-Selling DVDs, 2003

Titles are ranked by millions of units sold.

Finding Nemo	19.54
Lord of the Rings: The Two Towers	15.64
Pirates of the Caribbean	14.11
Harry Potter and the Chamber of Secrets	10.91
The Matrix Reloaded	10.08
My Big Fat Greek Wedding	8.87
The Lion King: Special Edition	8.68
Bruce Almighty	6.44
8 Mile	6.43
X2 X-Men United	6.31

Source: *USA TODAY*, January 8, 2004, p. 2A, from *Video Store* research.

★ 3421 ★
DVDs and Videos
SIC: 7812; NAICS: 51211
Best-Selling Fitness DVDs, 2093

Titles are ranked by unit sales.

Leslie Sansone: Walk Away the Pounds	168,000
The Method Pilates Target Specific	150,000
Pilates Conditioning for Weight Loss	117,000
Pilates for Dummies	110,000
Crunch: Pick Your Spot Pilates	105,000
Darrin's Dance Grooves	91,000
Cheer	80,000
The Firm: Total Body Super Cardio Mix	73,000
Yoga Conditioning for Weight Loss	72,000
The Method Pilates All in One	12,000

Source: *USA TODAY*, February 10, 2004, p. 5D.

★ 3422 ★
DVDs and Videos
SIC: 7812; NAICS: 51211
Best-Selling Sports DVDs, 2003

Data show unit sales.

Pumping Iron 25th Anniversary Edition	240,000
CKY4: The Latest & Greatest	170,000
Super Bowl XXXVII: Tampa Bay	125,000
ESPN's The Ultimate X	120,000
WWE: Ultimate Rick Flair Collection	110,000
WWE: Wrestlemania XIX	90,000

Continued on next page.

★ 3422 ★

[Continued]
DVDs and Videos
SIC: 7812; NAICS: 51211

Best-Selling Sports DVDs, 2003

Data show unit sales.

WWE From the Vault: Shawn Michaels . .	88,000
Mischief 3000 Episode 2: Import Street Racing	80,000
And 1 Mixtape Vol 6 (Street Basketball) . .	75,000
Entertainer's Basketball Classic at Rucker Park	70,000

Source: *USA TODAY*, January 30, 2004, p. 13D, from *Video Store* research.

★ 3423 ★

DVDs and Videos
SIC: 7812; NAICS: 51211

DVD and VHS Spending, 2002, 2005, 2007

DVD has become the primary home video format since its introduction in 1998. DVD took 72% of home software sales in 2002. There were 39 million DVD households in 2002 and 97 million households owning a VCR player. Home video spending is shown for 2002, 2005 and 2007. Figures for the final two years are projected.

	2002	2005	2007
DVD	$ 12.4	$ 24.9	$ 32.1
VHS	12.1	7.8	6.1

Source: *Deal Memo*, September 8, 2003, p. 8, from Veronis Suhler Stevenson, Adams Media Research, Video Software Dealers Association, and DVD Entertainment Group.

★ 3424 ★

DVDs and Videos
SIC: 7812; NAICS: 51211

DVD Sales by Genre, 2003

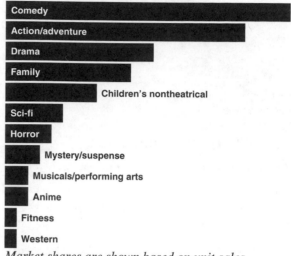

Market shares are shown based on unit sales.

Comedy	25.0%
Action/adventure	21.0
Drama	12.7
Family	11.2
Children's nontheatrical	7.7
Sci-fi	4.5
Horror	4.2
Mystery/suspense	2.6
Musicals/performing arts	2.0
Anime	1.8
Fitness	1.4
Western	1.2

Source: *Video Store*, January 18, 2004, p. 22, from *Video Store* market research.

★ 3425 ★
DVDs and Videos
SIC: 7812; NAICS: 51211
DVD Sales in Europe, 2003

Spending is shown in millions of dollars. The number of homes in Western Europe doubled to 56 million homes from 2002 to 2003.

United Kingdom . . . . $ 3,660
France 2,110
Germany 1,190
Holland 562
Spain 545
Italy 455

Source: *Daily Variety*, March 9, 2004, p. 12, from *Screen Digest*.

★ 3426 ★
DVDs and Videos
SIC: 7812; NAICS: 51211
DVD Sell-Through Market, 2003

Market shares are shown based on revenue for the first six months.

Warner Home Video 22.3%
Buena Vista Home Entertainment 17.1
Universal Studios Home Entertainment . . . 13.8
Columbia Tri-Star 11.0
20th Century Fox Home Entertainment . . . 10.8
Paramount Home Entertainment 9.4
MGM Home Entertainment 8.8
Other 6.8

Source: *DVD News*, November 6, 2003, p. 5.

★ 3427 ★
DVDs and Videos
SIC: 7812; NAICS: 51211
Largest Video Markets Worldwide

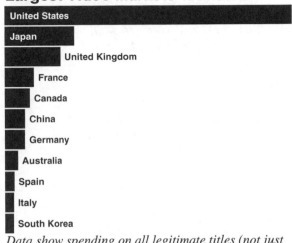

Data show spending on all legitimate titles (not just U.S. titles). North American had 56.6% of all DVD spending for the year. Total spending worldwide on VHS was $19.5 billion and for the popular DVD format $22.7 billion.

United States . . . . $ 19,827
Japan 4,797
United Kingdom 3,821
France 1,942
Canada 1,659
China 1,331
Germany 1,323
Australia 835
Spain 577
Italy 538
South Korea 524

Source: *Screen Digest*, November 2003, p. 329.

★ 3428 ★
DVDs and Videos
SIC: 7812; NAICS: 51211
Top DVD Distributors, 2003

Studios' shares are ranked by $16.3 billion in consumer spending from January 1 - December 28, 2003.

Warner 20.7%
Buena Vista 19.3
Universal 13.7
Columbia 11.3
Fox 11.1
Paramount 8.9

Continued on next page.

★ 3428 ★
[Continued]
DVDs and Videos
SIC: 7812; NAICS: 51211
Top DVD Distributors, 2003

Studios' shares are ranked by $16.3 billion in consumer spending from January 1 - December 28, 2003.

MGM	6.1%
Dreamworks	4.6
Other	8.9

Source: *Video Business*, January 12, 2004, p. 1, from *Video Business* research and studio sources and Rentrak Home Video Essentials.

★ 3429 ★
DVDs and Videos
SIC: 7812; NAICS: 334613
Top DVD Manufacturers in North America

Shares are shown based on Cinram's deal to buy the DVD and CD manufacturing operations of AOL Time Warner (known as Warner Advanced Media Operations) for $1.05 billion. More than half of the households in North America own at least one DVD player.

Technicolor Entertainment Services of California	41.0%
Cinram	35.0
Other	24.0

Source: *Canadian Business*, September 29, 2003, p. 52, from National Bank Financial.

★ 3430 ★
DVDs and Videos
SIC: 7812; NAICS: 51211
Top DVD Suppliers, 2003

Market shares are shown in percent.

	($ bil.)	Share
Warner	$ 4.51	20.11%
Buena Vista	4.39	19.60
Columbia TriStar	2.55	11.36
Fox	2.35	10.48
Universal	2.04	9.09
Paramount	1.70	7.57
MGM	1.14	5.09
DreamWorks	0.98	4.36

	($ bil.)	Share
Lions Gate	$ 0.98	4.35%
Other	1.79	7.99

Source: *Video Store*, January 18, 2004, p. 22, from *Video Store* market research.

★ 3431 ★
DVDs and Videos
SIC: 7812; NAICS: 51211
Top-Selling Titles, 2003

Titles are ranked by revenue in millions of dollars.

Finding Nemo	$ 398.3
Lord of the Rings: the Two Towers	305.4
Pirates of the Caribbean: Curse of the Black Pearl	259.7
Harry Potter and the Chamber of Secrets	218.1
My Big Fat Greek Wedding	164.8
The Indiana Jones Collection	158.1
The Lion King Special Edition	154.4
The Matrix Reloaded	151.0
Signs	140.0
Sweet Home Alabama	128.7

Source: *Video Business*, January 12, 2004, p. 1, from *Video Business* research from studio sources.

★ 3432 ★
DVDs and Videos
SIC: 7812; NAICS: 51211
Top-Selling Titles (Previously Viewed), 2003

Titles are ranked by revenue in millions of dollars.

Lord of the Rings: The Two Towers	$ 27.0
Chicago	25.9
Die Another Day	22.7
Catch Me If You Can	21.8
The Matrix Reloaded	20.0
Anger Management	19.9

Continued on next page.

★ **3432** ★

[Continued]
DVDs and Videos
SIC: 7812; NAICS: 51211

Top-Selling Titles (Previously Viewed), 2003

Titles are ranked by revenue in millions of dollars.

Maid in Manhattan	$ 19.3
Daddy Day Care	18.9
Bringing Down the House	18.9
Daredevil	18.3

Source: *Video Business*, December 28, 2003, p. 1, from *Video Store* market research.

★ **3433** ★

DVDs and Videos
SIC: 7812; NAICS: 51211

Top Title Rentals, 2003

Titles are ranked by revenue in millions of dollars.

The Bourne Identity	$ 79.2
Catch Me if You Can	75.5
Signs	75.0
Sweet Home Alabama	74.8
My Big Fat Greek Wedding	74.3
The Ring	68.9
How to Lose a Guy in 10 Days	66.2
Bringing Down the House	64.2
Maid in Manhattan	62.3
Two Weeks Notice	62.1

Source: *Video Business*, January 12, 2004, p. 1, from *Video Business* research from studio sources and Rentrak Home Video Essentials.

★ **3434** ★

DVDs and Videos
SIC: 7812; NAICS: 51211

Top VHS Distributors, 2003

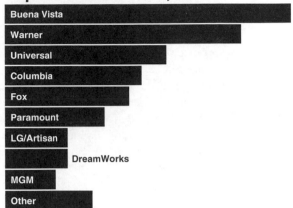

Studios' shares are ranked by $5.9 billion in consumer spending from January 1 - December 28, 2003.

Buena Vista	22.5%
Warner	19.1
Universal	12.9
Columbia	11.2
Fox	9.5
Paramount	7.9
LG/Artisan	5.1
DreamWorks	4.6
MGM	4.4
Other	7.4

Source: *Video Business*, January 12, 2004, p. 1, from *Video Business* research by studio sources and Rentrak Home Video Essentials.

★ **3435** ★

DVDs and Videos
SIC: 7812; NAICS: 51211

TV Shows on DVD

Old television shows are finding a new life on the increasingly popular DVD format. The table shows the most popular genres for shows.

	2001	2002
Sci-fi	19.03	28.46
Horror	8.25	15.15
Anime	5.03	8.30
Foreign	1.56	6.46

Source: *USA TODAY*, July 16, 2003, p. 4D, from *Video Store* market research.

★ 3436 ★
DVDs and Videos
SIC: 7812; NAICS: 51211
Vendors of TV Shows on DVD

For the first nine months of the year, the market for TV series on DVD saw roughly $450 million in revenues.

Fox Home Entertainment	40.2%
HBO/Warner Home Video	29.9
Buena Vista Home Entertainment	7.8
Paramount Home Entertainment	5.7
Other	16.4

Source: *DVD News*, October 30, 2003, p. 1, from DVD TV Conference and *Hollywood Reporter*.

★ 3437 ★
DVDs and Videos
SIC: 7812; NAICS: 51211
VHS Sales by Genre, 2003

Market shares are shown based on unit sales for November 2003.

Family	34.1%
Children's nontheatrical	21.6
Comedy	16.2
Action/adventure	9.0
Drama	5.4
Fitness	2.6
Musicals/performing arts	1.5
Other	9.6

Source: *Video Store*, December 28, 2003, p. 14.

★ 3438 ★
DVDs and Videos
SIC: 7812; NAICS: 51211
Video Industry Spending Worldwide

Worldwide spending on DVDs overtook the VHS format for the first time in 2002. ($22.7 billion to $19.6 billion). DVDs have become popular with users because they offer better sound and picture than the VHS tape format. DVDs also contain extra footage, director commentaries and other material that appeals to consumers. The average trade retail price of a DVD in 2002 was $14.00. For a VHS tape it was $7.80.

Retail DVD	39.2%
Rental VHS	27.2
Retail VHS	17.5
Rental DVD	12.7
Retail VCD	3.3
Rental VCD	0.1

Source: *Screen Digest*, November 2003, p. 329.

★ 3439 ★
Motion Pictures
SIC: 7812; NAICS: 51211
Domestic and Foreign Films in Canada

Total box office receipts increased from $855.5 million in 2001 to $949.0 million in 2003.

	2001	2002
Foreign	98.3%	97.3%
Canadian	1.7	2.7

Source: *Globe & Mail*, May 1, 2004, p. R1, from Telefilm Canada.

★ 3440 ★
Motion Pictures
SIC: 7812; NAICS: 51211
Home Video Content

VOD stands for video on demand. Figures are based on sales revenues in millions of dollars.

	2003	2005	2007
Home video sales	$ 18,709	$ 25,589	$ 25,834
Home video rental	10,201	9,530	8,122
VOD	410	1,412	2,984

Source: *CableWorld*, May 17, 2004, p. 20, from Forrester Research.

★ 3441 ★
Motion Pictures
SIC: 7812; NAICS: 51211

Illegal Downloading of Films

*Data show number of copies available for download-
ing as of November.*

Terminator 3: Rise of the Machines	62,827
Finding Nemo	57,801
S.W.A.T.	54,031
Out of Time	48,653
Bad Boys II	42,722
Once Upon a Time In Mexico	42,220
Jeepers Creepers 2	39,204
Pirates of the Caribeean	37,947
American Wedding	37,194

Source: *New York Times*, December 25, 2003, p. C1, from
BayTSP.

★ 3442 ★
Motion Pictures
SIC: 7812; NAICS: 51211

Leading Motion Picture Markets in Europe

Data show cinema admissions.

	1999	2002
France	153.6	185.1
U.K.	139.5	175.0
Spain	131.3	140.7
Italy	103.5	112.0
Netherlands	18.6	24.0
Belgium	21.9	22.8
Austria	15.0	19.3
Sweden	16.0	18.3
Ireland	12.4	17.3
Denmark	10.9	12.9
Finland	7.0	7.7
Luxembourg	1.3	1.4

Source: *Variety*, December 1, 2003, p. 3, from OBS.

★ 3443 ★
Motion Pictures
SIC: 7812; NAICS: 51211

Lowest Grossing Films, 2003

*The films with lowest domestic box office receipts are
shown through February 2004. Films are from the
top 132 films released for the year.*

Alex & Emma	$ 14.2
How to Deal	14.1
In America	13.3
Gods and Generals	12.9
House of 1000 Corpses	12.6
House of Sand and Fog	12.2
Confidence	12.2
Winged Migration	10.8
House of the Dead	10.2
Swimming Pool	10.1

Source: *Entertainment Weekly*, March 7, 2004, p. 42, from
EDI and *Variety*.

★ 3444 ★
Motion Pictures
SIC: 7812; NAICS: 51211

Men, Women and Movies

*Percent of attendance is shown for men and women
18-34 years of age.*

	Men	Women
R	31.0%	19.0%
PG-13	19.0	16.0
PG	5.0	12.0
G	3.0	15.0

Source: *Adweek*, November 24, 2003, p. 7, from Nielsen
Cinema Report.

★ 3445 ★
Motion Pictures
SIC: 7812; NAICS: 51211

Top Animated Films

*Films are ranked by box office receipts in millions of
dollars.*

Finding Nemo (2002)	$ 338.2
The Lion King (1994)	328.5
Shrek (2001)	267.7

Continued on next page.

★ 3445 ★
[Continued]
Motion Pictures
SIC: 7812; NAICS: 51211

Top Animated Films

Films are ranked by box office receipts in millions of dollars.

Monsters Inc. (2001)	$ 255.9
Toy Story 2 (1999)	245.9
Aladdin (1992)	217.4
Toy Story (1995)	191.8
Snow White (1937)	178.0
Ice Age (2002)	176.4
Beauty and the Beast (1991)	171.4

Source: *Wall Street Journal*, October 23, 2003, p. A1, from Exhibitor Relations Co.

★ 3446 ★
Motion Pictures
SIC: 7812; NAICS: 51211

Top Comic Book Movies

Films are ranked by box office receipts adjusted for 2003 dollars.

Spider-Man (2002)	$ 413.4
Superman (1978)	379.2
Batman (1989)	373.1
Men in Black (1997)	287.7
Batman Forever (1995)	222.4
Superman 2 (1981)	219.2
Batman Returns (1992)	213.8
Men in Black 2 (2002)	195.0
Teenage Mutant Ninja Turtles (1990) . . .	190.6
X-Men (2000)	168.3

Source: *USA TODAY*, April 25, 2003, p. 2A, from Nielsen EDI.

★ 3447 ★
Motion Pictures
SIC: 7812; NAICS: 51211

Top Domestic Box Office Leaders in France, 2003

A total of 174 million movie tickets were sold in France during 2003.

Taxi 3	6.15
Chouchou	3.90
Tais-Toi (Shut Up)	3.00
La Beuze	2.00
7 Years of Marriage	1.65

Source: *Hollywood Reporter*, January 20, 2003, p. 30.

★ 3448 ★
Motion Pictures
SIC: 7812; NAICS: 51211

Top Films in Australia, 2003

Films are ranked by box office gross 2003 sales in millions of Australian dollars.

Finding Nemo	$ 37.13
The Matrix Reloaded	33.62
Lord of the Rings: The Two Towers . . .	28.08
Pirates of the Caribbean	25.12
Bruce Almightly	20.47
Terminator 3: Rise of the Machines . . .	19.10
Chicago	19.00
Lord of the Rings: The Return of the King . .	18.99
Charlie's Angels: Full Throttle	18.90
The Matrix Revolutions	17.96

Source: *Film Journal International*, March 2004, p. 50.

★ 3449 ★
Motion Pictures
SIC: 7812; NAICS: 51211

Top Films in Canada, 2003

Films are ranked by gross receipts in millions of Canadian dollars.

Lord of the Rings: The Return of the King .	$ 37.79
Lord of the Rings: The Two Towers	35.50

Continued on next page.

★ 3449 ★

[Continued]
Motion Pictures
SIC: 7812; NAICS: 51211

Top Films in Canada, 2003

Films are ranked by gross receipts in millions of Canadian dollars.

The Matrix Reloaded	$ 33.06
Pirates of the Caribbean	32.37
Finding Nemo	26.14
X2: X-Men United	23.35
Bruce Almighty	20.71
Chicago	19.15
Matrix Revolutions	18.28
Terminator 3: Rise of the Machines	15.81

Source: "Canada BoxOffice." [online] from http://www.moviecitynews.com/columnists/klady/2003/2003_Canada.html [accessed March 19, 2004].

★ 3450 ★

Motion Pictures
SIC: 7812; NAICS: 51211

Top Films in China, 2002

Films are ranked by box office revenues in millions of yen. China's total box office revenues stood at 1.2 billion yen ($145 million) for the year. This is about 1.4% of Hollywood's total.

Hero	¥ 245
The Lord of the Rings	60
Harry Potter and the Chamber of Secrets	50
Star Wars: Episode II: Attack of the Clones	40
The Touch	27
The Lion Roars	23
Chinese Odyssey 2002	22
Ghosts	17
Together	14
Mighty Baby	10

Source: *China Business Review*, November/December 2003, p. 42, from Cinezoic Film and Television Corp.

★ 3451 ★

Motion Pictures
SIC: 7812; NAICS: 51211

Top Films in Hong Kong, 2002

Films are ranked by box office receipts in millions of dollars.

Infernal Affairs	$ 6.1
Harry Potter and the Chamber of Secrets	4.3
Spider-Man	3.7
Monsters Inc.	3.3
The Lord of the Rings: The Fellowship of the Ring	3.2
Minority Report	2.9
Marry a Rich Man	2.8
Hero	2.8
Men in Black II	2.7
My Left Eye Sees Ghosts	2.6

Source: *Variety*, February 17, 2003, p. S30, from *Variety*.

★ 3452 ★

Motion Pictures
SIC: 7812; NAICS: 51211

Top Films in New Zealand, 2003

Total box office receipts were $142.7 million in 2002, up steadily since 2000 when $106.3 million in tickers were sold.

The Lord of the Rings: Two Towers	$ 12.10
Harry Potter and the Chamber of Secrets	6.71
The Lord of the Rings: The Return of the King	6.40
Matrix Reloaded	6.39
Whale Rider	6.36
Finding Nemo	6.17
Pirates of the Caribbean	4.60
Terminator 3	4.07
X-Men 2	3.62
Charlie's Angles 2	3.54

Source: *AdMedia*, February 2004, p. 39.

★ 3453 ★
Motion Pictures
SIC: 7812; NAICS: 51211
Top Grossing Films, 2004

Films are ranked by box office receipts for the period January 6 - January 4, 2004.

Finding Nemo	$ 340
Pirates of the Caribbean: The Curse of the Black Pearl	305
The Lord of the Rings: The Return of the King	290
The Matrix Reloaded	282
Bruce Almighty	243
X2: Xmen United	215
Elf	171
Chicago	161
Terminator 3: The Rise of the Machiens	150
The Matrix Revolutions	138
Bad Boys 2	138

Source: *Variety*, January 12, 2004, p. A1.

★ 3454 ★
Motion Pictures
SIC: 7812; NAICS: 51211
Top Independent Films

Films are ranked by box office receipts for the period January 6, 2003 - January 4, 2004.

28 Days Later	$ 45
Bend It Like Beckham	33
The Pianist	32
Lost in Translation	32
Cabin Fever	22
Whale Rider	21
Deliver Us From Eva	17
Antwone Fisher	15
My Big Fat Greek Wedding	14
House of 1000 Corpses	13

Source: *Variety*, January 12, 2004, p. A1.

★ 3455 ★
Motion Pictures
SIC: 7812; NAICS: 51211
Top Movie Firms in Japan, 2002

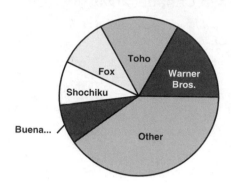

Market shares are shown based on total revenue of 196.7 billion yen.

Warner Bros.	16.8%
Toho	15.8
Fox	10.1
Shochiku	9.0
Buena Vista International	8.1
Other	40.2

Source: "Market Share Survey Report 2002." [online] from http://www.nni.nikkei.co.jp [accessed January 20, 2004], from Nikkei estimate and Motion Picture Producers Association of Japan.

★ 3456 ★
Motion Picture Libraries
SIC: 7819; NAICS: 512199
Largest Film Libraries

Studios are ranked by theatrical features.

Warner Bros.	6,600
Universal	5,000
Fox	4,200
MGM	4,100
Sony	3,500
Paramount	1,100
Disney	688

Source: *Variety*, April 9/, 204, p. 3, from studio figures.

★ 3457 ★
Film Distribution
SIC: 7822; NAICS: 51212
Leading Studios, 2004

Market shares are shown based on box office receipts for January 6, 2003 - January 4, 2004.

	($ bil.)	Share
Disney	$ 1,520	17.0%
Sony	1,210	13.0
Warner Bros.	1,160	13.0
Universal	1,080	12.0
New Line	924	10.0
Fox	801	9.0
Miramax	695	8.0
Paramount	650	7.0
MGM	364	3.0
DreamWorks	238	2.0
Other	514	6.0

Source: *Variety*, January 12, 2004, p. A1.

★ 3458 ★
Film Distribution
SIC: 7822; NAICS: 51212
Top Film Distributors in Canada, 2003

Market shares are shown in percent.

Alliance	23.3%
Buena Vista	13.3
Warner Bros.	12.9
Sony	12.5
Universal	11.2
Fox	9.2
Paramount	7.0
MGM	2.8
Other	4.7

Source: "Canada BoxOffice." [online] from http://www.moviecitynews.com/columnists/klady/2003/2003_Canada.html [accessed March 19, 2004].

★ 3459 ★
Film Distribution
SIC: 7822; NAICS: 51212
Top Film Distributors in France, 2002

Shares are shonw based on films distributed through March 31, 2002. The French film is seen as going through a difficult period after the collapse of the pay-TV market.

UFG (20th Century Fox, UGC)	13.9%
GBVI (Gaumont, Buena Vista)	13.5
Warner (Warner Brothers Pictures)	12.7
Other	59.9

Source: *Hollywood Reporter*, May 10, 2003, p. 39, from *ECRAN Total*.

★ 3460 ★
Film Distribution
SIC: 7822; NAICS: 51212
Top Film Distributors in Germany

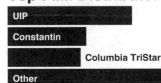

Market shares are shown in percent.

UIP	22.2%
Constantin	14.1
Columbia TriStar	13.4
Other	50.3

Source: *Hollywood Reporter*, May 11, 2002, p. 1.

★ 3461 ★
Film Distribution
SIC: 7822; NAICS: 51211

Top Film Distributors in Italy, 2002

Production is at its highest level in a decade. Both admissions and receipts are up. The industry is seeing some dangers in reduced budgets in TV broadcasts and promised tax breaks that have yet to appear.

Medusa	22.0%
Warner	11.3
United International Pictures	10.8
Other	55.9

Source: *Hollywood Reporter*, May 10, 2003, p. 39, from CINETEL.

★ 3462 ★
Film Distribution
SIC: 7822; NAICS: 51212

Top Film Distributors in South Korea, 2002

For the first time since 1997 the top film in the country was not locally produced (it was Lord of the Rings: The Two Towers). *Local filsm take 46% of the box office but have become expensive to produce.*

Cinema Services (Miramax, New Line)	22.4%
CJ Entertainment (Dreamworks)	17.6
Columbia TriStar	9.6
Other	50.4

Source: *Hollywood Reporter*, May 10, 2003, p. 39, from KOFIC.

★ 3463 ★
Film Distribution
SIC: 7822; NAICS: 51212

Top Film Distributors in Spain

Total attendance dropped 2% from 2002 to stand at 131.5 million in 2003. Ticket sales grew, however, to $780 million.

Buena Vista International	18.9%
UIP	17.5
Warner Sogefilms	14.4
Columbia TriStar	11.9
20th Century Fox	10.6
Aurum	6.5
Lauren	4.7
TriPictures	3.6

Filmax	3.1%
Other	8.8

Source: *Film Journal International*, March 2004, p. 47, from EDI Nielsen Spain.

★ 3464 ★
Film Distribution
SIC: 7822; NAICS: 51212

Top Film Distributors in the U.K., 2003

Shares are for January 6 - December 7, 2003.

BVI	28.3%
UIP	23.1
WB	11.7
CTSI	10.5
Fox	9.2
Entertainment	8.9
Pathe	2.1
Momentum	1.4
Other	4.8

Source: *Variety*, December 15, 2003, p. 29.

★ 3465 ★
Film Distribution
SIC: 7822; NAICS: 51212

Top Film Distributors Worldwide, 2003

Shares are shown in percent for leading film distributors based $9.5 billion gross receipts..

Buena Vista International	16.1%
United International Pictures	15.9
Warner Brothers	14.7
Columbia TriStar International	10.7
Fox	8.8
New Line Cinema	6.9
Miramax	4.8

Continued on next page.

★ 3465 ★

[Continued]
Film Distribution
SIC: 7822; NAICS: 51212

Top Film Distributors Worldwide, 2003

Shares are shown in percent for leading film distributors based $9.5 billion gross receipts..

Toho	3.0%
CJ/Cinema Service	1.6
Intermedia	1.3
Other	16.9

Source: "The Weekend Report" [Online] http://www.moviecitynews.com/columnists/klady/2003/ [accessed 03/19/04], 4, p. NA, from *MCN*.

★ 3466 ★

Film Distribution
SIC: 7822; NAICS: 51212

Top Independent Film Distributors in France

Market shares are shown in percent.

Pathe Distribution	16.8%
Bac Distribution	9.0
Metropolitan Filmexport	7.5
Mars Films	7.5
SND	1.7
Diaphana Distribution	1.0
Other	56.5

Source: *Variety*, October 28, 2002, p. 24.

★ 3467 ★

Movie Theaters
SIC: 7832; NAICS: 512131

Leading Movie Theater Operators in the U.K., 2002

Companies are ranked by number of screens. Admissions were at 175.9 million, the highest in 30 years.

	Screens	Share
Odeon Cinemas	609	17.90%
Warner Village	404	11.88

	Screens	Share
UGC	396	11.64%
UCI	355	10.44
Cine UK	323	9.49
Showcase	243	7.14
Ward Anderson	74	2.18
Ster Century	59	1.73
Apollo	56	1.65
Spean Bridge	31	0.91
City Screens	31	0.91
Other	821	24.13

Source: *Leisure Report*, February 2003, p. 17, from Crema Advertising Association.

★ 3468 ★

Movie Theaters
SIC: 7832; NAICS: 512131

Leading Multiplex Operators in Japan

Multiplex cinemas account for 6% of total screens. Over 60 companies have entered the market since the first multiplex opened in 1991. Market shares are shown based on total number of screens.

Warner Mycal	23.5%
Shochiku Multiplex	6.5
Corona	6.2
United Cinemas	5.9
Toho	5.9
Virgin Cinemas	5.7
AMC	5.2
Sasaki Kogyo	4.0
Tokyu Recreation	3.4
Other	33.7

Source: *Screen Digest*, April 2003, p. 125.

★ 3469 ★
Movie Theaters
SIC: 7832; NAICS: 512131
Movie Theater Industry

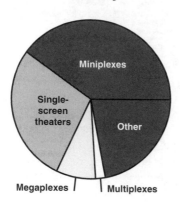

Multiplexes are theaters with 8 to 15 screens. Miniplexes have 2 to 7 screens. Megaplexes have 16 or more screens. The U.S. industry is shown in percent.

Miniplexes	40.0%
Single-screen theaters	28.0
Megaplexes	8.0
Multiplexes	2.4
Other	22.0

Source: *Hawaii Business*, November 2003, p. 72, from Motion Picture Association Worldwide Market Research.

★ 3470 ★
Movie Theaters
SIC: 7832; NAICS: 512131
Movie Theater Market in Fort Wayne, IN

Rave took the lion's share of the market within a year after its November 2001 opening in the Fort Wayne area. Regal Cinemas lost its controlling share.

Rave Motion Pictures	80.0%
Other	20.0

Source: *The News-Sentinel*, February 2, 2004, p. NA.

★ 3471 ★
Movie Theaters
SIC: 7832; NAICS: 512131
Top Film Exhibitors in Australia, 2002

Exhibitors are ranked by number of screens, which increased from 1,748 in 2000 to 1,900 in 2002. Box office receipts increased also: $372 million to $506 million during the same period. Star Wars Episode 2: Attack of the Clones was the top film for the year.

	Screens	Share
Village Cinemas	582	42.6%
Greater Union	457	33.5
Hoyts Cinemas	328	24.0

Source: *Hollywood Reporter*, May 10, 2003, p. 39, from Australian Film Commission, MPPA Australia.

★ 3472 ★
Movie Theaters
SIC: 7832; NAICS: 512131
Top Film Exhibitors in Germany, 2002

The entertainment market is in poor shape in Germany. The film industry has been focusing on blockbusters to the detriment of independent and art films.

	Screens	Shares
Cinestar (Kieft und Kieft)	534	51.5%
CinemaxX	356	34.3
UCI Kinowelt	148	14.2

Source: *Hollywood Reporter*, May 10, 2003, p. 39, from *Screen Digest*.

★ 3473 ★
Movie Theaters
SIC: 7832; NAICS: 512131
Top Film Exhibitors in Hong Kong, 2002

The industry has been suffering lately with both sites, numbers films produced and box office receipts, all in decline.

	Screens	Shares
Broadway	44	46.4%
UA Cinemas	40	42.1
Newport	11	11.6

Source: *Hollywood Reporter*, May 10, 2003, p. 39, from Kowland and New Territories Motion Picture Industry Association.

★ 3474 ★
Movie Theaters
SIC: 7832; NAICS: 512131
Top Film Exhibitors in Spain, 2002

Shares are by number of movie screens operated by each exhibitor. There were 140.7 million admissions generating $625.9 million in box office receipts.

	Screens	Share
CAEC	432	38.9%
CINESA	347	31.2
Yelmo	333	30.0

Source: *Hollywood Reporter*, May 10, 2003, p. 39, from ICAA, Spanish Film Academy.

★ 3475 ★
Movie Theaters
SIC: 7832; NAICS: 512131
Top Film Exhibitors in the U.K., 2002

Shares are by number of movie screens operated by each exhibitor. Total admissions increased from 142.5 million in 2000 to 175.9 million in 2002. Harry Potter and the Chamber of Secrets was the year's top film.

	Screens	Share
Odeon	608	35.6%
UGC	396	23.2
UCI	352	20.6
Warner Village	352	20.6

Source: *Hollywood Reporter*, May 10, 2003, p. 39, from *ACNielsen EDI*.

★ 3476 ★
Movie Theaters
SIC: 7832; NAICS: 512131
Top Movie Chains in Mexico

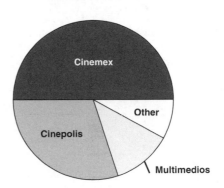

Market shares are shown in percent. According to Cinemark, attendance at movie theaters is down about 20%.

Cinemex	50.0%
Cinepolis	30.0
Multimedios	12.3
Other	7.7

Source: *America's Intelligence Wire*, October 9, 2003, p. NA.

★ 3477 ★
Movie Theaters
SIC: 7833; NAICS: 512132
Drive In Theaters by State

There were 405 drive-in theaters (with 639 screens) at the end of 2003. At the industry's high point in 1958 there were 4,063 theaters across the country.

	Drive-Ins	Share
Pennsylvania	35	8.64%
Ohio	35	8.64
New York	32	7.90
California	25	6.17
Indiana	22	5.43
Tennessee	14	3.46
Kentucky	14	3.46
Texas	13	3.21
Missouri	12	2.96
Colorado	12	2.96
Other	191	47.16

Source: *Research Alert*, October 3, 2003, p. 12, from United Drive-In Theatre Owners Association.

★ 3478 ★
Movie Rental Industry
SIC: 7841; NAICS: 53223
Largest Video Retailers Worldwide, 2001

Companies are ranked by number of outlets. Based on VHS and DVD sales, CCC generated $736 million in revenues and Blockbuster had $675 million.

Blockbuster	2,607
CCC	985
EMP	750
DVR	620
Video Ezy	460
Global Video	264
Videoland	218
Apollo	190
Choices	170
Sun Leisure	125

Source: *Video Store*, April 28, 2002, p. 26, from *Video Store* market research.

★ 3479 ★
Movie Rental Industry
SIC: 7841; NAICS: 53223
Online DVD Rental Market

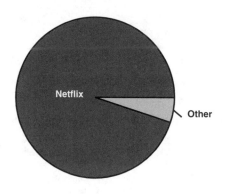

Market shares are shown in percent.

Netflix	95.0%
Other	5.0

Source: *U.S. News & World Report*, December 29, 2003, p. 64.

★ 3480 ★
Movie Rental Industry
SIC: 7841; NAICS: 53223
Online Video Rental

Market shares are shown in percent.

Netflix	90.0%
Other	10.0

Source: *Atlanta Journal Constitution*, September 2, 2003, p. NA.

★ 3481 ★
Video Game Rental Industry
SIC: 7841; NAICS: 53223
Leading Video Game Renters, 2003

Market shares are shown based on $776 million in rentals. Figures exclude previously viewed title game sales.

Blockbuster	38.7%
Independent rentailers	36.4
Hollywood Video	15.3
Movie Gallery	6.6
Other	3.0

Source: *Video Store*, April 25, 2004, p. 18, from *Video Store* Magazine Market Research.

SIC 79 - Amusement and Recreation Services

★ 3482 ★

Theatrical Entertainment

SIC: 7922; NAICS: 71111

Broadway Audiences

Total ticket sales in 2000-2001 season were 11.9 million, 11.0 million in 2001-2002 and 11.4 million in 2002-2003 season.

	2000-01	2001-02	2002-03
Out-of-town audience	56.2%	50.8%	55.0%
Other	43.8	49.2	45.0

Source: *USA TODAY*, November 20, 2003, p. 6D, from League of American Theaters and Producers.

★ 3483 ★

Theatrical Entertainment

SIC: 7922; NAICS: 71111

Leading Broadway Shows, 2003

A box office record was set in 2003 with grosses of $726.4 million, up over $21 million from 2002. Shows are ranked by cumulative grosses. Life X3, Salome and Long Day's Journey Into Night all opened and closed during the year and recouped their investment.

Gypsy	$ 27.1
The Boy From Oz	11.9
Long Day's Journey Into Night	11.3
Wicked	11.1
Avenue Q	7.8
Cat on a Hot Tin Roof	5.6
Life X 3	4.6
Salome	3.7
Wonderful Town	3.6
Golda's Balcony	2.8

Source: *Variety*, January 12, 2004, p. A1.

★ 3484 ★

Concerts

SIC: 7929; NAICS: 71113

Top Concerts in North America, 2003

Overall sales increased for the fifth straight year to $2.4 billion.

Bruce Springsteen and the E Street Band .	$ 115.9
Celine Dion	80.5
The Eagles	69.3
Fleetwood Mac	69.0
Cher	68.2
Simon & Garfunkel	64.5
Aerosmith & Kiss joint tour	64.0
Dixie Chicks	60.5
Billy Joel/Elton John joint tour	50.9
Summer Sanitarium (led by Metallica) . . .	48.8

Source: *Christian Science Monitor*, December 30, 2003, p. 20, from *Pollstar*.

★ 3485 ★
Sports Teams
SIC: 7941; NAICS: 711211

Largest Sports Franchises Worldwide

Manchester United	
New York Yankees	
Juventus	
A.C. Milan	
Washington Redskins	

The franchises are ranked by revenues in millions of dollars for 2003-2004.

Manchester United	$ 303.4
New York Yankees	294.2
Juventus (Italian Series A soccer)	263.4
A.C. Milan (Italian Series A soccer)	241.6
Washington Redskins (NFL)	238.6

Source: *BusinessWeek*, May 31, 2004, p. 13, from Deloitte.

★ 3486 ★
Sports Teams
SIC: 7941; NAICS: 711211

Leading Basketball Teams, 2002-2003

Teams are ranked by revenues in millions of dollars for the 2002-2003 season.

New York Knicks	$ 160
Los Angeles Lakers	149
Chicago Bulls	119
Dallas Mavericks	117
Phoenix Suns	109
Philadelphia 76ers	109
Sacramento Kings	102
Washington Wizards	98
Boston Celtics	97
Toronto Raptors	96

Source: *Forbes*, February 16, 2004, p. 66.

★ 3487 ★
Sports Teams
SIC: 7941; NAICS: 711211

Leading Football Teams, 2002-2003

Teams are ranked by revenues in millions of dollars.

Washington Redskins	$ 227
Dallas Cowboys	198
Houston Texans	193
New England Patriots	189
Cleveland Browns	174
Denver Broncos	171
Tampa Bay Buccaneers	168
Tennessee Titans	155
Baltimore Ravens	155
Pittsburgh Steelers	152

Source: *Forbes*, September 15, 2003, p. 82.

★ 3488 ★
Sports Teams
SIC: 7941; NAICS: 711211, 71131

Leading Soccer Clubs in Europe, 2002-2003

European football (soccer) clubs are big business. The top ten teams are listed by annual revenue in millions of Euros.

Manchester United	$ 251.4
Juventus	218.3
AC Milan	200.2
Real Madrid	192.6
Bayern Munich	162.7
Internazionale Milan	162.4
Arsenal	149.6
Liverpool	149.4
Newcastle United	138.9
Chelsea	133.8

Source: *Financial Times*, March 4, 2004, p. 7, from Sports Business Group at Deloitte.

★ 3489 ★
Sports Teams
SIC: 7941; NAICS: 711211, 71131

Most Sponsored Sports Worldwide, 2003

The most sponsored sports are ranked by value committed in millions of dollars.

Football	$ 1,921
Venues	840
Motorsports (other)	489
Formula 1	388
Olympics	319
Golf	319
Basketball	231
US football	215
Sailing/yachting	180
Rugby Union	125

Source: *Brand Strategy*, April 2004, p. 40, from *The World Sponsorship Monitor*.

★ 3490 ★
Horse Racing
SIC: 7948; NAICS: 711212, 711219

Leading Track Operators in the U.K.

Racecourse Holdings Trust

Chepstow

Arena Leisure

Companies are ranked by number of courses. The major independent courses are Ascot, Doncaster, Goodworld, Newbury and York.

Racecourse Holdings Trust	13
Chepstow	9
Arena Leisure	6

Source: *Leisure Report*, March 2004, p. 16.

★ 3491 ★
Gyms
SIC: 7991; NAICS: 71394

Largest Health/Fitness Chains in Germany

There were 713,460 members in non-franchise and franchise clubs as of December 2002. The health club industry is valued at 3.16 British pounds in 2002.

	Members	Share
Fitness Company	140,200	13.39%
Kieser Training	133,620	12.76
INJOY	94,320	9.01
TC Holdings	80,500	7.69
Elixia	77,600	7.41
Eisenhauer Training	28,350	2.71
TC Holdings	24,500	2.34
Fitness Park Pfitzenmeier	22,440	2.14
Future Sports	21,400	2.04
Kieser Training	18,374	1.75
Meridian	17,600	1.68
TEAM World of Fitness	13,000	1.24
Fitness Point	12,000	1.15
Selection Fitness	9,100	0.87
Other	354,096	33.82

Source: *Health Club Management*, June 2003, p. 57, from D&T analysis and corporate reports and DSSV.

★ 3492 ★
Health Clubs
SIC: 7991; NAICS: 71394

Leading Health Clubs/Chains

Companies are ranked by revenues in millions of dollars.

Bally Total	$ 968
24 Hour Fitness	934
Town Sports	319
LifeTime Fitness	192
The Wellbridge Co.	174
The Sports Club	122
TCA	90
Western Athletic Club	73
The Sport & Health Co.	71
Spectrum Clubs Inc.	65

Source: *Club Industry*, July 1, 2003, p. NA.

★ 3493 ★
Golf Courses
SIC: 7992; NAICS: 71391

Stand-Alone and Executive Golf Courses

Data show the states with the most stand-alone executive and par-3 courses. Nearly 28 million Americans were thought to play golf in 2001.

Florida	195
California	185
New York	94
Illinois	70
Minnesota	65
Pennsylvania	63
Ohio	63
Arizona	59
Wisconsin	57
Texas	56
Michigan	53
Indiana	46

Source: *Golf World Business*, January 2004, p. 61, from National Golf Foundation.

★ 3494 ★
Foosball Tables
SIC: 7993; NAICS: 339999

Coin-Operated Foosball Tables

The company has 60-80% of the market for coin-operated foosball, air hockey and pool tables.

Valley Dynamo	80.0%
Other	20.0

Source: *Play Meter*, August 2003, p. NA.

★ 3495 ★
Gaming Systems
SIC: 7993; NAICS: 339999

Gaming Systems Market

IGT and Acres Gaming each have less than 20% shares. IGT has 65% of the slot machine industry.

Alliance Gaming	45.0%
Aristocrat Gaming	25.0
Other	35.0

Source: *Knight Ridder/Tribune Business News*, July 1, 2003, p. NA.

★ 3496 ★
Slot Machines
SIC: 7993; NAICS: 339999

Slot Machine Market, 2002

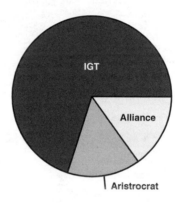

Market shares are shown in percent. Aristocrat and Alliance's shares are less than 15% of the industry.

IGT	70.0%
Aristrocrat	15.0
Alliance	15.0

Source: *Las Vegas Review-Journal*, August 27, 2003, p. NA.

★ 3497 ★
Slot Machines
SIC: 7993; NAICS: 71311

Slot Machine Market in North America

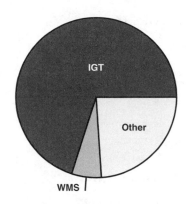

Market shares are shown in percent.

IGT	70.0%
WMS	6.0
Other	24.0

Source: *Crain's Chicago Business*, December 8, 2003, p. NA.

★ 3498 ★
Amusement Parks
SIC: 7996; NAICS: 71311

Amusement Park Markets

Revenues are in billions of dollars.

	2002	2004	2006
United States	$ 9.90	$ 10.60	$ 11.30
Asia/Pacific	5.30	5.80	6.90
Europe/Middle East/Africa . .	2.80	3.10	3.40
Canada	0.27	0.30	0.32
Latin America	0.24	0.25	0.27

Source: *Amusement Business*, July 7, 2003, p. 3, from *Entertainment and Media Outlook* and PricewaterhouseCoopers.

★ 3499 ★
Amusement Parks
SIC: 7996; NAICS: 71311

Leading Amusement Park Chains Worldwide, 2003

Parks are ranked by millions of visitors. The 50 most visited parks in North America saw a 1.5% drop in attendance. In Central and South America there was a 2% drop and in Europe an 8% drop during the same time period.

Walt Disney Attractions	96.96
Six Flags Inc.	48.17
Universal Studios Recreation Group	31.04
Anheuser-Busch	20.02
Cedar Fair Ltd.	14.65
Paramount Parks	13.64
Palance Entertainment	12.38
Grupo Magico Internacional	11.38
The Tussauds Group	10.00
Blackpool Pleasure Beach	8.40

Source: *Amusement Business*, December 22, 2003, p. 9.

★ 3500 ★
Amusement Parks
SIC: 7996; NAICS: 71311

Leading Amusement Parks in South/ Central America, 2003

Parks are ranked by millions of visitors.

Chapultec	2.80
Six Flags Mexico	2.45
Hopi Hari	2.00
Selva Magica	1.95
Playcenter	1.60
El Salitre Magico	1.52
Divertido	1.15
Parque de la Costa	0.73
Planeta Azul	0.60
Parque da Monica	0.56

Source: *Amusement Business*, December 22, 2003, p. 9.

★ 3501 ★
Amusement Parks
SIC: 7996; NAICS: 71311

Leading Amusement Parks in the Asia/Pacific Region, 2003

Parks are ranked by millions of visitors.

Tokyo Disneyland	13.18
Tokyo Disneysea	12.17
Universal Studios Japan	8.81
Everland	8.80
Lotte World	8.50
Hakkeijima Sea Paradise	5.30
Ocean Park	3.00
Huis Ten Bosch	2.84
Seoul Land	2.80
Suzuka	2.70

Source: *Amusement Business*, December 22, 2003, p. 9.

★ 3502 ★
Amusement Parks
SIC: 7996; NAICS: 71311

Leading Amusement Parks Worldwide, 2003

Magic Kingdom

Tokyo

Disneyland

Tokyo Disneysea

Disneyland Paris

Universal Studios Japan

Everland

Epcot

Lotte World

Disney-MGM Studios Theme Park

Other

Parks are ranked by millions of visitors. Total attendance at the top 50 parks was 247,061,884, down slightly from the previous year.

	(mil.)	Share
Magic Kingdom	14.04	5.68%
Tokyo (Japan) Disneyland	13.18	5.33
Disneyland	12.72	5.15
Tokyo Disneysea	12.17	4.93

	(mil.)	Share
Disneyland Paris	10.23	4.14%
Universal Studios Japan	8.81	3.57
Everland	8.80	3.56
Epcot	8.62	3.49
Lotte World	8.50	3.44
Disney-MGM Studios Theme Park	7.87	3.19
Other	142.14	57.53

Source: *Amusement Business*, December 22, 2003, p. 9.

★ 3503 ★
Amusement Parks
SIC: 7996; NAICS: 71311

Theme Park Attendance

Figures are in millions of visitors.

2002	92.4
2001	88.3
2000	84.6
1999	82.5
1998	82.1
1997	81.8
1996	78.7

Source: *USA TODAY*, December 4, 2003, p. D1, from Domestic Travel Market Report and Travel Industry Associaiton of America.

★ 3504 ★
Amusement Parks
SIC: 7996; NAICS: 71312, 71399

Top Theme/Amusement Parks in North America, 2003

Total attendance dropped 1.6% to 167.97 million but the industry saw revenues increase. Weather, economic conditions and increasing competition continue to drive the industry. Parks are ranked by millions of visitors.

	(mil.)	Share
The Magic Kingdom	14.04	8.36%
Disneyland	12.72	7.57
Epcot	8.62	5.13
Disney MGM Studios	7.87	4.69
Disney's Animal Kingdom	7.30	4.35
Universal Studios	6.85	4.08
Islands of Adventure	6.07	3.61

Continued on next page.

★ 3504 ★
[Continued]
Amusement Parks
SIC: 7996; NAICS: 71312, 71399

Top Theme/Amusement Parks in North America, 2003

Total attendance dropped 1.6% to 167.97 million but the industry saw revenues increase. Weather, economic conditions and increasing competition continue to drive the industry. Parks are ranked by millions of visitors.

	(mil.)	Share
Disney's California Adventure	5.31	3.16%
Seaworld Florida	5.20	3.10
Universal Studios Hollywood	4.57	2.72
Other	89.42	53.24

Source: *Amusement Business*, December 22, 2003, p. 9.

★ 3505 ★
Fairs
SIC: 7996; NAICS: 71399

Top Fairs in North America, 2003

Total attendance at fairs was 37.35 million. Parks are ranked by millions of visitors.

	(mil.)	Share
Conklin Shows	6.69	17.91%
Ray Cammack Shows	5.97	15.98
Strates Shows	2.83	7.58
Wade Shows	2.71	7.26
Murphy Bros. Exposition	2.42	6.48
Reithoffer Shows	2.40	6.43
Might Blue Grass Shows	2.24	6.00
Butler Amusements	1.83	4.90
Funtastic Shows	1.16	3.11
Other	9.10	24.36

Source: *Amusement Business*, December 22, 2003, p. 9.

★ 3506 ★
Stadiums
SIC: 7997; NAICS: 71394

Largest Sports Stadium Deals

| Reliant Energy |
| FedEx |
| American Airlines |
| Royal Philips Electronics |
| Minute Maid |

"Naming rights" is a new phenomenon. In 1998, there were only 3 naming rights deals. Contract values were worth $25 million. In 2004, there are 66 deals worth $3.6 billion. Deals are in millions of dollars.

Reliant Energy	$ 300
FedEx	205
American Airlines (American Airlines Center)	195
Royal Philips Electronics (Philips Arena)	185
Minute Maid (Minute Maid Park)	170

Source: *New York Times*, May 30, 2004, p. 4, from *Sports Business Journal*.

★ 3507 ★
Gambling
SIC: 7999; NAICS: 71321, 71329

Casino Market in Missouri

Market shares are shown in percent.

Ameristar	37.3%
Harrah's	32.7
Other	30.0

Source: *Kansas City Star*, December 12, 2003, p. NA, from Missouri Gaming Commission.

★ 3508 ★
Gambling
SIC: 7999; NAICS: 71321, 71329

Gambling Industry, 2002

Industries are ranked by gross revenues in millions of dollars. Gross gambling revenues, according to the source, "is the amount wagered minus the winnings returned to players, a true value of the economic value of gambling. CGR is the figure used to determine what a casino, racetrack, lottery or other gaming operation earns before taxes, salaries and other expenses are paid - the equivalent of sales not profit."

	($ mil.)	Share
Casinos	$ 28,100.0	40.90%
Lotteries	18,600.0	27.07
Indian reservations	14,200.0	20.67
Pari-mutuel	4,000.0	5.82
Charitable games and bingo	2,600.0	3.78
Card rooms	972.5	1.42
Legal bookmaking	116.2	0.17
Other	111.3	0.16

Source: "Industry Information." [online] from http://www.americangaming.org/industry/factsheets [May 10, 2004], from Christiansen Capital Advisors LLC.

★ 3509 ★
Gambling
SIC: 7999; NAICS: 71321, 71329

Gambling Market in the Czech Republic

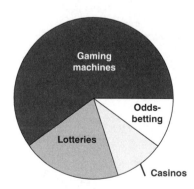

The country's odds-betting industry is worth $370 million a year. Figures show top methods of gaming.

Gaming machines	60.0%
Lotteries	20.0
Casinos	10.0
Odds-betting	10.0

Source: *The Prague Post*, March 25, 2020, p. NA.

★ 3510 ★
Gambling
SIC: 7999; NAICS: 71321, 71329

Indian Gaming Revenues

Indian gaming is the market leader in 19 of 29 states that have it. Indian casinos capture 75% of all gaming visits. Data show revenues in billions of dollars. New York may see revenues of $2 billion when its casinos open.

California	$ 5
Connecticut	2
Michigan	1

Source: *Indian Country Today*, July 9, 2003, p. NA.

★ 3511 ★
Gambling
SIC: 7999; NAICS: 71321, 71329

Largest Gambling Markets, 2002

Markets are ranked by gross revenues in millions of dollars. Shares are shown based on the top 40 markets.

	($ mil.)	Share
Las Vegas - Strip	$ 4,700.0	16.85%
Atlantic City, NJ	4,400.0	15.77
Chicagoland (IL, IN)	2,300.0	8.24
Connecticut (Indian)	2,000.0	7.17
Tunica, MS	1,100.0	3.94
Detroit, MI	1,100.0	3.94
Reno/Sparks, NV	916.8	3.29
Biloxi, MS	878.8	3.15
Southeast Indiana	841.7	3.02
Shreveport, LA	823.5	2.95
St. Louis (MO, IL)	804.7	2.88
Other	8,033.4	28.79

Source: "Industry Information." [online] from http://www.americangaming.org/industry/factsheets [May 10, 2004], from Innovation Group.

★ 3512 ★
Gambling
SIC: 7999; NAICS: 71321, 71329

Leading High Street Bookmakers in the U.K.

Companies are ranked by number of outlets. Some people do not like traditional bookmaking shops — what one person is quoted as describing as "shops that are full of men in flat caps smoking." Person-to-person onlne betting exchanges have become very popular.

Ladbrokes	1,890
William Hill	1,575
Coral	880
Stanley Leisure	650
Tote	400

Source: *Leisure Report*, June 2003, p. 16, from Association of British Bookmakers.

★ 3513 ★
Gambling
SIC: 7999; NAICS: 71321, 71329

The New Betting Exchange Market in the U.K., 2002

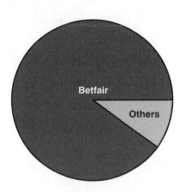

The betting exchange market is a subset of the gaming industry and covers online betting in which those placing bets are allowed to set their own odds. As a new form of gaming the market is dominated by one company.

Betfair	90.0%
Others	10.0

Source: *Evening Standard*, June 16, 2003, p. NA.

★ 3514 ★
Gambling
SIC: 7999; NAICS: 71321, 71329

Top Casino Companies, 2003

Companies are ranked by revenue in billions of dollars. Mandalay and MGM have announced plans to merge. Haraah's and Caesar's have discussed merging as well.

Caesars Entertainment	$ 4.5
Haraah's Entertainment	4.3
MGM Mirage	3.9
Mandalay Resort Group	2.5

Source: *USA TODAY*, July 15, 2004, p. B1, from Reuters Research.

★ 3515 ★
Sports
SIC: 7999; NAICS: 71392

National Ski Industry

The 2002-2003 ski industry saw its best year ever with 57.6 million visits. Largest resorts are defined as capacity of more than 12,000 vertical transport per hour.

	2002	2003
Largest resorts	48.1%	45.3%
Smallest resorts	16.4	17.7

Source: *The Aspen Times*, November 13, 2003, p. NA, from National Ski Areas Association.

★ 3516 ★
Sports
SIC: 7999; NAICS: 71392

Ski Industry in Canada

Nearly 15% of Canadians at least 12 years of age participate in one or more forms of skiing. Over 11 percent (11.5%) participate in Alpine skiing. This represents 3.05 million skiers, 30% of which are in Ontario and Quebec. Data show alpine and snowboarder visits.

	1995-96	2002-03
Quebec	5,783	6,976
BC, Yukon, Heli-Ski	4,256	5,500
Ontario	2,838	3,200
Alberta	2,220	2,400
Nova Scotia	265	230
New Brunswick	171	190

Continued on next page.

★ 3516 ★
[Continued]
Sports
SIC: 7999; NAICS: 71392

Ski Industry in Canada

Nearly 15% of Canadians at least 12 years of age participate in one or more forms of skiing. Over 11 percent (11.5%) participate in Alpine skiing. This represents 3.05 million skiers, 30% of which are in Ontario and Quebec. Data show alpine and snowboarder visits.

	1995-96	2002-03
Saskatchewan	155	108
Newfoundland	102	132
Manitoba	84	133
P.E.I.	17	18

Source: ''2003 Canadian Ski & Snowboard Industry Facts & Stats.'' [online] from http://www.canadianskicouncil.org [accessed May 24, 2004], from Canadian Ski Council.

★ 3517 ★
Sports
SIC: 7999; NAICS: 61162

Sport Travel Industry

The sports-travel industry includes everything from sponsoring teams, placing billboards in stadiums, and providing accomodations to teams. Such categories represent nearly $4 billion in spending.

Amateur	$ 1,100
Youth	1,000
Collegiate	1,000
Pro	340

Source: *Travel Weekly*, April 12, 2004, p. 1, from *Street & Smith Magazine*.

SIC 80 - Health Services

★ 3518 ★

Doctors

SIC: 8011; NAICS: 621111

Top Diagnoses from Doctors, 2003

According to the source the figures represent "projected number of patient visits specific to the diagnoses for which they are being treated by office-based physicians in the U.S. Excludes all post-operative visits and wellness exams."

	Visits (mil.)	Share
Essential hypertension	83.4	5.2%
Diabetes Mellitus w/o complications	38.9	2.4
Acute respiratory infection	30.2	1.9
Hyperlipidemia	26.9	1.7
Otitis Media	26.4	1.7
Depressive Disorder	21.1	1.3
Chronic Sinusitis	18.5	1.2
Asthma	18.0	1.1
Allergy Rhinitis	17.4	1.1
Acute Pharyngitis	16.7	1.1

Source: "Leading 10 Diagnoses by Total U.S. Patient Visits." [online] from http://www.imshealth.com [accessed April 15, 2004], from IMS Health.

★ 3519 ★

Prison Health Care Services

SIC: 8011; NAICS: 621111

Health Care Treatment in Jails

The nation's prison population grew 2.6% between 2001 and 2002. The rise in incarceration comes in part from the three-strikes law. Health care for prisoners is thought to be a $7 billion market, with 60% still handled by the government with the balance covered by the private sector.

American Service	23.0%
Correction Medical Services	17.0
Wexford Health Services	8.0
Other	52.0

Source: *Investor's Business Daily*, May 19, 2004, p. A6, from Avondale Partners.

★ 3520 ★

Cosmetic Surgery

SIC: 8062; NAICS: 62211

Leading Cosmetic Surgeries, 2003

Data show number of patients for each procedure. The most expensive procedure is a face lift which had an average doctor fee of $5283.

Nose reshaping	129,774
Eyelid surgery	46,308
Liposuction	32,092
Breast reduction	14,611
Face lift	12,760
Tummy tuck	5,584
Thigh lift	284
Buttock lift	251

Source: *New York Times*, April 15, 2004, p. 2, from American Society of Plastic Surgeons.

905

★ 3521 ★
Cosmetic Surgery
SIC: 8062; NAICS: 62211

Where Cosmetic Surgery is Performed

The number of surgical and nonsurgical procedures increased from 2.1 million to 8.3 million in 2003.

	1997	2002
Office	46.0%	52.0%
Hospitals	30.0	25.0
Freestanding surgical centers	23.0	23.0

Source: *Time*, March 1, 2004, p. 50.

★ 3522 ★
Cosmetic Surgery
SIC: 8062; NAICS: 62211

Who Gets Cosmetic Surgery, 2003

Lip augmentation saw a 21% growth from 2002-2003. Nose reshaping was the top surgery of 2003 with 356,554 surgeries.

35-50	40.0%
19-34	26.0
51-64	24.0
Other	10.0

Source: *Newsweek*, May 10, 2004, p. 85, from American Society of Plastic Surgeons.

★ 3523 ★
Hospitals
SIC: 8062; NAICS: 62211

Hospital Market for Roanoke and New River Valleys, VA

In the New River Valley and Radford, 29% of residents attended Carilion New River Medical Center while only 12% attended Carilion Roanoke Memorial Hospital or Carilion Roanoke Community Hospital.

Carilion Roanoke Memorial/Community Hospital	61.0%
Lewis-Gale Medical Center in Salem	31.0
Carilion Franklin Memorial Hospital	6.0
Other	2.0

Source: *The Roanoke Times*, November 2, 2003, p. 1, from Virginia Health Information data.

★ 3524 ★
Hospitals
SIC: 8062; NAICS: 62211

Hospital Market in Durham County, NC

Market shares are shown in percent.

Duke University Health Services	88.0%
Other	12.0

Source: *Triangle Business Journal*, March 19, 2004, p. NA.

★ 3525 ★
Hospitals
SIC: 8062; NAICS: 62211

Hospital Market in Rochester, NY

Rochester General and Park Ridge Hospital are discussing a merger to better compete with Strong Memorial. Market shares are shown in percent.

Strong Memorial Hospital	52.0%
Rochester General	33.0
Other	15.0

Source: *Rochester Democrat and Chronicle*, September 5, 2003, p. 1A.

★ 3526 ★
Hospitals
SIC: 8062; NAICS: 62211
Hospital Market in the Triad, NC

Figures show projected market shares upon the completion of a new Stokes-Reynolds hospital in King County. It would take a 30.5% share, compared to the 7.4% the Stokes-Reynolds hospital in Danbury has.

	2000	2005
Forsyth Medical Center	53.1%	48.7%
Main Baptist campus	27.1	10.9
Northern Hospital	6.0	4.3
Other	13.8	36.1

Source: *The Business Journal of the Greater Triad Area*, May 26, 2003, p. NA, from Baptist's projections.

★ 3527 ★
Hospitals
SIC: 8062; NAICS: 62211
Hospital Market in Yuma, AZ

The hospital is the community's sole provider.

Yuma Regional Medical Center	90.0%
Other	10.0

Source: *Bond Buyer*, May 7, 2004, p. 4.

★ 3528 ★
Hospitals
SIC: 8062; NAICS: 62211
Leading Health Care Providers in Eastern Massachusetts

Market shares are shown in percent.

Partners Healthcare Systems	20.7%
CareGroup Inc./Boston Medical Center	20.2
Other	59.1

Source: *Bond Buyer*, May 19, 2003, p. 4.

★ 3529 ★
Hospitals
SIC: 8062; NAICS: 62211
Leading Health Systems in Texas

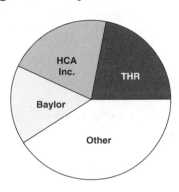

Market shares are shown in percent. THR stands for Texas Health Resources.

	2001	2002
THR	21.4%	22.0%
HCA Inc.	21.0	21.0
Baylor	16.4	15.7
Other	41.2	41.3

Source: *Health Care Strategic Management*, September 2003, p. 9.

★ 3530 ★
Hospitals
SIC: 8062; NAICS: 62211
Top Hospital Companies, 2002

Companies are ranked by share of total number of beds. Bed counts are based on the end of each company's fiscal year 2002.

HCA Inc.	38.0%
Tenet Healthcare	29.0
Universal Health Systems	10.0
Triad Hospitals	7.0
Health Management Associates Inc.	6.0
Community Health Systems	5.0
LifePoint Hospitals	3.0
Province Healthcare	2.0

Source: *Healthcare Financial Management*, October 2003, p. 20, from DGA Partners analysis of Bloomberg/CMS Health Care Industry Market Updata.

★ 3531 ★

Hospitals

SIC: 8062; NAICS: 62211

Top Hospital Groups, 2002

Figures refer to 567 for-profit hospitals.

HCA Inc.	31.0%
Tenet Healthcare	20.0
Universal Health Services	11.0
Community Health System	11.0
Triad Hospitals	10.0
Health Management Associates	8.0
LifePoint Hospitals	5.0
Province Healthcare	4.0

Source: *Health Care Food & Nutrition News*, February 2004, p. 1.

★ 3532 ★

Psychiatric Hospitals

SIC: 8063; NAICS: 62221

Inpatient Mental Health Service Providers

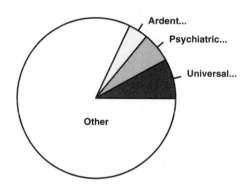

The number of private mental hospitals fell from 460 in 1995 to 255 in 2002. A number of hospitals came on the scene in the 1980s . However, when Medicare and Medicaid could not afford to pay the high fees many of these establishments had to close. Demand for mental health services is on the increase, in part because the stigma around such illnesses has been (largely) removed.

Universal Health Services	8.0%
Psychiatric Solutions	6.0
Ardent Health Services	4.0
Other	82.0

Source: *Investor's Business Daily*, July 27, 2004, p. A8, from J.P. Morgan.

★ 3533 ★

Clinical Testing Industry

SIC: 8071; NAICS: 621511

Clinical Testing Market

Market shares are shown in percent.

Hospitals	49.0%
Independents	39.0
Doctors' offices	12.0
Quest	11.0
LabCorp.	7.0

Source: *Business Week Online*, May 13, 2003, p. NA.

★ 3534 ★

Medical Laboratories

SIC: 8071; NAICS: 621511

The State of Stored Embryos

There were 396,526 embryos stored in storage at the end of April 2002. Other includes patient death and abandonment.

Family building	88.2%
Research	2.8
Donation to others	2.3
Other	6.7

Source: *Wall Street Journal*, November 21, 2003, p. B1, from Study by RAND and the Society of the Assisted Reproductive Technology (SART).

★ 3535 ★

Medical Research

SIC: 8071; NAICS: 621511

Cardiac Data Collection

Market shares of the core lab cardiac data collection industry are estimated.

eResearch	50.0%
Covance Inc.	25.0
Other	25.0

Source: *Investor's Business Daily*, September 26, 2003, p. A6, from company reports and Advest Inc.

★ 3536 ★
Dialysis Centers
SIC: 8092; NAICS: 621492
Kidney Dialysis Market

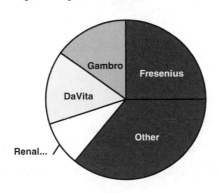

Market shares are shown in percent.

Fresenius	25.0%
Gambro	15.0
DaVita	15.0
Renal Care	9.0
Other	36.0

Source: *Investor's Business Daily*, May 25, 2004, p. A6.

★ 3537 ★
Medical Waste Disposal
SIC: 8099; NAICS: 621999
Clinical Waste Industry in Ireland

Market shares are shown in percent.

STG	90.0%
Other	10.0

Source: *Irish Times*, December 4, 2003, p. 19.

SIC 81 - Legal Services

★ 3538 ★

Legal Services

SIC: 8111; NAICS: 54111

Largest Law Firms in Japan

Nagashima Ohmo & Tsunematsu	
Mori Hamada & Matsumoto	
Nishimura & Partners	
Anderson Mori	
Asahi Koma Law Offices	

Firms are ranked by number of lawyers as of June 2003.

Nagashima Ohmo & Tsunematsu	159
Mori Hamada & Matsumoto	155
Nishimura & Partners	144
Anderson Mori	114
Asahi Koma Law Offices	113

Source: *Nikkei Weekly*, July 7, 2003, p. 6, from *Nikkei Financial Daily*.

★ 3539 ★

Legal Services

SIC: 8111; NAICS: 54111

Leading Law Firms, 2002

Firms are ranked by fee income in billions of dollars.

Skadden, Arps Meagher & Flom	$ 1.3
Baker & McKenzie	1.1
Latham & Watkin	0.9
Sidley Austin Brown & Wood	0.8
White & Case	0.7
Weil Gotschal & Manges	0.7

Shearman & Sterling	$ 0.7
Mayer Brown Rowe & Maw	0.7
McDermott Will & Emery	0.6
Davis Polk & Wardwell	0.6

Source: *Financial Times*, May 12, 2003, p. 13, from *Legal Week*.

★ 3540 ★

Legal Services

SIC: 8111; NAICS: 54111

Top Law Firms in Europe

Companies are ranked by global profits per equity partner by law firm operating in Europe.

Gianni Origoni	£ 1,400
Chiomenti	1,050
Bonelli Erede	1,050
Sullivan & Cromwell	1,010
Skadden Arps	898
Cleary Gottlieb	849
Weil Gotshal & Manges	840
Hengeler Mueller	834
Slaughter and May	819
Macfarlanes	773

Source: *Financial Times*, March 29, 2004, p. 19, from *The Lawyer*.

SIC 82 - Educational Services

★ 3541 ★
Schools
SIC: 8211; NAICS: 61111

Largest School Districts, 2001-2002

Figures show enrollment.

New York City, NY	1,049,831
Los Angeles, LA	735,058
Chicago, IL	437,418
Miami Dade County, FL	375,836
Broward County, FL	262,055
Clark County, NV	245,659
Houston, TX	210,950
Philadelphia, PA	197,083
Hawaii	184,546
Hillsborough County, FL	169,789

Source: *American School & University*, September 1, 2003, p. 1, from National Center for Education Statistics.

★ 3542 ★
Colleges
SIC: 8221; NAICS: 61131

Leading For-Profit Colleges

Apollo Group/University of Phoenix

Career Education Corp.

DeVry Inc.

Education Management Corp.

University of Phoenix Online

ITT Educational Services

Corinthian Colleges

Sylvan Learning Systems

Schools are ranked by revenues in millions of dollars. Apollo Group/University of Phoenix has the largest enrollment with 200,000 students. It offers degrees in business, technology, education, health care, and criminal justice.

Apollo Group/University of Phoenix	$ 1,300
Career Education Corp.	1,200
DeVry Inc.	680
Education Management Corp.	640
University of Phoenix Online	527
ITT Educational Services	525
Corinthian Colleges	517
Sylvan Learning Systems	460

Source: *BusinessWeek*, November 17, 2003, p. 72, from *BusinessWeek* research.

★ 3543 ★
Colleges
SIC: 8221; NAICS: 61131

Top Language Courses on College Campuses

Enrollment in sign language courses is up nearly 433% from 1998 (11,420 enrollment). Arabic is up 92.5% from the same year (5,505).

Italian	63,866
American Sign Language	60,849

Continued on next page.

★ 3543 ★
[Continued]
Colleges
SIC: 8221; NAICS: 61131

Top Language Courses on College Campuses

Enrollment in sign language courses is up nearly 433% from 1998 (11,420 enrollment). Arabic is up 92.5% from the same year (5,505).

Japanese	52,238
Chinese	34,153
Ancient Greek	20,858
Biblical Hebrew	14,469
Arabic	10,596
Modern Hebrew	8,619
Portugese	8,385
Korean	5,211

Source: *Christian Science Monitor*, December 16, 2003, p. 12, from Modern Language Association.

★ 3544 ★
Libraries
SIC: 8231; NAICS: 51412

Largest Libraries in the United States, 2002

Institutions are ranked by millions of volumes.

Library of Congress	28.68
Harvard University	14.68
Boston Public Library	14.61
Chicago Public Library	10.94
Yale University	10.70
The Public Library of Cincinnati & Hamilton County	9.82
University of Illinois - Urbana-Champaign	9.64
University of California - Berkeley	9.28
Queens Borough Public Library	9.15
County of Los Angeles Public Library	8.79

Source: "Nation's Largest Libraries." [online] from http://www.ala.org [accessed June 14, 2004], from American Library Association.

★ 3545 ★
Tutoring
SIC: 8299; NAICS: 611691, 61171

Tutoring Industry

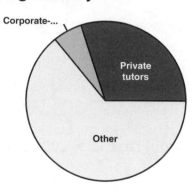

Annual spending on all forms of tutoring has been estimated to be $8 billion. Roughly 10% of students are thought to receive tutoring. Corporate-owned tutoring services include Huntington Learning Centers and Sylvan.

Private tutors	30.0%
Corporate-owned tutoring services	6.0
Other	64.0

Source: *Twin Cities*, November 30, 2003, p. NA.

SIC 83 - Social Services

★ 3546 ★
Child Care
SIC: 8351; NAICS: 62441

Leading Child Card Firms in North America, 2003

Organizations are ranked by licensed capacity.

KinderCare Learning Centers	167,000
Knowledge Learning Corporation	112,365
La Petite Academy	89,835
Bright Horizons Family Solutions	59,000
Childtime Learning Centers	52,000
Nobel Learning Centers	28,100
Child Care Network	15,881
Children's Courtyard	13,255
The Sunshine House	13,010
New Horizon Child Care	12,410

Source: *Child Care Information Exchange*, January/February 2004, p. 18.

★ 3547 ★
Child Care
SIC: 8351; NAICS: 62441

Leading Employer Child Card Firms, 2003

Organizations are ranked by licensed capacity.

Bright Horizons Family Solutions	57,000
Knowledge Learning Corporation	20,176
La Petite Academy	13,318
KinderCare Learning Centers	9,948
Hildebrandt Learning Centers	3,049
New Horizon Child Care	2,829
Children's Choice Learning Centers	2,325
The Children's Courtyard	2,220

Easter Seals Child Development	2,011
Children's Creative Learning Centers	1,650

Source: *Child Care Information Exchange*, September/October 2003, p. 24.

★ 3548 ★
Charities
SIC: 8399; NAICS: 813219, 813311, 813312

Largest Charities

Organizations are ranked by highest private donations. Figures are in millions of dollars.

American Red Cross	$ 1,700.0
Salvation Army	1,400.0
Gifts in Kind International	793.2
American Cancer Society	765.0
Fidelity Investments Charitable Gift Fund	735.5
Lutheran Services in America	723.3
YMCA of the USA	713.9
Nature Conservancy	628.3
University of Southern California	585.0
Feed the Children	546.9

Source: *Christian Science Monitor*, October 30, 2003, p. 20, from *Chronicle of Philanthropy*.

★ 3549 ★
Charities
SIC: 8399; NAICS: 813219, 813311, 813312

Largest Private Foundations

Foundations are ranked by assets in billions of dollars.

Bill & Melinda Gates Foundation	$ 24.1
Lilly Endowment	10.1
Ford Foundation	9.3

Continued on next page.

★ 3549 ★

[Continued]

Charities

SIC: 8399; NAICS: 813219, 813311, 813312

Largest Private Foundations

Foundations are ranked by assets in billions of dollars.

J. Paul Getty Trust	$ 8.6
Robert Wood Johnson Foundation	8.0
W.K. Kellogg Foundation	5.7
William and Flora Hewlett Foundation	5.0
David and Lucille Packard Foundation	4.8
John D. and Catherine MacArthur Foundation	3.8
Pew Charitable Trusts	3.7

Source: *USA TODAY*, March 11, 2004, p. 2B, from company reports.

★ 3550 ★

Charities

SIC: 8399; NAICS: 813219, 813311, 813312

Largest U.S. Charities

Groups are ranked by total income in millions of dollars.

The National Council of YMCAs	$ 4,271.7
American Red Cross	4,087.4
Catholic Charities	2,621.2
Salvation Army	2,160.1
Goodwill Industries International	2,055.2
United Jewish Communities	1,962.0
Boys & Girls Clubs of America	1,079.4
The Nature Conservancy	972.4
American Cancer Society Inc.	816.9
Gifts in Kind International	795.7
Fidelity Investments Charitable Gift Fund	758.2
Habitat for Humanity International	747.9

Source: *Christian Science Monitor*, November 24, 2003, p. 18, from *NonProfit Times* and *Chronicle of Philanthropy*.

★ 3551 ★

Charities

SIC: 8399; NAICS: 813219, 813311, 813312

Where We Donated, 2003

American individuals and corporations donated $240.72 billion to charities in 2003, up from $234 billion in 2002. This is the highest rate of growth since 2000, according to Giving USA.

	($ bil.)	Share
Religion	$ 86.39	35.89%
Education	31.59	13.12
Foundations	21.44	8.91
Health	20.89	8.68
Human services	18.89	7.85
Arts, culture and humanities	13.11	5.45
Public-society benefit (United Way)	12.13	5.04
Environment/animals	6.95	2.89
International affairs	5.30	2.20
Other	24.03	9.98

Source: *Christian Science Monitor*, June 21, 2004, p. 15, from Giving USA.

★ 3552 ★

Charities

SIC: 8399; NAICS: 813219, 813311, 813312

Who Gave to Charity, 2002

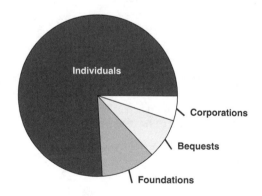

Total contributions gave $241 billion.

Individuals	76.0%
Foundations	11.0
Bequests	8.0
Corporations	5.0

Source: *U.S. News & World Report*, December 8, 2003, p. 50, from *Giving USA* and AAFRC Trust for Philanthopy.

★ 3553 ★
Charities
SIC: 8399; NAICS: 813219, 813311, 813312

Who Gave to Charity, 2003

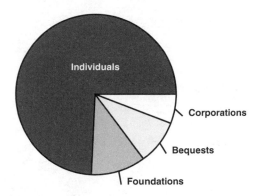

American individuals and corporations donated $240.72 billion to charities in 2003. This is the highest rate of growth since 2000, according to Giving USA.

	($ bil.)	Share
Individuals	$ 179.38	74.51%
Foundations	26.30	10.92
Bequests	21.60	8.97
Corporations	13.46	5.59

Source: *Christian Science Monitor*, June 21, 2004, p. 15, from Giving USA.

★ 3554 ★
Charities
SIC: 8399; NAICS: 813219, 813311, 813312

Who Receives Charitable Contributions, 2002

Total contributions reached $240.9 billion.

Religion	35.0%
Education	13.1
Unallocated giving	12.6
Foundations	9.1
Health	7.8
Human services	7.7
Art, culture, humanities	5.1
Public-society benefit	4.8
Environment/animals	2.7
International affairs	1.9

Source: "2003 by Type of Recipient Organization." [online] available from http://www.aafrc.org/bytypeof.html [December 9, 2003], from American Association of Fundraising Counsel Trust for Philanthopy and *Giving USA 2003*.

SIC 84 - Museums, Botanical, Zoological Gardens

★ 3555 ★

Art

SIC: 8412; NAICS: 71211, 71212

Art Auction Market in Switzerland

Switzerland ranks fifth in the world for trade in art. It has 2.3% of the industry or a market worth $697 million.

Christie's/Sotheby's/Phillip's	90.0%
Other	10.0

Source: "Fine Art and Antiques Market in Switzerland." [online] from http://www.usatrade.gov [accessed January 5, 2004], from U.S. Commercial Service, Tefaf, and European Fine Arts Association.

★ 3556 ★

Art

SIC: 8412; NAICS: 71211

Global Art Market, 2002

The U.K. is about to take the lead over the U.S., breaking that country's 20 year lead in the market. In the 1990s, the U.S. had about 70% of the fine art market. Shares are shown based on sales turnover are for the first half of the year.

United States	38.7%
United Kingdom	37.5
France	8.6
Germany	2.3
Italy	2.3
Switzerland	2.2
Other	8.3

Source: *Financial Times*, September 20, 2002, p. 23, from Artprice.com.

★ 3557 ★

Museums

SIC: 8412; NAICS: 71211, 71212

Busiest Museum Shows

Exhibitions are ranked by daily traffic. The Van Gogh and Gauguin exhibit at the Van Gogh Museum saw a total of 739,117 visitors, followed by the same show at the Art Institute of Chicago with 690,951 visitors.

Van Gogh and Gauguin (Van Gogh Museum)	6,719
Van Gogh and Gauguin (Art Institute of Chicago)	6,281
Masterpieces from the Prado Museum (Nat. Mus. Of Western Art)	5,616
Matisse/Picasso (Tate Museum)	4,671
Surrealist Revolution (Centres Georges Pompidou)	4,500
The Artists of the Pharoahs (Musee du Louvre)	4,285
The Secret Gallery and the Nude (Museo del Prado)	4,074
Andy Warhol (Tate Museum)	4,052
Treasures of Ancient Egypt (Nat. Gallery of Art)	4,026
Gerhard Richter (Mus. Of Modern Art) . . .	4,020

Source: *The Economist*, February 15, 2003, p. 78, from *The Art Newspaper*.

SIC 86 - Membership Organizations

★ 3558 ★
Horse Associations
SIC: 8621; NAICS: 81392

Leading Horse Associations

Membership figures for 2003 are forecasted.

	2001	2003
USA Equestrian	80,760	84,000
U.S. Dressage Federation	31,480	33,500
U.S. Trotting Association	30,166	25,000
National Cutting Horse Association	13,200	16,500
U.S. Eventing Association	13,091	13,500
U.S. Pony Clubs	12,559	12,500
National Reining Horse Association	11,000	12,500
Professional Rodeo Cowboys Association	9,000	9,000
American Endurance Ride Conference	5,691	6,000
International Pro Rodeo Association	3,500	3,500
American Driving Society	2,300	2,300
National Steeplechase Association	1,000	1,000

Source: *Equus*, November 2003, p. 48.

★ 3559 ★
Unions
SIC: 8631; NAICS: 81393

Union Membership by State

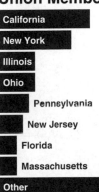

California
New York
Illinois
Ohio
Pennsylvania
New Jersey
Florida
Massachusetts
Other

Union membership has been on the decline in recent years. California is the home to nearly 2.4 million of the nation's union members.

	Members	Share
California	2,395,000	14.71%
New York	2,024,000	12.43
Illinois	999,000	6.14
Ohio	899,000	5.52
Pennsylvania	888,000	5.45
New Jersey	712,000	4.37
Florida	422,000	2.59
Massachusetts	420,000	2.58
Other	7,521,000	46.20

Source: ''Union Members by State in 2001.'' [online] from http://laborresearch.org/tables/mbrs_states.php [accessed June 14, 2004], from U.S. Bureau of Labor Statistics.

★ 3560 ★
Political Action Committees
SIC: 8651; NAICS: 81394

Leading PACs, 2001-2002

Groups are ranked by total receipts in millions of dollars as of July 9, 2003.

EMILY'S List	$ 22.68
Servie Employees International Union . . .	14.29
American Federation of Teachers	13.48
American Medical Assn	11.47
Teamsters Union	11.33
Intl. Brotherhood of Electrical Workers . . .	11.16
Laborers Union	10.70
National Rifle Assn.	10.50
American Fed. of State/County/Munic Employees	10.14
United Auto Workers	9.37
Assn. of Trial Lawyers of America	7.45
National Education Assn.	7.37

Source: "The Big Picture 2002 Cycle." [online] from http://www.opensecrets.org [accessed May 20, 2004], from Federal Election Committee.

★ 3561 ★
Churches
SIC: 8661; NAICS: 81311

Largest Churches in the United States, 2002

Denominations are ranked by number of members.

Roman Catholic Church	63.68
Southern Baptist Convention	15.96
United Methodist Church	8.34
Church of God in Christ	5.49
Church of Jesus Christ of Latter-Day Saints .	5.20
Evangelical Lutheran Church in America . .	5.12
National Baptist Convention of America Inc. .	3.50
Presbyterian Church	3.48
Assemblies of God	2.57
Lutheran Church - Missouri Synod	2.55

Source: "Largest 25 U.S. Churches, 2002." [online] from http://www.print.infoplease.com/ipa/A0001481.html [accessed June 14, 2004].

SIC 87 - Engineering and Management Services

★ 3562 ★

Design Services

SIC: 8710; NAICS: 54131, 54133

Leading Design Firms, 2002

Firms are ranked by design revenues in millions of dollars.

URS	$ 2,887.5
Bechtel	2,030.0
Fluor Corp.	1,959.9
Jacobs	1,896.8
AECOM Technology Corp.	1,726.1
Earth Tech	1,467.0
CH2M Hill Cos.	1,327.6
Parsons	1,269.2
ABB Lummus Global	899.5
Tetra Tech Inc.	862.0

Source: *ENR*, April 21, 2003, p. NA.

★ 3563 ★

Engineering Services

SIC: 8711; NAICS: 54133

Engineering Services Industry in Canada, 2001

The engineering services field saw revenues reach $7.5 billion for the year with 63% coming directly from construction/design revenues. Most engineering firms are small and privately held.

Ontario	36.0%
Quebec	22.0
Alberta	22.0
Other	20.0

Source: "Architecture, Construction and Engineering Services." [online] from http://www.usatrade.gov [accessed January 7, 2004], from U.S. Commercial Service.

★ 3564 ★

Architectural Services

SIC: 8712; NAICS: 54131

Architectural Billings

Diverse institutional includes justice, civic, religious and similar organizations.

Educational	24.1%
Diverse institutional	17.1
Office	14.2
Residential	12.1

Continued on next page.

★ 3564 ★
[Continued]
Architectural Services
SIC: 8712; NAICS: 54131
Architectural Billings

Diverse institutional includes justice, civic, religious and similar organizations.

Health care	11.3%
Retail	8.8
Industrial	3.4
Hospitality	1.8

Source: *Architectural Record*, February 2004, p. 70, from *2003 American Institute of Architects Firm Survey*.

★ 3565 ★
Architectural Services
SIC: 8712; NAICS: 54131
Architectural Industry in France

Top firms are Renzo Piano Building Workshop ($16 million), Les Architects CVZ ($10.8 million), Valode et Pistre ($10 million), Architectures Jean Nouvel ($8.4 million), Dupont ($8.1 million).

Residential condominium	27.0%
Offices/commercial outlets	17.0
Residential Homes	14.0
Schools	12.5
Other	29.5

Source: "Architectural, Construction and Engineering Services." [online] from http://www.usatrade.gov [accessed January 5, 2004], from U.S. Commercial Service.

★ 3566 ★
Architectural Services
SIC: 8712; NAICS: 54131
Leading Retail Design Firms

Firms are ranked by retail design fees in millions of dollars.

Callison Architecture	$ 47.97
Pavlik Design	40.25
MulvannyG2 Architecture	37.20
WD Partners	36.00
Carter & Burgess	34.73

Design Forum	$ 29.60
Miller Zell	24.00
Little Diversified Architectural Consulting	21.20
MCG Architecture	18.50

Source: *VM + SD*, March 2004, p. 31.

★ 3567 ★
Design Services
SIC: 8712; NAICS: 54131
Leading Design-Builder Firms

Firms are ranked by revenues in millions of dolalrs.

Bechtel	$ 7,610.0
Fluor Corp.	6,349.5
Jacobs	3,929.7
Foster Wheeler Ltd.	2,592.0
The Shaw Group Inc.	2,353.2
Black & Veatch	1,887.1
ABB Lummus Global	1,704.3
Washington Group International Inc.	1,570.7
Kellogg Brown & Root	1,379.0
Peter Kiewit Sons Inc.	1,281.9

Source: *ENR*, June 16, 2003, p. 42.

★ 3568 ★
Accounting Services
SIC: 8721; NAICS: 541211, 541219
Accounting Firms in France

Shares are for accounting firm services in France by type of service.

Audit	43.0%
Accounting	39.0
Tax	7.0
Management consulting	5.0
Other	6.0

Source: *The Accountant*, November 2003, p. 10.

★ 3569 ★
Accounting Services
SIC: 8721; NAICS: 541211, 541219

Accounting Industry in Europe

Data show fee splits.

Audit	29.0%
Accounting	27.0
Tax	18.0
Management consulting	8.0
Other	18.0

Source: *International Accounting Bulletin*, September 12, 2003, p. NA, from WAI and Lafferty.

★ 3570 ★
Accounting Services
SIC: 8721; NAICS: 541211, 541219

Accounting Services in South Africa, 2003

Distribution of industry fees is shown in percent.

Auditing	46.0%
Management consulting	14.0
Tax work	13.0
Accounting	8.0
Corporate finance	2.0
Legal work	1.0
Other	16.0

Source: *International Accounting Bulletin*, April 2, 2004, p. 6, from Lafferty.

★ 3571 ★
Accounting Services
SIC: 8721; NAICS: 541211, 541219

Leading Accounting Firms in Australia, 2003

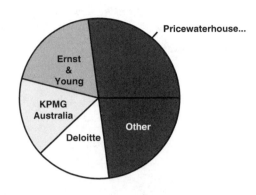

Market shares are shown in percent.

PricewaterhouseCoopers	27.0%
Ernst & Young	19.0
KPMG Australia	16.0
Deloitte	15.0
Other	23.0

Source: *International Accounting Bulletin*, November 7, 2003, p. 1, from WAI and Lafferty.

★ 3572 ★
Accounting Services
SIC: 8721; NAICS: 541211, 541219

Leading Accounting Firms in Spain

The industry's split is 32% auditing, 26% tax fees and the rest are from other sources. Market shares are shown in percent.

Deloitte	25.0%
PricewaterhouseCoopers	24.0
Ernst & Young	13.0
KPMG Spain	10.0
Other	28.0

Source: *International Accounting Bulletin*, September 12, 2003, p. NA, from WAI and Lafferty.

★ 3573 ★
Accounting Services
SIC: 8721; NAICS: 541211, 541219
Leading Auditing Firms in the U.K., 2002

Shares are based on auditing fees from companies in the Financial Times Stock Exchange (FTSE) 100.

PricewaterhouseCoopers	44.0%
KPMG	23.0
Deloitte	17.0
E&Y	16.0

Source: *The Accountant*, November 2003, p. 10.

★ 3574 ★
Accounting Services
SIC: 8721; NAICS: 541211, 541219
Public Auditing Market, 2002

Market shares are shown in percent.

PricewaterhouseCoopers	34.0%
Deloitte	24.0
Ernst & Young	23.0
KPMG	18.0
Other	1.0

Source: *The Accountant*, August 2003, p. 1, from General Accounting Office.

★ 3575 ★
Research
SIC: 8730; NAICS: 54191
Who Funds Research, 2004

Total funding was forecasted at $290.8 billion for 2004. Defense and homeland security are going to be major drivers in federal funding.

	($ mil.)	Share
Private industry	$ 181,140	62.28%
Federal government	89,370	30.73
Academia	11,380	3.91
Other non-profit	8,940	3.07

Source: *R&D*, January 2004, p. F3.

★ 3576 ★
Research
SIC: 8731; NAICS: 54171
Industrial Research Spending, 2003

Spending is shown in billions. The biotech category grew 16.4% in 2003. The category including radios and TV equipment fell 11.8% in 2003.

Pharmaceutical	$ 59.61
Motor vehicles	46.29
Telecom apparatus	22.79
Software	22.33
Radio/tv equipment	11.29
Electrical equipment	10.16
Aerospace	9.20
Computer/office equipment	8.35
Biotech	8.11

Source: *R&D*, January 2004, p. F3, from Schonfeld & Associates and *R&D*.

★ 3577 ★
Registered Agents
SIC: 8732; NAICS: 54172, 54191
Registered Agent Market in Delaware

The industry - which includes specialized legal research and services — is estimated to have annual revenues over $1 billion. CSC stands for Corporation Service Co. CT has 60% of the registered agent services industry in the country.

CT	35.0%
CSC	31.0
Other	34.0

Source: *The News Journal*, July 20, 2003, p. E1.

★ 3578 ★
Research
SIC: 8732; NAICS: 54172, 54191
Consumer Product Sales Analysis

Information Research Inc. has seen its share of supermarket, drug store and mass merchandiser sales erode over the last five years.

Information Resources Inc.	55.0%
A.C.Nielsen Corp.	45.0

Source: *Crain's Chicago Business*, February 23, 2004, p. 12.

★ 3579 ★
Research
SIC: 8732; NAICS: 54191

Leading Market Research Firms, 2002

Firms are ranked by U.S. only revenues in millions of dollars. Shares are shown based on the 187 firms and $5.98 billion in revenues (up 3.5% over 2001).

	($ mil.)	Share
VNU Inc.	$ 1,526.0	25.50%
IMS Health Inc.	488.0	8.15
Information Resources Inc.	411.5	6.88
Westat Inc.	341.9	5.71
The Kantar Group	312.7	5.23
Arbitron Inc.	241.9	4.04
NOP World	200.9	3.36
Taylor Nelson Sofres USA	191.9	3.21
NFO WorldGroup	168.4	2.81
Synovate	161.6	2.70
Ipsos	145.0	2.42
Maritz	123.5	2.06
Other	1,671.1	27.92

Source: *Marketing News*, June 9, 2003, p. 1, from Council of American Survey Research Organizations.

★ 3580 ★
Research
SIC: 8732; NAICS: 54191

Leading Market Research Firms Worldwide

Firms are ranked by revenues in millions of dollars.

VNU	$ 2,814.0
IMS Health Inc.	1,219.4
The Kantar Group	1,033.2
TNS	908.3
Information Resources Inc.	554.8
GfK Group	528.9
Ipsos Group	509.0
NFO WorldGroup Inc.	466.1
Westat Inc.	341.9
NOP World	320.0
Synovate	317.6

Source: *Marketing News*, August 18, 2003, p. H4.

★ 3581 ★
Research
SIC: 8732; NAICS: 54191

Patient Recruitment Industry

Data show market shares of industry-sponsored trials by type of site.

	($ mil.)	Share
Part-time site	$ 1,650	37.0%
AMC/MMC	1,570	35.0
Dedicated sites	1,040	22.0
SMOs	270	6.0

Source: *Applied Clinical Trials Supplement*, November 2003, p. 16, from CenterWatch 2003.

★ 3582 ★
Research
SIC: 8732; NAICS: 54191

Universities and Government Funding

The government dispensed $21.4 billion to universities in 2002. California universities saw the highest level of government funding with $1.73 billion in funds, followed by New York at $1.67 billion and Pennsylvania at $1.33 billion.

Health & Human Services	67.0%
National Science Foundation	11.0
Department of Defense	7.0
NASA	5.0
Department of Defense	4.0
Other	6.0

Source: *Wall Street Journal*, April 30, 2004, p. D8, from Rand Corp.

★ 3583 ★
Testing Laboratories
SIC: 8734; NAICS: 54138

Who Conducts Product Safety Tests

The company held a 100% share in the 1960s.

Underwriters Laboratories	50.0%
Other	50.0

Source: *Knight Ridder/Tribune News Service*, May 15, 2003, p. NA.

★ 3584 ★
Management Consulting Services
SIC: 8742; NAICS: 541613

Leading Consultants in Canada, 2002

IBM Global Services
EDS
CGI
Deloitte Touche Tohmatsu
Accenture
Deloitte Consulting
Cap Gemini Ernst & Young
Mercer Consulting Group
Fujitsu Consulting
Towers Perrin

Firms are ranked by consulting revenue in millions of dollars for fiscal year.

IBM Global Services	$ 2,158.0
EDS	884.0
CGI	230.0
Deloitte Touche Tohmatsu	156.0
Accenture	148.0
Deloitte Consulting	144.4
Cap Gemini Ernst & Young	138.0
Mercer Consulting Group	131.0
Fujitsu Consulting	114.0
Towers Perrin	79.5

Source: *Management Consultant International*, January 2003, p. 14, from estimates by source.

★ 3585 ★
Management Consulting Services
SIC: 8742; NAICS: 541613

Leading Consultants in Europe, 2002

Market shares are shown for fiscal year.

Cap Gemini Ernst & Young	13.3%
LogicaCMG	5.8
SAP	5.4
Atos Origin	4.7
T-Systems	4.5
Altran	3.2
TietoEnator	2.2
Gedas	1.6

Roland Berger	1.4%
Other	57.9

Source: *Management Consultant International*, May - June 2003, p. S11, from estimates by source.

★ 3586 ★
Management Consulting Services
SIC: 8742; NAICS: 541613

Leading Consultants in France

France has 16% of the European consulting market, placing behind Germany and the U.K. with 27% shares each.

Cap Gemini	$ 923.0
Accenture	522.2
IBM Global Services	492.5
Atos Origin	367.0
CSC	240.0
PwC Consulting	239.6
SchlumbergerSema	194.6
McKinsey & Co.	150.1
DTT	116.0
Syntegra France	90.6

Source: *Management Consultant International*, March 2003, p. S6, from estimates by source.

★ 3587 ★
Management Consulting Services
SIC: 8742; NAICS: 541613

Leading Management Consultants in the U.K., 2003

Consultants generated fee income of 10 billion pounds sterling. Market shares are shown in percent.

IBM	11.0%
Accenture	9.0
LogicaCMG	8.0
Deloitte	7.0
McKinsey	4.0
CGE&Y	4.0
Fujitsu	3.0
EDS	3.0
CSC	3.0
Other	48.0

Source: *Management Consultant International*, April 2004, p. 2, from source estimates.

★ 3588 ★
Management Consulting Services
SIC: 8742; NAICS: 541613

Leading Management Consulting Firms in Germany

Companies are ranked by domestic business in millions of euros.

McKinsey & Company Deutschland 580
Roland Berger Strategy Consultants 316
The Boston Consulting Group 258
Deloitte Consulting 215
A.T. Kearney 209
Booz Allen Hamilton 160
Mercer Consulting Group 125
IBM Unternehmensberatung 104
Arthur D. Little 85

Source: *Der Spiegel*, no. 8, 2004, p. 63, from Lunendonk.

★ 3589 ★
Public Relations Industry
SIC: 8743; NAICS: 54182

Public Relations Industry, 2002

Data are based on a survey of 214 firms. The top industries are shown based on revenues reported in the survey. New York City was the top market with $317.3 million in revenues, with Washington D.C. coming in second at $111.42 million.

Technology 31.0%
Consumer/retail 21.0
Healthcare 19.0
Government/non-profit 9.0
Financial products & services 6.0

Source: "2002 Public Relations Revenue and Performance Fact Sheet." [online] from http://www.prfirms.org [accessed May 17, 2004], from *Council of Public Relations Firms 2002 Rankings Survey.*

★ 3590 ★
Public Relations Industry
SIC: 8743; NAICS: 54182

Top Public Relations Firms, 2002

Firms are ranked by revenues in millions of dollars.

Edelman Public Relations Worldwide . . $ 136.30
The Ruder Finn Group 70.67
Incepta 70.19

Waggener Edstrom . . . .$ 58.44
Schwartz Communications Inc. 19.54
Campbell & Co. 19.48
Text 100 Public Relations 18.93
FD Morgan-Walke 14.73
DeVreis Public Relations 14.55
Gibbs & Soell 13.21
PR21 Inc. 11.29

Source: "2002 Rankings Survey." [online] from http://www.prfirms.org [accessed May 17, 2004], from *Council of Public Relations Firms 2002 Rankings Survey.*

★ **3591** ★

Prisons

SIC: 9223; NAICS: 92214

Top Prison Managers

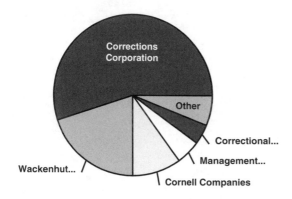

Market shares are shown based on capacity of the total privatized prison beds.

	Capacity	Share
Corrections Corporation of America	65,254	54.9%
Wackenhut Corrections Corp. . .	23,921	20.2
Cornell Companies	11,217	9.5
Management & Training Corp. . .	5,986	5.0
Correctional Services Corporation	5,124	4.3
Other	7,207	6.1

Source: "Lehman Brothers High Yield Bond." [online] from http://www.shareholder.com/cxw/download/lehman03242004.pdf [accessed April 14, 2004], from Corrections Corporation of America.

SIC 95 - Environmental Quality and Housing

★ 3592 ★

Environmental Services

SIC: 9510; NAICS: 92411, 92412

Leading Environmental Firms, 2002

Firms are ranked by sales in millions of dollars.

U.S. Filter Corp.	$ 5,600.0
Weston Solutions Inc.	349.4
The ERM Group	317.0
Duratek Inc.	291.5
BNFL Inc.	275.5
Malcolm Pirnie Inc.	224.9
ENSR International	168.9
Sevenson Environmental Services Inc.	166.1
Brown and Caldwell	165.0
LVI Services Inc.	148.2

Source: *ENR*, June 2, 2003, p. 58.

★ 3593 ★

Geotechnology

SIC: 9512; NAICS: 92412

Federal Geotechnology Spending

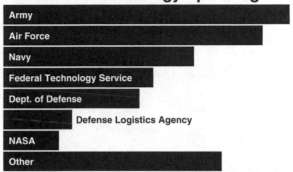

According to the source "a total of 117 federal agencies purchased a range of geotechnology products and services from 393 companies. Geotechnology is broadly defined to include related fields such as data conversion and digitizing, satellite and aerial imagery, environmental management and consulting, GIS consulting and application development, mapping services and professional engineering services."

Army	21.0%
Air Force	19.0
Navy	14.0
Federal Technology Service	11.0
Dept. of Defense	10.0
Defense Logistics Agency	5.0
NASA	4.0
Other	16.0

Source: *GEO World*, January 2004, p. 10, from Cary & Associates.

SIC 96 - Administration of Economic Programs

★ 3594 ★

Energy Department

SIC: 9631; NAICS: 92613

Leading Contractors for the Energy Department, 2002

Market shares are shown based on total spending of $18.9 billion.

University of California System	21.08%
Bechtel Group Inc.	13.61
Lockheed Martin Corp.	12.64
BNFL Inc.	8.52
McDermott Inc.	5.93
Battelle Memorial Institute	4.68
Fluro Corp.	4.51
University of Chicago	2.79
Brookhaven Science Assoc.	2.42
Honeywell Inc.	2.35
Other	21.47

Source: *Government Executive*, September 4, 2003, p. NA.

★ 3595 ★

Aerospace Contracting

SIC: 9661; NAICS: 92711

Leading Contractors for NASA, 2002

Boeing Co.
Lockheed Martin
California Institute of Technology
Northrop Grumman
Alliant Techsystems Inc.
Raytheon Co.
Comptuer Sciences Corp.
United Technologies Corp.
SAIC
QSS Group
Other

Market shares are shown based on total spending of $11.5 billion.

Boeing Co.	21.89%
Lockheed Martin	20.15
California Institute of Technology	12.26
Northrop Grumman	3.67
Alliant Techsystems Inc.	3.38
Raytheon Co.	2.25
Comptuer Sciences Corp.	1.85
United Technologies Corp.	1.59
SAIC	1.55
QSS Group	1.37
Other	30.04

Source: *Government Executive*, September 4, 2003, p. NA.

SIC 97 - National Security and International Affairs

★ 3596 ★
Air Force
SIC: 9711; NAICS: 92811

Leading Contractors for Air Force, 2002

Market shares are shown based on total spending of $45.3 billion.

Lockheed Martin	22.49%
Boeing Co.	19.47
Northrop Grumman Corp.	4.20
Raytheon Co.	3.83
United Technologies Corp.	3.79
TRW Inc.	2.16
L-3 Communications Corp.	1.86
Computer Sciences Corp.	1.60
North American Airlines	1.37
General Dynamics Corp.	1.16
Other	38.07

Source: *Government Executive*, September 4, 2003, p. NA, from General Services Administration.

★ 3597 ★
Army
SIC: 9711; NAICS: 92811

Leading Contractors for the Army, 2002

Market shares are shown based on total spending of $45 billion.

Lockheed Martin Corp.	7.62%
Raytheon Co.	5.65
Boeing Co.	5.37
General Dynamics Corp.	4.55
Carlyle Group	2.79
Computer Sciences Corp.	2.39
Northrop Grumman Corp.	2.10
United Technologies Corp.	1.98

Alliant Techsystems Inc.	1.32%
SAIC	1.21
Other	65.02

Source: *Government Executive*, September 4, 2003, p. NA.

★ 3598 ★
Defense
SIC: 9711; NAICS: 92811

Cities and Counterterrorism Aid

According to the source cities will share $500 million in new funding for first responders.

New York City, NY	$ 125.0
Washington D.C.	42.4
Chicago, IL	30.0
Houston, TX	23.8
Los Angeles, CA	18.9
San Francisco, CA	18.6
Seattle, WA	18.2
Boston, MA	16.7
Denver, CO	15.6
Philadelphia, PA	14.2

Source: *Christian Science Monitor*, May 30, 2003, p. 24, from U.S. Department of Homeland Security.

★ 3599 ★
Defense
SIC: 9711; NAICS: 92811

Defense Spending Leaders

Spending is shown in billions of dollars.

United States	$ 348.5
China	55.9
Russia	50.8
France	40.2
Japan	39.2
United Kingdom	37.3
Germany	33.3

Source: *U.S. News & World Report*, October 6, 2003, p. 32.

★ 3600 ★
Defense
SIC: 9711; NAICS: 92811

Homeland Security Spending

The 2005 budget for the U.S. Department of Homeland Security increased to $27.2 billion. $8.06 billion will be available to the private sector. The distribution of this spending is shown below. Figures are for fiscal years.

	2004	2005
Goods & equipment	45.0%	39.0%
Services	43.0	50.0
R&D	12.0	11.0

Source: *Military & Aerospace Electronics*, April 2004, p. 15, from Civitas Group.

★ 3601 ★
Defense
SIC: 9711; NAICS: 92811

Large Contracts in Iraq

Companies are ranked by value of contracts. Kellogg Brown & Root is involved in extinguishing oil well fires and reconstructing oil fields. Bechtel is involved in rebuilding power lines, improving sanitation services and roads. Parsons destroys weapons and rebuilds oil fields. International American Products and Perini are rebuilding Iraq's electrical systems. Perini also supplies good sand services to U.S. Central Command.

Kellogg Brown & Root (Halliburton)	$ 3,970
Bechtel Group	2,830
Parsons	880
Intenational American Products	528
Perini	525

Source: *BusinessWeek*, May 31, 2004, p. 78, from Center for Public Integrity.

★ 3602 ★
Defense
SIC: 9711; NAICS: 92811

Largest Arms Sellers

United States
Great Britain
Russia
France
China
Germany
Italy

Countries are ranked by arms sales in billions of dollars. Saudia Arabia was the leading purchaser of arms, spending roughly $5.2 billion.

	($ bil.)	Share
United States	$ 10.241	40.3%
Great Britain	4.700	18.5
Russia	3.100	12.2
France	1.800	7.1
China	0.800	3.1
Germany	0.500	2.0
Italy	0.400	0.0

Source: *Europe Intelligence Wire*, October 15, 2003, p. NA, from International Institute of Strategic Studies.

★ 3603 ★
Navy
SIC: 9711; NAICS: 92811

Leading Contractors for the Navy, 2002

Market shares are shown based on total spending of $45 billion.

Northrop Grumman	11.94%
General Dynamics Corp.	9.70
Boeing Co.	7.58
Lockheed Martin Corp.	7.48
Raytheon Co.	5.97
United Technologies Corp.	2.75
Bechtel Group Inc.	1.82
Carlyle Group	1.24
BAE Systems	1.21
General Electric Co.	1.17
Other	49.14

Source: *Government Executive*, September 4, 2003, p. NA.

SOURCE INDEX

This index is divided into *primary sources* and *original sources*. Primary sources are the publications where the market shares were found. Original sources are sources cited in the primary sources. Numbers following the sources are entry numbers, arranged sequentially; the first number refers to the first appearance of the source in *Market Share Reporter*. All told, 2,105 organizations are listed. Roman numerals indicate volume number.

Primary Sources

"$1 Billion North American Electric Heating Element Industry." [online] available from http://www.vdc-corp.com [accessed December 17, 2003], I-1642

"$1.3B Expected for Online Auto Ads." [online] from http://www.clickz.com/news/print.php/3101211 [accessed April 29, 2004], II-2479

20/20 Magazine, II-2139

"2002 Participation." [online] available at http://www.nsga.org/public/pages/index.cfm?pageid=150 [accessed November 1, 2003], II-2236

"2002 Public Relations Revenue and Performance Fact Sheet." [online] from http://www.prfirms.org [accessed May 17, 2004], II-3589

"2002 Rankings Survey." [online] from http://www.prfirms.org [accessed May 17, 2004], II-3590

"2003 by Type of Recipient Organization." [online] available from http://www.aafrc.org/bytypeof.html [December 9, 2003], II-3554

"2003 Canadian Ski & Snowboard Industry Facts & Stats." [online] from http://www.canadianskicouncil.org [accessed May 24, 2004], II-3516

"2003 Market Graphs." [online] available from http://www.biomet.com/financials/market_graphs.cfm, II-2096, 2101-2102, 2109

"2003 Romance Novel Sales Statistics." [online] available from http://www.rwanational.org [accessed December 1, 2003], I-916

"2003 Worldwide Mobile Phone Shipments up 29.7% in Fourth Quarter." [online] available from http://www.idc.com [accessed February 3, 2004], I-1769, 1781

"2003 Year in Review." [online] from http://www.diamondcomics.com/market_share.html [accessed March 19, 2004], I-886

2.5G-3G, I-1756

"4Q03 Seasonal Demand Helps Fuel Another Quarter." [online] available from http://www.idc.com [accessed February 9, 2004], I-1589

ABSA Bank Quarterly South African Economic Monitor, II-3019

The Accountant, II-3568, 3573-3574

Acquisitions Monthly, II-3115

Across the Board, I-1757

AdAgeGlobal, I-895

Adams Wine Handbook, I-524-525, 529-531, 535, 538-539, 543, 554

Adhesives Age, I-830

Adhesives & Sealants Industry, I-829, 953, 1326, 1328, 1330-1331

AdMedia, II-2517, 3452

"Admission Control and Video Surveillance." [online] from http://www.usatrade.gov [accessed January 5, 2004], I-1823

"Advanced Assistive Technology Market." [online] from http://www.export.gov [accessed May 4, 2004], II-2077

Advanced Ceramics Report, I-1413

Advanced Manufacturing Technology, I-1440, 1457-1458, 1559-1560, 2057

Advertising Age, I-730, 857, 862, 866-867, 879, 893, 896, 898, 902, 1253, 1687, 1947, II-2534, 2554, 2763, 3269-3272, 3306

"Advertising Services." [online] from http://www.export.gov [February 11, 2004], II-3279

Adweek, I-322, II-2478, 3265, 3444

Aerospace Daily, I-2007

Africa News, I-1409

African and Middle East Mobile Communications Report, II-2442

African Business, II-2956

Aftenposten, I-485

Aftermarket Business, I-1648, 1979, II-2722-2723, 2725-2727

Ag Lender, II-3087-3088

AgExporter, I-100, 394, 450, 631

Agra Europe, I-57

Agri Marketing, I-1060, 1084

"Industry Information." [online] from http:// www.americangaming.org/industry/factsheets [May 10, 2004], II-3508, 3511

"Information Technology and Telecommunications." [online] from http://www.bisnis.doc.gov [accessed May 10, 2004], I-1569, II-3334

Informationweek, II-3341

InfoStor, I-1603

"Infotrends/CP Ventures Releases Canadian Document Outsourcing Forecast." [online] from http:// www.capv.com [Press release May 19, 2004], I-944

Ink World, I-1335-1336

Inland Valley Daily Bulletin, I-8

Insurance Journal, II-3167, 3188, 3206, 3221

"Insurance Services." [online] from http:// www.usatrade.gov [accessed January 5, 2004], II-3144

"Intel Remains Leading Flash Memory Supplier." [online] from http://www.icinsights.com [Press release accessed Janaury 1, 2004], I-1830

Interavia, I-1761, 1786, 1997, 2012

Interior Design, II-3377

International Accounting Bulletin, II-3569-3572

International Construction, I-153, 179, 1515

International Food Ingredients, I-475

International Herald Tribune, I-1612, 1727, II-2407, 3317

International Petroleum Finance, II-2733

International Railway Journal, I-2024, 2026-2027

Internet Business Daily, II-2473

Internet Securities, I-1463

Internet Wire, I-1801, 1816

Investment Dealers' Digest, II-3107

Investment News, II-3114, 3118, 3154, 3244

Investor's Business Daily, I-4, 788, 941, 1069-1070, 1120, 1264, 1381, 1404, 1563-1564, 1568, 1606, 1650, 1772, 1776, 1809, 1815, 1832, 1850, 1852, 1854, 1856, 1860, 1874, 1876, 1878, 2038, II-2068, 2078, 2086, 2112, 2122, 2136, 2160, 2211, 2213, 2262, 2408, 2410, 2439, 2462, 2465, 2481, 2485, 2514, 2563, 2565, 3122, 3132, 3295, 3320, 3323, 3337, 3342-3343, 3345, 3348, 3350, 3353, 3355, 3360, 3363, 3519, 3532, 3535-3536

IPR Strategic Business Information Database, I-1780

Irish Times, II-3537

"Is it the Name?" [online] available from http://www.the managementor.com/kuniverse/kmailers_universe/ mktg_kmailers [accessed February 26, 2003], I-1538

Israel Diamonds, II-2166-2167

Izvestia, I-497

Japan Inc., II-2130, 3257

"Japan Wine Manual Annual Report." [online] from http://www.fas.usda.gov [accessed January 1, 2004], I-542

Jerusalem Post, I-302

Jewelers Circular Keystone, II-2169

Journal of Commerce, II-2298-2299, 2310

just-auto.com, I-1941, 1952

just-drinks.com, I-620

just-drinks.com (Management Briefing), I-519, 552-553, 563-567, 571, 574, 583-590, 610-611, 628

just-food.com (Management Briefing), I-211, 311, 313-315, 432, 480, II-2927

just-style.com (Management Briefing), I-734

Kansas City Star, II-3507

Kipliner's Personal Finance Magazine, II-2630

Knight Ridder/Tribune Business News, I-670, 760, 1128, 1437, 1552-1553, 1834, II-2128, 2230, 2274, 2280, 2303, 2804, 2917, 3396, 3495

Knight Ridder/Tribune News Service, I-70, II-2550, 3583

Knoxville News-Sentinel, I-323

Kommersant, I-334, 459, 1572

Korea Times, I-1935

"Korea's Faucet and Sanitary Ware Market" [online] http://www.export.gov/comm_svc/index.html [accessed March 30, 2004], I-178

"Korea's Faucet and Sanitaryware Market" [online] http://www.export.gov/comm_svc/index.html [accessed March 30, 2004], I-1423

"Korea's Television Homeshopping Industry." [online] from http://www.usatrade.gov [accessed February 1, 2004], II-2926

Landscape Managment, I-41, 95

"Largest 25 U.S. Churches, 2002." [online] from http:// www.print.infoplease.com/ipa/A0001481.html [accessed June 14, 2004], II-3561

Las Vegas Review-Journal, II-3496

Laser Focus World, I-1835-1836, 1839

Latin America Telecom, II-2452-2453

Latin Trade, I-1578, II-3123

Latincom, II-2496

LatinFinance, II-3120-3121

LCGC North America, II-2059

"Lead Statistics." [online] from http://www.ilzsg.org/ statistics.asp?pg=lead [accessed June 10, 2004], I-106

"Leading 10 Diagnoses by Total U.S. Patient Visits." [online] from http://www.imshealth.com [accessed April 15, 2004], II-3518

"Leading 20 Corporations by Total U.S. Dispensed Prescriptions." [online] from http://www.imshealth.com [accessed April 15, 2004], I-1095

"Leading Therapy Classes by Global Pharmaceutical Sales." [online] from http://www.imshealth.com [accessed April 15, 2004], I-1083, 1108

"Leasing Industry." [online] from http:// www.usatrade.gov [accessed January 5, 2004], II-3311

Lebensmittel Zeitung, I-1035, II-2716

The Ledger, I-329, 825

"Lehman Brothers High Yield Bond." [online] from

MMR, I-308-309, 327, 447, 466, 470, 626, 673, 835, 849, 856, 859, 861, 873, 1028, 1031, 1037-1039, 1046, 1048-1050, 1052-1053, 1056, 1115-1117, 1124, 1141-1142, 1150-1151, 1156, 1163, 1167, 1172-1175, 1188, 1198, 1200, 1206-1207, 1216-1217, 1227, 1238, 1240-1242, 1247, 1262, 1272, 1282, 1284, 1287, 1325, 1340, 1367, 1374-1375, 1450, 1682-1684, 1692, 1896, II-2076, 2089-2090, 2092-2093, 2149, 2157, 2260-2261, 2265, 2645, 2647, 2651, 2656, 2658, 2660-2662, 2664-2665, 2669, 2672-2677, 2679-2680, 2684-2689, 2694, 2701, 2847-2849, 2852-2853, 2855, 2857, 2865-2866, 2868-2870, 2872, 2875-2877, 2881-2884, 2891

"Mobile Applications Prompt Strong Growth in LED Market." [online] http://compoundsemiconductor.net/ [accessed April 5, 2004], I-1872

Mobile Games Analyst, II-2404

Mobile Messaging Analyst, I-1785, II-2403

Modern Brewery Age, I-508

Modern Casting, I-1442, 1456

Modern Healthcare, I-1094, II-3177

Modern Machine Shop, I-1473, 1527

Modern Materials Handling, I-1522, II-2069

Modern Plastics, I-1371

Modern Power Systems, I-1494

Modern Tire Dealer, I-1354, 1358-1359, 1361, 1364-1365, 1942, II-3414

Modesto Bee, I-546

Mondaq Business Briefing, II-2126

Money Marketing, II-3104

Montreal Gazette, II-2308

The Morning Call, I-775, II-2666

Mortgage Banking, II-3102-3103

Mortgage Servicing News, II-3096

Motor Trend, I-1900, 1972

"Motors and Generators in USA." [online] from http:// www.euromonitor.com [accessed June 9, 2004], I-1652

MSI, II-3344

"Mushrooms." [online] from http://ffas.usda.gov [accessed June 10, 2004], I-75

Music & Copyright, I-1733-1734, 1740, 1744, 1752, II-2799-2801

Music Trades, II-2176-2177, 2802

Music Week, II-2516

"Musical Instruments." [online] available from http:// www.usatrade.gov [accessed Janaury 5, 2004], II-2803

"Musical Instruments." [online] available from http:// www.usatrade.gov [accessed January 5, 2004], II-2174

Nashville Business Journal, II-2896

National Fisherman, I-98

National Floor Trends, I-1418, II-2254-2255, 2257

National Geographic, I-126

National Geographic Explorer, I-31

National Jeweler, II-2165, 2915

National Mortgage News, II-3099

National Petroleum News, I-1344

National Provisioner, I-222, 226-227, 230, 233

National Real Estate Investor, II-3237, 3255

National Underwriter, II-3141, 3209, 3227

"Nation's Largest Libraries." [online] from http:// www.ala.org [accessed June 14, 2004], II-3544

Nation's Restaurant News, II-2822-2825, 2828

Natural Gas Week, I-132, II-2572

"NeGeCo Implements." [online] from http:// www.suse.de [accessed May 5, 2004], I-708

"Network Security Market Eclipses $3B in 2003." [online] from http://wwww.srgresearch.com [Press release February 27, 2003], I-1814

Network World, I-1791

"New Directors for Distributors." [online] from http:// en-us.ergoline.de [Press release October 2003], II-2275

"New Leader in the Growing SHD Market." [online] from http://www.idc.com [Press release dated March 11, 2004], I-1595

New Media Age, II-2420, 2468, 2487

New Orleans CityBusiness, I-183, II-2331

"New Passenger Car Registrations by Manufacturer." [online] http://www.acea.be [Press Release: January 1, 2004], I-1923

"New Passenger Car Registrations by Market." [online] from http://www.acea.be [Press release February 12, 2004], I-1922

New York Diamonds, II-2170, 2916

New York Post, II-2798

New York Times, I-118, 149, 294, 513, 601, 697, 712, 728, 877, 1137, 1349-1350, 1391, 1445, 1475, 1570, 1602, 1625-1626, 1701, 1703, 1721-1722, 1738, 1753, 1799, 1821, 1861, 2004, II-2307, 2317-2318, 2321, 2329, 2334, 2360, 2362, 2415, 2419, 2450, 2463, 2469, 2471, 2494-2495, 2500, 2536, 2553, 2567, 2582, 2808, 2894, 2952, 2955, 3061, 3110, 3169-3171, 3252, 3282, 3302, 3322, 3330, 3367, 3372, 3441, 3506, 3520

New Zealand Forest Industries Magazine, I-781, 791

New Zealand Marketing Magazine, II-2705

The News Journal, II-3577

News-Press, II-2237

The News-Sentinel, II-3470

Newsday, II-3267

Newsweek, I-904, II-2203, 3522

Nikkei Weekly, I-273, 996, 1534, 1586, 1676, 2018, II-2223, 2349, 2501, 3538

Nonwovens Industry, I-718, 720, 836, 838-840, 850, 1015

Nordic Business Report, I-1777

"North American Electronic Connector Market." [online] from http://www.bishopassociates.com

Original Sources

1194, 1279, 1291, 1461-1462, 2625, II-2649
ACNielsen ChannelScan, II-2705
ACNielsen EDI, II-3475
ACNielsen Health and Beauty Care Category Performance Study, II-2840
ACNielsen MarketTrack, I-455
ACNielsen ScanTrack, I-202, 677
ACNielsen Strategic Planner, I-1023, 1158, 1205, II-2273
ACNielsen Wal-Mart Channel Service, I-200, 659
ACNielsen's Homescan Panel, I-208
Adams Handbook Advance 2003, I-524-525, 529-531
Adams Media, I-535, 538-539, 543, 554, II-3423
Adams Research Database, I-498, 556
Adhesives in Developing Regions, I-1326
AdRelevance, II-3302
ADVA Optical Networking, I-1813
Advertising Age research, II-2829, 3272, 3306
Advest Inc., II-3132, 3535
Advisen Inc., II-3190
Adweek Directory 2002, II-3299-3301
AEA statistics and company reports, II-2356
Aerostrategy, I-2012
A.G. Edwards & Sons Research, II-2583
AGB, II-2543
Agence France Presse, I-922
Agencia Nacional de Telecommunicacoes, II-2451
Agriculture Ministry, Japan, I-231
Air Transport Association, II-2331
Air Transport World research and direct reports, II-2314, 2326, 2375
Airclaims CASE database, I-2008-2011
Airports Council International, II-2367, 2369-2374
AIS's Managed Medicare and Medicaid Factbook, II-3179
Albemarle, I-1348
Alexander Brown, I-1564, 1650
Allan Woodburn Associates, I-1321
Alliance for the Polyurethane Industry, I-992
Allied Business Intelligence, II-3396
Almanac of China's Insurance, II-3156
A.M. Best & Co., II-3147, 3156, 3161-3166, 3184-3186, 3192, 3199, 3202-3205, 3207, 3210-3211, 3213-3220
A.M. Best Statement Products, II-3181-3183, 3191, 3193-3198
AMA Research, I-5, 786
Amer Tobacco, I-692
American Association of Fundraising Counsel Trust for Philanthopy, II-3554
American Banker, II-2952
American Kennel Club, I-90
American Library Association, II-3544
American Pet Product Manufacturers Association National Pet Owners Survey, I-31

American Plastics Council, I-998
American Public Transportation Association, II-2283
American Road & Transportation Builders Association, I-181
American Society of Plastic Surgeons, II-3520, 3522
American Veterinary Medical Association, I-93
American Wind Energy Association, I-1495, II-2578
AMR Research, II-3322, 3344, 3350
Anatel, II-2564
Annual Production Statistics of Pharmaceuticals Etc., II-2127
APGDat, II-2319
Appliance research, I-1664, 1670-1673, 1675, 1690
APW/Komitel, I-1585
Arbitron, II-2528
The Art Newspaper, II-3557
Artprice.com, II-3556
Asian Market Information & Development Company, I-806
Association des Constructeurs Europeens d'Automobiles, I-1922-1923
Association for Manufacturing Technology's Laser Systems Product Group, I-1837
Association of American Publishers, I-911
Association of American Railroads, II-2278-2279
Association of British Bookmakers, II-3512
Association of Canadian Advertisers, II-3279
Association of European Airlines, II-2363-2364
Association of Home Appliance Manufacturers, II-2785
Association of International Automobile Manufacturers of Canda, I-1927
Athens News Agency, II-3130
Atlanta Convention & Visitors Bureau, II-3376
ATM & Debit News EFT Data Book, 2004, I-1636
ATM & Debit News research, I-1632
Auckland 2004 Commercial Radio Measurement Surveys, II-2517
Audit Bureau of Circulations, I-876-877, 879, 881, 893, 898, 900, 903, 905
Australian Film Commission, MPPA Australia, II-3471
Australian Magazine Industry Review 2003-04, I-891
Australian Mobile Telecommunications Association, I-1778
Auto Outlook Inc., I-1924
Auto Rental News, II-3412
Autodata Corp., I-1911, 1915, 1943
Automatic Merchandiser State of the Industry Report, II-2929
Automotive News Data Center, I-1916, 1927-1928, 1945, 1947, 1958-1959
Automotive News research, I-1936, 1984
Automotive Resources Asia, I-1903
AutoPacific Group, I-1953

Source Index: Original

PLACE NAMES INDEX

This index shows countries, political entities, states and provinces, regions within countries, parks, airports, and cities. The numbers that follow listings are entry numbers; they are arranged sequentially so that the first mention of a place is listed first. The index shows references to more than 490 places. Roman numerals indicate volume number.

PRODUCTS, SERVICES, NAMES, AND ISSUES INDEX

This index shows, in alphabetical order, references to products, services, personal names, and issues covered in *Market Share Reporter*, 15th Edition. More than 2,600 terms are included. Terms include subjects not readily categorized as products and services, including such subjects as *aerospace* and *asthma*. The numbers that follow each term refer to entry numbers and are arranged sequentially so that the first mention is listed first. Roman numerals indicate volume number.

Products, Services, Names, and Issues Index

Products, Services, Names, and Issues Index

Products, Services, Names, and Issues Index

Products, Services, Names, and Issues Index

Products, Services, Names, and Issues Index

COMPANY INDEX

The more than 6,100 companies and institutions in this book are indexed here in alphabetical order. Numbers following the terms are entry numbers. They are arranged sequentially; the first entry number refers to the first mention of the company in *Market Share Reporter*. Although most organizations appear only once, some entities are referred to under abbreviations in the sources and these have not always been expanded. Roman numerals indicate volume number.

Company Index

Company Index

Bowater, I-813, 816, 819
Bowen Builders Group, I-156
Bowne & Co., I-947
BOX, II-3134
Boykin Lodging Co., II-3255
Boys & Girls Clubs of America, II-3550
BP, I-119, 124-125, 965, 1309-1310, 1344, 1346, II-2629, 3086
BP America Holding, II-2570
BP & Aral, II-2730-2731
BP Chemicals, I-964, 966
BP Pipelines North America, II-2377
BP Solar, I-1475-1476
BP Solvay, I-999-1000
BPH BPK2, II-3073
B.R. Lee Industries, I-1513
Bracco, II-2080
Brach's Confections, I-456
Bradco Supply Corp., II-2589
Bradesco, II-2962
Bradesco Seguros, II-3145
Bradesco Vida e Previdencia, II-3145
Bradshaw International, I-8
BradyGames, I-934
Branch Banking & Trust Co., II-2979, 2990, 2993, 3007, 3039, 3041
Branch Banking & Trust Co. of South Carolina, II-3020
Branch Banking & Trust Co. of Virginia, II-3037
Brandenburg Industrial Service Co., I-195
Brank's Home Security Inc., II-3369
Brant-Allen Industries, I-816
Brave, I-1588
Brayson Homes, I-156
Breed, I-777, 1985
Bremer Bank, II-2997, 3008, 3029
Brentwood Originals, I-768
The Brickman Group Ltd., I-95
Bricomarche, II-2612
Bridgestone, I-1003, 1352, 1355, 1357, 1360, 1362-1363, 3413
Bridgestone Sports, II-2222-2223
Bridgford Foods, I-418
Bright Dairy, I-246
Bright Dairy & Food Co., I-274
Bright Horizons Family Solutions, II-3546-3547
Brionne, I-1428
Bristol Myers Squibb, I-1032, 1094-1095, 1097, 1106-1107, 1110
Britannica Home Fashions, I-771
British Airways, II-2318, 2326, 2356, 2363-2364
British American Tobacco, I-704
British Bookshop, II-2910
British Petroleum, II-2733

British Polyethylene Industries, I-949
Broadcom, I-1770, 1846, 1850
Broadway, II-3473
Bronco Wine Co., I-532
Brook Mays / H&H, II-2802
Brookhaven Science Associates, II-3594
Brooks, II-2879, 2898
Brooks Brothers, II-2745
Brooks Pharmacy, II-2842
Brother, I-1621, 1626
Brown and Caldwell, II-3592
Brown & Jackson, II-2755
Brown & Williamson, I-697
Brown-Forman Beverages, I-539, 543, 577
Brown Jordan International, I-796
Brown Printing, I-945, 951
Bruegger's Bagel Bakery, II-2822
Brunnen, I-869
Bruno's, II-2640, 2648
Brunswick, I-2021
Bryco Arms, I-1488-1489, 1491
BSH, I-1675
BSkyB, II-2559
BT, II-2445-2446, 2499
Bubba Gump Shrimp, II-2836
Buckeye Technologies, I-718
Buckle, II-2759
Buckley Broadcasting, II-2520
Budget, II-3397, 3399-3406, 3408-3412
Buell, I-2037
Buena Vista, II-3428, 3430, 3434, 3458
Buena Vista Home Entertainment, II-3426, 3436
Buena Vista International, II-3455, 3463, 3465
Buffalo, I-1816-1817
Build-A-Mould Ltd., I-1524
Builders FirstSource, II-2589
Bulgarski Imoti, II-3155
Bulstrad DZK Life, II-3155
Bupa, II-3150
Burberry, I-12
Burger King, II-3278, 3293
Burlington Coat Factory, II-2754
Burlington Northern Santa Fe, II-2276
Burlington Resources Oil & Gas Co., I-119
Burrells/VMS, II-2550
Burt Toyota (CO), II-2721
Burton, II-2239
Busch's, II-2657
Bush Brothers, I-323
Bushmaster Firearms, I-1490
Butler Amusements, II-3505
Butler J Construction, I-167
Buy Music, II-2798

Buy.com, II-2793
BVI, II-3464
C&S Wholesale Grocers, II-2638
C&W, II-2445
C Brewer & Sons Ltd., II-2608
C-Town, II-2668
CA Comp Fund, II-3199
Cabcorp, I-618
Cabela's, II-2904-2905
Cablevision, II-2444, 2495, 2554
Cabot, I-1339
Cadbury Schweppes, I-450-451, 457, 459, 469, 480, 486-487, 609, 620-621
Cadbury Wedel, I-482
Cadence, II-3329
Cadmus Communications, I-951
CAE, I-2014
CAEC, II-3474
Caesars Entertainment, II-3514
Cafaro Co., II-3233
Cagle's Inc., I-82
Cainz, II-2613
Caisse Regionales, II-3098
Caisses d'Espargne, II-3067
Calabrian, I-984
California Earthquake, II-3182
California Institute of Technology, I-2044, II-3595
California Office of State Publishing, I-948
California Prune Packing, I-71
California State Auto Group, II-3184
Callaway Golf, II-2222, 2227
Callison Architecture, II-3377, 3566
Calloway's Nursery, II-2620
Cambria Mobel, I-801
Cambridge Homes, I-157
Camden National Bank, II-2992
Camino Real Foods, I-379
Campbell & Co., II-3590
Campbell Concrete of Nevada, I-191
Campbell Soup Co., I-264, 331, 338-339, 352
Campina Deutschland, I-289
Canadel Furniture, I-797
Canadian Firelog Co. Ltd., II-2264
Canadian National Railway, II-2276
Canadian Pacific Railway, II-2276
Canadian Tire, II-2616, 2907
Canal+, II-2540
Canal Plus Technologies, I-1762
Canal Satellite Digital, II-2559
Canandaigua Wine, I-532, 535, 539, 543
Candlewick, I-914
Candlewood Suites, II-3252
Candy, I-1672, 1690

Canfor, I-783, 815
Canon Inc., I-1545-1546, 1612, 1617, 1619, 1621-1624, 1626, 1628-1629, 1703-1705, 2143, II-2147, 2151, 2153, 3246
CanWest Global, I-14
Canyon Resources, I-108
Cap Gemini Ernst & Young, II-3363, 3365, 3584-3586
Capcom, II-2208
Capital, II-2516
Capital Ford, II-2721
Capital Group, II-3129
Capital One, II-3037, 3061, 3063, 3078, 3080, 3308
Capital Research & Management Co., II-3128
Capitol Federal Savings Bank, II-2989
Carbolite, I-460
Cardinal, II-2116
Career Education Corp., II-3542
CareerBuilder, II-2476
CareGroup Inc., II-3528
Caremark Rx, II-2894, 2896
CareSource, II-3179
Caretti Inc., I-188
Cargill Inc., I-201, 1168, II-2570
Cargill Turkey Products, I-87
Cargolux, II-2363-2364, 2368
Caribou Coffee, II-2808, 2821
Carilion Franklin Memorial Hospital, II-3523
Carilion Roanoke Memorial, II-3523
Carl Buddig & Co., I-228
Carlsberg, I-517, 519, 521
Carlson Hospitality, II-3253-3254
Carlson Wagonlit Travel, II-2384
Carlton Screen Advertising, II-3287
Carlyle Group, I-2045, II-3597, 3603
Carma Lbs Inc., I-1234
CarMax.com, II-2479
Carnival, II-2304
Carolina Beverage, I-621
Carolina First Bank, II-3020
Carolina Turkeys, I-87
Carpenter Co., I-769
Carpetright, II-2767
Carrabba's Italian Grill, II-2835
Carrefour, II-2622, 2633, 2637, 2642, 2649, 2659
Carriage House Imports, I-538
Carr's, I-438
Carson Products, I-1219
Carter & Burgess, II-3566
Carter Holt Harvey, I-855
The Cartoon Network, II-2555
Carvico, I-709
Cascades, I-818, 828
Case, I-1513

Company Index

Company Index

Company Index

Gorenje, I-1664

Gorenjska Banka d.d. Kranj, II-3018

Gorton's Corp., I-640

Gothic Landscape Inc., I-95

Goto Optical, II-2162

Grace, I-1348

Graco Children's Pdts. Inc., II-2259

Granador, I-324

Granite Bank, II-3003

Granite Construction Inc., I-180

Grasso, I-1551

GRAVE Bulgaria, II-3155

Graybar Electric, II-2590

Great Foods of America, I-251

Great Southern Bank, II-2981

Great Western Bank, II-3001, 3021

Greater Media, II-2519, 2522

Greater Union, II-3471

Green Bay Packaging, I-821, 824

Greene King, II-2839

Greenlink, I-1632

Greenpoint Bank, II-3006

Green's, I-399, 403

Greenvale Construction, I-167

Greer Farms, I-60

Grey Global Group, II-3271, 3273, 3275

Greystar Real Estate Partners, II-3234

Greystone Homes, I-164

Grimmway Farms, I-61

Group Automotive Inc., II-2720

Group Sense PDA Ltd., I-1597

Groupe Brandt, I-1671-1673, 1690

Groupe Danone, I-598

Grover, I-1512

Grubb & Ellis, II-3231

Gruner & Jahr USA (Bertelsmann), I-893

Grupo Durango, I-815

Grupo Magico Internacional, II-3499

Grupo Mexico, I-111

Grupo Nactional Provincial, II-3145

GS Battery, I-1881

GSC Enterprises, II-2595

GSK Pharmaceuticals, I-1100, 1103, 1254

Guangdong Wangda, I-822

Guangdong Yinzhou, I-822

Guaranty Bank, II-3026

Guardian Japan, I-1399

Gucci, I-12

Guckenheimer Enterprises, II-2814

Gudang Garam, I-701

Guerrero, I-687

Guest Inn, II-3238

Guest Services, II-2814

Guidant, II-2087

Guitar Center Inc., II-2802

Guizhou Satellite, II-2562

Gulf States Paper, I-823

Gulfstream, I-2001

Gulfstream Aerospace, I-1997

Gulfstream Coach Inc., I-1994

Gunze, I-758

Guranty Bank, II-2981

Gusdorf Canada, I-797

Gwaltney of Smithfield, I-221

GWR, II-2516

H&R, I-1488, 1490

H&R Block, II-3267-3268

H3G, II-2421

Haagen-Dazs, I-276

Haas, I-1526

Habitat for Humanity International, II-3550

Hagemeyer NA Holdings Inc., II-2593

Hagoromo Foods Corp., I-672

Haier, I-1643, 1663, 1668

Haier America, I-1667

Hain Celestial Group, I-665

Hakkeijima Sea Paradise, II-3501

Hakuhodo DY Holdings, II-3271, 3274

Hale Products, I-1549, 1558

Halifax, II-3046

Halliburton, I-1516, II-3601

Hallmark, I-956

Hallmark Technologies Inc., I-1524

Halsall, II-2190

Hampton Bay, I-1643

Hampton Inns, II-3256

Hana, II-3022

Hanaro, II-2497

Hancock Bank, II-2998

Hancock Bank of Louisiana, II-2991

Handmark, II-3320

Handspring, I-1599

Hanes, I-741

Hanjin Shipping, II-2298-2299, 2313

Hankook, I-1357, 1363-1364

Hankyu Express International, II-2386

Hannaford, II-2685

Hannover Re, II-3187, 3228-3229

Hansapanga Kindlustus, II-3157

Hansen Natural, I-621

Hanson, I-1411

Hanson Aggregates Midwest, I-139

Hapag-Lloyd, II-2298-2299

Happy Harry's, II-2892

Haraah's Entertainment, II-3514

Harbin Brewery Group, I-518

Company Index

Company Index

Company Index

National Powersport Auctions, II-3386
National Reining Horse Association, II-3558
National Rifle Assn., II-3560
National Riggers & Erectors Inc., I-192
National Science Foundation, II-3582
National Steeplechase Association, II-3558
National Tobacco Company, I-704
National Vision, II-2936
National Westminster (Royal Bank of Scotland), II-3379
NationsBank, II-3379, 3381
Nationwide, II-3046
Nationwide Corp., II-3166-3167, 3187
Nationwide Life Insurance Co., II-3154
Natural Gas Pipeline Co. of America, II-2581
Natural Lite, I-515
Nature Conservancy, II-3548, 3550
Natuzzi, I-796
NatWest, II-3046
Nautica, I-746
Navajo Agricultural Products Industry, I-60
Navigant International, II-2384
Navistar, I-1971
Navy Federal Credit Union, II-3047
NBBJ, II-3377
NBC, II-2536
NBC-TV (General Electric), II-2534
NBG, II-2980
N.C. Farm Bureau, II-3166
NC Numericable, II-2552
NCR, I-1632-1633, 1640
NCRIC Group, II-3220
ND, II-2387
NDS, I-1762, 1765
NEC, I-1441, 1454, 1582, 1586, 1589, 1591, 1624, 1773,
    1811, 1851, 1858-1859, 1862, 1864, II-2160, 2504,
    3353-3354
NEC Tokin, I-1890
Nedcor, II-3019
Nedcor Group, II-2956
Nedcor Investment Bank, II-3019
NEG Micron, I-1495
Neiman Marcus, II-2626, 2816
NEL, I-927
Neopost, I-1638
Neoware, I-1566, 1568
Neste-Petersburg, II-2732
Nestle, I-260-261, 272, 274-275, 301, 311-312, 321, 386,
    405, 450-451, 457-459, 465, 480, 482, 598, 652, II-3269
Nestle Prepared Foods, I-370, 372, 379
Nestle Purina Products, I-402
Nestle SA, I-201, 285, 500
Nestle Treasures, I-476
Nestle USA, I-205, 368, 371, 375, 456, 478

Nestle Waters North America, I-597, 609
Net, II-2564
Neta, I-1569
Netbank, II-2979
Netflix, II-2793, 3479-3480
Netgear, I-1629, 1816-1817
Netherlands Insurance Company (W.I.) Ltd., II-3154
NetJets, I-1998
NetLogic/SiberCore, I-1793
Netscreen, I-1815
Netto, II-2631
Network Applications, I-1603
Network Associates, II-3315-3316, 3318
Neumann Homes, I-157
Neutrogena Corp., I-1186, 1289
Nevada State Bank, II-3040
New Balance, I-1386, 1394-1395
New Belgium Brewing, I-524
New China Life, II-3156
New England Patriots, II-3487
New Haven Savings Bank, II-2971
New Horizon Child Care, II-3546-3547
New Horizons Worldwide, II-3391
New India, II-3146
New Jersey Resources, II-2570
New Line Cinema, II-3465
New Look, II-2755
New Plan Excel Realty Trust, II-3232-3233
New Skies Satellites, I-1788
New South FSB, II-2957
New World Mobility, II-2429
New York City (LIRR), I-2025
New York City (NYC Transit), I-2025
New York Community Bancorp, II-3378
New York Knicks, II-3486
New York Life Insurance Co., II-3154
New York Stock Exchange, II-3135, 3137
The New York Times Co., I-879
New York Water Taxi, II-2307
New York Yankees, II-3485
Newman's Own Inc., I-347
Newmark Homes, I-167
Newmont Mining, I-108, 110
Newport, I-768, II-3473
News Corp., I-15, II-2534, 2554
Newstalk ZB, II-2517
Next, II-2756, 2758
Nextel, II-2418-2419, 2431
NextGenTel, II-2505
NexTran, I-1632
Nextwave wireless licenses (Cingular Wireless), II-3385
NFO WorldGroup Inc., II-3579-3580
Nice Group, I-1129

Company Index

OSG, I-1531
Oshkosk Truck, I-1508
Osim (M) Sdn Bhd, I-812
Osotspa, I-602
Osram Sylvania, I-1693
Otis Spunkmeyer, I-408
Otsuka Pharmaceutical Co., I-619
Ottakar's, II-2910
Otto, II-2468
Outback Steakhouse, II-2823, 2834
Overnite Transportation, II-2287
Overture Services, II-2473
Owens-Illinois, I-978
Oxford, II-3171
OxyChem, I-1315
OxyMar, I-1315
OxyVinyls, I-993, 1315
Oxyvinyls LP, I-994
P&C, II-2650
P&O Logistics, II-2294
P&O Nedlloyd, II-2298-2299
P&O Ports, II-2311, 2313
Pabst Brewing, I-528
Paccar, I-1968, 1971
Pace, I-1723
Pace Micro Technology, I-1767, 1771
Pacific, I 890
Pacific Coast Feather, I-773
Pacific Coast Steel Inc., I-192
Pacific Group, II-3238
Pacific Northwest Bank, II-3038
Pacific Pools, I-196
Pacific Publications, I-891
Pacific Seafood Group, I-634
Pacific Sunwear, II-2759, 2903
Pacific Tomato Growers, I-59
PacifiCare, II-3169
Packaging Corp. of America, I-824
Packet 8, II-2495
Pactiv Corp., I-1369
Paddock Pool Construction Co., I-196, II-2951
Pakistan Tobacco Company, I-703
Palacio de Hierro, II-2753
Paladin, I-123
Palance Entertainment, II-3499
Palladium, II-2187
Palliser Furniture, I-797
Palm, I-1592, 1598-1599, 1756
Palm Bay Imports, I-540
Palm Beach Broadcasting, II-2529
Palm Harbor Homes, I-794
Palm/MDM, II-3320
Palmolive, I-1680

palmOne, I-1596, 1600
Pamplin Communications, II-2527
Pan, I-927
PAN Africa, II-3144
Pan American Silver, I-111
Panaflex, II-2146
Panafon Vodafone, II-2428
Panalpina, II-2399-2400
PanAmSat Corp., I-1788
Panasonic, I-1703, 1773, 1778, 1896
Panasonic Battery Co., I-1888-1889
Panda, II-3316
Panda Software, II-3315
Pannon, II-2430
The Pantry Inc., II-2629
Papa John's, II-2829
Papa Murphy's Take 'N Bake Pizza, II-2828
Papiers Stadacona, I-816, 819
Par Pharmaceutical, I-1064, 1109
Paramount, I-810, II-3179, 3428, 3430, 3434, 3456, 3458
Paramount Farms Inc., I-58, 73
Paramount Home Entertainment, II-3426, 3436
Paramount Parks, II-3499
Pardee Homes, I-164
Park View Federal Savings Bank, II-2969
Parker-Hannifin Corp., I-1003
Parkhouse Tire Inc., II-2728
Parmalat, I-259, 436
Parmalat Finanziaria SpA, I-284
Parque da Monica, II-3500
Parque de la Costa, II-3500
Parsons, II-3562, 3601
Parthus Ceva, I-1863
Partner Re, II-3229
Partners Healthcare Systems, II-3528
Pasco Beverage Group, I-328
Pasminco Ltd., I-111
Pasquinelli Construction Co., I-157
Pasquinelli Produce Co., I-60
Passumpsic Savings Bank, II-3036
Patelco Credit Union, II-3047
Paterson Zochonis, I-1145
Pathe Distribution, II-3464, 3466
Pathmark, II-2668, 2674, 2676-2677
Patientline, II-2556
Patio Pools & Spas, I-196, II-2951
Patriot Homes, I-794
Patterson, I-70
Pavlik Design Team, II-3377, 3566
Payless ShoeSource, II-2762-2763
PayPal, II-3380
P.C. Richard & Son, II-2784
PCX, II-3134

Company Index

Province Healthcare, II-3530-3531
Proxim, I-1817
Prudential Financial Inc., II-3118, 3301
Prudential Insurance Co. of America, II-3154, 3159
Prudential Mortgage Capital, II-3092
Prudential of America, II-3165
Prudhoe Bay, I-128
PSA, I-1944
PSA Group, I-1923, II-2311, 2313
PSA Peugeot Citroen, I-1930, 1936
PSC - Industrial Services, II-2587
PSI, I-1640
Psychiatric Solutions, II-3532
PT Djarum, I-701
PT HM Sampoerna, I-701
PTK, II-2732
The Public Library of Cincinnati & Hamilton County,
    II-3544
Publicis, II-3271, 3273, 3275, 3306
Publishers Printing/Publishers Press, I-951
Publix, II-2638-2639, 2644, 2648, 2653, 2658, 2670, 2673,
    2692, 2697, 2897
Pubmaster, II-2839
Pulliam Pools, II-2951
Pulse, I-1636
Pulte Homes, I-156-157, 159-161, 163-164, 166-169, 173
Punch Taverns, II-2838-2839
Purcell Tire & Rubber Co., II-2728, 3413
Puritan, I-741
Putnam, II-3105
Putnam County Bank, II-3041
PVS Chemicals, I-984
PZ Cussons, I-1278
Q-Cells, I-1475
Q-Telecom, II-2428
Qantas, II-2338
QDI, I-1871
QS Group, II-2755
QSS Group, II-3595
Quad/Graphics, I-945, 951-952
Quadrant AG, I-987
Quaker Oats, I-473
QualChoice, II-3179
Qualcomm, I-1846, 1851, 1861
Qualitest, I-1109
Quality Construction Products Plc, I-1415
Quality Food Centers, II-2694
Quam, II-2427
Quanta, I-1564
Quebecor Media, I-14
Quebecor World, I-936, 945-946, 951-952
Queens Borough Public Library, II-3544
Quest, II-3533

Quicklogic, I-1848
Quiznos, II-2833
QVC, II-2467, 2915, 3383
Qwest, I-1812, II-2447, 2454-2461
R-G Premier Bank, II-3015
Racecourse Holdings Trust, II-3490
RAD, I-1798
Radio One, II-2515, 2519, 2522, 2528, 2531
Radio Shack, II-2790
Radio Wawa, II-2523
Radio ZET, II-2523
Radiolinja, II-2424-2425
Rafidain, II-2988
RAG American Coal Holding, I-115
Ragu Foods, I-352
Raiffeisen Bank Croatia, II-2972
Raiffeisen Leasing, II-3091
Railworks Corp., I-195
Rainbow, II-2672
Raindance, II-3349
Raley's, II-2641, 2688
Ralph's, II-2688, 2691
Ralston Purina, I-399, 403, 405
RAM Systems GmbH, I-2045
Rambus, I-1863
Ranbaxy, I-1100
Randall's, II-2645, 2662
Randflex, I-1006
Random House, I-914, 921-924, 926
Randstad, II-3313
Ranger American, II-3369
Rational/IBM, II-3342
Rave Motion Pictures, II-3470
Ray Cammack Shows, II-3505
Raymond James, II-3114, 3118
Rayong Olefins, I-1316
Rayovac, I-1886, 1888-1889
Raytheon Aircraft, I-1997
Raytheon Co., I-2001-2002, 2042-2043, 2045,
    II-2050-2051, 2053-2054, 2390, 3362, 3595-3597, 3603
RBC Centura Bank, II-3007
RBS Group, II-3078
RCA, I-1700, 1896
R.D. Offutt Co., I-58
Re/Max, II-3301
Readers Digest (Australia), I-891
Reader's Digest Association, I-893
Ready Pac Foods, I-204, 681
Real Networks, II-2798
Reciprocal Group, II-3215
Reckitt Benckiser, I-1043, 1131, 1133, 1145, 1159, 1162,
    1277, II-3291
Recruit, I-875

Red Bull, I-609, 621
Red Chamber Co., I-634
Red Cross, I-1126
Red Dress, I-916
Red Lobster, II-2823, 2834, 2836
Red McCombs Automotive (TX), II-2721
Red Oval Farms (Kraft), I-438
Redback, I-1808, 1820
Redcats, II-3308
Reebok, I-728, 1386, 1394-1395
Reed Elsevier, I-893, 920
Reed Exhibitions, II-3388-3389
Reese's, I-460, 476
Reetsma, I-694
Regal Cinemas, II-3470
Regent, II-2116
Regions Bank, II-2957, 2960, 2979, 2991, 3020, 3025, 3087
REI, II-2904
Reinhart FoodService, II-2600
Reithoffer Shows, II-3505
Reko Intenational Group Inc., I-1524
Reliance Industries, I-1000, 1013, 1316
Reliant Energy, II-2574, 3506
Remicade, I-1070
Remington, I-1677, 1679
Remington Arms, I-1488, 1490
Renaissance Learning, II-3331-3332
Renal Care, II-3536
Renault, I-1905, 1920, 1928, 1944, 1950, 1973
Renault Nissan, I-1936
Renault Samsung, I-1935
Renesas Technology Corporation, I-1859, 1864
Renzo Piano Building Workshop, II-3565
ReplayTV, I-1721
Repsol, II-2730
Reptron Electronics Inc., II-2591
Republic, II-2963
Republic Bank & Trust Co., II-2990
Republic Services Inc., II-2587
Research in Motion, I-1596
Reser's Fine Foods, I-206
Residence Inn, II-3256
ResMed, II-2086
Respironics, II-2086
Restaurant Associates, II-2827
Restaurant Development Group, II-2827
Restaurants Unlimited, II-2827
Restonic, I-803
Retail, II-2596, 2738
Review Directories, I-940
Revlon Inc., I-1186, 1226, 1258
Rewe-Touristik, II-2395-2396

Rexel, II-2590
The Reyes Family, I-523
RF, II-2130
RF Micro Devices, I-1851
Rheinische BioEster, I-1342
Rhodes, II-2766
Rhodes International, I-418
Rhodia, I-984
Rich Products Corp., I-408
Rich-SeaPak Corp., I-206, 640
Richmond American Homes, I-156, 159, 164-165
Ricoh Corp., I-1760, II-2151, 2153
Ricoh Elemex, II-2163
Riddell, II-2234
Riggs Bank, II-3037, 3039
Rijecka Banka, II-2972
RIM, I-1599, 1769
Rio, I-1700
Rio Audio, I-1699
Rio Farms, I-61
Rio Tinto, I-111, 1445
Ritabell, II-2424
RiTdisplay, I-1876
Rite Aid, II-2841-2843, 2845-2846, 2849, 2851, 2853, 2856, 2858, 2861, 2864, 2866-2867, 2870, 2872, 2875, 2877-2878, 2880, 2882-2886, 2888, 2890-2893, 2900-2902
Riva, I-1434
Rival, I-1686
Rivella, I-324
Riverbend Sandler Pools, I-196
Riverdeep, II-3332
Riverside, II-2963
Rizal Commerical Bank, II-3027
R.J. Reynolds, I-697
RMC, I-1411
RMF FM, II-2523
RNS, II-3370
Roadway Express, II-2287-2288
Robert Bosch, I-1989-1990
Robert Dyas, II-2608
Robert Mondavi Winery, I-532, 543
Robert Wood Johnson Foundation, II-3549
Robinson, I-2007
Robinson Textiles, I-749
Robison-Prezioso Inc., I-186
Roche, I-1021, 1099, 1103, 1106, 1120
Roche-Syntex, I-1102
Rochester General, II-3525
Rockford Homes, I-158
Rockport, I-1379
Rockwood Realty, II-3236
Rocky, I-1380-1381

Rocky Mountain Bank, II-3000
Rodiguez Group, I-2019
Rogers Corp., I-14, 1764
Rohm and Haas, I-963, 1311, 1862
Roland Berger Strategy Consultants, II-3585, 3588
Rolls-Royce, I-1496, 2008, 2010-2011
Roman Catholic Church, II-3561
Romano's Macaroni Grill, II-2823, 2835
Rona, II-2616
Rooms To Go, II-2764, 2766, 2777
Roper, I-1659, 1662, 1669
Roquette, I-1168
Rose City Radio, II-2524
Rosemont Exposition Services, II-3387
Rosenbluth International, II-2384
Rosendin Electric Inc., I-187
Roslyn Bancorp, II-3378
Ross Stores, II-2734, 2754, 2757
Rossignol, II-2239
Rot-Front, I-459
Rothschild, II-3115, 3382
Rotring, I-869
Rottlund Homes, I-166, 168
Rough Guides, I-917
Roundy's, II-2671, 2696
The Rouse Co., II-3232-3233
Rousseau Farming Co., I-60
Route 66, I-741
Rover Computers, I-1572
Rowan, I-132
Rowe International, I-1698
Royal, I-1687
Royal Ahold, II-2622
Royal & SunAlliance, II-3150, 3181, 3190, 3196, 3202, 3205
Royal Bank of Scotland, II-2975, 3046, 3113, 3117, 3378-3379
Royal Canin, I-405
Royal Caribbean, II-2304
Royal Denship, I-2019
Royal Dutch Printing Ink Van Son, I-1336
Royal Dutch/Shell, I-125, 965, II-2733
Royal Mail, II-2296
Royal Numico, I-313-314, 321
Royal Philips Electronics, II-2134, 3506
Royal Toto Metal, I-1423
RPM Inc., I-1302-1303
RR Donnelley, I-936, 945-947, 951-952
RREEF, II-3241
Ruby Tuesday, II-2823, 2834
Rubycon Corporation, I-1867
The Ruder Finn Group, II-3590
Ruhrgas, II-2579

Ruiz Foods, I-379
RusAl, I-1444
Russell Stover, I-460, 478
Rustler, I-741
RWE, I-1475
RWE Power, II-2569
Ryan Inc. Central, I-194
Ryanair, II-2356
Ryan's Family Steak House, II-2825
Ryder Integrated Logistics, II-2287
The Ryland Group, I-173
Ryland Homes, I-156-157, 159, 162, 166, 168
S. Abraham & Sons, II-2595
S&F Concrete Construction, I-191
S-Group, II-2709
S. Lichtenberg, I-761
SAB Miller, I-510, 521
Saba, II-3324
Sabadell, II-3023
Sabic, I-999-1000
SABMiller, I-500, 517
Sabre, II-2387-2389
Saco & Biddeford, II-2992
Sacramento Kings, II-3486
Safeco, II-3161
Safety-Kleen Systems, II-2587
Safety National, II-3207
Safeway, II-2621, 2637-2639, 2645-2647, 2651, 2656, 2662, 2667, 2683, 2686, 2688, 2693-2694, 2700-2701, 2715, 2878, 2884, 2891, 2902, 2938-2939
Saft America Inc., I-1885
Saga Communications, II-2521
Sagawa Express, II-2293
Sahara, II-2348
SAIC, I-2044, II-3595, 3597
SAIC-Chery, I-1930
Sainsbury, II-2667, 2693, 2698, 2700, 2715, 2939
St. Anne Chemical, I-983
St. George, II-3064
St. George Bank, II-2961
Saint Gobain, I-978
St. Ives, I-949
St. Ives Burrups, I-947
St. Jude Medical, II-2087
St. Marys, I-819
St. Paul Cos., II-3181, 3190, 3196, 3199, 3202, 3207, 3217, 3219-3220
SAIPA Khodro, I-1932
Sakata Inx, I-1336
Saks, II-2626
Sakura Bank (Sumitomo Bank), II-3379
Salem Communications, II-2524
Salomon, II-2239

Company Index

THQ, II-2208-2210
THR, II-3529
Three J's Construction, I-163
Thriftway, II-2652
Thrifty, II-3398-3399, 3402, 3405, 3409, 3411
Thrunet, II-2497
Thule Holding, I-1472
Thyssen, I-1519
Thyssengas, II-2579
ThyssenKrupp Steel, I-1434
TI, I-1441, 1720, 1851
TIAA-CREF, II-3105, 3124
Tibbett & Britten Group, II-2285
Ticketmaster (USA Interactive), II-3380
Ticonderoga, II-2250
Ticor Title, II-3224
Tidel, I-1632
Tierone Bank, II-3001
TietoEnator, II-3585
Tiffany & Co., II-2915
Tiger, I-2039
Tillamook Country Creamery, I-249, 255
Tim Hortons, II-2821
Timberland, I-1380
Time Group, I-1589
Time Inc. South Pacific, I-891
Time Warner, I-926, II-2444, 2557, 2561, 3269
Time Warner Cable, II-2495
Times, II-2863
Tingyi (Cayman Islands) Holding Corp., I-670
Tip Top, II-2738
Tire Centers L.L.C. (Michelin), II-3413
Tire Distribution Systems Inc. (Bandag), II-3413
Tire Kingdom, II-2729
Tirecraft Auto Centers, II-2728
Tiscali, II-2406, 2499
Titan Peach Farms, I-71
TiVo, I-1721-1722
T.J. Maxx/Marshall's, II-2754
TJX Cos., II-2736, 2757, 2771, 2778
TK Maxx, II-2755
TMN, II-2433
TNS, II-3580
TNT, II-2289, 2292, 2360, 2555
TNT Logistics, II-2285
Toa Re, II-3230
Tobacco Central Inc., II-2933
Tobacco Outlet Plus, II-2933
Tobacco Superstore, II-2933
Toho, II-3455, 3465, 3468
TOK, I-1847
Tokai, I-1339
Tokai Pulp & Paper, I-865

Tokai-Rika, I-1983
Tokai Rubber Industries Ltd., I-1003
Tokio, II-3230
Tokuyama, I-1410
Tokyo Disneyland, II-3501-3502
Tokyo Disneysea, II-3501-3502
Tokyo Electron, I-1543, 1546
Tokyo Marine Co., II-2297
Tokyo Printing Ink, I-1336
Tokyo Steel Manufacturing, I-1431, 1438
Tokyopop, I-886-887
Tokyu Agency, II-3274
Tokyu Hands, II-2613
Tokyu Hotels, II-3259
Tokyu Recreation, II-3468
Tolko Industries, I-815
Toll Brothers, I-160, 173
Tom Thumb, II-2655
Tombstone Pizza Corp., I-375
Tomkins, I-1003
Tommy Hilfiger, I-739, 746, II-3286
Tomy, II-2190
Tony's Pizza, I-371
Tootsie Roll, I-465
Topa Equities Ltd., I-523
Toppan, I-1855
Toppes Tiles, II-2608
Topps, I-487, 942
Tops, II-2702
Toray Industries, I-995, 1013, 1015, 1017
Torch Offshore, I-183
Toronto (GO Transit) transit service, I-2025
Toronto Raptors, II-3486
Torrey Dobson Homes, I-156
Torrey Farms Inc., I-58
Torstar, I-14
Tosco Phillips, I-1309
Toshiba, I-1519, 1529, 1571-1572, 1574, 1579, 1586-1587,
    1590, 1596, 1599-1600, 1606, 1666, 1674, 1691,
    1709-1710, 1715, 1718, 1754, 1829-1830, 1843, 1851,
    1858, 1862, 1864, 1890, II-2134
Toshiba Carrier, I-1644
Toshiba-EMI, I-1743
Toshiba Machine, I-1540
Toshiba Matsushita Display Technology, I-1875
Toshiba Tungaloy, I-1531
Tostem, I-1480
Total, I-965
Total/FinaElf, I-1306, 1346, II-2730-2731
Tote, II-3512
Toto, I-1424, 1691
Towa Real Estate, I-176
Towers Perrin, II-3584

Company Index

Company Index

BRANDS INDEX

This index shows more than 3,040 brands—including names of periodicals, television programs, popular movies, and other "brand-equivalent" names. Each brand name is followed by one or more numerals; these are entry numbers; they are arranged sequentially, with the first mention of the brand shown first. Roman numerals indicate volume number.

Brands Index

Brands Index

Brands Index

Brands Index

Brands Index

Brands Index

APPENDIX I - INDUSTRIAL CLASSIFICATIONS
SIC COVERAGE

This appendix lists the Standard Industrial Classification codes (SICs) included in *Market Share Reporter*. A volume and page number are shown following each SIC category; the page shown indicates the first occurrence of an SIC. *NEC* stands for not elsewhere classified.

Agricultural Production - Crops

0110 Cash grains, p. I-11
0111 Wheat, p. I-11
0112 Rice, p. I-12
0115 Corn, p. I-12
0116 Soybeans, p. I-13
0119 Cash grains, nec, p. I-13
0131 Cotton, p. I-14
0132 Tobacco, p. I-15
0133 Sugarcane and sugar beets, p. I-16
0161 Vegetables and melons, p. I-16
0171 Berry crops, p. I-17
0172 Grapes, p. I-17
0173 Tree nuts, p. I-18
0175 Deciduous tree fruits, p. I-18
0179 Fruits and tree nuts, nec, p. I-19
0181 Ornamental nursery products, p. I-20
0182 Food crops grown under cover, p. I-20

Agricultural Production - Livestock

0214 Sheep and goats, p. I-21
0250 Poultry and eggs, p. I-21
0251 Broiler, fryer, and roaster chickens, p. I-22
0252 Chicken eggs, p. I-23
0253 Turkeys and turkey eggs, p. I-23
0279 Animal specialties, nec, p. I-24
0291 General farms, primarily animal, p. I-25

Agricultural Services

0740 Veterinary services, p. I-26
0751 Livestock services, exc. veterinary, p. I-26
0782 Lawn and garden services, p. I-26

Forestry

0811 Timber tracts, p. I-27

Fishing, Hunting, and Trapping

0910 Commercial fishing, p. I-28
0921 Fish hatcheries and preserves, p. I-29

Metal Mining

1000 Metal mining, p. I-30
1011 Iron ores, p. I-30
1021 Copper ores, p. I-30
1031 Lead and zinc ores, p. I-31
1041 Gold ores, p. I-31
1044 Silver ores, p. I-32

Coal Mining

1220 Bituminous coal and lignite mining, p. I-33

Oil and Gas Extraction

1311 Crude petroleum and natural gas, p. I-36
1321 Natural gas liquids, p. I-39
1381 Drilling oil and gas wells, p. I-39
1389 Oil and gas field services, nec, p. I-40

Nonmetallic Minerals, Except Fuels

1411 Dimension stone, p. I-41
1420 Crushed and broken stone, p. I-42
1422 Crushed and broken limestone, p. I-42
1423 Crushed and broken granite, p. I-43
1442 Construction sand and gravel, p. I-43
1450 Clay, ceramic, & refractory minerals, p. I-43
1475 Phosphate rock, p. I-44
1499 Miscellaneous nonmetallic minerals, p. I-44

General Building Contractors

1500 General building contractors, p. I-46
1521 Single-family housing construction, p. I-47
1522 Residential construction, nec, p. I-52
1531 Operative builders, p. I-52

Appendix I - Industrial Classifications

Primary Metal Industries

3312 Blast furnaces and steel mills, p. I-381
3315 Steel wire and related products, p. I-383
3316 Cold finishing of steel shapes, p. I-383
3317 Steel pipe and tubes, p. I-383
3321 Gray and ductile iron foundries, p. I-383
3334 Primary aluminum, p. I-384
3339 Primary nonferrous metals, nec, p. I-385
3341 Secondary nonferrous metals, p. I-386
3353 Aluminum sheet, plate, and foil, p. I-386
3357 Nonferrous wiredrawing & insulating, p. I-387
3360 Nonferrous foundries (castings), p. I-387

Fabricated Metal Products

3411 Metal cans, p. I-389
3421 Cutlery, p. I-389
3423 Hand and edge tools, nec, p. I-391
3429 Hardware, nec, p. I-392
3433 Heating equipment, except electric, p. I-392
3442 Metal doors, sash, and trim, p. I-394
3443 Fabricated plate work (boiler shops), p. I-394
3444 Sheet metalwork, p. I-394
3462 Iron and steel forgings, p. I-395
3465 Automotive stampings, p. I-395
3469 Metal stampings, nec, p. I-395
3479 Metal coating and allied services, p. I-395
3484 Small arms, p. I-396
3491 Industrial valves, p. I-397

Industry Machinery and Equipment

3511 Turbines and turbine generator sets, p. I-398
3519 Internal combustion engines, nec, p. I-399
3523 Farm machinery and equipment, p. I-399
3524 Lawn and garden equipment, p. I-402
3531 Construction machinery, p. I-402
3533 Oil and gas field machinery, p. I-404
3534 Elevators and moving stairways, p. I-404
3536 Hoists, cranes, and monorails, p. I-405
3537 Industrial trucks and tractors, p. I-405
3540 Metalworking machinery, p. I-406
3541 Machine tools, metal cutting types, p. I-406
3544 Special dies, tools, jigs & fixtures, p. I-408
3555 Printing trades machinery, p. I-409
3556 Food products machinery, p. I-409
3559 Special industry machinery, nec, p. I-409
3561 Pumps and pumping equipment, p. I-412
3563 Air and gas compressors, p. I-412
3565 Packaging machinery, p. I-413
3567 Industrial furnaces and ovens, p. I-413
3568 Power transmission equipment, nec, p. I-414
3569 General industrial machinery, nec, p. I-414
3571 Electronic computers, p. I-415

3572 Computer storage devices, p. I-424
3577 Computer peripheral equipment, nec, p. I-426
3578 Calculating and accounting equipment, p. I-431
3581 Automatic vending machines, p. I-433
3585 Refrigeration and heating equipment, p. I-434
3586 Measuring and dispensing pumps, p. I-434
3589 Service industry machinery, nec, p. I-435
3599 Industrial machinery, nec, p. I-435

Electronic and Other Electric Equipment

3600 Electronic & other electric equipment, p. I-436
3621 Motors and generators, p. I-436
3630 Household appliances, p. I-437
3631 Household cooking equipment, p. I-438
3632 Household refrigerators and freezers, p. I-438
3633 Household laundry equipment, p. I-440
3634 Electric housewares and fans, p. I-442
3635 Household vacuum cleaners, p. I-445
3639 Household appliances, nec, p. I-445
3643 Current-carrying wiring devices, p. I-446
3647 Vehicular lighting equipment, p. I-446
3651 Household audio and video equipment, p. I-447
3652 Prerecorded records and tapes, p. I-453
3661 Telephone and telegraph apparatus, p. I-460
3663 Radio & tv communications equipment, p. I-462
3669 Communications equipment, nec, p. I-468
3670 Electronic components and accessories, p. I-476
3672 Printed circuit boards, p. I-476
3674 Semiconductors and related devices, p. I-477
3675 Electronic capacitors, p. I-487
3678 Electronic connectors, p. I-487
3679 Electronic components, nec, p. I-487
3691 Storage batteries, p. I-490
3694 Engine electrical equipment, p. I-493
3695 Magnetic and optical recording media, p. I-493
3699 Electrical equipment & supplies, nec, p. I-494

Transportation Equipment

3711 Motor vehicles and car bodies, p. I-495
3713 Truck and bus bodies, p. I-510
3714 Motor vehicle parts and accessories, p. I-514
3715 Truck trailers, p. I-519
3716 Motor homes, p. I-519
3721 Aircraft, p. I-520
3724 Aircraft engines and engine parts, p. I-522
3728 Aircraft parts and equipment, nec, p. I-523
3731 Ship building and repairing, p. I-523
3732 Boat building and repairing, p. I-524
3743 Railroad equipment, p. I-525
3751 Motorcycles, bicycles, and parts, p. I-526
3761 Guided missiles and space vehicles, p. I-530
3792 Travel trailers and campers, p. I-532

Wholesale Trade - Nondurable Goods

5100   Wholesale trade - nondurable goods, p. II-670
5112   Stationery and office supplies, p. II-670
5122   Drugs, proprietaries, and sundries, p. II-670
5146   Fish and seafoods, p. II-671
5192   Books, periodicals, & newspapers, p. II-671
5199   Nondurable goods, nec, p. II-671

Building Materials and Garden Supplies

5211   Lumber and other building materials, p. II-672
5231   Paint, glass, and wallpaper stores, p. II-674
5251   Hardware stores, p. II-675
5261   Retail nurseries and garden stores, p. II-675

General Merchandise Stores

5300   General merchandise stores, p. II-677
5311   Department stores, p. II-678
5331   Variety stores, p. II-679

Food Stores

5411   Grocery stores, p. II-681
5421   Meat and fish markets, p. II-698
5431   Fruit and vegetable markets, p. II-698
5451   Dairy products stores, p. II-698

Automotive Dealers and Service Stations

5511   New and used car dealers, p. II-699
5531   Auto and home supply stores, p. II-699
5541   Gasoline service stations, p. II-701

Apparel and Accessory Stores

5600   Apparel and accessory stores, p. II-703
5611   Men's & boys' clothing stores, p. II-703
5621   Women's clothing stores, p. II-706
5641   Children's and infants' wear stores, p. II-707
5651   Family clothing stores, p. II-708
5661   Shoe stores, p. II-709

Furniture and Homefurnishings Stores

5712   Furniture stores, p. II-711
5713   Floor covering stores, p. II-712
5719   Misc. homefurnishings stores, p. II-712
5722   Household appliance stores, p. II-715
5731   Radio, tv, & electronic stores, p. II-717
5734   Computer and software stores, p. II-717
5735   Record & prerecorded tape stores, p. II-718
5736   Musical instrument stores, p. II-720

Eating and Drinking Places

5812   Eating places, p. II-721
5813   Drinking places, p. II-730

Miscellaneous Retail

5912   Drug stores and proprietary stores, p. II-731
5941   Sporting goods and bicycle shops, p. II-745
5942   Book stores, p. II-746
5943   Stationery stores, p. II-747
5944   Jewelry stores, p. II-748
5945   Hobby, toy, and game shops, p. II-748
5946   Camera & photographic supply stores, p. II-750
5949   Sewing, needlework, and piece goods, p. II-750
5961   Catalog and mail-order houses, p. II-750
5962   Merchandising machine operators, p. II-751
5984   Liquefied petroleum gas dealers, p. II-752
5992   Florists, p. II-752
5993   Tobacco stores and stands, p. II-752
5994   News dealers and newsstands, p. II-752
5995   Optical goods stores, p. II-753
5999   Miscellaneous retail stores, nec, p. II-753

Depository Institutions

6021   National commercial banks, p. II-757
6061   Federal credit unions, p. II-782
6081   Foreign bank & branches & agencies, p. II-782
6099   Functions related to deposit banking, p. II-782

Nondepository Institutions

6141   Personal credit institutions, p. II-784
6150   Business credit institutions, p. II-791
6159   Misc. business credit institutions, p. II-792
6162   Mortgage bankers and correspondents, p. II-792
6163   Loan brokers, p. II-793

Security and Commodity Brokers

6211   Security brokers and dealers, p. II-796
6231   Security and commodity exchanges, p. II-802
6289   Security & commodity services, nec, p. II-804

Insurance Carriers

6300   Insurance carriers, p. II-806
6311   Life insurance, p. II-809
6321   Accident and health insurance, p. II-811
6324   Hospital and medical service plans, p. II-814
6331   Fire, marine, and casualty insurance, p. II-816
6351   Surety insurance, p. II-823
6361   Title insurance, p. II-826
6371   Pension, health, and welfare funds, p. II-827
6399   Insurance carriers, nec, p. II-827

Insurance Agents, Brokers, and Service

6411 Insurance agents, brokers, & service, p. II-828

Real Estate

6512 Nonresidential building operators, p. II-829
6513 Apartment building operators, p. II-830
6531 Real estate agents and managers, p. II-831

Holding and Other Investment Offices

6712 Bank holding companies, p. II-833
6730 Trusts, p. II-833
6794 Patent owners and lessors, p. II-834
6798 Real estate investment trusts, p. II-834

Hotels and Other Lodging Places

7011 Hotels and motels, p. II-836

Personal Services

7221 Photographic studios, portrait, p. II-839
7231 Beauty shops, p. II-839
7261 Funeral service and crematories, p. II-839
7291 Tax return preparation services, p. II-840

Business Services

7311 Advertising agencies, p. II-842
7312 Outdoor advertising services, p. II-844
7313 Radio, tv, publisher representatives, p. II-844
7319 Advertising, nec, p. II-844
7323 Credit reporting services, p. II-850
7331 Direct mail advertising services, p. II-850
7334 Photocopying & duplicating services, p. II-851
7353 Heavy construction equipment rental, p. II-851
7359 Equipment rental & leasing, nec, p. II-852
7363 Help supply services, p. II-852
7372 Prepackaged software, p. II-853
7373 Computer integrated systems design, p. II-860
7375 Information retrieval services, p. II-863
7378 Computer maintenance & repair, p. II-864
7379 Computer related services, nec, p. II-864
7381 Detective & armored car services, p. II-864
7382 Security systems services, p. II-865
7383 News syndicates, p. II-865
7384 Photofinishing laboratories, p. II-866
7389 Business services, nec, p. II-866

Auto Repair, Services, and Parking

7514 Passenger car rental, p. II-872
7534 Tire retreading and repair shops, p. II-876
7538 General automotive repair shops, p. II-877

Miscellaneous Repair Services

7699 Repair services, nec, p. II-878

Motion Pictures

7812 Motion picture & video production, p. II-879
7819 Services allied to motion pictures, p. II-888
7822 Motion picture and tape distribution, p. II-889
7832 Motion picture theaters, ex drive-in, p. II-891
7833 Drive-in motion picture theaters, p. II-893
7841 Video tape rental, p. II-894

Amusement and Recreation Services

7922 Theatrical producers and services, p. II-895
7929 Entertainers & entertainment groups, p. II-895
7941 Sports clubs, managers, & promoters, p. II-896
7948 Racing, including track operation, p. II-897
7991 Physical fitness facilities, p. II-897
7992 Public golf courses, p. II-898
7993 Coin-operated amusement devices, p. II-898
7996 Amusement parks, p. II-899
7997 Membership sports & recreation clubs, p. II-901
7999 Amusement and recreation, nec, p. II-901

Health Services

8011 Offices & clinics of medical doctors, p. II-905
8062 General medical & surgical hospitals, p. II-905
8063 Psychiatric hospitals, p. II-908
8071 Medical laboratories, p. II-908
8092 Kidney dialysis centers, p. II-909
8099 Health and allied services, nec, p. II-909

Legal Services

8111 Legal services, p. II-910

Educational Services

8211 Elementary and secondary schools, p. II-911
8221 Colleges and universities, p. II-911
8231 Libraries, p. II-912
8299 Schools & educational services, nec, p. II-912

Social Services

8351 Child day care services, p. II-913
8399 Social services, nec, p. II-913

Museums, Botanical, Zoological Gardens

8412 Museums and art galleries, p. II-916

Appendix I - Industrial Classifications

Membership Organizations

Engineering and Management Services

Justice, Public Order, and Safety

Environmental Quality and Housing

Administration of Economic Programs

National Security and International Affairs

APPENDIX I - INDUSTRIAL CLASSIFICATIONS

NAICS COVERAGE

This appendix lists the North American Industrial Classification codes (NAICS) included in *Market Share Reporter*. A volume and page number are shown following each NAICS category; the page shown indicates the first occurrence of a NAICS.

Crop Production

111110 Soybean farming, p. I-13
111140 Wheat farming, p. I-11
111150 Corn farming, p. I-11
111160 Rice farming, p. I-12
111199 All other grain farming, p. I-13
111219 Other vegetable (exc potato) & melon, p. I-64
111331 Apple orchards, p. I-18
111332 Grape vineyards, p. I-17
111334 Berry (exc strawberry) farming, p. I-17
111335 Tree nut farming, p. I-18
111336 Fruit & tree nut combination farming, p. I-19
111339 Other noncitrus fruit farming, p. I-17
111411 Mushroom production, p. I-20
111421 Nursery & tree production, p. I-20
111422 Floriculture production, p. I-20
111910 Tobacco farming, p. I-15
111920 Cotton farming, p. I-14
111991 Sugar beet farming, p. I-16
111998 All other miscellaneous crop farming, p. I-183

Animal Production

112310 Chicken egg production, p. I-60
112320 Broilers & other chicken production, p. I-21
112330 Turkey production, p. I-23
112410 Sheep farming, p. I-21
112511 Finfish farming & fish hatcheries, p. I-29
112920 Horses & other equine production, p. I-25
112990 All other animal production, p. I-24

Fishing, Hunting & Trapping

114111 Finfish fishing, p. I-29
114112 Shellfish fishing, p. I-29

Agriculture & Forestry Support Acvities

115210 Support activities for animal production, p. I-26

Oil & Gas Extraction

211111 Crude petroleum & natural gas, p. I-36
211112 Natural gas liquid extraction, p. I-39

Mining (except Oil & Gas)

212111 Bituminous coal & lignite surface mining, p. I-33
212112 Bituminous coal underground mining, p. I-33
212210 Iron ore mining, p. I-30
212221 Gold ore mining, p. I-31
212222 Silver ore mining, p. I-32
212231 Lead ore & zinc ore mining, p. I-31
212234 Copper ore & nickel ore mining, p. I-30
212311 Dimension stone mining & quarrying, p. I-41
212312 Crushed & broken limestone, p. I-42
212313 Crushed & broken granite, p. I-43
212321 Construction sand & gravel mining, p. I-43
212324 Kaolin & ball clay mining, p. I-43
212325 Clay/ceramic/refractory minerals mining, p. I-43
212392 Phosphate rock mining, p. I-44
212399 All other nonmetallic mineral mining, p. I-44

Mining Support Activities

213111 Drilling oil & gas wells, p. I-39
213112 Support activities for oil & gas operations, p. I-40

Utilities

221111 Hydroelectric power generation, p. II-662
221112 Fossil fuel electric power generation, p. II-662
221113 Nuclear electric power generation, p. II-662
221119 Other electric power generation, p. II-662
221121 Electric bulk power transmn & control, p. II-662
221122 Electric power distribution, p. II-662
221210 Natural gas distribution, p. II-663

Building, Developing, & General Contracting

233210 Single family housing construction, p. I-46
233220 Multifamily housing construction, p. I-52
233310 Mfg & industrial building construction, p. I-46
233320 Commercial & institutional building, p. I-46

Heavy Construction

234110 Highway & street construction, p. I-54
234120 Bridge & tunnel construction, p. I-54
234910 Water, sewer, & pipeline construction, p. I-55
234920 Power & communication transmission line, p. I-55
234930 Industrial nonbuilding structure construction, p. I-55
234990 All other heavy construction, p. I-55

Special Trade Contractors

235110 Plumbing, heating, AC contractors, p. I-56
235210 Painting & wall covering contractors, p. I-56
235310 Electrical contractors, p. I-56
235410 Masonry & stone contractors, p. I-56
235610 Roofing, siding, & sheet metal contractors, p. I-57
235710 Concrete contractors, p. I-57
235910 Structural steel erection contractors, p. I-57
235920 Glass & glazing contractors, p. I-58
235930 Excavation contractors, p. I-58
235940 Wrecking & demolition contractors, p. I-58
235990 All other special trade contractors, p. I-58

Food Manufacturing

311111 Dog & cat food mfg, p. I-277
311212 Rice milling, p. I-108
311225 Fats & oils refining & blending, p. I-136
311230 Breakfast cereal mfg, p. I-60
311311 Sugarcane mills, p. I-122
311312 Cane sugar refining, p. I-122
311320 Chocolate mfg from cacao beans, p. I-107
311330 Confectionery mfg from purchased chocolate, p. I-61
311340 Nonchocolate confectionery mfg, p. I-123
311411 Frozen fruit, juice, & vegetable mfg, p. I-99
311412 Frozen specialty food mfg, p. I-62
311421 Fruit & vegetable canning, p. I-62
311422 Specialty canning, p. I-63
311423 Dried & dehydrated food mfg, p. I-95
311511 Fluid milk mfg, p. I-61
311512 Creamery butter mfg, p. I-73
311513 Cheese mfg, p. I-60
311514 Dry, condensed, evaporated dairy mfg, p. I-72
311520 Ice cream & frozen dessert mfg, p. I-61
311611 Animal (exc poultry) slaughtering, p. I-61
311612 Meat processed from carcasses, p. I-60
311615 Poultry processing, p. I-60
311711 Seafood canning, p. I-169

311712 Fresh & frozen seafood processing, p. I-171
311812 Commercial bakeries, p. I-61
311813 Frozen cakes, pies, & other pastries mfg, p. I-121
311821 Cookie & cracker mfg, p. I-60
311822 Flour mixes/dough from purchased flour, p. I-107
311823 Dry pasta mfg, p. I-179
311911 Roasted nuts & peanut butter mfg, p. I-135
311919 Other snack food mfg, p. I-176
311920 Coffee & tea mfg, p. I-61
311930 Flavoring syrup & concentrate mfg, p. I-169
311941 Mayonnaise/dressing/other sauce mfg, p. I-97
311942 Spice & extract mfg, p. I-182
311991 Perishable prepared food mfg, p. I-181
311999 All other miscellaneous food mfg, p. I-62

Beverage & Tobacco Product Manufacturing

312111 Soft drink mfg, p. I-60
312112 Bottled water mfg, p. I-137
312120 Breweries, p. I-136
312130 Wineries, p. I-60
312140 Distilleries, p. I-136
312221 Cigarette mfg, p. I-185
312229 Other tobacco product mfg, p. I-189

Textile Mills

313210 Broadwoven fabric mills, p. I-190
313230 Nonwoven fabric mills, p. I-192
313241 Weft knit fabric mills, p. I-207

Textile Product Mills

314110 Carpet & rug mills, p. II-581
314121 Curtain & drapery mills, p. I-204
314129 Other household textile product mills, p. I-204
314911 Textile bag mills, p. I-366

Apparel Manufacturing

315111 Sheer hosiery mills, p. I-191
315119 Other hosiery & sock mills, p. I-191
315211 Men's & boys' apparel contractors, p. I-194
315212 Women's/girls'/infants' apparel contractors, p. I-194
315221 Men's & boys' underwear & nightwear mfg, p. I-198
315223 Men's & boys' shirt (exc work shirt) mfg, p. I-196
315228 Men's & boys' other outerwear mfg, p. I-195
315231 Women's & girls' nightwear mfg, p. I-202
315232 Women's & girls' blouse & shirt mfg, p. I-201
315239 Women's & girls' other outerwear mfg, p. I-195
315991 Hat, cap, & millinery mfg, p. I-204

Leather & Allied Product Manufacturing

316211 Rubber & plastics footwear mfg, p. I-369
316213 Men's footwear (exc athletic) mfg, p. I-368
316214 Women's footwear (exc athletic) mfg, p. I-368
316219 Other footwear mfg, p. I-364
316991 Luggage mfg, p. I-371

Wood Product Manufacturing

321113 Sawmills, p. I-209
321911 Wood window & door mfg, p. I-211
321912 Cut stock, resawing lumber, & planing, p. I-209
321918 Other millwork (including flooring), p. I-210
321920 Wood container & pallet mfg, p. I-212
321991 Manufactured home (mobile home) mfg, p. I-212
321992 Prefabricated wood building mfg, p. I-212
321999 All other miscellaneous wood product mfg, p. I-209

Paper Manufacturing

322121 Paper (exc newsprint) mills, p. I-219
322122 Newsprint mills, p. I-220
322130 Paperboard mills, p. I-221
322211 Corrugated & solid fiber box mfg, p. I-222
322212 Folding paperboard box mfg, p. I-223
322214 Fiber can, tube, drum, & similar products mfg, p. I-222
322221 Coated & laminated paper & plastics film mfg, p. I-223
322222 Coated & laminated paper mfg, p. I-223
322223 Plastics, foil, & coated paper bag mfg, p. I-224
322233 Stationery, tablet, & related product mfg, p. I-233
322291 Sanitary paper product mfg, p. I-225
322299 All other converted paper product mfg, p. I-234

Printing & Related Support Activities

323110 Commercial lithographic printing, p. I-253
323114 Quick printing, p. II-851
323116 Manifold business forms printing, p. I-256
323117 Books printing, p. I-251
323122 Prepress services, p. I-256

Petroleum & Coal Products Manufacturing

324110 Petroleum refineries, p. I-357
324191 Petroleum lubricating oil & grease mfg, p. I-358

Chemical Manufacturing

325110 Petrochemical mfg, p. I-348
325120 Industrial gas mfg, p. I-260
325131 Inorganic dye & pigment mfg, p. I-257
325132 Synthetic organic dye & pigment mfg, p. I-257
325181 Alkalies & chlorine mfg, p. I-257
325182 Carbon black mfg, p. I-355
325188 All other basic inorganic chemical mfg, p. I-349

325192 Cyclic crude & intermediate mfg, p. I-257
325199 All other basic organic chemical mfg, p. I-348
325211 Plastics material & resin mfg, p. I-267
325212 Synthetic rubber mfg, p. I-268
325221 Cellulosic organic fiber mfg, p. I-270
325222 Noncellulosic organic fiber mfg, p. I-271
325320 Pesticide & other agricultural chemical mfg, p. I-351
325411 Medicinal & botanical mfg, p. I-272
325412 Pharmaceutical preparation mfg, p. I-272
325413 In-vitro diagnostic substance mfg, p. I-297
325414 Biological product (exc diagnostic) mfg, p. I-299
325510 Paint & coating mfg, p. I-344
325520 Adhesive mfg, p. I-352
325611 Soap & other detergent mfg, p. I-299
325612 Polish & other sanitation good mfg, p. I-307
325620 Toilet preparation mfg, p. I-279
325910 Printing ink mfg, p. I-354
325992 Photographic film & chemical mfg, p. II-557
325998 Other chemical product & preparation mfg, p. I-356

Plastics & Rubber Products Manufacturing

326111 Unsupported plastics bag mfg, p. I-224
326113 Unsupported plastics film & sheet, p. I-364
326121 Unsupported plastics profile shape mfg, p. I-366
326122 Plastics pipe & pipe fitting mfg, p. I-365
326130 Laminated plastics plate, sheet, & shape, p. I-365
326160 Plastics bottle mfg, p. I-365
326192 Resilient floor covering mfg, p. II-581
326199 All other plastics product mfg, p. I-366
326211 Tire mfg (exc retreading), p. I-360
326212 Tire retreading, p. II-876
326299 All other rubber product mfg, p. I-364

Nonmetallic Mineral Product Manufacturing

327111 Vitreous china bathroom accessories mfg, p. I-378
327121 Brick & structural clay tile mfg, p. I-376
327122 Ceramic wall & floor tile mfg, p. I-376
327124 Clay refractory mfg, p. I-377
327211 Flat glass mfg, p. I-373
327212 Other pressed & blown glass, p. I-374
327213 Glass container mfg, p. I-373
327215 Glass product mfg made of purchased glass, p. I-374
327310 Cement mfg, p. I-374
327331 Concrete block & brick mfg, p. I-376
327420 Gypsum product mfg, p. I-379
327910 Abrasive product mfg, p. I-380

Primary Metal Manufacturing

331111 Iron & steel mills, p. I-381
331210 Iron & steel pipe/tube mfg from purch steel, p. I-383
331221 Rolled steel shape mfg, p. I-383
331222 Steel wire drawing, p. I-383

Transportation Equipment Manufacturing

336111 Automobile mfg, p. I-495
336112 Light truck & utility vehicle mfg, p. I-495
336211 Motor vehicle body mfg, p. I-495
336212 Truck trailer mfg, p. I-519
336213 Motor home mfg, p. I-519
336214 Travel trailer & camper mfg, p. I-532
336312 Gasoline engine & engine parts mfg, p. I-514
336321 Vehicular lighting equipment mfg, p. I-446
336322 Other motor vehicle electrical equipment mfg, p. I-493
336330 Motor vehicle steering/suspension, p. I-514
336340 Motor vehicle brake system mfg, p. I-514
336350 Motor vehicle transmission/power train, p. I-514
336360 Motor vehicle seating & interior trim mfg, p. I-207
336370 Motor vehicle metal stamping, p. I-395
336399 All other motor vehicle parts mfg, p. I-399
336411 Aircraft mfg, p. I-520
336412 Aircraft engine & engine parts mfg, p. I-522
336413 Other aircraft parts mfg, p. I-523
336414 Guided missile & space vehicle mfg, p. I-530
336510 Railroad rolling stock mfg, p. I-525
336611 Ship building & repairing, p. I-524
336612 Boat building, p. I-524
336991 Motorcycle, bicycle, & parts mfg, p. I-526
336999 All other transportation equipment mfg, p. I-532

Furniture & Related Product Manufacturing

337121 Upholstered household furniture mfg, p. I-215
337122 Nonupholstered household furniture mfg, p. I-214
337124 Metal household furniture mfg, p. I-214
337125 Household furniture mfg, p. I-214
337127 Institutional furniture mfg, p. I-217
337211 Wood office furniture mfg, p. I-214
337214 Office furniture (exc wood) mfg, p. I-216
337910 Mattress mfg, p. I-216

Miscellaneous Manufacturing

339111 Laboratory apparatus & furniture mfg, p. II-536
339112 Surgical & medical instrument mfg, p. II-540
339113 Surgical appliance & supplies mfg, p. II-540
339114 Dental equipment & supplies mfg, p. II-551
339115 Ophthalmic goods mfg, p. II-553
339911 Jewelry (exc costume) mfg, p. II-561
339920 Sporting & athletic goods mfg, p. II-573
339931 Doll & stuffed toy mfg, p. II-564
339932 Game, toy, & children's vehicle mfg, p. II-564
339941 Pen & mechanical pencil mfg, p. II-579
339942 Lead pencil & art good mfg, p. II-579
339950 Sign mfg, p. II-580
339992 Musical instrument mfg, p. II-562
339993 Fastener, button, needle, & pin mfg, p. II-580
339994 Broom, brush, & mop mfg, p. II-580

339999 All other miscellaneous mfg, p. I-444

Wholesale Trade, Durable Goods

421130 Tire & tube wholesalers, p. II-668
421310 Lumber, plywood, millwork, & wood panel, p. II-668
421320 Brick, stone, & related construction material, p. II-668
421690 Electronic parts wholesaling, p. II-668
421810 Construction & mining equipment, p. II-669
421820 Farm & garden equipment wholesalers, p. II-669
421910 Sporting & recreational goods & supplies, p. II-669

Wholesale Trade, Nondurable Goods

422120 Stationery & office supplies wholesalers, p. II-670
422210 Drugs & druggists' sundries wholesalers, p. II-670
422410 General line grocery wholesalers, p. II-670
422460 Fish & seafood wholesalers, p. II-671
422920 Book, periodical, & newspaper wholesalers, p. II-671
422940 Tobacco & tobacco product wholesalers, p. II-670
422990 Other nondurable goods wholesalers, p. II-671

Motor Vehicle & Parts Dealers

441110 New car dealers, p. II-699
441310 Automotive parts & accessories stores, p. II-699
441320 Tire dealers, p. II-701

Furniture & Home Furnishings Stores

442110 Furniture stores, p. II-711
442210 Floor covering stores, p. II-712
442291 Window treatment stores, p. II-713
442299 All other home furnishings stores, p. II-712

Electronics & Appliance Stores

443111 Household appliance stores, p. II-715
443112 Radio, TV, & other electronics stores, p. II-717
443120 Computer & software stores, p. II-717
443130 Camera & photographic supplies stores, p. II-750

Bldg Material & Garden Equip & Supp Dealers

444110 Home centers, p. II-672
444120 Paint & wallpaper stores, p. II-675
444130 Hardware stores, p. II-675
444190 Other building material dealers, p. II-672
444210 Outdoor power equipment stores, p. II-669
444220 Nursery & garden centers, p. II-675

Food & Beverage Stores

445110 Supermarkets & other grocery stores, p. II-678
445120 Convenience stores, p. II-697
445210 Meat markets, p. II-698
445230 Fruit & vegetable markets, p. II-698

511199 All other publishers, p. I-252
511210 Software publishers, p. II-853

Motion Picture & Sound Recording Industries

512110 Motion picture & video production, p. II-879
512120 Motion picture & video distribution, p. II-889
512131 Motion picture theaters (exc drive-ins), p. II-891
512132 Drive-in motion picture theaters, p. II-893
512199 Other motion picture & video industries, p. II-888
512220 Integrated record production/distribution, p. I-453
512230 Music publishers, p. I-245

Broadcasting & Telecommunications

513111 Radio networks, p. II-649
513112 Radio stations, p. II-649
513120 Television broadcasting, p. II-653
513210 Cable networks, p. II-657
513220 Cable & other program distribution, p. II-657
513310 Wired telecommunications carriers, p. II-632
513321 Paging, p. II-622
513322 Cellular/other wireless telecommunications, p. II-622
513330 Telecommunications resellers, p. II-622

Information & Data Processing Services

514110 News syndicates, p. II-865
514120 Libraries & archives, p. II-912
514191 On-line information services, p. II-644

Credit Intermediation & Related Activities

522110 Commercial banking, p. II-757
522130 Credit unions, p. II-782
522210 Credit card issuing, p. II-784
522292 Real estate credit, p. II-792
522298 All other nondepository credit intermediation, p. II-791
522310 Mortgage & nonmortgage loan brokers, p. II-793
522320 Financial transaction processing activities, p. II-782
522390 Other credit intermediation activities, p. II-793

Security, Commodity Contracts & Like Activity

523110 Investment banking & securities dealing, p. II-796

Appendix I - Industrial Classifications

APPENDIX I - INDUSTRIAL CLASSIFICATIONS

ISIC COVERAGE

This appendix lists the International Standard Industrial Classification Codes (ISICs). Entries in the body of the book are arranged according to the Standard Industrial Classification (SIC) system of the U.S. Department of Commerce. Products may be located using either the SIC Coverage listing beginning on page 1091 or the Products, Services, and Issues Index beginning on page 971.

0110	Growing of crops; market gardening; horticulture		1511	Production, processing and preserving of meat and meat products
0111	Growing of cereals and other crops nec		1512	Processing and preserving of fish and fish products
0112	Growing of vegetables, horticultural specialties and nursery products		1513	Processing and preserving of fruits and vegetables
0113	Growing of fruits, nuts, beverage and spice crops		1514	Manufacture of vegetable and animal oils and fats
0120	Farming of animals		1520	Manufacture of dairy products
0121	Farming of cattle, sheep, goats, horses, asses, mules and hinnies; dairy farming		1530	Manufacture of grain mill products, starches and starch products, and prepared animal feeds
0122	Other animal farming; production of animal products nec		1531	Manufacture of grain mill products
0130	Growing of crops combined with farming of animals (mixed farming)		1532	Manufacture of starches and starch products
0140	Agricultural and animal husbandry service activities, except veterinary activities		1533	Manufacture of prepared animal feeds
			1540	Manufacture of other food products
0150	Hunting, trapping and game propagation including related service activities		1541	Manufacture of bakery products
			1542	Manufacture of sugar
0200	Forestry, logging, and related service activities		1543	Manufacture of cocoa, chocolate, and sugar confectionery
0500	Fishing, operation of fish hatcheries and fish farms; service activities incidental to fishing		1544	Manufacture of macaroni, noodles, couscous and similar farinaceous products
1010	Mining and agglomeration of hard coal		1549	Manufacture of other food products nec
1020	Mining and agglomeration of lignite		1550	Manufacture of beverages
1030	Extraction and agglomeration of peat		1551	Distilling, rectifying and blending of spirits; ethyl alcohol production from fermented materials
1110	Extraction of crude petroleum and natural gas		1552	Manufacture of wines
1120	Service activities incidental to oil and gas extraction excluding surveying		1553	Manufacture of malt liquors and malt
			1554	Manufacture of soft drinks; production of mineral waters
1200	Mining of uranium and thorium ores			
1310	Mining of iron ores		1600	Manufacture of tobacco products
1320	Mining of non-ferrous metal ores, except uranium and thorium ores		1710	Spinning, weaving and finishing of textiles
			1711	Preparation and spinning of textile fibers; weaving of textiles
1410	Quarrying of stone, sand and clay			
1420	Mining and quarrying, nec		1712	Finishing of textiles
1421	Mining of chemical and fertilizer minerals		1720	Manufacture of other textiles
1422	Extraction of salt		1721	Manufacture of made-up textile articles, except apparel
1429	Other mining and quarrying nec			
1510	Production, processing, and preservation of meat, fish, fruit, vegetables, oils and fats		1722	Manufacture of carpets and rugs

1107

1723 Manufacture of cordage, rope, twine and netting

1729 Manufacture of other textiles nec

1730 Manufacture of knitted and crocheted fabrics and articles

1810 Manufacture of wearing apparel, except fur apparel

1820 Dressing and dyeing of fur; manufacture of articles of fur

1910 Tanning and dressing of leather; manufacture of luggage, handbags, saddlery and harness

1911 Tanning and dressing of leather

1912 Manufacture of luggage, handbags and the like, saddlery and harness

1920 Manufacture of footwear

2010 Sawmilling and planning of wood

2020 Manufacture of products of wood, cork, straw and plaiting materials

2021 Manufacture of veneer sheets; manufacture of plywood, laminboard, particle board and other panels and boards

2022 Manufacture of builders' carpentry and joinery

2023 Manufacture of wood containers

2029 Manufacture of other products of wood; manufacture of articles of cork, straw and plaiting materials

2101 Manufacture of pulp, paper, and paperboard

2102 Manufacture of corrugated paper and paperboard and of containers of paper and paperboard

2109 Manufacture of other articles of paper and paperboard

2210 Publishing

2211 Publishing of books, brochures, musical books, and other publications

2212 Publishing of newspapers, journals, and periodicals

2213 Publishing of recorded media

2219 Other publishing

2220 Printing and service activities related to printing

2221 Printing

2222 Service activities related to printing

2230 Reproduction of recorded media

2310 Manufacture of coke oven products

2320 Manufacturer of refined petroleum products

2330 Processing of nuclear fuel

2410 Manufacture of basic chemicals

2411 Manufacture of basic chemicals, except fertilizers and nitrogen compounds

2412 Manufacture of fertilizers and nitrogen compounds

2413 Manufacture of plastics in primary forms and of synthetic rubber

2420 Manufacture of other chemical products

2421 Manufacture of pesticides and other agro-chemical products

2422 Manufacture of paints, varnishes, and similar coatings, printing ink and mastics

2423 Manufacture of pharmaceuticals, medicinal chemicals, and botanical products

2424 Manufacture of soap and detergents, cleaning and polishing preparations, perfumes and toilet preparations

2429 Manufacture of other chemical products nec

2430 Manufacture of man-made fibers

2510 Manufacture of rubber products

2511 Manufacture of rubber tires and tubes; retreading and rebuilding of rubber tires

2519 Manufacture of other rubber products

2520 Manufacture of plastic products

2610 Manufacture of glass and glass products

2690 Manufacture of non-metallic minerals products nec

2691 Manufacture of non-structural non-refractory ceramic ware

2692 Manufacture of refractory ceramic products

2693 Manufacture of structural non-refractory clay and ceramic products

2694 Manufacture of cement, lime and plaster

2695 Manufacture of articles of concrete, cement and plaster

2696 Cutting, shaping, and finishing of stone

2699 Manufacture of other non-metallic mineral products nec

2710 Manufacture of basic iron and steel

2720 Manufacture of basic precious and non-ferrous metals

2730 Casting of metals

2731 Casting of iron and steel

2732 Casting of non-ferrous metals

2810 Manufacture of structural metal products, tanks, reservoirs and steam generators

2811 Manufacture of structural metal products

2812 Manufacture of tanks, reservoirs and containers of metals

2813 Manufacture of steam generators, except central heating hot water boilers

2890 Manufacture of other fabricated metal products; metal working service activities

2891 Forging, pressing, stamping and roll-forming of metal; powder metallurgy

2892 Treatment and coating of metals; general mechanical engineering on a fee or contract basis

2893 Manufacture of cutlery, hand tools, and general hardware

2899 Manufacture of other fabricated metal products nec

2910   Manufacture of general purpose machinery

2911   Manufacture of engines and turbines, except aircraft, vehicle and cycle engines

2912   Manufacture of pumps, compressors, taps, and valves

2913   Manufacture of bearings, gears, gearing and driving elements

2914   Manufacture of ovens, furnaces and furnace burners

2915   Manufacture of lifting and handling equipment

2919   Manufacture of other general purpose machinery

2920   Manufacture of special purpose machinery

2921   Manufacture of agricultural and forestry machinery

2922   Manufacture of machine-tools

2923   Manufacture of machinery for metallurgy

2924   Manufacture of machinery for mining, quarrying and construction

2925   Manufacture of machinery for food, beverage, and tobacco processing

2926   Manufacture of machinery for textile, apparel and leather production

2927   Manufacture of weapons and ammunition

2929   Manufacture of other special purpose machinery

2930   Manufacture of domestic appliances nec

3000   Manufacture of office, accounting, and computing machinery

3110   Manufacture of electric motors, generators and transformers

3120   Manufacture of electricity distribution and control apparatus

3130   Manufacture of insulated wire and cable

3140   Manufacture of accumulators, primary cells, and primary batteries

3150   Manufacture of electric lamps and lighting equipment

3190   Manufacture of other electrical equipment nec

3210   Manufacture of electronic valves and tubes and other electronic components

3220   Manufacture of television and radio transmitters and apparatus for line telephony and line telegraphy

3230   Manufacture of television and radio receivers, sound or video recording or reproducing apparatus, and associated goods

3310   Manufacture of medical appliances and instruments and appliances for measuring, checking, testing, navigating, and other purposes, except optical instruments

3311   Manufacture of medical and surgical equipment and orthopedic appliances

3312   Manufacture of instruments and appliances for measuring, checking, testing, navigating, and other purposes, except industrial process control equipment

3313   Manufacture of industrial process control equipment

3320   Manufacture of optical instruments and photographic equipment

3330   Manufacture of watches and clocks

3410   Manufacture of motor vehicles

3420   Manufacture of bodies (coachwork) for motor vehicles; manufacture of trailers and semi-trailers

3430   Manufacture of parts and accessories for motor vehicles and their engines

3510   Building and repairing of ships and boats

3511   Building and repairing of ships

3512   Building and repairing of pleasure and sporting boats

3520   Manufacture of railway and tramway locomotives and rolling stock

3530   Manufacture of aircraft and spacecraft

3590   Manufacture of transport equipment nec

3591   Manufacture of motorcycles

3592   Manufacture of bicycles and invalid carriages

3599   Manufacture of other transport equipment nec

3610   Manufacture of furniture

3690   Manufacturing nec

3691   Manufacture of jewelry and related articles

3692   Manufacture of musical instruments

3693   Manufacture of sports goods

3694   Manufacture of games and toys

3699   Other manufacturing nec

3710   Recycling of metal waste and scrap

3720   Recycling of non-metal waste and scrap

4010   Production, collection, and distribution of electricity

4020   Manufacture of gas; distribution of gaseous fuels through mains

4030   Steam and hot water supply

4100   Collection, purification, and distribution of water

4510   Site preparation

4520   Building of complete constructions or parts thereof; civil engineering

4530   Building installation

4540   Building completion

4550   Renting of construction or demolition equipment with operator

5010   Sale of motor vehicles

5020   Maintenance and repair of motor vehicles

5030   Sale of motor vehicle parts and accessories

Appendix I - Industrial Classifications

5040	Sale, maintenance and repair of motorcycles and related parts and accessories
5050	Retail sale of automotive fuel
5110	Wholesale on a fee or contract basis
5120	Wholesale of agricultural raw materials, live animals, food, beverages and tobacco
5121	Wholesale of agricultural raw materials and live animals
5122	Wholesale of food, beverages, and tobacco
5130	Wholesale of household goods
5131	Wholesale of textiles, clothing, and footwear
5139	Wholesale of other household goods
5140	Wholesale of non-agricultural intermediate products, waste and scrap
5141	Wholesale of solid, liquid and gaseous fuels and related products
5142	Wholesale of metals and metal ores
5143	Wholesale of construction materials, hardware, plumbing and heating equipment and supplies
5149	Wholesale of other intermediate products, waste and scrap
5150	Wholesale of machinery, equipment, and supplies
5190	Other wholesale
5210	Non-specialized retail trade in stores
5211	Retail sale in non-specialized stores with food, beverages, or tobacco predominating
5219	Other retail sale in non-specialized stores
5220	Retail sale of food, beverages, and tobacco in specialized stores
5230	Other retail trade of new goods in specialized stores
5231	Retail sale of pharmaceutical and medical goods, cosmetic and toilet articles
5232	Retail sale of textiles, clothing, footwear, and leather goods
5233	Retail sale of household appliances, articles, and equipment
5234	Retail sale of hardware, paints and glass
5239	Other retail sale in specialized stores
5240	Retail sale of second-hand goods in stores
5250	Retail trade not in stores
5251	Retail sale via mail-order houses
5252	Retail sale via stalls and markets
5259	Other non-store retail sale
5260	Repair of personal and household goods
5510	Hotels; camping sites and other provision of short-stay accommodation
5520	Restaurants, bars and canteens
6010	Transport via railways
6020	Other land transport

6021	Other scheduled passenger land transport
6022	Other non-scheduled passenger land transport
6023	Freight transport by road
6030	Transport via pipelines
6110	Sea and coastal water transport
6120	Inland water transport
6210	Scheduled air transport
6220	Non-scheduled air transport
6300	Supporting and auxiliary transport activities; activities of travel agencies
6301	Cargo handling
6302	Storage and warehousing
6303	Other supporting transport activities
6304	Activities of travel agencies and tour operators; tourist assistance activities nec
6309	Activities of other transport agencies
6410	Post and courier activities
6411	National post activities
6412	Courier activities other than national post activities
6420	Telecommunications
6510	Monetary intermediation
6511	Central banking
6519	Other monetary intermediation
6559	Other financial intermediation nec
6590	Other financial leasing
6591	Financial leasing
6592	Other credit granting
6600	Insurance and pension funding, except compulsory social security
6601	Life insurance
6602	Pension funding
6603	Non-life insurance
6710	Activities auxiliary to financial intermediation, except insurance and pension funding
6711	Administration of financial markets
6712	Security dealing activities
6719	Activities auxiliary to financial intermediation nec
6720	Activities auxiliary to insurance and pension funding
7010	Real estate activities with own or leased property
7020	Real estate activities on a fee or contract basis
7110	Renting of transport equipment
7111	Renting of land transport equipment
7112	Renting of water transport equipment
7113	Renting of air transport equipment
7120	Renting of other machinery and equipment
7121	Renting of agricultural machinery and equipment

7122	Renting of construction and civil engineering machinery and equipment	7520	Provision of services to the community as a whole
7123	Renting of office machinery and equipment (including computers)	7521	Foreign affairs
7129	Renting of other machinery and equipment nec	7522	Defense activities
7130	Renting of personal and household goods nec	7523	Public order and safety activities
7210	Hardware consultancy	7530	Compulsory social security activities
7220	Software consultancy and supply	8010	Primary education
7230	Data processing	8020	Secondary education
7240	Database activities	8021	General secondary education
7250	Maintenance and repair of office, accounting and computing machinery	8022	Technical and vocational secondary education

7122　Renting of construction and civil engineering machinery and equipment

7123　Renting of office machinery and equipment (including computers)

7129　Renting of other machinery and equipment nec

7130　Renting of personal and household goods nec

7210　Hardware consultancy

7220　Software consultancy and supply

7230　Data processing

7240　Database activities

7250　Maintenance and repair of office, accounting and computing machinery

7290　Other computer related activities

7310　Research and experimental development on natural sciences and engineering (NSE)

7320　Research and experimental development on social sciences and humanities (SSH)

7410　Legal, accounting, bookkeeping, and auditing activities; tax consultancy; market research and public opinion polling; business and management consultancy

7411　Legal activities

7412　Accounting, book-keeping and auditing activities; tax consultancy

7413　Market research and public opinion polling

7414　Business and management consultancy activities

7420　Architectural, engineering and other technical activities

7421　Architectural and engineering activities and related technical consultancy

7422　Technical testing and analysis

7430　Advertising

7490　Business activities nec

7491　Labor recruitment and provision of personnel

7492　Investigation and security activities

7493　Building-cleaning activities

7494　Photographic activities

7495　Packaging activities

7499　Other business activities nec

7510　Administration of the State and the economic and social policy of the community

7511　General (overall) public service activities

7512　Regulation of the activities of agencies that provide health care, education, cultural service, and other social services, excluding social security

7513　Regulation of and contribution to more efficient operation of business

7514　Ancillary service activities for the Government as a whole

7520　Provision of services to the community as a whole

7521　Foreign affairs

7522　Defense activities

7523　Public order and safety activities

7530　Compulsory social security activities

8010　Primary education

8020　Secondary education

8021　General secondary education

8022　Technical and vocational secondary education

8030　Higher education

8090　Adult and other education

8510　Human health activities

8511　Hospital activities

8512　Medical and dental practice activities

8519　Other human health activities

8520　Veterinary activities

8530　Social work activities

8531　Social work with accommodation

8532　Social work without accommodation

9000　Sewage and refuse disposal, sanitation, and similar activities

9110　Activities of business, employers and professional organizations

9111　Activities of business and employers' organizations

9112　Activities of professional organizations

9120　Activities of trade unions

9190　Activities of other membership organizations

9191　Activities of religious organizations

9192　Activities of political organizations

9199　Activities of other membership organizations nec

9210　Motion picture, radio, television and other entertainment activities

9211　Motion picture and video production and distribution

9212　Motion picture projection

9213　Radio and television activities

9214　Dramatic arts, music, and other arts activities

9219　Other entertainment activities nec

9220　News agencies activities

9230　Library, archives, museums and other cultural activities

9231　Library and archives activities

9232　Museums activities and preservation of historical sites and buildings

9233　Botanical and zoological gardens and nature reserves activities

9240　Sporting and other recreational activities

Appendix I - Industrial Classifications

9241 Sporting activities

9249 Other recreational activities

9300 Other service activities

9301 Washing and (dry-) cleaning of textile and fur products

9302 Hairdressing and other beauty treatment

9303 Funeral and related activities

9309 Other service activities nec

9500 Private households with employed persons

9900 Extra-territorial organizations and bodies

APPENDIX I - INDUSTRIAL CLASSIFICATIONS

HARMONIZED CODE COVERAGE

This appendix lists the Harmonized Code Classifications (HCs). Entries in the body of the book are arranged according to the Standard Industrial Classification (SIC) system of the U.S. Department of Commerce. Products may be located using either the SIC Coverage listing beginning on page 1091 or the Products, Services, and Issues Index beginning on page 971.

01	Live animals
02	Meat and edible meat offal
03	Fish and crustaceans, mollusks and other aquatic invertebrates
04	Dairy produce; birds' eggs; natural honey, edible products of animal origin, not elsewhere specified or included
05	Products of animal origin, not elsewhere specified or included
06	Live trees and other plants; bulbs, roots, and the like; cut flowers and ornamental foliage
07	Edible vegetables and certain roots and tubers
08	Edible fruits and nuts; peel of citrus fruits or melons
09	Coffee, tea, mate, and spices
10	Cereals
11	Products of the milling industry; malt; starches; insulin; wheat gluten
12	Oil seeds and oleaginous fruits; miscellaneous grains, seeds, and fruits; industrial or medicinal plants; straw and fodder
13	Lac; gums, resins and other vegetable saps and extract
14	Vegetable plaiting materials; vegetable products not elsewhere specified or included
15	Animal or vegetable fats and oils and their cleavage products; prepared edible fats; animal or vegetable waxes
16	Preparation of meat, of fish, or of crustaceans, mollusks, or other aquatic invertebrates
17	Sugars and sugar confectionery
18	Cocoa and cocoa preparations
19	Preparations of cereals, flour, starch or milk; bakers' wares
20	Preparations of vegetables, fruits, nuts, or other parts of plants
21	Miscellaneous edible preparations

22	Beverages, spirits, and vinegar
23	Residues and waste from the food industries; prepared animal feed
24	Tobacco and manufactured tobacco substitutes
25	Salt; sulfur; earths and stone; plastering materials, lime and cement
26	Ores, slag, and ash
27	Mineral fuels, mineral oils and products of their distillation; bituminous substances; mineral waxes
28	Inorganic chemicals; organic or inorganic compounds of precious metals, of rare-earth metals, of radioactive elements, or of isotopes
29	Organic chemicals
30	Pharmaceutical products
31	Fertilizers
32	Tanning or dyeing extracts; tannins and their derivatives; dyes, pigments, and other coloring matter; paints and varnishes; putty and other mastics; inks
33	Essential oils and resinoids; perfumery, cosmetic or toilet preparations
34	Soaps; organic surface-active agents; washing preparations; lubricating preparations; artificial waxes; prepared waxes; polishing or scouring preparations; candles and similar articles; modeling pastes; "dental waxes," and dental preparations with a basis of plaster
35	Albuminoidal substances; modified starches; glues; enzymes
36	Explosives; pyrotechnic products; matches; pyrotechnic alloys; certain combustible preparations
37	Photographic or cinematographic goods
38	Miscellaneous chemical products
39	Plastics and articles thereof
40	Rubber and articles thereof
41	Raw hides and skins (other than furskins) and leather

42	Articles of leather; saddlery and harness; travel goods, handbags and similar containers; articles of animal gut (other than silkworm gut)
43	Furskins and artificial fur; manufactures thereof
44	Wood and articles of wood; wood charcoal
45	Cork and articles of cork
46	Manufacturers of stray, of esparto or of other plaiting materials; basketware and wickerwork
47	Pulp of wood or of other fibrous cellulosic material; waste and scrap of paper or paperboard
48	Paper and paperboard; articles of paper pulp, of paper, or of paperboard
49	Printed books, newspapers, pictures, and other products of the printing industry; manuscripts, typescripts, and plans
50	Silk
51	Wool; fine or coarse animal hair; horsehair yarn and woven fabric
52	Cotton
53	Other vegetable textile fibers; paper yarn and woven fabrics of paper yarn
54	Man-made filaments
55	Man-made staple fibers
56	Wadding, felt and nonwovens; special yarns; twine, cordage, ropes and cables and articles thereof
57	Carpets and other textile floor coverings
58	Special woven fabrics; tufted textile fabrics; lace; tapestries; trimmings; embroidery
59	Impregnated, coated, covered or laminated textile fabrics; textile articles of a kind suitable for industrial use
60	Knitted or crocheted fabrics
61	Articles of apparel and clothing accessories, knitted or crocheted
62	Articles of apparel and clothing accessories, not knitted or crocheted
63	Other made-up textile articles; needle craft sets; worn clothing and worn textile articles; rags
64	Footwear, gaiters and the like; parts of such articles
65	Headgear and parts thereof
66	Umbrellas, sun umbrellas, walking sticks, seatsticks, whips, riding crops and parts thereof
67	Prepared feathers and down and articles made of feathers or of down; artificial flowers; articles of human hair
68	Articles of stone, plaster, cement, asbestos, mica or similar materials
69	Ceramic products

70	Glass and glassware
71	Natural or cultured pearls, precious or semiprecious stones, precious metals; metals clad with precious metal, and articles thereof; imitation jewelry; coin
72	Iron and steel
73	Articles of iron or steel
74	Copper and articles thereof
75	Nickel and articles thereof
76	Aluminum and articles thereof
77	Reserved for possible future use
78	Lead and articles thereof
79	Zinc and articles thereof
80	Tin and articles thereof
81	Other base metals; cermets; articles thereof
82	Tools, implements, cutlery, spoons and forks, of base metal; parts thereof of base metal
83	Miscellaneous articles of base metal
84	Nuclear reactors, boilers, machinery and mechanical appliances; parts thereof
85	Electrical machinery and equipment and parts thereof; sound recorders and reproducers, television image and sound recorders and reproducers, and parts and accessories of such articles
86	Railway or tramway locomotives, rolling stock and parts thereof; railway or tramway track fixtures and fittings and parts thereof; mechanical (including electromechanical) traffic signalling equipment of all kinds
87	Vehicles, other than railway or tramway rolling stock, and parts and accessories thereof
88	Aircraft, spacecraft, and parts thereof
89	Ships, boats, and floating structures
90	Optical, photographic, cinematographic, measuring, checking, precision, medical or surgical instruments and apparatus; parts and accessories thereof
91	Clocks and watches and parts thereof
92	Musical instruments; parts and accessories of such articles
93	Arms and ammunition; parts and accessories thereof
94	Furniture; bedding, mattresses, mattress supports, cushions and similar stuffed furnishings; lamps and lighting fittings, not elsewhere specified or included; illuminated signs; illuminated nameplates and the like; prefabricated buildings
95	Toys, games, and sports equipment; parts and accessories thereof
96	Miscellaneous manufactured articles
97	Works of art, collectors' pieces and antiques

APPENDIX II

ANNOTATED SOURCE LIST

The following listing provides the names, publishers, addresses, telephone and fax numbers (if available), and frequency of publications for the primary sources used in *Market Share Reporter*.

2.5G-3G, IGI Group Inc., 320 Washington Street, Suite 302, Boston, MA 02135, *Telephone:* (617) 782-5033, *Fax:* (617) 782-5735.

20/20 Magazine, Jobson Publishing LLC, 100 Avenue of the Americas, New York, NY 10013-1678, *Telephone:* (212) 274-7000, *Fax:* (212) 431-0500, *Published:* 14x/yr.

A.M. Best Newswire, A. M. Best Company, Inc., Ambest Road, Oldwick, NJ 08858, *Telephone:* (908) 439-2200, *Published:* real-time.

ABSA Bank Quarterly South African Economic Monitor, 2nd Floor, Absa Towers North, 180 Commissioner Street, Johannesburg 2001

The Accountant, Lafferty Publications, IDA Tower, Pearse Street, Dublin 2, Ireland (353-1) 671-8022, *Fax:* (353-1) 671-8520, *Published:* monthly.

Acquisitions Monthly, Thomson Financial, 195 Broadway, New York, NY, 10007, *Telephone:* (646) 822-2000, *Published:* monthly.

Across the Board, The Conference Board, 845 Third Avenue, New York, NY 10022, *Telephone:* (212) 339-0345, *Fax:* (212) 836-9740, *Published:* bimonthly.

AdAge Global, Crain Communications Inc., 711 Third Avenue, New York, NY 10017-4036, *Telephone:* (212) 210-0100, *Fax:* (212) 210-0465, *Published:* daily, *Price:* $99 per year.

Adams Wine Handbook, Adams Beverage Group, 17 High Street 2nd Floor, Norwalk, CT 06851, *Telephone:* (203) 855-8499, *Fax:* (203) 855-9446, *Published:* yearly, *Price:* $545.

Adhesives Age, Crain Communications Inc., 711 Third Avenue, New York, NY 10017-4036, *Telephone:* (212) 210-0414, *Fax:* (212) 210-0200, *Published:* monthly.

Adhesives & Sealants Industry, BNP Media, P.O. Box 936, Lapeer, MI 48446, *Telephone:* (810) 664-0300, *Fax:* (810) 664-0036, *Published:* monthly.

AdMedia, P.O. Box 5544, Wellesley Street, Aukland, New Zealand, *Telephone:* 64-9-630 8940, *Fax:* 64-9-630 1046, *Published:* monthly, *Price:* $196 per year in New Zealand dollars.

Advanced Ceramics Report, International Newsletters, 9A Victoria Aquare, Droitwich, Wores WR9 8DE, United Kingdom, *Telephone:* 44 (0) 870 1657210.

Advanced Coatings & Surface Technology, Freedonia Group, 767 Beta Drive, Cleveland, OH 44143, *Telephone:* (440) 684-9611.

Advanced Manufacturing Technology, 209-3228 South Service Road, Burlington, Ontario Canada L7N 3H8, *Telephone:* (905) 634-2100.

Advertising Age, Crain Communications, Inc., 711 Third Avenue, New York, NY 10017-4036, *Telephone:* (212) 210-0100, *Fax:* (212) 210-0200, *Published:* weekly.

Adweek, VNU Business Publications USA, Inc., 200 Jackson Blvd., Suite 2700, Chicago, IL 60606 *Telephone:* (312) 583-5500, *Fax:* (312) 583-5502, *Published:* weekly.

Aerospace Daily, McGraw-Hill, 1200 G Street, Suite 922, Washington, D.C. 20005, *Telephone:* (609) 426-7070, *Fax:* (609) 426-7087, *Published:* daily.

Africa News, COMTEX, 625 N. Washington St., Suite 301, Alexandria, VA 22314, *Telephone:* (703) 820-2000, *Fax:* (703) 820-2005.

African and Middle East Mobile Communications Report, EMC, Mortimer House, 37/41 Mortimer Street, London, W1T 3JH, United Kingdom, *Telephone:* +44 (0) 207 017 5070, *Fax:* +44 (0) 207 017 5071, *Published:* bimonthly.

African Business, IC Publications, 7 Coldbath Square, London, EC1R 4LQ, *Telephone:* (00 44) (0) 20 7713 7711, *Fax:* (00 44) (0) 20 7713 7970, *Published:* monthly.

Aftenposten, Aftenposten Multimedia A/S, Oslo, Norway, *Telephone*: +47 22 86 30 00, *Published:* daily.

Aftermarket Business, Advanstar Communications, Inc., 7500 Old Oak Blvd., Cleveland, OH 44130-3343, *Published*: monthly.

Ag Lender, Doane Agricultural Services, 11701 Borman Drive, Suite 300, St. Louis, MO 63146-4193, *Telephone:* (314) 372-3520, *Fax:* (314) 569-1083.

AgExporter, U.S. Department of Agriculture, Foreign Agricultural Service, U.S. Government Printing Office, Superintendent of Documents, Stop SSOP, Washington, D.C. 20402-0001, *Telephone:* 1 (866) 512-1800, *Fax:* (202) 512-2250, *Published:* monthly.

Agra Europe, Agra Informa Ltd., 80 Calverley Road, Tunbridge Wells, Kent, TN1 2UN, United Kingdom, *Telephone:* +44 (0) 1892 533813, *Fax:* +44 (0) 1892 544895, *Published:* weekly.

Agri Marketing, Doane Agricultural Services, 11701 Borman Drive, Suite 300, St. Louis, MO 63146-4193, *Telephone:* (314) 569-2700, *Fax:* (314) 569-1083, *Published:* weekly.

Air Cargo World, Commonwealth Business Media, 1270 National Press Building, Washington D.C. 20045, *Telphone*: (202) 661-3387, *Fax:* (202) 783-2550 *Published*: monthly.

Air Conditioning, Heating and Refrigeration News, Business News Publishing Co., 2401 W. Big Beaver Road, Suite 700, Troy, MI 48084, *Telephone:* (248) 362-3700, *Fax:* (248) 362-0317 *Published:* weekly.

Air Transport World, ATW Media Group, 1350 Connecticut Ave. NW, Suite 902, Washington, D.C. 20036, *Telephone:* (202) 659-8500, *Fax:* (202) 223-1979. *Published:* monthly.

Airline Business, Reed Business Information, Quadrant House, Sutton, Surrey, SM2 5AS, United Kingdom, *Telephone:* +44 20 8652 4996, *Fax:* +44 20 8652 3814. *Published:* monthly.

Airline Financial News, PBI Media, 1201 Seven Locks Road, Suite 300, Potomac, MD 20854, *Telephone:* (301) 354-2000, *Fax:* (301) 309-3847, *Published:* biweekly.

The Albuquerque Tribune, P.O. Drawer T, 7777 Jefferson NE, Albuquerque, NM 87103, *Telephone:* (505) 823-7777, *Fax:* (505) 823-3689, *Published:* daily.

Alternative Investment News, New York, NY, *Telephone:* 1 (800) 715-9195.

America's Intelligence Wire, FT Publications Inc., 14 East 60th Street, New York, NY 21002, *Telephone:* (212) 752-4500, *Fax:* (212) 319-0704.

American Banker, The Thomson Corporation and American Banker, 1 State Street Plaza, New York, NY 10004, *Telephone:* (212) 803-8200, *Fax:* (212) 843-9600, *Published:* Mon. - Fri., *Price:* $895 per year.

American Ceramic Society Bulletin, American Ceramic Society, P.O. Box 6136, Westerville, OH 43086-6136, *Published:* monthly, *Price:* $75 per year for North American subscribers, $131 per year for international subscribers.

American Demographics, Primedia Business Magazines & Media, P.O. Box 2042, Marion, OH 43306-8142, *Telephone:* 1 1 (800) 529-7502, *Published:* monthly.

American Fruit Grower, Meister Publishing Company, 37733 Euclid Avenue, Willoughby, OH 44094-5992, *Published:* monthly, *Price:* $19.95 per year.

American Lawyer, 105 Madison Avenue, 7th Floor, New York, NY 10016, *Telephone:* 1 (800) 888-8300, *Fax:* (212) 481-8255, *Published:* monthly, *Price:* $298 per year in U.S.; $350 per year internationally.

American School & University, Primedia Business Magazines & Media, 2104 Harvell Circle, Bellevue, NE 68005,

Telephone: 1 (866) 505-7173, *Fax:* (402) 293-0741, *Published:* monthly.

American Shipper, Howard Publications Inc., 33 West Adams Street, Suite 600, P.O. Box 4728, Jacksonville, FL 32201, *Telephone:* (904) 365-2601. *Published:* monthly, *Price:* $60 per year; $5 per single copy.

American/Western Fruit Grower, Meister Media Worldwide, 37733 Euclid Avenue, Willoughby, OH 44094, *Telephone:* (440) 942-2000, *Fax:* (440) 942-0662.

Amusement Business, VNU eMedia Inc., 5055 Wilshire Blvd., Suite 600, Los Angeles, CA 90036, *Telephone:* (323) 525-2350, *Published:* weekly, *Price:* $129 per year.

Annuity Market News, The Thomson Corporation and Annuity Market News, 1 State Street Plaza, 27th Floor, New York, NY 10004, *Telephone:* (212) 803-8200, *Published:* monthly, *Price:* $1,100 per year in the U.S.; $1,200 per year internationally.

Apparel, VNU eMedia, Inc., 1500 Hampton Street, Suite 150, Columbia, SC 29201, *Telephone:* 1 (800) 845-8820, *Fax:* (803) 799-1461, *Published:* monthly.

Appliance, Dana Chase Publications Inc., 1110 Jorie Blvd., CS 9019, Oak Brook, IL 60522-9019, *Telephone:* (630) 990-3484, *Fax:* (630) 990-0078, *Published:* monthly.

Appliance Manufacturer, BNP Media, 5900 Harper Rd., Suite 105, Solon, OH 44139-1835, *Telephone:* (440) 349-3060, *Fax:* (440) 498-9121, *Published:* monthly.

Applied Clinical Trials Supplement, 859 Williamette St., Eugene OR 97401, *Telephone:* (541) 343-1200.

Appraisal Journal, Appraisal Institute, 550 West Van Buren Street, Suite 1000, Chicago, IL 60607, *Telephone:* (312) 335-4100, *Fax:* (312) 335-4400, *Published:* quarterly, *Price:* in US, $48 per year for nonmembers, $100 per year for libraries; in other countries, $90 per year for nonmembers, $140 per year for libraries.

Arable Farming, Ludgate House, 245 Blackfriars Road, London SE1 9UY.

Architectural Record, McGraw-Hill, Two Penn Plaza, New York, NY 10121-2288, *Telephone:* (212) 904-8594, *Fax:* (212) 904-4256.

Arizona Daily Star, 4850 South Park Avenue, Tucson, AZ 85714, *Telephone:* (520) 573-4511, *Published:* daily.

Arizona Republic, 200 East Van Buren Street, Phoenix, AZ 85004, *Telephone:* (602) 444-8000, *Published:* daily.

Arkansas Business, 201 E. Markham, P.O. Box 3686, Little Rock, AR 72203, *Telephone:* (501) 372-1443 Fax: (501) 375-7933, *Published:* weekly.

Asia Africa Intelligence Wire, FT Publications Inc., 14 East 60th Street, New York, NY 21002, *Telephone:* (212) 752-4500, *Fax:* (212) 319-0704.

Asia Pacific Intelligence Wire, FT Publications Inc., 14 East 60th Street, New York, NY 21002, *Telephone:* (212) 752-4500, *Fax:* (212) 319-0704.

Asia Pulse, Level 7, The AAP Centre, Locked Bag 21, Grosvenor Plaza, Sydney NSW 2000, Australia, *Telephone:* 61-2-9322-8634, *Fax:* 61-2-9322-8639, *Published:* real-time.

Asian Pacific Coatings Journal, Business Media, Queensway House, 2 Queensway, Redhill Surrey RH1 1QS, *Telephone:* (44) 1737 768-611, *Fax:* (44) 1737 855-477.

The Aspen Times, 310 East Main Street, Aspen, CO 81611, *Telephone:* (970) 925-3414, *Fax:* (970) 925-6240, *Published:* daily.

Assembly, BNP Media, 1050 Illinois Route 83, Suite 200, Bensenville, IL 60106-1096, *Telephone:* (630) 616-0200, *Fax:* (630) 227-0204.

Atlanta Business Chronicle, American City Business Journals, Inc., 1801 Peachtree Street, Suite 150, Atlanta, GA 30309, *Telephone:* (404) 249-1000, *Fax:* (404) 249-1048, *Published:* weekly, *Price:* $87 per year.

Atlanta Journal-Constitution, 72 Marietta St., NW Atlanta, GA 30303, *Telephone:* (404) 526 - 5151, *Published:* daily.

ATM & Debit News, One State Street Plaza, New York, NY 10004, *Telephone:* (800) 221-1809, *Fax:* (800) 235-5552.

Austin Chronicle, P.O. Box 49066, Austin, TX 78765, *Telephone:* (512) 454-5766, *Fax:* (512) 458-6910, *Published:* daily.

Australasian Business Intelligence, Level 2, 627 Chapel Street, South Yarra, VIC, 3141, *Telephone:* 03 9856 3900, *Fax:* 03 9856 3999.

The Australian, 2 Holt Street, Surrey Hills, NSW 2010, Australia, *Telephone:* (02) 9288 3000, *Fax:* (02) 9288 2250, *Published:* daily.

Auto Body Repair News, Advanstar Communications, 100 Monroe Street, Suite 1100, Chicago, IL 60603, *Telephone:* (312) 553-8900, *Fax:* (312) 553-8926, *Published:* monthly.

Auto Rental News, 3250 Challenger Street, Torrance, CA 90503, *Telephone:* 1 (888) 274-4580, *Fax:* (847) 647-8064.

Automatic Merchandiser, Johnson Hill Press Inc., 1233 Janesville Ave., Fort Atkinson, WI 53538, *Telephone:* (414) 563-6388, *Fax:* (414) 563-1699, *Published:* monthly.

Automotive Industries, 24901 Northwestern Highway, Suite 505, Southfield, MI 48075, *Telephone:* (248) 350-8199, *Fax:* (248) 350-2692, *Published:* monthly.

Automotive News, Crain Communications Inc., 1155 Gratiot Avenue, Detroit, MI 48207-2997, *Telephone:* (313) 446-6031, *Fax:* (313) 446-8030.

Automotive News Europe, Crain Communications Inc., Carbery, Mount Pleasant, Hartley, Wintney Hampshire, RG27 8PW, United Kingdom, *Telephone:* +44 1252 844 403, *Fax:* +44 1252 849 527.

Automotive News Fact Book, Crain Communications Inc., 1155 Gratiot Avenue, Detroit, MI 48207-2997, *Telephone:* (313) 446-6031, *Fax:* (313) 446-8030.

AVG, Meister Publishing Co., 37733 Euclid Ave., Willoughby, OH 44094-5992, *Telephone:* (216) 942-2000, *Fax:* (216) 942-0662, *Published:* monthly.

Aviation Daily, McGraw Hill Inc., 1200 G Street N.W., Suite 900, Washington, D.C., 20005, *Telephone:* (202) 383-2374, *Fax:* (202) 383-2438, *Published:* daily.

Aviation Week & Space Technology, McGraw Hill Inc., 1200 G Street N.W., Suite 900, Washington D.C., 20005, *Telephone:* (202) 383-2374, *Fax:* (202) 383-2438, *Published:* weekly.

B&T Weekly, Tower 2, 475 Victoria Avenue, Chatswood, NSW 2067, Australia, *Telephone:* +61 2 9422 2999, *Fax:* +61 2 9422 2949.

Baking & Snack, Sosland Publishing Co., 4800 Main St., Ste 100, Kansas City, MO 64112, *Telephone:* (816) 756-1000, *Fax:* (816) 756-0494, *Published:* monthly.

Baltimore Sun, 501 N. Calvert Street, P.O. Box 1377, Baltimore, MD 21278, *Telephone:* (410) 332-6000, *Published:* daily.

Bangkok Post, Post Publishing Company Ltd., Bankok Post Building, 136 Na Ranong Road, Klong Toey, Bangkok, Thailand 10110, *Telephone:* (662) 240-3700, *Fax:* (662) 671-3174, *Published:* daily.

Bank Marketing International, Lafferty Group, The Colonnades, 82, Bishops Bridge Road, London, England W2 6BB, *Telephone:* +44 (0) 207 563 5700, *Fax:* +44 (0) 207 563 5701.

Bank Technology News, Thomson Media, 1 State Street Plaza, 27th Floor, New York, NY 10004, *Telephone:* (212) 803-8200, *Published:* monthly.

The Banker, Financial Times Business Ltd., Tabernacle Court, 16-28 Tabernacle Street, London EC2A 4OD, *Telephone:* +44 (0) 20 7382 8000, *Published:* monthly, *Price:* $352 per year.

Baseline, 520 Broadway Street, Suite 230, Santa Monica, CA 90401, *Telephone:* (310) 393-9999, *Fax:* (310) 393-7799.

Batteries International, Euromoney Publications LLC, Euromoney Institutional Investor Plc, Nestor House, Playhouse Yard, London, England EC4U 5EX, *Published:* quarterly, *Price:* $175 US dollars per year.

Battery & EV Technology, Business Communications Company, Inc., 25 Van Zant Street, Norwalk, CT 06855-1781, *Telephone:* (203) 853-4266, *Fax:* (203) 853-0348.

Best Wire, A.M. Best Co. Inc., Ambest Rd., Oldwick, NJ 08858, *Telephone:* (908) 439-2200, *Published:* monthly.

Best's Review, A.M. Best Co. Inc., Ambest Rd., Oldwick, NJ 08858, *Telephone:* (908) 439-2200, *Published:* monthly.

Beverage Aisle, VNU Business Publications USA, Inc., 770 Broadway, New York, NY 10003, *Telephone:* (646) 654-5000, *Published:* monthly.

Beverage Dynamics, Adams Beverage Group, 17 High Street, 2nd Floor, Norwalk, CT 06851, *Telephone:* (203) 855-8499, *Fax:* (203) 855-9446, *Published:* bimonthly.

Beverage Industry, Stagnito Communications, 155 Pfingsten Road, Suite 205, Deerfield, IL 60015, *Telephone:* (847) 205-5660, *Fax:* (847) 205-5680, *Published:* monthly.

Beverage World, VNU Business Publications USA, Inc., 770 Broadway, New York, NY 10003, *Telephone:* (847) 763-9050, *Fax:* (847) 763-9037, *Published:* monthly.

Bicycle Retailer & Industry News, VNU Business Publications USA, Inc., 25431 Cabot Road, Suite 204, Laguna Hills, CA 92653, *Telephone:* (949) 206-1677, *Fax:* (949) 206-1675, *Published:* monthly.

Billboard, VNU Business Publications USA, Inc., 770 Broadway, New York, NY 10003, *Telephone:* (847) 763-9050, *Fax:* (847) 763-9037.

Birmingham Business Journal, 2140 11th Avenue South, Suite 205, Birmingham, AL 35205, *Telephone:* (205) 443-5600, *Fax:* (205) 322-0040, *Published:* weekly.

The Birmingham Post, Trinity Mirror Plc, One Canada Square, Canary Wharf, London E14 5AP, *Telephone:* 0121 236 3366.

The Blade, The Toledo Blade Company, 541 N. Superior St., Toledo, OH 43660, *Telephone:* (419) 724-6000, *Published*: daily.

Boersen, P.O. Box 11 09 32, 60044 Frankfort am Main, Dusseldorf Strabe 16, 60329.

Bond Buyer, Thomson Media, 1 State Street Plaza, 27th Floor, New York, NY 10004, *Telephone:* 1 (800) 221-1809, *Publication:* daily, *Price:* $1,997 per year.

The Bookseller, VNU Business Media Inc., Fifth Floor, Endeavor House, 189 Shaftesbury Avenue, London WC2H

8TJ, United Kingdom, *Telephone:* +44 (0) 20 7420 6006, *Fax:* +44 (0) 20 7420 6103, *Published:* weekly.

Boston Globe, The New York Times Company, 135 Morrissey Blvd., Boston, MA 02125, *Telephone:* (617) 929-2000, *Published:* daily.

Boston Herald, One Herald Square, P.O. Box 2096, Boston, MA 02106, *Telephone:* (617) 426-3000, *Published:* daily.

BP Report, 535 Madison Avenue, New York, NY 10022, *Telephone:* (212) 421-5010.

Brand Strategy, *Telephone*: +44 (0)20 7943 8173, *Published:* monthly.

Brandweek, VNU Business Publications USA, Inc., 770 Broadway, New York, NY 10003, *Telephone:* (646) 654-5000, *Published:* weekly, except no issue in the last week of Dec.

Broadcasting & Cable, Reed Business Information, 360 Park Avenue South, New York, NY 10010, *Telephone:* (646) 746-6400.

Broadcasting & Cable's TV International, Baskerville Communications Corp., 2455 Teller Rd., Thousand Oaks, CA 91320, *Published:* 24x/yr., *Price:* $495 per year.

The Budapest Sun, Northcliffe Newspapers, 1122 Budapest, Maros utca 12 Il. em., Telephone: (36-1) 489-4343, Fax: (36-1) 489-4344.

The Buffalo News, One News Plaza, PO Box 100, Buffalo, NY 14240, *Telephone:* (716) 842-1111, *Published:* daily.

Builder, Hanley-Wood LLC., One Thomas Circle, N.W., Suite 600, Washington, D.C. 20005, *Telephone:* (202) 452-0800, *Fax:* (202) 785-1974, *Published:* monthly.

Building Design & Construction, Reed Business Information, 2000 Clearwater Drive, Oak Brook, IL 60523, *Telephone:* (630) 288-8081, *Published:* monthly.

Building Products, Hanley-Wood LLC., One Thomas Circle, N.W., Suite 600, Washington, D.C. 20005, *Telephone:* (202) 452-0800, *Fax:* (202) 785-1974, *Published:* monthly.

The Burlington Free Press, Gannett Foundation, P.O. Box 10, Burlington, VT 05402, *Telephone:* (802) 863 3441, *Published:* daily.

Business & Commercial Aviation, McGraw-Hill, 1200 G Street, Suite 922, Washington, D.C. 20005, *Telephone:* (609) 426-7070, *Fax:* (609) 426-7087.

Business 2.0, One California Street, 29th Floor, San Francisco, CA, 94111.

Business Daily Update, *Published:* daily.

Business India, Living Media India, Connaught Place, New Delhi, India 11001, *Published:* weekly.

The Business Journal (Minneapolis-St. Paul), 527 Marquette Avenue, Suite 300, Minneapolis, MN 55402, *Telephone:* (612) 288-2100, *Fax:* (612) 288-2121.

The Business Journal of Portland, 851 SW Sixth Avenue #500, Portland, OR 97204, *Telephone:* (503) 274-8733, *Fax:* (503) 227-2650.

The Business Journal of the Greater Triad Area, 100 South Elm Street, Suite 400, Greensboro, NC 27401, *Telephone:* (336) 271-6539, *Fax:* (336) 574-3607.

Business Mexico, American Chamber of Commerce, A.C., Lucerna 78, Col. Juarez, DEL. Cuahtemoc, Mexico City, Mexico, *Telephone:* 705-0995, *Published:* monthly.

Business Record (Des Moines), 100 4th Street, Des Moines IA 50309, *Telephone:* (515) 288-3336, *Fax:* (515) 288-0309, *Published:* weekly.

Business Report, P.O. Box 1014, Johannesburg, South Africa, 2000, *Telephone:* +27 21 488 4911, *Published:* daily.

Business Review Weekly, Fairfax Business Media, GPO Box 55A, Melbourne, Australia 3001 VIC, *Telephone:* +61 3 9603 3888, *Fax:* +61 3 9603 3898, *Published:* weekly.

Business Standard, Nehru House, 4 Bahadur Shah Zafar Marg, New Delhi 11000 *Published:* daily.

Business Today, Living Media India Ltd., Hamilton House, 1-A Connaught Place, New Delhi 110001, India *Telephone:* 3352233, Ext. 165, 173, 179, *Fax:* 3352874.

Business Travel News, VNU Business Publications USA, Inc., 770 Broadway, New York, NY 10003, *Telephone:* (646) 654-4500.

BusinessWeek, McGraw-Hill Inc., 1221 Avenue of the Americas, New York, NY 10020. *Published:* weekly, *Price:* $45.97 per year in the U.S.; $94.95 CDN per year.

BusinessWeek Online, McGraw-Hill Inc., 1221 Avenue of the Americas, New York, NY 10020. *Published:* weekly.

Business Wire, 44 Montgomery Street, 39th Floor, San Francisco, CA 94104, *Telephone:* (415) 986-4422, *Published:* daily.

BusinessWorld, BusinessWorld Publishing Corp., 95 Balete Drive Extension, New Manila, Quezon City, *Telephone:* 727-0091 to 97, 411-0268 to 85, *Published:* weekdays.

Buyouts, Thomson Financial, 395 Hudson Street, 3rd Floor, New York, NY 10014, *Telephone:* 1 (888) 605-3385, *Fax:* (917) 408-5276.

Buyside, Adams Business Media, P.O. Box 320, Sonoma, CA 95476, *Telephone:* (707) 933-2800, *Fax:* (707) 933-2820.

C&EN, American Chemical Society, 1155 16th Street N.W., Washington, D.C., *Telephone:* (202) 872-4600, *Fax:* (202) 872-8127, *Published:* weekly, except last week in December.

Cabinet Maker, 1350 E. Touhy Avenue, Suite 105W, Des Plaines, IL 60018, *Telephone:* (847) 390-6700, *Fax:* (847) 390-7100.

CableWorld, PBI Media, LLC, 1201 Seven Locks Road, Suite 300, Potomac, MD 20854, *Telephone:* (301) 354-2000, *Published:* bimonthly.

Canadian Business, Rogers Media Inc., 1 Mount Pleasant Road, 11th Floor, Toronto, Ontario, Canada, M4Y 2Y5, *Telephone:* (416) 764-1200, *Price:* signature service, $34.95 for 26 issues; basic rate, $39.95; USA surface mail, $64.95 CDN; International air mail, $129.95 CDN.

Canadian Corporate News, 48 Yonge Street, 8th Floor, Toronto, Ontario, Canada M5E 1G6, *Telephone:* (416) 362-0885, *Fax:* (416) 362-6669.

Canadian Electronics, CLB Media Inc., 240 Edward Street, Aurora, Ontario, Canada L4G 3S9, *Telephone:* (905) 727-0077, *Fax:* (905) 727-0017.

Canadian Machinery and Metalworking, Rogers Media Inc., 1 Mount Pleasant Road, 7th Floor, Toronto, Ontario, Canada, M4Y 2Y5, *Fax:* (416) 764-1735 *Published:* monthly.

Canadian Packaging, Rogers Media Inc., 1 Mount Pleasant Road, 7th Floor, Toronto, Ontario, Canada, M4Y 2Y5, *Fax:* (416) 764-1755, *Published:* monthly.

Candy Business, Adams Business Media, 833 West Jackson, 7th Floor, Chicago, IL 60607, *Telephone:* (312) 846-4600, *Fax:* (312) 977-1042, *Published:* monthly.

Candy Industry, Stagnito Communications, 155 Pfingsten Road, Suite 205, Deerfield, IL 60015, *Telephone:* (847) 205-5660 Ext. 4039, *Fax:* (847) 205-5680, *Published:* monthly.

Capital Times, 1901 Fish Hatchery Road, Madison, WI 53708, *Telephone:* (608) 252-6400, *Fax:* (608) 252-6445, *Published:* daily, *Price:* $214.90 per year in Dane County, Wisconsin, $301.35 pcr year elsewhere in Wisconsin, $447.20 per year elsewhere in the U.S.

Cardiovascular Week, 2900 Paces Ferry Road, Atlanta GA 30339, *Telephone:* (770) 507-7777.

Cardline, Thomson Media, 1 State Street Plaza, 27th Floor, New York, NY 10004, *Telephone*: 1 (800) 221-1809.

Cards International, Faulkner & Grey, 11 Penn Plaza, New York, NY 10001.

Caribbean Business, Casiano Communications Inc., 1700 Avenue Fernández Juncos, San Juan, PR 00909-2938, *Telephone:* (787) 728-3000, *Fax:* (787) 268-1001, *Published:* weekly.

Carpets & Floorcovering Review, PPA, Queens House, 28 Kingsway, London WC2B 6JR, *Telephone*: 020 7400 7540.

Catalog Age, Primedia Business Magazines & Media, 11 River Bend Drive South, P.O. Box 4242, Stamford, CT 06907-0242, *Fax:* (203) 358-5823, *Published:* 13x/yr.

Caterer & Housekeeper, Quadrant House, The Quadrant, Sutton, Surrey, United Kingdom SM2 5AS, *Telephone:* 020 8652 3221, *Published:* weekly.

CED, Reed Business Information, 8778 S. Barrons Blvd., Highlands Ranch, CO 80129-2345, *Telephone:* (303) 470-4800, *Fax:* (303) 470-4890.

Ceramic Industry, BNP Media, 6075 B Glick Rd., Powell, OH 43065, *Telephone:* (614) 789-1880, *Fax:* (614) 760-5922, *Published:* monthly.

CFO, 111 W. 57th Street, 12th Floor, New York, NY 10019, *Telephone:* (212) 459-3004, *Fax:* (212) 459-3007.

Chain Drug Review, Racher Press, 220 5th Ave, New York, NY 10001, *Telephone:* (212) 213-6000, *Fax*: (212) 725-3961, *Published:* 21x/yr.

Chain Leader, Reed Business Information, 2000 Clearwater Drive, Oak Brook, IL 60523, *Telephone:* (630) 288-8242, *Fax:* (630) 288-8215, *Published:* monthly.

Chain Store Age, 425 Park Avenue, New York, NY 10022, *Telephone:* 1 (800) 216-7117, *Published:* monthly.

Charlotte Business Journal, 120 W Morehead St., Suite 200, Charlotte, NC 28202, *Telephone:* (704) 973-1100, *Fax:* (704) 973-1102, *Published:* weekly, *Price:* $78 for 1 year, $130 for 2 years, $175 for 3 years.

Chemical Market Reporter, Reed Business Information, Quadrant House, The Quadrant, Sutton, Surrey, United Kingdom SM2 5AS, *Telephone:* 020 8652 3500, *Fax:* 020 8652 8932, *Published:* weekly.

Chemical Week, Chemical Week Associates, 110 William Street, New York, NY 10038, *Telephone:* (212) 621-4900, *Fax:* (212) 621-4800, *Published:* weekly, except four combination issues (total of 49 issues), *Price:* $159 per year in the U.S.; $180 per year in Canada.

Chemist & Druggist, Pharmacy United Kingdom, *Telephone:* 00 377-97704175.

Chicago Tribune, 435 N. Michigan Ave., Chicago, IL 60611, *Telephone:* 1 (800) 874-2863. *Published:* daily.

Chief Executive, 110 Summit Avenue, Montvale, NJ 07645, *Telephone:* (201) 930-5959, *Fax:* (201) 930-5956, *Published:* monthly.

Child Care Information Exchange, Exchange Press Inc., P.O. 3249, Redmond, WA 98073, *Telephone:* (425) 883-9394, *Fax:* (425) 867-5217, *Published:* bimonthly, *Price:* $38 per year.

Children's Business, Fairchild Publications, 7 W 34th St., New York, NY 10001, *Telephone:* (212) 630-4520, *Fax:* (212) 630-4511, *Published:* bimonthly.

China Business Review, China Business Forum, 1818 N St., NW Ste 500, Washington D.C. 20036, *Telephone:* (202) 429-0340, *Fax:* (202) 833-9027, *Published:* bimonthly.

China Economic Review, SinoMedia Ltd., Units C & D, 9/F., Neich Tower, 128 Gloucester Road, Wanchai, Hong Kong, *Telephone:* +86 21 5385-8955, *Published:* monthly.

China Telecom, 31, Jinrong Street Xicheng District, Beijing, China, 100032, *Telephone:* 86-10-58501688, *Fax:* 86-10-58501060.

Chinese Markets for Cement Additives, Asia Market Information & Development Company, *Published:* annually.

Chinese Markets for Coated Fabrics, Asia Market Information & Development Company, *Published:* annually.

Chinese Markets for Home Office Furniture, Asia Market Information & Development Company, *Published:* annually.

Chinese Markets for Laundry Care Products, Asia Market Information & Development Company, *Published:* annually.

Chinese Markets for Printers, Asia Market Information & Development Company, *Published:* annually.

The Christian Science Monitor, Christian Science Publishing Society, One Norway St., Boston, MA 02115, *Telephone:* (617) 450-2000, *Published:* daily, except weekends and holidays.

Cincinnati Enquirer, 50 Broad Street, Suite 1130a, Columbus, OH 43215, *Telephone:* (614) 224-4640.

The Cincinnati Post, E.W. Scripps Co., 125 E Court St., Suite 500, Cincinnati, OH 45202, *Telephone:* (513) 352-2000, *Fax:* (513) 621-3962.

Circuits Assembly, UP Media Group, P.O. Box 35646, Tulsa, OK 74153-0646, *Fax:* (918) 496-9465.

CircuiTree, BNP Media, 755 West Big Beaver, Ste 100, Troy, MI 48084, *Telephone:* (248) 362-3700.

Client Server News, G2 Computer Intelligence, 323 Glen Cove, Sea Cliff, NY 11579, *Telephone:* (516) 759-7025, *Fax:* (516) 759-7025, *Published:* weekly.

Club Industry, Intertec Publishing, 9800 Metcalf Avenue, Overland Park, KS 66282, *Telephone:* (913) 967-1300, *Published:* monthly.

CNET Asia, CNET Networks Asia Pacific Ptc Ltd., 8 Shenton Way, #15-02, Temasek Tower, Singapore 068811, *Telephone:* (65) 6227 5755, *Fax:* (65) 6224 5755.

Coatings World, 70 Hilltop Road, Ramsey, NJ 07466, *Telephone:* (201) 825-2552, *Fax:* (201) 825-0553.

Colorado Springs Business Journal, 31 E. Platte Avenue, Suite 300, Colorado Springs, CO 80903.

Columbus Business First, 303 West Nationwide Blvd., Columbus, OH 43215, *Telephone:* (614) 461-4040, *Fax:* (614) 365-2780, *Published:* weekly, *Price:* $86 per year.

Columbus Dispatch, 34 S. Third St., Columbus, OH 43215, *Telephone:* (614) 461-5000, *Published:* daily.

Commercial Appeal, E. W. Scripps, 425 Union Ave., Memphis, TN, *Telephone:* (901) 529-2666.

Commercial Carrier Journal, Capital Cities/ABC/Chilton Co., Chilton Way, Radnor, PA 19089, *Telephone:* (215) 964-4000, *Fax:* (215) 964-4981.

Commercial Motor, Reed Business Information, 360 Park Avenue South, New York, NY 10010, *Telephone:* (646) 746-6400.

Commercial Property News, VNU Business Publications USA, Inc., 770 Broadway, New York, NY 10003, *Telephone:* (646) 654-5000.

Communications & Electronic Report, Interfax, Denver, CO *Telephone:* (303) 368-1421, *Fax:* (303) 368-1458.

Community Pharmacy, CMP Information, Sovereign House, Sovereign Way, Tunbridge, Kent, United Kingdom TW9 1RW, *Telephone:* 01732 377269, *Fax:* 01732 377538.

Company Van, DMG World Media, 2141 West Orangewood Ave, building 8 Suite B, Orange, CA 92868, *Telephone:* (714) 978-8888, *Fax:* (800) 442-7469.

Computer Graphics World, PennWell, 98 Spit Brook Rd, Nashua, NH 03062, *Telephone:* (603) 891-0123, *Published:* monthly.

Computer Reseller News, CMP Media, One Jericho Plaza, Jericho, NY 11753, *Published:* weekly, *Price:* $199 per year in the U.S.; $224 per year in Canada.

Computer Workstations, Worldwide Videotex, *published:* monthly.

Computergram International, ComputerWire Inc., 150 Post Street, Suite 520, San Francisco, CA 94108, *Telephone:* (415) 274-8290, *Fax:* (415) 274-8281, *Published:* 5 times a week.

Computerwoche, Brabanter Str. 4, 80805 Munchen, *Telephone:* (089) 36086-175 (-170), *Fax:* (089) 36086-175 (-170).

Computerworld, 500 Old Connecticut Path, Framingham, MA 01701, *Telephone:* (508) 879-0700, *Published:* weekly.

Concrete Construction, Hanley-Wood LLC, One Thomas Circle NW, Suite 600, Washington D.C. 20005, *Telephone:* (202) 452-0800, *Fax:* (202) 785-1974, *Published:* monthly.

Concrete Products, Primedia Business Magazines & Media, 29 N Wacker Drive, Chicago, IL 60606, *Telephone:* (312) 609-4296, *Fax:* (913) 514-36107.

Construction Equipment, Reed Business Information, 2000 Clearwater Drive, Oak Brook, IL 60523-8809, *Telephone:* (630) 288-8141.

Consumers' Research Magazine, *Published:* monthly.

Contract Flooring Journal, 102 Queens Road, Tunbridge Wells, Kent, United Kingdom TN4 9JU, *Telephone:* +44 (0) 1892 680816, *Fax:* +44 (0) 1892 543046, *Published:* monthly.

Contract Journal, Reed Business Information, Quadrant House, Sutton, Surrey, SM2 5AS, United Kingdom.

Contractor's Business Management Report, Institute of Management and Administration, 3 Park Avenue, 30th Floor, New York, NY 10016, *Telephone:* (212) 244-0360, *Fax:* (212) 564-0465, *Published:* monthly, *Price:* $269 per year.

Convenience Store News, VNU Business Publications USA, Inc., 770 Broadway, New York, NY 10003, *Telephone:* (847) 763-9050, *Fax:* (847) 763-9037, *Published:* 15x/yr.

Converting Magazine, Reed Business Information, 2000 Clearwater Drive, Oak Brook, IL 60523, *Telephone:* (630) 288-8530, *Fax:* (630) 288-8536, *Published:* monthly.

Corn and Soybean Digest, Primedia Business Magazines & Media, 7900 International Drive, Suite 300, Minneapolis, MN, *Telephone:* (952) 851-9329, *Fax:* (952) 851-4601, *Published:* 11x/yr.

Cosmetics & Toiletries Household Products Marketing News in Japan, Pacific Research Consulting, Oskar Consulting, 862 Manor Way, Los Altos, CA 94024, *Telephone:* (650) 625-1780, *Fax:* (650) 625 - 1779.

Cosmetics International, 307 Linen Hall, 162/168 Regent Street, London, W1R 5TB, *Telephone:* (020) 7434-1530, *Fax:* (020) 7437-0915.

Cosmetics Magazine, Rogers Media, One Mount Pleasant Road, 7th fl, Toronto, Ontario, Canada.

Country Reports, Central European Business Ltd., *Telephone:* 44 (0) 171 209 2369, *Published:* 4x/yr.

Country ViewsWire, Economist Intelligence Unit, 15 Regent Street, London, SW1Y 4LR, *Telephone:* +44 (0) 20 7830 1007, *Fax:* +44 (0) 20 7830 1023, *Published:* daily.

Crain's Chicago Business, Crain Communications Inc., 360 N. Michigan Ave., Chicago, IL 60611, *Telephone:* (312) 649-5411, *Fax:* (312) 280-3150.

Crain's Cleveland Business, Crain Communications Inc., 700 W. St. Clair, Suite 310, Cleveland, OH 44113, *Telephone:* (216) 522-1383.

Crain's Detroit Business, Crain Communications Inc., 1155 Gratiot Ave., Detroit, MI 48207-3187, *Telephone:* 1 (888) 909-9111. *Published:* weekly, except semiweekly the fourth week in May.

Crain's New York Business, Crain Communications, Inc., 711 Third Ave., New York, NY 10017, *Telephone:* 1 (888) 909-9111, *Published:* weekly.

Cranes Today, *Telephone*: +44 (0) 208 269 7779, *Fax:* +44 (0) 208 269 7803.

Crop Production, U.S. Government Printing Office, Superintendent of Documents, Washington D.C. 20402, *Telephone:* (202) 720-2127, *Published:* yearly.

Current Events, 200 First Stamford Place, P.O. Box 120023, Stamford, CT 06912.

Dagens Naeringslivr, Gjorwellsgatan 30, Stockholm, Sweden, *Published:* daily.

Daily Business Review, 330 Clematis Street, Via Jardin, Suite 114, West Palm Beach, FL 33401, *Telephone:* (561) 820-2060, *Fax:* (561) 820-2077.

The Daily Deal, The Deal LLC, 105 Madison Avenue, New York, NY 10016, *Telephone:* (212) 313- 9200.

Daily Herald, Paddock Publishing Inc., P.O. Box 280, Arlinton Heights, IL 60006-0280, *Telephone:* (847) 427-4300.

Daily News Record, Cahners Publishing Co., 275 Washington St., Newton, MA 02158, *Telephone:* (617) 558-4243, *Fax:* (617) 558-4759, *Published:* 2x/mo.

Daily News, through Knight Ridder/Tribune Business News, 790 National Press Building, Washington D.C. 20045, *Telephone:* (202) 383-6134, *Fax:* (202) 393-2460, *Published:* daily.

The Daily Oklahoman, P.O. Box 25125, Oklahoma City, OK 73125, *Telephone:* (405) 478-7171 or 1 (877) 987-2737.

Daily Record, 1 Central Quay, Glasgow G3 8DA, *Telephone:* 0141 309 3000.

The Daily Telegraph, 1 Canada Square, Canary Wharf, London E14 5AR, *Telephone:* +44 (0) 20 75 38 5000, *Published:* daily.

Daily Variety, Reed Business Information, 5700 Wilshire Blvd., Suite 120, Los Angeles, CA 90036, *Telephone:* (323) 857-6600.

Dairy Farmer, United Business Media, Sovereign Way, Tonbridge, Kent, United Kingdom TN9 1RW.

Dairy Field, Stagnito Communications Inc., 155 Pfingsten Road, Suite 205, Deerfield, IL 60015, *Telephone:* (847) 205-5660, *Fax:* (847) 205-5680.

Dairy Foods, 1050 IL Route 83, Suite 200, Bensenville, IL 60106, *Telephone:* (630) 694-4341, *Fax:* (630) 227-0527, *Published:* monthly, except semimonthly in Aug.

Dairy Industries International, Paulton House, 8 Shepherdess Walk, London England Telephone: (020) 7251 6499, Fax: (020) 7608 2215.

Dallas Morning News, 508 Young Street, Dallas, TX 75202, *Telephone:* (214) 977-8222, *Published:* daily.

Datamonitor Industry Market Research, Datamonitor USA, 1 Park Avenue, 14th Floor, New York, NY 10016-5802.

Dayton Business Journal, 137 N. Main St., Suite 800, Dayton, OH 45402-1772, *Telephone:* (937) 222-6900, *Fax:* (937) 222-9967.

Deal Memo, Informa Media, Mortimer House, 37-41 Mortimer Street, London, W1T 3JH, *Telephone:* +44 (0) 20 7017 5533, *Fax:* +44 (0) 7017 4783, *Published:* 24x/yr.

Dealernews, Advanstar Communications Inc., 1700 E Dyer Rd., Ste. 250, Santa Ana, CA 92705, *Telephone:* (714) 252-5300, *Fax:* (714) 261-9790, *Published:* monthly.

Dealerscope, North American Publishing Co., 401 N Broad St, Philadelphia, PA 19108.

Decision Distribution, Groupe Tests, 26, rue d'Oradour sur glane, 75015 Paris, Telephone: 33 (0) 1 4424-3001, Fax: 33 (0) 14026-0401.

The Denver Post, 1560 Broadway, Denver, CO 80202, Telephone: (303) 820-1010, *Published*: daily.

Detroit Free Press, Knight-Ridder, Inc., 600 Fort, Detroit, MI 48226, *Telephone:* (313) 222-6400, *Published:* daily.

Detroit News, Detroit News Inc., 615 W. Lafayette, Detroit, MI 48226, *Telephone:* (313) 222-2300, *Published:* daily.

Dialogue, Diamond Comics Distributors, 1966 Greenspring Drive, Suite 300, Timmonium, MD 21093, Telephone: (410) 560-7100, *Published:* monthly.

Diamond Intelligence Briefs, *Published:* 20x/yr.

Diesel Progress North American Edition, Diesel & Gas Turbine Publications, 20855 Watertown Road, Suite 220, Waukesha, WI 53186, *Telephone:* (262) 832-5000, *Fax:* (262) 832-5075.

Display & Design Ideas, *Telephone:* (847) 763-9050, *Published:* monthly.

Distribucion Actualidad, Ip Mark, *Telephone:* 913 159845.

DM News, Courtenay Communications Corporation, 100 Avenue of the Americas, New York, NY 10013, *Telephone:* (212) 925-7300, *Fax:* (212) 925-8752.

DNR, Fairchild Publications, 7 West 34th Street, New York, NY 10001-8191, *Telephone:* 1 (800) 360-1700.

Do-It-Yourself-Retailing, National Retail Hardware Assn., 5822 W. 74th St., Indianapolis, IN 46278-1756, *Telephone:* (317) 297-1190, *Fax:* (317) 328-4354, *Published:* monthly, *Price:* $8; $2 single *issue.*

Dolan's Virginia Business Observer, 300 E Main St., Suite 170, Norfolk VA 235101737, *Telephone:* (757) 6273766.

Dominion Post, 1251 Earl L Core Road, Morgantown, WV 26505-6298, *Telephone:* (304) 292-6301, *Fax:* (304) 292-3704.

Drug Cost Management Report, AIS, 1100 7th Street NW, Suite 300, Washington, D.C. 20036, *Telephone:* 1 (800) 521-4323.

Drug Store News, Lehbhar-Friedman Inc., 425 Park Ave, New York, NY 10022, *Telephone:* 1 (800) 216-7117, *Published:* 2x/mo.

Drug Topics, Advanstar Medical Economics, 5 Paragon Drive, Montvale, NJ 07645-1742, *Telephone:* (973) 847-5314, *Fax:* (973) 847-5303.

DSN Retailing Today, Lebharr-Friedmann Inc., 425 Park Ave., New York, NY 10022, *Telephone:* 1 (800) 216-7117.

Duty-Free News International, Euromoney, Nestor House, Playhouse Yard, London EC4V 5EX, United Kingdom, *Published:* 22x/yr.

DVD News, M2 Communications, P.O. Box 475 Coventry CV1 1ZB, *Telephone:* 44 (0) 24 7623 8200.

DVD Report, 1201 Seven Locks Road, Suite 300, Potomac, MD 20854, *Telephone:* (301) 354-2000.

E&MJ, Regency Tower, Suite 708, 9550 Regency Square Blvd., Jacksonville, FL 32225, *Published:* monthly.

Eagle Times, 11 Main St., Springfield, VT 05156, *Telephone:* (802) 885-2162.

East Africa Intelligence Wire, FT Publications Inc., 14 East 60th Street, New York, NY 21002, *Telephone:* (212) 752-4500, *Fax:* (212) 319-0704.

East Bay Business Times, 6160 Stoneridge Mall Road, Suite 300, Pleasanton, CA 94588, *Telephone:* (925) 598-1830, *Fax:* (925) 598-1840, *Price:* $74 per year.

EBN, Cahners Publishing Co., 275 Washington, Newton, MA 02158-1630, *Telephone:* (617) 964-3030, *Fax:* (617) 558-4470.

Echos, 46 Street Boétie, 75381 Paris Cedex 08, France, *Telephone:* 01-49-53-65-65, *Fax:* 01-45-61-48-92.

The Economist,111 West 57th Street, New York NY 10019, *Telephone*: (212) 541-0500, *Fax:* (212) 541-9378, *Published:* weekly.

Econtent, Online Inc., 213 Danbury Rd., Wilton, CT 06897-4007, *Telephone:* (203) 761-1466, *Fax:* (203) 761-1444.

Editor & Publisher, VNU Business Publications USA, Inc., 770 Broadway, New York, NY 10003-9595, *Telephone:* 1 (800) 336-4380, *Fax:* (646) 654-5370.

EDN, Reed Business Information, 275 Washington, Newton, MA 02458.

Educational Marketer, Simba Information, PO Box 4234, 11 River Bend Drive South, Stamford, CT 06907-0234, *Telephone:* (203) 358-4100, *Fax:* (203) 358-5824, *Published:* 36x/yr.

Electric and Hybrid Vehicles Today, 119 S. Fairfax St., Alexandria VA 22314.

Electric Light & Power, PennWell, 1421 S Sheridan Road, Tulsa, OK 74112, *Telephone:* (918) 832-3161, *Published:* monthly.

Electrical Wholesaling, One IBM Plaza, 330 N. Wabash Ave., #2300, Chicago, IL 60611, *Telephone:* (312) 840-8422, *Fax:* (312) 840-8432, *Published:* monthly.

Electronic Business, Reed Business Information, 275 Washington, Newton, MA 02158-1630, *Telephone:* (617) 630-3815, *Fax:* (617) 558-4621.

Electronic Buyers News, CMP Media, 600 Community Drive, Manhasset, NY 11030.

Electronic Design, Penton Media, Inc., 1300 E. 9th St., Cleveland, OH 44114, *Telephone:* 1 (800) 249-8365.

Electronic Education Report, Simba Information, PO Box 4234, 11 River Bend Drive South, Stamford, CT 06907-0234.

Electronic Engineering Times, CMP Publications, 600 Community Drive, Manhasset, NY 11030, *Telephone:* (516) 562-5000, *Fax:* (516) 562-5995.

Electronic Gaming Business, PBI Media, 1201 Seven Locks Road, Suite 300, Potomac, MD 20854, *Telephone:* (301) 354-2000, *Published:* 25x/yr.

Electronic Information Report, Simba Information, P.O. Box 4234 11 River Bend Drive South, Stamford, CT 06907-0234, *Telephone:* (203) 358-4100, *Fax:* (203) 358-5824, *Published:* 46x/yr, *Price:* $659 per year.

Electronic Materials Update, Business Communications Company, Inc., 25 Van Zant Street, Norwalk, CT 06855-1781, *Telephone:* (203) 853-4266, *Fax:* (203) 853-0348, *Published:* monthly, *Price:* $500 per year.

Electronic News, Reed Business Information, 275 Washington Street, Newton, MA 02458, *Telephone:* (617) 558-4624, *Fax:* (617) 558-4621, *Published:* weekly, except last week of Dec.

Electronic Packaging & Production, Reed Business Information, 2000 Clearwater Drive, Oak Brook, IL 60523, *Telephone:* (630) 288-8000, *Fax:* (630) 288-8843.

Electronic Payments International, Lafferty, The Colonnades, 82 Bishops Bridge Road, London, W2 6BB, United Kingdom, *Telephone:* +44 (0) 207 563 5700, *Fax:* +44 (0) 207 563 5701.

Electronic Publishing, PennWell Publishing, 1421 S. Sheridan, Tulsa OK 74112, *Telephone:* (918) 835-3161, *Fax:* (800) 331-4463.

Electronics Weekly, Reed Business Information, Quadrant House, The Quadrant, Sutton, Surrey, United Kingdom SM2 5AS, *Telephone:* 020 8652 3500, *Fax:* 020 8652 8932.

Embroidery Monogram Business, 1115 Northmeadow Parkway, Roswell, GA 30076, *Telephone:* (770) 291-5534, *Fax:* (770) 777-8733, *Published:* monthly.

Energy User News, BNP Media, 1428-30 Midland Ave. #8, Bronxville, NY 10708, *Telephone:* (914) 776-9241, *Fax:* (914) 776-5217.

ENR , McGraw-Hill Inc., Fulfillment Manager, ENR, P.O. Box 518, Highstown, NJ 08520, *Telephone:* (609) 426-7070 or (212) 512-3549, *Fax:* (212) 512-3150, *Published:* weekly, *Price:* $89 per year in U.S.; $75 per year in Canada. Single copies $5 in U.S.

Entertainment Marketing Letter, EMP Communications, 160 Mercer St, 3rd Floor, New York, NY 10012-3212, *Telephone:* (212) 941-0099, *Fax:* (212) 941-1622.

Entertainment Weekly, Time-Warner Inc., 1675 Broadway, New York, NY 10019, *Published:* weekly.

Equus, 656 Quince Orchard Road, Suite 600, Gaithersburg, MD 20878, *Telephone:* (301) 977-3900, *Fax:* (301) 990-9015, *Published:* monthly.

Estates Gazette, United Kingdom, *Telephone:* 01444 445335, *Fax:* 01444 445567.

Eurofood, Agra Informa Ltd., 80 Calerley Road, Tunbridge Wells, Kent, TN1 2UN, United Kingdom, *Telephone:* +44 (0) 1892 533813, *Fax:* +44 (0) 1892 544895

Euromoney, Euromoney Publications PLC, Nestor House, Playhouse Yard, London EC4V 5EX, *Published:* monthly.

Europe Agri, Europe Information Service, Brussels, *Published:* 11X/yr.

Europe Intelligence Wire, FT Publications Inc., 14 East 60th Street, New York, NY 21002, *Telephone:* (212) 752-4500, *Fax:* (212) 319-0704.

European Banker, Lafferty Publications, The Colonnades, 82 Bishops Bridge Road, London W2 6BB, *Telephone:* +44 (0) 207 563 5700, *Fax:* +44 (0) 207 563 5701, *Published:*weekly.

European Chemical News, Reed Business Information, Quadrant House, The Quadrant, Sutton, Surrey, SM2 5AS, United Kingdom, *Telephone:* +44 20 8652 8147, *Fax:* +44 20 8652 3375, *Published:* weekly.

European Cosmetic Markets, Wilmington Publishing, 6-14 Underwood St, London N1 7JQ, *Telephone:* +44 (0) 20 7549-8626, *Fax:* +44 (0) 20 7549-8622.

European Rubber Journal, Crain Communications Ltd., 34 Southwark, Bridge Road, London SE19E1, *Telephone:* (44) 207 457 1400, *Published:* monthly, except August.

European Telecom, *Published:* 250x/yr.

EuropeMedia, Informa Telecoms & Media Group, Mortimer House, 37-41 Mortimer Street, London W1T 3JH, *Telephone:* +44 (0) 20 7017 5533, *Fax:* +44 (0) 20 7017 4783.

The Evening Standard, Associated New Media, Northcliffe House, 2 Derry Street, London W8 5TT, *Telephone:* 020 7938 6000

Expansion, 14, Poissonnière boulevard, 75308 Paris Cedex 09, France, *Telephone:* 01 53 24 40 40, *Fax:* 01 53 24 41 05.

Export America, U.S. Government Printing Office, Superintendent of Documents, P.O. Box 371954, Pittsburg, PA 15250-7954, *Telephone:* (202) 512-1800, *Fax:* (202) 512-2250.

Far Eastern Economic Review, Review Publishing Company Limited, GPO Box 160, Hong Kong, *Telephone:* (852) 2508 4338, *Fax:* (852) 2503 1549, *Published*: weekly.

Fayetteville Observer, 458 Whitfield St., P.O. Box 849, Fayetteville, NC 28302, *Telephone:* (910) 323-4848, *Fax:* (910) 433-3431, *Published:* daily.

Feedstuffs, Miller Publishing Co., 12400 Whitewater Dr., Ste. 160, Minnetonka, MN 55343, *Telephone:* (952) 931-0211, *Fax:* (952) 938-1832, *Published:* weekly.

Fertilizer International, British Sulfur Publishing, 31 Mount Pleasant, London WC1X0AD, *Telephone:* +44 20 7903 2147, *Fax:* +44 20 7903 2172, *Published:* bimonthly, *Price:* $440 per year.

Fiber Optics Weekly Update, IGI Group Inc., 320 Washington Street, Suite 302, Boston, MA 02135, *Telephone:* 1 (800) 323-1088 or (617) 782-5033, *Fax:* (617) 782-5735, *Published:* weekly, *Price:* $695 per year.

Film Journal International, VNU eMedia, Inc., 770 Broadway, 6th Floor, New York, NY 10003, *Published:* monthly.

Finance and Commerce, Dolan Media, 615 S. 7th St, Minneapolis MN 55415, *Published:* daily.

The Financial Express, Indian Express Newspapers, C-6, Qutab Institutional Area, New Delhi -110 016, India, *Telephone:* +91-11-26531111, *Fax:* +91-11-26511615

Financial News, 2nd Floor, Stapleton House, 29-33 Scrutton Street, London EC2A 4HU, *Telephone:* +44 (0) 20 7426 3333, *Fax:* +44 (0) 20 7426 9554, *Published:* weekly.

Financial Post, 300-1450 Don Mills Road, Don Mills, Ontario, Canada M3B 3R5, *Telephone:* (416) 383-2300, *Fax:* (416) 383-2443.

Financial Times, FT Publications Inc., 14 East 60th Street, New York, NY 21002, *Telephone:* (212) 752-4500, *Fax:* (212) 319-0704, *Published:* daily, except for Sundays and holidays, *Price:* $425 per year.

Fleet Equipment, Transportation Communications, LLC, 2615 Three Oaks Rdl, Suite 1B, Cary, IL 60013, *Telephone:* (847) 359-6100, *Fax:* (847) 639-9542.

Flexible Packaging, Stagnito Communications, Inc., 155 Pflingsten Road, Suite 205, Deerfield, IL 60015, *Telephone:* (847) 205-5660, ext. 4020, *Published:* monthly.

Flight International, Reed Business Information, 333 N. Fairfax Street, Suite 301, Alexandria, VA 22314, *Telephone:* (703) 836-3448, *Fax:* (703) 836-8344.

Florida Times-Union, 1 Riverside Ave., Jacksonville, FL 32202, *Telephone:* (904) 359-4111, *Published:* daily.

Florida Today, 1 Gannett Plaza, Melbourne, FL 32940, *Telephone:* (321) 242-3500, *Published:* daily.

Florida Trend, Trend Magazines, 490 First Avenue South, Saint Petersburg, FL 33701, *Telephone:* (727) 821-5800, *Published:* monthly.

Folio, Primedia Inc., 249 W 17th Street, 3rd Floor, New York, NY 10011.

Food & Drink Weekly, Sparks Companies, Inc., 775 Ridge Lake Blvd., Suite 400, Memphis, TN 38120-9403, *Telephone:* (901) 766-4600, *Fax:* (901) 766-4402.

Food & Drug Packaging, Stagnito Communications Inc., 155 Pflingsten Rd, Suite 205, Deerfield, IL 60015, *Telephone:* (847) 205-5660, *Fax:* (847) 205-5680, *Published:* monthly, *Price:* $85.20 per year in U.S.; $150.20 internationally.

Food & Agriculture Report, Interfax, *Telephone:* (303) 368-1421, *Fax:* (303) 368-1458.

Food Engineering & Ingredients, Reed Business Information, P.O. Box 4, 7000 BA Doetinchen, The Netherlands, *Telephone:* +31 314 349498.

Food Engineering, 901 S. Bolmar Street, Suite P, West Chester, PA 19382, *Telephone:* (610) 436-4220.

Food in Canada, Rogers Media Inc., One Mount Pleasant Rd, 7th Floor, Toronto, Ontario, Canada M4Y 2Y5, *Telephone:* (416) 764-1522, *Fax:* (416) 764-1755, *Published:* monthly.

Food Ingredient News, Business Communications Company, Inc., 25 Van Zant Street, Norwalk, CT 06855-1781, *Telephone:* (203) 853-4266, *Fax:* (203) 853-0348.

Food Institute Report, Food Insitute, One Broadway Elmwood Park, NJ 07407, *Telephone:* (201) 791-5570, *Fax:* (201) 791-5222.

Food Management, Penton Media, 1300 E. 9th Street, Cleveland, OH 44114, *Telephone:* (216) 696-7000, *Fax:* (216) 696-1752, *Published:* monthly.

Food Processing, Putman Media, 555 West Pierce Rd., Suite 301, Itasca, IL 60143, *Telephone:* (630) 467-1300, *Fax:* (630) 467-1179, *Published:* monthly.

Footwear News, Fairchild Publications, 7 W. 34th Street, New York, NY 10001, *Telephone:* (212) 630-4000, *Published:* weekly.

Forbes, Forbes, Inc., 60 Fifth Avenue, New York, NY 10011, *Telephone:* 1 (800) 888-9896, *Published:* 27x/yr., *Price:* $54 per year in U.S.; $95 per year in Canada (includes GST).

Forbes Global, Forbes, Inc., P.O. Box 494 Haywards Heath, RH16 3GQ, United Kingdom, *Fax:* +44 (0) 1444 445562.

Forest Products Journal, Forest Products Society, 2801 Marshall Ct, Madison, WI 53705-2295, *Telephone:* (608) 231-1361, *Fax:* (608) 231-2152.

Fortune, Time Inc., Time & Life Building, Rockefeller Center, New York, NY 10020-1393, *Published:* twice monthly, except two issues combined into a single issue at year-end, *Price:* $139.72 per year in U.S.

Frankfurter Allgemeine, D-60267, Frankfurt, Germany.

The Fresno Bee, 1626 E Street, Fresno, CA 93786-0001, *Telephone:* (559) 441-6111 or 1 (800) 877-7300, *Fax:* (559) 441-6499, *Published:* daily.

Frozen and Chilled Foods, DMG Business Media, *Published:* monthly.

Frozen Food Age, Cygnus Business Media, 445 Broad Hollow Road, Melville, NY 11747, *Telephone:* (631) 845-2700 ext. 208, *Fax:* (631) 845-2723 *Published:* monthly.

Furniture Manufacturer, Polygon Media, Tubs Hill House, London Road, Seven Oaks, Kent TN13 1BY, *Telephone:* (44) 1732 - 4700 35, *Fax:* (44) 1732-47 0049.

Furniture Today, Reed Business Information, P.O. Box 2754, High Point, NC 27261-2754, *Telephone:* (336) 605-0121, *Fax:* (336) 605-1143, *Published:* weekly.

Games Analyst, Informa Media Group, Mortimer House, 37-41 Mortimer Street, London W1T 3JH, *Published:* monthly.

The Gazette, Freedom Colorado Information, 30 S. Prospect St., Colorado Springs, CO 80903, *Telephone*: (719) 632-5511, *Published:* daily.

GEO World, Adams Business Media, 833 West Jackson Blvd., 7th Floor, Chicago, IL 60607, *Telephone:* (312) 846-4608, *Fax:* (312) 846-4634.

Global Cosmetic Industry, Allured Publishing Corporation, P.O. Box 380, Mount Morris, IL 60154-0506, *Telephone:* (815) 734-1225, *Fax:* (815) 734-5887.

Global Fund News, Institutional Investor, *Telephone:* 1 (800) 715-9195.

Global Mobile, Informa Group, Mortimer House, 37-41 Mortimer Street, London W1T 3JH, *Telephone:* 44 (0)20 7017 5000.

Global Refining & Fuels Report, Hart Energy Publishing, LP, 4545 Post Oak Place Dr., Suite 210, Houston, TX 77027, *Telephone:* (713) 993-9320, *Fax:* (713) 840-8585, *Published:* biweekly, *Price:* $975 per year.

Globe and Mail, 444 Front St. W., Toronto, ON, Canada M5V 2S9, *Telephone:* (416) 585-5000, *Fax:* (416) 585-5085, *Published:* Mon.-Sat. (Morn.).

Globes Online, 53 Etzel Street, Rishon Le-Zion 75706, Israel, *Telephone:* 972 3 953 8611, *Fax:* 972 3 952 5971, *Published:* daily.

Golf World, Golf Digest Companies, 20 Westport Rd., P.O. Box 850, Wilton, CT 06897, *Telephone:* (203) 761-5100 or 1 (800) 962-5513.

Golf World Business, Golf Digest Companies, 20 Westport Rd., P.O. Box 850, Wilton, CT 06897, *Telephone:* (203) 761-5100 or 1 (800) 962-5513.

Gourmet Retailer, 3301 Ponce de Leon Blvd., Suite 300, Coral Gables, FL 33134, *Telephone:* (847) 763-9050.

Governing, Congressional Quarterly, Inc., 1100 Connecticut Ave., NW, Suite 1300, Washington, D.C. 20036.

Government Executive, 1501 M. St. NW, Suite 300, Washington, D.C. 20005, *Telephone:* (202) 739-8500, *Fax:* (202) 739-8511.

Grand Rapids Press, 155 Michigan St. NW, Grand Rapids, MI, 49503 *Published:* daily.

Graphic Arts Monthly, Reed Business Information, 360 Park Avenue South, New York, NY 10010, *Telephone:* (646) 746-7321.

Greater Baton Rouge Business Report, Louisiana Business, 445 North Blvd., Suite 210, Baton Rouge, LA 70802, *Telephone:* (225) 928-1700, *Fax:* (225) 923-3448, *Published:* biweekly.

Grocer's Review, GR Publishing Ltd., Level 2, 16 York St. Parnell, P.O. Box 3990, Shortland St., Auckland 1001, New Zealand, *Telephone:* +649-307 9748, *Fax:* +649-307 9744.

Grocer, William Reed Publishing Ltd., Broadfield Park, Crawley, RH11 9RT, United Kingdom, *Telephone:* +44 (0) 1293 613400.

Grocery Headquarters, Trend Publishing, Inc., One East Erie, Suite 401, Chicago, IL 60611, *Telephone:* (312) 654-2300, *Fax:* (312) 654-2323, *Published:* monthly.

The Guardian, 3-7 Ray Street, London EC1R 3DR, *Telephone:* 020-7278 2332, *Published:* daily.

Haaretz, 21 Schocker St., P.O. Box 233, Tel Aviv 61001, Israel, *Telephone:* 972-3-5121212, *Published:* daily except Saturday.

Handelsbatt, Germany, *Telephone:* 01805 365 365.

HandelsZeitung, Seestrasse, Postfach, CH 8027 Zurich, Telephone: 0041 (0) 1288 3500.

Hartford Courant, 285 Broad Street, Hartford, CT 06115, *Published:* daily, *Price:* $234 per year.

Hawaii Business, 1000 Bishop Street, Suite 405, Honolulu, HI 96813, *Telephone:* (808) 537-9500, *Fax:* (808) 537-6455, *Published:* monthly.

Health Care Food & Nutrition News, Aspen Publishers, 1185 Avenue of the Americas, New York, NY 10036, *Telephone:* (212) 597-0200, *Fax:* (212) 597-0338.

Health Care Strategic Management, 11211 E. Araphoe Rd, Suite 101, Centennial, CO 80112-3851..

Health Club Management, Leisure Media Co. Ltd., Portmill House, Portmill Lane, Hitchin Herts SG5 1DJ, United Kingdom, *Telephone:* +44 (0) 1462 431385

Healthcare Financial Management, 2 Westbrook Corporate Center, Suite 700, Westchester, IL 60154-5700, *Telephone:* 1 (800) 252-4362 or (708) 531-9600, *Fax:* (708) 531-0032.

Healthcare Purchasing News, 7650 So. Tamiami Trail Suite Suite 10, Sarasota, FL 34231, *Telephone*: (941) 927-9345, *Fax:* (941) 927-9588.

The Hearing Journal, Lippincott Williams & Wilkins, PO Box 1620, Hagerstown MD 21741, *Telephone:* (301) 223-2300 or 1 (800) 638-3030, *Fax:* (301) 223-2400, *Published:* monthly, *Price:* $110 per year for individuals, $132 per year for institutions.

The Herald, 200 Renfield Street, Glasgow, Scotland G2 3QB, *Telephone:* 0141 302 7000, *Fax:* 0141 302 7171, *Published:* daily.

Herald Sun, P.O. Box 14999, Melbourne City MC, 8001, Australia, *Telephone:* (03) 9292 2000, *Published:* daily.

HFN, Fairchild Publications, 7 W. 34th Street, New York, NY 10001, *Telephone:* (212) 630-4000, *Published:* weekly.

Hindu Business Line, India, *Telephone:* 91-44-28413344, *Fax:* 91-44-28415325, *Published:* daily.

Hollywood Reporter, 5055 Wilshire Blvd, 6th Fl, Los Angeles, CA 90036, *Telephone:* (323) 525-2000, *Fax:* (323) 525-2377, *Published:* weekdays.

Home Accents Today, Reed Business Information, 7025 Albert Pick Rd., Suite 200, Greensboro, NC 27409.

Home Channel News, Lebhar-Friedman Inc., 425 Park Avenue, New York, NY 10022, *Telephone:* (212) 756-5000, *Published:* 22x/yr.

Home Channel News NewsFax, Lebhar-Friedman Inc., 425 Park Avenue, New York, NY 10022, *Telephone:* (212) 756-5000, *Published:* 22x/yr.

Home Textiles Today, Reed Business Information, 360 Park Avenue South, New York, NY 10010, *Telephone:* (646) 746-7290, *Fax:* (646) 746-7300.

Honolulu Star Bulletin, Oahu Publications, 7 Waterfront Plaza, Suite 210, 500 Ala Moana, Honolulu, HI 96813, *Telephone:* (808) 529-4700.

Horizont, B2B On-Line GmbH, Mainzer Landstr. 251, D-60326 Frankfurt, Main.

Hospital Materials Management, The Business Word, Inc., 11211 E. Arapahoe Rd., Suite 101, Centennial, CO 80112-3851, *Telephone:* 1 (800) 328-3211 or (303) 290-8500, *Fax:* (303) 290-9025, *Published:* monthly, *Price:* $284 per year.

Hospitality, Reed Business Information, Tower 2, 475 Victoria Ave., Chatswood, NSW, Australia 2067, *Telephone:* +61 2 9422 2666, *Fax:* +61 2 9422 2633.

Hotel & Motel Management, Advanstar Communications, Inc., 7500 Old Oak Blvd., Cleveland, OH 44130, *Telephone:* (440) 891-2674, *Fax:* (440) 891-3120.

Household and Personal Products Industry, Rodman Publishing, 17 S. Franklin Turnpike, Box 555, Ramsey, NJ 07446, *Telephone:* (201) 825-2552, *Fax:* (201) 825-0553, *Published:* monthly.

Houston Chronicle, 801 Texas Ave., Houston, TX 77002, *Telephone*: (713) 220-7171, *Fax:* (713) 220-6677.

Hydrocarbon Processing, Gulf Publishing Co., 2 Greenway Plaza, Suite 1020, Houston, TX 77046, *Telephone:* (713) 529-4301, *Fax:* (713) 520-4433.

Ice Cream Reporter, *Published:* monthly.

ID Sales Pro, VNU Business Media, 770 Broadway, New York, NY 10003, *Telephone:* (646) 654-5000.

Idaho Business Review, 200 North Fourth Street, Suite 300, Boise, ID 83702, *Telephone:* (208) 336-3768, *Fax:* (208) 336-5534.

The Idaho Statesman, Gannett Co. Inc., 1200 N. Curtis Road, Boise, Idaho 83706, *Telephone:* (208) 377-6200 or 1 (800) 635-8934, *Published:* daily.

Implement & Tractor, Agra USA, P.O. Box 1420, Clarksdale, MS 38614, *Telephone:* (601) 624-8503, *Fax:* (601) 627-1977, *Published:* monthly, *Price:* $33 in the U.S. and Canada; $90 internationally.

In-Plant Graphics, North American Publishing Company, 401 North Broad Street, Philadelphia, PA 19108.

Indian Country Today, 3059 Seneca Turnpike, Canastota, NY 13032, *Telephone:* (315) 829-8393, *Fax:* (315) 829-8028, *Price:* $48 in the U.S.; $83 in Canada and Mexico; $227 per year elsewhere.

Indianapolis Business Journal, IBJ Corp., 41 E. Washington St., Indianapolis, IN 46204-3592, *Telephone:* (317) 634-6200, Fax: (317) 263-5060, *Published:* weekly, *Price:* $74 per year.

The Indianapolis Star, Gannett Inc., 307 N. Pennsylvania St., Indianapolis, IN 46204, *Telephone:* (317) 444-4000.

Indonesian Commercial Newsletter, PT Data Consult, Divisi EDP, *Telephone:* (021) 3904711-3901880.

Industrial Distribution, Reed Business Information, 275 Washington Street, Newton, MA 02458, *Telephone:* (617) 964-3030, *Published:* monthly.

Industrial Paint & Powder, 1050 IL Route 83, Suite 200, Bensenville, IL 60106, *Published:* monthly.

The Industry Standard, Internet Industry Publishing, 315 Pacific Ave., San Francisco, CA 94111-1701, *Telephone*: (415) 733-5400, *Fax:* (415) 733-5401, *Published:* weekly.

Industries in Transition, Business Communications Company, Inc., 25 Van Zant Street, Norwalk, CT 06855-1781, *Telephone:* (203) 853-4266, *Fax:* (203) 853-0348, *Published:* monthly.

Informationweek, CMP Media, 600 Community Drive, Mahassat, NY 11030, *Telephone:* (516) 562-5000, *Fax:* (516) 562-5036.

InfoStor, PennWell, 98 Spit Brook Rd., Nashua, NH 03062, *Telephone:* (603) 891-0123.

Ink World, 70 Hilltop Road, Ramsey NJ 07446, *Telephone:* (201) 825-2552, *Fax:* (201) 825-0553.

Inland Valley Daily Bulletin, 2041 E. Fourth St., Ontario, CA 91764, *Telephone:* (909) 987-6397, *Fax:* (909) 466-0235.

Insurance Journal, Wells Publishing, 1214 E. Colorado Blvd., Suite 206, Pasadena, CA 91106, *Telephone:* (626) 792-5209, *Fax:* (626) 792-5219.

Interavia, Swissair Centre, 31 Route de l'Aeroport, P.O. Box 437, 1215 Geneva 15 Switzerland, *Telephone:* (902) 788-2788, *Published:* monthly, *Price:* $128 per year.

Interavia Business & Technology, Swissair Centre, 31 Route de l'Aeroport, P.O. Box 437, 1215 Geneva 15 Switzerland, *Telephone:* (902) 788-2788, *Published:* bimonthly.

Interior Design, Reed Business Information, 360 Park Avenue South, New York, NY 10010, *Telephone:* (646) 746-6400.

International Accounting Bulletin, Lafferty, The Colonnades, 82 Bishops Bridge Road, London W2 6BB, United Kingdom, *Telephone:* +44 (0) 207 563 5700, *Fax:* +44 (0) 207 563 5701.

International Construction, KHL Group Limited, Southfields, Southview Road, Wadhurst, East Sussex, TN5

6TP, United Kingdom, *Telephone:* +44 (0) 1892 784088, *Fax:* +44 (0) 1892 784086.

International Food Ingredients, Tower Publishing, Tower House, Lathkill Street, Leicestershire LE16 9EF, United Kingdom, *Published:* bimonthly.

International Herald Tribune, 6 bis rue des Graviers, 92521 Neuilly Cedex, France.

International Petroleum Finance, 5 East 37th Street, 5th Floor, New York, NY 10016-2807, *Telephone:* (212) 532-1112, *Fax:* (212) 532-4479, *Published:* monthly.

International Railway Journal, Summons-Boardman Publishing Corporation, 345 Hudson Street, New York, NY 10014-4590, *Telephone:* (212) 620-7200, *Fax:* (212) 633-1165, *Published:* monthly.

Internet Business Daily, M2 Communications, P.O. Box 475, Coventry CV1 1ZB, United Kingdom.

Internet Securities, Comtex, 625 N. Washington St., Suite 301, Alexandria VA 22314, *Telephone:* (703) 820-2000, *Fax:* (703) 820-2005.

Internet Wire, 5757 W. Century Blvd., 3rd Floor, Los Angeles, CA 90045, *Telephone:* (310) 846-3712, *Fax:* (310) 846-3702.

Investment Dealers' Digest, Thomson Media, 1 State Street Plaza, 26th Floor, New York, NY 10004, *Telephone:* 1 (800) 221-1809 or (212) 803-8333, *Published:* weekly.

Investment News, 711 Third Avenue, Third floor, New York, NY 10017, *Telephone:* (212) 210-0759, *Fax:* (212) 210-0117.

Investor's Business Daily, P.O. Box 661750, Los Angeles, CA 90066-8950, *Published:* daily, except weekends and holidays, *Price:* $128 per year.

IPR Strategic Business Information Database, Info-Prod Research Ltd., 11 Kehilat Saloniki St., Tel Aviv 69513, Israel, *Telephone:* +972-3-6448977, *Fax:* +972-3-6448981.

Irish Times, 4th Floor, Ballast House, Aston Quay, Dublin 2, Ireland, *Telephone:* +353 1 4727103, *Published:* daily.

Israel Diamonds, P.O. Box 3237, Ramat Gan 52131, Israel, *Telephone:* (972) 3 751-2165/6, *Fax:* (972) 3 575-2201.

Izvestia, Moscow, Russia.

Japan Inc., Japan Inc. Communications, Inc., Odakyu Minami-Aoyama Building 10F, 7-8-1 Minami Aoyama, Minato-ku Tokyo 107-0062, Japan, *Telephone:* +813-3499-2099, *Fax:* +813-3499-3109.

Jerusalem Post, Palestine Post Ltd., The Jerusalem Post Building, P.O. Box 81, Jerusalem 91000, Israel, *Telephone:* 972-2-5315666, *Fax:* 972-2-5389527, *Published:* daily except Saturdays and national and religious holidays.

Jewelers Circular Keystone, Reed Business Information, 1018 West Ninth Avenue, King of Prussia, PA 19406, *Fax:* (610) 205-1139.

Journal of Commerce, Commonwealth Business Media, 400 Windsor Corporate Center, 50 Millstone Road, Suite 200, East Windsor, NJ 08520-1415, *Telephone:* 1 (800) 221-5488, *Published:* weekly.

just-auto.com, Aroq Ltd., Seneca House, Buntsford Park Road, Bromsgrove, Worcs B6O 3DX, United Kingdom.

just-drinks.com, Aroq Ltd., Seneca House, Buntsford Park Road, Bromsgrove, Worcs B6O 3DX, United Kingdom.

just-food.com, Aroq Ltd., Seneca House, Buntsford Park Road, Bromsgrove, Worcs B6O 3DX, United Kingdom.

just-style.com, Aroq Ltd., Seneca House, Buntsford Park Road, Bromsgrove, Worcs B6O 3DX, United Kingdom.

Kansas City Star, Knight Ridder, 1729 Grand Blvd., Kansas City, MO 64108, *Telephone:* (816) 234-4000, *Fax:* (816) 234-4100, *Published:* daily.

Kiplinger's Personal Finance Magazine, Kiplinger Washington Editors, Inc., 1729 H Street NW, Washington D.C. 20006, *Telephone:* 1 (800) 544-0155, *Published:* monthly.

Knight Ridder/Tribune Business News, 790 National Press Building, Washington D.C. 20045, *Telephone:* (202) 383-6134, *Fax:* (202) 393-2460, *Published:* daily.

Knoxville News-Sentinel, 2332 News Sentinel Drive, Knoxville, TN 37921-5961, *Telephone:* (865) 523-3131.

Kommersant, East View Publications, 3020 Harbor Lane, Minneapolis, MN 55447.

Korea Times, The Korea Times Co. Ltd., 17-11 Chunghak-dong, Chongro-ku, Seoul 110-792, *Telephone:* (02) 724-2340/54.

Landscape Management, Advanstar Communications, 131 West First Street, Duluth, MN 55802-2065, *Telephone:* 1 (800) 346-0085 ext. 129, *Fax:* (218) 723-9223, *Price:* $46 per year in the U.S. and its possessions; $76 per year in Canada and Mexico; $148 elsewhere.

Las Vegas Review-Journal, 1111 W. Bonanza Road, P.O. Box 70, Las Vegas, NV 89125, *Telephone:* (702) 383-0211, *Published:* daily.

Laser Focus World, PennWell, 98 Spit Brook Rd., Nashua, NH 03062, *Telephone:* (603) 891-0123, *Published:* monthly.

Latin America Telecom, IGI Group, 320 Washington, Suite 302, Boston, MA 02135, *Telephone:* 1 (800) 323-1088, *Fax:* (617) 782-5735.

Latin Trade, Latin America Media Management LLC., 200 South Bicauyne Blvd., Suite 1150, Miami, FL 33131, *Published:* monthly.

Latincom, Baskerville, Informa United Kingdom, Sheepen Place, Colchester, Essex, CO3 3LP, United Kingdom, *Telephone:* +44 (0) 20 7017 5537, *Fax:* +44 (0) 20 7017 4783.

LatinFinance, 2121 Ponce de Leon Boulevard, Suite 1020, Coral Gables, FL 33134, *Telephone:* (305) 448-6593, *Fax:* (305) 448-0718, *Price:* $235 in the U.S.; $255 internationally.

LCGC North America, Advanstar Communications, Inc., Woodbridge Corporate Plaza, 485 Route 1 South, Building F, First Floor, Iselin, NJ 08830, *Telephone:* (732) 225-9500, *Fax:* (732) 225-0211.

Lebensmittel Zeitung, Mainzer Landstr. 251, D-60326 Frankfurt/Main.

The Ledger, 300 West Lime Street, Lakeland, FL 33802, *Telephone:* (863) 802-7323, *Published:* daily.

Leisure Report, William Reed Publishing Ltd., Broadfield Park, Crawley, West Sussex RH11 9RT, United Kingdom, *Telephone:* +44 (0) 1293 613400.

Lexington Herald-Leader, Knight Ridder, 35 S. Market Street, San Jose, CA 95113.

Lifelong Learning Market Report, Simba Information, Inc., P.O. Box 4234, 11 River Bend Drive South, Stamford, CT 00907-0234, *Telephone:* (203) 358-4100, *Fax:* (203) 358-5824, *Published:* 24x/yr., *Price:* $599 per year.

Lightwave, PennWell, 98 Spit Brook Rd., Nashua, NH 03062, *Telephone:* (603) 891-0123.

Long Island Business News, 2150 Smithtown Ave., Ronkonkoma, New York 11779.

Los Angeles Business Journal, Los Angeles, CA 92005-0001, *Telephone:* 1 (800) 404-5225.

Los Angeles Business Wire, 12121 Wilshire Blvd., Suite 1000, Los Angeles, CA 90025, *Telephone:* (310) 820-9473 or 1 (800) 237-8212, *Fax:* (310) 820-7363.

Los Angeles Times, 202 West 1st Street, Los Angeles, CA 90012, *Telephone:* (213) 237-5000.

*LP/Gas, Adva*nstar Communications, 7500 Old Oak Blvd., Cleveland, OH 44130, *Telephone:* (218) 723-9477, *Fax:* (218) 723-9437.

LSA Libre Service Actualites, Group Industry Services Information, 12-14 rue Mederic 75017, Paris, France, *Telephone:* 01 56 79 41 00

M2 Best Books, M2 Communications, P.O. Box 475, Coventry CV1 1ZB, United Kingdom.

M2 Presswire, M2 Communications Ltd., P.O. Box 505, Coventry CV1 1ZQ, United Kingdom, *Telephone:* +44 (0) 24 76 238 200, *Fax:* +44 (0) 24 76 238 211, *Price:* $160.

Managed Care Week, Atlantic Information Services, Inc., 1100 17th Street, NW, Suite 300, Washington, D.C. 20036, *Telephone:* (202) 775-9008 or 1 (800) 521-4323, *Published:* weekly, *Price:* $614 per year.

Managed Healthcare Executive, 7500 Old Oak Blvd, Cleveland, OH 44130, *Telephone:* (440) 891-2765, *Fax:* (440) 891-2683.

Management Consultant International, Kennedy Information, One Phoenix Mill Lane, 5th Floor, Petersborough, NH 03458, *Telephone:* (603) 924-1006 or 1 (800) 531-0007, *Fax:* (603) 924-4034, *Published:* monthly, Price: $1,110 per year.

Manufacturing & Technology News, P.O. Box 36, Annandale, VA 22003, *Telephone:* (703) 750-2664, *Fax:* (703) 750-0064, *Published:* biweekly.

The Marion Star, Gannett Inc., 150 Court Street, Marion, OH 43302, *Telephone:* (740) 387-0400, *Published:* daily.

Marketing News, American Marketing Assn., 250 S. Wacker Dr., Ste. 200, Chicago, IL 60606-5819, *Telephone:* (312) 993-9517, *Fax:* (312) 993-7540, *Published:* biweekly.

Marketing Week, Centaur Communications Ltd., 50 Poland Street, London W1F 7AX, *Telephone:* +44 (0) 20 7292 3711

Marketing, Rogers Media Inc., One Mount Pleasant Rd., 7th Floor, Toronto, Ontario, Canada, M4Y 2Y5, *Telephone:* (416) 764-2000, *Fax:* (416) 764-1519.

Masonry Construction, Hanley Wood, LLC, One Thomas Circle, NW, Suite 600, Washington, D.C. 20005, *Telephone:* (202) 452-0800, *Fax:* (202) 785-1974.

Meat Retailer, Stagnito Communications, Inc., 155 Pfingsten Road, Suite 205, Deerfield, IL 60015, *Telephone:* (847) 205-5660, *Fax:* (847) 205-5680, *Published:* 9x/yr., *Price:* $65 per year in U.S.; $120 per year internationally.

Med Ad News, Engel Publishing Partners, 828A Newtown-Yardley Road, Newtown, PA 18940 *Telephone:* (215) 867-0044, *Fax:* (215) 867-0053.

Mediaweek, VNU Business Publications USA, Inc., 770 Broadway, 7th Floor, New York, NY 10003, *Telephone:* (646) 654-7601, *Fax:* (646) 654-5351, *Published:* weekly.

Medical Device Technology, Octo Media, Lamb House, Church Street, Chiswick, London W4 2PD, *Telephone:* +44 (0) 20 8987 0900, *Fax:* +44 (0) 20 8987 0949

Medical Devices & Surgical Technology Week, 2900 Paces Ferry Road, Atlanta GA 30339, *Telephone:* (770) 507-7777.

Medical Marketing & Media, CPS Communications, 7200 West Camino Real, Ste. 215, Boca Raton, FL 33433, *Telephone:* (561) 368-9301, *Fax:* (561) 368-7870, *Published:* monthly, *Price:* $96 per year.

Medical Textiles, International Newsletters Ltd., 9A Victoria Square, Droitwich, Worcs, WR9 8DE, United Kingdom, *Telephone:* +44 (0) 870 1657210, *Fax:* +44 (0) 870 1657212, *Published:* monthly, *Price:* $569 per year.

MEED - Middle East Economic Digest, Tower House, Sovereign Park, Market Harborough, LE16 9EF, United Kingdom, *Telephone:* +44 (0) 1858 438837, *Fax:* +44 (0) 1858 461739.

Mergers & Acquisitions, Securities Data Publishing, 40 West 57th Street, New York, NY 10019.

Mergers & Acquisitions Report, Thomson Media, 1 State Street Plaza, 27th fl, New York, NY 10004, *Telephone:* (212) 803-8200.

Metals & Mining Report, Interfax, Russia *Telephone:* 7 095 250 9840, *Fax:* 7 095 250 9727.

Metalworking Insiders Report, Gardner Publications, Inc., P.O. Box 107, Larchmont, NY 10538, *Telephone:* (914) 834-2300, *Published:* 24x/yr., *Price:* $449 per year in North America; $579 per year elsewhere.

Michelin Fact Book 2001, Place des Carmes-Dechaux 63040 Clermont-Fd., France.

Middle East North Africa Financial Network, 39 Abu Sufian Street, P.O. Box 940192, Amman, 11194, Jordan, *Telephone:* ++962 6 5690450/4, *Fax:* ++962 6 5666680.

Military & Aerospace Electronics, PennWell, 98 Spit Brook Rd., Nashua, NH 03062, *Telephone:* (603) 891-0123, *Published:* monthly.

Milwaukee Journal-Sentinel, Journal/Sentinel Inc., P.O. Box 661, Milwaukee, WI 53201, *Telephone:* (414) 224-2000, *Published:* Mon-Sat.

Min's B to B, Access Intelligence, LLC, 1201 Seven Locks Road, Suite 300, Potomac, MD 20854, *Telephone:* (301) 354-2000, *Published*: 48x/yr., *Price*: $795 per year.

Mining Engineering, Society for Mining, Metallurgy and Exploration Inc., 8307 Shafer Parkway, P.O. Box 625002, Littleton, CO 80127-102, *Telephone*: (303) 973-9550, *Fax*: (303) 973-3845, *Published:* monthly.

Mississippi Business Journal, Ventura Publications Inc., Jackson, MS, *Telephone:* (601) 364-1000, *Price:* $54.95 per year.

MMR, Racher Press, 220 5th Ave., New York, NY 1001, *Telephone:* (212) 213-6000, *Fax*: (212) 213-6101, *Published*: biweekly.

Mobile Games Analyst, Baskerville, Informa United Kingdom, Sheepen Place, Colchester, Essex, CO3 3LP, United Kingdom, *Telephone:* +44 (0) 20 7017 5537, *Fax:* +44 (0) 20 7017 4783.

Mobile Messaging Analyst, Baskerville, Informa United Kingdom, Sheepen Place, Colchester, Essex CO3 3LP, United Kingdom, *Telephone:* +44 (0) 20 7017 5537, *Fax:* +44 (0) 20 7017 4783.

Modern Brewery Age, 50 Day Street, P.O. Box 55550, Norwalk, CT 06856, *Telephone:* (203) 853-6015, *Fax*: (203) 853-8175.

Modern Casting, American Foundrymen's Society, 505 State St., Des Plaines, IL 60016-8399, *Telephone:* (847) 824-0181, *Fax:* (847) 824-7848.

Modern Healthcare, 360 N. Michigan Avenue, 5th Floor, Chicago, IL 60601-3806, *Telephone:* (312) 649-5350, *Published:* weekly.

Modern Machine Shop, Gardner Publications, Inc., 6915 Valley Avenue, Cincinnati, OH 45244, *Telephone:* (513) 527-8800, *Fax:* (513) 527-8801.

Modern Materials Handling, Reed Business Information, 275 Washington St, Newton, MA 02458, *Telephone:* (617) 964-3030, *Fax:* (617) 558-4327.

Modern Plastics, Canon Communications LLC, 11444 W. Olympic Blvd., Suite 900, Los Angeles, CA 90064, *Telephone:* (310) 445-4200.

Modern Power Systems, United Kingdom, *Telephone*: +44 (0) 20 8269 7766, *Fax:* +44 (0) 8269 7804.

Modern Tire Dealer, 341 White Pond Drive, Akron, OH 44320, *Telephone:* (330) 867-4401, *Fax:* (330) 867-0019, *Published:* monthly.

Modesto Bee, McClatchy Newspapers, 1325 H Street, Modesto, CA 95352.

Mondaq Business Briefing, London, England, *Telephone:* +44 (0) 20 8544 8300, *Fax:* +44 (0) 20 8544 8340.

Money Marketing, Centaur Communications Limited, St. Giles House, 50 Poland Street, London W1V 4AX.

Montreal Gazette, 1010 St. Catherine St. West, Suite 200, Montreal, Quebec H3B 5L1, Canada, *Telephone:* (514) 987-2222.

The Morning Call, 101 North 6th St., Allentown, PA 18101, Telephone: (610) 820-6500, *Published:* daily, *Price:* $221 per year.

Mortgage Banking, Mortgage Bankers Assn of America, 1125 15th St. NW, Washington D.C. 20005, *Telephone*: (202) 861-6500, *Fax:* (202) 872-0186, *Published:* monthly.

Mortgage Servicing News, Thomson Financial Mortgage Publications, 1 State Street Plaza, 27th Floor, New York, NY 10004, *Fax:* (212) 292-5216.

Motor Trend, Primedia, Inc., 260 Madison Ave., New York, NY *Telephone:* (212) 726-4300, *Fax:* (917) 256-0025, *Published*: monthly.

MSI, MSI Computer Corporation, 901 Canada Court, City of Industry, CA 91748, *Telephone*: (626) 913-0828, *Fax:* (626) 913-0818.

Music & Copyright, Informa, Mortimer House, 37-41 Mortimer Street, London W1T 3JH, United Kingdom.

Music Trades, 80 West St., Englewood, NJ 07631, *Telephone:* (201) 871-1965, *Fax:* (201) 871-0455, *Published:* monthly.

Music Week, CMP Information, Tower House, Sovereign Park, Market Harborough, Leicestershire, LE16 9EF, United Kingdom.

Nashville Business Journal, 344 Fourth Avenue North, Nashville, TN 37219, *Telephone*: (615) 248-2222, *Fax*: (615) 248-6246.

Nation's Restaurant News, New York, NY, *Telephone*: (212) 756-5129, *Fax*: (212) 756-5215.

National Fisherman, Diversified Business Communications, 121 Free Street, Portland, ME 04101, *Telephone:* (207) 842-5608, *Fax*: (207) 842-5609.

National Floor Trends, 22801 Ventura Blvd, #115, Woodland Hills, CA 91364, *Telephone:* (818) 224-8035, *Fax:* (818) 224-8042.

National Geographic, National Geographic Society, 1145 17th Street N.W., Washington, D.C. 20036-4688, *Telephone:* 1 (800) 647-5463, *Published:* monthly.

National Geographic Explorer, National Geographic Society, 1145 17th Street N.W., Washington, D.C. 20036-4688, *Telephone*: 1 (800) 647-5463, *Published*: monthly.

National Jeweler, VNU Business Publications USA, Inc., 770 Broadway, Fifth Floor, New York, NY 10003-9595, *Published:* biweekly.

National Mortgage News, Thomson Corporation, 1 State Street Plaza, 27th Floor, New York, NY 10004, *Fax:* (212) 292-5216.

National Petroleum News, Adams Business Media, 833 West Jackson, 7th Floor, Chicago, IL 60607, *Telephone*: (312) 846-4600, *Fax*: (312) 977-1042.

National Provisioner, Stagnito Communications, 155 Pfingsten Road, Suite 205, Deerfield, IL 60015, *Telephone:* (847) 205-5660, *Fax:* (847) 205-5680.

National Real Estate Investor, Primedia Business Magazines & Media, 2104 Harvell Circle, Bellvue, NE 68005, *Telephone*: (402) 505-7173, *Fax:* (402) 293-0741.

National Underwriter, The National Underwriter Co., 505 Gest St., Cincinnati, OH 45203, *Telephone:* 1 (800)

543-0874, *Fax:* 1 (800) 874-1916, *Published:* weekly, except last week in December, *Price:* $98 per year in U.S.

Natural Gas Week, Energy Intelligence, 5 East 37th Street, 5th Floor, New York, NY 10016-2807, *Telephone:* (212) 532-1112, *Fax:* (212) 532-4479.

Network World, Network World Inc., 118 Turnpike Road, Southborough, MA 01772-9108, *Telephone:* (508) 460-3333, *Fax:* (508) 460-1192, *Published:* weekly.

New Media Age, Centaur Communications Ltd., 50 Poland St., London W1F 7AX, *Published:* weekly.

New Orleans CityBusiness, New Orleans Publishing Group, 111 Veterans Blvd., Suite 1440, Metairie, LA 70005, *Telephone:* (504) 834-9292, *Fax:* (504) 832-3550.

New York Diamonds, Reed Business Information, 360 Park Avenue South, New York, NY 10010, *Telephone*: (646) 746-6400, *Published*: bimonthly.

New York Post, 1211 Avenue of the Americas, New York, NY 10036-8790, *Telephone:* (212) 930-8000.

The New York Times, New York Times Co., 229 W. 43rd St., New York, NY 10036, *Telephone:* (212) 556-1234. *Published:* daily.

New Zealand Forest Industries Magazine, Profile Publishing Limited, Level 2, Suite 1, 72 Dominion Rd., Mt. Eden, Auckland, New Zealand, *Telephone:* +64 9 630 8940, *Fax:* +64 9 630 1046.

New Zealand Marketing Magazine, Profile Publishing Limited, Level 2, Suite 1, 72 Dominion Rd., Mt. Eden, Auckland, New Zealand, *Telephone:* +64 9 630 8940, *Fax:* +64 9 630 1046.

The News Journal, Gannett Inc., 950 West Basin Road, New Castle, DE 19720, *Telephone:* (302) 324-2500 or 1 (800) 235-9100, *Published:* daily.

News-Press, Gannett, 2442 Dr. MLK Jr. Blvd., Fort Myers, FL 33901, *Telephone:* (239) 335-0200.

The News-Sentinel, 2332 News Sentinel Drive, Knoxville, TN 37921-5761, *Telephone:* (865) 523-3131, *Published:* daily.

Newsday, 235 Pinelawn Rd., Melville, NY 11747-4250.

Newsweek, 251 W. 57th St., New York, NY 10019, *Published:* weekly.

Nikkei Weekly, 1-9-5 Otemachi, Chiyoda-ku, Tokyo, 100-8666 Japan, *Telephone:* +81-3-5255-2312, *Fax:* +81-3-5255-2631.

Nonwovens Industry, Rodman Publishing, 17 S. Franklin Turnpike, P.O. Box 555, Ramsey, NJ 07446, *Telephone:* (201) 825-2552, *Fax:* (201) 825-0553, *Published:* monthly, *Price:* $48, or free to qualified subscribers.

Nordic Business Report, M2 Communications Ltd., P.O. Box 505, Coventry CV1 1ZQ, United Kingdom, *Published:* biweekly.

North American Mobile Communications Report, EMC Publications, Mortimer House, 37-41 Mortimer Street, London W1T 3JH, *Telephone:* +44 (0) 207 017 5070, *Fax:* +44 (0) 207 017 5071, *Published*: quarterly.

NTT Topics, Kyodo News International, 50 Rockerfeller Plaza, Suite 803, New York, NY 10020, *Telephone:* (212) 397-3723, *Fax:* (212) 397-3721.

Nursery Retailer, Brantwood Publications, 2410 Northside Dr., Clearwater, FL 33761, *Telephone:* (727) 786-9771, *Fax:* (727) 786-9772, *Published:* 6x/yr.

Nutraceuticals International, Marketletter Publications Limited, 54-55 Wilton Road, London SW10 1DE, *Telephone:* +44 20 7828 7272, *Fax:* +44 20 7828 0415, *Published*: monthly.

Nutraceuticals World, 70 Hilltop Road, Ramsey, NJ 07446, *Telephone:* (201) 825-2552, *Fax:* (201) 825-0553.

The Oakland Press, 48 W. Huron, Pontiac, MI 48342, *Telephone:* (248) 745-4700, *Published:* daily.

Office Products International, Mondiale Corporation Ltd., Nestor House, Playhouse Yard, London EC4V 5EX, *Telephone:* +44 (0) 20 7236 0389, *Fax:* +44 (0) 20 7236 0393, *Published*: monthly.

Oil & Fats International, DMG World Media, 2141 West Orangewood Ave, Building 8 Suite B, Orange, CA 92868, *Telephone:* 1 (714) 978-8888, *Fax:* 1 (714) 978-2422.

Oil & Gas Investor, Hart Energy Publishing LP, 4545 Post Oak Place Drive, Suite 210, Houston, TX 77027, *Telephone:* (713) 993-9320, *Fax:* (713) 840-8585, *Published:* monthly.

Oil and Gas Journal, 1700 West Loop South, Suite 1000, Houston, TX 77027, *Telephone:* (713) 621-9720, *Fax:* (713) 963-6285.

Oil Express, 1255 Hwy 70, Suite 32N Lakewood, NJ 08701, *Telephone:* (732) 901-8800, *Published:* weekly.

On Wall Street, Thomson Corporation, 1 State Street Plaza, 27th Floor, New York, NY 10004, *Fax:* (212) 292-5216.

Online Reporter, G2 Computer Intelligence Inc., 323 Glen Cove Avenue, Sea Cliff, NY 11579, *Telephone:* (516) 759-7025, *Fax*: (516) 759-7028, *Published:* weekly, *Price:* $595 per year.

Optistock Market Watch, Access Media Group, LLC, 11 Campus Boulevard, Suite 100, Newtown Square, PA 19073, *Telephone:* (610) 492-1046, *Price:* $100 per year.

Optoelectronics Report, PennWell, 98 Spit Brook Rd., Nashua, NH 03062, *Telephone:* (603) 891-0123, *Published*: 24x/yr., *Price*: $295 per year.

Orange County Register, 625 N Grand Ave, P.O. Box 11626, Santa Ana, CA 92701, *Telephone:* (877) 469-7344.

Orbis, Foreign Policy Research Institute, 1528 Walnut St., Suite 610, Philadelphia, PA 19102, *Telephone:* (215) 732-3774, *Fax:* (215) 732-4401, *Published:* quarterly.

The Oregonian, 1320 S.W. Broadway, Portland, OR 97201, *Telephone:* (503) 221-8100, *Published:* daily.

Package Printing, North American Publishing Company, 401 North Broad Street, Fifth Floor, Philadelphia, PA 19108.

Packaging Digest, Reed Business Information, 2000 Clearwater Drive, Oak Brook, IL 60523, *Telephone:* (630) 288-8000, *Fax:* (630) 288-8750, *Published:* monthly.

The Palm Beach Post, 2751 S. Dixie Highway, West Palm Beach, FL 33405, *Telephone*: (561) 820-4663 or 1 (800) 926-7678, *Published:* daily.

Paper, Film & Foil Converter, Primedia Business Magazines & Media, 330 N. Wabash, Suite 2300, Chicago, IL 60611-3698, *Telephone:* (312) 595-1080 or 1 (800) 458-0479, *Fax:* (312) 840-8455, *Published:* monthly.

Paperboard Packaging, Advanstar Communications Inc., 131 West First Street, Duluth, MN 55802, *Telephone:* (218) 723-9200, *Fax:* (218) 723-9437, *Published:* monthly.

Passive Component Industry, Paumanok Group, 130 Preston Executive Drive, Suite 101, Cary, NC 27513, *Telephone:* (919) 468-0384 or 1 (800) 862-3328, *Fax:* (919) 468-0386, *Published:* 6x/yr.

Pensions & Investments, Crain Communications Inc., 711 Third Avenue, New York, NY 10017, *Telephone:* (212) 210-0100, *Fax:* (212) 210-0117, *Published:* 26x/yr., *Price:* $229 per year.

Petroleum Finance Week, Hart Energy Publishing, LP, 4545 Post Oak Place Drive, Suite 210, Houston, TX 77027, *Telephone:* (713) 993-9320, *Fax:* (713) 840-8585, *Published:* 50x/yr., *Price:* $1097 per year.

Pharma Marketletter, Marketletter Publications Ltd., 54-55 Wilton Road, London SW1V 1DE, *Telephone:* +44 (0) 20 7828 7272, *Fax:* +44 (0) 20 7828 0415.

Pharmaceutical Executive, Advanstar Communications, 485 Route 1 South, Building F, 1st Floor, Iselin, NJ 08830, *Telephone:* (732) 225-9500, *Fax:* (732) 596-0053.

Philadelphia Business Journal, 400 Market Street, Suite 1200, Philadelphia, PA 19106, *Telephone:* (215) 238-1450, *Published:* weekly.

Philadelphia Inquirer, Philadelphia Newspapers Inc., 400 N. Broad St., Box 8263, Philadelphia, PA 19101, *Telephone:* (215) 854-2000, *Published:* daily.

Photo District News, VNU Business Publications USA, Inc., 770 Broadway, 7th Floor, New York, NY 10003, *Telephone:* (646) 654-5780, *Fax:* (646) 654-5813, *Published:* monthly.

Photo Marketing, 3000 Picture Place, Jackson, MI 49201, *Telephone:* (517) 788-8100, *Fax:* (517) 788-8371, *Published:* monthly, *Price:* $50 per year.

Photo Marketing Newsline, 3000 Picture Place, Jackson, MI 49201, *Telephone:* (517) 788-8100, *Fax:* (517) 788-8371.

Pipeline & Gas Journal, Oildom Publishing Company of Texas Inc., 1160 Dairy Ashford St., #610, Houston, TX 77079-3014, *Telephone:* (281) 558-6930, *Fax:* (281) 558-7029, *Published:* monthly.

Pittsburgh Post-Gazette, 34 Blvd of the Allies, Pittsburgh, PA 15222, *Telephone:* 1 (800) 228-6397, *Published:* daily, *Price:* $143 per year.

Pittsburgh Tribune-Review, D.L. Clark Bldg., 503 Martindale St., 3rd Floor, Pittsburgh, PA 15212, *Telephone:* (412) 320-7914, *Published:* daily.

Pizza Marketing Quarterly, 605 Edison Street, Oxford, MS 38655, *Telephone:* (662) 234-5481, *Fax:* (662) 234-0665.

Plain Dealer, Plain Dealer Plaza, 1801 Superior Avenue, Cleveland, OH 44114-2198, *Published:* weekly.

Plastics News, Crain Communications Inc., 1725 Merriman Road, Akron, OH 44313-5283, *Telephone:* (330) 836-9180, *Fax:* (330) 836-2322, *Published:* weekly, *Price:* $69 in the U.S.; $129 in Canada; $177 in Mexico; $287 elsewhere.

Plastics Technology, SPG Media Limited, Brunel House, 55-57 North Wharf Road, London W2 1LA, *Telephone:* +44 (0) 20 7915 9957, *Fax:* +44 (0) 20 7915 9958, *Published:* monthly.

Play Meter, 6600 Fleur De Lis Drive, New Orleans, LA 70124, *Telephone:* (504) 488-7003 or (888) 473-2376, *Fax:* (504) 488-7083, *Published:* 13x/yr., *Price:* $60 per year in the U.S. and Canada; $150 per year elsewhere.

Poland Business News, Interfax, *Telephone:* 42 02 2287, Fax: 42 02 2287 4110.

Polymers Paint Colour Journal, DMG Media, *Telephone:* (44) 1737 855079.

Pool & Spa News, Hanley-Wood, LLC, One Thomas Circle, NW, Suite 600, Washington D.C. 20005, *Telephone:* (202) 452-0800, *Fax:* (202) 785-1974.

Post and Courier, 134 Columbus Street, Charleston, SC 29403-4800, *Telephone:* (843) 577-7111, *Published:* daily.

Post-Standard, Clinton Square, P.O. Box 4915, Syracuse, NY 13221-4915, *Telephone:* (315) 470-0011, *Published:* daily.

Poultry - Production and Value, United States Department of Agriculture, National Agricultural Statistics Service, U.S. Government Printing Office, Washington, D.C.

PR Newswire, PR Newswire Association LLC, 810 7th Avenue, 35th Floor, New York, NY, *Telephone:* (212) 596-1500 or 1 (800) 832-5522.

The Prague Post, Stepanska 20, Prague 1, 110 00, Czech Republic, *Telephone:* +420 (0)2 9633 4400, *Fax:* +420 (0)2 9633 4450, *Published:* daily.

Prepared Foods, BNP Media, 1050 IL Route 83, Suite 200, Bensenville, IL 60106.

PrimeZone Media Network, 5200 West Century Blvd., Suite 470, Los Angeles, CA 90045, *Telephone:* (310) 642-6930, *Fax:* (310) 642-6933.

Print Week, Haymarket Business Publications, 174 Hammersmith Road, London W6 7JP, *Telephone:* 020 8267 4397, *Fax:* 020 8267 4455.

Printed Circuit Design & Manufacture, UP Media Group, 2018 Powers Ferry Center, Suite 600, Atlanta, GA 30339, *Telephone:* (678) 589-8800, *Fax:* (678) 589-8850, *Published:* monthly.

Printing Impressions, North American Publishing Company, 401 North Broad Street, Fifth Floor, Philadelphia, PA 19108, *Telephone:* (215) 238-5300, *Fax:* (215) 238-5457, *Published:* weekly.

Private Label Buyer, Stagnito Communications, 155 Pfingsten Road, Suite 205, Deerfield, IL 60015, *Telephone:* (847) 205-5660, *Fax:* (847) 205-5680, *Published:* monthly, *Price:* $85.18 per year in the U.S.; $180.18 per year internationally.

Private Placement Market, Thomson Media, One State Street Plaza, 27th Floor, New York, NY 10004, *Telephone:* (212) 803-8200.

PROCESS Chemical and Pharmaceutical Engineering, Vogel Life Science Media, Max-Plank-Str., 7/9 97082 Wurzburg, Germany, *Telephone:* +49-9 31-418-2665, Fax: +49-9 31-418-2750, *Published:* quarterly.

Process Heating, BNP Media, 1910 Cochran Road, Suite 450, Pittsburgh, PA 15220.

Products Finishing, 6915 Valley Avenue, Cincinnati, OH 45244, *Telephone:* (513) 527-8800 or 1 (800) 950-8020, *Fax:* (513) 527-8801.

Professional Builder, Reed Business Information, 2000 Clearwater Drive, Oak Brook, IL 60523, *Telephone:* (630) 288-8072, *Fax:* (630) 288-8075, *Published:* monthly.

Professional Candy Buyer, Adams Business Media, 10225 Berea Road, Suite B, Cleveland, OH 44102, *Telephone:* (216) 631-8200, *Fax:* (216) 631-8210, *Published:* bi-monthly.

Professional Carwashing & Detailing Online, National Trade Publications Inc., 13 Century Hill Drive, Latham, NY 12110, *Telephone:* (578) 783-1281, *Fax:* (518) 783-1386.

Progressive Grocer, VNU Business Publications USA, Inc., 770 Broadway, New York, NY 10003, *Published:* monthly.

Prosales, Hanley-Wood, LLC, One Thomas Circle, NW, Suite 600, Washington D.C. 20005, *Telephone:* (202) 452-0800, *Fax:* (202) 785-1974.

Providence Journal, 75 Fountain St., Providence, RI 02902, *Telephone:* (401) 277-7000, *Published*: daily.

Publishers Weekly, Reed Business Information, 360 Park Avenue South, New York, NY 10010, *Telephone*: (646) 746-6758, *Fax:* (646) 746-6631.

Puget Sound Business Journal, 801 2nd Avenue, Suite 210, Seattle, WA 98104, *Telephone:* (206) 583-0701, *Fax:* (206) 447-8510, *Published:* weekly.

Pulp & Paper, Paperloop, 4 Alfred Circle, Bedford, MA 01730, *Telephone:* 1 (866) 271-8525, *Fax:* (818) 487-4550, *Published:* monthly.

Purchasing, Reed Business Information, 275 Washington Street, Newton, MA 02458-1630, *Fax:* (617) 558-4327.

Quick Frozen Foods International, EW Williams Publishing Co., 2125 Center Ave., Ste. 305, Fort Lee, NJ 07024, *Telephone:* (201) 592-7007, *Fax:* (201) 592-7171, *Published:* monthly.

R&D, Reed Business Information, 100 Enterprise Drive, Suite 600, Box 912, Rockaway, NJ 07866-0912, *Telephone:* 1 (800) 222-0289, *Published:* monthly.

R&D Directions, Engel Publishing, 820 Bean Tavern Road, West Trenton, NJ 08628, *Telephone:* (609) 530-0044, *Fax:* (609) 530-1274, *Published:* 10x/yr.

Railway Age, Simmons-Boardman Publishing, 345 Hudson St., New York, NY 10014, *Telephone:* (212) 620-7200, *Fax:* (212) 633-1165, *Published:* monthly.

RCR Wireless News, RCR Publications, 777 East Speer Blvd., Denver, CO 80203-4214, *Telephone*: (303) 733-2500.

Reactions, Euromoney Institutional Investor Plc, Nestor House, Playhouse Yard, London EC4V 5EX, *Telephone:* +44 (0) 20 7779 8888, *Published:* monthly.

Reading Eagle, P.O. Box 582, 345 Penn St., Reading, PA 19603-0582, *Telephone*: (610) 371-5000, *Published:* daily.

Real Estate Alert, 5 Marine View Plaza, Ste. 301, Hoboken, NJ 07030-5795, *Telephone:* (201) 659-1700, *Fax:* (201) 659-4141, *Published:* weekly.

Realtor Magazine, 430 N Michigan Ave, Chicago, IL 60611-4087, *Telephone:* 1 (800) 874-6500, *Published:* monthly.

The Record, North Jersey Media Group, 150 River Street, Hackensack, NJ 07601-7172, *Telephone:* (201) 646-4100, *Fax*: (201) 646-4135, *Published*: daily.

Refrigerated & Frozen Foods, Stagnito Communications, 155 Pfingsten Road, Suite 205, Deerfield, IL 60015, *Telephone*: (847) 205-5660, *Fax*: (847) 205-5650, *Published*: monthly.

Register-Guard, Summer Oaks Center, 3500 Chad Drive, Eugene, OR 97440-2188, *Telephone*: (541) 485-1234.

Reinforced Plastics, Elsevier Science, P.O. Box 945, New York, NY 10159-0945, *Telephone*: (212) 633-3680, *Fax*: (212) 633-3680.

Reinsurance Magazine, Incisive Media Investments Ltd., WDIS, Freepost LON20586, Southale UB1 2BR, United Kingdom, *Telephone:* +44 (0) 20 8606 7516, *Fax:* +44 (0) 20 8606 7303, *Published:* bimonthly.

Reno Gazette-Journal, 955 Kuenzli Lane, Reno, NV 89500, *Published:* daily.

Research Alert, EPM Communications, 160 Mercer Street, 3rd Floor, New York, NY 10012.

Research Studies, Freedonia Group, 767 Beta Drive, Cleveland, OH 44143, *Telephone:* (440) 684-9600, *Fax:* (440) 646-0484.

The Reserve Bank of New Zealand, 2 The Terrace, PO Box 2498, Wellington, New Zealand, *Telephone:* 64 4 472 2029, *Fax:* 64 4 473 8554.

Restaurant & Institutions, Reed Business Information, 2000 Clearwater Drive, Oak Brook, IL 60523, *Telephone:* (630) 288-8242, *Fax:* (630) 288-8225, *Published:* 2x/mo.

Restaurant Business, VNU Business Publications USA, Inc., 770 Broadway, New York, NY 10003, *Published:* 18x/yr.

Retail Banker International, Lafferty, The Colonnades, 82 Bishops Bridge Road, London W2 6BB, *Telephone*: +44 (0) 207 563 5700, *Fax:* +44 (0) 207 563 5701.

Retail Merchandiser, VNU Business Publications USA, Inc., 770 Broadway, New York, NY 10003.

Retail Traffic, Primedia, Inc., 249 W. 17th Street, New York, NY 10011, *Telephone:* (212) 462-3600, *Fax:* (212) 367-8345.

Retail Week, 3rd Floor, 33-39 Bowling Green Lane, London EC1R 0DA, *Telephone*: +44 (0) 20 7505 8000, *Fax:* +44 (0) 20 7520 3529.

Risk Management, Risk Insurance Management Society, Inc., 655 Third Avenue, Second Floor, New York, NY 10017-5637, *Telephone:* (212) 286-9364, *Fax:* (212) 922-0716, *Published:* monthly.

The Roanoke Times, 201 W. Campbell Ave., P.O. Box 2491, Roanoke, VA 24010-2491, *Telephone:* 1 (800) 346-1234, *Published:* daily.

Rochester Democrat and Chronicle, Gannett Co., 55 Exchange Blvd., Rochester, NY 14614, *Telephone*: (585) 232-7100 or 1 (800) 767-7539.

Rock Products, Primedia, Inc., 9800 Metcalf Ave., Overland Park, KS 66212, *Telephone:* (913) 341-1300, *Fax:* (913) 967-1898.

Rocky Mountain News, E.W. Scripps Co., 100 Gene Amole Way, Denver, CO 80204, *Telephone:* (303) 892-2527, *Fax:* (303) 892-2368, *Published:* daily.

Roofing Contractor, BNP Media, 2401 W. Big Beaver Rd., Suite 700, Troy, MI 48084, *Telephone:* (248) 362-3700, *Fax:* (248) 362-0317.

Rubber & Plastics News, Crain Communications Inc., 1725 Merriman Road, Akron, OH 44313-5251, *Telephone:* (330) 836-9180, *Fax:* (330) 836-2831, *Published:* weekly.

Rubber World, P.O. Box 5451, 1867 W. Market St., Akron, OH 44313-6901, *Telephone:* (330) 864-2122, *Fax:* (330) 864-5298.

Rural Cooperatives, Rural Business-Cooperative Service, U.S. Department of Agriculture, 1400 Independence Avenue, SW Stop 0705, Washington D.C. 20250-9410, *Telephone:* (202) 720-5964, *Published:* bimonthly.

RV Business, P.O. Box 17126, North Hollywood, CA 91615-9925, *Published:* monthly.

Sacramento Bee, 2100 Q Street, Sacramento, CA 95816, *Telephone:* (916) 321-1000.

Saigon Times Magazine, Saigon, Vietnam, *Published:* weekly.

St. Louis Business Journal, American City Business Journals, Inc., One Metropolitan Square, Suite 2170, St. Louis, MO 63102, *Telephone:* (314) 421-6200, *Fax:* (314) 621-5031, *Published:* weekly.

St. Louis Post Dispatch, 900 Tucker Blvd., St. Louis, MO 63101, *Telephone:* (314) 340-8000 or 1 (800) 365-0820, *Published:* daily.

Saint Paul Pioneer Press, Knight Ridder, 345 Cedar Street, St. Paul, MN 55101, *Telephone:* (651) 222-1111 or 1 (800) 950-9080, *Published:* daily.

St. Petersburg Times, 490 First Avenue, St. Petersburg, FL 33701, *Telephone:* (727) 893-8111, *Fax:* (727) 893-8675, *Published:* daily.

San Antonio Business Journal, 70 NE Loop 410, Suite 350, San Antonio, TX 78216, *Telephone:* (210) 341-3202, *Fax:* (210) 341-3031, *Published:* weekly.

San Antonio Express-News, 400 3rd Street, San Antonio, TX 78287-2171, *Telephone:* (210) 250-3000, *Published:* daily.

San Diego Union-Tribune, P.O. Box 12091, San Diego, CA 92112-0191, *Telephone:* (619) 299-3131 or 1 (800) 244-6397, *Published:* daily.

San Fernando Valley Business Journal, Woodland Hills, CA 91367, *Telephone:* (818) 676-1750.

San Francisco Chronicle, Hearst Communications, 901 Mission St., San Francisco, CA 94103-2988, *Telephone:* (415) 777-1111, *Fax:* (415) 536-5178.

San Jose Mercury News, Knight Ridder, 750 Ridder Park Drive, San Jose, CA 95190, *Telephone:* (408) 920-5000, *Fax:* (408) 288-8060, *Published:* daily.

Sarasota Herald-Tribune, 801 S. Tamiami Trail, Sarasota, FL 34236, *Telephone:* (941) 953-7755, *Fax:* (941) 957-5276.

Satellite News, 800 Siesta Way, Sonoma, CA 95476, *Telephone:* (707) 939-9306, *Fax:* (707) 939-9235.

Screen Digest, Global Media Intelligence, Lymehouse Studios, 38 Georgiana Street, London NW1 0EB, *Telephone:* +44 (0) 20 7424 2820, *Fax:* +44 (0) 20 7424 2838, *Published:* weekly.

Seafood Business, Diversified Business Communications, 121 Free Street, P.O. Box 7437, Portland, ME 04112-7437, *Telephone:* (207) 842-5500, *Fax:* (207) 842-5503, *Published:* monthly.

Seattle Post-Intelligence, 101 Elliott Ave. W., Seattle, WA 98119, *Telephone:* (206) 448-8000, *Published:* daily.

Seattle Times, P.O. Box 70, Seattle WA 98111, *Telephone:* (206) 464-2111, *Published:* daily.

Securities Industry News, Thomson Corporation, 1 State Street, 27th Floor, New York, NY 10004, *Telephone:* 1 (888) 280-4820, *Fax:* (301) 545-4836.

Security Director's Report, The Institute of Management and Administration, 3 Park Avenue, 30th Floor, New York, NY 10016, *Telephone:* (212) 244-0360, *Fax:* (212) 564-0465, *Published:* monthly, *Price:* $259 per year.

Security Distribution & Marketing, BNP Media, 1050 IL Route 83, Suite 200, Bensenville, IL 60106, *Telephone*: (630) 616-0200, *Fax*: (630) 227-0214, *Published*: monthly.

Shooting Industry, FMG Publications, 12345 World Trade Drive, San Diego, CA 92128, *Telephone*: (858) 605-0254, *Published*: monthly, *Price*: $25 per year in U.S; $45 per year internationally.

Shopping Center World, Primedia Business Magazines and Media, 6151 Powers Ferry Road, Suite 200, Atlanta, GA 30339, *Telephone*: (770) 955-2500, *Fax*: (770) 618-0204.

Signs of the Times, ST Publications, 407 Gilbert Avenue, Cincinnati, OH 45202, *Telephone:* (513) 421-2050 or 1 (800) 925-1110, *Fax*: (513) 421-5144, *Published*: 13x/yr., *Price:* $39 per year in U.S.; $59 per year in Canada; $62 per year elsewhere.

Snack Food & Wholesale Bakery, Stagnito Communications, 155 Pfingsten Road, Suite 205, Deerfield, IL 60015, *Telephone*: (847) 205-5660, *Fax:* (847) 205-5680, *Published:* monthly, *Price:* $85.06 per year in U.S., $150.06 per year internationally.

Soap & Cosmetics, 110 William Street, New York, NY 10038, *Telephone:* (212) 621-4900, *Fax:* (212) 621-4800.

Soap, Perfumery & Cosmetics, Wilmington Publishing Ltd., Wilmington House, 2 Maidstone Road, Sidcup, DA14 5H2, Kent, United Kingdom, *Telephone:* 020 8269 7700, *Fax:* 020 8269 7733, *Published*: monthly.

Soap, Perfumery & Cosmetics Asia, Wilmington Publishing Ltd., Wilmington House, 2 Maidstone Road, Sidcup, DA14 5H2, Kent, United Kingdom, *Telephone:* 020 8269 7700, *Fax:* 020 8269 7733, *Published:* 4x/yr.

Solid State Technology, PennWell, 98 Spit Brook Rd., Nashua, NH 03062, *Telephone:* (603) 891-0123, *Published:* monthly.

South American Business Information, COMTEX News, 625 N. Washington St, Suite 301, Alexandria, VA 22314, *Telephone:* (703) 820-2000, *Fax:* (703) 820 - 2005.

Specialty Chemicals, DMG World Media, Business Media, Queensway House, 2 Queensway, Redhill Surrey RH1 1QS, *Telephone:* 44 1737 768611, *Fax:* 44 1737 855477.

Spectroscopy, Advanstar Communications, 485 Route One South, Building F, Iselin, NJ 08830, *Telephone:* (732) 225-9500, *Fax:* (732) 225-0211, *Published:* monthly.

Spiegel, Spiegel Verlag Rudolf Augstein, Verlag Brandstwiete, 20457 Hamburg, *Telephone:* 040 3007 - 2455, *Fax:* 040 3007 - 3094.

Spokesman-Review, 999 West Riverside Avenue, Spokane, WA 99201, *Telephone:* (509) 459-5000, *Published:* daily.

Sporting Goods Business, VNU Business Publications USA, Inc., 770 Broadway, New York, NY 10003, *Published:* monthly.

Springfield News-Leader, Gannett Co., 651 Boonville, Springfield, MO 65806, *Telephone:* (417) 836-1100 or 1 (800) 695-1969, *Published:* daily.

The Star-Ledger, 1 Star-Ledger Plaza, Newark, NJ 07102-1200, *Telephone:* (973) 392-4141.

Star Tribune, 425 Portland Ave., Minneapolis, MN 55488, *Telephone:* (612) 673-4000.

Statesman Journal, 280 Church St NE, Salem, OR 97301.

Stone World, BNP Media, 210 Route 4 East, Suite 311, Paramus, NJ 07652, *Telephone:* (201) 291-9001, *Fax:* (201) 291-9002.

Stores, National Retail Federation, 325 7th Street, NW, Suite 1100, Washington D.C. 20004, *Telephone:* (202) 626-8101, *Published*: monthly.

Strategy, Brunico Communications Inc., Suite 500, 366 Adelaide St. W., Toronto, Ontario, Canada M5V 1R9, *Telephone:* (416) 408-2300, *Fax:* (416) 408-0870.

Successful Farming, Meredith Corporation, P.O. Box 37466, Boone, IA 50037-0466, *Telephone:* (515) 246-6952 or 1 (800) 374-3276, *Published:* monthly.

The Sunday Times, Times Newspapers, P.O. Box 495, Virginia Street, London E19XY.

Supermarket News, Fairchild Publications, 7 W. 34th St., New York, NY 10001, *Telephone:* 1 (800) 204-4515, *Fax:* (212) 630-4760, *Published:* weekly.

Supply House Times, BNP Media, 1050 IL Route 83, Suite 200, Bensenville, IL 60106, *Telephone*: (630) 616-0200.

Surgical Litigation & Law Weekly, 2900 Paces Ferry Road, Atlanta GA 30339, *Telephone:* (770) 507-7777.

Sydney Morning Herald, 201 Sussex Street, Sydney 2000, Australia, *Telephone*: (02) 9282-2833, *Published:* daily.

Taipei Times, Nanking East Rd., Sec. 2, #137, 5 Fl., Taipei, Taiwan, ROC-104, *Telephone:* +886-2-2518-2728, *Fax:* +886-2-2518-9159, *Published:* daily.

Taiwan Economic News, China Economic News Service.

The Tampa Tribune, 200 S. Parker St., Tampa, FL 33606, *Telephone:* (813) 259-8010 or 1 (800) 527-2773, *Published:* daily.

Tarifica Alert, Access Intelligence, LLC, 24-25 Scala Street, London W1T 2HP, United Kingdom, *Telephone:* +44 207 692 5292, *Fax:* +44 207 692 5293, *Published:* weekly.

Technology Decisions, P.O. Box 14367, Cincinnati, OH 45250-0361, *Telephone:* 1 (800) 543-0874, *Fax:* (859) 692-2246, *Published:* monthly.

Telecom Asia, Advanstar Asia Pacific Group, 26/F Pacific Plaza, 410 Des Voeux Road West, Hong Kong, *Telephone:* +852 2559 2772, *Fax:* +852 2559 7002, *Published:* monthly.

Telecommunications Americas, P.O. Box 3255, Northbrook, IL 60065-3255, *Telephone:* (847) 291-5216, *Fax:* (847) 291-4816.

Telephony, Primedia Business Magazines & Media, One IBM Plaza, Suite 2300, Chicago, IL 60611, *Telephone:* (312) 595-1080 or 1 (800) 458-0479, *Fax:* (312) 595-0295.

Television Asia, Reed Business Information, The Signature, 51 Changi Business Park, Central 2, #07-01, Singapore 4860066, *Telephone:* (65) 6789 2234, *Fax:* (65) 6789 1141.

Textile World, Billian Publishing, 2100 Powers Ferry Road, Atlanta, GA 30339, *Telephone:* (770) 955-5656, *Fax:* (770) 952-0669.

Time, Time, Inc., Time & Life Bldg., Rockefeller Center, New York, NY 10020-1393, *Telephone:* 1 (800) 843-8463, *Published:* weekly, *Price:* $72.24 per year.

Time Canada, Time Inc., 175 Bloor Street East, Suite 602 North Tower, Toronto, Ontario, Canada M4W 3R8, *Telephone:* 1 (800) 668-9934, *Fax:* (416) 929-0019, *Published:* weekly.

The Times, 601 W. 45th Avenue, Munster, IN 46321, *Telephone:* (219) 933-3200, *Fax:* (219) 933-3249, *Published:* daily.

Times Colonist, CanWest Global Communications Corp., 2621 Douglas Street, Victoria, British Columbia, Canada V8T 4M2, *Telephone:* (250) 380-5211, *Fax:* (250) 380-5353, *Published:* daily.

Times Dispatch, Media General, Inc., 300 E. Franklin Street, Richmond, VA 23219, *Telephone:* (804) 649-6000 or 1 (800) 468-3382, *Published:* daily.

Tire Business, Crain Communcations, Inc., 1725 Merriman Rd., Ste. 300, Akron, OH 44313-5283, *Telephone:* (330) 836-9180, *Fax:* (330) 836-1005.

Tobacco Europe, DMG World Media, Business Media, Queensway House, 2 Queensway, Redhill Surrey RH1 1QS, *Telephone:* 44 1737 768611, *Fax:* 44 1737 855477.

Tobacco Outlet Business, 6401 Carmel Road, Suite 205, Charlotte, NC 28226, *Telephone:* (704) 341-5969, *Fax:* (704) 541-1981, *Published:* bimonthly, *Price:* $45 per year.

Tobacco Retailer, Adams Business Media, Inc., 833 West Jackson, Floor 7, Chicago, IL 60607, *Telephone:* (847) 550-0207, *Fax:* (847) 550-0253, *Published:* bimonthly.

Toronto Star, One Yonge Street, Toronto, Ontario, Canada M5E 1E6, *Telephone:* (416) 367-2000, *Published:* daily.

Town Talk, Gannett Co. Inc., 1201 Third Street, Alexandria, LA 71306, *Telephone:* (318) 487-6397 or 1 (800) 523-8391, *Fax:* (318) 487-6315, *Published:* daily.

Toy Industries of Europe, Avenue des Arts 58, B-1000 Brussels, Belgium, *Telephone:* 32-2-732 7040, *Fax:* 32-2-736 9068.

Tradeshow Week, Reed Business Information, 5700 Wilshire Boulevard, Suite 120, Los Angeles, CA 90036-5804, *Telephone:* (323) 965-2093, *Fax:* (323) 965-5334.

Traffic World, 1270 National Press Building, Washington, D.C. 20045, *Telephone:* (202) 783-1101, *Published:* weekly.

Trailer/Body Builders, Primedia Business Magazines & Media, 2104 Harvell Circle, Bellevue, NE 68005, *Telephone*: (402) 505-7173 or 1 (866) 505-7173, *Fax:* (402) 293-0741.

Trailer Body Business, Tunnell Publications, P.O. Box 66010, Houston, TX 77266.

Training, VNU Business Publications USA, Inc., 50 South Ninth Street, Minneapolis, MN 55402, *Telephone:* (612) 333-0471 or 1 (800) 328-4329, *Fax:* (612) 333-6526, *Published:* monthly, *Price*: $78 per year.

Trains, Kalmbach Publishing Co., P.O. Box 1612, Waukesha, WI 53187-1612, *Telephone:* (262) 796-8776, *Fax:* (262) 796-1142, *Published:* monthly, *Price*: $59.40 per year.

Transportation & Distribution, Penton Media, Inc., The Penton Media Building, 1300 E. 9th Street, Cleveland, OH 44114, *Telephone:* (216) 696-7000, *Fax:* (216) 696-1752.

Travel Retailer International, Raven Fox Cohen Publishing, 263 New Bedford Road, Luton, Bedfordshire LU3 1LW, United Kingdom, *Telephone:* 01582459050.

Travel Trade Gazette United Kingdom & Ireland, 7th Floor, Ludgate House, 245 Blackfriars Road, London SE1 9UY, *Telephone:* +44 (0) 20 7921 8029.

Travel Weekly, Reed Business Information, Quadrant House, The Quadrant, Sutton, Surrey SM2 5AS, United Kingdom, *Telephone:* 020-8652 3799, *Fax:* 020-8652 3956.

Triangle Business Journal, 1305 Navaho Drive, Suite 100, Raleigh, NC 27609, *Telephone:* (919) 878-0010, *Fax:* (919) 790-6885, *Published:* weekly, *Price:* $74 per year.

Tribune Business News, Knight Ridder, 790 National Press Building, Washington D.C. 20045-1601, *Telephone:* (202) 383-6134.

TV International, Baskerville, Informa UK, Sheepen Place, Cochester, Essex, CO3 3LP, United Kingdom, *Telephone:* +44 (0) 20 7017 5537, *Fax:* +44 (0) 20 7017 4783.

Twin Cities, Pioneer Press, 345 Cedar Street, St. Paul, MN 55101, *Telephone*: (651) 222-1111 or 1 (800) 950-9080, *Published:* daily.

Underground Construction, Oildom Publishing Co. of Texas, 1160 Dairy Ashford, Suite 610, Houston, TX 77079, *Telephone:* (281) 558-6930, *Fax:* (281) 558-7029, *Published:* monthly.

United Kingdom Retail Briefing, Mintel International Group Ltd, 213 W. Institute Place, Suite 208, Chicago, IL 60610, *Telephone:* (312) 932-0400, *Fax:* (312) 932-0469.

United Kingdom Retail Report, Retail Intelligence, Adelaide Hall, 3 Adelaide Street, Dun Laoghaire, Co. Dublin, *Telephone*: +353 1 2300322, *Fax:* +353 1 2300629, *Published*: monthly, *Price*: $1,085 per year.

U.S. Geological Survey, Mineral Commodity Summaries, U.S. Department of the Interior, U.S. Geological Survey National Center, 12201 Sunrise Valley Drive, Reston, VA 20192, *Telephone:* (703) 648-4000, *Published:* yearly.

U.S. News & World Report, 1050 Thomas Jefferson Street NW, Washington D.C. 20007, *Telephone:* (202) 955-2000, *Published:* weekly.

U.S. Transportation Construction Market Report, American Road & Transportation Builders Association, The ARTBA Building, 1010 Massachusetts Avenue, N.W., Washington, D.C. 20001-5402, *Telephone:* (202) 289-4434, *Published*: monthly, *Price*: $300 per report.

Urban Land, Urban Land Institute, 1025 Thomas Jefferson Street, NW, Suite 500 West, Washington D.C. 20007, *Telephone*: 1 (800) 321-5011 or (202) 624-7000, *Fax:* (202) 624-7140.

Urban Land Europe, ULI Europe, 29 Gloucester Place, London W1U 8HX, *Telephone*: +44-0-207-792-6022, *Fax:* +44-0-792-4656.

Urethanes Technology, Crain Communications Ltd, 34 Southwark Bridge Road, London SE1 9EU, *Telephone*: +44 (0) 20 7457 1400, *Fax:* +44 (0) 20 7457 1440, *Published:* bi-monthly.

US Banker, Thomson Media, 1 State Street Plaza, 27th Floor, New York, NY 10004, *Telephone:* (212) 803-8200.

USA TODAY, Gannett Co., 7950 Jones Branch Drive, McLean, VA 22108-0605, *Telephone:* 1 (800) 872-0001, *Published:* Mon.-Fri.

Utah Business, Olympus Publishers, 1245 E. Brickyard Rd., Suite 90, Salt Lake City, UT 84106, *Telephone:* (801) 568-0114, *Fax:* (801) 568-0812, *Published:* monthly.

Variety, Reed Business Information, 5700 Wilshire Blvd., Suite 120, Los Angeles, CA 90036, *Telephone:* (323) 857-6600.

Video Business, Reed Business Information, 5700 Wilshire Blvd., Suite 120, Los Angeles, CA 90036, *Telephone:* (323) 857-6600, *Fax:* (323) 965-2423, *Published:* weekly.

Video Store, Advanstar Communications Inc., 201 Sandpoint Ave., Ste 600, Santa Ana, CA 92707-8700, *Telephone:* (714) 513-8400 or 1 (800) 854-3112, *Fax:* (714) 513-8680.

Vietnam Economic Times, FT Publications Inc., 14 East 60th Street, New York, NY 21002, *Telephone:* (212) 752-4500, *Fax:* (212) 319-0704.

The Virginian Pilot, 150 West Brambleton Avenue, Norfolk, VA 23510, *Telephone:* (757) 446-2000.

Vision Monday, Jobson Publishing LLC, 100 Avenue of the Americas, New York, NY 10013-1678, *Telephone:* (212) 274-7000, *Fax:* (212) 274-0392, *Published:* monthly.

Vision Systems Design, PennWell, 98 Spit Brook Rd., Nashua, NH 03062, *Telephone:* (603) 891-0123, *Published:* monthly.

VM + SD, ST Publications, 407 Gilbert Avenue, Cincinnati, OH 45202, *Telephone:* (513) 421-2050 or 1 (800) 925-1110, *Fax:* (513) 421-5144.

Wall Street Journal, Dow Jones & Co. Inc., 200 Liberty St., New York, NY 10281, *Telephone:* (212) 416-2000. *Published:* Mon.-Fri.

Walls & Ceiling, BNP Media, 2401 West Big Beaver Road, Suite 700, Troy, MI 48084, *Telephone:* (248) 362-3700, *Fax:* (248) 382-5103.

WARD's Dealer Business, Primedia Business Magazines & Media, 3000 Town Center, Suite 2750, Southfield, MI 48075, *Telephone:* (248) 357-0800, *Fax:* (248) 357-0810, *Published:* monthly.

Warsaw Rzeczpospolita in Polish, Warsaw, Poland.

The Washington Post, The Washington Post, 1150 15th St., N.W., Washington, D.C. 20071, *Published:* daily.

Washington Technology, Post-Newsweek Tech Media Group, 10 G Street, N.E., Washington, D.C. 20002, *Telephone:* (202) 772-2500, *Fax:* (202) 772-2511, *Published:* 24x/yr.

Waste Age, Primedia Business Magazines & Media, 6151 Powers Ferry Road, Suite 200, Atlanta, GA 30339, *Telephone:* (770) 955-2500, *Fax:* (770) 618-0204, *Published:* monthly.

Waste News, Crain Communications, Inc., 1725 Merriman Road, Akron, OH 44313, *Telephone:* (330) 836-9180, *Fax:* (330) 836-1692.

Water and Waste Water International, PennWell, 1421 S. Sheridan Road, Tulsa, OK 74112, *Telephone:* (918) 835-3161 or 1 (800) 331-4463, *Published*: 9x/yr., *Price*: $180 per year.

Water World, PennWell, 1421 S. Sheridan Road, Tulsa, OK 74112, *Telephone:* (918) 835-3161 or 1 (800) 331-4463, *Published:* 11x/yr., *Price*: $35 per year in the U.S.; $45 per year in Canada and Mexico; $50 per year elsewhere.

Waterbury Republican-American, 389 Meadow Street, Waterbury, CT 06702, *Telephone:* (203) 574-3636, *Published:* Mon.-Sat.

WattPoultryUSA, WATT Publishing, 122 S. Wesley Ave., Mt. Morris, IL 61054, *Telephone:* (815) 734-4171, *Fax:* (815) 734-5679.

The Weekend Australian, News Limited, Level 3, 2 Holt St., Surrey Hills NSW 2010, Australia, *Telephone*: +61 2 9288 3000.

Weekly Petroleum Argus, Argus Media Ltd., 93 Shepperton Road, London N1 3DF, *Telephone*: +44 (0) 20 7359 8792, *Fax*: +44 (0) 20 7359 6661.

Welding Design & Fabrication, Penton Media, Inc., The Penton Media Building, 1300 E. 9th Street, Cleveland, OH 44114, *Telephone:* (216) 696-7000, *Fax:* (216) 696-1752, *Published:* monthly.

Wine & Spirit Industry Marketing, Adams Beverage Group, 420 South Palm Canyon Drive, 2nd Floor, Palm Springs, CA 92260, *Telephone:* (630) 762-8709, *Published:* yearly, *Price:* $325 per year.

Wine Handbook, Adams Beverage Group, 420 South Palm Canyon Drive, 2nd Floor, Palm Springs, CA 92260, *Telephone:* (630) 762-8709, *Published:* yearly, *Price:* $595 per year.

Wines & Vines, Hiaring Co., 1800 Lincoln Ave., San Rafael, CA 94901-1298, *Telephone:* (415) 453-9700, *Fax:* (415) 453-2517, *Published:* monthly, *Price:* $32 per year in U.S.; $50 per year internationally.

Winston-Salem Journal, 418 N. Marshall St., Winston-Salem, NC 27101, *Telephone:* (336) 727-7211 or 1 (800) 642-0925, *Published:* daily.

Wireless Data News, Access Intelligence, LLC, 1201 Seven Locks Road, Suite 300, Potomac, MD 20854, *Telephone:* (301) 354-2000, *Published:* biweekly, *Price:* $997 per year.

Wireless News, M2 Communications, P.O. Box 475, Coventry CV1 1ZB, United Kingdom.

Wood & Wood Products, Vance Publishing Corp., P.O. Box 1400, Lincolnshire, IL 60069, *Telephone:* (847) 634-4347, *Fax:* (847) 634-4374, *Published:* monthly, except semimonthly in March.

Wood Based Panels International, Polygon Media, Tubs Hill House, London Road, Sevenoaks, Kent TN13 1BY, United Kingdom, *Telephone:* +44 (0) 1371 865072, *Fax:* +44 (0) 1732 470049, *Published:* bimonthly.

Wood Markets Monthly, Aktrin Wood Information Center, 164 S. Main St., P.O. Box 898, High Point, NC 27261, *Telephone:* (336) 841-8535, *Fax:* (336) 841-5435, *Published:* monthly, *Price:* $395 per year.

Workboat, Diversified Business Comm., 121 Free Street, P.O. Box 7437, Portland ME 04112-7437, *Telephone:* (207) 842-5500, *Fax:* (207) 842-5503.

World CDMA Report, EMC Publishing, Mortimer House, 37/41 Mortimer Street, London, W1T 3JH, United Kingdom, *Telephone*: +44 (0) 207 017 5070, *Fax:* +44 (0) 207 017 5071.

World Gas Intelligence, Energy Intelligence, 5 East 37th Street, 5th Floor, New York, NY 10016-2807, *Telephone:* (212) 532-1112, *Fax*: (212) 532-4479, *Published:* weekly.

World Oil, Gulf Publishing, 2 Greenway Plaza, Suite 1070, PO Box 2608, Houston, TX 77242, *Telephone:* (713) 529-4301, *Fax:* (713) 520-4433.

World Poultry, Reed Business Information, Hanzestraat 1, 7006 RH Doetinchem, The Netherlands.

World Tobacco, DMG Business Media Ltd, Queensway House, 2 Queensway Redhill, Surrey RH1 1QS, United Kingdom, *Telephone:* 0 1737 855294, *Fax:* 0 1737 761989, *Published:* bimonthly.

World Trade, 23421 South Point Dr, Suite 280, Laguna Hills, CA 92653, *Telephone:* (949) 830-1340, *Fax:* (949) 830-1328.

Worldsources Online, Published by FDCH e-Media, 4200 Forbes Blvd, Suite 200, Lanham, MD 20706.s.

WWD, Fairchild Publications, 7 West 34th Street, New York, NY 10001, *Telephone:* (212) 630-4000, *Published:* Mon.-Fri., Price: $99 per year.

Yellow Pages & Directory Report, Simba Information Inc., P.O. Box 4234, 11 River Bend Drive South, Stanford, CT 06907-0234, *Telephone:* (203) 358-4100, *Fax:* (203) 358-5824.

Yonhap News Agency Korea, Yonhap News Agency, 85-1, Susong-dong, Jongro-gu, Seoul, Korea, *Fax:* 82-2-389-3463.